T0275799

Categories for Types

Categories for Types

Roy L. Crole

S.E.R.C. Research Fellow,
Imperial College, London

CAMBRIDGE
UNIVERSITY PRESS

Published by the Press Syndicate of the University of Cambridge
The Pitt Building, Trumpington Street, Cambridge CB2 1RP
40 West 20th Street, New York, NY 10011–4211, USA
10 Stamford Road, Oakleigh, Melbourne 3166, Australia

© Cambridge University Press 1993

First published 1993

British Library cataloguing in publication data available

Library of Congress cataloguing in publication data available

ISBN 0 521 45092 6 hardback
ISBN 0 521 45701 7 paperback

Transferred to digital printing 2002

To Andrew M. Pitts

Contents

Preface

During the Michaelmas term of 1990, while at the University of Cambridge Computer Laboratory, the opportunity arose to lecture on categorical models of lambda calculi. The course consisted of sixteen lectures of about one hour's duration twice a week for eight weeks, and covered much of the material in this book, but excluded higher order polymorphism and some of the category theory. The lectures were delivered to an audience of computer scientists and mathematicians, with an emphasis on presenting the material to the former. It was kindly suggested by the Cambridge University Press that these lectures might form the core of a textbook, and the original suggestion has now been realised as "Categories for Types."

What are the contents of "Categories for Types"? I will try to answer this question for those who know little about categorical type theory. In Chapter 1, we begin with a discussion of ordered sets. These are collections of things with an order placed on the collection. For example, the natural numbers form a set $\{1, 2, 3 \ldots\}$ with an order given by $1 \leq 2 \leq 3 \leq \ldots$ where $\leq$ means "less than or equal to." A number of different kinds of ordered set are defined, and results proved about them. Such ordered sets then provide a stock of examples of categories. A category is a very general mathematical world and various different sorts of mathematical structures form categories. It is precisely because of this generality that apparently diverse properties of different mathematical structures can be seen as instances of the same property from the point of view of category theory. A categorical property might be thought of as a specification of a property which may hold of categories in general, but a particular mathematical structure (particular category) may be shown to yield a specific implementation of this property. We give the definition of a category in Chapter 2, show how various categories are related and give many examples. We then go on to describe some results about categories, using material on ordered sets to give gentle introductions to the categorical results. Chapters 1 and 2 contain (most of) the background mathematical machinery used in the remainder of "Categories for Types." Chapter 3 begins by showing how the definition of a category is related to certain underlying principles of syntax formation, giving us a first glance of the connections of category theory with type theory in particular and computer science in general. We

show how a particular kind of formal syntactic language is intimately related
to a particular kind of category theory—the study of such correspondences is
known as categorical type theory. In Chapter 4 we introduce a functional type
theory based on the simply typed λ-calculus. This is a formal syntactic language which can be viewed as a very basic programming language. Once again
we show a connection between a language (this time functional type theory)
and a particular kind of category theory, thus further developing the theme of
categorical type theory. We use the category theory to prove a result about
functional type theory which says (in a certain sense) that the functional type
theory has given us a richer programming language than that of Chapter 3,
but that the things we can actually express and prove in the richer language
are the same as those in the language of the previous chapter. In Chapter 5 the
idea of polymorphism is introduced. In certain programming languages, one
needs to write a different sorting algorithm to sort a list of numbers or a list
of words. However, the essence of the process of sorting is the same for both
kinds of list. A polymorphic language allows one sorting program to work for
both lists. We give a formal language which incorporates the basic feature of
polymorphism, and once again describe the category theory which corresponds
to this language. We give a full account of two examples of categorical models
of second order polymorphism. Finally, in Chapter 6, we enrich the polymorphic capabilities of the language from Chapter 5. In this new language we
are able to write programs which involve not only the usual syntax of simple
functional languages but also a syntax which allows programs to be written
involving types and type constructors. Once again we discuss categorical models, examples of such models, and also the precise correspondence between the
type theory and category theory.

I have tried to maintain a balance between presenting material rapidly
with a minimum of background discussion on the one hand, and proceeding
too slowly with obvious points on the other hand. Categorical type theory
often involves many "routine" calculations: because this work is intended as
an introductory textbook, which might even be used for undergraduate courses,
I often present some of these computations in detail. Note also that because
this book is aimed at both computer scientists and mathematicians, some
discussions may seem laboured to one group and not the other. Although I
have included some background discussions which motivate definitions, I have
decided to keep these to a minimum. I hope that the reader will put in time
to flesh out the material which this book provides. In most cases where new
topics are introduced, I have tried to give simple definitions and examples
which are then followed by the more general cases; I think this is appropriate

for a working textbook of this nature.

I have included a small number of exercises throughout the book. They fall (roughly) into three categories (no pun(s) intended):

• routine exercises which may appear anywhere (often asking the reader to verify details omitted from the text);

• less routine exercises which may appear anywhere; and

• further exercises which are given at the ends of chapters.

Mathematics in general and theoretical computer science in particular are very much *doing* subjects, and to understand them requires an active role on the part of the student. To make full use of this book it is essential that at least some of the exercises are attempted. When easy details need to be filled in to make everything crystal clear, but may (for example) involve a lengthy calculation, this will often be brought to the reader's attention with an exercise. Of course, the attentive reader will always ensure that details are understood before progressing with the text, but I think it appropriate in a working student textbook to point out occasionally that technical details are missing from the text and should be worked out. In general, the routine exercises are intended to reinforce the basic contents of the material presented in the book. The exercises given at the end of some chapters cover all topics which have been discussed up to that point in the book. I have not given large numbers of problems. Students often find it difficult to select tasks when given a large collection of exercises; and if the questions are too easy very little will be learned. Thus I have presented a small number of problems which will make (some) readers stop to think. Experience suggests this is a good approach to learning. Finally, the text will often say "it is easy to see that..." Sometimes this will be very true, but at other times this is code for "a short exercise," meaning that the reader will have to scribble with pencil and paper for a minute or so in order to understand fully what is going on.

I have to thank a number of people. I single out one person for special mention, namely Andrew Pitts, who introduced me to categorical type theory and from whom I have probably learnt more about the subject matter of this book than from anyone else. For this reason I dedicate "Categories for Types" to him. He has been a constant source of inspiration and I am indebted to him for the many discussions we have had over recent years. An anonymous referee provided a number of very useful comments and suggestions for improvements to a draft version (they will be pleased to see that certain "fatuous mottos" have been removed). Samson Abramsky has always shown a keen interest in the project and has provided encouragement and advice at all stages. Mark Dawson kept the machines running and patiently answered some of my more naive questions about the Unix system. Peter Freyd provided some inspiration for me to finish "Categories for Types" during the latter stages of production. Paul Taylor has given me more help than I deserve with typesetting in LaTeX and the diagrams in "Categories for Types" are drawn using his Commutative Diagrams package. He has also provided help with a number of mathematical questions and ensured that there was never a dull moment at Imperial College. I have had very useful technical conversations with Martin Hyland and Eugenio Moggi who have helped greatly in smoothing out parts of the presentation. John Harrison, Eike Ritter and Joshua Ross gave me detailed comments on draft versions which led to significant improvements in the presentation. A number of other people have contributed towards the production of this book by way of discussion, past lecture notes or simply enthusiasm, including Bart Jacobs, Peter Johnstone, Luke Ong, Edmund Robinson, Wesley Phoa and Steve Vickers. The category theory reading group at Imperial College proved a useful test-bed for parts of the book and I have had useful comments from Dave Clark, Abbas Edalat, Lindsay Errington, Simon Gay, Martin Köhler, David Lillie, Ian Mackie, Nick Merriam, Raja Nagarajan and Mark Ryan. Last, but by no means least, I thank my parents for their encouragement.

I am grateful to David Tranah of the Cambridge University Press for suggesting that I write this book, and to Roger Astley for helping efficiently with all stages of the production. Thanks also to the copy editors who did a very thorough and professional job. Let me conclude by emphasising that the blame for any errors which remain in "Categories for Types" must lie solely at my feet.

Advice for the Reader

Uses of "Categories for Types"

This text is intended to be a student textbook which primarily provides an introduction to (a particular kind of) categorical type theory, but which should also be useful as a reference to those mathematicians and computer scientists pursuing research in related areas. It is envisaged that it could provide the basis for a course of lectures aimed at advanced undergraduate or beginning graduate students. Given the current content of typical British undergraduate mathematics and computer science courses, it is difficult to describe an exact audience at whom the book is aimed. For example, the material on ordered sets should be readily accessible to first and second year undergraduates and indeed I know of courses which contain elements of such topics. However, the material on category theory, while probably accessible to good third year undergraduate students, does require a certain amount of mathematical maturity. Perhaps it is better suited to graduate students in their early stages. Chapters 3 and 4 are probably of second and third year undergraduate level respectively, assuming that the requisite category theory has been assimilated. The final two chapters are probably better suited to first year graduates. In summary, as well as serving as a textbook for (graduate) students, I hope "Categories for Types" will provide a useful reference for those conducting research into areas involving categorical type theory and program semantics. I have included a comprehensive index which will provide a quick route to definitions.

It is difficult to say what prerequisites are necessary to read the book. On the mathematical front, a solid understanding of basic algebra and set theory will be needed. Technically a bright student should be able to follow the material knowing little else, but in practice it will help to have some acquaintance with elementary mathematics such as group theory and vector spaces. Anyone reading this advice who knows little or nothing of these things should not be deterred from trying to get to grips with categorical type theory; understanding such topics is not essential. One of the difficulties of learning category theory is having a sufficient stock of examples of categories and this problem is accentuated in the case of computer scientists. I have tried to make the majority of examples appeal to computer scientists, but I have also included some mainstream mathematical examples to make the book appeal to mathematicians and logicians. On the computer science front, it will help if the reader is familiar with elementary logic, λ-calculus, functional programming, type inference systems and the principles of polymorphism to the level found in good British undergraduate courses. The most essential topic is λ-calculus, especially the notion of variable binding. However, this book contains all necessary formal definitions and the mature reader should find the text very much self-contained on the computer science front.

Interdependence of Chapters

The picture below gives an indication of how material in later chapters of "Categories for Types" depends on earlier material.

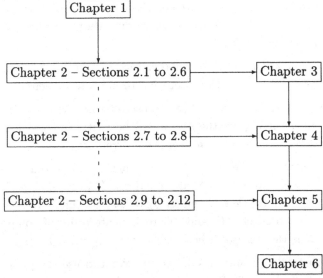

Chapters 1 and 2 on domain theory and category theory respectively might be readable in themselves if the reader has a little knowledge of the other topic. For a reader with knowledge of category theory, the remaining Chapters 3 to 6 concerning type theory are technically self-contained, but in practice it would be almost impossible to follow their contents without understanding the preceding material. Note that it is not necessary to understand all of the category theory in Chapter 2 in order to follow the chapters on type theory. I have (within reason) only included material in earlier chapters which will be put to use in later chapters.

Notational Conventions

This section is aimed particularly at computer scientists. In essence, the message is that apart from the formal syntactical systems which appear, mathematical notation will be informal. For example, given sets X and Y, we can define a function f to be a subset $f \subseteq X \times Y$ (where $X \times Y$ is the set of pairs of elements of X and Y) for which given any $x \in X$ there is a unique $y \in Y$ with $(x,y) \in f$. Formally we have to give sets X and Y and then talk of the function between them. Informally we will just talk of a function f, and then say that f has source X and target Y to mean that $f \subseteq X \times Y$. Other abuses of formal set theory will appear throughout the text, but of course in practice this aids understanding of the essential details; things can always be formalised once one knows what is going on.

• We will write (for example) $[x_1, \ldots, x_n]$ for a list of n objects, and will allow the context of discussion to indicate the nature of the length of the list; thus the previous list will usually be finite because n is commonly used as a symbol for a finite natural number. Of course such conventions will be made clear at appropriate points in the text.

• Vector notation will be used to abbreviate lists. Thus $[x_1, \ldots, x_n]$ will be denoted $\vec{x}$, leaving the context of discussion to indicate the length of the list.

• Sometimes we leave superscripts and subscripts off symbols. For example, the identity function id_X on the set X will be written id providing we can deduce the source and target of id from the current discussion.

• We will often say "let $f, g: X \to Y$ be functions" to mean that X and Y are sets and $f: X \to Y$ and $g: X \to Y$ are functions. If $f: X \to Y$, $g: Y \to Z$ and $h: Z \to Z'$ are functions, we write either gf or $g \circ f$ for functional composition. We may also use brackets "(" and ")" to indicate order of composition, so $h(gf): X \to Z'$ is the function whose value at $x \in X$ is $h(gf(x)) \in Z'$.

• We will abbreviate "if and only if" to iff. We also use the phrase "just in case" to mean iff. We will often write implications and bi-implications using proofrules. So if we have a mathematical sentence

$$\langle \text{Statement1} \rangle \quad \text{implies} \quad \langle \text{Statement2} \rangle$$

this will often be written
$$\frac{\langle \text{Statement1} \rangle}{\langle \text{Statement2} \rangle}$$

and

$$\langle \text{Statement1} \rangle \quad \text{iff} \quad \langle \text{Statement2} \rangle$$

will be written

$$\frac{\langle \text{Statement1} \rangle}{\langle \text{Statement2} \rangle}$$

• Throughout "Categories for Types" we will use the informal notion of a *commutative diagram*. We will not give any formal definition of such diagrams, but leave the reader to understand the ideas from a few examples.

Suppose that we are given set-theoretic functions

$$f : A \longrightarrow B \qquad\qquad g : B \longrightarrow D$$
$$h : A \longrightarrow C \qquad\qquad k : C \longrightarrow D$$

for which $gf = kh : A \to D$, that is the composition of f and g equals the composition of h and k. We can illustrate this with a diagram

$$
\begin{array}{ccc}
A & \xrightarrow{\;f\;} & B \\
{\scriptstyle h}\big\downarrow & & \big\downarrow {\scriptstyle g} \\
C & \xrightarrow[\;k\;]{} & D
\end{array}
$$

and we refer to the diagram as commutative to mean that the paths round the diagram indicated by arrows (in this case the paths mean functional composition) are equal.

If $a \in A$ is an element of A, we could also draw a diagram

$$
\begin{array}{ccc}
a & \longmapsto & f(a) \\
\big\downarrow & & \big\downarrow \\
h(a) & \longmapsto & k(h(a)) = g(f(a))
\end{array}
$$

to indicate that the compositions gf and kh are equal.

• We will sometimes use the symbols $-$ and $+$ to indicate "blank space" in order to give definitions of functions. This is best illustrated by example. Let $\mathbb{N}$ be the set of natural numbers. Then

$$(-) * (+) : \mathbb{N} \times \mathbb{N} \longrightarrow \mathbb{N}$$

is the function which maps any $(n, m) \in \mathbb{N} \times \mathbb{N}$ to $n * m$ where $*$ indicates multiplication. Also, if n_0 is a fixed natural number, the function

$$n_0 * (+) : \mathbb{N} \longrightarrow \mathbb{N}$$

maps any $m \in \mathbb{N}$ to $n_0 * m$.

1 Order, Lattices and Domains

1.1 Introduction

DISCUSSION 1.1.1   We shall begin by giving an informal description of some of the topics which appear in Chapter 1. The central concept is that of an ordered set. Roughly, an ordered set is a collection of items some of which are deemed to be greater or smaller than others. We can think of the set of natural numbers as an ordered set, where, *for example*, 5 is greater than 2, 0 is less than 100, 1234 is less than 12687 and so on. We shall see later that one way in which the concept of order arises in computer science is by regarding items of data as ordered according to how much information a certain data item gives us. Very crudely, suppose that we have two programs P and P' which perform identical tasks, but that program P is defined (halts with success) on a greater number of inputs than does P'. Then we could record this observation by saying that P is greater than P'. These ideas will be made clearer in Discussion 1.5.1. We can perform certain operations on ordered sets, for example we have simple operations such as maxima and minima (the maximum of 5 and 2 in the ordered set of natural numbers is 5), as well as more complicated ones such as taking suprema and infima. If the reader has not met the idea of suprema and infima, then he will find the definitions in Discussion 1.2.7. We shall meet examples of ordered sets with given properties; for example, the set of real numbers has the property that the infimum and supremum of any bounded non-empty subset of reals always *exist* (bounded means that every element of the subset is less than a given fixed real and greater than another fixed real). As well as discussing ordered sets in themselves, we shall want to talk about relations between ordered sets and in particular this will include different varieties of function. We will also need to understand the idea that functions *themselves* can be ordered. As an example, consider the function f on the natural numbers which sends n to $n+1$, and g which sends n to $n+4$. Then on every argument, the result of g is greater than that of f, and so we can regard g as greater than f. This completes the informal description of the contents of this chapter. To summarise, Chapter 1 deals with ordered sets, the properties they may have, and relations and functions between ordered sets.

Before beginning in earnest, we shall give a slightly more formal description of the contents of Chapter 1. The account begins with Discussion 1.2.1, which

contains a short and terse summary of background material on sets and functions. The idea is simply to fix notation and ideas, and the summary is not a
leisurely exposition. We will not introduce every basic mathematical concept
that we will be using, but simply give some basic definitions just to give the
reader some familiarity with notation and style. For example, while "function"
is given a formal definition below (and fixes our notation for functions), it is
certainly assumed that the reader has some knowledge of functions, and knows
the meaning of injective and surjective function (for which we adopt no special
notation). Once the summary is complete, we proceed with discussions of the
basic definitions and properties of ordered sets. Different kinds of order are
discussed, and concepts such as maximum, greatest element, join and Hasse
diagram are defined. We also define the notion of monotone function. With
this, we are able to consider some of the most common structures which arise
in the theory of ordered sets, such as lattices, Heyting lattices and Boolean
lattices. Some basic examples are given, along with some very simple representation theorems which provide information about the way such ordered sets
arise. In particular, we describe the idea of a closure system, which gives examples of ordered sets in which the order is given by subset inclusion. Finally
we move on to domain theory, once again giving simple examples and proving
representation theorems. We also give a number of technical results whose use
will only be seen in the later chapters of this book, where domains will provide
mathematical models of type theories.

1.2   Ordered Sets

DISCUSSION 1.2.1   We begin with a summary of basic naive set theory. If
A and X are sets, we write $A \subseteq X$ to mean A is a subset of X, and $A \subseteq^f X$
to mean that A is a finite subset. A *total function* between a set X and a
set Y is a subset $f \subseteq X \times Y$ for which given any $x \in X$ there is a unique
$y \in Y$ such that $(x, y) \in f$. Given $x \in X$ we write $f(x)$ for the unique y such
that $(x, y) \in f$. It will often be convenient to write $x \mapsto f(x)$ to indicate that
$(x, f(x)) \in f$; for example, if $\mathbb{R}$ is the set of real numbers, then the function f
between $\mathbb{R}$ and $\mathbb{R}$, given by $r \mapsto r^2$, is formally the subset

$$\{(r, r^2) \mid r \in \mathbb{R}\} \subseteq \mathbb{R} \times \mathbb{R}.$$

Often we shall say that f is a function $X \to Y$ and write $f: X \to Y$ in place of
$f \subseteq X \times Y$. We shall say (informally) that X and Y are the *source* and *target*
of the function f. A function $f: X \to X$ with identical source and target is
called an *endofunction* on X. Given functions $f: X \to Y$ and $g: Y \to Z$, we

write gf or $g \circ f$ for the function $X \to Z$ defined by $x \mapsto g(f(x))$. A *partial function* between X and Y is a subset $f \subseteq X \times Y$ such that given any elements $(x, y) \in f$ and $(x, y') \in f$ then $y = y'$. If $(x, y) \in f$, we write $f(x)$ for y. If $f: X \to Y$ is a partial function, and given $x \in X$ there is no $y \in Y$ for which $(x, y) \in f$, then we say that f is *undefined* at x, or sometimes simply say that $f(x)$ is undefined. If $f: X \to Y$ is a function and $S \subseteq X$ is a subset of X, then we shall sometimes use the notation $f(S)$ to represent the set $\{ f(s) \mid s \in S \}$. If X and Y are any two sets, then the set $X \setminus Y \stackrel{\text{def}}{=} \{ x \in X \mid x \notin Y \}$ is the *set difference* of Y from X. If X is a set, then $|X|$ will denote the *cardinality* (size) of X. A *binary relation* R on a set X is any subset $R \subseteq X \times X$. If $x, y \in X$, then we will write xRy for $(x, y) \in R$. R is *reflexive* if for any $x \in X$ we have xRx; *symmetric* if whenever $x, y \in X$ then xRy implies yRx; *transitive* if for any $x, y, z \in X$, whenever we have xRy and yRz then xRz; and *anti-symmetric* if whenever $x, y \in X$, xRy and yRx imply x and y are identical. R is an *equivalence relation* if it is reflexive, symmetric and transitive. Given an equivalence relation R on X, the *equivalence class* of $x \in X$ is the set $[x] \stackrel{\text{def}}{=} \{ y \mid y \in X, xRy \}$. We write X/R for the set of equivalence classes $\{ [x] \mid x \in X \}$. This completes the summary, and we now move on to the definition of ordered sets.

A *preorder* on a set X is a binary relation $\leq$ on X which is reflexive and transitive. The relation $\leq$ will sometimes be referred to informally as the *order relation* on the set X. It will sometimes be convenient to write $x \geq y$ for $y \leq x$. If at least one of $x \leq y$ and $y \leq x$ holds, then x and y are said to be *comparable*. If neither relation holds, then x and y are *incomparable*. A *preordered* set $(X, \leq)$ is a set equipped with a preorder, that is to say we are given a set (in this case X) along with a preorder $\leq$ on the set X; the set X is sometimes called the *underlying* set of the preorder $(X, \leq)$. Where confusion cannot result, we refer to the preordered set X, or sometimes just the preorder X. The preorder X is said to be *discrete* if any two distinct elements of X are incomparable. If $x \leq y$ and $y \leq x$ then we shall write $x \cong y$ and say that x and y are *isomorphic* elements. Note that we can regard $\cong$ as a relation on X, which is in fact an equivalence relation. If $(X, \leq_X)$ is a preorder, we shall write $S \subseteq X$ to mean that the set S is a subset of the underlying set of X. Of course, we can regard S as a preordered set $(S, \leq_S)$ by restricting the order relation on X to S; more precisely, if $s, s' \in S$, then $s \leq_S s'$ iff $s \leq_X s'$. We shall then say that S has the *restriction order* inherited from X. However, we shall limit the force of the judgement $S \subseteq X$ to mean that S is simply a subset of the underlying set of X. The notation $x \leq S$ will mean that for each $s \in S$, $x \leq s$.

A *partial order* on a set X is a binary relation $\leq$ which is reflexive, transitive and anti-symmetric. A set X equipped with a partial order is called a *partially ordered* set, or sometimes a *poset*. Thus a poset is a preorder which is anti-symmetric. If $x, y \in X$, where X is a poset, then we shall write $x < y$ to mean that $x \leq y$ and $x \neq y$. Given a preorder X then the set of equivalence classes $X/\cong$ can be given a partial ordering by setting $[x] \leq [y]$ iff $x \leq y$ for all $x, y \in X$. The poset $X/\cong$ is called the *poset reflection* of X.

REMARK 1.2.2   We shall use informal pictures, known as *Hasse diagrams*, to describe *partially* ordered sets. *Roughly*, in order to illustrate a finite poset pictorially, we select a distinct point $P(x)$ of the Euclidean plane $\mathbb{R}^2$ for each element x of the poset X and draw a small circle at $P(x)$. If $x < y$ in X and there is no $z \in X$ with $x < z < y$ we draw a line segment $l(x, y)$ joining the circle at $P(x)$ to the circle at $P(y)$, such that the second coordinate of $P(x)$ is strictly less than the second coordinate of $P(y)$. Ensure also that the circle at $P(z)$ does not intersect $l(x, y)$ if z is different from x and y. For example, consider the poset X with underlying set $\{a, b, c\}$ where $a \leq c$, $b \leq c$, $a \leq a$, $b \leq b$ and $c \leq c$. We can draw the Hasse diagram

to represent X. Finally, note that while we can only use this procedure sensibly for finite posets, in practice we shall draw "Hasse diagrams" of infinite posets, making the exact meaning of the picture clear with accompanying mathematics.

EXAMPLES 1.2.3

(1) The set of natural numbers, $\mathbb{N}$, with the usual increasing order is a poset. We will refer to this poset as the *vertical natural numbers*. Although this is an infinite poset, we can draw a diagram to represent it:

(2) See Figure 1.1. Examples (a) and (b) are both finite posets. Example (c) shows that the order in a finite poset can be quite involved. (d) is the poset

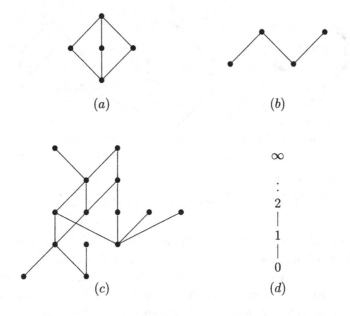

Figure 1.1: Some Examples of Posets.

which is "a copy of the natural numbers (as in example (1)) with a top element added." We will refer to this poset as the *topped* vertical natural numbers. The underlying set of the poset is $\{0, 1, 2, 3, \ldots, \infty\}$.

(3) The set $\{A \mid A \subseteq X\}$ of subsets of a set X is often written as $\mathcal{P}(X)$ and is called the *powerset* of X. The powerset is a poset with order given by inclusion of subsets, $A \subseteq B$. The order is certainly anti-symmetric, for if A and A' are subsets of X where $A \subseteq A'$ and $A' \subseteq A$, then $A = A'$. Reflexivity and transitivity are clear.

(4) Given preorders X and Y, their *cartesian product* has underlying set

$$X \times Y \stackrel{\text{def}}{=} \{(x, y) \mid x \in X, y \in Y\}$$

with order given *pointwise*, that is $(x, y) \leq (x', y')$ iff $x \leq x'$ and $y \leq y'$.

(5) If X is a preorder, then X^{op} is the preorder with underlying set X and order given by $x \leq^{op} y$ iff $y \leq x$ where $x, y \in X$. We usually call X^{op} the *opposite* preorder of X. Of course any poset is certainly also a preorder. The following Hasse diagram is a picture of the opposite of the poset (b):

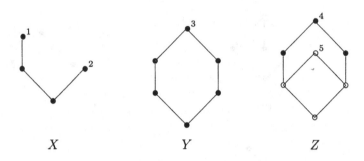

Figure 1.2: Illustrating some Definitions.

DISCUSSION 1.2.4   We now give some more definitions. Suppose that X is a preorder and A is a subset of X. An element $x \in X$ is an *upper bound* for A if for every $a \in A$ we have $a \leq x$ (or we can just write $A \leq x$, using the informal notation given in Discussion 1.2.1). An element $x \in X$ is a *lower bound* for A if $x \leq A$. An element $x \in X$ is a *greatest element* of A if it is an upper bound of A which belongs to A; x is a *least element* of A if it is a lower bound of A and belongs to A. An element $a \in A$ is *maximal* if for every $b \in A$ we have $a \leq b$ implies that $a \cong b$. An element $a \in A$ is *minimal* if for every $b \in A$ we have $b \leq a$ implies that $b \cong a$. We can prove a useful little result about greatest and least elements:

PROPOSITION 1.2.5   Let X be a preordered set and A a subset of X. Then greatest and least elements of A are unique up to isomorphism if they exist.

PROOF   Let a and a' be greatest elements of A. By definition, a is an upper bound of A, and also $a' \in A$. Hence $a' \leq a$. Similarly $a \leq a'$. Hence $a \cong a'$. The proof for least elements is essentially the same.   □

EXAMPLES 1.2.6

(1) Consider the posets illustrated in Figure 1.2. Of course, any poset is certainly a preorder, and we consider examples of the above definitions. In poset X the elements 1 and 2 are maximal. In poset Y, the element 3 is a maximal element which is the greatest element of Y. In poset Z, element 4 is greatest and maximal in Z and 5 is maximal in the subset of Z indicated by the light circles.

(2) Consider the poset of natural numbers $\mathbb{N}$ with its usual increasing order and the subset $S \stackrel{\text{def}}{=} \{25, 65, 100\}$. Examples of lower bounds for S are 0, 10 and 25, and examples of upper bounds are 100, 105, 1253 and 245.

DISCUSSION 1.2.7 The notions of upper bound, maximal element and so on give us mathematical tools for the description of the structure of preordered sets. The reader is probably familiar with the everyday notions of maximum and minimum, and our definitions of greatest and least elements correspond to such notions. Unfortunately, such ideas are not quite general enough for our purposes. We shall now define the concept of meet and join which is a generalisation of the notion of maximum and minimum.

Let X be a preordered set and $A \subseteq X$. A *join* of A, if such exists, is a least element in the set of upper bounds for A. A join is sometimes called the *least upper bound* or a *supremum*. A *meet* of A, if it exists, is a greatest element in the set of lower bounds for A. A meet is sometimes called the *greatest lower bound* or *infimum*. Note that meets and joins are defined as greatest and least elements; so from Proposition 1.2.5 we know that meets and joins are determined up to isomorphism if they exist. If the subset A has at least one join, then we will write $\bigvee A$ for a choice of one of the joins of A. Similarly, if the subset A has at least one meet, then we will write $\bigwedge A$ for a choice of one of the meets of A. If we wish to draw attention to the ordered set with respect to which a join and meet are being taken (in this case X) we shall write $\bigvee_X A$ and $\bigwedge_X A$ respectively. Note that the join is characterised by the property that for every $x \in X$ we have $\bigvee A \leq x$ iff $A \leq x$; this amounts to a formal statement that a join is by definition a least element in a set of upper bounds. Using the notation described on page xvi, we could also say that $\bigvee A$ is a join for the subset $A \subseteq X$ if for every $x \in X$ we have

$$\frac{\bigvee A \leq x}{A \leq x}$$

Similarly, $\bigwedge A$ is a meet of a subset A of X if for every $x \in X$ we have

$$\frac{x \leq \bigwedge A}{x \leq A}$$

Some special points deserve attention.

• Let X be a non-empty discrete preorder X, and $A \subseteq X$ a non-empty subset. Then A only has a meet or join if A is a singleton set. Clearly, for any $x \in X$, we have $\bigwedge \{x\} = x$ and $\bigvee \{x\} = x$.

• Consider the empty set, $\varnothing \subseteq X$. Then $\bigvee \varnothing$, if such exists, is written $\bot$ and is called a *bottom* of X. Note that a bottom element satisfies the property that for any $x \in X$ we have $\bot \leq x$. Similarly, $\bigwedge \varnothing$, if such exists, is written $\top$ and is called the *top* of X; it satisfies $x \in X$ implies $x \leq \top$.

• Consider a two element subset $\{a, b\} \subseteq X$. Write $a \vee b$ for $\bigvee \{a, b\}$ and call this a (binary) join of a and b. Similarly $a \wedge b$ is a (binary) meet of a and b. If we unravel the definitions, it can be seen that binary joins are characterised by the property that for every $x \in X$ we have $a \vee b \leq x$ iff $a \leq x$ and $b \leq x$; and binary meets by asking that for any $x \in X$ we have $x \leq a \wedge b$ iff $x \leq a$ and $x \leq b$.

EXERCISE 1.2.8   Make sure you understand the definition of meet and join in a preorder X. Think of some simple finite preordered sets in which meets and joins do not exist. Now suppose that X is a poset (and thus also a preorder). Show that meets and joins in a poset are unique if they exist.

DISCUSSION 1.2.9   A subset C of a preorder X is called a *chain* if for every $x, y \in C$ we have $x \leq y$ or $y \leq x$. We shall often simply refer to a chain in X. C is called an ω-*chain* if its elements can be indexed by the natural numbers, say $C \stackrel{\text{def}}{=} \{x_n \mid n \in \mathbb{N}\}$. C is an *anti-chain* if for every $x, y \in C$ then $x \leq y$ iff $x \geq y$. A subset D of X is called *directed* if every finite subset of D has an upper bound in D. Note that we regard the empty set as finite; thus any directed subset is non-empty by definition. We say the poset X is *directed* if any finite subset of X has an upper bound in X. A subset I of a preorder X is *inductive* if given a directed subset $D \subseteq X$ for which $D \subseteq I$ then $\bigvee_X D \in I$. We shall say that a preorder X is a *chain* or *anti-chain* if the underlying set X is such. Given a subset A of a preorder X, then the *up-set* of A is defined to be $A{\uparrow} \stackrel{\text{def}}{=} \{x \in X \mid x \geq A\}$ and the *down-set* is $A{\downarrow} \stackrel{\text{def}}{=} \{x \in X \mid x \leq A\}$. So the up-set of A is the set of all upper bounds of A, and the down-set of A is the set of all lower bounds of A. We shall write $x{\downarrow}$ for $\{x\}{\downarrow}$ and $x{\uparrow}$ for $\{x\}{\uparrow}$, where $x \in X$.

REMARK 1.2.10   This example shows why we take care with definitions involving subsets of preorders and posets. Let $X \stackrel{\text{def}}{=} \{1, 2, \ldots, n, n{+}1, \ldots, \infty, \top\}$ be the poset with partial order "generated" by

$$1 \leq 2 \leq 3 \leq 4 \leq 5 \ldots \leq \infty \leq \top.$$

Let $I \stackrel{\text{def}}{=} X \setminus \{\infty\}$ and let $D \stackrel{\text{def}}{=} X \setminus \{\infty, \top\}$, and refer to Figure 1.3. If we preorder I with the restriction order from X (so that I is a copy of the topped

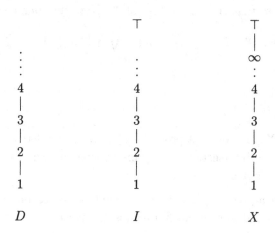

Figure 1.3: A Subset of a Poset which is not Inductive.

vertical natural numbers) then $\bigvee_I D$ exists in the preorder I and is $\top$ with respect to this order; *but I is not an inductive subset of* X because $\bigvee_X D = \infty$ which is not an element of I. It is sometimes tempting for beginners to glance at a *subset* such as I and think it must be inductive with the restriction order. See also Example 1.3.3.

EXERCISE 1.2.11   Let C and C' be chains. Show that the set of pairs (c, c'), where $c \in C$ and $c' \in C'$, is also a chain when ordered lexicographically. Show that the set of pairs with the pointwise order is a chain just in case at most one of C or C' has more than one element.

DISCUSSION 1.2.12   The existence of meets and joins for certain kinds of subsets of preordered sets is known as completeness and cocompleteness respectively. If P is a property of a subset A of the preorder X, and meets exist for all such subsets A, then we say that X is *P-complete*; dually X is *P-cocomplete* if joins exist for subsets A with property P. For example, suppose that X has binary meets and a top element. Then by induction it is easy to see that X has meets of all finite subsets, and we say that X is *finitely* complete. If X has joins of all directed subsets then it is said to be *directed* cocomplete, and if X has joins of ω-chains it is said to be ω-cocomplete. If X has meets or joins of *all* subsets then it is said to be *complete* or *cocomplete* respectively. We can give a very useful result which states that a preorder X is complete if and only if it is cocomplete:

LEMMA 1.2.13   A preorder X has all meets just in case it has all joins.

PROOF   Suppose that A is any subset of X. Note that one has

$$\bigwedge A \overset{\text{def}}{=} \bigvee \{x \mid x \in X \text{ and } x \leq A\} \quad \text{and} \quad \bigvee A \overset{\text{def}}{=} \bigwedge \{x \mid x \in X \text{ and } A \leq x\}.$$

$\square$

EXAMPLES 1.2.14

(1) Given a set X, the powerset poset $\mathcal{P}(X)$ is both complete and cocomplete. Meets are given by intersections and joins by unions. The top element is of course X and the bottom element $\varnothing$.

(2) Suppose that a preorder X is finitely complete and cocomplete, that is to say X has meets and joins of all finite subsets. We regard the empty subset as being finite and thus X has top and bottom elements.

DISCUSSION 1.2.15   We now turn our attention to notions of relations between preordered sets, and in particular to functional relations. If we talk of a function between the preordered sets X and Y we shall simply mean that we are given a function between the underlying sets. Such a function is said to be *monotone* if for $x, y \in X$ we have $x \leq y$ implies $f(x) \leq f(y)$; and *antitone* if $x \leq y$ implies $f(y) \leq f(x)$. We often refer to such a monotone function as a *homomorphism of preorders*. Roughly one thinks of a homomorphism as a function which preserves structure; in the case of a preorder, this structure is just the order relation. A monotone function may alternatively be called an *order preserving* function. f is said to *reflect order* if given any $x, y \in X$, $f(x) \leq f(y)$ implies $x \leq y$. The posets X and Y are *isomorphic* if there are monotone functions $f \colon X \to Y$ and $g \colon Y \to X$ for which $gf = id_X$ and $fg = id_Y$. The monotone function g is an *inverse* for f; and likewise f is an inverse for g. We say that f is an *isomorphism* if such an inverse g exists. The set $X \Rightarrow Y$ is defined to have elements the monotone functions with source X and target Y, that is functions $X \to Y$. This set can be regarded as a preorder by defining a relation $f \leq g$ iff given any $x \in X$ we have $f(x) \leq g(x)$, where $f, g \colon X \to Y$. This ordering is often referred to as the *pointwise* order. We have the following proposition:

PROPOSITION 1.2.16   The identity function on any preordered set is monotone, and the composition of two monotone functions is another monotone function. Now let X, Y and Z be preordered sets. The composition function

$$\circ \colon (Y \Rightarrow Z) \times (X \Rightarrow Y) \to (X \Rightarrow Z)$$

sending the pair $(g, f) \in (Y \Rightarrow Z) \times (X \Rightarrow Y)$ to $gf \in X \Rightarrow Z$ is itself a monotone function between preordered sets. Finally, any function $f: X \times Y \to Z$ is monotone iff it is monotone in each variable separately, which is to say that given any $x, x' \in X$ and $y, y' \in Y$, then

$$x \leq x' \text{ implies } f(x, y) \leq f(x', y)$$

and

$$y \leq y' \text{ implies } f(x, y) \leq f(x, y').$$

PROOF   Follows by a routine manipulation of the definitions.   □

EXAMPLES 1.2.17

(1) Let $f: X \to Y$ be a set-theoretic function between sets X and Y. Then there is a monotone function $f^{-1}: \mathcal{P}(Y) \to \mathcal{P}(X)$ where given $B \subseteq Y$ we define $f^{-1}(B) \overset{\text{def}}{=} \{x \in X \mid f(x) \in B\}$.

(2) Take $\mathbb{R}$ to be the set of reals with their usual ordering. Then the function $f: \mathbb{R} \to \mathbb{R}$ defined by $f(x) = x^3$ is monotone.

EXERCISES 1.2.18

(1) Complete the proof of Proposition 1.2.16.

(2) Let X and Y be preorders and $X \times Y$ their cartesian product. Check that there are monotone functions $\pi_X: X \times Y \to X$, $(x, y) \mapsto x$ and $\pi_Y: X \times Y \to Y$, $(x, y) \mapsto y$ where $(x, y) \in X \times Y$. Now verify that given monotone functions $f: Z \to X$ and $g: Z \to Y$ where Z is any given preorder, there is a unique monotone function $m: Z \to X \times Y$ for which $f = \pi_X m$ and $g = \pi_Y m$.

(3) Find a counterexample to the following statement. A monotone function $f: X \to Y$ between posets X and Y which is a bijection is necessarily an isomorphism.

(4) Let X be a poset and define a relation on the set X by saying that $x \prec y$ just in case $x < y$ and there is no $z \in X$ for which $x < z < y$. Now let X be any set and Y be a poset. Let $X \Rightarrow Y$ be the poset of functions $X \to Y$ ordered pointwise. Show that $f \prec g$ (where $f, g \in X \Rightarrow Y$) iff

(a) There is $\hat{x} \in X$ for which $f(\hat{x}) \prec g(\hat{x})$ in Y, and

(b) $f(x) = g(x)$ for each $x \in X \setminus \{\hat{x}\}$.

Now let X be a finite poset, and $X \Rightarrow Y$ the poset of *monotone* functions $X \to Y$. Show that $f \prec g$ iff (a) and (b) remains true, with this new definition of $X \Rightarrow Y$.

1.3   Basic Lattice Theory

DISCUSSION 1.3.1   In this section we shall describe some examples of posets which have additional structure and which feature in concrete examples of categorical structures which model functional type theories. For each kind of poset we shall give its formal definition, some examples, and certain elementary theorems which will give further examples.

A *lattice* is a poset which has finite meets and joins. A *complete lattice* is a poset which has arbitrary meets and joins. A poset X which has finite meets is called a *meet-semilattice*; a *join-semilattice* is defined analogously. We shall want to consider functional relations between such structures; those we consider will usually preserve structure and are known in general as *homomorphisms*. Thus a *homomorphism of lattices* is a function $f\colon X \to Y$ (with X and Y lattices) which preserves finite meets and joins, that is $f(x \wedge y) = f(x) \wedge f(y)$ and $f(x \vee y) = f(x) \vee f(y)$ and also $f(\top) = \top$ and $f(\bot) = \bot$. Note that such a function is automatically monotone. A *homomorphism of complete lattices* is a function $f\colon X \to Y$ (with X and Y complete lattices) which preserves meets and joins (and hence is monotone). A *sublattice* A of a lattice X is a subset $A \subseteq X$ for which given any finite subset $F \subseteq^f A$ we have $\bigvee_X F \in A$ and $\bigwedge_X F \in A$. Note that this definition is tantamount to saying that if A is regarded as a poset by restricting order from X, then $\bigwedge_X F = \bigwedge_A F$ and $\bigvee_X F = \bigvee_A F$. Given a sublattice A of a lattice X, if we regard A as a lattice with the restriction order from X, then the inclusion function $i\colon A \to X$ is a homomorphism of lattices. If A and X are lattices, $A \subseteq X$ as sets, and the inclusion $i\colon A \to X$ is a homomorphism of lattices, then A is a sublattice of X.

REMARK 1.3.2   Because $x \wedge y = x$ and $x \vee y = y$ just in case $x \leq y$ in a poset X, one only needs to check the existence of binary meets and joins of non-comparable pairs of elements of X to see that X is a lattice (as well as checking that X has top and bottom elements). Note also that a complete lattice has top and bottom elements (being the join and meet of the empty subset).

REMARK 1.3.3   Note that if $A \subseteq X$ and X is a lattice, then it is possible for A to be a lattice with respect to the restriction ordering from X without being a sublattice. An example is given by the Hasse diagram of a lattice in Figure 1.4, where the black discs indicate a subset which is a lattice under the restriction order, but not a sublattice.

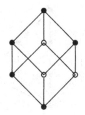

Figure 1.4: A Subset which is not a Sublattice.

EXAMPLES 1.3.4

(1) $\mathbb{N}$, $\mathbb{Z}$, $\mathbb{Q}$, $\mathbb{R}$ are lattices with their usual order, where binary meets and joins are given by taking minima and maxima; for example in $\mathbb{N}$, $3 \wedge 5 = \min\{3, 5\} = 3$. If we adjoin a top and bottom to the set $\mathbb{R}$ to obtain $\mathbb{R}^* \stackrel{\text{def}}{=} (\mathbb{R} \cup \{\infty\} \cup \{-\infty\}, \leq)$ where for every $r \in \mathbb{R}$ we have $-\infty \leq r \leq \infty$, then $\mathbb{R}^*$ is a complete lattice due to the completeness axiom for R. Here, of course, ∞ and $-\infty$ are the top and bottom elements of $\mathbb{R}$ respectively. Similarly any closed interval $[r_1, r_2] \subseteq \mathbb{R}$ is a complete lattice when its order is inherited from $\mathbb{R}$.

(2) The power set $\mathcal{P}(X)$ of a set X is a complete lattice with the inclusion order, with meets and joins given by intersection and union. The top element is X and the bottom element is $\varnothing$.

(3) The down sets $\{A\!\!\downarrow \mid A \subseteq X\}$ of a poset X form a complete lattice via intersection and union.

(4) The topped vertical natural numbers form a lattice.

(5) The poset $(\mathbb{N}, |)$ (where we put $m \mid n$ iff there is some $k \in \mathbb{N}$ for which $n = km$ and km means multiplication of k and m) is a lattice in which the meet of m and n is the least common multiple $\text{lcm}\{m, n\}$ and the join is given by greatest common divisor $\gcd\{m, n\}$. In fact $(\mathbb{N}, |)$ is a complete lattice: see page 18.

(6) Let G be a group. Then $(Sub(G), \subseteq)$, the poset of subgroups of G ordered by inclusion, is a lattice in which, given subgroups H and K of G, we have $H \wedge K = H \cap K$ and $H \vee K = \langle H \cup K \rangle$, where the latter is the subgroup generated by the union of the underlying sets of H and K. Also the poset of normal subgroups $(NSub(G), \subseteq)$ is a lattice where in this case join is given by $H \vee K = HK$, where $HK = \{hk \mid h \in H, k \in K\}$ is well known to be a

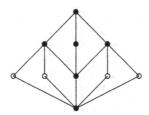

Figure 1.5: Subgroups of the Dihedral Group of Order 8.

normal subgroup of G. For example, the Hasse diagram in Figure 1.5 shows
the lattice of subgroups of the dihedral group of order 8, in which we have
used black discs to indicate the normal subgroups.

(7) If X and Y are (complete) lattices, their binary *cartesian product* is the
set $X \times Y$ of pairs of elements, ordered pointwise. Then $X \times Y$ is a (complete)
lattice with meets and joins calculated pointwise. In a similar way we can
consider the cartesian product of a finite number (say n) of lattices $X_1 \times \ldots \times X_n$.

(8) Let S be any set and X a poset. Then the set of functions $S \Rightarrow X$ with
source S and target (the underlying set of) X is a (complete) lattice whenever
X is a (complete) lattice, with $S \Rightarrow X$ ordered pointwise. It is easy to see that
meets and joins are calculated pointwise. For example, if $f, g \in S \Rightarrow X$ then
for any $x \in X$ we have $(f \wedge g)(x) = f(x) \wedge g(x)$.

The next lemma lists some useful elementary facts about lattices.

LEMMA 1.3.5   Any lattice X satisfies the following laws, where x, y and z
are taken to be any elements of X.

(i) $x \wedge x = x = x \vee x$ (idempotency).

(ii) $x \wedge y = y \wedge x$ and $x \vee y = y \vee x$ (commutativity).

(iii) $x \wedge (y \wedge z) = (x \wedge y) \wedge z$ and $x \vee (y \vee z) = (x \vee y) \vee z$ (associativity).

(iv) $x \wedge (x \vee y) = x \vee (x \wedge y) = x$ (absorption).

(v) $x \leq y$ iff either $x \wedge y = x$ or $x \vee y = y$.

(vi) If $y \leq z$ then $x \wedge y \leq x \wedge z$ and $x \vee y \leq x \vee z$ (monotonicity).

(vii) $(x \wedge y) \vee (x \wedge z) \leq x \wedge (y \vee z)$ and $x \vee (y \wedge z) \leq (x \vee y) \wedge (x \vee z)$.

(viii) $x \leq z$ implies $x \vee (y \wedge z) \leq (x \vee y) \wedge z$.

PROOF   The proof is an easy application of the properties of meets and joins. For example, to prove (viii), note that $y \leq x \vee y$ implies $y \wedge z \leq (x \vee y) \wedge z$; and $x \leq x \vee y$ and the hypothesis imply $x \leq (x \vee y) \wedge z$.   □

DISCUSSION 1.3.6   Let X be a set and let $\mathcal{F}$ be a set of subsets of X. $\mathcal{F}$ is called a *closure system* on X if

• $\bigcap \{A_i \mid i \in I\} \in \mathcal{F}$ for every non-empty set of subsets $\{A_i \mid i \in I\} \subseteq \mathcal{F}$, and

• $X \in \mathcal{F}$.

Then we have

PROPOSITION 1.3.7   A set of subsets $\mathcal{F}$ of a set X which is a closure system can be regarded as a poset via inclusion, and this poset is a complete lattice.

PROOF   From Lemma 1.2.13 it is sufficient to prove that $\mathcal{F}$ has a top element and meets of non-empty subsets. Let $\mathcal{S} \stackrel{\text{def}}{=} \{A_i \mid i \in I\}$ be a non-empty subset of $\mathcal{F}$. As $\bigcap \mathcal{S} \in \mathcal{F}$ and for each $j \in I$ we have $\bigcap \mathcal{S} \subseteq A_j$ it follows that $\bigcap \mathcal{S}$ is a lower bound for $\mathcal{S}$. If B is another lower bound, then clearly $B \subseteq \bigcap \mathcal{S}$. Hence $\mathcal{F}$ is a complete lattice with meets given by intersections, where of course we can deduce from Lemma 1.2.13 that

$$\bigvee \mathcal{S} = \bigcap \{B \in \mathcal{F} \mid A_i \subseteq B \text{ each } i \in I\}.$$

X is the top element of $\mathcal{F}$.   □

DISCUSSION 1.3.8   Let X be a set and $A \subseteq X$ a subset. A function

$$C \colon \mathcal{P}(X) \to \mathcal{P}(X), \qquad A \mapsto \overline{A},$$

is called a *closure operator* on X if for all $A, B \subseteq X$,

• $A \subseteq \overline{A}$,

• $A \subseteq B$ implies $\overline{A} \subseteq \overline{B}$, and

• $\overline{\overline{A}} = \overline{A}$.

A subset A of X is called *closed* if $\overline{A} = A$.

PROPOSITION 1.3.9   Let C be a closure operator on a poset X. Then the set

$$\mathcal{F}_C \stackrel{\text{def}}{=} \{A \subseteq X \mid \overline{A} = A\}$$

of closed subsets of X is a closure system and hence is a complete lattice, where given any (non-empty) subset $\{A_i \mid i \in I\} \subseteq \mathcal{F}_C$ we have

$$\bigwedge \{A_i \mid i \in I\} \;=\; \bigcap \{A_i \mid i \in I\}, \text{ and}$$

$$\bigvee \{A_i \mid i \in I\} \;=\; \overline{\bigcup \{A_i \mid i \in I\}}.$$

Conversely, if $\mathcal{F}$ is a closure system on X and $A \subseteq X$, then

$$\overline{A} \stackrel{\text{def}}{=} \bigcap \{B \in \mathcal{F} \mid A \subseteq B\}$$

defines a closure operator $C_{\mathcal{F}}$ on the set X. Moreover, these assignments are mutually inverse, that is to say $\mathcal{F} = \mathcal{F}_{C_{\mathcal{F}}}$ and $C = C_{\mathcal{F}_C}$.

PROOF   Let us check that if C is a closure operator on X, then $\mathcal{F}_C$ is a closure system. Given a non-empty subset $\mathcal{S} \stackrel{\text{def}}{=} \{A_i \mid i \in I\} \subseteq \mathcal{F}_C$, we have $\bigcap \mathcal{S} \subseteq A_i$ for every $i \in I$ and thus

$$\overline{\bigcap \mathcal{S}} \subseteq \bigcap \{\overline{A_i} \mid i \in I\} = \bigcap \{A_i \mid i \in I\} = \bigcap \mathcal{S}$$

which is to say $\bigcap \mathcal{S} \in \mathcal{F}_C$. It is clear that $X \in \mathcal{F}_C$. Thus from Proposition 1.3.7 $\mathcal{F}_C$ is a complete lattice.

Next we check the specified formulae for meets and joins. That meets exist as specified is trivial. We check the existence of joins. Given $\mathcal{S} \stackrel{\text{def}}{=} \{A_i \mid i \in I\} \subseteq \mathcal{F}_C$, certainly $\overline{\bigcup \mathcal{S}} \in \mathcal{F}_C$, and this is clearly an upper bound for $\mathcal{S}$. If $B \in \mathcal{F}_C$ is an upper bound for $\mathcal{S}$, then $\overline{\bigcup \mathcal{S}} \subseteq \overline{B} = B$, showing $\overline{\bigcup \mathcal{S}}$ is least. Hence $\overline{\bigcup \mathcal{S}}$ is the join of $\mathcal{S}$, as asserted.

The converse, and that the assignments are mutually inverse, is a simple task in set theory.   □

EXERCISE 1.3.10   Fill in the details of the proof of Proposition 1.3.9.

EXAMPLES 1.3.11

(1) The families of (the underlying sets of) subgroups and normal subgroups, $Sub(G)$ and $NSub(G)$, of a group G are closure systems on (the underlying set of) G.

(2) The set $\{ \sim \mid \sim \, \subseteq X \times X \}$ of equivalence relations on a set X is a closure system. It is easy to see that an intersection of equivalence relations is another equivalence relation.

(3) The linear and convex subspaces of a real vector space are each closure systems on the vector space. (Strictly we should take underlying sets to match the definition of closure system).

(4) Let X be a poset and $\mathcal{I}(X)$ the set of inductive subsets of X; then $\mathcal{I}(X)$ is a closure system. The closure operator $C_{\mathcal{I}(X)} \colon \mathcal{P}(X) \to \mathcal{P}(X)$ takes any subset A of (the underlying set of) X to the smallest inductive subset of X which contains A.

(5) The subrings of a ring R and also the set of ideals of R form closure systems.

(6) Let X be a topological space. The closed subsets of X are a closure system on (the underlying set of) X. Of course there is a closure operator on X taking a subset of X to its topological closure. By Proposition 1.3.9, such a closure system is a complete lattice with joins given by closure of unions.

DISCUSSION 1.3.12   Let X be a poset. If C is a finite chain in X we say that C has *length* n if $|C| = n + 1$. If every chain in X is of finite length, then X has *no infinite chains*. X satisfies the *ascending chain condition* (ACC) if given any sequence of elements of the form $(x_n \mid n \in \mathbb{N})$ in X for which $x_n \leq x_{n+1}$, then there is some $n_0 \in \mathbb{N}$ for which $x_{n_0} = x_{n_0+1} = \ldots$ The dual statement is the *descending chain condition* (DCC). We shall now give a few results which show how completeness can be characterised in terms of (ACC) and (DCC). The astute reader who knows some formal set theory will see that we are going to gloss over the axiom of choice and I hope this will not offend too many people.

LEMMA 1.3.13   A poset X satisfies (ACC) iff every non-empty subset A of X has a maximal element.

PROOF

($\Rightarrow$) Let $A \subseteq X$ be non-empty and suppose for a contradiction that A has no maximal element. We can argue informally as follows. Let $x_1 \in A$. By hypothesis, there is $x_2 \in A$ such that $x_1 < x_2$. But as x_2 is also not maximal in A we can find $x_3 \in A$ for which $x_1 < x_2 < x_3$. Inductively (strictly, invoking the axiom of choice) this gives us an infinite chain $x_1 < x_2 < x_3 \ldots$ in A which contradicts (ACC).

($\Leftarrow$) If there is a chain that does not satisfy (ACC), then it certainly has no maximal element.   □

THEOREM 1.3.14   A poset X has no infinite chains iff it satisfies both (ACC) and (DCC).

PROOF

($\Rightarrow$) This way is clear.

($\Leftarrow$) Conversely suppose that X satisfies (ACC) and (DCC) and has an infinite chain, say C. Then C is non-empty, with maximal element $x_1 \in C$ using Lemma 1.3.13. As C is a chain it is easy to see that x_1 is a greatest element for C. Now let $x_2 \in C \setminus \{x_1\}$ be greatest (we can do this for $C \setminus \{x_1\}$ is a non-empty chain; thus Lemma 1.3.13 applies) and in general let x_{n+1} be greatest in $C_{n+1} \stackrel{\text{def}}{=} C \setminus \{x_1, \ldots, x_n\}$. Then we can deduce (strictly, invoking the axiom of choice) that $(x_n \mid n \in \mathbb{N})$ is an infinite (descending) sequence of elements in X, which contradicts the (DCC). □

THEOREM 1.3.15   Let X be a lattice. Then

(i) If X satisfies (ACC), then for every non-empty subset A of X, there is a finite subset $F \subseteq X$ for which $\bigvee A = \bigvee F$.

(ii) If X satisfies (ACC) then it is complete. Dually X is complete if it satisfies (DCC).

(iii) If X has no infinite chains then it is complete.

PROOF

(i) Consider $B \stackrel{\text{def}}{=} \{\bigvee F \mid F \subseteq A, F \text{ is finite}\}$ where A is a given non-empty subset of X; note that B is well defined and non-empty. So by Lemma 1.3.13 there is a maximal element m of B, say $m = \bigvee F_0$. Claim $m = \bigvee A$. To see this, note that if $a \in A$, then $\bigvee F_0 \leq \bigvee(F_0 \cup \{a\})$ implying that $m = \bigvee(F_0 \cup \{a\})$ by maximality and hence $a \leq m$. Suppose now $A \leq x$; then $m = \bigvee F_0 \leq \bigvee A \leq x$, completing the proof.

(ii) Note that (i) implies that (the lattice) X has joins of all non-empty subsets and is therefore complete. Dually, we would have that X has meets of all non-empty subsets and is therefore complete.

(iii) Immediate from Theorem 1.3.14.

□

EXAMPLE 1.3.16   The lattice $(\mathbb{N}, |)$ is complete. It has a top element $0 \in \mathbb{N}$. It also satisfies (DCC). For if $(n_i \mid i \in \mathbb{N})$ is an infinite descending sequence of elements in $(\mathbb{N}, |)$ then we must have an infinite descending chain in $(\mathbb{N}, \leq)$ where $\leq$ is the vertical ordering. Contradiction.

DISCUSSION 1.3.17   We end this section by giving some simple results concerning the distributive and modular lattices. These lattices have pleasant properties which aid the manipulation of meets and joins. Let X be a lattice. Then X is *distributive* if it satisfies $x \wedge (y \vee z) = (x \wedge y) \vee (x \wedge z)$ for all x, y, z in X. X is called *modular* if $x \leq z$ implies $x \vee (y \wedge z) = (x \vee y) \wedge z$.

REMARK 1.3.18   From Lemma 1.3.5, parts (vii) and (viii), we see that in order to check that a lattice is distributive or modular it is only necessary to check that an inequality holds.

LEMMA 1.3.19   For any lattice X the following conditions are equivalent:

(i) For every $x, y, z \in X$ we have $x \wedge (y \vee z) = (x \wedge y) \vee (x \wedge z)$,

(ii) For every $x, y, z \in X$ we have $x \vee (y \wedge z) = (x \vee y) \wedge (x \vee z)$,

(iii) For every $x, y, z \in X$ we have $x \wedge (y \vee z) \leq (x \wedge y) \vee z$. ·

PROOF   Throughout we use the results of Lemma 1.3.5. If (i) holds then

$$x \wedge (y \vee z) = (x \wedge y) \vee (x \wedge z) \leq (x \wedge y) \vee z$$

which is (iii). If (iii) holds, then we have

$$x \wedge (y \vee z) \leq x \wedge [(x \wedge y) \vee z] \leq (x \wedge z) \vee (x \wedge y), \qquad (*)$$

namely one half of (i). To see $(*)$, note that by using monotonicity of $x \wedge (-)$ on the hypothesis (iii) we obtain the first inequality. We can also use (iii) to deduce that

For every $x, y, z \in X$ we have $x \wedge (y \vee z) \leq (x \wedge z) \vee y$.

and then use this deduction to obtain the second inequality of $(*)$. The other half of (i) holds via Lemma 1.3.5. That (ii) iff (iii) is a similar argument.   □

EXAMPLES 1.3.20

(1) The poset $\mathcal{P}(X)$ is distributive. For if A, B and C are subsets of X, it follows from simple naive set theory that $A \cap (B \cup C) = (A \cap B) \cup (A \cap C)$.

(2) Any poset which is a chain is distributive.

(3) The complete lattice $(\mathbb{N}, |)$ is distributive.

(4) For any group G, the set of normal subgroups with the inclusion order $NSub(G)$ is modular. For let H, K, N be normal subgroups of G. By Lemma 1.3.5, it is enough to prove that if $N \subseteq H$ then $H \wedge (K \vee N) \subseteq (H \wedge K) \vee N$. Suppose that $g \in H \wedge (K \vee N)$ and thus $g \in H$ and $g = kn$ for $k \in K$ and $n \in N$. Note $k = gn^{-1} \in H$ and so we are done.

(5) The lattice of subspaces of a vector space is also modular; the proof of this fact is similar to that for the lattice of normal subgroups.

(6) If X is a distributive lattice then $S \Rightarrow X$, the functions from S to X with the pointwise order, is a distributive lattice.

1.4   Boolean and Heyting Lattices

DISCUSSION 1.4.1   In this section we introduce the notions of Boolean and Heyting lattices. A Boolean lattice is, roughly, a distributive lattice for which there is an operation on elements which mimics the notion of complementation in a powerset (recall that if $A \in \mathcal{P}(X)$ then the complement of A in $\mathcal{P}(X)$ is the set difference $X \setminus A$ of A from X). Readers may have met the notion of Boolean lattice from undergraduate or even school circuit theory, but this will not concern us here. A Heyting lattice can be viewed as a primitive model of functional type theory, as we shall see in Chapter 4. In this section we simply concentrate on the basic theory of Boolean and Heyting lattices.

Take a lattice X and let $x \in X$. An element $a \in X$ satisfying $a \wedge x = \bot$ and $a \vee x = \top$ is called a *complement* of x. The next proposition shows that, in a distributive lattice, such complements are unique.

PROPOSITION 1.4.2   Let X be a distributive lattice and $x, y, z \in X$. Then there is at most one $a \in X$ for which $x \wedge a = y$ and $x \vee a = z$.

PROOF   Suppose that $a' \in X$ also satisfies the hypotheses. We have

$$
\begin{aligned}
a &= a \wedge (a \vee x) \\
  &= a \wedge z \\
  &= a \wedge (x \vee a') \\
  &= (a \wedge x) \vee (a \wedge a') \\
  &= y \vee (a \wedge a').
\end{aligned}
$$

But $y \leq a$ and $y \leq a'$ and so $a = a \wedge a'$. Similarly $a' = a \wedge a'$ and so $a = a'$. $\square$

DISCUSSION 1.4.3   A *Boolean lattice* X is a distributive lattice, which also has complements of all elements. We write $\neg x$ for the complement of x where $x \in X$. Note that it makes sense to talk of *the* complement of x, because Proposition 1.4.2 implies that complements are unique if they exist. The next lemma states some laws which are true of all Boolean lattices, and are analogues of the well known De Morgan rules which hold for powersets.

LEMMA 1.4.4   In a Boolean lattice X, we have for all $x, y \in X$,

(i) $\neg\neg x = x$,

(ii) $\neg(x \wedge y) = \neg x \vee \neg y$, and

(iii) $\neg(x \vee y) = \neg x \wedge \neg y$.

PROOF   Note that both $\neg\neg x$ and x are complements of the element $\neg x$ in X. Then use Proposition 1.4.2 to deduce that (i) holds. There is of course a well defined function $\neg \colon X \to X$ (and (i) shows that it is a bijection). In fact this function is antitone. To prove this, one shows that if $x \leq y$ in X then $\neg y = \neg y \wedge \neg x$, by showing that $\neg y \wedge \neg x$ is a complement of y and thus equals $\neg y$. But $\neg y = \neg y \wedge \neg x$ implies $\neg y \leq \neg x$, as required. Then (ii) and (iii) follow from the fact that $\neg$ is an antitone bijective endofunction on X.   □

EXAMPLES 1.4.5

(1) Let X be a set and define, for $A \subseteq X$, $\neg A \stackrel{\text{def}}{=} X \setminus A$. Then $\mathcal{P}(X)$ is a Boolean lattice. (Recall that $X \setminus A$ is the set difference of A from X).

(2) The collection of finite and cofinite subsets of a set X,

$$\{A \subseteq X \mid A \text{ is finite or } X \setminus A \text{ is finite}\}$$

is a Boolean lattice in which $\neg A \stackrel{\text{def}}{=} X \setminus A$.

(3) The subsets of a topological space X which are both open and closed is a Boolean lattice in which $\neg A \stackrel{\text{def}}{=} X \setminus A$, where A is a closed and open subset of X.

(4) Let us write Ω for the poset with a two point underlying set $\{\bot, \top\}$ for which $\bot \leq \top$. We call this the *Sierpinski* poset. Then the cartesian product of a finite number of copies of Ω, $\Omega \times \ldots \times \Omega$, is a Boolean lattice.

(5) The set of idempotents of any commutative ring R is a Boolean lattice. An *idempotent* of R is an element r for which $r^2 = r$. We order the idempotents by setting $r \leq s$ iff $rs = r$. Then the Boolean lattice operations are given by $r \wedge s \stackrel{\text{def}}{=} rs$, $r \vee s \stackrel{\text{def}}{=} r + s - rs$ and $\neg r \stackrel{\text{def}}{=} 1 - r$. We leave the verification to the reader.

DISCUSSION 1.4.6   A *Heyting lattice* X is a lattice in which for each pair of elements $y, z \in X$ there is an element $y \Rightarrow z \in X$ such that

$$x \le y \Rightarrow z \qquad \text{iff} \qquad x \wedge y \le z.$$

We call $y \Rightarrow z$ the *Heyting implication* of y and z.

LEMMA 1.4.7   In a Heyting lattice X, the Heyting implication of y and z is unique.

PROOF   Suppose that a and a' are two candidates for the element $y \Rightarrow z \in X$. Then $a \le a$ implies $a \wedge y \le z$ implies $a \le a'$; the converse is similar.   □

PROPOSITION 1.4.8   Every Boolean lattice is a Heyting lattice.

PROOF   Let X be a Boolean lattice, $x, y \in X$, and define $x \Rightarrow y \overset{\text{def}}{=} \neg x \vee y$. Then $z \le \neg x \vee y$ implies

$$
\begin{aligned}
z \wedge x &\le (\neg x \vee y) \wedge x \\
&= (\neg x \wedge x) \vee (y \wedge x) \\
&= \bot \vee (y \wedge x) \\
&\le y,
\end{aligned}
$$

and $z \wedge x \le y$ implies $\neg x \vee y \ge \neg x \vee (z \wedge x) \ge (\neg x \vee z) \wedge (\neg x \vee x) \ge z$.   □

PROPOSITION 1.4.9

(i) A Heyting lattice X is distributive.

(ii) Any finite distributive lattice X is a Heyting lattice.

(iii) A Heyting lattice X is a Boolean lattice iff for all $x \in X$, $\neg\neg x = x$, where we define $\neg x \overset{\text{def}}{=} x \Rightarrow \bot$.

PROOF

(i) Recall Lemma 1.3.5 which tells us that $(x \wedge y) \vee (x \wedge z) \le x \wedge (y \vee z)$. Then note that

$$x \Rightarrow ((x \wedge y) \vee (x \wedge z)) \ge (x \Rightarrow (x \wedge y)) \vee (x \Rightarrow (x \wedge z)) \ge y \vee z$$

which amounts to $(x \wedge y) \vee (x \wedge z) \ge x \wedge (y \vee z)$, and so X is distributive.

(ii) Take x and y and define $x \Rightarrow y \overset{\text{def}}{=} \bigvee \{u \in X \mid u \wedge x \leq y\}$. Then $z \wedge x \leq y$ implies $z \leq x \Rightarrow y$ is immediate. If $z \leq x \Rightarrow y$ then

$$z \wedge x \leq \bigvee \{u \wedge x \mid u \wedge x \leq y\} \leq y$$

follows from distributivity (and the finiteness of X).

(iii) ($\Rightarrow$) This way is part (i) of Lemma 1.4.4.

($\Leftarrow$) Conversely, we have just seen that X is distributive, and

$$x \wedge \neg x = x \wedge (x \Rightarrow \perp) = \perp$$

is trivial. There is a well defined function $\neg \colon X \to X$ given by $x \mapsto \neg x$ and it is easy to check that it is antitone and bijective. Thus it follows that De Morgan's rules (ii) and (iii) of Proposition 1.4.4 hold (but here in the Heyting lattice X). Hence $\top = \neg(x \wedge \neg x) = \neg x \vee x$ as required.

$\square$

EXAMPLES 1.4.10

(1) Let X be a chain with top and bottom elements; so X is a lattice in which meet and join are given by greatest and least elements. Then X is Heyting with

$$x \Rightarrow y \;=\; \begin{cases} \top & \text{if } x \leq y \\ y & \text{otherwise} \end{cases}$$

where $x, y \in X$. Note that X is not a Boolean lattice, for $\neg\neg x = \top$ for all $x \in X$: see Proposition 1.4.9.

(2) Take X an infinite set and let $\mathcal{F}$ be the set of finite subsets of X along with X itself. Then $\mathcal{F}$ is a sublattice of $\mathcal{P}(X)$ and so is distributive. But $\mathcal{F}$ is not Heyting. For if $F \subseteq X$ is a finite subset then the set $\{Y \mid Y \cap F = \varnothing\}$ has no largest member and so $F \Rightarrow \varnothing$ cannot exist.

EXERCISES 1.4.11

(1) Let X be any poset with finite meets. Prove that X is a Boolean lattice iff for all $x \in X$, there is $\bar{x} \in X$ such that for all $y \in X$ we have

$$x \leq y \qquad \text{iff} \qquad x \wedge \bar{y} = b$$

for some fixed $b \in X$.

(2) Let X be a Heyting lattice, and for each $x \in X$ make the definition $\neg x \overset{\text{def}}{=} x \Rightarrow \perp$. Prove that for any $x, y \in X$, $\neg(x \vee y) = \neg x \wedge \neg y$ and $\neg\neg(x \wedge y) = \neg\neg x \wedge \neg\neg y$.

1.5   Elementary Domain Theory

DISCUSSION 1.5.1   The concept of a domain pervades the theory of semantics of programming languages, yet there is unfortunately no (fixed) formal
definition of a domain. A *domain* in computer science has come to mean a
poset which has some kind of cocompleteness property, that is, joins of various
kinds are required to exist. For example, ωcpos and dcpos may be referred
to as domains. Domains arose from attempts to give semantics to recursively
defined procedures, and we now give a summary of (some of) the key ideas.

Suppose that we have a recursive procedure P which takes elements of a
datatype D and returns elements of a datatype D'. Now let us model this
procedure P as a function $[P]$, from a set $[D]$ which models D to a set $[D']$
which models D'. Suppose that we have a sequence of data items $\{d_i \mid i \in \mathbb{N}\}$
each of which yields more information about another data item d—we can
think of the approximations as successive recursions of the procedure P. We
might then model this by taking $[D]$ to be a poset, in which the poset order is
a representation of the notion of data approximation. In this case, if we have a
chain, say $\{[d_i] \mid i \in I\}$ in $[D]$, modelling the approximations to the data item
d, then the join of the chain should exist and be thought of as modelling the
total information given by the approximations. In this case, $[D]$ would then
be ω-cocomplete. If we perform more iterations of P, we might hope to get a
more accurate output. In our model, this would be tantamount to asking the
function $[P]$ to be monotone. Further, if the chain $\{[d_i] \mid i \in \mathbb{N}\}$ is thought of
as modelling the series of approximations (datatypes) $\{d_i \mid i \in \mathbb{N}\}$ to the data
item d modelled by $\bigvee\{[d_i] \mid i \in \mathbb{N}\}$, we could ask that the data item given by
the output approximations $\{P(d_i) \mid i \in \mathbb{N}\}$ (resulting from applying P to the
input approximations) is the same as the data item $P(d)$ (given by applying
P to the data item given by all of the input approximations). In our model,
this would mean that $[P]$ should preserve joins of ω-chains.

$$\bigvee\{[P]([d_i]) \mid i \in \mathbb{N}\} = [P](\bigvee\{[d_i] \mid i \in \mathbb{N}\}).$$

The use of domain theory in computer science arose from these very tentative
and tenuous thoughts; but it has proved to be a very powerful tool. Let us
now move on to some more theory.

We shall refer to directed cocomplete partial orders as *dcpos* and to ω-
chain cocomplete partial orders as ω*cpos*. A *homomorphism of dcpos* X and
Y, $f: X \to Y$, is a function which preserves the structure of X, which is to say
f is monotone and if $D \subseteq X$ is directed, then $f(\bigvee D) = \bigvee f(D)$ where the join
on the right hand side exists for f is monotone. A *homomorphism of ωcpos* is

defined analogously. A homomorphism of dcpos (ωcpos) will also be referred to as a *continuous* (ω-*continuous*) function between dcpos (ωcpos). If X and Y both have least elements then any function $f: X \to Y$ is said to be *strict* if $f(\bot) = \bot$. If X is a dcpo then the set A is a *sub-dcpo* of X if $A \subseteq X$, and given any subset $D \subseteq A$ where D is directed in X, then $\bigvee_X D \in A$. Thus if A is a sub-dcpo of X and A is given the restriction order from X, then the inclusion $i: A \to X$ is a continuous function. Note also that if A and X are dcpos, $A \subseteq X$, and $i: A \to X$ is continuous, then the set A is a sub-dcpo of X.

REMARK 1.5.2　Let X be a poset and D a *directed* subset of X. If the join of D in X exists we shall write $\bigsqcup_X D$ for it, rather than $\bigvee_X D$. This notation will be useful in later chapters when directed sets will play a crucial role, and it will be convenient to distinguish directed joins form other kinds of join. Note that part of the force of the judgement $\bigsqcup_X D$ is that the set D is directed.

EXAMPLES 1.5.3

(1) Any complete lattice is certainly a dcpo and an ωcpo.

(2) Any anti-chain is a dcpo and any poset satisfying (ACC) is a dcpo.

(3) The poset of subgroups $Sub(G)$ of any group G is a dcpo. For let $\mathcal{H} \subseteq Sub(G)$ be a directed subset of subgroups of G, say $\mathcal{H} \stackrel{\text{def}}{=} \{H_i \mid i \in I\}$. If $\bigcup \mathcal{H}$ is a subgroup of G then it is clearly the join of $\mathcal{H}$. But if $g, h \in \bigcup \mathcal{H}$ then $g \in H_i$ and $h \in H_j$ for some $i, j \in I$, implying that $gh^{-1} \in H_k$ for some $k \in I$ because $\mathcal{H}$ is directed. So of course $gh^{-1} \in \bigcup \mathcal{H}$, and so $\bigcup \mathcal{H}$ is indeed in $Sub(G)$.

(4) Given a poset X and a closure operator C on X, the set of closed subsets of X with the inclusion order is a dcpo.

EXERCISE 1.5.4　Let I be a directed poset, X a poset, and $f: I \times I \to X$, $(i, j) \mapsto x_{(i,j)}$ a monotone function. Put

$$x = \bigvee\{\bigvee\{x_{(i,j)} \mid j \in I\} \mid i \in I\}$$
$$x' = \bigvee\{\bigvee\{x_{(i,j)} \mid i \in I\} \mid j \in I\}$$
$$x'' = \bigvee\{x_{(i,i)} \mid (i, i) \in I \times I\}$$

Show that if the join x (x') exists, then so do the joins x' and x'' (x and x''), and they are all equal.

PROPOSITION 1.5.5　Let X and Y be dcpos (ωcpos). Then the set $X \Rightarrow Y$ of continuous functions $X \to Y$ with the pointwise order (which is to say that $f \leq g$ iff for every $x \in X$ we have $f(x) \leq g(x)$ in Y) is a dcpo (ωcpo).

PROOF   Let $\{f_i \mid i \in I\}$ be a directed subset of $X \Rightarrow Y$. Define a function $f: X \to Y$ by setting $f(x) \stackrel{\text{def}}{=} \bigsqcup\{f_i(x) \mid i \in I\}$, well defined because Y is a dcpo. Certainly the function f is the required join provided that it is continuous; but f is continuous because each f_i is. More precisely, f is continuous if

$$\bigsqcup\{\bigsqcup\{f_i(d) \mid d \in D\} \mid i \in I\} = \bigsqcup\{\bigsqcup\{f_i(d) \mid i \in I\} \mid d \in D\}$$

for all directed subsets D of X. This equality follows from Exercise 1.5.4.   □

EXERCISES 1.5.6

(1) Suppose that D is an ωcpo with a bottom element, and that $f: D \to D$ is a continuous function. A *fixpoint* of f is an element $x \in D$ for which $x = f(x)$. A *least* fixpoint of f is such an x for which given any other fixpoint d of f, $x \leq d$. Prove that f always has a least fixpoint and find an explicit definition of it; recognise that any such least fixpoint is unique. *Hint: think about the action of f on the bottom element $\bot$ of D.*

(2) Let D be an ωcpo with least element. From the previous exercise there is a well defined function $Y: (D \Rightarrow D) \to D$ for which given $f \in D \Rightarrow D$, $Y(f)$ is the (unique) least fixpoint of f. Using Proposition 1.5.5 we see that $D \Rightarrow D$ is an ωcpo. Prove that the function Y is continuous.

DISCUSSION 1.5.7   It is time to give some definitions which will be crucial to the formulation of domain-theoretic models of polymorphism. Suppose that X is a poset. An element $e \in X$ is said to be *compact* if whenever $D \subseteq X$ is a directed subset and the join $\bigsqcup D$ exists with $e \leq \bigsqcup D$, then there is some $d \in D$ for which $e \leq d$. We shall write X° for the set of compact elements of X. A subset B of a poset X is a *basis* of compact elements if $B \subseteq X^\circ$ and every compact element of X is the join of a finite number of elements of B. (Compare this with the notion of a basis of a topological space). The poset X is said to be *algebraic* if for each $x \in X$, the set $\{e \in X^\circ \mid e \leq x\}$ is directed in X, its join exists, and moreover $x = \bigsqcup\{e \in X^\circ \mid e \leq x\}$. The poset X is *bounded cocomplete* if given $S \subseteq X$ and $x \in X$ such that $S \leq x$ (that is, S has an upper bound) then the join of S in X exists. It will be useful to have the following alternative characterisation of bounded cocompleteness, which should help to make the definition a little more tractable.

PROPOSITION 1.5.8   A poset X is bounded cocomplete just in case it has all non-empty meets.

PROOF

($\Rightarrow$) Take $S \subseteq X$ non-empty. Then

$$\bigwedge S = \bigvee \{x \in X \mid x \leq S\}$$

by Lemma 1.2.13, which exists because the set $\{x \in X \mid x \leq S\}$ has upper bound $s \in S$.

($\Leftarrow$) Suppose that $S \subseteq X$ and S has an upper bound. Then

$$\bigvee S = \bigwedge \{x \in X \mid S \leq x\}$$

exists because it is a meet of a non-empty set. $\qquad\square$

EXAMPLES 1.5.9

(1) The topped vertical natural numbers $X \overset{\text{def}}{=} \mathbb{N} \cup \{\infty\}$ has $X^\circ = \mathbb{N}$, and X is certainly algebraic.

(2) For any set X, the compact elements of the poset $\mathcal{P}(X)$ are the subsets of finite cardinality. Also $\mathcal{P}(X)$ is algebraic.

(3) If G is a group, the finitely generated subgroups of G are the compact elements of $Sub(G)$.

(4) If V is any vector space, the finite dimensional subspaces of V are the compact elements of $Sub(V)$, the poset of subspaces of V.

(5) The set of real numbers $\mathbb{R}$ with its usual order does not have any compact elements.

(6) Let X be a poset with finite cardinality. Then every element of X is compact.

DISCUSSION 1.5.10   Let X be a set and $\mathcal{F}$ a set of subsets of X. Then $\mathcal{F}$ is said to be an *algebraic closure system* if

• it is a closure system, and

• given any directed subset $\mathcal{D} \subseteq \mathcal{F}$ (where we regard $\mathcal{F}$ as a poset via inclusion), then $\bigcup \mathcal{D} \in \mathcal{F}$.

A closure operator C on a set X is said to be *algebraic* if for all subsets $A \subseteq X$,

$$\overline{A} = \bigcup \{\overline{B} \mid B \subseteq A, |B| \text{ is finite}\}$$

where $|B|$ is the cardinality of B. This definition will allow us to produce some more examples of algebraic posets.

PROPOSITION 1.5.11   Let C be an algebraic closure operator on a set X and write $\mathcal{F}_C$ for the set of closed subsets of X. Then $\mathcal{F}_C$ is an algebraic complete lattice in which $A \in \mathcal{F}$ is compact iff $A = \overline{Y}$ for some $Y \subseteq X$ with $|Y|$ finite.

PROOF   Appealing to Proposition 1.3.9, we already have $\mathcal{F}_C$ is a complete lattice. We begin by showing that joins of directed subsets of $\mathcal{F}_C$ are given by unions. From Proposition 1.3.9, we know that if $\mathcal{S} \subseteq \mathcal{F}_C$ then $\bigvee \mathcal{S} = \overline{\bigcup \mathcal{S}}$. Suppose that $\mathcal{S} \overset{\text{def}}{=} \{A_i \mid i \in I\}$ is a directed subset of $\mathcal{F}_C$. We show that $\overline{\bigcup \mathcal{S}} = \bigcup \mathcal{S}$. For if

$$x \in \overline{\bigcup \mathcal{S}} = \bigcup \{\overline{B} \mid B \subseteq \bigcup \mathcal{S}, |B| \text{ is finite}\},$$

then $x \in \overline{B} \subseteq A_j \subseteq \bigcup \mathcal{S}$, because for any $B \subseteq \bigcup \mathcal{S}$ we have $|B|$ finite implies $B \subseteq A_j$ for some $j \in I$.

Next we prove the stated characterisation of compact elements. Let $Y \subseteq X$, $|Y|$ be finite and $\overline{Y} \subseteq \bigcup \mathcal{S} = \bigcup \mathcal{S}$. Then $Y \subseteq \bigcup \mathcal{S}$ and so $Y \subseteq A_j$ for some $j \in I$, implying $\overline{Y} \subseteq \overline{A_j} = A_j$ and thus showing that $\overline{Y}$ is compact. Conversely, take $A \in \mathcal{F}_C$ compact. It is immediate from the definition of algebraic closure operator that $A \subseteq \overline{Y}$ with $Y \subseteq A$ and $|Y|$ finite. So $A = \overline{Y}$.

Finally, if we look at the definition of algebraic closure system, it is now clear that to prove $\mathcal{F}_C$ is an algebraic complete lattice, it is sufficient to prove

$$\{E \in \mathcal{F}_C^\circ \mid E \subseteq A\} = \{\overline{B} \mid B \subseteq A, |B| \text{ finite}\}$$

for any given $A \in \mathcal{F}_C$. That these sets are equal, and indeed directed subsets of $\mathcal{F}_C$, follows by a routine argument. $\square$

THEOREM 1.5.12

(i) Let $\mathcal{F}$ be an algebraic closure system on a set X. Then $\mathcal{F}$ is an algebraic complete lattice.

(ii) Let X be an algebraic complete lattice and define $X_x \overset{\text{def}}{=} \{e \in X^\circ \mid e \leq x\}$. Then $\mathcal{F} \overset{\text{def}}{=} \{X_x \mid x \in X\}$ is an algebraic closure system which regarded as a poset is isomorphic to X.

PROOF

(i) From Proposition 1.3.9 we know that $\mathcal{F}$ is a complete lattice, and that $\mathcal{F} = \mathcal{F}_{C_\mathcal{F}}$. So appealing to Proposition 1.5.11, all we need is that $C_\mathcal{F}$ is an algebraic closure operator. This amounts to proving that

$$\bigcap \{L \in \mathcal{F} \mid A \subseteq L\} = \bigcup \{\bigcap \{L \in \mathcal{F} \mid B \subseteq L\} \mid B \subseteq A, |B| \text{ finite}\}$$

for every $A \subseteq X$. Note that the right hand side is well defined, because it is a directed union of elements of $\mathcal{F}$ which certainly belongs to $\mathcal{F}$ for $\mathcal{F}$ is an algebraic closure system; we omit the details.

(ii) It is simple calculation to see that $\mathcal{F}$ is a closure system. Defining a function $f: X \to \mathcal{F}$ by $f(x) \stackrel{\text{def}}{=} X_x$ it is then quite easy to verify that f preserves and reflects order, and is bijective. Hence X and $\mathcal{F}$ are isomorphic.

We shall verify that $\mathcal{F}$ is an *algebraic* closure system; to do this let $\{X_{x(i)} \mid i \in I\}$ be a directed subset of $\mathcal{F}$. Because f reflects order, $D \stackrel{\text{def}}{=} \{x(i) \mid i \in I\}$ is a directed subset of X. Set $\hat{x} \stackrel{\text{def}}{=} \bigsqcup D$. Note that, as D is directed,

$$e \in X_{\hat{x}} \quad \text{iff} \quad e \in X^{\circ} \text{ and } e \leq x(i) \text{ for some } i \in I \ (e \text{ compact in } X)$$

$$\text{iff} \quad e \in X_{x(i)}.$$

These last observations imply $\bigcup\{X_{x(i)} \mid i \in I\} = X_{\hat{x}} \in \mathcal{F}$, as required.

$\square$

DISCUSSION 1.5.13 The remaining results of this chapter are rather technical in nature, and by themselves serve little purpose. However, they will be crucial in Chapters 5 and 6 where they will be used to verify that certain domain-theoretic structures form models of polymorphic type theories. The reader can safely move on to the next chapter at this point, returning to this chapter as required.

LEMMA 1.5.14 Let X and Y be algebraic complete lattices and suppose that monotone functions $l: X \to Y$ and $r: Y \to X$ are such that for all $x \in X$ and $y \in Y$,

$$\frac{l(x) \leq y}{x \leq r(y)}$$

Then r is continuous iff l preserves the compactness of elements of X.

PROOF

($\Rightarrow$) Suppose that r is continuous. Take $e \in X^{\circ}$ and suppose that $l(e) \leq \bigsqcup\{y_i \mid i \in I\}$. It is simple to see that $e \leq rl(e) \leq \bigsqcup\{r(y_i) \mid i \in I\}$ and so $e \leq r(y_{i_0})$ for some $i_0 \in I$, that is $l(e) \leq y_{i_0}$. Thus $l(e)$ is compact.

($\Leftarrow$) Certainly $r(y) = \bigvee\{x \in X \mid l(x) \leq y\}$. In fact slightly more is true, namely

$$r(y) = \bigsqcup\{x \in X^{\circ} \mid x \leq r(y)\} = \bigsqcup\{x \in X^{\circ} \mid l(x) \leq y\}.$$

Take a directed subset $\{y_i \mid i \in I\}$ of Y; in order to verify the continuity of r we need to check that

$$\underbrace{\bigsqcup\{x \in X° \mid l(x) \leq \bigsqcup\{y_i \mid i \in I\}\}}_{A} = \underbrace{\bigsqcup\{\bigsqcup\{x \in X° \mid l(x) \leq y_i\} \mid i \in I\}}_{B}.$$

For any $x \in X°$ and $i \in I$ with $l(x) \leq y_i$ then $l(x) \leq \bigsqcup\{y_j \mid j \in I\}$. Hence

$$\bigsqcup\{x \in X° \mid l(x) \leq y_i\} \leq \bigsqcup\{x \in X° \mid l(x) \leq \bigsqcup\{y_j \mid j \in I\}\} = \bigsqcup A$$

and thus

$$\bigsqcup B = \bigsqcup\{\bigsqcup\{x \in X° \mid l(x) \leq y_i\} \mid i \in I\} \leq \bigsqcup A.$$

Thus to show that $\bigsqcup A = \bigsqcup B$, it is now enough to show that for any element $a \in A$, there is $b \in B$ with $a \leq b$. Take $\hat{x} \in X°$ for which $l(\hat{x}) \leq \bigsqcup\{y_i \mid i \in I\}$. Then by hypothesis $l(\hat{x})$ is compact in Y, and so $l(\hat{x}) \leq y_{i_0}$ for some $i_0 \in I$. Thus we have $\hat{x} \leq \bigsqcup\{x \in X° \mid l(x) \leq y_{i_0}\} \in B$. Thus r is continuous.   □

LEMMA 1.5.15   Let $f: X \to Y$ be a monotone function between complete lattices. f preserves all joins just in case f preserves finite joins and directed joins.

PROOF   A routine manipulation of the definitions.   □

EXERCISE 1.5.16   Work through the details of the proof of Lemma 1.5.15.

DISCUSSION 1.5.17   We shall need the following definition. Suppose that X is a join-semilattice. Then a subset $I \subseteq X$ is an *ideal* if I is closed under finite joins and is down closed. More precisely,

• $\perp_X \in I$,

• $x, y \in I$ implies $x \vee y \in I$, and

• $x' \leq x \in I$ implies $x' \in I$.

We have the following proposition:

PROPOSITION 1.5.18   Suppose that X is a join-semilattice and let us write

$$\overline{X} \stackrel{\text{def}}{=} \{I \subseteq X \mid I \text{ is an ideal}\}.$$

Then the set $\overline{X}$ of ideals of X is an algebraic complete lattice when regarded as a poset via inclusion. If A is an algebraic complete lattice and $f: X \to A$ is a monotone function which preserves finite joins, then the function

$$\hat{f}: \overline{X} \to A \qquad\qquad I \mapsto \bigsqcup_A\{f(x) \mid x \in I\}$$

preserves all joins in $\overline{X}$. Moreover, if Y is also a join-semilattice, and $f\colon X \to Y$ is monotone and preserves finite joins, then there is a function

$$\overline{f}\colon \overline{X} \to \overline{Y} \qquad\qquad I \mapsto \bigcup\{f(x)\!\downarrow \mid x \in I\}$$

which preserves all joins in $\overline{X}$ and preserves the compactness of elements of $\overline{X}$. We shall call $\overline{f}$ the *ideal lifting*.

PROOF   To show that $\overline{X}$ is a complete lattice, we show that $\overline{X}$ has all meets. The bottom element is $\{\bot_X\}$. If $\{I_s \mid s \in S\} \subseteq \overline{X}$ is a nonempty subset of $\overline{X}$, then $\bigcap\{I_s \mid s \in S\} \in \overline{X}$, as we now check. $\bot_X \in I_s$ for each $s \in S$, and if $x, y \in \bigcap\{I_s \mid s \in S\}$, then x and y are in each ideal I_s, implying that $x \wedge y$ is in each ideal; thus $\bigcap\{I_s \mid s \in S\}$ is closed under finite joins. It is equally trivial to verify that $\bigcap\{I_s \mid s \in S\}$ is down closed. Finally, it is simple to check that this intersection has to be the required meet.

We remark that if $\{I_s \mid s \in S\} \subseteq \overline{X}$ is a directed subset, then

$$\bigcup\{I_s \mid s \in S\} \in \overline{X},$$

implying that directed joins in $\overline{X}$ are given by set-theoretic union. The only thing to comment on is the closure of the union under binary join. If $x, y \in \bigcup\{I_s \mid s \in S\}$, then $x \in I_s$ and $y \in I_{s'}$ for some $s, s' \in S$. By directedness, $\{I_s, I_{s'}\} \subseteq I_{s''}$ for some $s'' \in S$. It follows easily that $x \vee y \in \bigcup\{I_s \mid s \in S\}$.

We use this remark to check the algebraicity of $\overline{X}$. In fact the compact elements of $\overline{X}$ are precisely the ideals of the form $(\bigvee F)\!\downarrow$ where $F \subseteq^f X$ is a finite subset of X; if $F \subseteq^f X$ then certainly $\bigvee F$ exists in X, so this makes sense. If this is the case, then the algebraicity of $\overline{X}$ is virtually immediate; let us see that this characterisation of the compact elements is correct:

($\Rightarrow$) Let $F \subseteq^f X$ and suppose that $(\bigvee F)\!\downarrow \subseteq \bigcup\{I_s \mid s \in S\}$ where

$$\{I_s \mid s \in S\} \subseteq \overline{X}$$

is a directed subset. Clearly $F \subseteq^f (\bigvee F)\!\downarrow$, and by directedness there is some s with $F \subseteq^f I_s$. Thus it follows that $(\bigvee F)\!\downarrow \subseteq I_s$, and so $(\bigvee F)\!\downarrow$ is compact in $\overline{X}$.

($\Leftarrow$) Certainly if $E \in \overline{X}$ is a compact element, then

$$E \subseteq \bigcup\{(\bigvee F)\!\downarrow \mid F \subseteq^f E\},$$

implying there is some $F \subseteq^f E$ for which $E \subseteq (\bigvee F)\!\downarrow$. Hence $E = (\bigvee F)\!\downarrow$, as required.

For the next part of the proof, it will be helpful to show that the binary join of ideals I and J in $\overline{X}$ is given by

$$K = I \vee J \stackrel{\text{def}}{=} \bigcup\{(x \vee y)\!\downarrow \mid x \in I, y \in J\}.$$

To see that K is closed under binary joins, take $z \leq x \vee y$ and $z' \leq x' \vee y'$ for some $x, x' \in I$ and $y, y' \in J$. Then $\{z, z'\} \leq (x \vee x') \vee (y \vee y')$ from which we deduce binary joins exist in K because I and J both have binary joins. The remaining details which show that K is an ideal and is $I \vee J$ are omitted.

To see that $\widehat{f}$ preserves all joins, we appeal to Lemma 1.5.15. First we check that $\widehat{f}$ preserves directed joins. Take a directed subset $D = \{I_s \mid s \in S\} \subseteq \overline{X}$; we have to verify that

$$\underbrace{\bigsqcup\{f(x) \mid x \in \bigcup D\}}_{U} \;=\; \bigsqcup\{\bigsqcup\{f(x) \mid x \in I_s\} \mid s \in S\}$$
$$=\; \underbrace{\bigsqcup\{f(x) \mid s \in S, x \in I_s\}}_{V}.$$

To show that $V \leq \bigsqcup U$, take $f(x)$ for any $s \in S$ and $x \in I_s$ (that is $f(x) \in V$). Then $x \in \bigsqcup D = \bigcup D$, so $f(x) \in U \leq \bigsqcup U$. To show that $U \leq \bigsqcup V$ is equally easy.

Now we check that $\widehat{f}$ preserves finite joins. First note that

$$\widehat{f}(\{\perp_X\}) = \bigsqcup\{f(\perp_X)\} = f(\perp_X) = \perp_A.$$

It remains to see that $\widehat{f}$ preserves binary joins. Given ideals I and J, and the above construction of $I \vee J$, we need

$$\bigsqcup\{f(z) \mid z \in \bigcup\{(x \vee y)\!\downarrow \mid x \in I, y \in J\}\} =$$
$$\bigsqcup\{f(x) \mid x \in I\} \vee \bigsqcup\{f(y) \mid y \in J\}.$$

This equality is easy to verify and we omit the details.

Note that the function $\downarrow \colon Y \to \overline{Y}$, where $y \mapsto y\!\downarrow$, is well defined, monotone and preserves finite joins; from this we can define $\overline{f} \stackrel{\text{def}}{=} \widehat{\downarrow \circ f}$. It only remains to check that $\overline{f}$ preserves compactness of elements of $\overline{X}$. Using the characterisation of compact elements of $\overline{X}$ given in the proof, we have

$$\overline{f}((\textstyle\bigvee F)\!\downarrow) = \bigcup\{f(e)\!\downarrow \mid e \in (\textstyle\bigvee F)\!\downarrow\} = (f(\textstyle\bigvee F))\!\downarrow$$

and so we are done. $\square$

COROLLARY 1.5.19   Suppose that X and Y are algebraic complete lattices, and that $f: X \to Y$ is a function preserving all joins and also compactness of elements of X. Then there is an isomorphism $\theta: \overline{X^\circ} \cong X: \theta^{-1}$ (similarly for Y), and moreover the following diagram commutes

$$
\begin{array}{ccc}
\overline{X^\circ} & \xrightarrow{\;\overline{f}\;} & \overline{Y^\circ} \\
\theta \uparrow\downarrow \theta^{-1} & & \theta \uparrow\downarrow \theta^{-1} \\
X & \xrightarrow{\;f\;} & Y
\end{array}
$$

where we note that the set X° of compact elements of X is a join-semilattice.

PROOF   It is simple to verify that X° (similarly Y°) is a join-semilattice; hence f restricts to a function $f: X^\circ \to Y^\circ$ and there is an ideal lifting $\overline{f}: \overline{X^\circ} \to \overline{Y^\circ}$. We define $\theta: \overline{X^\circ} \to X$ by the assignment $I \mapsto \bigvee I$ and $\theta^{-1}: X \to \overline{X^\circ}$ by the assignment $x \mapsto \{e \in X^\circ \mid e \le x\}$ where $x \in X$. It is routine to verify that these functions are well defined, and that the above diagram commutes. $\square$

EXERCISE 1.5.20   Fill in the details of the proof of Corollary 1.5.19.

DISCUSSION 1.5.21   We end this chapter with a definition which will be used throughout the remainder of this book. A *Scott domain* is a dcpo *with a bottom element* which is also bounded cocomplete and algebraic.

EXERCISE 1.5.22   Think of as many examples of Scott domains as you can—draw pictures of your domains.

1.6   Further Exercises

(1) Consider the poset $D = \{(A, B) \mid A \subseteq \mathbb{N}, B \subseteq \mathbb{N}, A \cap B = \varnothing\}$ ordered as a pointwise subset of $\mathcal{P}(\mathbb{N}) \times \mathcal{P}(\mathbb{N})$. Describe both the finite elements and maximal elements of D. Prove that D is a dcpo. Let P be the poset with underlying set $\{\bot, 1, 2\}$ where 1 and 2 are incomparable and $\bot$ is a bottom element. Prove that $D \cong \mathbb{N} \Rightarrow P$, where $\mathbb{N} \Rightarrow P$ is the set of *all* functions $\mathbb{N} \to P$ ordered pointwise.

(2) Let X be any poset. A subset $S \subseteq X$ is a *poset-ideal* of X if S is directed in X and also $S = \bigcup\{s\downarrow \mid s \in S\}$. Write $\overline{X}$ for the set of poset-ideals of X. A dcpo F is called a *free dcpo generated by X* if there is a monotone function

$\iota\colon X \to F$ for which given any other monotone function $\phi\colon X \to C$ where C is a dcpo, then there is a unique continuous function $\bar{\phi}\colon F \to C$ such that $\phi = \bar{\phi}\iota$:

(a) If X is a join-semilattice, show that the set of ideals of X coincides with the set of poset-ideals of X.

(b) Given a poset X, show that any two free dcpos generated by X are isomorphic.

(c) Show that the set of poset-ideals of X is a dcpo when ordered by inclusion, and that the function $\gamma\colon X \to \overline{X}$ given by $\gamma(x) \overset{\text{def}}{=} \{y \in X \mid y \le x\} = x{\downarrow}$ is well defined, and is both order preserving and order reflecting. Show that $\overline{X}$ is the smallest dcpo which contains as a subset the set $\gamma(X)$. *Hint: show that if I is any poset-ideal of X, then $I = \bigcup\{y \in X \mid \exists x \in I.y \le x\}$.*

(d) Show that $\overline{X}$ is a free dcpo generated by X.

(3) Let D and E be ωcpos with least elements and $f\colon D \times E \to D$ and $g\colon D \times E \to E$ continuous functions. Let $h\colon D \times E \to D \times E$ be the function defined by $(d, e) \mapsto (f(d, e), g(d, e))$ where $(d, e) \in D \times E$. Show that h is a continuous function (and hence has a least fixpoint: see Exercises 1.5.6).

Now consider the functions $\phi_e\colon D \to D$, $d \mapsto f(d, e)$, one for each $e \in E$. Show that they are continuous, and hence that each has a least fixpoint $Y(\phi_e) \in D$. Show that the function $\psi\colon E \to E$, $e \mapsto g(Y(\phi_e), e)$ is continuous, and hence has a least fixpoint $Y(\psi)$.

Finally prove that $(Y(\phi_{Y(\psi)}), Y(\psi)) \in D \times E$ is the least fixpoint of h.

(4) Let X be a Heyting lattice and call an element $x \in X$ *regular* if $\neg\neg x = x$ where $\neg x \overset{\text{def}}{=} x \Rightarrow \bot$. Show that the set of regular elements of X is a Boolean lattice. *Hint: Exercise 1.4.11 (2) will be useful.*

(5) Let X be an algebraic complete lattice, and Y a complete sublattice. Prove that Y is also algebraic.

(6) (a) Let X be a complete lattice and $f\colon X \to X$ be a monotone function. Define
$$\hat{x} \overset{\text{def}}{=} \bigvee\{x \in X \mid x \le f(x)\}.$$
Prove that $f(\hat{x})$ is an upper bound for the set $\{x \in X \mid x \le f(x)\}$. Deduce that $\hat{x}$ is a fixpoint for f, that is $f(\hat{x}) = \hat{x}$.

(b) Let X be a poset. A *lower segment* of X is a subset $A \subseteq X$ for which if $a \in A$ and $x \in X$, then $x \leq a$ implies $x \in A$. An *upper segment* is defined similarly. Now suppose that X is isomorphic to a lower segment of a poset Y, and that Y is isomorphic to an upper segment of X. Let $f: X \to Y$ be the obvious function arising from the first isomorphism, and $g: Y \to X$ the obvious function arising from the second isomorphism. By considering the set of lower segments of X (say $L(X)$) and the function $\theta: L(X) \to L(X)$ defined by $\theta(A) \stackrel{\text{def}}{=} X \setminus g(Y \setminus f(A))$, show that there is a bijection $h: X \to Y$ of the underlying sets of X and Y for which given any $x, y \in X$ where $x < y$, then either $h(x) < h(y)$ or else $h(x)$ and $h(y)$ are incomparable. *Hint: use Part (a), and be careful to check all the details.*

(7) Suppose that X and Y are any sets, and that $f: X \to Y$ is any set function. We can define a function $f^{-1}: \mathcal{P}(Y) \to \mathcal{P}(X)$ by setting

$$f^{-1}(B) \stackrel{\text{def}}{=} \{x \in X \mid f(x) \in B\}$$

for $B \subseteq Y$ and a function $\exists f: \mathcal{P}(X) \to \mathcal{P}(Y)$ by setting

$$\exists f(A) \stackrel{\text{def}}{=} \{f(a) \mid a \in A\}$$

for $A \subseteq X$. Now suppose that X and Y are dcpos and let $\mathcal{I}(X)$ denote the inductive subsets of X (similarly for Y). Note that for any continuous function $f: X \to Y$ between dcpos, there is a function $f^*: \mathcal{I}(Y) \to \mathcal{I}(X)$ defined by $f^*(I) \stackrel{\text{def}}{=} \{x \in X \mid f(x) \in I\}$ which can be viewed as the restriction of $f^{-1}: \mathcal{P}(Y) \to \mathcal{P}(X)$ to inductive subsets. Finally note that there is a function $f_!: \mathcal{I}(X) \to \mathcal{I}(Y)$ which is defined by

$$f_!(I) \stackrel{\text{def}}{=} \bigcap \{J \in \mathcal{I}(Y) \mid \exists f(I) \subseteq J\}.$$

where formally $\exists f(I)$ is $\exists f$ applied to the underlying set of I.

The *Beck-Chevalley condition* says that for any continuous function $f: X \to Y$ and dcpo Z, the diagram

$$
\begin{array}{ccc}
\mathcal{I}(Z \times Y) & \xrightarrow{\ \pi_! \ } & \mathcal{I}(Y) \\
{\scriptstyle (id_Z \times f)^*}\downarrow & & \downarrow{\scriptstyle f^*} \\
\mathcal{I}(Z \times X) & \xrightarrow[\ \pi'_! \ ]{} & \mathcal{I}(X)
\end{array}
$$

commutes, where π and π' are coordinate projections.

(a) Verify that the definitions of f^{-1} and $\exists f$ make sense.

(b) Check that f^* is well defined and can be seen as a restriction of f^{-1} to inductive subsets.

(c) Verify that $f_!$ is well defined.

(d) Show that in fact the Beck-Chevalley condition does *not* hold. *Hint: write down the Beck-Chevalley condition for the case* $f\colon \{*\} \to Y$, *where (say)* $f(*) \stackrel{\text{def}}{=} y$. *Unravel the definitions of the functions in the commutative square, and conclude a certain property (say* (†)) *of the function* $\exists\pi\colon \mathcal{P}(Z \times Y) \to \mathcal{P}(Y)$ *when restricted to inclusive subsets. Consider the dcpos A and B with underlying set* $\mathbb{N} \cup \{\infty\}$, A *discrete and B the topped vertical natural numbers. By considering a certain dcpo constructed from A and B and assuming* (†), *obtain a contradiction.*

1.7   Pointers to the Literature

Birkhoff's [Bir67] contains much of the basic theory of lattices. A short account of very basic lattice theory can be found in [Coh79]. An excellent textbook introduction to ordered sets can be found in [DP90]. This book covers most of the contents of our Chapter 1 and much more besides. The "Compendium of Continuous Lattices," [GHK+80], gives a state-of-the-art account of the theory of continuous lattices as it stood up to about 1980. This work will be found particularly useful to those interested in the kind of lattice and domain theory which is used in type theory semantics. Grätzer aimed to give a survey of lattice theory in the 1960's, and his book [Gra71] was intended as the first part of this program. However, due in part to a rapid development of lattice theory shortly after the early 1960's, such a survey became a virtually impossible task. Grätzer published [Gra78] in 1978 which is a monograph of the core concepts of lattice theory. Johnstone's book [Joh82] gives a fast paced account of basic lattice theory and covers much, much more. The concept of locale, a lattice which mimics the defining properties of a topological space, pervades the book, in which a variety of representation theorems are proved. Dana Scott and Christopher Strachey pioneered the use of lattices for the denotational semantics of programming languages. The papers [Sco69a], [Sco69b], [Sco70a], [Sco70b], [Sco71], [Sco76], [Sco82] and [SS71] make interesting historical reading. A simple account of locale theory, along with much of the material covered in our Chapter 1, can be found in [Vic89]. This book is aimed at computer scientists.

2   A Category Theory Primer

2.1   Introduction

DISCUSSION 2.1.1   A category consists of a pair of collections, namely a collection of "structures" together with a collection of "relations between the structures." Let us illustrate this with some informal examples of categories.

• The collection of all sets (thus each set is an example of one of the structures referred to above), together with the collection of all set-theoretic functions (the functions are the relations between the structures).

• The collection of all posets (each poset is a structure), together with all monotone functions (the monotone functions are the relations between the structures).

• The collection of all finite dimensional vector spaces, together with all linear maps.

• The set of real numbers $\mathbb{R}$ (in this case each structure is just a real number $r \in \mathbb{R}$), together with the relation of order $\leq$ on the set $\mathbb{R}$. Thus given two structures $r, r' \in \mathbb{R}$, there is a relation between them just in case $r \leq r'$.

All categories have this basic form, that is, consist of structures and relations between the structures: the structures are usually referred to as the objects of the category and the relations between the structures as morphisms. It is important to note that the objects of a category do not have to be sets (in the fourth example they are real numbers) and that the morphisms do not have to be functions (in the fourth example they are instances of the order relation $\leq$). Of course, there are some precise rules which define exactly what a category is, and we shall come to these shortly: the reader may care to look at the definition of a category given in Discussion 2.2.1 while also reading the remainder of this introduction. For the time being we continue with a broad discussion of the aims of category theory, that is, the general study of categories. Category theory looks at properties which are common to different categories. It is often the case that the specification of a property of a category can be set out in very general terms, but that the implementation of this property in particular categories varies greatly. Let us look at an example. We have said that the collection of all sets and functions forms a category; consider the following property of this "category:"

(*Property* CP) *Given* any two sets A and B, *then* there is a set P and functions $\pi \colon P \to A$, $\pi' \colon P \to B$ *such that* the following condition holds: given any functions $f \colon C \to A$, $g \colon C \to B$ with C any set, then there is a unique function $h \colon C \to P$ making the diagram

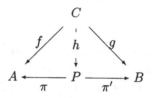

commute. End of definition of (*Property* CP).

Let us investigate an instance of (*Property* CP) in the case of two given sets A and B. Suppose that $A \overset{\text{def}}{=} \{a, b\}$ and $B \overset{\text{def}}{=} \{c, d, e\}$. Let us take P to be $A \times B \overset{\text{def}}{=} \{(x, y) \mid x \in A, y \in B\}$ and the functions π and π' to be coordinate projection to A and B respectively, and see if (P, π, π') makes the instance of (*Property* CP) for the given A and B hold. Let C be any other set and $f \colon C \to A$ and $g \colon C \to B$ be any two functions. Define the function $h \colon C \to P$ by $z \mapsto (f(z), g(z))$. We leave the reader to verify that indeed $f = \pi h$ and $g = \pi' h$, and that h is the only function for which these equations hold with the given f and g. Now define $P' \overset{\text{def}}{=} \{1, 2, 3, 4, 5, 6\}$ along with functions $p \colon P' \to A$ and $q \colon P' \to B$ where

$$p(1), \quad p(2), \quad p(3) = a \qquad\qquad q(1), \quad q(4) = c$$
$$p(4), \quad p(5), \quad p(6) = b \qquad\qquad q(2), \quad q(5) = d$$
$$q(3), \quad q(6) = e$$

In fact (P', p, q) also makes the instance of (*Property* CP) for the given A and B hold true. To see this, one can check by enumerating six cases that there is a unique function $h \colon C \to P'$ for which $f = ph$ and $g = qh$ (for example, if $x \in C$ and $f(x) = a$ and $g(x) = d$ then we must have $h(x) = 2$, and this is one case).

Now notice that there is a bijection between P (the cartesian product

$$\{(a, c), (a, d)(a, e), (b, c), (b, d), (b, e)\}$$

of A and B) and P'. In fact any choices for the set P can be shown to be bijective. It is very often useful to determine sets up to bijection rather than worry about their elements or "internal make up," so we might consider taking (*Property* CP) as a definition of cartesian product of two sets and think of the P and P' in the example above as two implementations of the notion of cartesian product of the sets A and B. Of course (*Property* CP) only makes sense when talking about the collection of sets and functions; we can give a definition of cartesian product for an arbitrary category which becomes (*Property* CP) for the "category" of sets and functions.

Category theory looks at properties enjoyed by categories which may be described using an abstract definition of a category and not particular examples of categories. Such a property is called a categorical property. Very roughly, such properties depend on the external behaviour of objects in categories, and not the internal make up of the objects. For example, if we take an instance of (*Property* CP) for sets A and B as the new definition of the cartesian product of A and B, then we have shifted our viewpoint away from the structures of our category (sets) and towards the relations between the structures (functions). The traditional definition of cartesian product is given in terms of the elements of the *sets* A and B, and the new definition is given solely in terms of *functions* involving A and B. It is the emphasis of relations between objects in categories, rather than the objects themselves, which allows us to make definitions which do not (explicitly) depend on the internal make up of the objects.

Now that we have painted an informal picture of a category, and described the idea of a categorical property, we can move on to an account of the contents of Chapter 2. We begin with a formal definition of a category and give a number of examples of the concept. Next, the notion of functor is given, which is a mapping between categories. We give examples of functors and introduce a little more notation. This is followed by the definition of natural transformation; such a gadget can be thought of as a mapping between functors. The concepts of category, functor and natural transformation are the three most basic notions of category theory. Using these three ideas, we give an account of ways of regarding two categories as being "essentially the same," namely isomorphism and equivalence. These notions of similarity are based on the idea that two bijective sets are similar, as are two isomorphic groups. We follow this with the Yoneda lemma, which will turn out to be a very useful tool indeed when discussing the semantics of type theories. We give an account of cartesian closed categories, which are particular kinds of categories not wholly dissimilar from the category of sets and functions, and which will give us categorical models of functional type theory. Next we define the idea of an adjunction between functors and give a number of results about adjoint functors. There is a discussion of the idea of a limit and colimit in a category. These are categorical generalisations of the notion of meets and joins in a preordered set. Finally, we give some basic definitions of strict indexed categories. Let us now move on to a formal definition of a category.

2.2   Categories and Examples

DISCUSSION 2.2.1   We begin with a definition of a category. A *category* C is specified by the following data:

• A collection $ob\,C$ of entities called *objects*. An object will often be denoted by a capital letter such as A, B, C...

• A collection $mor\,C$ of entities called *morphisms*. A morphism will often be denoted by a small letter such as f, g, h...

• Two operations assigning to each morphism f its *source* $src(f)$ which is an object of C and its *target* $tar(f)$ also an object of C. We shall write $f\colon src(f) \longrightarrow tar(f)$ to indicate this, or perhaps $f\colon A \to B$ where $A = src(f)$ and $B = tar(f)$. Sometimes we shall just say "let $f\colon A \to B$ be a morphism of C" to mean f is a morphism of C with source A and target B.

• Morphisms f and g are *composable* if $tar(f) = src(g)$. There is an operation assigning to each pair of composable morphisms f and g their *composition* which is a morphism denoted by $g \circ f$ or just gf and such that $src(gf) = src(f)$ and $tar(gf) = tar(g)$. So for example, if $f\colon A \to B$ and $g\colon B \to C$, then there is a morphism $gf\colon A \to C$. There is also an operation assigning to each object A of C an *identity* morphism $id_A\colon A \to A$. These operations are required to be *unitary*

$$id_{tar(f)} \circ f \;=\; f$$
$$f \circ id_{src(f)} \;=\; f$$

and *associative*, that is given morphisms $f\colon A \to B$, $g\colon B \to C$ and $h\colon C \to D$ then

$$(hg)f \;=\; h(gf).$$

It is time to give some examples of categories. We adopt the convention of using calligraphic letters to denote categories, using an abbreviation of the names of the objects of the category, or occasionally the morphisms of a category. This convention should become clear with the following examples.

EXAMPLES 2.2.2

(1) The category of sets and total functions, Set. The objects of the category are sets and the morphisms are triples (A, f, B) where A and B are sets and $f \subseteq A \times B$ is a subset of the cartesian product of A and B giving rise to a total function. The source and target operations are defined by $src(A, f, B) \stackrel{\text{def}}{=} A$

and $tar(A, f, B) \stackrel{\text{def}}{=} B$. Suppose that we have another morphism (B, g, C). Then $tar(A, f, B) = src(B, g, C)$, and the composition is given by

$$(B, g, C) \circ (A, f, B) = (A, gf, C)$$

where gf is the usual composition of the functions f and g. Finally, if A is any set, the identity morphism assigned to A is given by (A, id_A, A) where $id_A \subseteq A \times A$ is the identity function. We leave the reader to check that composition is an associative operation and that composition by identities is unitary. Informally, the morphisms of *Set* are functions in the usual set theoretic sense together with a *specified* source and target. From now on we shall not give such a formal account of our examples of categories.

(2) The category of sets and partial functions, *Part*. The objects are sets and the morphisms are partial functions equipped with a specified source and target. The definition of composition is the expected one, namely given $f: A \rightarrow B$, $g: B \rightarrow C$, then for each element a of A, $gf(a)$ is defined with value $g(f(a))$ if both $f(a)$ and $g(f(a))$ are defined, and is otherwise not defined.

(3) The category of ωcpos, *ωCPO*. Recall Section 1.5. The objects of *ωCPO* are ωcpos and the morphisms of *ωCPO* are set functions $f: X \rightarrow Y$ (where X and Y are ωcpos) which are monotone and preserve joins of ω-chains, that is the ω-continuous functions. Readers familiar with standard denotational semantics of programming languages will recognise the category *ωCPO*.

(4) The category of dcpos, *DCPO*. Its definition is essentially the same as for *ωCPO*, with objects the dcpos and morphisms the continuous functions.

(5) Any preordered set $(X, \leq)$ may be viewed as a category. Recall from Section 1.2 that a preorder $\leq$ on a set X is a reflexive, transitive relation on X. The objects are the elements of the set X and the morphisms instances of the order relation; formally the collection of morphisms is the set of pairs of the form (x, y) where $x, y \in X$ and $x \leq y$. $(X, \leq)$ forms a category with identity morphisms (x, x) for each object x (because $\leq$ is reflexive) and composition $(y, z) \circ (x, y) \stackrel{\text{def}}{=} (x, z)$ (because $\leq$ is transitive). Note for x and y elements of X, there is at most one morphism from x to y according to whether $x \leq y$ or not.

(6) A *discrete* category is one for which the only morphisms are identities. So a very simple example of a discrete category is given by regarding any set as a category in which the objects are the elements of the set, there is an identity morphism for each element, and there are no other morphisms.

(7) A *semigroup* (S, b) is a set S together with an associative binary operation $b: S \times S \rightarrow S$, $(s, s') \mapsto ss'$. An *identity element* for a semigroup S is some

(necessarily unique) element e of S such that for all $s \in S$ we have $es = se = s$. A *monoid* (M, b, e) is a semigroup (M, b) with identity element e. For example, addition on the natural numbers, $(\mathbb{N}, +, 0)$, is a monoid. For another example, if X is a set and X^* is the set of lists of elements of X which have finite length, then any such X^* gives rise to a monoid $(X^*, concat, [\,])$ with list concatenation as the binary operation and with the empty list $[\,]$ as identity element. This monoid is sometimes called the *Kleene closure* of the set X. We can now describe the category of monoids, $\mathcal{M}on$. The category $\mathcal{M}on$ has objects consisting of all monoids, and morphisms which are functions preserving the monoid multiplication. Thus a monoid morphism f between monoids M and M' is a function $f: M \to M'$ between the underlying sets, for which $f(mn) = f(m)f(n)$ where m and n are elements of M.

(8) Given a category $\mathcal{C}$, we may define the *opposite category* $\mathcal{C}^{op}$. The collection of objects of $\mathcal{C}^{op}$ is the same as the collection of objects of $\mathcal{C}$. The collection of morphisms of $\mathcal{C}^{op}$ is the same as the collection of morphisms of $\mathcal{C}$. If f is a morphism of $\mathcal{C}^{op}$ (and thus by definition a morphism of $\mathcal{C}$), then the source $src(f)$ of f in $\mathcal{C}^{op}$ is defined to be the target $tar(f)$ of f in $\mathcal{C}$. Also, the target of f in $\mathcal{C}^{op}$ is the source of f in $\mathcal{C}$. (Thus $f: A \to B$ is a morphism in $\mathcal{C}^{op}$ just in case $f: B \to A$ is a morphism in $\mathcal{C}$). The identity on an object A in $\mathcal{C}^{op}$ is defined to be id_A in $\mathcal{C}$. Finally we need to define composition in $\mathcal{C}^{op}$. If $f: A \to B$ and $g: B \to C$ are morphisms in $\mathcal{C}^{op}$, then $f: B \to A$ and $g: C \to B$ are morphisms in $\mathcal{C}$. Hence f and g are composable in $\mathcal{C}$, with composition $f \circ g: C \to A$. We define the composition of f and g in $\mathcal{C}^{op}$ to be the morphism $f \circ g$.

(9) If we are given a preorder X which we regard as a category, then the opposite category X^{op} is precisely the opposite preorder of X.

(10) The category $\mathcal{P}re\mathcal{S}et$ has objects preorders and morphisms the monotone functions; the category $\mathcal{P}\mathcal{O}\mathcal{S}et$ has objects posets and morphisms the monotone functions.

(11) The category of lattices $\mathcal{L}at$ has objects lattices and morphisms the lattice homomorphisms—see Section 1.3.

(12) The category $\mathcal{C}\mathcal{L}at$ has objects the complete lattices and morphisms the complete lattice homomorphisms—see Section 1.3.

(13) The category $\mathcal{B}\mathcal{L}at$ has objects Boolean lattices and morphisms Boolean lattice homomorphisms. By definition, a morphism of Boolean lattices is a function $f: X \to Y$ between Boolean lattices which preserves finite meets and joins (that is f is a lattice homomorphism) and preserves complementation.

However, it is easy to see that any lattice homomorphism between Boolean lattices automatically preserves complements. Thus a Boolean lattice homomorphism $X \to Y$ is just a lattice homomorphism.

(14) The category $\mathcal{HLat}$ has objects the Heyting lattices and morphisms Heyting lattice homomorphisms. A Heyting lattice homomorphism $f: X \to Y$ between Heyting lattices is a function preserving finite meets and joins and preserving Heyting implications. So if $x, x' \in X$, then

$$f(x \Rightarrow x') = f(x) \Rightarrow f(x').$$

(15) We shall write $\mathcal{ACLat}$ for the category whose objects are algebraic complete lattices and whose morphisms are complete lattice homomorphisms; note that in this example, the morphisms are not required to preserve a certain part of the structure of the objects of the category, that is, compact elements are not necessarily mapped to compact elements.

(16) The category of Scott domains $\mathcal{SDom}$ has objects Scott domains and morphisms continuous functions.

(17) The category $\mathcal{CJSLat}$ has objects the complete join-semilattices and morphisms functions preserving all joins. Note that a complete join-semilattice is indeed a complete lattice, but that a function which preserves all joins need not preserve all meets. Thus $\mathcal{CJSLat}$ has the same objects as $\mathcal{CLat}$ but different morphisms.

(18) Let C be a category and B an object of C. The *slice of C by B*, denoted by C/B, is the category whose objects are morphisms $f: A \to B$ in C, and whose morphisms $g: f \to f'$ are those morphisms $g: src(f) \to src(f')$ in C for which $f = f'g$. It is often helpful to view such objects and morphisms as a commutative diagram:

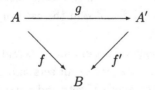

Similarly we can define the *coslice*, B/C. This has objects which are morphisms $f: B \to A$ in C and morphisms $g: f \to f'$ are morphisms $g: tar(f) \to tar(f')$ in C for which $f' = gf$.

(19) Suppose that C and D are categories. Then the *product* of C and D, $C \times D$, has objects pairs (C, D) where C is an object of C and D an object of D. The

morphisms $(C, D) \rightarrow (C', D')$ are pairs of morphisms (f, g) where $f \colon C \rightarrow C'$ and $g \colon D \rightarrow D'$ with composition given (as expected) coordinatewise.

(20) Any monoid (M, b, e) yields a category where there is one object M, the morphisms are elements of the monoid, and composition and identity arise from the monoid operations. So if m and m' are elements of M and hence morphisms $m, m' \colon M \rightarrow M$, then their composition is $b(m, m') \colon M \rightarrow M$. N.B. *Every monoid can be viewed as a category; do not confuse this fact with the definition of the category* Mon.

EXERCISE 2.2.3   Understand how each of the informal descriptions of categories given in Examples 2.2.2 can be formalised to fit the definition of a category given in Discussion 2.2.1.

DISCUSSION 2.2.4   Before moving on to Section 2.3, we shall define the notion of a subcategory. Very informally, we can think of a subcategory $\mathcal{D}$ of a category $\mathcal{C}$ as having classes of objects and morphisms which are subclasses of those of $\mathcal{C}$, such that $\mathcal{D}$ is itself a category. An analogy is the definition of a subgroup H of G where the set H is a subset of G and H is closed under the group operations of G. Now let us make a formal definition of subcategory.

A *subcategory* $\mathcal{D}$ of a category $\mathcal{C}$ is defined by specifying:

• A subclass of the objects of $\mathcal{C}$ which are the objects of $\mathcal{D}$, and a subclass of the morphisms of $\mathcal{C}$ which are the morphisms of $\mathcal{D}$.

• For any morphism f of $\mathcal{D}$, the source and target of f in $\mathcal{C}$ are objects of $\mathcal{D}$, and these are taken as the source and target of f in $\mathcal{D}$. Thus the collection of morphisms $A \rightarrow B$ in $\mathcal{D}$ is a subcollection of the morphisms $A \rightarrow B$ in $\mathcal{C}$.

• For every object D of $\mathcal{D}$, the identity id_D of $\mathcal{C}$ is a morphism of $\mathcal{D}$.

• If $f \colon A \rightarrow B$ and $g \colon B \rightarrow C$ in $\mathcal{D}$, then the composition gf in $\mathcal{C}$ is a morphism of $\mathcal{D}$ and is the composition of f and g in the category $\mathcal{D}$.

EXAMPLE 2.2.5   The category *FSet* of finite sets and functions between finite sets is a subcategory of the category of all sets and functions, *Set*. In turn, *Set* is a subcategory of the category of sets and partial functions, *Part*.

EXERCISE 2.2.6   Understand that the definition of subcategory does indeed give rise to a category. Think about the ways in which the subcategories defined in Example 2.2.5 arise, especially comparing the sets of functions $A \rightarrow B$ for fixed A and B in each of *FSet*, *Set* and *Part*.

2.3 Functors and Examples

DISCUSSION 2.3.1   A function $f: X \to Y$ can be thought of as a relation between two sets. We can also think of the function f as specifying an element of Y for each element of X; from this point of view, f is rather like a program which outputs a value $f(x) \in Y$ for each $x \in X$. We could say that a functor is to a pair of categories as a function is to a pair of sets. Roughly, a functor from a category C to a category D is an assignment which sends each object of C to an object of D, and each morphism of C to a morphism of D. This assignment has to satisfy some rules. For example, the identity on an object A of C is sent to the identity in D on the object FA, where the functor sends the object A in C to FA in D. Further, if two morphisms in C compose, then their images under the functor must compose in D. Very informally, we might think of the functor as "preserving the structure" of C. Let us move to the formal definition of a functor.

A *functor* F between categories C and D, written as $F: C \to D$, is specified by

• an operation taking objects A in C to objects FA in D, and

• an operation sending morphisms $f: A \to B$ in C to morphisms $Ff: FA \to FB$ in D,

for which $F(id_A) = id_{FA}$, and whenever the composition of morphisms gf is defined in C we have $F(gf) = Fg \circ Ff$. Note that $Fg \circ Ff$ is defined in D whenever gf is defined in C, that is, Ff and Fg are composable in D whenever f and g are composable in C.

REMARK 2.3.2   Sometimes we shall give the specification of a functor F by writing the operation on an object A as $A \mapsto FA$ and the operation on a morphism f, where $f: A \to B$, as $f: A \to B \mapsto Ff: FA \to FB$. Provided that everything is clear, we shall sometimes even say "the functor $f: C \to D$ is defined by an assignment

$$f: A \longrightarrow B \quad \mapsto \quad Ff: FA \longrightarrow FB$$

where $f: A \to B$ is any morphism of C." We shall refer informally to C as the source of the functor F, and to D as the target of F.

EXAMPLES 2.3.3

(1) Let C be a category. The *identity* functor id_C is defined by $id_C(A) \overset{\text{def}}{=} A$ where A is an object of C and $id_C(f) \overset{\text{def}}{=} f$ where f is a morphism of C.

(2) We have seen (page 42) that the Kleene closure A^* of a set A gives rise to a monoid via list concatenation. Hence we may define a functor $F: Set \to Mon$ by taking the operation on objects to be $FA \stackrel{\text{def}}{=} A^*$ and an operation on morphisms $Ff \stackrel{\text{def}}{=} map(f)$, where $map(f): A^* \to B^*$ is defined by

$$map(f)([a_1, \ldots, a_n]) = [f(a_1), \ldots, f(a_n)],$$

with $[a_1, \ldots, a_n]$ any element of A^*. Being our first example of a functor, we give explicit details of the verification that F is indeed a functor. To see that $F(id_A) = id_{A^*}$ note that

$$
\begin{aligned}
F(id_A)([a_1, \ldots, a_n]) &\stackrel{\text{def}}{=} map(id_A)([a_1, \ldots, a_n]) \\
&= id_{A^*}([a_1, \ldots, a_n]) \\
&\stackrel{\text{def}}{=} id_{FA}([a_1, \ldots, a_n]),
\end{aligned}
$$

and to see that $F(gf) = Fg \circ Ff$ where $A \xrightarrow{f} B \xrightarrow{g} C$ note that

$$
\begin{aligned}
F(gf)([a_1, \ldots, a_n]) &\stackrel{\text{def}}{=} map(gf)([a_1, \ldots, a_n]) \\
&= [gf(a_1), \ldots, gf(a_n)] \\
&= map(g)([f(a_1), \ldots, f(a_n)]) \\
&= map(g)(map(f)([a_1, \ldots, a_n])) \\
&= Fg \circ Ff([a_1, \ldots, a_n]).
\end{aligned}
$$

(3) Given a set A, recall that the powerset $\mathcal{P}(A)$ is the set of subsets of A. We can define a functor $\mathcal{P}: Set \to Set$ which is given by

$$f: A \to B \quad \mapsto \quad f_*: \mathcal{P}(A) \to \mathcal{P}(B),$$

where $f: A \to B$ is a function and f_* is defined by $f_*(A') \stackrel{\text{def}}{=} \{f(a') \mid a' \in A'\}$ where $A' \in \mathcal{P}(A)$. We call $P: Set \to Set$ the *covariant powerset* functor.

(4) We can define a functor $\mathcal{P}: Set^{op} \to Set$ by setting

$$f: B \to A \quad \mapsto \quad f^{-1}: \mathcal{P}(B) \to \mathcal{P}(A),$$

where $f: A \to B$ is a function in Set, and the function f^{-1} is defined by $f^{-1}(B') \stackrel{\text{def}}{=} \{a \in A \mid f(a) \in B'\}$ where $B' \in \mathcal{P}(B)$. Note that the source of the functor $\mathcal{P}$ is the *opposite* of the category of sets and functions; we refer to $\mathcal{P}$ as the *contravariant powerset* functor.

(5) Given functors $F:\mathcal{C} \to \mathcal{C}'$ and $G:\mathcal{D} \to \mathcal{D}'$, the *product functor*

$$F \times G: \mathcal{C} \times \mathcal{D} \to \mathcal{C}' \times \mathcal{D}'$$

is defined in the expected coordinatewise manner.

(6) The functors between two preorders A and B regarded as categories are precisely the monotone functions from A to B.

(7) A functor between monoids is a monoid homomorphism, where we are regarding a monoid as a category with one object.

(8) Given a set function $f:A \to B$, we can define $\exists f:\mathcal{P}(A) \to \mathcal{P}(B)$ by setting $\exists f(A') = \{f(a) \mid a \in A'\}$ where $A' \in \mathcal{P}(A)$. This gives rise to the *existential image functor* by regarding the posets $\mathcal{P}(A)$ and $\mathcal{P}(B)$ as categories (via the inclusion order) and noting that $\exists f$ is then a monotone function. We can also define $\forall f:\mathcal{P}(A) \to \mathcal{P}(B)$ by setting $\forall f(A') \overset{\text{def}}{=} \{y \in B \mid f^{-1}(\{y\}) \subseteq A'\}$ for each $A' \in \mathcal{P}(A)$. We call the functor $\forall f$ the *universal image functor*.

(9) Given a slice category $\mathcal{C}/B$, we may define a functor $U:\mathcal{C}/B \to \mathcal{C}$ as follows. Suppose that $f:A \to B$ is an object of the slice category, and that $h:f \to f'$ is a morphism of the slice. We set $Uf \overset{\text{def}}{=} A$ and $Uh \overset{\text{def}}{=} h$:

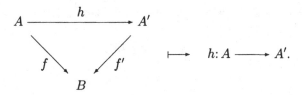

(10) Let X and Y be dcpos and $f:X \to Y$ be a continuous function. Then there is a functor $\mathcal{I}(f):\mathcal{I}(Y) \to \mathcal{I}(X)$ where $\mathcal{I}(X)$ is the set of inductive subsets of X, regarded as a category with the inclusion order (and similarly for $\mathcal{I}(Y)$). Let us specify $\mathcal{I}(f)$; if $B \in \mathcal{I}(Y)$ we define

$$\mathcal{I}(f)(B) \overset{\text{def}}{=} f^{-1}(B) \overset{\text{def}}{=} \{x \in X \mid f(x) \in B\}.$$

It is easy to check that $\mathcal{I}(f)(B)$ is an inductive subset of X; for if $D \subseteq f^{-1}(B)$ and D is a directed subset of X then the monotonicity of f implies $f(D) \subseteq Y$ is directed. But clearly $f(D) \subseteq B$ and hence we can deduce $f(\bigvee D) \in B$ from the fact that f is continuous, implying $\bigvee D \in f^{-1}(B)$. So $\mathcal{I}(f)$ is well defined and it is easy to see that $\mathcal{I}(f)$ is a monotone function $\mathcal{I}(Y) \to \mathcal{I}(X)$. Hence it is immediate that $\mathcal{I}(f)$ can be regarded as a functor.

(11) Let $F:\mathcal{C} \to \mathcal{D}$ be any functor. Then we can define a functor $F^{op}:\mathcal{C}^{op} \to \mathcal{D}^{op}$ which sends an object A of $\mathcal{C}^{op}$ to FA in $\mathcal{D}^{op}$, and a morphism $f:A' \to A$ in $\mathcal{C}^{op}$ to $Ff:FA' \to FA$ in $\mathcal{D}^{op}$.

(12) Given categories C and $\mathcal{D}$ and an object D of $\mathcal{D}$, the *constant* functor $\tilde{D}\colon C \to \mathcal{D}$ sends any object A of C to D and any morphism $f\colon A \to B$ of C to $id_D\colon D \to D$.

(13) Let $F\colon C \to \mathcal{D}$ be a functor and D an object of $\mathcal{D}$. Then the *under-cone* category $(D \downarrow F)$ has objects (f, A) where A is an object of C and $f\colon D \to FA$ is a morphism of $\mathcal{D}$. A morphism $g\colon (f, A) \to (f', B)$ is a morphism $g\colon A \to B$ for which the following diagram commutes:

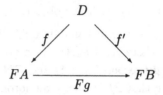

The *over-cone* category $(F \downarrow D)$ is defined similarly.

(14) Suppose that $F\colon C \to \mathcal{D}$ and $G\colon C' \to \mathcal{D}$ are functors. Then we define the *comma* category $(F \downarrow G)$ to have objects which are triples (A, f, A') where A and A' are objects of C and C' respectively and $f\colon FA \to GA'$ is a morphism of $\mathcal{D}$. A morphism $(A, f, A') \to (B, f', B')$ is a pair (g, h) where $g\colon A \to B$ in C and $h\colon A' \to B'$ in C' for which the following diagram commutes:

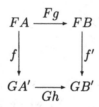

(15) Let $\mathcal{G}rp$ be the category of groups and group homomorphisms. The *forgetful* functor $U\colon \mathcal{G}rp \to \mathcal{S}et$ sends a group to its underlying set and a group homomorphism to its underlying function.

EXERCISES 2.3.4

(1) Check that the definitions given in Examples 2.3.3 make sense and do indeed define functors between categories.

(2) Let us say that a category C is *tiny* if the collection of objects forms a set and C is discrete; prove that a category C is tiny iff given any category $\mathcal{D}$ with a set of objects $ob\,\mathcal{D}$ and any set function $f\colon ob\,C \to ob\,\mathcal{D}$, then f extends uniquely to a functor $F\colon C \to \mathcal{D}$. (Extends means that if A is an object of C, then $FA = f(A) \in ob\,\mathcal{D}$.)

DISCUSSION 2.3.5 We shall end this section with a few definitions. A morphism $f: A \to A$ with equal source and target is called an *endomorphism*. A pair of morphisms f and g for which $src(f) = src(g)$ and $tar(f) = tar(g)$ are said to be *parallel* and this will be written $f, g: A \to B$. A functor with common source and target categories is called an *endofunctor*. Now let $F: \mathcal{C} \to \mathcal{D}$ be any functor. We say that F is *faithful* if given a parallel pair of morphisms $f, g: A \to B$ in $\mathcal{C}$ for which $Ff = Fg$, then $f = g$. We say that F is *full* if given objects A and B in $\mathcal{C}$ and a morphism $g: FA \to FB$ in $\mathcal{D}$, then there is some $f: A \to B$ in $\mathcal{C}$ for which $Ff = g$.

As an example, consider the functor $U: \mathcal{M}on \to \mathcal{S}et$ which takes monoids and monoid homomorphisms to their underlying sets and set functions respectively. Then U is faithful but not full. The functor $U: \mathcal{G}rp \to \mathcal{M}on$ which takes groups and group homomorphisms to their underlying monoids is both full and faithful.

Suppose that $\mathcal{D}$ is a subcategory of the category $\mathcal{C}$. We say that $\mathcal{D}$ is a *full* subcategory if the inclusion functor $i: \mathcal{D} \to \mathcal{C}$ is full (the definition of the inclusion functor is the expected one). Note that this is just saying that the morphisms $A \to B$ in $\mathcal{D}$ are exactly the morphisms $A \to B$ in $\mathcal{C}$. We say that $\mathcal{D}$ is a *lluf* subcategory of $\mathcal{C}$ if the collection of objects of $\mathcal{D}$ coincides with that for $\mathcal{C}$.

2.4 Natural Transformations and Examples

Not content with just the notion of a relation between categories, we now consider the notion of a relation between functors.

Let $\mathcal{C}$ and $\mathcal{D}$ be categories and $F, G: \mathcal{C} \to \mathcal{D}$ be functors. Then a *natural transformation* α from F to G, written $\alpha: F \to G$, is specified by an operation which assigns to each object A in $\mathcal{C}$ a morphism $\alpha_A: FA \to GA$ in $\mathcal{D}$, such that for any morphism $f: A \to B$ in $\mathcal{C}$, we have $Gf \circ \alpha_A = \alpha_B \circ Ff$, that is, the following diagram commutes:

$$
\begin{array}{ccc}
FA & \xrightarrow{\;\alpha_A\;} & GA \\
{\scriptstyle Ff}\downarrow & & \downarrow{\scriptstyle Gf} \\
FB & \xrightarrow[\;\alpha_B\;]{} & GB
\end{array}
$$

The morphism α_A is called the *component* of the natural transformation α at A. We shall also write $\alpha: F \to G: \mathcal{C} \to \mathcal{D}$ to indicate that α is a natural transformation between the functors $F, G\colon \mathcal{C} \to \mathcal{D}$. If we are given such a natural transformation, we shall refer to the above commutative square by saying "consider naturality of α in A at $f\colon A \to B$."

EXAMPLES 2.4.1

(1) Recall the functor $F\colon \mathcal{S}et \to \mathcal{M}on$ (see page 46) which takes a set to its Kleene closure. We can define a natural transformation $rev\colon F \to F$ which has components $rev_A\colon A^* \to A^*$ defined by

$$rev_A([a_1, \ldots, a_n]) \stackrel{\text{def}}{=} [a_n, \ldots, a_1]$$

where A is a set and $[a_1, \ldots, a_n] \in A^*$. It is trivial to see that this does define a natural transformation:

$$Ff \circ rev_A([a_1, \ldots, a_n]) = [f(a_n), \ldots, f(a_1)] = rev_B \circ Ff([a_1, \ldots, a_n]).$$

(2) Take a fixed set X and define a functor $F_X\colon \mathcal{S}et \to \mathcal{S}et$ by the operation $F_X(A) \stackrel{\text{def}}{=} (X \Rightarrow A) \times X$ on objects and the operation $F_X(f) \stackrel{\text{def}}{=} (f \circ -) \times id_X$ on morphisms (see page xvii) where A is any set and f is any function. Here, $X \Rightarrow A$ is the set of functions from X to A, $(X \Rightarrow A) \times X$ is a cartesian product of sets, and $(f \circ -) \times id_X$ denotes a cartesian product of functions. Then we can define a natural transformation $ev\colon F_X \to id_{\mathcal{S}et}$ by setting $ev_A(g, x) \stackrel{\text{def}}{=} g(x)$ where $(g, x) \in (X \Rightarrow A) \times X$. To see that we have defined a natural transformation ev with components $ev_A\colon (X \Rightarrow A) \times X \to A$ let $f\colon A \to B$ be a set function, $(g, x) \in (X \Rightarrow A) \times X$ and note that

$$
\begin{aligned}
(id_{\mathcal{S}et}(f) \circ ev_A)(g, x) &= f(ev_A(g, x)) \\
&= f(g(x)) \\
&= ev_B(fg, x) \\
&= ev_B(F_X(f)(g, x)) \\
&= (ev_B \circ F_X(f))(g, x).
\end{aligned}
$$

(3) Let $\mathcal{V}ec$ be the category of vector spaces over a (fixed) field K. Write V^* for the set of linear maps from V into K. Then there is a functor $(-)^*\colon \mathcal{V}ec^{op} \to \mathcal{V}ec$, which is defined by

$$f\colon U \longrightarrow V \quad \longmapsto \quad f^*\colon U^* \xrightarrow{\ \theta \,\mapsto\, \theta f\ } V^*$$

where $f\colon U \to V$ is any morphism of $\mathcal{V}ec^{op}$ and $\theta \in U^*$ is any linear map. Thus there is a functor $(-)^{**}\colon \mathcal{V}ec \to \mathcal{V}ec$ which is defined by

$$f\colon V \longrightarrow U \quad \longmapsto \quad f^{**}\colon V^{**} \xrightarrow{\ (\chi \,\mapsto\, (\theta \,\mapsto\, \chi(f^*(\theta))))\ } U^{**}$$

where $\chi \in V^{**}$ is any linear map. For each vector space V there is a linear map $\alpha_V: V \to V^{**}$ given by $\alpha_V(v)(\theta) \overset{\text{def}}{=} \theta(v)$ where $v \in V$ and $\theta \in V^*$. It is easy to check that the diagram

$$
\begin{array}{ccc}
V & \xrightarrow{\alpha_V} & V^{**} \\
{\scriptstyle f}\downarrow & & \downarrow{\scriptstyle f^{**}} \\
U & \xrightarrow[\alpha_U]{} & U^{**}
\end{array}
$$

commutes, where $v \in V$:

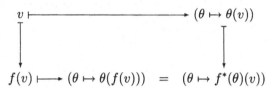

$$
\begin{array}{ccc}
v & \longmapsto & (\theta \mapsto \theta(v)) \\
\downarrow & & \downarrow \\
f(v) \longmapsto (\theta \mapsto \theta(f(v))) & = & (\theta \mapsto f^*(\theta)(v))
\end{array}
$$

and hence that the α_V define a natural transformation $\alpha: id_{\mathcal{V}ec} \to (-)^{**}$.

DISCUSSION 2.4.2   It will be convenient to introduce some notation for dealing with methods of "composing" functors and natural transformations. Let $\mathcal{C}$ and $\mathcal{D}$ be categories and let F, G, H be functors from $\mathcal{C}$ to $\mathcal{D}$. Also let $\alpha: F \to G$ and $\beta: G \to H$ be natural transformations. We can define a natural transformation $\beta\alpha: F \to H$ by setting the components to be $(\beta\alpha)_A \overset{\text{def}}{=} \beta_A\alpha_A$. For clarity we will sometimes write $\beta \circ \alpha$ instead of $\beta\alpha$. This yields a category $[\mathcal{C}, \mathcal{D}]$ with objects functors from $\mathcal{C}$ to $\mathcal{D}$, morphisms natural transformations between such functors, and composition as given above. $[\mathcal{C}, \mathcal{D}]$ is called the *functor category* of $\mathcal{C}$ and $\mathcal{D}$.

    We end this discussion with a little more notation. Suppose that $\alpha: F \to G: \mathcal{D} \to \mathcal{E}$ is a natural transformation, and that $I: \mathcal{C} \to \mathcal{D}$ and $J: \mathcal{E} \to \mathcal{F}$ are functors. Then we can define a natural transformation $\alpha_I: FI \to GI: \mathcal{C} \to \mathcal{E}$ by setting components to be $(\alpha_I)_C \overset{\text{def}}{=} \alpha_{IC}$ where C is an object of $\mathcal{C}$, and a natural transformation $J\alpha: JF \to JG: \mathcal{D} \to \mathcal{F}$ by setting components $(J\alpha)_D \overset{\text{def}}{=} J(\alpha_D)$ where D is an object of $\mathcal{D}$.

EXAMPLE 2.4.3   Note that we may define a functor

$$
Ev : \mathcal{C} \times [\mathcal{C}, \mathcal{S}et] \longrightarrow \mathcal{S}et
$$

where $Ev(A, F) \overset{\text{def}}{=} FA$ and $Ev(g, \mu) \overset{\text{def}}{=} \mu_{A'} \circ Fg = F'g \circ \mu_A$ with $g: A \to A'$ and $\mu: F \to F'$. Such a functor Ev is usually referred to as an *evaluation* functor.

EXERCISES 2.4.4

(1) Given categories $\mathcal{C}$ and $\mathcal{D}$, verify that the functor category $[\mathcal{C}, \mathcal{D}]$ as defined in Discussion 2.4.2 is indeed a category.

(2) Verify that the definitions given in Discussion 2.4.2 do indeed yield natural transformations. Further, given a diagram of categories and functors

$$ \mathcal{C} \xrightarrow{\;\;I\;\;} \mathcal{D} \xrightarrow{\;F,G,H\;} \mathcal{E} \xrightarrow{\;\;J\;\;} \mathcal{F} $$

and natural transformations $\alpha \colon F \to G$ and $\beta \colon G \to H$, show that $J(\beta \circ \alpha) = J\beta \circ J\alpha$ and $(\beta \circ \alpha)_I = \beta_I \circ \alpha_I$. Note: make sure you understand in which categories the compositions are defined.

2.5 Isomorphisms and Equivalences

DISCUSSION 2.5.1   Of course, the basic idea of isomorphism is that isomorphic objects are "essentially the same." In the case of *Set*, two sets X and Y are isomorphic just in case there is a bijection between them. This means that either there is a function $f \colon X \to Y$ which is injective and surjective, or, equivalently, there are functions $f \colon X \to Y$ and $g \colon Y \to X$ which are mutually inverse. We can use the idea that a pair of mutually inverse functions in the category *Set* gives rise to bijective sets to define the notion of isomorphism in an arbitrary category.

A morphism $f \colon A \to B$ in a category $\mathcal{C}$ is said to be an *isomorphism* if there is some $g \colon B \to A$ for which $fg = id_B$ and $gf = id_A$. We shall say that g is an *inverse* for f and that f is an inverse for g. Given objects A and B in $\mathcal{C}$, we say that A is *isomorphic* to B and write $A \cong B$ if such a mutually inverse pair of morphisms exists, and we say that the pair of morphisms *witnesses* the fact that $A \cong B$. Note that there may be many such pairs. In the category determined by a partially ordered set, the only isomorphisms are the identities, and in a preorder X with $x, y \in X$ we have $x \cong y$ iff $x \leq y$ and $y \leq x$. Note that in this case there can be only one pair of mutually inverse morphisms witnessing the fact that $x \cong y$.

An isomorphism in a functor category is referred to as a *natural isomorphism*. If there is a natural isomorphism between the functors F and G, then we shall say that F and G are *naturally isomorphic*.

EXERCISES 2.5.2

(1) Let $\mathcal{C}$ be a category and let $f: A \to B$ and $g, h: B \to A$ be morphisms. If $fh = id_B$ and $gf = id_A$ show that $g = h$. Deduce that any morphism f has a *unique* inverse if such exists.

(2) Let $\mathcal{C}$ be a category and $f: A \to B$ and $g: B \to C$ be morphisms. If f and g are isomorphisms, show that gf is too. What is its inverse?

LEMMA 2.5.3   Let $\alpha: F \to G: \mathcal{C} \to \mathcal{D}$ be a natural transformation. Then α is a natural isomorphism just in case each component α_C is an isomorphism in $\mathcal{D}$. More precisely, if we are given a natural isomorphism α in $[\mathcal{C}, \mathcal{D}]$ with inverse β, then each β_C is an inverse for α_C in $\mathcal{D}$; and if given a natural transformation α in $[\mathcal{C}, \mathcal{D}]$ for which each component α_C has an inverse (say β_C) in $\mathcal{D}$, then the β_C are the components of a natural transformation β which is the inverse of α in $[\mathcal{C}, \mathcal{D}]$.

PROOF   Direct calculations from the definitions.   □

EXERCISE 2.5.4   Do the proof of Lemma 2.5.3. Be careful to note precisely what the lemma is saying.

DISCUSSION 2.5.5   We emphasised at the start of this chapter that we were interested in the way structures behaved and not so much in their internal make-up. To this end we might expect that the judgement "A and B are isomorphic in $\mathcal{C}$" is more important than the judgement "A and B are equal in $\mathcal{C}$." Indeed, the development of category theory has shown this to be the case. This leads us to the notion of equivalence of categories. If two categories are equivalent, then the rough idea is that we can write down a one to one correspondence between isomorphism classes of objects obtained from the categories. Let us give the precise definition.

Two categories $\mathcal{C}$ and $\mathcal{D}$ are *equivalent* if there are functors $F: \mathcal{C} \to \mathcal{D}$ and $G: \mathcal{D} \to \mathcal{C}$ together with natural isomorphisms $\epsilon: FG \cong id_\mathcal{D}$ and $\eta: id_\mathcal{C} \cong GF$. We say that F is an *equivalence* with an *inverse equivalence* G and denote the equivalence by $F: \mathcal{C} \simeq \mathcal{D}: G$.

EXAMPLE 2.5.6   Let us look at an example of equivalent categories. Recall $\mathcal{P}art$, the category of sets and partial functions, and write 1 for a singleton set. Recall also the definition of a coslice category. Then it is the case that $\mathcal{P}art \simeq 1/Set$. Note that an object of $1/Set$ is a function $f: 1 \to A$ where A is a set (and hence in particular A is non-empty); this amounts to a giving a pair (A, a) where $a \in A$, and a is sometimes referred to as the distinguished element of A. A morphism $g: (A, a) \to (B, b)$ amounts to a function $g: A \to B$ for which $b = g(a)$, that is g preserves the distinguished element of A.

We pause to consider the intuition behind the equivalence. Any partial function $f: A \to B$ can be regarded as a total function $\bar{f}: A \cup \{*\} \to B \cup \{*\}$ (choose $*$ such that $* \notin A$ and $* \notin B$) where

$$\bar{f}(\xi) \;=\; \begin{cases} f(\xi) \text{ if } \xi \in A \text{ and } f(\xi) \text{ is defined} \\ * \text{ otherwise} \end{cases}$$

for any $\xi \in A \cup \{*\}$; and of course $A \cup \{*\}$ $(B \cup \{*\})$ can be viewed as a set with a distinguished element. Conversely, any total function whose source is a set with a distinguished element can be seen to give rise to a partial function.

Now we look more formally at the equivalence of $\mathcal{P}art$ and $1/\mathcal{S}et$. Let (X, x_0) and (Y, y_0) be objects of $1/\mathcal{S}et$, and $f: (X, x_0) \to (Y, y_0)$ a morphism. Define a functor $F: 1/\mathcal{S}et \to \mathcal{P}art$ by setting $F(X, x_0) \stackrel{\text{def}}{=} X \setminus \{x_0\}$ and

$$Ff(x) \;\stackrel{\text{def}}{=}\; \begin{cases} f(x) \text{ provided } f(x) \neq y_0 \\ \text{undefined otherwise} \end{cases}$$

where of course $x \in X \setminus \{x_0\}$ and $Ff: X \setminus \{x_0\} \to Y \setminus \{y_0\}$.

Let $g: X \to Y$ be a partial function. Define a functor $G: \mathcal{P}art \to 1/\mathcal{S}et$ by setting $GX \stackrel{\text{def}}{=} (X \cup \{X\}, X)$ and

$$Gg(\xi) \;\stackrel{\text{def}}{=}\; \begin{cases} g(\xi) \text{ if } \xi \neq X \text{ and } g(\xi) \in Y \text{ is defined} \\ Y \text{ otherwise} \end{cases}$$

where of course $Gg: X \cup \{X\} \to Y \cup \{Y\}$ and $\xi \in X \cup \{X\}$. Then one can check that this does give rise to an equivalence of categories.

EXERCISES 2.5.7

(1) Investigate the notion of equivalence of preorders regarded as categories. Draw some pictures of equivalent preorders.

(2) Complete a detailed verification of the equivalence given in Example 2.5.6.

(3) The slice category $\mathcal{S}et/B$ is often referred to as the category of B-indexed families of sets with functions preserving the indexing. To see this, note that a function $f: X \to B$ gives rise to the family of sets $(f^{-1}(b) \mid b \in B)$, and the family of sets $(X_b \mid b \in B)$ gives rise to the function

$$f: \{(x, b) \mid x \in X_b, b \in B\} \to B$$

where $f(x, b) \overset{\text{def}}{=} b$. Note that we can regard the set B as a discrete category; then there is an equivalence between the functor category $[B, Set]$ and the slice Set/B. Formulate this equivalence carefully and prove that your definitions really do give an equivalence.

2.6 Products and Coproducts

DISCUSSION 2.6.1   The notion of a "product of two objects in a category" can be viewed as an abstraction of the idea of a cartesian product of two sets. As we mentioned in Section 2.1, the definition of a cartesian product of sets is an "internal" one; we specify the elements of the product in terms of the elements of the sets from which the product is composed. However, as we have seen, there is a property of the cartesian product which characterises it *up to set-theoretic bijection*. The internal make up of two bijective sets may be very different, but their properties may well be very similar. We can now give the formal definition of a binary product of two objects of a category.

A *binary product* of objects A and B in a category $\mathcal{C}$ is specified by

• an object $A \times B$ of $\mathcal{C}$, together with

• two *projection* morphisms $\pi_A : A \times B \to A$ and $\pi_B : A \times B \to B$,

for which given any object C and morphisms $f : C \to A$, $g : C \to B$, there is a unique morphism $\langle f, g \rangle : C \to A \times B$ for which $\pi_A \langle f, g \rangle = f$ and $\pi_B \langle f, g \rangle = g$.

We shall refer simply to a binary product $A \times B$ instead of the triple $(A \times B, \pi_A, \pi_B)$, without explicit mention of the projection morphisms, much as it is common practice to speak of a group G rather than $(G, \circ, e)$. The data for a binary product is more readily understood as a commutative diagram, where we have written $\exists!$ to mean "there exists a unique":

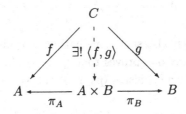

Given a binary product $A \times B$ and morphisms $f : C \to A$ and $g : C \to B$, the unique morphism $\langle f, g \rangle : C \to A \times B$ (making the above diagram commute) is called the *mediating* morphism for f and g. We shall say that the category $\mathcal{C}$ *has binary products* if there is a product in $\mathcal{C}$ of any two objects A and B, and that $\mathcal{C}$ has *specified* binary products if there is a given canonical choice of binary product for each pair of objects. For example, *Set* has specified binary products by setting $A \times B \stackrel{\text{def}}{=} \{(a,b) \mid a \in A, b \in B\}$ with projections given by the usual set-theoretic projection functions. Talking of *specified* binary products is a reasonable thing to do, by virtue of the next result.

LEMMA 2.6.2   A binary product of A and B in a category $\mathcal{C}$ is unique up to isomorphism if it exists.

PROOF   Suppose that (P, p_A, p_B) and (P', p'_A, p'_B) are two candidates for the binary product. Then we have $\langle p_A, p_B \rangle : P \to P'$ by applying the defining property of (P', p'_A, p'_B) to the morphisms $p_A : P \to A$, $p_B : P \to B$, and $\langle p'_A, p'_B \rangle : P' \to P$ exists from a similar argument. So we have diagrams of the form

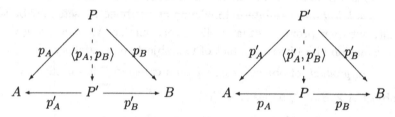

But then $f \stackrel{\text{def}}{=} \langle p'_A, p'_B \rangle \langle p_A, p_B \rangle : P \to P$ and one can check that $p_A f = p_A$ and that $p_B f = p_B$, that is f is a mediating morphism for the binary product (P, p_A, p_B); we can picture this as the following commutative diagram:

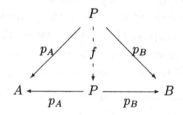

But it is trivial that id_P is also such a mediating morphism, and so uniqueness implies $f = id_P$. Similarly one proves that $\langle p_A, p_B \rangle \langle p'_A, p'_B \rangle = id_{P'}$, to deduce $P \cong P'$ witnessed by the morphisms $\langle p_A, p_B \rangle$ and $\langle p'_A, p'_B \rangle$. $\square$

DISCUSSION 2.6.3   The notion of binary product has an extension to set-indexed families of objects.

Given a family of objects $(A_i \mid i \in I)$ in a category $\mathcal{C}$ where I is a set, a *product* of the family of objects is specified by

• an *object* $\Pi_{i \in I} A_i$ in $\mathcal{C}$, and

• for every $j \in I$, a morphism $\pi_j \colon \Pi_{i \in I} A_i \to A_j$ in $\mathcal{C}$ called the jth *product projection*,

such that for any object C and family of morphisms $(f_i \colon C \to A_i \mid i \in I)$, there is a unique morphism $\langle f_i \mid i \in I \rangle \colon C \to \Pi_{i \in I} A_i$ for which given any $j \in I$, we have $\pi_j \langle f_i \mid i \in I \rangle = f_j$. We shall say that $\langle f_i \mid i \in I \rangle$ is the *mediating morphism* for the family $(f_i \mid i \in I)$.

REMARK 2.6.4 In the definition of product, for any family $(A_i \mid i \in I)$ we speak of *a* product and not *the* product. This is because a product is unique only up to isomorphism, and the proof that this is the case mimics that for binary products (Lemma 2.6.2). We shall sometimes speak of a product $\Pi_{i \in I} A_i$ without explicit mention of the product projections.

EXAMPLES 2.6.5

(1) A *terminal object* 1 of a category $\mathcal{C}$ has the property that for any object C of the ambient category, there is a unique morphism $!_C \colon C \to 1$. Note that such an object is unique up to isomorphism. For suppose that both 1 and $1'$ are terminal objects of $\mathcal{C}$. Then there is a unique morphism $!_{1'} \colon 1' \to 1$, and a unique morphism $!_1 \colon 1 \to 1'$. Thus by composition there is a morphism $!_{1'} \circ !_1 \colon 1 \to 1$. But 1 is a terminal object, and so we must have $!_{1'} \circ !_1 = id_1$, because there has to be a unique morphism $!_1 \colon 1 \to 1$ and this must therefore be the identity. Similarly $!_1 \circ !_{1'} = id_{1'}$ and thus $1 \cong 1'$ as required. Note that this kind of argument using uniqueness properties is prevalent in category theory.

(2) A product of an empty family of objects (that is a family indexed by the empty set) in a category $\mathcal{C}$ is given by a terminal object. The first clause of the definition of product says we are given an object of $\mathcal{C}$, say 1, and the remainder of the definition reduces to saying that for each object C there is a unique morphism $C \to 1$. A singleton set is an example of a terminal object in the category *Set*.

(3) A *global element* of an object A in a category $\mathcal{C}$ is any morphism $1 \to A$. What are global elements in the category *Set*?

(4) Now let $I = \{1, 2\}$. A product of a family (A_1, A_2) of two objects is just a binary product of A_1 and A_2 as defined on page 55. We usually denote the product $\Pi_{i \in \{1,2\}} A_i$ by $A_1 \times A_2$ and write $\langle f_1, f_2 \rangle$ for any mediating morphism $\langle f_i \mid i \in \{1, 2\} \rangle$.

(5) When I is a finite set we shall speak of a finite product. If $I = \{1, \ldots, n\}$ we shall sometimes write $A_1 \times \ldots \times A_n$ or $\Pi_1^n A_i$ for the product of $(A_i \mid i \in I)$.

We shall sometimes abuse notation and allow n to be 0 in the notation $\Pi_1^n A_i$. Thus $\Pi_1^0 A_i$ will indicate a product of no objects, that is, a terminal object.

DISCUSSION 2.6.6   A category C *has* products of set-indexed families of objects if there is always a product for any such family. C has *specified* products of set-indexed families of objects if it has products and there is always a specified canonical choice. We shall say that C has *finite* products if it has products of finite families of objects. We shall see that such categories with finite products arise naturally in the semantics of algebraic type theory. It will be useful to have a little additional notation for dealing with such categories. Let C be a category with finite products and take morphisms $f: A \to B$ and $f': A' \to B'$. We write $f \times f': A \times A' \to B \times B'$ for the morphism $\langle f\pi, f'\pi' \rangle$ where $\pi: A \times A' \to A$ and $\pi': A \times A' \to A'$. The uniqueness condition of mediating morphisms means that in general one has

$$id_A \times id_{A'} = id_{A \times A'} \quad \text{and} \quad (g \times g')(f \times f') = gf \times g'f',$$

where $g: B \to C$ and $g': B' \to C'$.

EXERCISES 2.6.7

(1) Show that a category C has finite products just in case it has binary products and a terminal object.

(2) Let C be a category with finite products and let

$$
\begin{array}{lll}
l: X \to A & f: A \to B & g: A \to C \\
h: B \to D & k: C \to E &
\end{array}
$$

be morphisms of C. Show that $(h \times k) \circ \langle f, g \rangle = \langle hf, kg \rangle$ and $\langle f, g \rangle \circ l = \langle fl, gl \rangle$.

(3) Investigate the notion of a binary product in a category C^{op}.

DISCUSSION 2.6.8   A coproduct is a dual notion of product. For example, a binary coproduct of a pair of objects in a category C is given by the binary product of the objects in the opposite category C^{op}. With this definition, readers should provide a definition of binary coproduct for themselves, and check their conclusion with the following definition.

A *binary coproduct* of objects A and B in a category C is specified by

• an object $A + B$ of C, together with

• two *insertion* morphisms $\iota_A: A \to A + B$ and $\iota_B: B \to A + B$, such that for each pair of morphisms $f: A \to C$, $g: B \to C$ there exists a unique morphism $[f, g]: A + B \to C$ for which $[f, g]\iota_A = f$ and $[f, g]\iota_B = g$. We can picture this definition through the following commutative diagram:

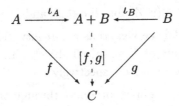

We can extend this definition to the notion of a coproduct of a set-indexed family of objects. Given a family of objects $(A_i \mid i \in I)$ in a category $\mathcal{C}$, where I is a set, a *coproduct* is specified by the following data:

- An object $\Sigma_{i \in I} A_i$ in $\mathcal{C}$, and

- for every $j \in I$, a morphism $\iota_j: A_j \to \Sigma_{i \in I} A_i$ called the *jth coproduct inser-tion*,

such that for any object C and any family of morphisms $(f_i: A_i \to C \mid i \in I)$ there is a unique morphism $[f_i \mid i \in I]: \Sigma_{i \in I} A_i \to C$ for which given any $j \in I$, we have $[f_i \mid i \in I]\iota_j = f_j$.

REMARK 2.6.9   In the definitions of products and coproducts there is always a clause which contains a phrase "there exists a unique ... satisfying ..." We will see that definitions involving the existence of unique gadgets which satisfy certain properties pervades category theory. Such properties are known as *universal* properties.

EXERCISE 2.6.10   Prove that the coproduct of any set-indexed family of objects is unique up to isomorphism if it exists.

EXAMPLES 2.6.11

(1) An object 0 of a category $\mathcal{C}$ is called *initial* if there is a unique morphism $!_A: 0 \to A$ for each object A of $\mathcal{C}$. Note that such an object is unique up to isomorphism. Then a coproduct of an empty family of objects of $\mathcal{C}$ (that is a family indexed by the empty set) is an initial object for $\mathcal{C}$, and the reader should verify this.

(2) In the category *Set*, the binary coproduct of sets A and B is given by their disjoint union together with the obvious insertion functions. We can define

the disjoint union $A \uplus B$ of A and B as the union $(A \times \{A\}) \cup (B \times \{B\})$ with the insertion functions

$$\iota_A : A \to A \uplus B \leftarrow B : \iota_B$$

where ι_A is defined by $a \mapsto (a, A)$ for all $a \in A$, and ι_B is defined analogously.

(3) Suppose that X is a lattice viewed as a category. Then the top of X is a terminal object, the bottom of X an initial object, and finite meets and joins are finite products and coproducts respectively.

(4) The category $\mathcal{POS}et$ has binary products through the pointwise order on the cartesian product of (the underlying sets of) posets X and Y, together with the monotone set-theoretic projection functions. Also, any one point poset is a terminal object.

DISCUSSION 2.6.12   In a category with finite products we can show that for any objects A, B and C that there is an isomorphism $A \times (B \times C) \cong (A \times B) \times C$. Moreover, we can show that both the left hand side and the right hand side of this isomorphism are products of the triple (A, B, C). One might loosely say that $A \times (B \times C)$, $(A \times B) \times C$ and $A \times B \times C$ each satisfy the same specification, but are implemented differently. In concrete examples, the internal make up of these objects will be different, but they will each have similar external properties.

If C and $\mathcal{D}$ are categories with finite products, then the functor $F : C \to \mathcal{D}$ *preserves finite products* if for any finite family of objects $(A_1, \ldots, A_n)$ in C the morphism

$$m \overset{\text{def}}{=} \langle F\pi_i \mid i \in I \rangle : F(A_1 \times \ldots \times A_n) \to FA_1 \times \ldots \times FA_n$$

is an isomorphism, where of course $F\pi_j : F(A_1 \times \ldots \times A_n) \to FA_j$ is F applied to the projection π_j for each $j \in I$. Note that there may be witnesses other than m to the above isomorphism; we refer to m as the *canonical* isomorphism. In the case that $n = 0$ we say that F *preserves terminal objects*, that is the unique morphism $F(1_C) \to 1_\mathcal{D}$ is an isomorphism where 1_C and $1_\mathcal{D}$ are the terminal objects of C and $\mathcal{D}$ respectively. A finite product preserving functor F is *strict* if the above isomorphisms are identities.

EXERCISE 2.6.13   Find an example of a functor $F : C \to \mathcal{D}$ for which

$$F(A \times B) \cong FA \times FB$$

in $\mathcal{D}$ for all pairs of objects A and B in C, but such that F does not preserve binary products. *Hint: think about countably infinite sets.*

Note: *All the category theory required to read Chapter 3 has now been covered.*

2.7 The Yoneda Lemma

DISCUSSION 2.7.1   We learn in a first course in set theory that the collection of all sets cannot be a set but is in fact a proper class. In category theory we have to deal with collections which are large in a very real sense. Questions of size are important, but we do not delve into formal details here. We shall, however, make the following definition.

A category C is *small* if its morphisms can be indexed by a set; note that this implies the collection of objects of C is a set. C is *locally small* if for any pair of objects A and B the collection of morphisms from A to B can be indexed by a set. This set is usually written $Hom_C(A, B)$ or $C(A, B)$. For example, if X is a preorder viewed as a category, then

$$X(x, y) \;=\; \begin{cases} \{*\} & \text{if } x \leq y \\ \varnothing & \text{otherwise} \end{cases}$$

where $x, y \in X$ and $\{*\}$ is a one point set. Most categories that one meets in everyday use are indeed locally small. However, functor categories are not always so. If C is small and D is locally small, then $[C, D]$ is locally small. This is because the components of the natural transformations in $[C, D]$ are indexed by the objects of C and this collection is a set by hypothesis. More precisely, to give a natural transformation $\alpha: F \to G$, we have to give a morphism $\alpha_C: FC \to GC$ in D for each object C of C. Thus there is a candidate for such a natural transformation α for every function

$$ob\,C \longrightarrow \bigcup \{D(FC, GC) \mid C \in ob\,C\}$$

and there is certainly a set of such functions. If C and D are locally small then $[C, D]$ need not be locally small.

Now it is time to introduce some more notation. Let A and B be objects of a locally small category C. We can define a functor

$$C(-, +): C^{op} \times C \to Set$$

by taking any morphism $(f, g): (A, B) \to (A', B')$ in $C^{op} \times C$ to the set-theoretic function

$$C(f, g): C(A, B) \to C(A', B')$$

where $C(f, g)(h) = ghf$ for each morphism $h: A \to B$. (Note that f is a morphism $A' \to A$ in C). We can also define a functor

$$C(A, +): C \to Set.$$

As expected, this functor takes objects B of $\mathcal{C}$ to the set $\mathcal{C}(A, B)$, and if $g: B \to B'$ is a morphism of $\mathcal{C}$ then the functor $\mathcal{C}(A, +)$ takes $g: B \to B'$ to the function $\mathcal{C}(A, g): \mathcal{C}(A, B) \to \mathcal{C}(A, B')$ defined by setting $\mathcal{C}(A, g)(h) \overset{\text{def}}{=} gh$, where $h: A \to B$. Similarly, we can define a functor $\mathcal{C}(-, B): \mathcal{C}^{op} \to \mathcal{S}et$. We shall also write H^A for the functor $\mathcal{C}(A, +)$ and H_B for the functor $\mathcal{C}(-, B)$, when the category to which we are referring is clear. If $h: C \to C'$ is a morphism of $\mathcal{C}$ then $H^A h: H^A C \to H^A C'$ will be written as $H_h^A: H_C^A \to H_{C'}^A$, with a similar notation adopted for H_B. Finally, we shall write

$$H: \mathcal{C}^{op} \to [\mathcal{C}, \mathcal{S}et]$$

for the functor which sends $f: A' \to A$ to $H^f: H^A \to H^{A'}$. The functor H is often called the *Yoneda embedding* of $\mathcal{C}^{op}$ into the functor category $[\mathcal{C}, \mathcal{S}et]$. There is also a functor $H: \mathcal{C} \to [\mathcal{C}^{op}, \mathcal{S}et]$ defined in a similar fashion, that is by the assignment

$$f : A \longrightarrow A' \quad \mapsto \quad H_f : H_A \longrightarrow H_{A'}$$

where $f: A \to A'$ is a morphism of $\mathcal{C}$.

Now suppose that we are given functors $F: \mathcal{C} \to \mathcal{D}$ and $G: \mathcal{D} \to \mathcal{C}$ between locally small categories $\mathcal{C}$ and $\mathcal{D}$. Then there are functors

$$\mathcal{D}^{op} \times \mathcal{C} \xrightarrow{\ id \times F\ } \mathcal{D}^{op} \times \mathcal{D} \xrightarrow{\ \mathcal{D}(-,+)\ } \mathcal{S}et$$

$$\mathcal{D}^{op} \times \mathcal{C} \xrightarrow{\ G^{op} \times id\ } \mathcal{C}^{op} \times \mathcal{C} \xrightarrow{\ \mathcal{C}(-,+)\ } \mathcal{S}et$$

and the compositions will usually be written as $\mathcal{D}(-, F+)$, $\mathcal{C}(G-, +)$ respectively. See page 47 for the definition of G^{op}: the omission of the "op" in the notation $\mathcal{C}(G-, +)$ arises from the fact that the action of the functor G^{op} is essentially to "apply G." If A is an object of $\mathcal{D}$ and B an object of $\mathcal{C}$, then there are obvious functors $\mathcal{D}(A, F+): \mathcal{C} \to \mathcal{S}et$ and $\mathcal{C}(G-, B): \mathcal{D}^{op} \to \mathcal{S}et$.

The reader should take time to familiarise himself with the notation which has just been introduced. All of the concepts involved are easy, and simply require a little familiarity to use them smoothly. Of course, the obvious question to ask is why such diverse notation has been introduced. The answer is simply that in various situations one of the above terminologies may be easier and clearer to manipulate. We urge the reader to read and understand the notation thoroughly, for the remainder of this section makes heavy use of it.

Let us finish this discussion with the definition of a representable functor. Given a functor $F: \mathcal{C} \to \mathcal{S}et$ where $\mathcal{C}$ is locally small, we say that F is *representable* if there is an object A of $\mathcal{C}$ for which we can find a natural isomorphism

$H^A \cong F$. We say that a pair (a, A) where $a \in FA$ is a *representation* of F if the natural transformation $\Psi \colon H^A \to F$ which has components $\Psi_B \colon \mathcal{C}(A, B) \to FB$ given by $\Psi_B(f) \overset{\text{def}}{=} Ff(a)$ is a natural isomorphism, where $f \colon A \to B$ is any morphism of $\mathcal{C}$.

EXAMPLE 2.7.2 To give some feel for the definition we look at a concrete example. Recall that the set of subsets of a given set X, $\mathcal{P}(X)$, is in bijection with the set of functions from X to a two point set $\{0, 1\}$. For if we think of 1 as meaning true and 0 as meaning false, then given a subset X' of X and an element $x \in X$, we can ask whether it is true or not that $x \in X'$. Thus we can see that a two point set can represent (or code) information about subset membership. We can use the idea of a representable functor to formalise these ideas. In fact it is the case that the contravariant powerset functor $\mathcal{P} \colon Set^{op} \to Set$ is represented by $(\{1\}, \{0, 1\})$. The natural transformation $\Psi \colon H^{\{0,1\}} \to \mathcal{P}$ has components

$$\Psi_X : Set(X, \{0, 1\}) \xrightarrow{\quad \chi \mapsto \mathcal{P}(\chi)(\{1\}) \overset{\text{def}}{=} \chi^{-1}(\{1\}) \quad} \mathcal{P}(X)$$

where X is any set and $\chi \colon X \to \{0, 1\}$ is a function. It is easy to check that Ψ is a natural isomorphism.

DISCUSSION 2.7.3 We are now in a position to state and prove the Yoneda lemma. On first reading, this material may feel rather heavy. However, the Yoneda lemma is an indispensable tool which every category theorist should carry in his kit and be able to use. We shall make use of the Yoneda lemma when discussing the semantics of datatypes in later chapters. Roughly, the Yoneda lemma says that for a locally small category $\mathcal{C}$ and a functor $F \colon \mathcal{C} \to Set$, if we choose any object A of $\mathcal{C}$, there is a bijection between the elements of FA and natural transformations from H^A to F.

LEMMA 2.7.4 Let $\mathcal{C}$ be a locally small category, $F \colon \mathcal{C} \to Set$ a functor and A an object of $\mathcal{C}$. Then the collection $Nat(H^A, F)$ of natural transformations $H^A \to F$ is a set and so we can define a functor

$$Nat(H^-, +) : \mathcal{C} \times [\mathcal{C}, Set] \longrightarrow Set$$

as follows. The morphism $(g, \mu) \colon (A, F) \to (A', F')$ in $\mathcal{C} \times [\mathcal{C}, Set]$ is taken to the function

$$Nat(H^g, \mu) \colon Nat(H^A, F) \to Nat(H^{A'}, F')$$

which is defined by $Nat(H^g, \mu)(\alpha) \stackrel{\text{def}}{=} \mu \circ \alpha \circ H^g$ where $\alpha \colon H^A \to F$ is a natural transformation. Recall also (page 51) the evaluation functor

$$Ev : \mathcal{C} \times [\mathcal{C}, Set] \longrightarrow Set.$$

Then there is a natural isomorphism $\Phi \colon Nat(H^-, +) \cong Ev \colon \Psi$. If A is an object of $\mathcal{C}$, this amounts to saying that there is an isomorphism (set-theoretic bijection)

$$\Phi_{(A,F)} : Nat(H^A, F) \cong FA : \Psi_{(A,F)}$$

and this isomorphism is natural in (A, F).

PROOF   In the first part of the proof, we show that for each A and F there is a bijective assignment between $Nat(H^A, F)$ and FA, establishing that $Nat(H^A, F)$ is indeed a set and thus $Nat(H^-, +)$ is well defined. We can define an assignment

$$\Phi_{(A,F)} : Nat(H^A, F) \longrightarrow FA$$

by setting $\Phi_{(A,F)}(\alpha) \stackrel{\text{def}}{=} \alpha_A(id_A)$ for $\alpha \colon H^A \to F$ a natural transformation, and define an assignment

$$\Psi_{(A,F)} : FA \longrightarrow Nat(H^A, F)$$

by setting $\Psi_{(A,F)}(a)_B(f) \stackrel{\text{def}}{=} Ff(a)$ where $a \in FA$, B is an object of $\mathcal{C}$, $\Psi_{(A,F)}(a)_B$ is the component of the natural transformation $\Psi_{(A,F)}(a)$ at B, and $f \colon A \to B$ is a morphism in $\mathcal{C}$, where of course $\Psi_{(A,F)}(a)_B \colon \mathcal{C}(A, B) \to FB$. Note that one has to check that $\Psi_{(A,F)}(a)$ *is* a natural transformation. We urge the reader to do this.

Now we check that assignments $\Phi_{(A,F)}$ are isomorphisms (bijections) with inverses given by the $\Psi_{(A,F)}$. One way round, we check that $\Psi_{(A,F)}\Phi_{(A,F)} = id_{Nat(H^A, F)}$. To see this, first note that $\Psi_{(A,F)}\Phi_{(A,F)}(\alpha) = \Psi_{(A,F)}(\alpha_A(id_A))$. Then we have

$$\Psi_{(A,F)}(\alpha_A(id_A))_B(f) \;=\; Ff(\alpha_A(id_A))$$
$$because\ \alpha\ is\ natural \;=\; \alpha_B(H^A_f(id_A))$$
$$=\; \alpha_B(f \circ id_A)$$
$$=\; \alpha_B(f).$$

Thus the components of $\Psi_{(A,F)}(\alpha_A(id_A))$ are the same as those of α which is to say that the natural transformations $\Psi_{(A,F)}\Phi_{(A,F)}(\alpha)$ and α are identical, as required.

For the other way we check that $\Phi_{(A,F)}\Psi_{(A,F)} = id_{FA}$. Let $a \in FA$; then we have

$$
\begin{aligned}
\Phi_{(A,F)}\Psi_{(A,F)}(a) &= \Phi_{(A,F)}(\Psi_{(A,F)}(a)) \\
&= \Psi_{(A,F)}(a)_A(id_A) \\
&= (F(id_A))(a) \\
&= a.
\end{aligned}
$$

Hence we have established a bijection between the set FA and the collection $Nat(H^A, F)$, implying that the latter is indeed a set.

In fact the functions $\Phi_{(A,F)}$ and $\Psi_{(A,F)}$ give rise to natural isomorphisms Φ and Ψ. We shall check that $\Phi : Nat(H^-, +) \longrightarrow Ev$ is a natural transformation, that is the diagram

$$
\begin{array}{ccc}
Nat(H^A, F) & \xrightarrow{\;\;\Phi_{(A,F)}\;\;} & FA \\
{\scriptstyle Nat(H^g, \mu)}\big\downarrow & & \big\downarrow{\scriptstyle F'g\, \circ\, \mu_A} \\
Nat(H^{A'}, F') & \xrightarrow[\;\;\Phi_{(A',F')}\;\;]{} & F'A'
\end{array}
$$

commutes, where $(g,\mu) : (A,F) \to (A',F')$ is a morphism in $\mathcal{C} \times [\mathcal{C}, Set]$. Let α be a natural transformation from H^A to F. Then we have

$$
\begin{aligned}
(\Phi_{(A',F')} \circ Nat(H^g, \mu))(\alpha) &= \Phi_{(A',F')}(Nat(H^g, \mu)(\alpha)) \\
&= \Phi_{(A',F')}(\mu \circ \alpha \circ H^g) \\
\textit{by definition of } \Phi_{(A',F')} &= (\mu \circ \alpha \circ H^g)_{A'}(id_{A'}) \\
&= (\mu_{A'} \circ \alpha_{A'} \circ H^g_{A'})(id_{A'}) \\
&= (\mu_{A'} \circ \alpha_{A'})(H^g_{A'}(id_{A'})) \\
&= (\mu_{A'} \circ \alpha_{A'})(H^A_g(id_A)) \\
&= (\mu_{A'} \circ \alpha_{A'} \circ H^A_g)(id_A) \\
\textit{naturality of } \alpha &= (\mu_{A'} \circ Fg \circ \alpha_A)(id_A) \\
\textit{naturality of } \mu &= (F'g \circ \mu_A \circ \Phi_{(A,F)})(\alpha).
\end{aligned}
$$

But now we are done, for Lemma 2.5.3 implies that Ψ must be a natural transformation which is an inverse for Φ. $\qquad\square$

EXAMPLE 2.7.5   It is instructive to see how the Cayley representation theorem for groups arises as a special case of the Yoneda lemma. Let G be a group; so G can be regarded as a category with one object $\star$ and a morphism $g\colon \star \to \star$ for each element $g \in G$. Consider the functor $F\colon G \to Set$ given by

$$g\colon \star \longrightarrow \star \qquad \mapsto \qquad \tau_g\colon G \to G$$

in which the function τ_g is defined by $\tau_g(h) \stackrel{\text{def}}{=} hg$ for all $h \in G$. Let us show that there is a subgroup

$$Nat(H^\star, F) \subseteq Perm(G) \tag{1}$$

where $Perm(G)$ is the group of permutations on the (underlying set of) G, and the set $Nat(H^\star, F)$ is regarded as a group via composition of natural transformations. To see that every natural transformation $H^\star \to F$ is a permutation on G, note that a natural transformation $\alpha\colon H^\star \to F$ is determined by a function $\alpha_\star\colon G(\star, \star) \to F(\star)$, that is (overloading the notation) a function $\alpha\colon G \to G$. The naturality of α tells us that it is a bijection on G; for example if $h \in G$, and if $e \in G$ is the identity element we have

$$\alpha(\alpha(e)^{-1}\, h) = \alpha(e)\, \alpha(e)^{-1}\, h = h$$

and so α is surjective; injectivity is proved similarly. Applying the Yoneda lemma to the functor F, we find that there is a bijection of sets

$$G \xrightarrow{\;\cong\;} Nat(H^\star, F) \qquad g \mapsto \tau_g \tag{2}$$

which is in fact an isomorphism of groups. Putting (1) and (2) together we see that G *is isomorphic to a subgroup of permutations on* G, which is Cayley's representation theorem.

EXERCISES 2.7.6

(1) Verify that Ψ in Example 2.7.2 is a natural isomorphism.

(2) Verify that the Yoneda embedding $H\colon \mathcal{C} \to [\mathcal{C}^{op}, Set]$ is a full and faithful functor for any locally small category $\mathcal{C}$.

(3) Let X be a preorder and let $F\colon X \to Set$ be a functor where we will write $x \mapsto Fx$ for the operation on objects and $x \le y \quad \mapsto \quad f_{x,y}\colon Fx \to Fy$ for the operation on morphisms.

(a) If Fx is the empty set $\varnothing$, what can we say about $x \in X$?

(b) Let $a \in X$. Show that to give a natural transformation $\alpha\colon H^a \to F$ is to give an element $e_x \in Fx$ for each $x \in X$ satisfying $a \le x$, such that $f_{x,y}(e_x) = e_y$ whenever $y \in X$ and $x \le y$.

(c) Investigate the Yoneda lemma in this situation.

2.8 Cartesian Closed Categories

DISCUSSION 2.8.1   We begin by giving some intuition behind the idea of cartesian closed categories. Consider the category Set. Given sets A and B, the collection of functions $A \to B$ is again a *set*, written $Set(A, B)$ using the notation of the previous section. Thus $Set(A, B)$ is actually an object of the ambient category Set. In a cartesian closed category C, for any objects A and B, there is an object $A \Rightarrow B$ of C which has properties making it "resemble" the collection of morphisms $A \to B$ in C. Also, in the category Set, for every pair of sets A and B, there is a *function* $ev: (A \Rightarrow B) \times A \to B$ defined by $ev(f, a) \overset{\text{def}}{=} f(a)$, for any $f: A \to B$ and $a \in A$, which "*evaluates a function at an argument.*" Bearing this in mind, let us now give the formal definition.

A category C is a *cartesian closed category* if it has finite products, and for any objects B and C there is an object $B \Rightarrow C$ and morphism

$$ev: (B \Rightarrow C) \times B \to C$$

such that for any $f: A \times B \to C$ there is a unique morphism $\lambda(f): A \to (B \Rightarrow C)$ such that $f = ev \circ (\lambda(f) \times id_B)$. This is another example of a universal property. In this definition, the object $B \Rightarrow C$ is called the *exponential* of B and C and $\lambda(f)$ is the *exponential mate* of f. We shall also write $g^\star \overset{\text{def}}{=} ev \circ (g \times id_B)$ for any morphism $g: A \to (B \Rightarrow C)$.

EXAMPLES 2.8.2

(1) We shall see later on that cartesian closed categories arise as natural models of functional type theory. For the time being we simply hint at this fact with our first example of a cartesian closed category. The category Set is a cartesian closed category. A specified choice of terminal object is $\{\varnothing\}$ and (specified) binary products are given by set-theoretic cartesian product. The exponential of A and B is the set of functions from A to B. The function $ev: (A \Rightarrow B) \times A \to B$ is given by $ev(f, a) = f(a)$, where $a \in A$ and $f: A \to B$ is a function. Then given any $f: X \times A \to B$ we may define $\lambda(f): X \to (A \Rightarrow B)$ by letting $\lambda(f)(x)(a) = f(x, a)$ for each $x \in X$ and $a \in A$. It is easy to check that $f = ev(\lambda(f) \times id)$ and that $\lambda(f)$ is the unique function which satisfies this equation. Now we can begin to see the connection with functional type theory. In Set, $\lambda(f)$ may be regarded as a "curried" version of the function f.

(2) The category Cat of small categories is cartesian closed, with the exponential of C and D being given by the functor category $[C, D]$. Note that $[C, D]$ *is* another small category.

(3) A Heyting lattice viewed as a category is indeed cartesian closed, with Heyting implications as exponentials. In fact such a lattice also has finite coproducts.

(4) The category of Scott domains and continuous functions, $SDom$, is cartesian closed. This is tricky to prove, and so we state the example as a proposition.

PROPOSITION 2.8.3   The category $SDom$ is cartesian closed.

PROOF   Finite products are given as would be expected. The underlying set of a product of Scott domains is the product of the underlying sets, and the order is given pointwise. Now let B and C be two Scott domains. The exponential of B and C is given by the set of continuous functions $B \to C$ with the pointwise order (so given $f, g: B \to C$ then $f \le g$ iff $f(b) \le g(b)$ holds in C for each $b \in B$), which we shall denote by $B \Rightarrow C$. The morphism $ev: (B \Rightarrow C) \times B \to C$ is given by the continuous function defined by $ev(f, b) \overset{\text{def}}{=} f(b)$. Given any continuous function $f: A \times B \to C$ we define $\lambda(f): A \to (B \Rightarrow C)$ by setting $\lambda(f)(a)(b) \overset{\text{def}}{=} f(a, b)$. It is easy to verify that these definitions make sense. The only thing which is not clear is that $B \Rightarrow C$ is indeed a Scott domain. If $F \subseteq B \Rightarrow C$ is a directed subset, then $\bigsqcup_{B \Rightarrow C} F$ is given by $(\bigsqcup_{B \Rightarrow C} F)(b) \overset{\text{def}}{=} \bigsqcup_C \{f(b) \mid f \in F\}$ for each $b \in B$. One can check bounded cocompleteness similarly. It remains to verify that $B \Rightarrow C$ is algebraic. Let us define a continuous function $[b, c]: B \to C$ for each $b \in B^\circ$ and $c \in C^\circ$ by setting (for $x \in B$)

$$[b, c](x) = \begin{cases} c & \text{if } b \le x \\ \bot & \text{otherwise} \end{cases}$$

Note: As a convenient notation, whenever we write $[b, c]$ it will be implicit that $b \in B^\circ$ and $c \in C^\circ$. We shall characterise the compact elements of $B \Rightarrow C$ and prove algebraicity at the same time; in fact the compact elements of $B \Rightarrow C$ are precisely those continuous functions of the form $f \overset{\text{def}}{=} [b_1, c_1] \vee \ldots \vee [b_n, c_n]$ for finite $n \in \mathbb{N}$ where $c_i \le f(b_i)$ for each $1 \le i \le n$; the join exists because $B \Rightarrow C$ is bounded cocomplete, and one can check that f is indeed a continuous function. First we show that

$$\{\bigvee_{i=1}^{n} [b_i, c_i] \mid n \in \mathbb{N}, c_j \le \bigvee_{i=1}^{n} [b_i, c_i](b_j), 1 \le j \le n\} \subseteq (B \Rightarrow C)^\circ. \tag{1}$$

Suppose that $\bigvee_{i=1}^{n} [b_i, c_i] \le \bigsqcup F$ for $F \subseteq B \Rightarrow C$. Then for any j where $1 \le j \le n$ we have $c_j \le \bigvee_{i=1}^{n} [b_i, c_i](b_j) \le \bigsqcup \{f(b_j) \mid f \in F\}$ implying that $c_j \le f_j(b_j)$ for some $f_j \in F$, because c_j is compact. Hence $[b_j, c_j] \le f_j$ for any j, so that the directedness of F implies that there is $f \in F$ for which $\bigvee_{i=1}^{n} [b_i, c_i] \leq f$. Thus $\bigvee_{i=1}^{n} [b_i, c_i]$ is compact and so (1) holds. Now we show

$$(B \Rightarrow C)^{\circ} \subseteq \{ \bigvee_{i=1}^{n} [b_i, c_i] \mid n \in \mathbb{N}, c_j \leq \bigvee_{i=1}^{n} [b_i, c_i](b_j), 1 \leq j \leq n \}. \qquad (2)$$

In order to do this, we claim that given any continuous function $f \colon B \to C$,

$$f = \bigsqcup \{ \bigvee_{i=1}^{n} [b_i, c_i] \mid n \in \mathbb{N}, c_i \leq f(b_i), 1 \leq i \leq n \}. \qquad (3)$$

If $x \in B$ then $\bigvee_{i=1}^{n} [b_i, c_i](x) \leq \bigvee_{j \in J \subseteq \{1,\ldots,n\}} c_j \leq f(x)$ where we have set $J \overset{\text{def}}{=} \{ i \in \mathbb{N} \mid b_i \leq x \}$. So

$$\bigsqcup \{ \bigvee_{i=1}^{n} [b_i, c_i] \mid n \in \mathbb{N}, c_i \leq f(b_i), 1 \leq i \leq n \} \leq f.$$

To show that

$$f \leq \bigsqcup \{ \bigvee_{i=1}^{n} [b_i, c_i] \mid n \in \mathbb{N}, c_i \leq f(b_i), 1 \leq i \leq n \}$$

consider the following. Take $x \in B$ where $x = \bigsqcup \{ b \in B^{\circ} \mid b \leq x \}$ by algebraicity of B. By continuity of f it is sufficient to show that whenever $\hat{b} \in B^{\circ}$ with $\hat{b} \leq x$, then

$$f(\hat{b}) \leq \bigsqcup \{ \bigvee_{i=1}^{n} [b_i, c_i](x) \mid n \in \mathbb{N}, c_i \leq f(b_i), 1 \leq i \leq n \}.$$

Certainly

$$\bigvee \{ [b, c] \mid b \in B^{\circ}, c \in C^{\circ}, c \leq f(b) \} \leq$$

$$\bigsqcup \{ \bigvee_{i=1}^{n} [b_i, c_i] \mid n \in \mathbb{N}, c_i \leq f(b_i), 1 \leq i \leq n \}$$

and so it is sufficient to prove that

$$f(\hat{b}) \leq \bigvee \{ [b, c](x) \mid b \in B^{\circ}, c \in C^{\circ}, c \leq f(b) \}.$$

But using the algebraicity of C we have $f(\hat{b}) = \bigsqcup \{ c \in C^{\circ} \mid c \leq f(\hat{b}) \}$ and so all we need to show is that if $\hat{c} \leq f(\hat{b})$ for compact $\hat{c}$ and $\hat{b}$ then

$$\hat{c} \leq \bigvee \{ [b, c](x) \mid b \in B^{\circ}, c \in C^{\circ}, c \leq f(b) \}.$$

But this is immediate, for if $\hat{b} \leq x$ then $\hat{c} = [\hat{b}, \hat{c}](x)$, showing (3). Hence if $f \in (B \Rightarrow C)^{\circ}$, from (3) we must have $f = \bigvee_{i=1}^{n} [b_i, c_i]$, showing (2). Note that (1), (2) and (3) together prove algebraicity. This completes the verification that $\mathcal{SDom}$ is a cartesian closed category. $\square$

DISCUSSION 2.8.4   In the case that C is a locally small category we can give a slightly different definition of the notion of being cartesian closed. Let us introduce some more notation, and then present the equivalent definition as Proposition 2.8.5. Let C be a locally small category with finite products, let A, A', B and C be objects of C and $g: A' \to A$ a morphism. Define a functor $F: C^{op} \to Set$ as follows, where $f: A \times B \to C$ is any morphism in C:

$$g: A' \longrightarrow A \quad \longmapsto \quad Fg: C(A \times B, C) \xrightarrow{\ f \mapsto f(g \times id_B)\ } C(A' \times B, C).$$

Note that we shall often write $C(- \times B, C): C^{op} \to Set$ for this functor. Recall that the functor $C(- \times B, C)$ is representable if there is an object $B \Rightarrow C$ in C^{op} for which there is a natural isomorphism

$$C(- \times B, C) \cong C^{op}(B \Rightarrow C, -) \stackrel{\text{def}}{=} C(-, B \Rightarrow C).$$

Now we have the proposition

PROPOSITION 2.8.5   Suppose that C is a locally small category with finite products and that B and C are objects of C. If the functor $C(- \times B, C)$ is representable by some object $B \Rightarrow C$ for all such B and C, then C is a cartesian closed category with exponentials given by $B \Rightarrow C$. Conversely, if C is a locally small cartesian closed category, the functor $C(- \times B, C)$ is well defined and represented by the exponential $B \Rightarrow C$ for all such B and C.

PROOF

($\Rightarrow$) Suppose that $C(- \times B, C)$ is represented by $B \Rightarrow C$ (for every pair of objects B and C of C), where, say, we have a natural isomorphism denoted by

$$\Phi : C(- \times B, C) \cong C(-, B \Rightarrow C) : \Psi.$$

We write

$$\lambda(-) : C(A \times B, C) \rightleftarrows C(A, B \Rightarrow C) : (-)^*$$

for the components of the natural isomorphisms at A, that is we write $\lambda(-)$ for Φ_A and $(-)^*$ for Ψ_A. Thus given a morphism $f: A \times B \to C$ in C there is a morphism $\lambda(f): A \to (B \Rightarrow C)$ in C. Unravelling the definition of naturality in A at $\lambda(f)$ we get the following commutative diagram:

$$
\begin{array}{ccc}
C(B \Rightarrow C, B \Rightarrow C) & \xrightarrow{\ (-)^*\ } & C((B \Rightarrow C) \times B, C) \\[2mm]
\Big\downarrow{\scriptstyle C(\lambda(f), B \Rightarrow C)} & & \Big\downarrow{\scriptstyle C(\lambda(f) \times B, C)} \\[2mm]
C(A, B \Rightarrow C) & \xrightarrow[\ (-)^*\ ]{} & C(A \times B, C)
\end{array}
$$

Setting $ev \overset{\text{def}}{=} (id_{B \Rightarrow C})^*$, and using commutativity, we get

$$[\mathcal{C}(\lambda(f), B \Rightarrow C)(id_{B \Rightarrow C})]^* = \mathcal{C}(\lambda(f) \times B, C)(ev)$$

that is $\lambda(f)^* = f = ev(\lambda(f) \times id_B)$. Thus $\mathcal{C}$ is a cartesian closed category provided $\lambda(f)$ is the *unique* morphism $A \to (B \Rightarrow C)$ satisfying $f = ev(\lambda(f) \times id_B)$ for each $f: A \times B \to C$. To see that this is the case, first note that for any morphism $g: A \to (B \Rightarrow C)$ we have $g^* = ev(g \times id_B)$, which follows from naturality of $\lambda(-)$. Now suppose also $h: A \to (B \Rightarrow C)$ is another candidate for $\lambda(f)$. Then $h = \lambda(h^*) = \lambda(ev(h \times id_B)) = \lambda(f)$ showing uniqueness of $\lambda(f)$.

($\Leftarrow$) Now suppose that $\mathcal{C}$ is a locally small cartesian closed category. Then we claim that $\mathcal{C}(- \times B, C)$ is represented by the object $B \Rightarrow C$. Let us define a natural isomorphism

$$\Phi : \mathcal{C}(- \times B, C) \cong \mathcal{C}^{op}(B \Rightarrow C, -) \overset{\text{def}}{=} \mathcal{C}(-, B \Rightarrow C) : \Phi^{-1}$$

by appealing to Lemma 2.5.3, that is, we shall define isomorphisms (bijections)

$$\lambda(-) : \mathcal{C}(A \times B, C) \rightleftarrows \mathcal{C}(A, B \Rightarrow C) : (-)^*$$

which are the components of Φ and Φ^{-1}. In fact $\lambda(-)$ is given by exponential mate in $\mathcal{C}$, and if $g: A \to (B \Rightarrow C)$ then $g^* \overset{\text{def}}{=} ev(g \times id_B)$. From the universal property of exponential mates, it is easy to see that we have defined a bijection of sets, for example note that

$$g^* = ev(g \times id_B) = ev(\lambda(g^*) \times id_B)$$

implying that $\lambda(g^*) = g$, and if $f: A \times B \to C$ we can show $\lambda(f)^* = f$ similarly. We also need to see that the bijection is natural in A, which in the case of $\lambda(-) \overset{\text{def}}{=} \Phi_A$ amounts to the diagram

$$
\begin{array}{ccc}
\mathcal{C}(A \times B, C) & \overset{\lambda(-)}{\longrightarrow} & \mathcal{C}(A, B \Rightarrow C) \\
{\scriptstyle \mathcal{C}(g \times B, C)} \downarrow & & \downarrow {\scriptstyle \mathcal{C}(g, B \Rightarrow C)} \\
\mathcal{C}(A' \times B, C) & \underset{\lambda(-)}{\longrightarrow} & \mathcal{C}(A', B \Rightarrow C)
\end{array}
$$

commuting, where $g: A' \to A$ in $\mathcal{C}$. To see this, take $f: A \times B \to C$ and note that

$$\mathcal{C}(g \times B, C)(f) \overset{\text{def}}{=} f(g \times id_B) = ev(\lambda(f) \times id_B)(g \times id_B) = ev(\lambda(f)g \times id_B)$$

implying that $\lambda(f)g = \lambda(f(g \times id_B))$ from the universal property. Thus we have shown $\mathcal{C}(g, B \Rightarrow C)(\lambda(f)) = \lambda(\mathcal{C}(g \times B, C)(f))$ as required. $\qquad \square$

EXERCISE 2.8.6   Prove that the category $\mathcal{DCPO}$ is cartesian closed. Be sure to check all of the details carefully.

DISCUSSION 2.8.7   We end this section with some notation which will prove useful when giving semantics to type theories. Let $\mathcal{C}$ be a cartesian closed category. We can define a functor $(-) \Rightarrow (+): \mathcal{C}^{op} \times \mathcal{C} \to \mathcal{C}$ by the assignment

$$(f, g): (A, B) \longrightarrow (A', B') \quad \mapsto \quad f \Rightarrow g: (A \Rightarrow B) \longrightarrow (A' \Rightarrow B')$$

where $(f, g): (A, B) \longrightarrow (A', B')$ is of course a morphism of $\mathcal{C}^{op} \times \mathcal{C}$, $A \Rightarrow B$ and $A' \Rightarrow B'$ are exponentials in $\mathcal{C}$, and we define $f \Rightarrow g \overset{\text{def}}{=} \lambda(g \circ ev \circ (id_{A \Rightarrow B} \times f))$. Given an object A of $\mathcal{C}$ we can similarly define functors $A \Rightarrow (-): \mathcal{C} \to \mathcal{C}$ and $(-) \Rightarrow A: \mathcal{C}^{op} \to \mathcal{C}$.

Let $F: \mathcal{C} \to \mathcal{D}$ be a functor between cartesian closed categories which preserves finite products. We say that F *preserves* exponentials if the exponential mate of

$$F(A \Rightarrow B) \times FA \overset{\cong}{\longrightarrow} F((A \Rightarrow B) \times A) \overset{F(ev)}{\longrightarrow} FB$$

is an isomorphism $\lambda(F(ev) \circ \cong): F(A \Rightarrow B) \to (FA \Rightarrow FB)$ and we call this witness the *canonical* isomorphism. We shall also refer to such an F as a *cartesian closed* functor. A cartesian closed functor F is *strict* if (it is a finite product preserving functor) and $\lambda(F(ev) \circ \cong) = id_{FA \Rightarrow FB}$.

EXERCISES 2.8.8

(1) Formulate precisely the definitions of the functors $A \Rightarrow (-): \mathcal{C} \to \mathcal{C}$ and $(-) \Rightarrow A: \mathcal{C}^{op} \to \mathcal{C}$, where A is an object of a cartesian closed category $\mathcal{C}$.

(2) Let $\mathcal{C}$ be a cartesian closed category and $f: A \to B$ and $g: B \to (C \Rightarrow D)$ be morphisms of $\mathcal{C}$. Show that $(gf)^{*} = g^{*}(f \times id_{C})$.

(3) Let $f: A \times B \to C$ and $g: C \to D$ be morphisms of a cartesian closed category. Show that $\lambda(gf) = (id_B \Rightarrow g)\lambda(f)$.

(4) Let A be an object of a cartesian closed category $\mathcal{C}$. Show that $A \Rightarrow (-)$ preserves finite products.

(5) Formulate the notion of a finite coproduct preserving functor and show that $A \times (-): \mathcal{C} \to \mathcal{C}$ is such a functor *provided* that $\mathcal{C}$ is cartesian closed.

Note: *All the category theory required to read Chapter 4 has now been covered.*

2.9 *Monics, Equalisers, Pullbacks and their Duals*

DISCUSSION 2.9.1   We begin by considering the notion of monic and epic morphisms. Roughly, a monic morphism is the categorical analogue of an injective function, and an epic morphism is the categorical analogue of a surjective function. However, the reader should note that this comparison is not as strict as one might hope, as we shall see in later examples. Let us now give the formal definitions.

A morphism $f: A \to B$ in a category $\mathcal{C}$ is *monic* if given any morphisms $g, h: C \to A$ for which $fg = fh$, then $g = h$. We denote a monic morphism by $f: A \rightarrowtail B$. In the categories $\mathcal{S}et$, $\mathcal{M}on$, $\omega\mathcal{CPO}$, and $\mathcal{G}rp$, the monic morphisms are precisely the morphisms whose underlying set functions are injective. In a preorder X regarded as a category, all morphisms are monic. A morphism $f: A \to B$ in a category $\mathcal{C}$ is *epic* if given any morphisms $g, h: B \to C$ such that $gf = hf$, then $g = h$. We denote an epic morphism by $f: A \twoheadrightarrow B$. An epic morphism is the dual notion of a monic morphism in the sense that a morphism $e: A \to B$ in a category $\mathcal{C}$ is epic just in case $e: B \to A$ is a monic morphism in $\mathcal{C}^{op}$.

In $\mathcal{S}et$, a morphism is epic just in case it is surjective. It is clear that a surjective function is epic. Conversely, suppose that f is not surjective and consider

$$A \xrightarrow{\;f\;} B \underset{h}{\overset{g}{\rightrightarrows}} \{0,1\}$$

where for $b \in B$, g is defined by $b \mapsto 0$, and h is defined by

$$h(b) \;=\; \begin{cases} 0 & \text{if } b \in f(A) \\ 1 & \text{otherwise} \end{cases}$$

Then $g \neq h$, but $gf = hf$ implying that f is not epic. One can also check that a morphism in $\mathcal{S}et$ is injective just in case it is monic. Unfortunately, such a correspondence does not always hold, as we now see. In the category $\mathcal{R}ng$ of commutative rings and ring homomorphisms, the canonical inclusion $i: \mathbb{Z} \to \mathbb{Q}$ is epic but is clearly not surjective. To see the former, suppose that

$$\mathbb{Z} \xrightarrow{\;i\;} \mathbb{Q} \underset{h}{\overset{g}{\rightrightarrows}} R$$

is commutative. Recall that any ring homomorphism $h: \mathbb{Q} \to \mathbb{R}$ is determined by its effect on $\mathbb{Z}$; to wit we have for $q = m/n \in \mathbb{Q}$:

$$h(q) = h(m/1)h(n/1)^{-1} = h(i(m))h(i(n))^{-1} = g(i(m))g(i(n))^{-1} = g(q).$$

Hence $g = h$.

Equalisers can be thought of as a categorical notion of an equationally defined subset. Given the functions $f, g\colon \mathbb{R} \times \mathbb{R} \to \mathbb{R}$ given by $(x, y) \mapsto x^2 + y^2$ and $(x, y) \mapsto 1$ for each $(x, y) \in \mathbb{R} \times \mathbb{R}$, the equaliser for f and g is the subset of $\mathbb{R} \times \mathbb{R}$ given by

$$\{(x, y) \in \mathbb{R} \times \mathbb{R} \mid x^2 + y^2 = 1\}.$$

Now for the definition of equalisers.

An *equaliser* for a pair of morphisms $f, g\colon A \to B$ in a category $\mathcal{C}$ is given by a morphism $e\colon E \to A$ such that

- $fe = ge$ and

- given any $h\colon C \to A$ with $fh = gh$, there is a unique $k\colon C \to E$ for which $h = ek$.

It may be helpful to view this data in diagrammatic form:

The notion of a coequaliser is dual to that of an equaliser in the following sense. A *coequaliser* for a pair of morphisms $f, g\colon A \to B$ in a category $\mathcal{C}$ is given by an equaliser for the pair of morphisms $f, g\colon B \to A$ in the category $\mathcal{C}^{op}$.

EXAMPLE 2.9.2   In *Set* an equaliser for $f, g\colon A \to B$ is given by the inclusion $\{a \in A \mid f(a) = g(a)\} \to A$.

EXERCISES 2.9.3

(1) Show how to construct the equaliser of any two continuous functions in the category $\mathcal{DCPO}$. Prove that your construction works.

(2) Write down a full definition of a coequaliser similar to that given for an equaliser.

(3) We construct coequalisers in the category *Set*. First, some background ideas. Let B be a set, and R a relation on B, that is a subset $R \subseteq B \times B$. The *equivalence relation generated by* R is the smallest equivalence relation $\sim\, \subseteq B \times B$ such that $R \subseteq\, \sim$. Now suppose that $f, g\colon A \to B$ are two functions. Then there is a relation on B given by $S \overset{\text{def}}{=} \{(f(a), g(a)) \in B \times B \mid a \in A\}$.

(a) Let R be a relation on a set B. Define

$$R^{op} \overset{\text{def}}{=} \{(b', b) \in B \times B \mid (b, b') \in R\},$$

and $\Delta \overset{\text{def}}{=} \{(b, b) \mid b \in B\}$. Now set $R_0 \overset{\text{def}}{=} R \cup \Delta \cup R^{op}$, and set

$$R_{i+1} \overset{\text{def}}{=} \{(b, b'') \in B \times B \mid \exists b' \in B. \ (b, b') \in R_i \text{ and } (b', b'') \in R_i\}$$

for each $i \in \mathbb{N}$. Show that the set $\sim \overset{\text{def}}{=} \bigcup\{R_i \mid i \in \mathbb{N}\}$ is the equivalence relation generated by R.

(b) By thinking about the definition of a coequaliser in $\mathcal{S}et$, the relation S, and quotients by equivalence relations, construct a coequaliser for f and g in $\mathcal{S}et$.

(4) Let $\mathcal{C}$ be any category and let all objects and morphisms which appear in this exercise lie in $\mathcal{C}$. Let $f: A \to B$ be any morphism. We say that f is a *split monic* if there is a morphism $g: B \to A$ for which $gf = id_A$, and that f is a *regular* monic if it occurs as an equaliser, that is, one can find an equaliser in $\mathcal{C}$ of the form

$$A \xrightarrow{\ f\ } B \underset{k}{\overset{h}{\rightrightarrows}} C$$

For the following problems, let $A \xrightarrow{f} B \xrightarrow{g} C$ be a composable pair of morphisms.

(a) Show that both split monics and regular monics are monics.

(b) Show that if f and g are monic (split monic) then gf is monic (split monic).

(c) Show that if gf is monic (split monic) then f is monic (split monic).

(d) Show that if gf is regular monic and g monic, then f is regular monic.

DISCUSSION 2.9.4   Finally we define the notion of a pullback. A *pullback* for a pair of morphisms $f: A \to C$ and $g: B \to C$ in a category $\mathcal{C}$ is given by

• an object $A \times_C B$ of $\mathcal{C}$, together with

• morphisms $p_A: A \times_C B \to A$ and $p_B: A \times_C B \to B$ for which $f \circ p_A = g \circ p_B$,

such that given any two morphisms $h: D \to A$ and $k: D \to B$ in $\mathcal{C}$ for which $f \circ h = g \circ k$, there is a unique morphism $m: D \to A \times_C B$ for which $p_A \circ m = h$

and $p_B \circ m = k$. We can picture these data in a diagram:

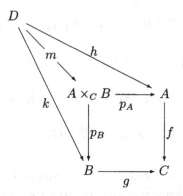

We say that p_A *is a pullback of* g *along* f and that p_B *is a pullback of* f *along* g. A *pushout* for a pair of morphisms $f: C \to A$ and $g: C \to B$ in a category $\mathcal{C}$ is given by a pullback of $f: A \to C$ and $g: B \to C$ in the category $\mathcal{C}^{op}$.

EXAMPLE 2.9.5   We look at pullbacks in *Set*. Given functions $f: A \to C$ and $g: B \to C$ a pullback is given by the pair of morphisms $\pi_1: P \to A$ and $\pi_2: P \to B$ where

$$P \overset{\text{def}}{=} \{(a, b) \in A \times B \mid f(a) = g(b)\},$$

$\pi_1(a, b) = a$ and $\pi_2(a, b) = b$.

To see that this gives us a pullback, take functions $h: D \to A$ and $k: D \to B$ such that $fh = gk$. Then there is certainly a unique well defined function $e: D \to P$ for which $\pi_1 e = h$ and $\pi_2 e = k$, given by $e(d) \overset{\text{def}}{=} (h(d), k(d))$ where $d \in D$.

EXERCISE 2.9.6   Suppose that

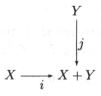

is a binary coproduct diagram in *Set*. What is the pullback?

We finish this section with a lemma that we shall need later on.

LEMMA 2.9.7   A pullback of a monic morphism is a monic morphism. More precisely, given a category $\mathcal{C}$, morphisms $f: A \to C$ and $m: B \rightarrowtail C$, and a pullback

$$
\begin{array}{ccc}
P & \xrightarrow{\;g\;} & B \\
\downarrow{\scriptstyle m'} & & \downarrow{\scriptstyle m} \\
A & \xrightarrow[\;f\;]{} & C
\end{array}
$$

then m' is monic.

PROOF   Suppose that $h, k: D \to P$ are morphisms for which $m'h = m'k$. Then both h and k factor $m'k$ through m', and because m is monic both h and k factor gh through g, implying that $h = k$ from the uniqueness property of pullbacks.   □

2.10   Adjunctions

DISCUSSION 2.10.1   We shall illustrate the concept of adjunction in the situation where categories are preorders and the functors are monotone functions. Given preorders X and Y, then the monotone function $f: X \to Y$ has a *left adjoint* if there exists a monotone function $l: Y \to X$ for which given any $x \in X$ and $y \in Y$ then $y \le f(x)$ iff $l(y) \le x$. The function f has a *right adjoint* if there exists a monotone function $r: Y \to X$ for which given any $x \in X$ and $y \in Y$ we have $f(x) \le y$ iff $x \le r(y)$. An *adjunction* between preorders X and Y is a pair of monotone functions f and g for which f is a left adjoint to g (or equivalently g is a right adjoint to f), written $(f \dashv g)$. We have the following propositions which illustrate the properties of adjoints; we shall write $X \Rightarrow Y$ for the set of monotone functions $X \to Y$, regarded as a preorder with the pointwise ordering.

PROPOSITION 2.10.2   Suppose that $f \in X \Rightarrow Y$ and $g \in Y \Rightarrow X$ where X and Y are preorders. Then $(f \dashv g)$ iff $id_X \le gf$ in $X \Rightarrow X$ and $fg \le id_Y$ in $Y \Rightarrow Y$.

PROOF

($\Rightarrow$) Suppose that $(f \dashv g)$. Then for all $x \in X$, we have $f(x) \le f(x)$ implying that $x \le g(f(x))$, that is $id_X \le gf$. Proving $fg \le id_Y$ is similar.

($\Leftarrow$) Conversely, suppose that the inequalities of the proposition hold. Suppose that $f(x) \le y$. Then $x \le g(f(x)) \le g(y)$ using monotonicity of g, that is $x \le g(y)$. That $x \le g(y)$ implies $f(x) \le y$ is equally easy.   □

PROPOSITION 2.10.3   A monotone function $f: X \to Y$ has a right adjoint iff there is a function $r: Y \to X$ such that

• for all $y \in Y$ we have $f(r(y)) \leq y$, and

• for all $x \in X$ and $y \in Y$ we have $f(x) \leq y$ implies $x \leq r(y)$.

Each value $r(y)$ is determined uniquely up to isomorphism by the stated conditions.

PROOF

   ($\Rightarrow$) Suppose that f has a right adjoint r. It is clear that this r will do for the r of the proposition.

   ($\Leftarrow$) Suppose now that we are given such an r. The only thing to prove is that r is monotone, for if this is so, the conditions of the proposition imply that $(f \dashv r)$. Take $y \leq y'$ in Y. Then $f(r(y)) \leq y \leq y'$ implying that $r(y) \leq r(y')$. □

PROPOSITION 2.10.4   Let X and Y be preorders. Suppose that $f, f' \in X \Rightarrow Y$ and $g, g' \in Y \Rightarrow X$ with $(f \dashv g)$ and $(f' \dashv g')$. Then $f \leq f'$ iff $g' \leq g$ and similarly $f' \leq f$ iff $g \leq g'$. Thus we have $f \cong f'$ iff $g \cong g'$. This implies that an adjoint to a monotone function is unique up to isomorphism; and if X and Y are in fact posets, then the adjoints are unique.

PROOF   Suppose that $g' \leq g$. Then $f \circ id_X \leq f(g'f') \leq (fg)f' \leq id_Y \circ f'$ implying $f \leq f'$. The other facts are proved similarly. □

PROPOSITION 2.10.5   Suppose that we are given preorders and monotone functions

$$X \xrightarrow[\;g\;]{\;f\;} Y \xrightarrow[\;k\;]{\;h\;} Z$$

for which $(f \dashv g)$ and $(h \dashv k)$. Then $(hf \dashv gk)$.

PROOF   For all $x \in X$ and $z \in Z$, we have $h(f(x)) \leq z$ iff $f(x) \leq k(z)$ iff $x \leq g(k(z))$. □

THEOREM 2.10.6   Let $f: X \to Y$ be a monotone function between preorders X and Y. If f has a right adjoint then f preserves all joins which exist in X. Dually, if f has a left adjoint then f preserves all meets which exist in X.

PROOF   Let $A \subseteq X$, $y \in Y$, and suppose that $\bigvee A$ exists in X. Then for every $y \in Y$ we have $f(\bigvee A) \leq y$ iff $\bigvee A \leq r(y)$ iff $A \leq r(y)$ iff $f(A) \leq y$. Hence $\bigvee f(A)$ exists and is isomorphic to $f(\bigvee A)$ as asserted. The dual result is proved similarly.   □

DISCUSSION 2.10.7   The theorem which follows is known as the *adjoint functor theorem for preorders*. It is a very useful result, giving conditions for the existence of left and right adjoints to monotone functions.

THEOREM 2.10.8   Let $f: X \to Y$ be a monotone function between preorders and suppose that X has all joins. Then f has a right adjoint if it preserves them. Dually, if X has all meets then f has a left adjoint if it preserves them.

PROOF   Define a function $r: Y \to X$ by setting $r(y) \stackrel{\text{def}}{=} \bigvee \{x \in X \mid f(x) \leq y\}$ for each $y \in Y$, and r is well defined by hypothesis. We show that r satisfies the hypotheses of Proposition 2.10.3. Now, f preserves joins, and so

$$f(r(y)) \cong \bigvee \{f(x) \mid x \in X, f(x) \leq y\}$$

implying that $f(r(y)) \leq y$. Let $x \in X$ and $y \in Y$ be given, and suppose that $f(x) \leq y$. Then certainly $x \leq r(y)$, and so r is a right adjoint. If f preserves all meets, the construction of a left adjoint for f is similar.   □

EXAMPLES 2.10.9

(1) Let $1 \stackrel{\text{def}}{=} \{*\}$ be the preorder with $* \leq *$, a terminal object in $\mathcal{PreSet}$. Given a preorder X, the unique function $!_X: X \to 1$ (which is trivially monotone) has a left adjoint iff X has a bottom element and a right adjoint iff X has a top element. As this is the first example, we spell out the easy details. Suppose $!_X$ has a left adjoint $l: 1 \to X$. Then for all $x \in X$ we have $* \leq !_X(x)$ implying $l(*) \leq x$. Hence $l(*)$ is a bottom element of in X. Conversely, if $\bot$ is a bottom element of X, defining $l(*) \stackrel{\text{def}}{=} \bot$ gives a left adjoint to $!_X$.

(2) Let X be a preorder with binary meets and joins. There is a monotone function $\Delta: X \to X \times X$ given by $\Delta(x) \stackrel{\text{def}}{=} (x, x)$. Then we have $(\vee \dashv \Delta \dashv \wedge)$ where $\wedge: X \times X \to X$ takes a pair of elements to their meet (and similarly for $\vee$).

(3) Let $f: X \to Y$ be a function. Recall the functors (monotone functions)

$$f^{-1}: \mathcal{P}(Y) \to \mathcal{P}(X) \qquad \exists f: \mathcal{P}(X) \to \mathcal{P}(Y) \qquad \forall f: \mathcal{P}(X) \to \mathcal{P}(Y)$$

(see Examples 1.2.17 and Examples 2.3.3). Then we have $(\exists f \dashv f^{-1} \dashv \forall f)$. For example, let $A \subseteq X$ and $B \subseteq Y$. Suppose $B \subseteq \forall f(A)$. Then for each

$b \in B$ we have $f^{-1}(\{b\}) \subseteq A$, implying that $f^{-1}(B) \subseteq A$. Also, $f^{-1}(B) \subseteq A$ implies $B \subseteq \forall f(A)$ is immediate, and so $(f^{-1} \dashv \forall f)$. That $(\exists f \dashv f^{-1})$ is similar.

(4) Let D be a dcpo and $\mathcal{I}(D)$ the set of inductive subsets. One can check that meets are calculated in $\mathcal{I}(D)$ by taking intersections in $\mathcal{P}(D)$. It follows that the inclusion $\mathcal{I}(D) \to \mathcal{P}(D)$ preserves all meets and so has a left adjoint using Theorem 2.10.8. Indeed, the left adjoint $l : \mathcal{P}(D) \to \mathcal{I}(D)$ is given by $l(A) \stackrel{\text{def}}{=} \bigcap \{ I \in \mathcal{I}(D) \mid A \subseteq I \}$ for every $A \in \mathcal{P}(D)$.

(5) Take a morphism $f : D \to E$ in $\mathcal{DCPO}$. Then the function $f^{-1} : \mathcal{P}(E) \to \mathcal{P}(D)$ restricts to give a monotone function $f^* : \mathcal{I}(E) \to \mathcal{I}(D)$. This has a left adjoint $l : \mathcal{I}(D) \to \mathcal{I}(E)$ where given $I \in \mathcal{I}(D)$,

$$l(I) \stackrel{\text{def}}{=} \bigcap \{ J \in \mathcal{I}(E) \mid f(I) \subseteq J \}.$$

f^* does not in general have a right adjoint—can you prove this?

DISCUSSION 2.10.10   We now move on to the definition of adjoint functor. The *forgetful* functor $U : \mathcal{Mon} \to \mathcal{Set}$ taking a monoid to its underlying set, and the functor $(-)^* : \mathcal{Set} \to \mathcal{Mon}$ taking a set to its Kleene closure, are related in a certain way which we now describe.

Given a monoid M and a set A any function $g : A \to UM$ corresponds to a unique monoid morphism $\widehat{g} : A^* \to M$. Indeed, there is a bijection

$$\widehat{(-)} : \mathcal{Mon}(A^*, M) \cong \mathcal{Set}(A, UM) : \overline{(-)}$$

given by

$$g : A \longrightarrow UM \quad \longmapsto \quad \widehat{g} : A^* \xrightarrow{[a_1, \ldots, a_n] \mapsto g(a_1) \ldots g(a_n)} M,$$

$$f : A^* \longrightarrow M \quad \longmapsto \quad \overline{f} : A \xrightarrow{a \mapsto f([a])} UM.$$

and one can check that this bijection gives rise to a natural isomorphism

$$\Phi : \mathcal{Set}(-, U(+)) \cong \mathcal{Mon}((-)^*, +) : \mathcal{Set}^{op} \times \mathcal{Mon} \to \mathcal{Set}$$

where at any object (A, M) of $\mathcal{Set}^{op} \times \mathcal{Mon}$ we have $\Phi_{(A,M)} \stackrel{\text{def}}{=} \widehat{(-)}$ and (say) $(\Phi^{-1})_{(A,M)} \stackrel{\text{def}}{=} \overline{(-)}$. This is an example of an adjunction between the functors $(-)^*$ and U.

EXERCISE 2.10.11   Check the naturality of the isomorphism.

DISCUSSION 2.10.12   Now we give a formal definition of adjunction.

Let $F:\mathcal{C} \to \mathcal{D}$ and $G:\mathcal{D} \to \mathcal{C}$ be two functors. We say that F is *left adjoint* to G or that G is *right adjoint* to F if given any objects A of $\mathcal{C}$ and B of $\mathcal{D}$ we have

- a bijection between morphisms $FA \to B$ in $\mathcal{D}$ and $A \to GB$ in $\mathcal{C}$, which we shall illustrate diagrammatically as

$$\frac{f:FA \to B}{\overline{f}:A \to GB} \qquad\qquad \frac{g:A \to GB}{\widehat{g}:FA \to B}$$

and moreover

- this bijection is *natural in A and B*, which by definition means that given morphisms $a:A' \to A$ in $\mathcal{C}$ and $b:B \to B'$ in $\mathcal{D}$ we have

$$\overline{b \circ f \circ Fa} = Gb \circ \overline{f} \circ a \quad \text{and} \quad (Gb \circ g \circ a)^{\wedge} = b \circ \widehat{g} \circ Fa.$$

It may be helpful to picture the naturality thus:

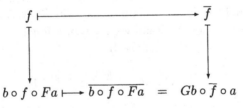

and

If F is left adjoint to G then we write $(F \dashv G)$. An *adjunction* consists of a pair of adjoint functors F and G together with a *choice* of natural bijection. We shall refer to $\overline{f}$ as the *mate* of f across the adjunction; similarly $\widehat{g}$ is the *mate* of g.

REMARK 2.10.13   Suppose that functors F and G are adjoint as in Discussion 2.10.12 and that $\mathcal{C}$ and $\mathcal{D}$ are *locally small*. To say that F is left adjoint to G (that is, there is a bijection between the morphisms $FA \to B$ and $A \to GB$, and this bijection is natural in A and B) is equivalent to saying that there is a natural isomorphism between the functors

$$\mathcal{C}(-, G(+)), \quad \mathcal{D}(F(-), +) : \mathcal{C}^{op} \times \mathcal{D} \longrightarrow \mathcal{S}et$$

which are well defined because of local smallness. In practise, this overloading of the word "natural" should not cause problems.

EXAMPLES 2.10.14

(1) For a fixed set A, the functor $A \times (-) \colon Set \to Set$ has a right adjoint $Set(A, -) \colon Set \to Set$. For given sets B and C, functions $f \colon B \to Set(A, C)$ correspond bijectively to functions $g \colon A \times B \to C$ (what is the bijection?) and the bijection is certainly natural in B and C.

(2) We have $((-)^* \dashv U)$ as described above in Discussion 2.10.10. Recall that A^* is the free monoid on A, for each set A.

(3) It is often the case that functors which arise through the creation of freely generated mathematical structures possess right adjoints which forget about the additional structure. Another example of this phenomenon is the construction of a vector space generated by a set X. Let $F \colon Set \to Vec_K$ be the functor which takes a set X to the vector space generated by X. Recall that a vector in FX is a formal finite linear combination $\Sigma_{i \in n} k_i x_i$ where the x_i are elements of X and the k_i are scalars in the field K, with addition and scalar multiplication defined in the usual way. Given a function $f \colon X \to Y$ then the linear map $Ff \colon FX \to FY$ is defined by

$$Ff(\Sigma_{i \in n} k_i x_i) \stackrel{\text{def}}{=} \Sigma_{i \in n} k_i f(x_i).$$

There is also a functor $U \colon Vec_K \to Set$ which sends a vector space V to its underlying set of vectors. Suppose that $g \colon X \to UV$ is a function. Then it is not difficult to see that g has a *unique extension* to a linear map $\widehat{g} \colon FX \to V$. The assignment $g \mapsto \widehat{g}$ has an inverse: given a linear map $f \colon FX \to V$, f restricts to a function $\overline{f} \colon X \to UV$. Thus we have a bijection

$$\overline{(-)} : Set(X, UV) \rightleftharpoons Vec_K(FX, U) : \widehat{(-)}$$

which we can check is natural in the required sense.

(4) The *diagonal functor* $\Delta \colon Set \to Set \times Set$ taking a function $f \colon A \to B$ to $(f, f) \colon (A, A) \to (B, B)$ has right and left adjoints Π and Σ taking any morphism $(f, g) \colon (A, A') \to (B, B')$ of $Set \times Set$ to $f \times g \colon A \times A' \to B \times B'$ and $f + g \colon A + A' \to B + B'$ respectively. Here, $f + g$ is the function defined to be $[\iota_B f, \iota_{B'} g]$ where

$$\iota_B : B \to B + B' \leftarrow B' : \iota_{B'}.$$

This example remains valid if we replace Set by any category $\mathcal{C}$, where we leave the reader to define the diagonal functor $\Delta \colon \mathcal{C} \to \mathcal{C} \times \mathcal{C}$.

(5) The category *Cat* has objects all small categories and morphisms functors between them. Then the functor $ob: Cat \to Set$ which sends a small category to its underlying set of objects has a left adjoint *dis*, where *dis* sends a set A to its corresponding *discrete category* (a discrete category is one in which the only morphisms are the identities). ob also has a right adjoint *ind* which maps a set A to the indiscrete category with objects the elements of A and precisely one morphism $a \to b$ for each pair (a, b) of elements of A. The functor $dis: Set \to Cat$ also has a left adjoint *con* which maps each small category C to the set $con\, C$ of connected components of C. By definition, $con\, C \overset{\text{def}}{=} ob\mathcal{C}/\equiv$ where $\equiv$ is the equivalence generated by $\prec$ where $A \prec B$ just in case there is a morphism $A \to B$. We make this more explicit. Define a bijection

$$\overline{(-)}: Set(con\, C, B) \cong Cat(\mathcal{C}, dis\, B): \widehat{(-)}$$

as follows. Suppose that C is an object of $\mathcal{C}$, and $u: C \to C'$ is a morphism of $\mathcal{C}$ and $f: con\, C \to B$. Then we set $\overline{f}(C) \overset{\text{def}}{=} f[C]$ where $[C]$ is the equivalence class of C under $\equiv$, and $\overline{f}(u) \overset{\text{def}}{=} id: f[C] \to f[C']$. If now $F: \mathcal{C} \to dis\, B$ is a functor, then $\widehat{F}([C]) \overset{\text{def}}{=} FC$. One can check that we have given a bijection, natural in the required sense. Summarising we have $(con \dashv dis \dashv ob \dashv ind)$.

(6) If we have an equivalence $F: \mathcal{C} \simeq \mathcal{D}: G$ then it is the case that each functor is both left and right adjoint to the other. For example, to see that $(F \dashv G)$, we define a bijection between morphisms $FA \to B$ and morphisms $A \to GB$ by

$$\frac{f: FA \to B}{G(f) \circ \eta_A: A \cong GFA \to GB}$$

and

$$\frac{g: A \to GB}{\epsilon_B \circ F(f): FA \to FGB \cong B}$$

where $\epsilon: FG \cong id_{\mathcal{D}}$ and $\eta: id_{\mathcal{C}} \cong GF$. It is an easy exercise to verify naturality.

(7) Recall the definition of cartesian closed category given in Discussion 2.8.1. In fact there is another formulation of cartesian closed category which turns out to be equivalent to the earlier definition. We shall state this as a proposition:

PROPOSITION 2.10.15   Let $\mathcal{C}$ be a category with finite products. The existence of a right adjoint R to the functor $(-) \times B: \mathcal{C} \to \mathcal{C}$ for each object B of $\mathcal{C}$, is equivalent to the definition of cartesian closed category in Discussion 2.8.1.

PROOF

($\Rightarrow$) Suppose that $\mathcal{C}$ satisfies the data of the proposition. Given an object B of $\mathcal{C}$, let R be the right adjoint of $(-) \times B$, and set $B \Rightarrow C \overset{\text{def}}{=} R(C)$ for any object C of $\mathcal{C}$. Given a morphism $f: A \times B \to C$ we define $\lambda(f): A \to (B \Rightarrow C)$ to be the mate of f across the given adjunction. The morphism

$$ev: (B \Rightarrow C) \times B \to C$$

is the mate $(id_{B \Rightarrow C})^*$ of the identity $id_{B \Rightarrow C}: (B \Rightarrow C) \to (B \Rightarrow C)$. Next, we need to show that $ev(\lambda(f) \times id_B) = f$. This follows directly from the naturality of the adjunction; we consider naturality in A and C at the morphisms $\lambda(f): A \to (B \Rightarrow C)$ and $id_C: C \to C$:

$$
\begin{array}{ccc}
id_{B \Rightarrow C} & \longmapsto & ev \\
\uparrow & & \uparrow \\
R(id_C) \circ id_{B \Rightarrow C} \circ \lambda(f) \longmapsto \lambda(f)^* & = & id_C \circ ev \circ (\lambda(f) \times id_B)
\end{array}
$$

that is $f = ev(\lambda(f) \times id_B)$. We let the reader show that $\lambda(f)$ is the unique morphism satisfying the latter equation.

($\Leftarrow$) Conversely, suppose that $\mathcal{C}$ is a cartesian closed category as originally defined. Let B be an object of $\mathcal{C}$. We shall define a right adjoint to $(-) \times B$ which we denote by $B \Rightarrow (-)$, by setting

$$c : C \longrightarrow C' \quad \mapsto \quad B \Rightarrow c \overset{\text{def}}{=} \lambda(c \circ ev): (B \Rightarrow C) \to (B \Rightarrow C'),$$

for each morphism $c: C \to C'$ of $\mathcal{C}$. We define a bijection giving rise to an adjunction by declaring the mate of $f: A \times B \to C$ to be $\lambda(f): A \to (B \Rightarrow C)$ and the mate of $g: A \to (B \Rightarrow C)$ to be

$$g^* \overset{\text{def}}{=} ev(g \times id_B): A \times B \to C.$$

It remains to verify that we have defined a bijection which is natural in the required sense. We only check one part of naturality. Let $a: A' \to A$ and $b: B \to B'$ be a morphism of $\mathcal{C}$. Then

$$
\begin{aligned}
ev \circ ((\lambda(b \circ ev)\lambda(f)a) \times id) &= ev \circ (\lambda(b \circ ev) \times id) \circ (\lambda(f)a \times id) \\
&= b \circ ev \circ (\lambda(f)a \times id) \\
&= b \circ f \circ (a \times id)
\end{aligned}
$$

implying that $\lambda(b \circ f \circ (a \times id)) = (B \Rightarrow b) \circ \lambda(f) \circ a$. $\square$

EXERCISES 2.10.16

(1) Fill in all of the missing details of Examples 2.10.14. Verify in detail the proof of Proposition 2.10.15 working out all the missing stages. In particular verify that a bijection was indeed defined in the final part of the proof and the other naturality equation.

(2) Is it possible to extend the chain of adjunctions in Example 5 at either end?

PROPOSITION 2.10.17

(i) Let $G: \mathcal{D} \to \mathcal{C}$ be a functor. Then G has a left adjoint iff for each object A of $\mathcal{C}$ there is an initial object in the under-cone category $(A \downarrow G)$.

(ii) Let $F: \mathcal{C} \to \mathcal{D}$ be a functor. Then F has a right adjoint iff for each object B of $\mathcal{D}$ there is a terminal object in the over-cone category $(F \downarrow B)$.

PROOF   For (i):

($\Rightarrow$) Suppose a left adjoint $F: \mathcal{C} \to \mathcal{D}$ exists and let A be an object of $\mathcal{C}$. Define the morphism $\eta_A \stackrel{\text{def}}{=} \overline{id_{FA}}: A \to GFA$ corresponding to id_{FA} under the adjunction. Suppose that we are given a morphism $g: A \to GB$ in $\mathcal{C}$. Let this correspond to $\hat{g}: FA \to B$ under the adjunction. Then from naturality we have

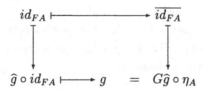

$$
\begin{array}{ccc}
id_{FA} & \longmapsto & \overline{id_{FA}} \\
\big\uparrow & & \big\uparrow \\
\hat{g} \circ id_{FA} & \longmapsto \ \ g \ \ = & G\hat{g} \circ \eta_A
\end{array}
$$

It follows from the bijection that $\hat{g}$ is the *unique* morphism for which we have

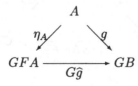

$$
\begin{array}{ccc}
& A & \\
\eta_A \swarrow & & \searrow g \\
GFA \xrightarrow[\;\;G\hat{g}\;\;]{} & & GB
\end{array}
$$

that is η_A is initial in $(A \downarrow G)$.

($\Leftarrow$) Suppose that for each object A of $\mathcal{C}$, there is an object B of $\mathcal{D}$ for which $\eta_A: A \to GB$ is initial in $(A \downarrow G)$. We define the functor F by taking FA to be B, and given a morphism $f: A \to A'$ in $\mathcal{C}$ we set Ff to be the unique morphism $Ff: FA \to FA'$ making the diagram

$$
\begin{array}{ccc}
A & \xrightarrow{\;f\;} & A' \\
{\scriptstyle \eta_A}\downarrow & & \downarrow{\scriptstyle \eta_{A'}} \\
GFA & \xrightarrow[GFf]{} & GFA'
\end{array}
$$

commute. Of course we need to check that this definition does yield a functor. We can see this is the case from the commutative diagrams

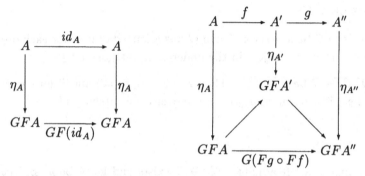

together with the universal property of the initial objects η_A, $\eta_{A'}$ and $\eta_{A''}$. Now we define a bijection for the adjunction. Given $f: FA \to B$ we set $\bar{f} \stackrel{\mathrm{def}}{=} Gf \circ \eta_A: A \to GB$ and given $g: A \to GB$ we define $\hat{g}: FA \to B$ using the initiality of η_A. It is simple to see that this *is* a bijection by directly unravelling the definitions. It remains to verify naturality. Suppose that we are given morphisms $a: A' \to A$ and $b: B \to B'$. Let $g: A \to GB$. We have to see that $b \circ \hat{g} \circ Fa = (Gb \circ g \circ a)^{\wedge}$. By the universal property of the initial object $\eta_{A'}$, we just need to see that the diagram

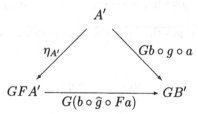

commutes. We have

$$
Gb \circ G\hat{g} \circ GFa \circ \eta_{A'} = Gb \circ G\hat{g} \circ \eta_A \circ a = Gb \circ g \circ a
$$

where we have used the definition of Fa followed by the definition of $\hat{g}$. The other naturality equation is proved similarly, and the proof of (ii) is dual to the proof of (i).   □

COROLLARY 2.10.18   If the left adjoint of a given functor exists then it is
unique up to canonical natural isomorphism.

PROOF   Suppose that we are given a functor $G: \mathcal{D} \to \mathcal{C}$ and let $F, F': \mathcal{C} \to \mathcal{D}$
be two choices for the left adjoint. For any object A of $\mathcal{C}$ the objects (FA, η_A)
and $(F'A, \eta'_A)$ (as defined in the proof of Proposition 2.10.17) are both initial
in the under-cone category $(A \downarrow G)$ and so there is a unique isomorphism
$\alpha_A: (FA, \eta_A) \to (F'A, \eta'_A)$. It follows that $\alpha_A: FA \to F'A$ is an isomorphism
in $\mathcal{D}$ and in fact such a collection of morphisms α_A gives rise to a natural
isomorphism $\alpha: F \to F'$. To see the naturality, take a morphism $f: A \to A'$ in
$\mathcal{C}$ and consider the following diagram:

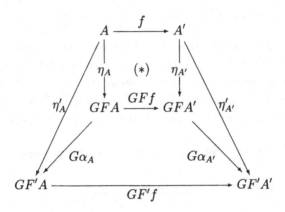

Note that the left and right triangles commute using the definition of α, and the
square $(*)$ along with the outer trapezium both commute from the naturality of
the bijection arising from the adjoints F and F' to G along with the definition
of the η_A. This implies that both $G\alpha_{A'} \circ GFf$ and $GF'f \circ G\alpha_A$ are factorisations
of $\eta'_{A'} f$ through η_A. The initiality of η_A in $(A \downarrow G)$ implies that $\alpha_{A'} \circ Ff =
F'f \circ \alpha_A$, as required.   □

EXAMPLES 2.10.19

(1) Let $\mathcal{D}$ be a subcategory of a category $\mathcal{C}$ and write $\iota: \mathcal{D} \to \mathcal{C}$ for the inclusion
functor. Then we say that $\mathcal{D}$ is a *reflective* subcategory of $\mathcal{C}$ if the functor ι has
a left adjoint $L: \mathcal{C} \to \mathcal{D}$. We refer to L as a *reflection* functor and to the values
of L as *reflections*. Note that using Proposition 2.10.17, it follows that $\mathcal{D}$ is a
reflective subcategory of $\mathcal{C}$ if it is a subcategory, and moreover for each object
C of $\mathcal{C}$ there is a morphism $\eta_C: C \to LC$ in $\mathcal{C}$ with the following universal
property: given any object D of $\mathcal{D}$ and morphism $f: C \to D$ in $\mathcal{C}$, there exists

a unique morphism $\hat{f} \colon LC \to D$ in $\mathcal{D}$ making the following triangle

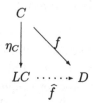

commute.

(2) We say that $\mathcal{D}$ is a *coreflective* subcategory of $\mathcal{C}$ if (it is a subcategory and) the inclusion functor $\iota \colon \mathcal{D} \to \mathcal{C}$ has a right adjoint.

(3) The category $\mathcal{A}b$ of Abelian groups is a full reflective subcategory of the category $\mathcal{G}rp$ of groups. What is the reflection functor?

EXERCISE 2.10.20   Recall that $\mathcal{L}at$ is the category of lattices and lattice homomorphisms. Let $\mathcal{D}$ be the category of complete lattices together with morphisms which preserve finite meets and arbitrary joins. Show that $\mathcal{D}$ is a (non-full) reflective subcategory of $\mathcal{L}at$. *Hint: consider Proposition 1.5.18; in fact the reflection of a lattice X in $\mathcal{D}$ is the poset of ideals of X.*

PROPOSITION 2.10.21   Suppose that we are given functors

$$\mathcal{C} \underset{G}{\overset{F}{\rightleftarrows}} \mathcal{D} \underset{K}{\overset{H}{\rightleftarrows}} \mathcal{E}$$

for which $(F \dashv G)$ and $(H \dashv K)$. Then we have $(HF \dashv GK)$.

PROOF   Morphisms $HFA \to B$ in $\mathcal{E}$ correspond bijectively to morphisms $FA \to KB$ in $\mathcal{D}$ and the latter correspond bijectively to morphisms $A \to GKB$ in $\mathcal{C}$. Both of these bijections are natural in A and B.   □

COROLLARY 2.10.22   Suppose that we are given a commutative diagram of categories and functors, and that all of the functors have left adjoints. Then the corresponding diagram of left adjoints commutes up to natural isomorphism.

PROOF   Suppose we have a commutative diagram of functors

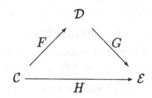

which have left adjoints $(F' \dashv F)$, $(G' \dashv G)$ and $(H' \dashv H)$. Then by Proposition 2.10.21 we have $(G'F' \dashv GF = H)$. By Corollary 2.10.18 there is a natural isomorphism $G'F' \cong H'$. The result follows by splitting the given commutative diagram into appropriate commutative triangles. $\qquad\square$

DISCUSSION 2.10.23   Suppose that we are given an adjunction between a pair of functors $F: \mathcal{C} \to \mathcal{D}$ and $G: \mathcal{D} \to \mathcal{C}$. Writing

$$\frac{f: FA \to B}{\overline{f}: A \to GB} \qquad\qquad \frac{g: A \to GB}{\widehat{g}: FA \to B}$$

for the adjunction, we put $\eta_A \overset{\text{def}}{=} \overline{id_{FA}}: A \to GFA$ and $\epsilon_B \overset{\text{def}}{=} \widehat{id_{GB}}: FGB \to B$. Thus for each A in $\mathcal{C}$, η_A is a choice of initial object in the under-cone category $(A \downarrow G)$, and we can check that ϵ_B is a choice of terminal object in the over-cone category $(F \downarrow B)$ for each B in $\mathcal{D}$. For each morphism $f: A \to B$ of $\mathcal{C}$ one can check, using the naturality of the bijection arising from the adjunction, that the diagram

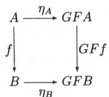

commutes, and so the η_A give rise to a natural transformation $\eta: id_{\mathcal{C}} \to GF$, and this is called the *unit* of the adjunction $(F \dashv G)$. Dually, we have a natural transformation $\epsilon: FG \to id_{\mathcal{D}}$ and this is called the *counit* of the adjunction. This discussion leads to the following propositions:

PROPOSITION 2.10.24   Suppose that we are given functors $F: \mathcal{C} \to \mathcal{D}$ and $G: \mathcal{D} \to \mathcal{C}$. Then to give an adjunction $(F \dashv G)$ is equivalent to *either* of

(i) There is a natural transformation $\eta: id_{\mathcal{C}} \to GF$ such that given any object A in $\mathcal{C}$, the morphism $\eta_A: A \to GFA$ is an initial object in the under-cone category $(A \downarrow G)$.

(ii) There is a natural transformation $\epsilon: FG \to id_{\mathcal{D}}$ such that given any object B in $\mathcal{D}$, the morphism $\epsilon_B: FGB \to B$ is a terminal object in the over-cone category $(F \downarrow B)$.

PROOF   Follows from Proposition 2.10.17 and Discussion 2.10.23. $\qquad\square$

PROPOSITION 2.10.25   Suppose that we are given functors $F: \mathcal{C} \to \mathcal{D}$ and $G: \mathcal{D} \to \mathcal{C}$. Then to give an adjunction $(F \dashv G)$ is equivalent to specifying natural transformations $\eta: id_{\mathcal{C}} \to GF$ and $\epsilon: FG \to id_{\mathcal{D}}$ such that the diagrams

both commute.

PROOF

($\Rightarrow$) Suppose we have an adjunction $(F \dashv G)$. Define η and ϵ as in Discussion 2.10.23. It remains to prove that the diagrams of the proposition commute. For an object A of $\mathcal{C}$ and an object B of $\mathcal{D}$ we have

$$
\begin{aligned}
id_{FA} &= \widehat{\widetilde{id_{FA}}} & id_{GB} &= \widetilde{\widehat{id_{GB}}} \\
&= \widehat{\eta_A} & &= \widetilde{\epsilon_B} \\
&= \epsilon_{FA} \circ F\eta_A & &= G\epsilon_B \circ \eta_{GB}
\end{aligned}
$$

and so we are done.

($\Leftarrow$) Suppose that we are given such η and ϵ. Define a correspondence of morphisms as follows:

$$
\frac{f: FA \to B}{\overline{f} \stackrel{\text{def}}{=} Gf \circ \eta_A : A \to GFA \to GB}
\qquad
\frac{g: A \to GB}{\widetilde{g} \stackrel{\text{def}}{=} \epsilon_B \circ Fg : FA \to FGB \to B}
$$

It is easy to check that this definition yields a natural bijection giving an adjunction.   □

PROPOSITION 2.10.26   Suppose that $G: \mathcal{D} \to \mathcal{C}$ has a left adjoint F with counit $\epsilon: FG \to id_{\mathcal{D}}$. Then

(i) G is faithful iff ϵ_B is epic for each object B of $\mathcal{D}$.

(ii) G is full and faithful iff ϵ_B is an isomorphism for each object B of $\mathcal{D}$.

PROOF

(i) ($\Rightarrow$) Suppose G is faithful. Let $f, g: B \to C$ be two morphisms in $\mathcal{D}$ for which $f\epsilon_B = g\epsilon_B$. Under the adjunction, $f\epsilon_B$ corresponds to $Gf: GB \to GC$ and similarly $g\epsilon_B$ to Gg implying that $Gf = Gg$ and hence $f = g$.

($\Leftarrow$) Suppose ϵ_B is epic; showing G faithful is a reverse of the argument used in ($\Rightarrow$).

(ii) ($\Rightarrow$) Suppose G is full and faithful. We have $\eta_{GB} = Gh: GB \to GFGB$ for some $h: B \to FGB$ and hence $id_{FGB} = \widehat{Gh} = h\epsilon_B$. Therefore

$$id_B\epsilon_B = \epsilon_B h\epsilon_B = (\epsilon_B h)\epsilon_B$$

and so $id_B = \epsilon_B h$ because ϵ_B is epic using (i).

($\Leftarrow$) Suppose ϵ_B is an isomorphism. From (i) we just need to show that G is full. Suppose that $f: GB \to GC$ in $\mathcal{C}$. Then we have

$$f = G\widehat{f} \circ \eta_{GB} = G\widehat{f} \circ G(\epsilon_B^{-1}) = G(\widehat{f} \circ \epsilon_B^{-1}),$$

implying that G is full as claimed.

$\square$

2.11 *Limits and Colimits*

DISCUSSION 2.11.1   First, some definitions. Throughout this section, we shall refer to functors $\mathbb{I} \to \mathcal{C}$ in which $\mathbb{I}$ is certainly small and possibly even finite as *diagrams* of shape $\mathbb{I}$. The *constant diagram* on A (where A is an object of $\mathcal{C}$) is just the constant functor $\tilde{A}: \mathbb{I} \to \mathcal{C}$ which sends all objects of $\mathbb{I}$ to A and all morphisms of $\mathbb{I}$ to id_A. Let $\Delta: \mathcal{C} \to [\mathbb{I}, \mathcal{C}]$ be the functor which sends an object A of $\mathcal{C}$ to the constant diagram $\tilde{A}$ on A and a morphism $f: A \to B$ of $\mathcal{C}$ to the natural transformation $\Delta f: \tilde{A} \to \tilde{B}$ with components $(\Delta f)_I \stackrel{\text{def}}{=} f$ where I is an object of $\mathbb{I}$.

Products, equalisers and pullbacks are all examples of the notion of limit. We could do without explicit mention of the former examples, just talking of limits of certain kinds, but it is best to get used to the ideas involved by looking first at simple examples. Let us have a look at the definition of a limit. Suppose that $D: \mathbb{I} \to \mathcal{C}$ is any diagram. Then we say that a *limit for the diagram D* is given by a terminal object in the over-cone category $(\Delta \downarrow D)$. Note that this formal definition will become clearer in the following discussion. By carefully unravelling the definition, we see that an object in $(\Delta \downarrow D)$ is given by an object C of $\mathcal{C}$ together with a natural transformation $k: \Delta C \to D$, which amounts to giving a family of morphisms $(k_I: C \to DI \mid I \in \mathbb{I})$ in $\mathcal{C}$ (here we write just $I \in \mathbb{I}$ for $I \in ob\,\mathbb{I}$: note that $\mathbb{I}$ is small) such that for each morphism $\alpha: I \to J$ in $\mathbb{I}$ the following triangle commutes:

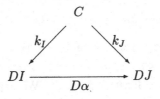

Such a family of morphisms which satisfies the above commuting triangle is called a *cone over* D and C is the *vertex* of the cone. So now we can get a more hands-on picture of a limit. A limit of the diagram $D : \mathbb{I} \to C$ is given by an object $\varprojlim D$ of C together with a family of morphisms

$$(k_I : \varprojlim D \to DI \mid I \in \mathbb{I})$$

which form a cone over D with vertex $\varprojlim D$, such that given any other cone $(h_I : C \to DI \mid I \in \mathbb{I})$ over D with vertex C there is a unique morphism $m : C \to \varprojlim D$ making the following triangle commute for each $I \in \mathbb{I}$:

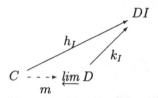

We sometimes refer to m as a *mediating* morphism.

We said that products are an instance of the notion of limit. Consider the discrete category $\mathbb{I} \overset{\text{def}}{=} \{0,1\}$ with two objects, and a diagram $D : \mathbb{I} \to C$. So D essentially picks out two objects $A \overset{\text{def}}{=} D0$ and $B \overset{\text{def}}{=} D1$ of C. Then a limit of D in C consists of an object $\varprojlim D = P$ of C together with morphisms $k_0 : P \to A$ and $k_1 : P \to B$, such that given any two morphisms $h_0 : C \to A$ and $h_1 : C \to B$, there is a unique morphism $m : C \to P$ for which $k_0 m = h_0$ and $k_1 m = h_1$. This is certainly a binary product of the objects A and B.

As well as considering the notion of a limit, it is useful to be able to say when a category has all limits of a certain form. For example, a lattice has *all finite* meets and joins and both meets and joins are examples of limits. We say that C has *limits of shape* $\mathbb{I}$ if the functor Δ has a right adjoint, and we shall write $\varprojlim : [\mathbb{I}, C] \to C$ for such a right adjoint if one exists (recall that an adjoint functor is determined up to isomorphism if it exists). If we know that for each diagram $D : \mathbb{I} \to C$ there is a specified choice of limit in C, this leads to a canonical choice of the functor $\varprojlim$. If D is any object of $[\mathbb{I}, C]$ then $\varprojlim D$ is the object of C arising from the specified limit $(k_I : \varprojlim D \to DI \mid I \in \mathbb{I})$ of D in C. Now we shall define $\varprojlim$ on morphisms of $[\mathbb{I}, C]$; let $\alpha : D \to D'$ be any such morphism. Then there is a cone over D' with vertex $\varprojlim D$ given by

$$(\alpha_I \circ k_I : \varprojlim D \to DI \to D'I \mid I \in \mathbb{I})$$

and so from the universal property of limits there is a unique morphism $m : \varprojlim D \to \varprojlim D'$ for which $k_I' \circ m = \alpha_I \circ k_I$ at every $I \in \mathbb{I}$ (the morphisms k_I' arising from the specified limit of D' in C). We define $\varprojlim(\alpha) \overset{\text{def}}{=} m$.

To illustrate this definition, let $\mathcal{C}$ be some category, $\mathbf{2} \overset{\text{def}}{=} \{0,1\}$ be the discrete category with two objects and so $\Delta \colon \mathcal{C} \to [\mathbf{2}, \mathcal{C}]$ is the functor which sends an object A of $\mathcal{C}$ to the constant diagram $\tilde{A}$ on A of shape $\mathbf{2}$ and sends morphisms $f \colon A \to A'$ of $\mathcal{C}$ to the natural transformation $\Delta f \colon \tilde{A} \to \tilde{A}'$ with components $(\Delta f)_B \overset{\text{def}}{=} f \colon A \to A'$ for each object B of $\mathcal{C}$. Then $\mathcal{C}$ *has binary products just in case the functor* Δ *has a right adjoint*.

For suppose that $R \colon [\mathbf{2}, \mathcal{C}] \to \mathcal{C}$ is a right adjoint to Δ. Take objects B and C in $\mathcal{C}$, and define the functor $F \colon \mathbf{2} \to \mathcal{C}$ which takes 0 to B and 1 to C. Then the adjunction says we have a bijection between natural transformations $\alpha \colon \Delta A \to F$ and morphisms $h \colon A \to RF$

$$\frac{\alpha \colon \Delta A \to F}{h \colon A \to RF}$$

and that the *bijection* is natural in A and F. But to give a natural transformation $\Delta A \to F$ is to give two morphisms $A \to B$ and $A \to C$, and so we see that the data amounts to a bijection between pairs of morphisms $(f,g) \colon (A,A) \to (B,C)$ and morphisms $h \colon A \to RF$ and the bijection is natural in A and (B,C):

$$\frac{(f,g) \colon (A,A) \to (B,C)}{h \colon A \to RF} \;\; \overline{(-)} \qquad \frac{h \colon A \to RF}{(f,g) \colon (A,A) \to (B,C)} \;\; \widehat{(-)}$$

Suppose that id_{RF} corresponds to $(\pi_B, \pi_C) \colon (RF, RF) \to (B,C)$ under the bijection:

$$\frac{id_{RF} \colon RF \to RF}{(\pi_B, \pi_C) \overset{\text{def}}{=} (id_{RF})^{\wedge} \colon (RF, RF) \to (B,C)}$$

Then (RF, π_B, π_C) is a binary product of B and C. To see this we need to show that if we are given $f \colon A \to B$ and $g \colon A \to C$, there is a unique morphism $h \colon A \to RF$ for which $\pi_B h = f$ and $\pi_C h = g$. Define h corresponding to (f,g) under the bijection, that is $h \overset{\text{def}}{=} \overline{(f,g)}$. Then applying naturality in A at the morphism $h \colon A \to RF$ we have

$$
\begin{array}{ccc}
id_{RF} & \longmapsto & \widehat{id_{RF}} \\
\downarrow & & \downarrow \\
id_{RF} \circ h & \longmapsto & \widehat{h} = \widehat{id_{RF}} \circ \Delta h
\end{array}
$$

that is

$$(f,g) = \widehat{\overline{(f,g)}} = (\pi_B, \pi_C) \circ \Delta h = (\pi_B, \pi_C) \circ (h,h)$$

and so h is a mediating morphism. To see uniqueness, suppose also $\pi_B h' = f$ and $\pi_C h' = g$ for an appropriate morphism h. Then both h and h' correspond to (f, g) under the bijection, implying $h = h'$. We leave it to the reader to see that existence of binary products in C implies the existence of a right adjoint to Δ.

EXERCISE 2.11.2   Work carefully through the details of Discussion 2.11.1. In particular, if C is a category with specified limits for all diagrams D, verify that the canonical definition of $\varprojlim \colon [\mathbb{I}, C] \to C$ is a good one and that $\varprojlim$ is indeed a functor.

EXAMPLES 2.11.3

(1) If $\mathbb{I}$ is a (small) discrete category, then limits of shape $\mathbb{I}$ amount to products of set-indexed families of objects, and correspond to the definition of binary product in the case that $\mathbb{I}$ has two objects.

(2) Let $\mathbb{I}$ be the category

$$0 \rightrightarrows 1$$

which has just two objects and two parallel non-identity morphisms. So a diagram of shape $\mathbb{I}$ in C is just a parallel pair of morphisms in C, say $f, g \colon A \to B$, and a cone over this diagram is a pair of morphisms

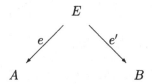

for which $fe = e' = ge$. But this is just equivalent to giving a morphism $e \colon E \to A$ for which $fe = ge$; the e' is redundant. We can draw a commutative diagram:

$$E \xrightarrow{\ e\ } A \underset{g}{\overset{f}{\rightrightarrows}} B$$

Now suppose that this cone is a limit for the diagram $f, g \colon A \to B$. If we are given any other cone, say $h \colon C \to A$ for which $fh = gh$, then there must be a unique morphism $k \colon C \to E$ such that $h = ek$. So this limit is in fact an equaliser.

(3) Let $\mathbb{I}$ be the category

and so a diagram of shape $\mathbb{I}$ in $\mathcal{C}$ is given by a pair of morphisms $f: A \to C$ and $g: B \to C$. A cone for this diagram is given by a triple of morphisms h, k and c where

$$
\begin{array}{ccc}
P & \xrightarrow{\ h\ } & A \\
{\scriptstyle k}\downarrow & \searrow^{c} & \downarrow{\scriptstyle f} \\
B & \xrightarrow[\ g\ ]{} & C
\end{array}
$$

in which $fh = c = gk$; so specifying the morphism c is redundant. A limit for a diagram of shape $\mathbb{I}$ is of course a pullback.

(4) Suppose that $\mathbb{I}$ is the empty category. Then $[\mathbb{I}, \mathcal{C}]$ is the category $\mathbf{1}$ which has one object (say D) and one morphism. In this case $\Delta: \mathcal{C} \to [\mathbb{I}, \mathcal{C}]$ is the functor taking all objects of $\mathcal{C}$ to the unique object of $\mathbf{1}$ and all morphisms of $\mathcal{C}$ to the identity in $\mathbf{1}$. One can check that $(\Delta \downarrow D)$ is isomorphic to $\mathcal{C}$ and hence that a limit for D is a terminal object for $\mathcal{C}$.

EXERCISE 2.11.4   Let $\mathbb{I}$ be the category

$$
0 \rightrightarrows 1 \longrightarrow 2
$$

with three objects and three non-identity morphisms as shown in the diagram. Describe a limit for a diagram $D: \mathbb{I} \to \mathcal{L}at$ where $\mathcal{L}at$ is the category of lattices and lattice homomorphisms. Prove that your description is indeed a limit.

DISCUSSION 2.11.5   The category $\mathcal{C}$ has *colimits of shape* $\mathbb{I}$ if the functor $\Delta: \mathcal{C} \to [\mathbb{I}, \mathcal{C}]$ has a left adjoint, and we write $\varinjlim$ for the left adjoint if it exists. A *colimit for a diagram* $D: \mathbb{I} \to \mathcal{C}$ is an initial object in the under-cone category $(D \downarrow \Delta)$. Note that an object in the category $(D \downarrow \Delta)$ is given by an object C in $\mathcal{C}$ together with a natural transformation $k: D \to \Delta C$, that is a family of morphisms $(k_I: DI \to C \mid I \in \mathbb{I})$ such that for each morphism $\alpha: I \to J$ in $\mathbb{I}$ the following diagram commutes:

$$
\begin{array}{ccc}
DI & \xrightarrow{\ D\alpha\ } & DJ \\
& {\scriptstyle k_I}\searrow \quad \swarrow{\scriptstyle k_J} & \\
& C &
\end{array}
$$

Such a family of morphisms is called a *cone under D with vertex C*. Unravelling the definition we see that a colimit for the diagram $D: \mathbb{I} \to \mathcal{C}$ is given by an object $\varinjlim D$ of $\mathcal{C}$ together with a family of morphisms $(k_I: DI \to \varinjlim D \mid I \in \mathbb{I})$

for which given any cone $(h_I \colon DI \to C \mid I \in \mathbb{I})$ under D with vertex C, there is a unique morphism $m \colon \underrightarrow{\lim} D \to C$ satisfying $m \circ k_I = h_I$ for each object I of $\mathbb{I}$. We sometimes refer to m as a *mediating* morphism.

EXAMPLES 2.11.6

(1) If $\mathbb{I}$ is empty, then a colimit of shape $\mathbb{I}$ in $\mathcal{C}$ is an initial object in $\mathcal{C}$.

(2) If $\mathbb{I}$ is the discrete two object category, a colimit of shape $\mathbb{I}$ is a binary coproduct.

(3) A colimit over the category

$$0 \rightrightarrows 1$$

is a coequaliser; compare this with the original definition of coequaliser.

(4) Colimits over the category

are pushouts; again, compare with the original definition.

DISCUSSION 2.11.7   Let $\mathcal{C}$ be a category and let $D \colon \mathbb{I} \to \mathcal{C}$ be a diagram; recall that by definition $\mathbb{I}$ is a small category. Let $\Delta \colon \mathcal{C} \to [\mathbb{I}, \mathcal{C}]$ have a right (left) adjoint in each of the following cases; we summarise previous definitions and make some new ones:

• If $\mathbb{I}$ is the empty category then $\mathcal{C}$ *has a terminal (initial) object.*

• If $\mathbb{I}$ is the discrete two object category, then $\mathcal{C}$ *has binary products (coproducts).*

• If $\mathbb{I}$ has two objects and a parallel pair of distinct non-identity morphisms, then we say that $\mathcal{C}$ *has all equalisers (coequalisers).*

• If $\mathbb{I}$ has three objects, and two distinct non-identity morphisms with a common target, then we say $\mathcal{C}$ *has all pullbacks (pushouts).*

• If $\mathbb{I}$ is any finite discrete category, then we say that $\mathcal{C}$ *has all finite products (coproducts).*

• If $\mathbb{I}$ is any small discrete category, we say $\mathcal{C}$ *has all small products (coproducts).*

• If $\mathbb{I}$ is any finite category, we say that $\mathcal{C}$ is *finitely complete (cocomplete)* or *has all finite limits (colimits)*.

• If $\mathbb{I}$ is any small category, we say that $\mathcal{C}$ is *small complete (cocomplete)* or *has all small limits (colimits)*.

If there is a canonical choice of limit (colimit) in a category $\mathcal{C}$ for any diagram $D: \mathbb{I} \to \mathcal{C}$ then we say that $\mathcal{C}$ has *specified* limits (colimits). Note also that the property of having all small products as defined above is exactly the same as having products of set-indexed families of objects. The next theorem shows how limits can be built up from simpler categorical constructs:

THEOREM 2.11.8

(i) If a category $\mathcal{C}$ has all small products and equalisers then $\mathcal{C}$ has all small limits.

(ii) If $\mathcal{C}$ has all finite products and equalisers then $\mathcal{C}$ has all finite limits.

(iii) If $\mathcal{C}$ has pullbacks and a terminal object then $\mathcal{C}$ has all finite limits.

PROOF

(i) Let $D: \mathbb{I} \to \mathcal{C}$ be a diagram where $\mathbb{I}$ is a small category. Consider the products

$$A \stackrel{\text{def}}{=} \Pi_{I \in ob\,\mathbb{I}} DI \qquad\qquad B \stackrel{\text{def}}{=} \Pi_{f \in mor\,\mathbb{I}} D(tar(f)).$$

We define a pair of morphisms $s, t: A \to B$ by setting

$$s \stackrel{\text{def}}{=} \langle \pi_{tar(f)} \mid f \in \mathbb{I} \rangle \qquad \text{and} \qquad t \stackrel{\text{def}}{=} \langle Df \circ \pi_{src(f)} \mid f \in \mathbb{I} \rangle$$

and then we form the equaliser $e: E \to A$ of s and t. Consider the family of morphisms $(k_I \stackrel{\text{def}}{=} \pi_I e: E \to DI \mid I \in \mathbb{I})$. Then this family is a cone over D with vertex E. To see this, take $f: I \to J$ in $\mathbb{I}$ and note that

$$Df \circ k_I = Df \circ \pi_I \circ e = \pi_f \circ t \circ e = \pi_f \circ s \circ e = \pi_J \circ e = k_J$$

where $\pi_f: B \to D(tar(f))$. This cone is in fact a limit for D. For suppose that $(h_I: C \to DI \mid I \in \mathbb{I})$ is any other cone over D with vertex C. Then there is a morphism $h \stackrel{\text{def}}{=} \langle h_I \mid I \in \mathbb{I} \rangle: C \to A$ and one can check that $sh = th$. Thus using the existence property of an equaliser, there is $k: C \to E$ for which

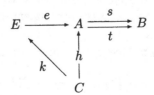

commutes. Hence $ek = h$ implying that $\pi_I \circ ek = h_I$ that is $k_I \circ k = h_I$ as required. The uniqueness of k follows from the universal property of the equaliser $e: E \to A$.

(ii) Proof exactly as for (i) with $\mathbb{I}$ finite.

(iii) We can define finite products inductively from a terminal object (say 1) and binary products. But the binary product of A and B is given as the pullback of $!_A: A \to 1$ and $!_B: B \to 1$ where $!$ denotes a unique morphism. The equaliser of a pair of morphisms $f, g: A \to B$ is given by the pullback

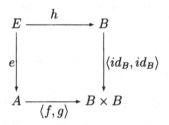

The result follows from (ii).

$\square$

LEMMA 2.11.9   Let $\mathcal{C}$, $\mathbb{I}$ and $\mathcal{E}$ be three categories where $\mathbb{I}$ is small. If $\mathcal{C}$ has limits of shape $\mathbb{I}$ then so does $[\mathcal{E}, \mathcal{C}]$.

PROOF   Let $D: \mathbb{I} \to [\mathcal{E}, \mathcal{C}]$ be a diagram of type $\mathbb{I}$. By currying, we can regard the functor D as a functor $D: \mathbb{I} \times \mathcal{E} \to \mathcal{C}$, and for each object E of $\mathcal{E}$ there is a functor $D(-, E): \mathbb{I} \to \mathcal{C}$ defined in the expected manner, and similarly a functor $D(I, +): \mathcal{E} \to \mathcal{C}$ for each object I of $\mathbb{I}$. Let

$$(k(E)_I: \varprojlim D(-, E) \to D(I, E) \mid I \in \mathbb{I})$$

be a limit of $D(-, E)$ for each E. If we are given a morphism $e: E \to E'$ in $\mathcal{E}$, then the family of morphisms

$$(D(I, e) \circ k(E)_I : \varprojlim D(-, E) \longrightarrow D(I, E) \longrightarrow D(I, E') \mid I \in \mathbb{I})$$

forms a cone over $D(-, E')$ and hence there is a morphism $\varprojlim D(-, E) \to \varprojlim D(-, E')$ denoted by, say, $\varprojlim D(-, e)$. One can also check that the uniqueness properties of limits imply that the assignment $+ \mapsto \varprojlim D(-, +)$ gives rise to a functor $\varprojlim D(-, +): \mathcal{E} \to \mathcal{C}$, and that the family of morphisms $k(E)_I$ (as E runs over objects of $\mathcal{E}$) induces a natural transformation

$$k(+)_I: \varprojlim D(-, +) \to D(I, +)$$

for each object I of $\mathbb{I}$. In fact one can also check that the family

$$(k(+)_I : \varprojlim D(-,+) \to D(I,+) \mid I \in \mathbb{I})$$

forms a cone over the functor D with vertex $\varprojlim D(-,+)$ and that this is the required limit. □

DISCUSSION 2.11.10 It will be useful for us to describe some properties that functors may enjoy. The reader will be familiar with the idea of a function between posets which (for example) preserves and reflects order. The properties of functors we now describe are based on similar ideas. Throughout the following definitions let $F : \mathcal{C} \to \mathcal{E}$ be a functor and $D : \mathbb{I} \to \mathcal{C}$ a diagram.

(i) We say that F *preserves* limits of shape $\mathbb{I}$ if given a limit

$$(k_I : \varprojlim D \to DI \mid I \in \mathbb{I})$$

for D, the cone

$$(Fk_I : F \varprojlim D \to FDI \mid I \in \mathbb{I})$$

is a limit for FD.

(ii) We say that F *reflects* limits of shape $\mathbb{I}$ if given any cone

$$(k_I : L \to DI \mid I \in \mathbb{I})$$

in $\mathcal{C}$ for which the cone $(Fk_I : FL \to FDI \mid I \in \mathbb{I})$ is a limit of $FD : \mathbb{I} \to \mathcal{E}$, then $(k_I : L \to DI \mid I \in \mathbb{I})$ is in fact a limit for D.

(iii) We say that F *creates* limits of shape $\mathbb{I}$ if given any limit

$$(k'_I : \varprojlim FD \to FDI \mid I \in \mathbb{I})$$

for the diagram $FD : \mathbb{I} \to \mathcal{E}$, then there is a unique cone $(k_I : L \to DI \mid I \in \mathbb{I})$ over D for which $\varprojlim FD = FL$ and $k'_I = Fk_I$ and the cone is a limit for D.

The definition of F *preserves, reflects* and *creates* colimits of shape $\mathbb{I}$ is similar and omitted.

EXAMPLES 2.11.11

(1) Show that the definition of a functor which preserves limits of shape **n**, where **n** is a finite discrete category with $n \in \mathbb{N}$ objects, coincides with the definition of a functor which preserves finite products.

(2) Let C and $\mathcal{E}$ be categories and let E be an object of $\mathcal{E}$. Then the functor $Ap: [\mathcal{E}, C] \to C$ given by "evaluation at E" preserves any limits which exist in $[\mathcal{E}, C]$.

(3) The forgetful functors on $\mathcal{G}rp$, $\mathcal{A}b$ and $\mathcal{T}op$ to the category $\mathcal{S}et$ all preserve limits, but only the third preserves colimits. Here, $\mathcal{A}b$ is the category of Abelian groups and homomorphisms, and $\mathcal{T}op$ is the category of topological spaces and *topologically* continuous functions.

(4) Theorem 2.11.8 remains true if we replace every instance of "C has" by "C has and F preserves" in the statement of the theorem.

DISCUSSION 2.11.12   In the remainder of this section we prove some results which are categorical analogues of earlier results for preordered sets. We shall see that things are not quite as straightforward when preorders are replaced by categories. The basic aim of the results is to give conditions for the existence of a left adjoint of a given functor, and also to examine when a given functor will preserve limits. The reader should compare Theorem 2.11.13 with Theorem 2.10.6, and Theorems 2.11.16 and 2.11.20 (which are "adjoint functor theorems" for categories) with Theorem 2.10.8 (the adjoint functor theorem for preorders).

THEOREM 2.11.13   Suppose that the functor $G: \mathcal{E} \to C$ has a left adjoint. Then G preserves all limits which exist in $\mathcal{E}$. Dually, if G has a right adjoint then G preserves all colimits which exist in $\mathcal{E}$.

PROOF   We shall consider the result in two ways, depending on what limits exist. Firstly,

Suppose that C and $\mathcal{E}$ have all limits of shape $\mathbb{I}$. Consider the diagrams

$$
\begin{array}{ccc}
[\mathbb{I}, \mathcal{E}] & \xleftarrow{\ F_* \ } & [\mathbb{I}, C] \\
\Delta \uparrow & (1) & \uparrow \Delta \\
\mathcal{E} & \xleftarrow{\ F \ } & C
\end{array}
\qquad\qquad
\begin{array}{ccc}
[\mathbb{I}, \mathcal{E}] & \xrightarrow{\ G_* \ } & [\mathbb{I}, C] \\
\underleftarrow{\lim} \downarrow & (2) & \downarrow \underleftarrow{\lim} \\
\mathcal{E} & \xrightarrow{\ G \ } & C
\end{array}
$$

in which we have $(F \dashv G)$, the functors F_* and G_* are given by postcomposition with F and G, and also $(\Delta \dashv \underleftarrow{\lim})$. Note that the diagram (1) commutes by definition of the functors, and hence that (2) commutes up to isomorphism using Corollary 2.10.22.

Now let $D: \mathbb{I} \to \mathcal{E}$ be a given diagram with limit $(k_I: \varprojlim D \to DI \mid I \in \mathbb{I})$.
We have to show that $(Gk_I: G(\varprojlim D) \to GDI \mid I \in \mathbb{I})$ is a limit in $\mathcal{C}$. Let
$(h_I: A \to GDI \mid I \in \mathbb{I})$ be a cone over GD in $\mathcal{C}$. Then the naturality of the
bijection associated with the adjunction $(F \dashv G)$ means that there is a cone
$(\widehat{h_I}: FA \to DI \mid I \in \mathbb{I})$. To see this, take a morphism $f: I \to J$ in $\mathbb{I}$ and note
that $\widehat{h_J} = [(GDf) \circ h_I]^\wedge = Df \circ \widehat{h_I}$. Hence there must be a unique morphism
$k: FA \to \varprojlim D$ for which $k_I \circ k = \widehat{h_I}$ for all objects I of $\mathbb{I}$. This gives us a
unique morphism $\overline{k}: A \to G \varprojlim D$ such that for all objects I of $\mathbb{I}$, $Gk_I \circ \overline{k} = h_I$.
□

We shall need a couple of lemmas before proving our first "adjoint functor
theorem."

LEMMA 2.11.14   Let $G: \mathcal{E} \to \mathcal{C}$ be a functor. Suppose that $\mathcal{E}$ has and G
preserves limits of shape $\mathbb{I}$. Then for any object A of $\mathcal{C}$, the under-cone category
$(A \downarrow G)$ has limits of shape $\mathbb{I}$, and moreover the forgetful functor $U: (A \downarrow G) \to \mathcal{E}$ preserves them.

PROOF   Let $\overline{D}: \mathbb{I} \to (A \downarrow G)$ be a diagram of shape $\mathbb{I}$. It is easy to see that
$\overline{D}$ consists of a diagram $D = U\overline{D}: \mathbb{I} \to \mathcal{E}$, together with a cone with vertex A
over the diagram GD in $\mathcal{C}$, say $(h_I: A \to GDI \mid I \in \mathbb{I})$: draw a sketch to see
this. Let $(k_I: \varprojlim D \to DI \mid I \in \mathbb{I})$ be a limit for the diagram D. Using the
hypothesis, a limit for GD is given by the cone $(Gk_I: G \varprojlim D \to GDI \mid I \in \mathbb{I})$
and hence there is a unique morphism $k: A \to G \varprojlim D$ for which the diagram

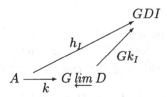

commutes. We claim that the object $(k, \varprojlim D)$ of $(A \downarrow G)$ is a candidate for
$\varprojlim \overline{D}$, that is, the family

$$(k_I: (k, \varprojlim D) \to (h_I, DI) \mid I \in \mathbb{I})$$

is a limit for $\overline{D}$. The verification of this is routine and omitted: one needs to
take a cone

$$(h'_I: (g, C) \to (h_I, DI) \mid I \in \mathbb{I})$$

and verify that there is a unique morphism $k': (g, C) \to (k, \varprojlim D)$ for which
$k_I \circ k' = h'_I: (g, C) \to (h_I, DI)$. That U preserves limits is immediate.   □

LEMMA 2.11.15   Suppose that C is locally small and complete. Then C has an initial object iff there is a set of objects of C, say $\{A_x \mid x \in X\}$, such that for every object B of C there is a morphism $j_x : A_x \to B$.

PROOF

($\Rightarrow$) Suppose C has an initial object. Call the initial object 0 and take the set of objects of C to be $\{0\}$; the result is immediate.

($\Leftarrow$) Suppose that $\{A_x \mid x \in X\}$ satisfies the hypothesis. Consider the morphism

$$j_x \pi_x : \Pi_{x \in X} A_x \to A_x \to B$$

which exists by completeness of C. Consider the diagram in C which consists of one object $\Pi_{x \in X} A_x$ together with all endomorphisms of the product; this is a small diagram because C is locally small. Now take the limit of this diagram giving us a morphism $l : L \to \Pi_{x \in X} A_x$ and hence a morphism $j_x \circ \pi_x \circ l : L \to B$ for every object B of C. Suppose that there are two morphisms $f, g : L \to B$. We can form the equaliser $e : B' \to L$ of f and g, note that there is a morphism $j'_x \pi_x : \Pi_{x \in X} A_x \to B'$ and thus observe that $lej'_x \pi_x$ is an endomorphism of the product $\Pi_{x \in X} A_x$. As l is a cone over the diagram of all endomorphisms of $\Pi_{x \in X} A_x$, we have $l = l(ej'_x \pi_x l)$ which implies that $ej'_x \pi_x l = id_L$ using the universal property of the limit L. So e is split implying that $f = g$. Hence L is initial. $\square$

Now we have the first of our results, known as *Freyd's adjoint functor theorem.*

THEOREM 2.11.16   Suppose that we are given a functor $G : \mathcal{E} \to C$ where $\mathcal{E}$ is locally small and complete. Then G has a left adjoint iff G preserves all small limits and for each object A of C there is a set of morphisms

$$\{f_x : A \to GB_x \mid x \in X\}$$

such that for any morphism $g : A \to GC$ there is a morphism $h_x : B_x \to C$ for which the diagram

$$
\begin{array}{ccc}
 & A & \\
f_x \downarrow & \searrow^{g} & \\
GB_x & \xrightarrow[Gh_x]{} & GC
\end{array}
$$

commutes. The condition which such a set of morphisms satisfies is called the *solution set condition.*

PROOF

($\Rightarrow$) If G has a left adjoint then it preserves limits using Theorem 2.11.13, and the solution set condition holds because the unit $\eta_A \colon A \to GFA$ is initial in $(A \downarrow G)$ for each object A of $\mathcal{C}$.

($\Leftarrow$) Note that the category $(A \downarrow G)$ is small (for $\mathcal{E}$ is locally small) and complete using Lemma 2.11.14. It is easy to verify that it satisfies the conditions of Lemma 2.11.15 and hence that $(A \downarrow G)$ has an initial object. We are done by appealing to Proposition 2.10.17. $\qquad\square$

EXAMPLE 2.11.17   Consider the forgetful functor $U \colon \mathcal{G}rp \to \mathcal{S}et$. The category of groups, $\mathcal{G}rp$, is locally small and complete, and U preserves all small limits. It remains to verify the solution set condition in order to use Theorem 2.11.16 to see the existence of a left adjoint to U. But if we are given any function $g \colon A \to UG$ where A is a set and G is a group, note that this function factors through the inclusion $i \colon U\langle im(G)\rangle \to UG$ where $\langle im(G)\rangle$ is the subgroup of G generated by the image $\{g(a) \mid a \in A\}$ of A in UG. Note that the cardinality of $\langle im(G)\rangle$ is less than $|\omega| \times |A|$ and that up to isomorphism there is only a set of groups of any given cardinality; in particular note that the cardinal number $|\omega| \times |A|$ is independent of the group G. As G runs over all groups, the collection of groups $\langle im(g)\rangle$ as g runs over the functions $A \to UG$ gives rise to a *set* of isomorphism classes. The set of functions $A \to UH$, where H runs over a set of representatives, satisfies the solution set condition.

DISCUSSION 2.11.18   Given a category $\mathcal{C}$, a *subobject* of an object A of $\mathcal{C}$ is a monic $A' \rightarrowtail A$. We write $Sub(A)$ for the category *of subobjects* which is defined to be the full subcategory of the slice $\mathcal{C}/A$ whose objects are the subobjects of A. Note that $Sub(A)$ is a preorder; if the diagram

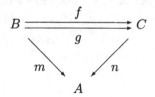

commutes, then n monic implies that $f = g$. We say that a category $\mathcal{C}$ is *well powered* if $Sub(A)$ is equivalent to a small category for each object A of $\mathcal{C}$. Note that $\mathcal{S}et$ is well powered, for each monic $B \rightarrowtail A$ is isomorphic to an inclusion $A' \subseteq A$, and there is only a set of such inclusions, that is a set of subsets of A. The same is true for the categories $\mathcal{G}rp$ and $\mathcal{T}op$ of groups and topological spaces.

Given a category $\mathcal{C}$, we call a collection of objects $\mathcal{O}$ of $\mathcal{C}$ a *coseparating* collection if for any parallel pair of morphisms $f, g: A \to B$ in $\mathcal{C}$ with f not equal to g there is an object O of $\mathcal{O}$ and morphism $h: B \to O$ of $\mathcal{C}$ for which hf is not equal to hg.

With this, we can now state and prove the special adjoint functor theorem after one final lemma.

LEMMA 2.11.19   Let a functor $F: \mathcal{C} \to \mathcal{E}$ preserve any pullbacks which exist in $\mathcal{C}$. Then F preserves monics.

PROOF   Let $m: A \rightarrowtail B$ be a monic morphism in $\mathcal{C}$ and let $f, g: C \to FA$ be morphisms of $\mathcal{E}$ for which $Fm \circ f = Fm \circ g$. That m is monic implies

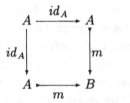

is a pullback in $\mathcal{C}$. The image under F is a pullback by hypothesis, and using this we see that there is a unique factorisation of both f and g through id_{FA}, implying $f = g$.   □

THEOREM 2.11.20   Suppose that the category $\mathcal{E}$ is locally small and complete, well powered, and has a coseparating *set*. Suppose also that $\mathcal{C}$ is a locally small category. Then any functor $G: \mathcal{E} \to \mathcal{C}$ which preserves all small limits has a left adjoint.

PROOF   First, fix an object X of $\mathcal{C}$. Let $\{E_i \mid i \in I\}$ be a coseparating set for $\mathcal{E}$, and write F for the set $\bigcup\{\mathcal{C}(X, GE_i) \mid i \in I\}$ indexing the morphisms $f: X \to GE_i$ in $\mathcal{C}$ for all $i \in I$. Set $S \overset{\text{def}}{=} \Pi_{f \in F} E_i$. G preserves the product S and so the set F induces a unique morphism $\theta: X \to GS$ for which the diagram

$$
\begin{array}{ccc}
 & GE_i & \\
 & \nearrow \quad \uparrow {\scriptstyle G\pi_f} & \\
 {\scriptstyle f} & & \\
X & \cdots\cdots\rightarrow & GS \\
 & {\scriptstyle \theta} &
\end{array}
$$

commutes. Among the subobjects $S' \rightarrowtail S$ there may be some for which θ factors through $GS' \rightarrowtail GS$. Note that the latter morphism is a monic by appealing to Lemma 2.11.19. Hence there can be at most one factorisation of θ through $GS' \rightarrowtail GS$. Pick a representative set, say $\{m_\beta : S_\beta \rightarrowtail S \mid \beta \in B\}$, of subobjects of S for which this factorisation exists, and write $f_\beta : X \to GS_\beta$ for the mediating morphism (so $\theta = Gm_\beta \circ f_\beta$).

By completeness of $\mathcal{E}$, we take the limit of the diagram which consists of the object S and the morphisms $S_\beta \rightarrowtail S$, say

$$j \stackrel{\text{def}}{=} S_0 \xrightarrow{\ n_\beta\ } S_\beta \xrightarrowtail{\ m_\beta\ } S.$$

G preserves this limit, and so there is a unique morphism k making the following diagram commute:

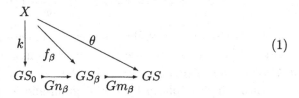

(1)

We shall aim to prove that $k : X \to GS_0$ is initial in the under-cone category $(X \downarrow G)$. Suppose that $g : X \to GY$ is another object in $(X \downarrow G)$. Set $H \stackrel{\text{def}}{=} \bigcup \{\mathcal{E}(Y, E_i) \mid i \in I\}$, and set $T \stackrel{\text{def}}{=} \Pi_{h \in H} E_i$. Then there is a morphism $\phi : Y \rightarrowtail T$ for which $\pi_h \circ \phi = h$. It is easy to check that ϕ is indeed a monic morphism using the fact that $\{E_i \mid i \in I\}$ is a coseparating set. Noting also that $Gh \circ g : X \to GE_i$ is in F, then we can form the morphism $\psi : S \to T$ for which $\pi_h \circ \psi = \pi_{Ghog}$. Finally note that G preserves the limit (product) $(\pi_h : T \to E_i \mid h \in H)$ and so there is a unique morphism $\overline{k}$ making

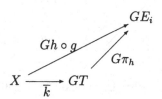

commute. In fact we can check that $\overline{k} = G\phi \circ g$ and $\overline{k} = G\psi \circ \theta$ (the easy calculation is omitted). Form the limit

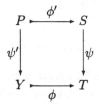

and once again using the fact that G preserves limits, together with the fact that $G\phi \circ g = G\psi \circ \theta$, we have

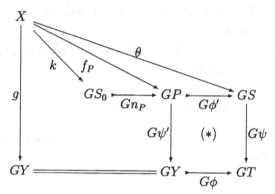

where f_P exists because $(*)$ is a pullback square, and hence $P \in \{S_\beta \mid \beta \in B\}$ implying that $n_P \colon S_0 \rightarrowtail P$ exists—see (1). Hence we have the existence of a morphism $\psi'n_P \colon (k, S_0) \to (g, Y)$ where to see this one needs to check that f_P is a (unique) mediating morphism for the diagram above. It remains to see that $\psi'n_P$ is unique. Suppose there are two such morphisms, p and q. Then form the equaliser diagram

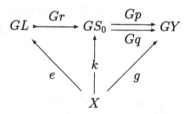

which leads to another equaliser diagram as G preserves limits:

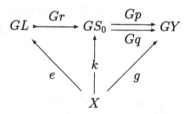

The mediating morphism e exists by appeal to the definition of p and q. Hence we have $\theta = Gj \circ k = G(jr) \circ e$, that is $L \in \{S_\beta \mid \beta \in B\}$ via $jr\colon L \rightarrowtail S$, and so from the construction of S_0 there is a morphism $n_L \colon S_0 \rightarrowtail L$ for which $j = (jr)n_L$. But j is monic so $id_{S_0} = rn_L$, and thus $id_L = n_Lr$ because r too is monic. Thus $S_0 \cong L$ implying $p = q$. $\square$

2.12   Strict Indexed Categories

DISCUSSION 2.12.1   We begin this section with a discussion of indexed categories. Strictly speaking, what we shall call an indexed category should more properly be described as a *strict* indexed category; we shall ask that certain diagrams commute up to strict equality, whereas these diagrams are traditionally only required to commute up to (canonical) isomorphism. Let $\mathcal{C}at$ be the category of small categories and functors. Then a *C-indexed category* $\mathbb{C}$ is by definition a functor $\mathbb{C}: C^{op} \to \mathcal{C}at$. One should think of the category C as a form of indexing collection; so each object I of C is an "index" for a category $\mathbb{C}I$. The category C is usually referred to as the *base* of the C-indexed category $\mathbb{C}$, and given an object I of C, the category $\mathbb{C}I$ is called the *fibre* of $\mathbb{C}$ at I. Not surprisingly, we can perform the game of defining notions of functor and natural transformation between indexed categories. Before doing this, we remark that if $f: J \to I$ is a morphism of C, then we shall write f^* for the functor $\mathbb{C}f$, that is $f^* \stackrel{\text{def}}{=} \mathbb{C}f: \mathbb{C}I \to \mathbb{C}J$. The functors f^* are known as *reindexing* functors.

Now we define a functor between indexed categories. Let $\mathbb{C}$ and $\mathbb{D}$ be C-indexed categories. Then a *C-indexed functor* α is a natural transformation $\alpha: \mathbb{C} \to \mathbb{D}$; thus by definition, for any morphism $f: J \to I$ in C, the diagram

$$
\begin{array}{ccc}
\mathbb{C}I & \xrightarrow{\alpha_I} & \mathbb{D}I \\
{\scriptstyle f^*}\downarrow & & \downarrow{\scriptstyle f^*} \\
\mathbb{C}J & \xrightarrow[\alpha_J]{} & \mathbb{D}J
\end{array}
$$

commutes. We sometimes say (informally) that the component functors commute with the reindexing functors, and we shall sometimes write $\alpha: \mathbb{C} \to \mathbb{D}: C^{op} \to \mathcal{C}at$ to denote the above data.

Next we can define a natural transformation between C-indexed functors. Suppose that both α and α' are C-indexed functors between the C-indexed categories $\mathbb{C}$ and $\mathbb{D}$. Then a *C-indexed natural transformation* $\delta: \alpha \to \alpha'$ is given by a natural transformation $\delta_I: \alpha_I \to \alpha'_I$ for each object I of C for which given any morphism $f: J \to I$ in C the diagram

$$
\begin{array}{ccc}
& \overset{\alpha_I}{\longrightarrow} & \\
\mathbb{C}I\ \ {\downarrow \delta_I} & & \mathbb{D}I \\
& \underset{\alpha'_I}{\longrightarrow} & \\
{\scriptstyle f^*}\downarrow & & \downarrow{\scriptstyle f^*} \\
& \overset{\alpha_J}{\longrightarrow} & \\
\mathbb{C}J\ \ {\downarrow \delta_J} & & \mathbb{D}J \\
& \underset{\alpha'_J}{\longrightarrow} &
\end{array}
\qquad (*)
$$

commutes, which is to say that for each $f: J \to I$ we have $(\delta_J)_{f^*} = f^* \delta_I$. We refer to the commuting square $(*)$ as the *intreid* condition. This is just saying (by definition—refer to page 51) that for each object A of $\mathbb{C}I$ we have $(\delta_J)_{f^*A} = f^*((\delta_I)_A)$, where

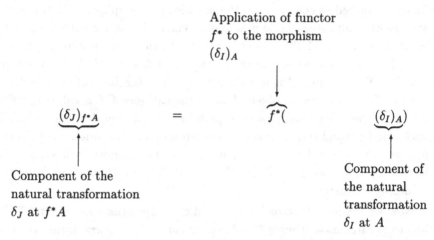

So far, our discussion has revolved around the notion of indexed categories, functors and natural transformations, $\mathbb{C}$, α, δ, relative to a fixed base category C. Now we shall consider the situation where the base category is allowed to change. To make our definitions tidy, we shall actually define a new category $\mathbb{ICat}$. An object of $\mathbb{ICat}$ is given by a functor $\mathbb{C}: C^{op} \to Cat$ where C is any category, that is the objects of $\mathbb{ICat}$ are indexed categories. Then given any other indexed category $\mathbb{D}: \mathcal{D}^{op} \to Cat$, a morphism $\mathbb{C} \to \mathbb{D}$ in $\mathbb{ICat}$ is given by a pair (α, F) where $F: C \to \mathcal{D}$ is a functor and α is a C-indexed functor $\alpha: \mathbb{C} \to \mathbb{D}F^{op}$; we can draw a diagram thus:

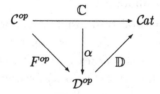

Suppose that we are given morphisms $(\alpha, F): \mathbb{C} \to \mathbb{D}$ and $(\alpha', F'): \mathbb{D} \to \mathbb{E}$. Then the composition of (α, F) and (α', F') is given by

$$(\alpha', F')(\alpha, F) \stackrel{\text{def}}{=} (\alpha'_F \circ \alpha, F'F) : \mathbb{C} \to \mathbb{E}.$$

The identity morphism at an object $\mathbb{C}$ is given by $(id_{\mathbb{C}}, id_C)$ where of course a component of $id_{\mathbb{C}}: \mathbb{C} \to \mathbb{C}$ at any object I of C is the identity functor $id_{\mathbb{C}I}$ on the fibre $\mathbb{C}I$, and id_C is the identity functor on the category C.

We can now mimic the definition of a functor category in the indexed setting. Let $\mathbb{C}$ and $\mathbb{D}$ be C-indexed and $\mathcal{D}$-indexed categories respectively.

We shall define a new category $[\mathbb{C}, \mathbb{D}]$ as follows. The objects of $[\mathbb{C}, \mathbb{D}]$ are morphisms of indexed categories $(\alpha, F) \colon \mathbb{C} \to \mathbb{D}$. Then given another object (α', F'), a morphism $(\delta, \chi) \colon (\alpha, F) \to (\alpha', F')$ in the category $[\mathbb{C}, \mathbb{D}]$ is given by a natural transformation $\chi \colon F \to F'$, and a $\mathcal{C}$-indexed natural transformation

$$\delta : \alpha \to (\chi_{(-)})^* \alpha' : \mathbb{C} \to \mathbb{D} F^{op}.$$

Such a δ is often referred to as a *modification*. The notation perhaps requires a word of explanation. The component of the natural transformation $(\chi_{(-)})^* \alpha' \colon \mathbb{C} \to \mathbb{D} F^{op}$ at an object I of $\mathcal{C}$ is given by the composition of functors

$$\mathbb{C} I \xrightarrow{\alpha_I'} \mathbb{D} F' I \xrightarrow{\chi_I^*} \mathbb{D} F I$$

where of course $\chi_I \colon FI \to F'I$ is a morphism of $\mathcal{D}$ and $\chi_I^* \overset{\text{def}}{=} \mathbb{D}(\chi_I) \colon \mathbb{D} F' I \to \mathbb{D} F I$. Let us now define composition in the category $[\mathbb{C}, \mathbb{D}]$. Take morphisms

$$(\delta, \chi) : (\alpha, F) \longrightarrow (\alpha', F') \qquad \text{and} \qquad (\delta', \chi') : (\alpha', F') \longrightarrow (\alpha'', F'').$$

We set

$$(\delta', \chi')(\delta, \chi) \overset{\text{def}}{=} ((\chi_{(-)})^* \delta'_{(-)} \circ \delta_{(-)}, \chi'\chi) : (\alpha, F) \longrightarrow (\alpha'', F'').$$

Once again, a word of explanation about notation is in order. The component of the $\mathcal{C}$-indexed natural transformation $(\chi_{(-)})^* \delta'_{(-)} \circ \delta_{(-)} \colon \alpha \to (\chi'\chi_{(-)})^* \alpha''$ at an object I of $\mathcal{C}$ is given by the composition of natural transformations

$$\alpha_I \xrightarrow{\delta_I} \chi_I^* \alpha_I' \xrightarrow{\chi_I^* \delta_I'} \chi_I^* \chi_I'^* \alpha_I'' \overset{\text{def}}{=} (\chi'\chi)_I^* \alpha_I''.$$

We have to check that this is well defined, that is the appropriate instance of the intreid condition (diagram (*)) holds—see page 107. So let $f \colon J \to I$ be a morphism of $\mathcal{C}$ and then we have:

$$
\begin{aligned}
(\chi_J^* \delta_J' \circ \delta_J)_{f^*} &\overset{\text{def}}{=} \chi_J^*((\delta_J')_{f^*}) \circ (\delta_J)_{f^*} \\
(*) \ \textit{for } \delta' \quad &= \quad \chi_J^*((F'f)^* \delta_I') \circ (\delta_J)_{f^*} \\
(*) \ \textit{for } \delta \quad &= \quad \chi_J^*((F'f)^* \delta_I') \circ (Ff)^* \delta_I \\
(-)^* \ \textit{is functorial} \quad &= \quad (F'f \circ \chi_J)^* \delta_I' \circ (Ff)^* \delta_I \\
\chi \colon F \to F' \ \textit{is a natural transformation} \quad &= \quad (\chi_I \circ Ff)^* \delta_I' \circ (Ff)^* \delta_I \\
(-)^* \ \textit{is functorial} \quad &= \quad (Ff)^* \chi_I^* \delta_I' \circ (Ff)^* \delta_I \\
(Ff)^* \ \textit{is a functor} \quad &= \quad (Ff)^* (\chi_I^* \delta_I' \circ \delta_I).
\end{aligned}
$$

The identity morphism at (α, F) is given by $(id_{\alpha_{(-)}}, id_F)$.

EXERCISE 2.12.2   Verify the above calculations which ensure that our definitions of composition of morphisms in the categories $\mathcal{ICat}$ and $[\mathbb{C}, \mathbb{D}]$ make sense. Also check that the definitions of identity are good.

DISCUSSION 2.12.3   When discussing categorical models of type theories in later chapters, we shall not only wish to talk about equivalences of categories, but also of indexed categories. We shall now define the notion of equivalence of indexed categories and then prove a little proposition which shows that what is a slightly unwieldy notion in fact amounts to a very simple idea. So let $\mathbb{C}$ be a C-indexed category and $\mathbb{D}$ be a D-indexed category; then we shall say that $\mathbb{C}$ is *equivalent* to $\mathbb{D}$, written $\mathbb{C} \simeq \mathbb{D}$, if there are morphisms

$$(\alpha, F) : \mathbb{C} \rightleftarrows \mathbb{D} : (\beta, G)$$

in $\mathcal{ICat}$ such that there are isomorphisms

$$(\alpha, F)(\beta, G) \cong (id_{\mathbb{D}}, id_{\mathcal{D}}) \qquad \text{in} \qquad [\mathbb{D}, \mathbb{D}],$$
$$(\beta, G)(\alpha, F) \cong (id_{\mathbb{C}}, id_{\mathcal{C}}) \qquad \text{in} \qquad [\mathbb{C}, \mathbb{C}].$$

We shall investigate this definition by proving the following proposition.

PROPOSITION 2.12.4   Let $\mathbb{C}$ be a C-indexed category and let $\mathbb{D}$ be a D-indexed category, for which there is an equivalence $\mathbb{C} \simeq \mathbb{D}$. Then the base categories C and D are equivalent, as are the fibres $\mathbb{C}I$ and $\mathbb{D}FI$ at an object I of C, that is

$$C \simeq D \qquad \text{and} \qquad \mathbb{C}I \simeq \mathbb{D}FI.$$

PROOF   Let us consider the isomorphism $(\beta, G)(\alpha, F) \cong (id_{\mathbb{C}}, id_{\mathcal{C}})$. Unravelling the definitions, we are given morphisms

$$(\delta, \eta^{-1}) \;\; : \;\; (\beta_F \circ \alpha, GF) \longrightarrow (id_{\mathbb{C}}, id_{\mathcal{C}})$$
$$(\rho, \eta) \;\; : \;\; (id_{\mathbb{C}}, id_{\mathcal{C}}) \longrightarrow (\beta_F \circ \alpha, GF)$$

in the category $[\mathbb{C}, \mathbb{C}]$ for which

$$(\delta, \eta^{-1})(\rho, \eta) \overset{\text{def}}{=} ((\eta_{(-)})^* \delta_{(-)} \circ \rho_{(-)}, \eta^{-1}\eta) = (id_{id_{\mathcal{C}(-)}}, id_{id_{\mathcal{C}}}), \qquad (1)$$

and

$$(\rho, \eta)(\delta, \eta^{-1}) \overset{\text{def}}{=} ([(\eta^{-1})_{(-)}]^* \rho_{(-)} \circ \delta_{(-)}, \eta\eta^{-1}) = (id_{(\beta_F \circ \alpha)_{(-)}}, id_{GF}). \qquad (2)$$

This means that we have $\eta^{-1}\eta = id_{id_{\mathcal{C}}}$ and $\eta\eta^{-1} = id_{GF}$ where

$$GF \xrightarrow[\eta]{\eta^{-1}} id_{\mathcal{C}} \qquad \text{and} \qquad F : \mathcal{C} \rightleftarrows \mathcal{D} : G$$

that is $GF \cong id_{\mathcal{C}}$. If we apply a similar procedure to the data in the proposition concerning the isomorphism in $[\mathbb{D}, \mathbb{D}]$, which, say, is witnessed by morphisms

$$(\mu, \epsilon) \ : \ (\alpha_G \circ \beta, FG) \longrightarrow (id_{\mathbb{D}}, id_{\mathcal{D}}),$$
$$(\nu, \epsilon^{-1}) \ : \ (id_{\mathbb{D}}, id_{\mathcal{D}}) \longrightarrow (\alpha_G \circ \beta, FG),$$

it will follow that $FG \cong id_{\mathcal{D}}$, and thus we have $\mathcal{C} \simeq \mathcal{D}$ as required.

We can also deduce from (1) and (2) that if I is an object of $\mathcal{C}$, then

$$\eta_I^* \delta_I \circ \rho_I = id_{id_{\mathcal{C}I}} \tag{3}$$

and

$$(\eta^{-1})_I^* \rho_I \circ \delta_I = id_{\beta_{FI} \circ \alpha_I}. \tag{4}$$

Note that the second of these equations implies that

$$\rho_I \circ \eta_I^* \delta_I = id_{\eta_I^* \circ \beta_{FI} \circ \alpha_I}, \tag{5}$$

where

$$id_{\mathcal{C}I} \xrightarrow[\eta_I^* \delta_I]{\rho_I} \eta_I^* \circ \beta_{FI} \circ \alpha_I$$

and

$$\alpha_I : \mathbb{C}I \rightleftarrows \mathbb{D}FI : \eta_I^* \circ \beta_{FI}.$$

Now we are in a position to see that the fibres $\mathbb{C}I$ and $\mathbb{D}FI$ are equivalent. Firstly, note that (3) and (5) imply that

$$(\eta_I^* \circ \beta_{FI}) \circ \alpha_I \cong id_{\mathbb{C}I}. \tag{6}$$

We will have shown that $\mathbb{C}I \simeq \mathbb{D}FI$ if we can also prove

$$\alpha_I \circ (\eta_I^* \circ \beta_{FI}) \cong id_{\mathbb{D}FI}. \tag{7}$$

To see (7), note that by following a similar argument to the one just given, but for the isomorphism in $[\mathbb{D}, \mathbb{D}]$, we can also deduce that $id_{\mathbb{D}J} \cong (\epsilon^{-1})_J^* \circ \alpha_{GJ} \circ \beta_J$, where J is an object of $\mathcal{D}$, this latter equation being an analogue of (6). Thus

$$id_{\mathbb{D}FI} \cong (\epsilon^{-1})_{FI}^* \circ \alpha_{GFI} \circ \beta_{FI}.$$

The base categories are equivalent, and thus $(F \dashv G)$, and we use Proposition 2.10.25 to deduce that $\epsilon_{FI} \circ F\eta_I = id_{FI}$. This implies $(\epsilon^{-1})_{FI} = F\eta_I$, and so we have

$$id_{\mathbb{D}FI} \cong (F\eta_I)^* \circ \alpha_{GFI} \circ \beta_{FI}. \tag{8}$$

Now we just need to note that the following diagram commutes, where we are using naturality of α at I in $\eta_I : I \to GFI$:

$$
\begin{array}{ccc}
\mathbb{C}I & \xrightarrow{\quad \alpha_I \quad} & \mathbb{D}FI \\
{\scriptstyle \eta_I^*} \uparrow & & \downarrow {\scriptstyle (F\eta_I)^*} \\
\mathbb{C}GFI & \xrightarrow[\quad \alpha_{GFI} \quad]{} & \mathbb{D}FGFI
\end{array}
$$

This diagram together with (8) implies (7), as required.   □

EXERCISE 2.12.5   Verify that (5) holds, which is a very simple exercise using the definitions. Derive also the analogue of (6). Make sure you understand the essence of the proof.

DISCUSSION 2.12.6   This discussion is devoted to a description of a certain categorical construction which is (among many others) due to Grothendieck. Recall the category *Cat* of small categories and functors, introduced on page 83, and suppose that $F : \mathcal{C} \to Cat$ is a functor. The (covariant) Grothendieck construction builds a category $\mathbb{G}(F)$ and a functor $\pi_F : \mathbb{G}(F) \to \mathcal{C}$ out of the functor F. In the category $\mathbb{G}(F)$

• objects are pairs (C, A) where C is an object of $\mathcal{C}$ and A is an object of FC, and

• a morphism $(C, A) \to (C', A')$ is a pair (u, f) where $u : C \to C'$ is a morphism of $\mathcal{C}$ and $f : Fu(A) \to A'$ is a morphism of FC'.

It is clear what identities in $\mathbb{G}(F)$ look like, and composition is more or less as expected. To be clear, if we are given morphisms $(u, f) : (C, A) \to (C', A')$ and $(v, g) : (C', A') \to (C'', A'')$ in $\mathbb{G}(F)$, then the composition is given by

$$(v, g) \circ (u, f) \overset{\text{def}}{=} (vu, g \circ Fv(f)) : (C, A) \longrightarrow (C'', A'').$$

The functor $\pi_F : \mathbb{G}(F) \to \mathcal{C}$ is given by the assignment

$$(u, f) : (C, A) \longrightarrow (C', A') \quad \longmapsto \quad f : C \to C'.$$

The (contravariant) Grothendieck construction builds a functor $\pi_F : \mathbb{G}(F) \to \mathcal{C}$ from a functor $F : \mathcal{C}^{op} \to Cat$. In the category $\mathbb{G}(F)$

• objects are pairs (C, A) where C is an object of $\mathcal{C}$ and A is an object of FC, and

• a morphism $(C, A) \to (C', A')$ is a pair (u, f) where $u: C \to C'$ is a morphism of $\mathcal{C}$ and $f: A \to Fu(A')$ is a morphism of FC.

It is easy to check that $\mathbb{G}(F)$ really is a category in the case of the (contravariant) Grothendieck construction, and the projection functor $\pi_F: \mathbb{G}(F) \to C$ is again given by "projection to the first coordinate."

We shall make use of the Grothendieck construction in later chapters when we give domain-theoretic models of certain polymorphic type theories. We remark that the construction will also apply (by analogy) to a functor $F: \mathcal{C} \to \mathcal{P}$ where $\mathcal{P}$ is some subcategory of the category $\mathcal{POSet}$ where we regard each poset as a category.

EXERCISE 2.12.7   Let $\mathcal{C}$ be a category and $F: \mathcal{C} \to \mathcal{S}et$ a functor. By regarding every set as a discrete category and every function as a functor between such categories, use the Yoneda lemma to prove that $(H \downarrow F)^{op}$ and $\mathbb{G}(F)$ are equivalent categories, where $H: \mathcal{C}^{op} \to [\mathcal{C}, \mathcal{S}et]$ is the Yoneda embedding.

2.13 Further Exercises

(1) Let $\mathcal{S}$ be the category of non-empty sets and set functions. Define a functor $\mathcal{P}: \mathcal{S} \to \mathcal{S}$ by sending $f: X \to Y$ in $\mathcal{S}$ to the function

$$\mathcal{P}(f): \mathcal{P}(X) \to \mathcal{P}(Y) \qquad A \mapsto f(A) \stackrel{\text{def}}{=} \{f(a) \mid a \in A\}.$$

Show that there is no natural transformation $\alpha: \mathcal{P} \to id_{\mathcal{S}}$.

(2) (a) Let $F: \mathcal{C} \to \mathcal{D}$ and $G: \mathcal{D} \to \mathcal{E}$ be functors. Show that F is faithful if GF is faithful. Show also that if GF is full and G faithful, then F is full.

(b) Suppose that $F, G: \mathcal{C} \to \mathcal{D}$ are functors which are naturally isomorphic. Show that F is full iff G is full and that F is faithful iff G is faithful.

(c) Suppose that $F: \mathcal{C} \to \mathcal{D}$ and $G: \mathcal{D} \to \mathcal{C}$ are functors and that GF is naturally isomorphic to $id_{\mathcal{C}}$. Show that F is faithful.

(3) Let X and Y be dcpos, $Y_\perp$ have underlying set $\{[y] \mid y \in Y\} \cup \{\perp\}$ with order $\perp \leq y$, and $y \leq y'$ iff $[y] \leq [y']$ (so informally $Y_\perp$ is Y with a least element added, and is also a dcpo). Let $i: Y \to Y_\perp$ be the continuous function given by $i(y) \stackrel{\text{def}}{=} [y]$. Let $\mathcal{I}(D)$ mean the set of inductive subsets of a dcpo D regarded as a category, and consider the functor

$$(id_X \times i)^{-1} : \mathcal{I}(X \times Y_\perp) \longrightarrow \mathcal{I}(X \times Y) \quad I \mapsto \{(x, y) \in X \times Y \mid (x, [y]) \in I\}.$$

Check that $(id_X \times i)^{-1}$ is well defined. Show that it has both left and right adjoints, giving explicit formulae for their definitions.

(4) Show that the pushout of an epic morphism is another epic morphism. More precisely, show that given morphisms $e: A \twoheadrightarrow B$ and $g: A \to C$ in a category for which the pushout exists, then the pushout is of the form

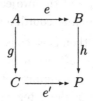

(5) Show that projections for binary products are not necessarily epic and that insertions for binary coproducts are not necessarily monic.

(6) Show that the category $[\mathcal{C}^{op}, Set]$, known as the category of *presheaves* on $\mathcal{C}$, is a cartesian closed category which has pullbacks. *Hint: you may find exponentials in $[\mathcal{C}^{op}, Set]$ tricky to construct. If $F, G: \mathcal{C}^{op} \to Set$, suppose that $F \Rightarrow G: \mathcal{C}^{op} \to Set$ exists, apply the Yoneda lemma to $F \Rightarrow G$, and think about the definition of cartesian closure of $[\mathcal{C}^{op}, Set]$.*

(7) Let $\mathcal{C}$ be a category for which every slice is a cartesian closed category. Show that the slice of any slice is cartesian closed. Show also that every slice of $\mathcal{C}$ has finite limits. *Hint: use Theorem 2.11.8 part (ii).*

(8) In this exercise we show how to construct limits and colimits in the category *Set*.

(a) Let $\mathbb{I}$ be a small category and $D: \mathbb{I} \to Set$ a functor. Write $\varprojlim D$ for the set of families of the form $(x_I \mid I \in \mathbb{I})$ such that

- $x_I \in DI$, and
- if $\alpha: I \to J$ is a morphism of $\mathbb{I}$ then $D\alpha(x_I) = x_J$.

Define a function $\pi_I: \varprojlim D \to DI$ for each object I of $\mathbb{I}$ by $(x_I \mid I \in \mathbb{I}) \mapsto x_I$. Prove that $(\pi_I: \varprojlim D \to DI \mid I \in \mathbb{I})$ is a limit for the diagram D.

(b) We define a *filtered* category $\mathcal{C}$ to be a category for which

- there is at least one object in $\mathcal{C}$;
- for any objects A and B of $\mathcal{C}$ there is an object C, and morphisms $A \to C$ and $B \to C$, and
- for any morphisms $f, g: A \to B$ in $\mathcal{C}$ there is a morphism $h: B \to C$ for which $hf = hg$.

Thus filteredness is the categorical analogue of directedness (of a poset): draw some diagrams of the definition. Now let $\mathbb{I}$ be small and filtered and $D\colon \mathbb{I} \to \mathit{Set}$ a functor. Let U be the disjoint union of the sets DI as I runs over the objects of $\mathbb{I}$; formally $U \stackrel{\text{def}}{=} ob\,\mathbb{I} \times \bigcup \{DI \mid I \in \mathbb{I}\}$. Define a relation on U by asking that $(I, x) \sim (J, y)$ just in case there is an object K of $\mathbb{I}$ and morphisms $\alpha\colon I \to K$, $\beta\colon J \to K$ for which $D\alpha(x) = D\beta(y)$ in DK. Prove that $\sim$ is an equivalence relation. Set $\varinjlim D \stackrel{\text{def}}{=} U/\sim$ and define a function $\iota_I\colon DI \to \varinjlim D$ by $x \mapsto [x]$ where $x \in DI$. Prove that $(\iota_I\colon DI \to \varinjlim D \mid I \in \mathbb{I})$ is a (filtered) colimit for D.

(c) Let $D\colon \mathbb{I} \to \mathit{Set}$ be a diagram. Again let U be the disjoint union of the DI and define a relation R on U by asking that $(I, x)R(J, y)$ just in case there is a morphism $\alpha\colon I \to J$ in $\mathbb{I}$ for which $y = D\alpha(x)$. Let $\sim$ be the equivalence relation generated by R, write $\varinjlim D \stackrel{\text{def}}{=} U/\sim$, and let $\iota_I\colon DI \to \varinjlim D$ map elements to their equivalence classes as in (b). Prove that this gives rise to a colimit for D.

(9) Let $\mathcal{C}$ be a category and $\mathcal{O}$ a class of objects of $\mathcal{C}$. The category $\mathcal{C}$ is said to be *balanced* if every morphism which is both monic and epic is an isomorphism. We say that $\mathcal{O}$ is a *separating class* for $\mathcal{C}$ if given $f, g\colon A \to B$ in $\mathcal{C}$ with $f \neq g$, then there is some O in $\mathcal{O}$ and $h\colon O \to A$ for which $fh \neq gh$. We say that $\mathcal{O}$ is a *detecting class* if given any morphism $f\colon A \to B$ in $\mathcal{C}$ for which given any O in $\mathcal{O}$ each morphism $O \to B$ factors uniquely through f, then f is an isomorphism.

(a) If $\mathcal{C}$ is balanced, show that any separating class is a detecting class.

(b) If $\mathcal{C}$ has all equalisers, show that any detecting class is a separating class.

(10) Suppose that $F\colon \mathcal{C} \to \mathcal{D}$ and $G\colon \mathcal{D} \to \mathcal{C}$, and we are given an adjunction $(F \dashv G)$ with unit η and counit ϵ. Let A be an object of $\mathcal{C}$. Prove that the following conditions are equivalent:

(a) $F\eta_A$ is an isomorphism for all A,

(b) ϵ_{FA} is an isomorphism for all A,

(c) $G\epsilon_{FA}$ is an isomorphism for all A, and

(d) $GF\eta_A = \eta_{GFA}$ for all A.

Formulate four more conditions which are dual to the above conditions, and prove that your four new conditions are equivalent. Are they equivalent themselves to conditions (a) to (d)?

(11) Let $\mathcal{C}$ be a cartesian closed category and $T\colon \mathcal{C} \to \mathcal{C}$ any endofunctor. Define, for each object C of $\mathcal{C}$, an endofunctor $C \times T(-)$ on $\mathcal{C}$ by sending

$f: A \to B$ to $id_C \times Tf: C \times TA \to C \times TB$. Define similarly an endofunctor $T(C \times -)$. Suppose also that there is a natural transformation $\tau^C: C \times T(-) \to T(C \times -)$ for each C, for which the diagram

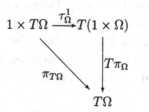

$$1 \times T\Omega \xrightarrow{\tau^1_\Omega} T(1 \times \Omega)$$

with $\pi_{T\Omega}$ and $T\pi_\Omega$ to $T\Omega$

commutes, where 1 is the (specified) terminal object of C. Finally, let there be a morphism $\sigma: T\Omega \to \Omega$ in C. Consider the following:

(FPO1) Given any morphism $f: TA \to A$ in C, there is a unique morphism $\overline{f}: \Omega \to A$ for which the diagram

$$
\begin{array}{ccc}
T\Omega & \xrightarrow{\sigma} & \Omega \\
{\scriptstyle T\overline{f}}\downarrow & & \downarrow{\scriptstyle \overline{f}} \\
TA & \xrightarrow{f} & A
\end{array}
$$

commutes.

(FPO2) Given any object C of C, and morphism $f: C \times TA \to A$ in C, there is a unique morphism $\overline{f}: C \times \Omega \to A$ for which the diagram

$$
\begin{array}{ccc}
C \times T\Omega & \xrightarrow{id_C \times \sigma} & C \times \Omega \\
{\scriptstyle \langle \pi_C, T\overline{f} \circ \tau^C_\Omega \rangle}\downarrow & & \downarrow{\scriptstyle \overline{f}} \\
C \times TA & \xrightarrow{f} & A
\end{array}
$$

commutes.

Prove that property (FPO1) holds of C just in case property (FPO2) holds of C.

(12) (a) Let X be a Boolean lattice. Prove that for $x, y \in X$ we have $x \leq y$ iff $x \wedge \neg y = \bot$.

(b) Recall Proposition 1.4.8 which says that every Boolean lattice X is a Heyting lattice. Use this result, along with Theorem 2.10.6, to deduce that for any $x \in X$, the monotone function $x \wedge (-): X \to X$ preserves all joins in X.

(c) Let X be Boolean lattice. We call an element $a \in X$ an *atom* if (it is not bottom and) for all $x \in X$, whenever $\bot \neq x \leq a$ then $x = a$. We write X^* for the set of atoms of X. We call a Boolean lattice *atomic* if given any non-bottom element $x \in X$, there is an atom a for which $a \leq x$.

We show that $\mathcal{P}(X^*) \cong X$ for any *complete* atomic Boolean lattice X. Define two functions by

$$\phi \; : \; X \longrightarrow \mathcal{P}(X^*) \qquad\qquad x \mapsto \{a \in X^* \mid a \leq x\}$$
$$\psi \; : \; \mathcal{P}(X^*) \longrightarrow X \qquad\qquad S \mapsto \bigvee S.$$

See that ϕ and ψ are monotone. Use (a) to show that $\psi\phi = id_X$. Use (b) to show that $\phi\psi = id_{\mathcal{P}(X^*)}$.

(d) If S is any set, what are the atoms of $\mathcal{P}(S)$? Show that $S \cong (\mathcal{P}(S))^*$.

(e) The category $\mathcal{C\!At\!B\!L\!at}$ has objects the complete atomic Boolean lattices and morphisms those functions which preserve all meets and joins. Prove that $\mathcal{C\!At\!B\!L\!at} \simeq \mathcal{S}et^{op}$, making use of the above results.

(13) Let $\pi : \mathcal{E} \to \mathcal{B}$ be any functor. An object E of $\mathcal{E}$ is *above* an object I of $\mathcal{B}$ if $\pi E = I$. A morphism f of $\mathcal{E}$ is *above* a morphism α of $\mathcal{B}$ if $\pi f = \alpha$. A morphism in $\mathcal{E}$ above an identity in $\mathcal{B}$ is said to be *vertical*. Every object I of $\mathcal{B}$ determines a category $\mathcal{E}(I)$ consisting of the objects above I and vertical morphisms, called the *fibre* of $\pi : \mathcal{E} \to \mathcal{B}$ at I.

A morphism $c : E \to C$ in $\mathcal{E}$ is *cartesian* if given any morphism γ in $\mathcal{B}$ with c above γ and any morphism $f : E' \to C$ in $\mathcal{E}$ with $\pi f = \gamma \circ \beta$ in $\mathcal{B}$, then there is a unique morphism $g : E' \to E$ in $\mathcal{E}$ above β with $f = cg$.

The functor $\pi : \mathcal{E} \to \mathcal{B}$ is a *fibration* if for every object C of $\mathcal{E}$ and morphism $\gamma : I \to \pi C$ in $\mathcal{B}$, there is a cartesian morphism $c : E \to C$ above γ. We call c a *cartesian lifting* of γ. Given any object C of $\mathcal{E}$, write $\bar{\gamma} : \gamma^*(C) \to C$ for the cartesian lifting of γ. A choice of $\bar{\gamma}$ for each $\gamma : I \to \pi C$ is called a *cleavage*. A fibration equipped with a given cleavage is called a *cloven* fibration.

(a) Let $\mathcal{F}am$ be the category with objects $(A_i \mid i \in I)$ indexed families of sets, and a morphism $f : (A_i \mid i \in I) \to (B_j \mid j \in J)$ is given by a function $\alpha : I \to J$ together with a family of functions

$$(f_i : A_i \to B_{\alpha(i)} \mid i \in I).$$

Let $\pi : \mathcal{F}am \to \mathcal{S}et$ be the functor mapping $(A_i \mid i \in I)$ to (the set) I and let π have the obvious definition on morphisms.

(i) Given a set I, verify that the fibre $\mathcal{F}am(I)$ is equivalent to the category $[I, \mathcal{S}et]$.

(ii) Verify that f is a cartesian morphism if each f_i is an isomorphism. Think about the fact that f essentially performs a pure reindexing of sets.

(iii) Prove that the functor $\pi: \mathcal{F}am \to \mathcal{S}et$ which maps families to their indexing sets is a fibration.

(b) Let $\pi: \mathcal{E} \to \mathcal{B}$ be a cloven fibration. Show that there is a functor $\alpha^*: \mathcal{E}(I) \to \mathcal{E}(J)$ for every $\alpha: J \to I$ in $\mathcal{B}$. *Hint: think about the definitions of fibration and cartesian lifting.*

(c) Let $\pi: \mathcal{E} \to \mathcal{B}$ be a cloven fibration. π is said to be *split* if $id_I^* = id_{\mathcal{E}(I)}$ and $(\alpha\beta)^* = \alpha^*\beta^*$, where $\alpha: J \to I$ and $\beta: K \to J$ are morphisms of $\mathcal{B}$.

(i) Formulate a notion of morphism between split fibrations by thinking about functors which preserve cleavages. Hence define the category $\mathcal{SF}ib$ of split fibrations.

(ii) Prove that the Grothendieck construction applied to an indexed category $\mathbb{C}: \mathcal{C}^{op} \to \mathcal{C}at$ produces a split fibration $\pi: \mathbb{G}(\mathbb{C}) \to \mathcal{C}$.

(iii) Hence prove that the categories $\mathcal{SF}ib$ and $\mathcal{IC}at$ are equivalent.

2.14 Pointers to the Literature

We begin by describing some of the research papers in which the original concepts of category theory can be found. The first notions of category, functor and natural transformation were introduced by Eilenberg and Mac Lane in [EM42] and [EM45]. The idea that cartesian products are an instance of a form of universal property first appears in [Mac48] and [Mac50]. The primeval ideas for the concept of adjunction appear in [Bou48] in which a description of "universal construction" can be found. However, there does not seem to have been an explicit definition of adjunction until Kan's paper [Kan58]. The categorical form of the adjoint functor theorem is due to Freyd and appears in his [Fre64]. The general description of limit can also be found in Kan's [Kan58], but the underlying ideas had been studied before 1958, and mathematicians had worked implicitly with particular *kinds* of limit.

Now we move on to a description of useful textbooks. These are given in alphabetical order of authors. Our first reference is in some respects a book which bears resemblance (in content rather than style) to "Categories for Types," namely Asperti and Longo's text [AL91]. Most of our Chapter 2 appears in the first half of Asperti and Longo. Material on internal category theory can be found in Asperti and Longo, which is highly relevant to a complete understanding of models of polymorphism, and this material is not covered in "Categories for Types." Most of the ideas of basic category theory

can be found in the book [BW90] by Barr and Wells, along with a few more
advanced topics. Much of the content of Chapter 2 of "Categories for Types"
appears in [BW90], but Barr and Wells present the material with more background discussion and at a slower pace. It is a textbook aimed at advanced
undergraduates and early postgraduates, and is a book solely concerned with
category theory. What still remains a classic reference for category theory
is Mac Lanes's [Mac71]. This graduate textbook covers much of the *general*
category theory used by computer scientists; published in 1971 it never men-
tions computer science as a discipline and its examples are from mainstream
mathematics, but it remains an excellent textbook. Material is covered at a
moderate to fast pace. Our Chapter 2 is much like a distilled version of the first
four chapters of [Mac71]. McLarty's [McL91] covers much of our Chapter 2,
excluding the Yoneda lemma. McLarty also covers some of the underlying
foundational questions which arise in category theory, as well as basic topos
theory. This book is written with logicians in mind, and so it should also
appeal to computer scientists. The book [Pie91] by Pierce is an elementary
introduction to category theory written for an audience of computer scientists.
The contents are similar to our Chapter 2.

3 Algebraic Type Theory

3.1 Introduction

DISCUSSION 3.1.1   The fundamental idea of algebraic type theory is to provide a formal framework for reasoning using the usual rules of equality. Simple algebraic type theory is far removed from the syntax and rules of real programming languages, but it is a good starting point from which to motivate and explain the ideas of categorical semantics. To a first approximation, algebraic type theory involves three entities, which will be called types, terms and equations. Think of a type as a collection of items (terms) having some common property, and an equation as a judgement that any two items (terms) are essentially the same. We aim to define the notion of a theory in algebraic type theory. Recall that the general idea of a theory is that one has some basic assumptions, usually referred to as axioms, and some rules for deducing theorems from the axioms. Thus a theory in algebraic type theory consists of a given collection of types, terms and equations, where the equations are the axioms of the theory. The theorems are the equations which one is able to deduce from the axioms using the rules of algebraic type theory. These rules say that equations may be manipulated according to the rules of reflexivity, transitivity and symmetry. So, for example, if a term t equals a term s, then we may deduce that the term s equals the term t, and this is the idea of symmetry.

Let us now give an informal summary of Chapter 3. We begin by defining the syntax of algebraic type theory. This syntax will be presented using a collection of formal rules, much as we describe the syntax of any programming language. The syntax is based on a given collection of types and function symbols, known as a signature. For example, a signature for the syntax of arithmetic might have a type of natural numbers, and function symbols which play the role of zero (thought of as a function which takes any argument and returns zero), the successor function, and primitive recursion. Next we show how to define an algebraic theory. We describe the syntactic form of an equation in an algebraic theory, and how to derive theorems from given axioms. This completes the syntactic presentation of algebraic theories, and so we move on to consider semantics. After reviewing traditional set-theoretic semantics, in which types are interpreted as sets and terms as elements of sets (for example, in the syntax for arithmetic, the type of natural numbers might be interpreted as the set N of natural numbers, the constant zero as $0 \in \mathbb{N}$ and so on), we describe a categorical semantics for algebraic theories. In this setting, types are interpreted as objects in a category and terms are interpreted as morphisms. In fact we shall see that the kind of category which is suitable for this purpose is a category with finite products. We give some examples of algebraic theories and suitable categories for interpreting the theories. A model of an algebraic theory is an interpretation of the terms in a category with finite products, in which the morphisms interpreting the terms t and s appearing in an axiom $s = t$ are equal morphisms in the category. We prove a soundness result, which says that if we are given a model of an algebraic theory, and $s = t$ is now a theorem derived from the axioms of the theory, then the morphisms interpreting s and t are indeed equal. We then show that for each algebraic theory Th we can construct a category $Cl(Th)$ with finite products out of the syntax of the theory, and that there is a model of the theory in this category. Further, we show that every category with finite products $\mathcal{C}$ gives rise to an algebraic theory $Th(\mathcal{C})$. These two processes are mutually inverse (for example there is an equivalence of categories $\mathcal{C} \simeq Cl(Th(\mathcal{C}))$). It is for this reason that we can regard algebraic theories and categories with finite products as "essentially the same" and moreover think of a category with finite products as a syntax free presentation of an algebraic theory. The study of relationships of this kind is known as *categorical type theory:*

Categorical Type Theory ─────────────────────────

Type Theory $\left\{ \begin{array}{l} Th \text{-----------} \rightarrow Cl(Th) \\ Th(\mathcal{C}) \leftarrow \text{-----------} \mathcal{C} \end{array} \right\}$ **Category Theory**

$$Cl(Th(\mathcal{C})) \simeq \mathcal{C}$$
$$Th(Cl(Th)) \simeq Th$$

3.2 Definition of the Syntax

DISCUSSION 3.2.1   We define the notion of algebraic signature for algebraic type theory. Think of an algebraic signature as specifying some basic data from which we will build types and terms. An *algebraic signature*, *Sg*, is specified by

• a collection of *types*,

- a collection of *function symbols* each of which has an *arity* which is a natural number (possibly 0), and

- a *sorting* for each function symbol f which is a list of $a + 1$ types (say $[\alpha_1, \ldots, \alpha_a, \alpha]$) and will be written $f: \alpha_1, \ldots, \alpha_a \to \alpha$, where a is the arity of f. In the case that a function symbol k has arity 0, we shall write the sorting of k as $k: \alpha$, and refer to k as a *constant* function symbol.

To simplify notation, we will often write "let $f: \alpha_1, \ldots, \alpha_a \to \alpha$ be a function symbol" from which it will be implicit that f is the actual function symbol, that f has arity a, and the sorting of f is (formally) the list $[\alpha_1, \ldots, \alpha_a, \alpha]$. We assume that we are given a countably infinite stock of *variables*, say $Var = \{x, y, \ldots\}$. The *raw terms* are then given by the following BNF grammar:

$$M ::= x \mid k \mid f(\underbrace{M, \ldots, M}_{\text{length } a}).$$

Here x is any variable, k any constant function symbol, and f is any function symbol of non-zero arity a.

REMARK 3.2.2   Note that the sorting of a function symbol does not play a role in the definition of the raw terms. One should think of the raw terms as expressions in a programming language which are not necessarily well typed.

DISCUSSION 3.2.3   Informally, think of the raw terms in the following ways:

- x is a variable (!),

- k is a language constant, and

- $f(M_1, \ldots, M_a)$ is an expression which is the application of f to a arguments.

EXAMPLES 3.2.4   We give an example of an algebraic signature and some raw terms generated from it. Let the types be *nat* and *bool*, and the function symbols be $0: nat$, $p: nat, nat \to nat$, $t: bool$, $f: bool$, $\neg: bool \to bool$. If x, y and z are variables, then examples of raw terms are:

x	t	$p(x, y)$	$\neg(z)$	0
	$p(0, \neg(x))$	$\neg(p(x, x))$	$p(p(x, x), p(y, z))$	

The types here should be thought of as the natural numbers and booleans, and the terms as zero, binary addition, truth, falsity and negation of truth. Later on, we will give rules for deriving "well typed" or "well formed" raw terms which makes use of the sorting of function symbols; so $p(0, \neg(x))$ is an example of an "improperly typed raw term," because the second argument of p should take a natural number and not a boolean term.

DISCUSSION 3.2.5   We now have to define a notion of substitution of raw terms for free variables. To do this, we first define the notion of free variables of a raw term. Intuitively, think of free variables as "holes" in a raw term into which we can "slot" other raw terms. For the simple systems of algebraic type theory the free variables of a raw term are just the variables which "appear in" the raw term. More formally, the set of *free* variables of a raw term M is defined by structural induction:

- $fv(x) \stackrel{\text{def}}{=} \{x\}$ where x is a variable,

- $fv(k) \stackrel{\text{def}}{=} \varnothing$ where k is a constant function symbol, and

- $fv(f(M_1, \ldots, M_a)) \stackrel{\text{def}}{=} fv(M_1) \cup \ldots \cup fv(M_a)$ where f is a function symbol of non-zero arity a.

We define the *substitution* of a raw term N for a variable x in another raw term M, written $M[N/x]$, by induction on the structure of M as follows:

- $x[N/x] \stackrel{\text{def}}{=} N$,

- $y[N/x] \stackrel{\text{def}}{=} y$ where y is a variable distinct from x,

- $k[N/x] \stackrel{\text{def}}{=} k$ where k is a constant function symbol, and

- $f(M_1, \ldots, M_a)[N/x] \stackrel{\text{def}}{=} f(M_1[N/x], \ldots, M_a[N/x])$ where f is a function symbol of non-zero arity a.

If $\vec{x} \stackrel{\text{def}}{=} [x_1, \ldots, x_n]$ is a finite list of n *distinct* variables, and $\vec{N} \stackrel{\text{def}}{=} [N_1, \ldots, N_n]$ is a list of n raw terms, then the *simultaneous substitution* of the raw terms $\vec{N}$ for the variables $\vec{x}$ in another raw term M, written $M[\vec{N}/\vec{x}]$ or sometimes even $M[N_1/x_1, \ldots, N_n/x_n]$, is defined in a manner analogous to $M[N/x]$ and we leave the reader to supply the formal definition. Note that substitution has to be treated with care, as the next exercise shows.

EXERCISES 3.2.6   Let M, N and N' be any raw terms for a given algebraic signature Sg, and x, y and z distinct variables.

(1) Show that substitution is well defined, that is, $M[N/x]$ *is* another raw term.

(2) Show that in general the raw term $M[N/x, N'/y]$ is not syntactically identical to the raw term $M[N/x][N'/y]$.

(3) Show that $M[N/x, N'/y]$ is however identical to $M[N[z/y]/x][N'/y][y/z]$ where $z \notin fv(M) \cup fv(N) \cup fv(N')$.

We can now define a type assignment system, which will generate a collection of well typed raw terms. To do this, we need a few more definitions. A *context*

Variables ───────────────────────────────

$$Sg \; \triangleright \; \Gamma, x{:}\,\alpha, \Gamma' \vdash x{:}\,\alpha$$

Function Symbols ───────────────────────

$$\frac{}{Sg \; \triangleright \; \Gamma \vdash k{:}\,\alpha} \; (k{:}\,\alpha)$$

$$\frac{Sg \; \triangleright \; \Gamma \vdash M_1{:}\,\alpha_1 \quad \ldots \quad Sg \; \triangleright \; \Gamma \vdash M_a{:}\,\alpha_a}{Sg \; \triangleright \; \Gamma \vdash f(M_1,\ldots,M_a){:}\,\alpha} \; (f{:}\,\alpha_1,\ldots,\alpha_a \to \alpha)$$

Figure 3.1: Proved Terms Generated from an Algebraic Signature.

is a finite list of (variable, type) pairs, usually written as

$$\Gamma = [x_1{:}\,\alpha_1, \ldots, x_n{:}\,\alpha_n],$$

where the variables x_i are required to be distinct. We shall say (informally) that (for example) the variable x_1 *appears* in Γ and (for example) the type α_n *appears* in Γ. We shall denote concatenation of contexts by juxtaposition, such as Γ, Γ' or $\Gamma, x{:}\,\alpha, \Gamma'$. We shall use the word *judgement* to mean "syntactical expression." A judgement of the form $\Gamma \vdash M{:}\,\alpha$ (where Γ is a context, M is a raw term and α is a type) is called a *term-in-context*. Informally, think of the raw term M as a program, and the variables which appear in the context Γ as an environment for M. We shall now define a certain class of judgements of the form $Sg \; \triangleright \; \Gamma \vdash M{:}\,\alpha$ where $\Gamma \vdash M{:}\,\alpha$ is a term-in-context; we refer to $Sg \; \triangleright \; \Gamma \vdash M{:}\,\alpha$ as a *proved term*. Formally, the *proved terms* are generated by the rules given in Figure 3.1. Informally, think of the raw term M in the judgement $Sg \; \triangleright \; \Gamma \vdash M{:}\,\alpha$ as a well typed program. We can also think of the free variables of M as program identifiers, and we shall see that every free variable must appear in the context Γ.

REMARK 3.2.7   We shall always assume that the hypothesis and conclusion of any rule for introducing syntactical constructs are both well formed; thus (for example) it is implicit in the rule which introduces $Sg \; \triangleright \; \Gamma \vdash k{:}\,\alpha$ that Γ is a context, even though we do not say so explicitly. Recall that $\Gamma, x{:}\,\alpha, \Gamma'$ is our informal notation for the concatenation of contexts $\Gamma, [x{:}\,\alpha]$ and Γ'. Thus if $\Gamma, x{:}\,\alpha, \Gamma'$ appears in an instance of the rule **Variables**, the variable x cannot appear in Γ or Γ'. Further, any variable appearing in Γ is not x and cannot appear in Γ'.

REMARK 3.2.8 Of course, the terms-in-context which appear as part of the judgements $Sg \ \triangleright \ \Gamma \vdash M : \alpha$ form a sub-class of all of the terms-in-context; the formal symbol $Sg \ \triangleright$ is indicating that $\Gamma \vdash M : \alpha$ is in this sub-class, and reminds us that we are working with respect to the signature Sg. In practise, we shall often refer to a proved term $\Gamma \vdash M : \alpha$, rather than writing the more cumbersome $Sg \ \triangleright \ \Gamma \vdash M : \alpha$, when it is clear to which signature we are referring.

DISCUSSION 3.2.9 Now let us begin to think about how to manipulate proved terms. Informally, it should not matter what the order of the (variable, type) pairs is in a context Γ. Also, it is reasonable to be able to add more variables to a context of a proved term to produce another proved term. We might say that "declaring more identifiers for the program M will not affect the well formedness of M; and the order of declaration is also unimportant." Finally, we can give rules for the substitution of raw terms. Let us make these ideas precise.

We can derive rules for the permutation of contexts (altering the order of (variable, type) pairs), and weakening of contexts (adding variables to contexts). Let π be a permutation of the first n positive integers. If $\Gamma = [x_1 : \alpha_1, \ldots, x_n : \alpha_n]$ then write $\pi\Gamma$ for the context $[x_{\pi(1)} : \alpha_{\pi(1)}, \ldots, x_{\pi(n)} : \alpha_{\pi(n)}]$. Also write $\Gamma \subseteq \Gamma'$ if Γ is a sublist of Γ'. The next few results formalise some of our intuitions. The proofs are easy, but we shall spell out the proof of the first result in detail to illustrate the techniques involved.

LEMMA 3.2.10 A derived rule is

$$\frac{Sg \ \triangleright \ \Gamma \vdash M : \alpha}{Sg \ \triangleright \ \pi\Gamma \vdash M : \alpha}$$

PROOF We induct on the derivation of the judgement $Sg \ \triangleright \ \Gamma \vdash M : \alpha$, giving separate cases according to the rules in Figure 3.1 for introducing such judgements.

(*Case* $Sg \ \triangleright \ \Gamma \vdash M : \alpha$ *is* $Sg \ \triangleright \ \Gamma, x : \alpha, \Gamma' \vdash x : \alpha$): We have to show that $Sg \ \triangleright \ \overline{\Gamma}, x : \alpha, \overline{\Gamma'} \vdash x : \alpha$, where $\overline{\Gamma}, x : \alpha, \overline{\Gamma'}$ is any permutation of the list $\Gamma, x : \alpha, \Gamma'$. But this is the case, being an instance of the rule **Variables**.

(*Case* $Sg \ \triangleright \ \Gamma \vdash M : \alpha$ *is* $Sg \ \triangleright \ \Gamma \vdash f(M_1, \ldots, M_a) : \alpha$): We can assume inductively that the lemma holds for the proved terms which appear in the hypothesis of the rule **Function Symbols**, that is $Sg \ \triangleright \ \pi\Gamma \vdash M_i \colon \alpha_i$ for each i; but now we can just apply the rule **Function Symbols** to these hypotheses to deduce that $Sg \ \triangleright \ \pi\Gamma \vdash f(M_1, \ldots, M_a) \colon \alpha$, as required. $\qquad \Box$

LEMMA 3.2.11   If $\Gamma \subseteq \Gamma'$ then a derived rule is

$$\frac{Sg \ \triangleright \ \Gamma \vdash M \colon \alpha}{Sg \ \triangleright \ \Gamma' \vdash M \colon \alpha}$$

PROOF   Induction on the derivation of the judgement $Sg \ \triangleright \ \Gamma \vdash M \colon \alpha$. $\quad \Box$

With this, we can prove a simple lemma which tells us how we may substitute raw terms in other raw terms.

LEMMA 3.2.12   A derived rule for forming proved terms is

$$\frac{Sg \ \triangleright \ \Gamma, x \colon \alpha, \Gamma' \vdash N \colon \beta \quad Sg \ \triangleright \ \Gamma \vdash M \colon \alpha}{Sg \ \triangleright \ \Gamma, \Gamma' \vdash N[M/x] \colon \beta}$$

PROOF   We use induction on the derivation of the judgement

$$Sg \ \triangleright \ \Gamma, x \colon \alpha, \Gamma' \vdash N \colon \beta$$

appealing to Lemma 3.2.11 in the case when N is x. Recall also Remark 3.2.7.
$\qquad \Box$

PROPOSITION 3.2.13   Suppose that Γ is a context and that M is a raw term. If we are able to derive $Sg \ \triangleright \ \Gamma \vdash M \colon \alpha$ and $Sg \ \triangleright \ \Gamma \vdash M \colon \alpha'$ then the types α and α' are identical.

PROOF   Use induction on the derivation of $Sg \ \triangleright \ \Gamma \vdash M \colon \alpha$. $\qquad \Box$

DISCUSSION 3.2.14   In view of Proposition 3.2.13, we might say that the rules in Figure 3.1 define a type assignment system, in the sense that for any given context Γ, if $Sg \ \triangleright \ \Gamma \vdash M \colon \alpha$ for some raw term M, then α is the unique type which may appear "after the colon." We refer informally to α as the type of M.

EXERCISES 3.2.15

(1) Work through the details of the proofs of Lemmas 3.2.11 and 3.2.12, and Proposition 3.2.13. Prove that if $Sg \ \triangleright \ \Gamma \vdash M \colon \alpha$ where Sg is an algebraic signature, then the free variables of M, $fv(M)$, appear in Γ.

(2) Let Sg be an algebraic signature, let $x_1 \colon \alpha_1, \ldots, x_n \colon \alpha_n \vdash N \colon \beta$ be a proved term, and $\Gamma \vdash M_i \colon \alpha_i$ proved terms for each i. Prove that $Sg \triangleright \Gamma \vdash N[\vec{M}/\vec{x}] \colon \beta$.

3.3 Algebraic Theories

DISCUSSION 3.3.1   We now set up a formal system in which we can assert the equality of raw terms. In fact we shall define a class of such systems, each known as an algebraic theory, and each of which has a collection of axioms and rules for deducing theorems from the axioms. Suppose that Sg is an algebraic signature. An *equation-in-context* takes the form $\Gamma \vdash M = M' : \alpha$ where $\Gamma \vdash M : \alpha$ and $\Gamma \vdash M' : \alpha$ are proved terms generated from Sg. Formally, an *algebraic theory*, Th, is a pair (Sg, Ax) where Sg is an algebraic signature and Ax is a collection of equations-in-context formed using Sg. We refer to the equations-in-context in Ax as *axioms* and we shall indicate that $\Gamma \vdash M = M' : \alpha$ is an axiom by writing $Ax \ \triangleright \ \Gamma \vdash M = M' : \alpha$. The *theorems* of the theory Th comprise the collection of judgements of the form $Th \ \triangleright \ \Gamma \vdash M = M' : \alpha$ (where $\Gamma \vdash M = M' : \alpha$ is an equation-in-context) generated by the rules in Figure 3.2.

REMARK 3.3.2   It is clear from the definition of theorem that the equations-in-context which appear as part of the judgement $Th \ \triangleright \ \Gamma \vdash M = M' : \alpha$ form a sub-class of the collection of all equations-in-context. We shall refer to a theorem $\Gamma \vdash M = M' : \alpha$ to mean that we can derive $Th \ \triangleright \ \Gamma \vdash M = M' : \alpha$ when it is clear to which algebraic theory we are referring.

EXAMPLES 3.3.3

(1) We begin with the algebraic theory of groups; we assume the reader is acquainted with elementary group theory. The algebraic signature of the theory of groups is given by

• one type G,

• three function symbols $\circ, i, e$, and

• sortings $\circ \colon G, G \to G$, $i \colon G \to G$ and $e \colon G$.

The axioms are given by the following equations-in-context:

(a) $x \colon G \vdash \circ(e, x) = x \colon G$

(b) $x \colon G \vdash \circ(x, e) = x \colon G$

(c) $x \colon G \vdash \circ(i(x), x) = e \colon G$

(d) $x \colon G \vdash \circ(x, i(x)) = e \colon G$

(e) $x \colon G, y \colon G, z \colon G \vdash \circ(\circ(x, y), z) = \circ(x, \circ(y, z)) \colon G$.

Of course, (a) and (b) are the formal axioms for identities, (c) and (d) axioms for inverses and (e) is associativity of the group multiplication. The axioms

Axioms

$$Ax \; \triangleright \; \Gamma \vdash M = M' \colon \alpha$$
$$\overline{Th \; \triangleright \; \Gamma \vdash M = M' \colon \alpha}$$

Equational Reasoning

$$\frac{Sg \; \triangleright \; \Gamma \vdash M \colon \alpha}{Th \; \triangleright \; \Gamma \vdash M = M \colon \alpha} \qquad \frac{Th \; \triangleright \; \Gamma \vdash M = M' \colon \alpha}{Th \; \triangleright \; \Gamma \vdash M' = M \colon \alpha}$$

$$\frac{Th \; \triangleright \; \Gamma \vdash M = M' \colon \alpha \quad Th \; \triangleright \; \Gamma \vdash M' = M'' \colon \alpha}{Th \; \triangleright \; \Gamma \vdash M = M'' \colon \alpha}$$

Permutation

$$\frac{Th \; \triangleright \; \Gamma \vdash M = M' \colon \alpha}{Th \; \triangleright \; \pi\Gamma \vdash M = M' \colon \alpha} \quad \text{(where } \pi \text{ is a permutation)}$$

Weakening

$$\frac{Th \; \triangleright \; \Gamma \vdash M = M' \colon \alpha}{Th \; \triangleright \; \Gamma' \vdash M = M' \colon \alpha} \quad \text{(where } \Gamma \subseteq \Gamma')$$

Substitution

$$\frac{Th \; \triangleright \; \Gamma, x \colon \alpha \vdash N = N' \colon \beta \quad Th \; \triangleright \; \Gamma \vdash M = M' \colon \alpha}{Th \; \triangleright \; \Gamma \vdash N[M/x] = N'[M'/x] \colon \beta}$$

Figure 3.2: Theorems Generated from an Algebraic Theory.

look more familiar if we write (for example) $x \circ y$ for $\circ(x, y)$. We say that $x \circ y$ is a syntactically sugared version of $\circ(x, y)$, meaning that the former is easier to read than the latter.

(2) The algebraic theory of meet semilattices has

- one type L, and
- function symbols $\top: L$ and $\wedge: L, L \to L$.

The axioms of the theory (also syntactically sugared) are

(a) $x: L, y: L \vdash x \wedge y = y \wedge x: L$

(b) $x: L, y: L, z: L \vdash x \wedge (y \wedge z) = (x \wedge y) \wedge z: L$

(c) $x: L \vdash x \wedge x = x: L$

(d) $x: L \vdash x \wedge \top = x: L$.

3.4 Motivating a Categorical Semantics

DISCUSSION 3.4.1   We motivate the categorical approach to the semantics of algebraic type theory. Traditionally, the judgements of algebraic type theory built up from an algebraic signature would have been defined rather differently from our approach in Section 3.2, and we review this here. For each type α take a countably infinite set $Var^\alpha \stackrel{\mathrm{def}}{=} \{x_1^\alpha, x_2^\alpha, \ldots\}$ of variables (we assume that such sets of variables are disjoint for different types α) and define the terms of the algebraic type theory by the rules

$$\frac{x \in Var^\alpha}{x: \alpha} \qquad \qquad k: \alpha \qquad \qquad \frac{M_1: \alpha_1, \ldots, M_a: \alpha_a}{f(M_1, \ldots, M_a): \beta}$$

where $k: \alpha$ and $f: \alpha_1, \ldots, \alpha_a \to \beta$ are function symbols. A set-theoretic semantics would then be defined by giving a set $[\![\alpha]\!]$ for each type α, an element $[\![k]\!] \in [\![\alpha]\!]$ for each constant $k: \alpha$ and a function of the form $[\![f]\!]: [\![\alpha_1]\!] \times \ldots \times [\![\alpha_n]\!] \to [\![\beta]\!]$ for each function symbol $f: \alpha_1, \ldots, \alpha_n \to \beta$. An environment for the theory is essentially a function which assigns a meaning to each of the variables. More precisely an environment ρ is a function

$$\rho: \bigcup \{Var^\alpha \mid \alpha \text{ is a type}\} \to \bigcup \{[\![\alpha]\!] \mid \alpha \text{ is a type}\}$$

where $\rho(x^\alpha) \in [\![\alpha]\!]$ for $x^\alpha \in Var^\alpha$. Given such an environment ρ, we assign a meaning to the terms by setting $[\![x^\alpha]\!] \stackrel{\mathrm{def}}{=} \rho(x^\alpha)$ and

$$[\![f(M_1, \ldots, M_n)]\!] \stackrel{\mathrm{def}}{=} [\![f]\!]([\![M_1]\!], \ldots, [\![M_n]\!]),$$

so in general if $M:\alpha$ then $[\![M]\!] \in [\![\alpha]\!]$.

There are at least two thoughts about this approach. The first is that each of the types must be interpreted by non-empty sets and that we must restrict to a set of types. For if any of the $[\![\alpha]\!]$ were empty, or we had a proper class of types, then we would not be able to define the function ρ. The second thought is that the semantics is specified in terms of elements of sets. Of course, we might consider replacing the sets by some mathematical object which has an underlying set-theoretic structure. But we would be in a much stronger position if we could interpret our syntax in a more general setting, such as a category. We have seen that categories are very general mathematical structures, and that category theory is a powerful organisational tool, but are categories suitable worlds in which to interpret syntactical systems such as algebraic theories?

Let us consider the first thought. We can think of a term as giving rise to a function with the variables of the term taking input data and the effect of the term on such data as the output. With this perspective, we can give a meaning to the types by assigning sets to them, and a meaning to the terms as functions. With due regard for this interpretation of the syntax, we should abandon type tagged variables and present the syntax using proved terms, as we did in Section 3.2. Thus a proved term

$$x_1:\alpha_1,\ldots,x_n:\alpha_n \vdash M:\beta$$

will now be modelled by a function $f: A_1 \times \ldots \times A_n \to B$, where we think of the n input variables of M being modelled by an element of the cartesian product $A_1 \times \ldots \times A_n$. We can now interpret types by non-empty sets, because we no longer need to define the environment ρ. Now let us think about terms M with exactly one free variable; thus $x:\alpha \vdash M:\beta$, for example, where $fv(M) = \{x\}$. We tacitly assume that we are only dealing with function symbols of arity 1. We shall try to generalise our set-theoretic model using as few assumptions as possible. Suppose we model α and β by "objects" A and B about which we make no assumptions. A function is a form of relation; so let us model $x:\alpha \vdash M:\beta$ as a "relation" between A and B about which we make no assumptions; we write $A \to B$ for this. Now let us think about how our syntactic term language is built up. The crucial point is that terms are built up by *substitution*, in the sense that a raw term $f(M)$ is precisely $f(x)[M/x]$. We now think about the process of substitution in general. Suppose that we have proved terms $x:\alpha \vdash M:\beta$ and $y:\beta \vdash N:\gamma$. We have seen that there is a derived proved term $x:\alpha \vdash N[M/y]:\gamma$—so how should we model this? Let us just say for the moment that whatever models this term depends on how we model $x: \alpha \vdash M: \beta$ and $y: \beta \vdash N: \gamma$. We can write this as

$$\frac{[\![x: \alpha \vdash M: \beta]\!] = A \xrightarrow{m} B \qquad [\![y: \beta \vdash N: \gamma]\!] = B \xrightarrow{n} C}{[\![x: \alpha \vdash N[M/y]: \gamma]\!] = A \xrightarrow{\Box(n,m)} C}$$

where $\Box(n, m)$ is some relation depending on n and m. What about the order of substitution of terms for term variables? Let $z: \gamma \vdash L: \delta$ be a further proved term (where we tacitly assume that x, y and z are distinct variables). Well, both of the proved terms

$$x: \alpha \vdash (L[N/z])[M/y]: \delta \qquad \text{and} \qquad x: \alpha \vdash L[N[M/y]/z]: \delta$$

are syntactically the same (caution—why is this?). So the relations which model them ought to be the same too, namely $A \xrightarrow{\Box(\Box(l,n),m)} C$ and $A \xrightarrow{\Box(l,\Box(n,m))} C$, and we will write $\Box(\Box(l, n), m) = \Box(l, \Box(n, m))$ to indicate this. Now we shall take a step backward and think about how proved terms with exactly one variable are formed. We will have to model $x: \alpha \vdash x: \alpha$ as a relation $A \xrightarrow{\star_A} A$. If we think about how the substitution of terms for variables is modelled, then we deduce that if $E \xrightarrow{e} A$ and $A \xrightarrow{m} B$ then $\Box(\star_A, e) = e$ and $\Box(m, \star_A) = m$. A proved term $x: \alpha \vdash f(M): \beta'$, where $f: \beta \to \beta'$ is a function symbol, is the proved term $x: \alpha \vdash f(y')[M/y']: \beta'$, and so will be modelled by the relation $A \xrightarrow{\Box(r,m)} B'$, where B' models β' and we *specify* that the proved term $x: \beta \vdash f(x): \beta'$ is modelled by $B \xrightarrow{r} B'$. Now we summarise our deductions, writing $n \circ m$ for $\Box(n, m)$ and id_A for $\star_A$:

- Types are interpreted by "objects," say $A, B \ldots$

- Proved terms are interpreted by "relations," say $A \xrightarrow{m} B \ldots$

- For each object A there is a relation id_A.

- Given relations $A \xrightarrow{m} B$ and $B \xrightarrow{n} C$, there is a relation $A \xrightarrow{nom} C$.

- Given relations $E \xrightarrow{e} A$ and $A \xrightarrow{m} B$, then we have $id_A \circ e = e$ and $m \circ id_A = m$.

- For any $A \xrightarrow{m} B$, $B \xrightarrow{n} C$ and $C \xrightarrow{l} D$, we have $l \circ (n \circ m) = (l \circ n) \circ m$.

Note that the above summary amounts to the specification of a category. Thus we have deduced, subject to certain primitive assumptions about how to model function symbols and substitution, that we can model algebraic type theory in which exactly one variable appears in a term, in an arbitrary *category*. In such a category, *the substitution of raw terms for variables will be interpreted by composition of morphisms*; because of the importance of this idea,

---

Interpreting Substitution by Composition ─────────

Here, $x: \alpha \vdash M: \beta$ and $x: \gamma \vdash M': \alpha$ are terms of an algebraic type theory, and $[\![x: \alpha \vdash M: \beta]\!]$ and $[\![x: \gamma \vdash M': \alpha]\!]$ are morphisms of a category $\mathcal{C}$ interpreting the proved terms.

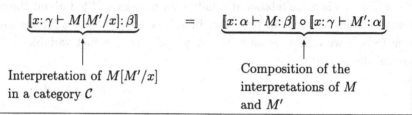

$$\underbrace{[\![x: \gamma \vdash M[M'/x]: \beta]\!]}_{} \qquad = \qquad \underbrace{[\![x: \alpha \vdash M: \beta]\!] \circ [\![x: \gamma \vdash M': \alpha]\!]}_{}$$

Interpretation of $M[M'/x]$ in a category $\mathcal{C}$

Composition of the interpretations of M and M'

Figure 3.3: A Basic Principle of Categorical Type Theory.

we give a special summary—see Figure 3.3. Following our intuitions about more than one variable appearing in a term M, we will model a proved term $x_1: \alpha_1, \ldots, x_n: \alpha_n \vdash M: \beta$ in a category with *finite products* as a morphism of the form $m: A_1 \times \ldots \times A_n \to B$; this will be formalised in Section 3.5.

EXERCISE 3.4.2   Work through the details of Section 3.4. Try to think of as many ways as possible in which syntax behaves and how it should be modelled. Can you think of ways of modelling contexts of variables in a category which do not involve finite products?

3.5 Categorical Semantics

DISCUSSION 3.5.1   Let us now formalise Section 3.4. Let $\mathcal{C}$ be a category with finite products and let Sg be an algebraic signature. A *structure*, **M**, in $\mathcal{C}$ for Sg is specified by giving

- for every type α of Sg an object $[\![\alpha]\!]$ of $\mathcal{C}$,

- for every constant function symbol $k: \alpha$, a global element $[\![k]\!]: 1 \to [\![\alpha]\!]$, and

- for every function symbol $f: \alpha_1, \ldots, \alpha_n \to \beta$ of Sg a morphism

$$[\![f]\!]: [\![\alpha_1]\!] \times \ldots \times [\![\alpha_n]\!] \to [\![\beta]\!].$$

If we wish to draw attention to the particular structure **M**, we will write $[\![-]\!]_\mathbf{M}$ in place of $[\![-]\!]$. Given a context $\Gamma = [x_1: \alpha_1, \ldots, x_n: \alpha_n]$ we set $[\![\Gamma]\!] \overset{\text{def}}{=}$

Variables ──

$$\llbracket \Gamma, x{:}\,\alpha, \Gamma' \vdash x{:}\,\alpha \rrbracket \stackrel{\mathrm{def}}{=} \pi{:}\, \llbracket \Gamma \rrbracket \times \llbracket \alpha \rrbracket \times \llbracket \Gamma' \rrbracket \to \llbracket \alpha \rrbracket$$

Function Symbols ────────────────────────────────

$$\frac{}{\llbracket \Gamma \vdash k{:}\,\alpha \rrbracket \stackrel{\mathrm{def}}{=} \llbracket k \rrbracket \circ \,!{:}\, \llbracket \Gamma \rrbracket \to 1 \to \llbracket \alpha \rrbracket} \quad (k{:}\,\alpha)$$

$$\frac{\llbracket \Gamma \vdash M_1{:}\,\alpha_1 \rrbracket \stackrel{\mathrm{def}}{=} m_1{:}\, \llbracket \Gamma \rrbracket \to \llbracket \alpha_1 \rrbracket \quad \cdots \quad \llbracket \Gamma \vdash M_a{:}\,\alpha_a \rrbracket \stackrel{\mathrm{def}}{=} m_a{:}\, \llbracket \Gamma \rrbracket \to \llbracket \alpha_a \rrbracket}{\llbracket \Gamma \vdash f(M_1, \ldots, M_a) \rrbracket \stackrel{\mathrm{def}}{=} \llbracket f \rrbracket \circ \langle m_1, \ldots, m_a \rangle{:}\, \llbracket \Gamma \rrbracket \to (\Pi_1^a \llbracket \alpha_i \rrbracket) \to \llbracket \alpha \rrbracket}$$

Figure 3.4: Categorical Semantics for the Proved Terms Generated by an Algebraic Signature.

$\llbracket \alpha_1 \rrbracket \times \ldots \times \llbracket \alpha_n \rrbracket$. Then for every proved term $\Gamma \vdash M{:}\,\alpha$ we shall specify a morphism

$$\llbracket \Gamma \vdash M{:}\,\alpha \rrbracket{:}\, \llbracket \Gamma \rrbracket \to \llbracket \alpha \rrbracket$$

in $\mathcal{C}$. The semantics of proved terms is specified inductively using the rules for generating proved terms and the definition appears in Figure 3.4. One of the most basic results about the categorical semantics of algebraic type theory is that substitution of a term for a variable in a term is interpreted by composition of morphisms, and indeed this is what we would expect given our discussion in Section 3.4. More precisely, we have the following

LEMMA 3.5.2   Let $\Gamma' \vdash N{:}\,\beta$ be a proved term where

$$\Gamma' = [x_1{:}\,\alpha_1, \ldots, x_n{:}\,\alpha_n]$$

and let $\Gamma \vdash M_i{:}\,\alpha_i$ be proved terms for $i = 1$ to n. Then one can show that $\Gamma \vdash N[\vec{M}/\vec{x}]{:}\,\beta$ is a proved term and further that

$$\llbracket \Gamma \vdash N[\vec{M}/\vec{x}]{:}\,\beta \rrbracket = \llbracket \Gamma' \vdash N{:}\,\beta \rrbracket \circ \langle \llbracket \Gamma \vdash M_1{:}\,\alpha_1 \rrbracket, \ldots, \llbracket \Gamma \vdash M_n{:}\,\alpha_n \rrbracket \rangle$$

where $N[\vec{M}/\vec{x}]$ denotes simultaneous substitution.

PROOF   By induction on the derivation of the judgement $\Gamma' \vdash N{:}\,\beta$.   □

3.6   Categorical Models and the Soundness Theorem

DISCUSSION 3.6.1   Let $\mathbf{M}$ be a structure for a algebraic signature Sg in a category C with finite products. Given an equation-in-context $\Gamma \vdash M = M' \colon \alpha$ we say that $\mathbf{M}$ *satisfies* the equation-in-context if $[\![\Gamma \vdash M \colon \alpha]\!]$ and $[\![\Gamma \vdash M' \colon \alpha]\!]$ are equal morphisms in C. We say that $\mathbf{M}$ is a *model* of an algebraic theory $Th = (Sg, Ax)$ if it satisfies all of the equations-in-context in Ax, and say that the structure $\mathbf{M}$ satisfies the axioms of the theory Th. We shall also refer to the satisfaction of theorems by a structure $\mathbf{M}$.

EXAMPLES 3.6.2   The algebraic theory of commutative monoids has an algebraic signature Sg with one type α and two function symbols $+ \colon \alpha, \alpha \to \alpha$ and $e \colon \alpha$, together with the following axioms (written using an informal "infix" notation):

(1) $x \colon \alpha, y \colon \alpha, z \colon \alpha \vdash (x + y) + z = x + (y + z) \colon \alpha$

(2) $x \colon \alpha, y \colon \alpha \vdash x + y = y + x \colon \alpha$

(3) $x \colon \alpha \vdash x + e = x \colon \alpha$.

So a model of this theory in a category with finite products is specified by giving an object M of C, and morphisms $+ \colon M \times M \to M$ and $e \colon 1 \to M$ such that the three axioms are satisfied. This means that the following diagrams commute:

$$
\begin{array}{ccc}
M \times M \times M & \xrightarrow{\ \langle \pi_1, +\, \circ\, \langle \pi_2, \pi_3 \rangle \rangle\ } & M \times M \\[2pt]
{\scriptstyle \langle +\, \circ\, \langle \pi_1, \pi_2 \rangle, \pi_3 \rangle} \big\downarrow & & \big\downarrow {\scriptstyle +} \\[2pt]
M \times M & \xrightarrow[\ +\ ]{\qquad\qquad\qquad} & M
\end{array}
$$

$$
\begin{array}{ccc}
M \times M \xrightarrow{\ \langle \pi_2, \pi_1 \rangle\ } M \times M & \qquad & M \xrightarrow{\ \langle id_M, e \circ\, ! \rangle\ } M \times M \\[2pt]
{}_{+}\searrow \qquad \swarrow_{+} & & {}_{id_M}\searrow \qquad \swarrow_{+} \\[2pt]
M & & M
\end{array}
$$

where $! \colon M \to 1$ is the unique morphism to the terminal object. For example, addition on the natural numbers is a model in the category *Set*. Formally, M is $\mathbb{N}$, $+ \colon \mathbb{N} \times \mathbb{N} \to \mathbb{N}$ is addition, and $e \colon \{*\} \to \mathbb{N}$ is the function where $e(*) = 0$ (a one point set is a terminal object of *Set*).

DISCUSSION 3.6.3   Intuitively, the soundness theorem says that if a structure in some category $\mathcal{C}$ with finite products satisfies the axioms of an algebraic theory, then it will also satisfy the theorems of the algebraic theory. More precisely, we have

THEOREM 3.6.4   Let $\mathcal{C}$ be a category with finite products, *Th* an algebraic theory and **M** a model of *Th* in $\mathcal{C}$. Then **M** satisfies any theorem of *Th*.

PROOF   We need to show that if $\Gamma \vdash M = M' \colon \alpha$ is a theorem, then the morphisms $[\![\Gamma \vdash M \colon \alpha]\!]$ and $[\![\Gamma \vdash M' \colon \alpha]\!]$ are equal in $\mathcal{C}$. We can prove this by showing that if **M** satisfies any equation-in-context appearing in the hypothesis of any of the rules given on page 128 for deriving theorems, then **M** satisfies the conclusion. To see that this is the case for **Equational Reasoning** is easy. To prove soundness for the **Substitution** rule we have to make use of Lemma 3.5.2. **Permutation** is also quite easy. We shall just give details for the case of **Weakening**. Let us suppose that $\Gamma \vdash M = M' \colon \alpha$ and that $\Gamma \subseteq \Gamma'$; we need to show that $[\![\Gamma \vdash M \colon \alpha]\!] = [\![\Gamma \vdash M' \colon \alpha]\!]$ implies that $[\![\Gamma' \vdash M \colon \alpha]\!] = [\![\Gamma' \vdash M' \colon \alpha]\!]$. Let $\Gamma = [x_1 \colon \alpha_1, \ldots, x_n \colon \alpha_n]$, and so $\Gamma' \vdash x_i \colon \alpha_i$ are proved terms. Then we have

$$
\begin{aligned}
[\![\Gamma' \vdash M \colon \alpha]\!] \quad &= \quad [\![\Gamma' \vdash M[\vec{x}/\vec{x}] \colon \alpha]\!] \\
\textit{using Lemma 3.5.2} \quad &= \quad [\![\Gamma \vdash M \colon \alpha]\!]\langle [\![\Gamma' \vdash x_1 \colon \alpha_1]\!], \ldots, [\![\Gamma' \vdash x_n \colon \alpha_n]\!]\rangle \\
\textit{using the hypothesis} \quad &= \quad [\![\Gamma \vdash M' \colon \alpha]\!]\langle [\![\Gamma' \vdash x_1 \colon \alpha_1]\!], \ldots, [\![\Gamma' \vdash x_n \colon \alpha_n]\!]\rangle \\
\textit{using Lemma 3.5.2} \quad &= \quad [\![\Gamma' \vdash M' \colon \alpha]\!].
\end{aligned}
$$

$\square$

EXERCISE 3.6.5   This exercise illustrates why we only deal with equations-in-context. We define a theory *Th* which has an algebraic signature *Sg* whose types are given by

• *bool* and *hegel*, and

the function symbols are given by

• $t \colon bool$, $f \colon bool$, $\neg \colon bool \rightarrow bool$, $\sharp \colon hegel \rightarrow bool$ and $\wedge, \vee \colon bool, bool \rightarrow bool$.

The axioms, *Ax*, consist of the following equations-in-context:

(a) $\vdash \neg(t) = f \colon bool$

(b) $\vdash \neg(f) = t \colon bool$

(c) $x \colon bool \vdash \wedge(\neg(x), x) = f \colon bool$

(d) $x: bool \vdash \vee(\neg(x), x) = t: bool$

(e) $x: bool \vdash \vee(x, x) = x: bool$

(f) $x: bool \vdash \wedge(x, x) = x: bool$

(g) $y: hegel \vdash \neg(\sharp(y)) = \sharp(y): bool$.

We can then deduce (using an informal notation)

$$
\begin{aligned}
Th \rhd \quad y: hegel \vdash t \;&=\; \vee(\neg(\sharp(y)), \sharp(y)): bool \\
&=\; \vee(\sharp(y), \sharp(y)): bool \\
&=\; \sharp(y): bool \\
&=\; \wedge(\sharp(y), \sharp(y)): bool \\
&=\; \wedge(\neg(\sharp(y), \sharp(y))): bool \\
&=\; f: bool
\end{aligned}
$$

that is $Th \rhd \quad y: hegel \vdash t = f: bool$.

(1) Write down a model **M** of Th in the category Set in which $[\![hegel]\!] \overset{\text{def}}{=} \varnothing$ and $[\![bool]\!] \overset{\text{def}}{=} \{\perp, \top\}$.

(2) Consider a traditional presentation of the theory Th with tagged variables $\{x_1^{hegel}, x_2^{hegel}, \ldots\}$ (and similarly for $bool$) and terms $M: \alpha$ as defined on page 129. In this setting we derive equations $M = M': \alpha$ without contexts of variables, using the rules of equational reasoning. Thus (as above) we can deduce that $t = f: bool$. Write down the environment style model (say **M'**) of Th in Set which mimics **M**. Show that $[\![t: bool]\!]_{\mathbf{M'}}$ does not equal $[\![f: bool]\!]_{\mathbf{M'}}$ in the set $[\![bool]\!]_{\mathbf{M'}}$. So this is an *unsound* conclusion.

(3) The soundness theorem shows that with our system of equations-in-context we have

$$[\![y: hegel \vdash t: bool]\!] = [\![y: hegel \vdash f: bool]\!] : [\![hegel]\!] \longrightarrow 1 \longrightarrow [\![bool]\!]$$

in any categorical model. Show that in particular this holds in **M**.

(4) Think about the fact that the interpretation of types by empty sets leads to unsound conclusions when working with equations without contexts.

(5) Write down a *formal* deduction tree for $Th \rhd \quad y: hegel \vdash t = f: bool$. Use a large sheet of paper for this!

3.7 Categories of Models

DISCUSSION 3.7.1   Now we turn our attention to relations between models of a given theory *Th* in a given category $\mathcal{C}$. In fact we shall define a notion of homomorphism between two models. Roughly a homomorphism will consist of morphisms (relations) between the interpretation of a type of *Th* in the two models, such that these morphisms commute with the interpretation of the function symbols in the two models.

Let **M** and **N** be models of an algebraic theory *Th* in a category $\mathcal{C}$ with finite products. A *homomorphism* $h: \mathbf{M} \to \mathbf{N}$ is specified by giving a collection of morphisms $h_\alpha: [\![\alpha]\!]_\mathbf{M} \to [\![\alpha]\!]_\mathbf{N}$ for each type α, such that for each function symbol $f: \alpha_1, \ldots, \alpha_a \to \alpha$ one has the following commutative diagram:

$$
\begin{array}{ccc}
[\![\alpha_1]\!]_\mathbf{M} \times \ldots \times [\![\alpha_a]\!]_\mathbf{M} & \xrightarrow{[\![f]\!]_\mathbf{M}} & [\![\beta]\!]_\mathbf{M} \\
\Big\downarrow{\scriptstyle h_{\alpha_1} \times \ldots \times h_{\alpha_a}} & & \Big\downarrow{\scriptstyle h_\beta} \\
[\![\alpha_1]\!]_\mathbf{N} \times \ldots \times [\![\alpha_a]\!]_\mathbf{N} & \xrightarrow[{[\![f]\!]_\mathbf{N}}]{} & [\![\beta]\!]_\mathbf{N}
\end{array}
$$

We refer to the h_α as the *components* of the homomorphism h.

Let $\mathcal{C}$ be a category with finite products and *Th* an algebraic theory. Then the *category of models* of *Th* in $\mathcal{C}$, written $\mathcal{M}od(Th, \mathcal{C})$, has

• objects the models of *Th* in $\mathcal{C}$ and

• morphisms the homomorphisms of models of *Th* in $\mathcal{C}$.

The identity $id: \mathbf{M} \to \mathbf{M}$ has components $id_\alpha \stackrel{\text{def}}{=} id_{[\![\alpha]\!]_\mathbf{M}}$ and the components of a composition hh' are $(hh')_\alpha \stackrel{\text{def}}{=} h_\alpha h'_\alpha$. We shall also need another new category. Let $\mathcal{C}$ and $\mathcal{D}$ be categories with finite products. The category $\mathcal{FP}(\mathcal{C}, \mathcal{D})$ has objects the finite product preserving functors and morphisms natural transformations.

We intend to show that for a given theory *Th*, we can find a category $Cl(Th)$, such that for all categories with finite products $\mathcal{D}$ there is a natural equivalence

$$\mathcal{FP}(Cl(Th), \mathcal{D}) \simeq \mathcal{M}od(Th, \mathcal{D}).$$

The idea is that we can regard a model of a theory as a functor, and vice versa, thus enabling us to view questions about models of algebraic type theories as questions about functors. Often this leads to a better understanding of the problem and yields a neat categorical solution. Before doing this we need a little more technical machinery. Given a finite product preserving functor $F: \mathcal{C} \to \mathcal{D}$ we shall define a functor

$$F_*: \mathcal{M}od(Th, \mathcal{C}) \to \mathcal{M}od(Th, \mathcal{D})$$

as follows. Let $\mathbf{M}$ be an object of $\mathcal{M}od(Th, \mathcal{C})$. $F_*\mathbf{M}$ is defined by putting $[\![\alpha]\!]_{F_*\mathbf{M}} \stackrel{\text{def}}{=} F[\![\alpha]\!]_{\mathbf{M}}$ where α is a type of Th and setting $[\![f]\!]_{F_*\mathbf{M}}$ to be given by the composition

$$[\![\alpha_1]\!]_{F_*\mathbf{M}} \times \ldots \times [\![\alpha_n]\!]_{F_*\mathbf{M}} \cong F([\![\alpha_1]\!]_{\mathbf{M}} \times \ldots \times [\![\alpha_n]\!]_{\mathbf{M}}) \stackrel{F[\![f]\!]_{\mathbf{M}}}{\longrightarrow} F[\![\beta]\!]_{\mathbf{M}}$$

where $f: \alpha_1, \ldots, \alpha_n \to \beta$ is a function symbol of Th and $\cong$ is the canonical isomorphism. Let $h: \mathbf{M} \to \mathbf{N}$ be a morphism of $\mathcal{M}od(Th, \mathcal{C})$. Then F_*h is given by $(F_*h)_\alpha \stackrel{\text{def}}{=} F(h_\alpha)$. We have to be sure that such a definition makes sense, that is $F_*h: F_*\mathbf{M} \to F_*\mathbf{N}$ really is a homomorphism of models. Given a proved term $\Gamma \vdash M: \alpha$ one can show by induction that the morphism $[\![\Gamma \vdash M: \alpha]\!]_{F_*\mathbf{M}}$ is given by the composition

$$[\![\alpha_1]\!]_{F_*\mathbf{M}} \times \ldots \times [\![\alpha_n]\!]_{F_*\mathbf{M}} \cong F([\![\alpha_1]\!]_{\mathbf{M}} \times \ldots \times [\![\alpha_n]\!]_{\mathbf{M}}) \stackrel{F[\![\Gamma \vdash M: \alpha]\!]_{\mathbf{M}}}{\longrightarrow} F[\![\alpha]\!]_{\mathbf{M}}.$$

If we are given proved terms $\Gamma \vdash M: \alpha$ and $\Gamma \vdash N: \alpha$ for which $[\![\Gamma \vdash M: \alpha]\!]_{\mathbf{M}} = [\![\Gamma \vdash N: \alpha]\!]_{\mathbf{M}}$ then certainly $[\![\Gamma \vdash M: \alpha]\!]_{F_*\mathbf{M}} = [\![\Gamma \vdash N: \alpha]\!]_{F_*\mathbf{M}}$. Thus if $\mathbf{M}$ is a model of Th in $\mathcal{C}$ then $F_*\mathbf{M}$ is a model of Th in $\mathcal{D}$ and we can conclude that we have a good definition of F_* on objects. The reader is left to check that F_* is well defined on morphisms.

The definition of F_* is our first item of technical machinery; now we give the second. If $\phi: F \to G$ is a natural transformation between finite product preserving functors F and G then we can define a homomorphism $\phi_*\mathbf{M}: F_*\mathbf{M} \to G_*\mathbf{M}$ of models which has components $\phi_{[\![\alpha]\!]_{\mathbf{M}}}: F[\![\alpha]\!]_{\mathbf{M}} \to G[\![\alpha]\!]_{\mathbf{M}}$ at the type α of Th. We will verify that $\phi_*\mathbf{M}$ is indeed a homomorphism of models. By definition, we need to check that the following diagram commutes:

$$
\begin{array}{ccccc}
\Pi_1^n F[\![\alpha_i]\!]_{\mathbf{M}} & \xrightarrow{\langle F\pi_1, \ldots, F\pi_n \rangle^{-1}} & F(\Pi_1^n[\![\alpha_i]\!]_{\mathbf{M}}) & \xrightarrow{F[\![f]\!]_{\mathbf{M}}} & F[\![\beta]\!]_{\mathbf{M}} \\
\Big\downarrow{\scriptstyle \times_1^n \phi_{[\![\alpha_i]\!]_{\mathbf{M}}}} & (1) & \Big\downarrow{\scriptstyle \phi_{\Pi_1^n[\![\alpha_i]\!]_{\mathbf{M}}}} & (2) & \Big\downarrow{\scriptstyle \phi_{[\![\beta]\!]_{\mathbf{M}}}} \\
\Pi_1^n G[\![\alpha_1]\!]_{\mathbf{M}} & \xrightarrow[\langle G\pi_1, \ldots, G\pi_n \rangle^{-1}]{} & G(\Pi_1^n[\![\alpha_i]\!]_{\mathbf{M}}) & \xrightarrow[G[\![f]\!]_{\mathbf{M}}]{} & G[\![\beta]\!]_{\mathbf{M}}
\end{array}
$$

It is immediate from the naturality of ϕ that (2) commutes. We shall check that (1) also commutes. Note that

$$\langle G\pi_1, \ldots, G\pi_n \rangle \circ \phi_{\Pi_1^n[\![\alpha_i]\!]_{\mathbf{M}}} = \langle G\pi_1 \circ \phi_{\Pi_1^n[\![\alpha_i]\!]_{\mathbf{M}}}, \ldots, G\pi_n \circ \phi_{\Pi_1^n[\![\alpha_n]\!]_{\mathbf{M}}} \rangle$$

$$= \langle \phi_{[\alpha_1]_{\mathbf{M}}} \circ F\pi_1, \ldots, \phi_{[\alpha_n]_{\mathbf{M}}} \circ F\pi_n \rangle$$

$$= (\phi_{[\alpha_1]_{\mathbf{M}}} \times \ldots \times \phi_{[\alpha_n]_{\mathbf{M}}}) \circ \langle F\pi_1 \ldots F\pi_n \rangle.$$

Let $\mathcal{C}$ and $\mathcal{D}$ be fixed categories with finite products, and let $\mathbf{M}$ be any model of a fixed algebraic theory Th in $\mathcal{C}$. We define a family of *modelling functors*

$$Ap_{\mathbf{M}} \colon \mathcal{FP}(\mathcal{C}, \mathcal{D}) \to \mathcal{M}od(Th, \mathcal{D})$$

by setting $Ap_{\mathbf{M}}(F) \overset{\text{def}}{=} F_*\mathbf{M}$ and $Ap_{\mathbf{M}}(\phi) \overset{\text{def}}{=} \phi_*\mathbf{M}$, where $\phi \colon F \to G$ is a natural transformation between finite product preserving functors. It is the notion of modelling functor which we shall use in the next section to set up an equivalence between categories of models and categories of finite product preserving functors.

3.8 Classifying Category of an Algebraic Theory

DISCUSSION 3.8.1   A classifying category for an algebraic theory Th can be thought of as a category with finite products which is in some sense the smallest such category in which Th can be modelled soundly. We shall see later that the classifying category arises through a formal construction using the syntax of the theory Th. The reader should compare this section with the idea of a freely generated vector space or group on a given set—compare the set to the algebraic theory Th and the freely generated gadgets to the classifying category.

Let Th be an algebraic theory. A category $Cl(Th)$ with finite products is called the *classifying* category of Th if there is a model $\mathbf{G}$ of Th in $Cl(Th)$ for which given any category $\mathcal{D}$ with finite products, the modelling functor

$$Ap_{\mathbf{G}} \colon \mathcal{FP}(Cl(Th), \mathcal{D}) \longrightarrow \mathcal{M}od(Th, \mathcal{D})$$

is an equivalence. Such a model $\mathbf{G}$ will be called *generic* and its corresponding modelling functor the *generic* modelling functor. We shall see that such classifying categories are unique up to equivalence and that they play the role described at the start of Discussion 3.8.1. We shall then give an example of a classifying category and in Theorem 3.8.6 show that every algebraic theory has a classifying category.

PROPOSITION 3.8.2   Let Th be an algebraic theory and $Cl(Th)$ a category with finite products for which there is a model $\mathbf{G}$ of Th in $Cl(Th)$. Suppose that given any category $\mathcal{D}$ with finite products there is an equivalence

$$Ap_{\mathbf{G}} \colon \mathcal{FP}(Cl(Th), \mathcal{D}) \longrightarrow \mathcal{M}od(Th, \mathcal{D}).$$

Then it is the case that whenever $Cl(Th)'$ and $\mathbf{G}'$ also have the above property there is an equivalence $Eq\colon Cl(Th) \simeq Cl(Th)'$ for which $Eq_*\mathbf{G} \cong \mathbf{G}'$.

PROOF   Given the equivalence $Ap_\mathbf{G}$, we can show that for any model $\mathbf{M}$ of Th in $\mathcal{D}$ there is a finite product preserving functor $F\colon Cl(Th) \to \mathcal{D}$ for which $F_*\mathbf{G} \cong \mathbf{M}$: we can just take $F \overset{\text{def}}{=} Ap_\mathbf{G}^{-1}\mathbf{M}$. To see this, we have by hypothesis a natural isomorphism $Ap_\mathbf{G}Ap_\mathbf{G}^{-1} \cong id_{\mathcal{M}od(Th,\mathcal{D})}$ implying that there is a natural isomorphism $Ap_\mathbf{G}(Ap_\mathbf{G}^{-1}(\mathbf{M})) \cong \mathbf{M}$ in $\mathcal{M}od(Th,\mathcal{D})$; that $F_*\mathbf{G} \cong \mathbf{M}$ follows from the definition of $Ap_\mathbf{G}$. It is also not too difficult to see that any two such F are naturally isomorphic. For if we are given another choice $\overline{F}$, then $F_*\mathbf{G} \cong \overline{F}_*\mathbf{G}$. Using the definition of $Ap_\mathbf{G}$ and applying its inverse, we get $F \cong \overline{F}$.

Hence, using instances of these properties of $Ap_\mathbf{G}$ and $Ap_{\mathbf{G}'}$, we may define functors $Eq\colon Cl(Th) \to Cl(Th)'$ and $Eq^{-1}\colon Cl(Th)' \to Cl(Th)$ for which there are natural isomorphisms $Eq_*\mathbf{G} \cong \mathbf{G}'$ and $Eq_*^{-1}\mathbf{G}' \cong \mathbf{G}$, giving one part of the proposition. It follows from the definitions that $(Eq^{-1} \circ Eq)_*\mathbf{G} = Eq_*^{-1}(Eq_*(\mathbf{G}))$ and $(id_{Cl(Th)})_*\mathbf{G} \cong \mathbf{G}$; using the observations of the first paragraph we deduce that $Eq^{-1} \circ Eq \cong id_{Cl(Th)}$. It is equally easy to check that we have $Eq \circ Eq^{-1} \cong id_{Cl(Th)'}$ and thus we have the required equivalence.   □

COROLLARY 3.8.3   For any model $\mathbf{M}$ of an algebraic theory Th in a category $\mathcal{D}$ with finite products, there is a functor $F\colon Cl(Th) \to \mathcal{D}$ which preserves finite products, for which the composition of the semantics of Th given by the generic model $\mathbf{G}$ in $Cl(Th)$ with the functor F yields the semantics given to Th by the model $\mathbf{M}$, up to isomorphism. This may be seen pictorially as

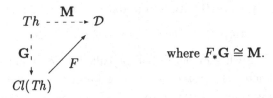

where $F_*\mathbf{G} \cong \mathbf{M}$.

Moreover F is unique up to isomorphism. It is because of this universal property that the model $\mathbf{G}$ is referred to as the generic model and that $Cl(Th)$ is the "smallest" category with finite products in which there is a model of Th.

PROOF   Follows from the first part of the proof of Proposition 3.8.2.   □

EXAMPLE 3.8.4   We shall give an example of a classifying category of an algebraic theory. In order to do this we shall define the category of finite sets and multirelations. This category $\mathcal{FSMR}$ is given by the following data. The objects are finite sets X and the morphisms $R: X \to Y$ are functions $R: X \times Y \to \mathbb{N}$. The composition of R, and $S: Y \to Z$, is given by the function $SR: X \times Z \to \mathbb{N}$ which we define by $SR(x,z) \stackrel{\text{def}}{=} \Sigma_{y \in Y} R(x,y) S(y,z)$ where the latter is a finite sum of products of natural numbers. The identity on X is given by the function $id_X: X \times X \to \mathbb{N}$ where

$$id_X(x,x') \stackrel{\text{def}}{=} \begin{cases} 1 \text{ if } x = x' \\ 0 \text{ otherwise.} \end{cases}$$

It is simple to see that the category $\mathcal{FSMR}$ has finite products. The terminal object is the empty set $\varnothing$. The (specified) product of objects X and Y consists of the object P which is the disjoint union of X and Y (let us define this to be $(X \times \{0\}) \cup (Y \times \{1\})$) together with projections $\pi_1: P \to X$ and $\pi_2: P \to Y$ which are given by the functions $\pi_1: P \times X \to \mathbb{N}$ and $\pi_2: P \times Y \to \mathbb{N}$ where

$$\pi_1(p,x) \stackrel{\text{def}}{=} \begin{cases} 1 \text{ if } p = (x,0) \\ 0 \text{ otherwise} \end{cases} \qquad \pi_2(p,y) \stackrel{\text{def}}{=} \begin{cases} 1 \text{ if } p = (y,1) \\ 0 \text{ otherwise} \end{cases}$$

We shall now write $X \uplus Y$ for the disjoint union of X and Y.

Let Th be the algebraic theory of commutative monoids, as defined on page 134. Then there is a model $\mathbf{G}$ of Th in $\mathcal{FSMR}$ where the type α is interpreted by the object $[\![\alpha]\!]_{\mathbf{G}} \stackrel{\text{def}}{=} \{*\}$ of $\mathcal{FSMR}$ (that is a one point set), the function symbol $+$ is interpreted by the morphism $[\![+]\!]_{\mathbf{G}}: \{*\} \times \{*\} \to \{*\}$ which is given by the function $[\![+]\!]_{\mathbf{G}}: (\{*\} \uplus \{*\}) \times \{*\} \to \mathbb{N}$ which is constant with value 1. Finally, e is interpreted by the morphism $[\![e]\!]_{\mathbf{G}}: \varnothing \to \{*\}$ which is given by the unique function $\varnothing \times \{*\} \cong \varnothing \to \mathbb{N}$. We shall simply refer to this model of Th as a monoid in the category $\mathcal{FSMR}$. As we shall see, this particular monoid is generic.

Now let $\mathcal{D}$ be any category with finite products and $\mathbf{M}$ any model in $\mathcal{D}$ of the theory of commutative monoids. We shall now write $(M, +, e)$ for the interpretation $([\![\alpha]\!], [\![+]\!], [\![e]\!])$ of the theory of commutative monoids specified by $\mathbf{M}$. It is hoped that this overloading of notation will clarify rather than confuse the technical details. Our aim is to prove that the modelling functor

$$Ap_{\mathbf{G}} : \mathcal{FP}(\mathcal{FSMR}, \mathcal{D}) \longrightarrow \mathcal{M}od(Th, \mathcal{D})$$

gives rise to an equivalence of categories; thus from Proposition 3.8.2, $\mathcal{FSMR}$ is $Cl(Th)$ up to equivalence. Define a functor

$$Ap_{\mathbf{G}}^{-1} : \mathcal{M}od(Th, \mathcal{D}) \to \mathcal{FP}(\mathcal{FSMR}, \mathcal{D})$$

by the following prescription, where $R\colon X \to Y$ is any morphism of $\mathcal{FSMR}$. We shall define

$$Ap_{\mathbf{G}}^{-1}(\mathbf{M})\colon \mathcal{FSMR} \to \mathcal{D}$$

to be the functor whose action on the object X is given by $Ap_{\mathbf{G}}^{-1}(\mathbf{M})(X) \overset{\text{def}}{=} \Pi_{x \in X} M$ where the notation means the finite product of one copy of M for each element x of X. To define the action of $Ap_{\mathbf{G}}^{-1}(\mathbf{M})$ on the morphism R we have to give a morphism $Ap_{\mathbf{G}}^{-1}(\mathbf{M})(R)\colon \Pi_{x \in X} M \to \Pi_{y \in Y} M$ in $\mathcal{D}$. In order to do this, we note that up to isomorphism there is a morphism $+_n\colon M \times \ldots \times M \to M$ for which the source is a finite product of n copies of M where $+_n$ is defined using $+\colon M \times M \to M$. With this, the yth component of $Ap_{\mathbf{G}}^{-1}(\mathbf{M})(R)$ is given by

$$\Pi_{x \in X} M \overset{\theta}{\longrightarrow} \Pi_{x \in X} M \overset{+_{|X|}}{\longrightarrow} M$$

(that is $\pi_y \circ Ap_{\mathbf{G}}^{-1}(\mathbf{M})(R) = +_{|X|} \circ \theta$) where the xth component of the morphism θ is given by

$$\Pi_{x \in X} M \overset{\langle \pi_x, \ldots, \pi_x \rangle}{\longrightarrow} \Pi_1^{R(x,y)} M \overset{+_{R(x,y)}}{\longrightarrow} M$$

where π_x is the xth projection of the product $\Pi_{x \in X} M$. This completes the definition of the functor $Ap_{\mathbf{G}}^{-1}$ on objects $\mathbf{M}$ of $\mathcal{M}od(Th, \mathcal{D})$. Suppose that $h\colon \mathbf{M} \to \mathbf{N}$ is a homomorphism of models; then the natural transformation $Ap_{\mathbf{G}}^{-1}(h)\colon Ap_{\mathbf{G}}^{-1}(\mathbf{M}) \to Ap_{\mathbf{G}}^{-1}(\mathbf{N})$ has components

$$Ap_{\mathbf{G}}^{-1}(h)_X \overset{\text{def}}{=} h_\alpha \times \ldots \times h_\alpha\colon \Pi_{x \in X} M \to \Pi_{x \in X} N$$

where we have written $N \overset{\text{def}}{=} [\![\alpha]\!]_{\mathbf{N}}$. Note that we have to check that $Ap_{\mathbf{G}}^{-1}(\mathbf{M})$ is indeed a finite product preserving functor and that $Ap_{\mathbf{G}}^{-1}(h)$ is a natural transformation. All these details form the next exercise.

EXERCISES 3.8.5

(1) Verify that $\mathcal{FSMR}$ is a category with finite products.

(2) Write down the action of the functor $Ap_{\mathbf{G}}$.

(3) Write down a formal definition of $+_n$.

(4) Verify that $Ap_{\mathbf{G}}^{-1}(\mathbf{M})$ preserves finite products and that $Ap_{\mathbf{G}}^{-1}(h)$ is a natural transformation.

(5) Prove the required equivalence of categories.

THEOREM 3.8.6   Every algebraic theory Th has a classifying theory $Cl(Th)$. A classifying category can be constructed from the syntax of Th and we shall refer to it as the *canonical* classifying category of the theory Th.

PROOF   We begin with some notation. Let $\alpha_1, \ldots, \alpha_n$ and β be fixed types. Then we define $(\Gamma \mid M)$ to be an equivalence class of pairs (Γ, M) where

- $\Gamma = [x_1 : \alpha_1, \ldots, x_n : \alpha_n]$ is a context where the types appearing in Γ are the given $\alpha_1, \ldots, \alpha_n$,

- M is a raw term for which $Sg \rhd \Gamma \vdash M : \beta$, and

- the equivalence relation is defined by $(\Gamma, M) \sim (\Gamma', M')$ just in case $Th \rhd \Gamma \vdash M = M'[\vec{x}/\vec{x'}] : \beta$ where $\vec{x}$ are the variables in Γ and $\vec{x'}$ the variables in Γ'.

The objects of $Cl(Th)$ are finite lists of types from the algebraic signature Sg of Th, for example $\vec{\alpha} \overset{\text{def}}{=} [\alpha_1, \ldots, \alpha_n]$. The morphisms with source $\vec{\alpha}$ and target $\vec{\beta}$, where $\beta \overset{\text{def}}{=} [\beta_1, \ldots, \beta_m]$ and both $\vec{\alpha}$ and $\vec{\beta}$ are non-empty lists, are given by finite lists of the form

$$[(\Gamma \mid M_1), \ldots, (\Gamma \mid M_m)] : \vec{\alpha} \to \vec{\beta}$$

where the types $\vec{\alpha}$ appear in Γ and we have $Sg \rhd \Gamma \vdash M_j : \beta_j$ for $1 \le j \le m$. Such a list will be written $(\Gamma \mid \vec{M})$ (take care with this abbreviation). We leave the reader to consider what happens if $\vec{\alpha}$ or $\vec{\beta}$ is empty. It is clear that $([x_1 : \alpha_1, \ldots, x_n : \alpha_n] \mid \vec{x})$ is the identity morphism on $\vec{\alpha}$. Now consider the morphisms $(\Gamma \mid \vec{M}) : \vec{\alpha} \to \vec{\beta}$ and $(\Gamma' \mid \vec{N}) : \vec{\beta} \to \vec{\gamma}$. The composition $(\Gamma' \mid \vec{N}) \circ (\Gamma \mid \vec{M}) : \vec{\alpha} \to \vec{\gamma}$ is given by $[(\Gamma \mid N_1[\vec{M}/\vec{y}]), \ldots, (\Gamma \mid N_l[\vec{M}/\vec{y}])]$ where $\vec{y}$ are the variables in Γ'. Of course we must verify that the composition is well defined: these details are left to the reader. The terminal object of $Cl(Th)$ is the empty list $[]$ and binary products are given by list concatenation.

The generic model $\mathbf{G}$ of Th in $Cl(Th)$ is given by putting $[\![\alpha]\!]_{\mathbf{G}} \overset{\text{def}}{=} [\alpha]$ where α is a type of Sg and $[\![f]\!]_{\mathbf{G}} \overset{\text{def}}{=} (\Gamma \mid f(x_1, \ldots, x_n))$ where $f : \alpha_1 \ldots \alpha_n \to \beta$ is a function symbol of Sg and $\Gamma \overset{\text{def}}{=} [x_1 : \alpha_1, \ldots, x_n : \alpha_n]$. The proof is completed by showing that the modelling functor

$$Ap_{\mathbf{G}} : \mathcal{FP}(Cl(Th), \mathcal{D}) \longrightarrow \mathcal{M}od(Th, \mathcal{D}),$$

given by the assignment

$$\phi : F \longrightarrow F' \quad \mapsto \quad \phi_* \mathbf{G} : F_* \mathbf{G} \longrightarrow F'_* \mathbf{G}$$

is an equivalence for all categories $\mathcal{D}$ with finite products. We write $Ap_{\mathbf{G}}^{-1}$ for the proposed inverse equivalence. Suppose that $\mathbf{M}$ is an object of $\mathcal{M}od(Th, \mathcal{D})$. We define a product preserving functor $Ap_{\mathbf{G}}^{-1} \mathbf{M} : Cl(Th) \to \mathcal{D}$ by setting

$$(\Gamma \mid \vec{M}) : \vec{\alpha} \longrightarrow \vec{\beta} \longmapsto$$

$$\begin{cases} \langle [\![\Gamma \vdash M_1 : \beta_1]\!]_{\mathbf{M}}, \ldots, [\![\Gamma \vdash M_m : \beta_m]\!]_{\mathbf{M}} \rangle : \Pi_1^n [\![\alpha_i]\!]_{\mathbf{M}} \longrightarrow \Pi_1^m [\![\beta_j]\!]_{\mathbf{M}} \\ \text{if } \vec{\beta} \text{ is non-empty} \\[6pt] ! : \Pi_1^n [\![\alpha_i]\!]_{\mathbf{M}} \to 1 \quad \text{otherwise.} \end{cases}$$

Rather than verify formally that $Ap_{\mathbf{G}}^{-1}\mathbf{M}$ preserves finite products, we shall just check that it preserves the product $[\alpha, \alpha'] \times [\beta]$; the formal proof that the functor preserves all finite products follows an identical procedure. Set $\Gamma \stackrel{\text{def}}{=} [x\colon \alpha, x'\colon \alpha', y\colon \beta]$, and so there are projections

$$[(\Gamma \mid x), (\Gamma \mid x')]\colon [\alpha, \alpha', \beta] \longrightarrow [\alpha, \alpha'] \qquad [(\Gamma \mid y)]\colon [\alpha, \alpha', \beta] \longrightarrow [\beta]$$

in $Cl(Th)$. We need to show that the morphism

$$\langle Ap_{\mathbf{G}}^{-1}\mathbf{M}([(\Gamma \mid x), (\Gamma \mid x')]), Ap_{\mathbf{G}}^{-1}\mathbf{M}([(\Gamma \mid y)]) \rangle :$$
$$Ap_{\mathbf{G}}^{-1}\mathbf{M}([\alpha, \alpha', \beta]) \longrightarrow (Ap_{\mathbf{G}}^{-1}\mathbf{M}([\alpha, \alpha']) \times Ap_{\mathbf{G}}^{-1}\mathbf{M}([\beta]))$$

is an isomorphism in $\mathcal{D}$, that is

$$\langle\langle \pi_{[\alpha]_{\mathbf{M}}}, \pi_{[\alpha']_{\mathbf{M}}} \rangle, \pi_{[\beta]_{\mathbf{M}}} \rangle : [\alpha]_{\mathbf{M}} \times [\alpha']_{\mathbf{M}} \times [\beta]_{\mathbf{M}} \longrightarrow ([\alpha]_{\mathbf{M}} \times [\alpha']_{\mathbf{M}}) \times [\beta]_{\mathbf{M}}$$

is an isomorphism in $\mathcal{D}$. This is certainly the case with inverse given by $\langle \pi p, \pi' p, p' \rangle$ where we have projections

$$\pi\colon [\alpha]_{\mathbf{M}} \times [\alpha']_{\mathbf{M}} \to [\alpha]_{\mathbf{M}}$$
$$\pi'\colon [\alpha]_{\mathbf{M}} \times [\alpha']_{\mathbf{M}} \to [\alpha']_{\mathbf{M}}$$
$$p\colon ([\alpha]_{\mathbf{M}} \times [\alpha']_{\mathbf{M}}) \times [\beta]_{\mathbf{M}} \to ([\alpha]_{\mathbf{M}} \times [\alpha']_{\mathbf{M}})$$
$$p'\colon ([\alpha]_{\mathbf{M}} \times [\alpha']_{\mathbf{M}}) \times [\beta]_{\mathbf{M}} \to [\beta]_{\mathbf{M}}$$

in $\mathcal{D}$.

Now let $h\colon \mathbf{M} \to \mathbf{N}$ be a morphism of $\mathcal{M}od(Th, \mathcal{D})$. We define the natural transformation $Ap_{\mathbf{G}}^{-1}h\colon Ap_{\mathbf{G}}^{-1}\mathbf{M} \to Ap_{\mathbf{G}}^{-1}\mathbf{N}$ by setting

$$(Ap_{\mathbf{G}}^{-1}h)_{\vec{\alpha}} \stackrel{\text{def}}{=} \times_1^n h_{\alpha_i} : \Pi_1^n [\alpha_i]_{\mathbf{M}} \longrightarrow \Pi_1^n [\alpha_i]_{\mathbf{N}}.$$

We need to check that $Ap_{\mathbf{G}}^{-1}h$ is a natural transformation, that is given a morphism $(\Gamma \mid \vec{M})\colon \vec{\alpha} \to \vec{\beta}$ in $Cl(Th)$, the diagram

$$
\begin{array}{ccc}
\Pi_1^n [\alpha_i]_{\mathbf{M}} & \xrightarrow{\langle [\Gamma \vdash M_1\colon \beta_1]_{\mathbf{M}}, \ldots, [\Gamma \vdash M_m\colon \beta_m]_{\mathbf{M}} \rangle} & \Pi_1^m [\beta_j]_{\mathbf{M}} \\
{\scriptstyle \times_1^n h_{\alpha_i}} \downarrow & & \downarrow {\scriptstyle \times_1^m h_{\beta_j}} \\
\Pi_1^n [\alpha_i]_{\mathbf{N}} & \xrightarrow[\langle [\Gamma \vdash M_1\colon \beta_1]_{\mathbf{N}}, \ldots, [\Gamma \vdash M_m\colon \beta_m]_{\mathbf{N}} \rangle]{} & \Pi_1^m [\beta_j]_{\mathbf{N}}
\end{array}
$$

commutes. This will certainly be the case if given any morphism $(\Gamma \mid M)\colon \vec{\alpha} \to [\beta]$ we have $h_\beta \circ [\Gamma \vdash M\colon \alpha]_{\mathbf{M}} = [\Gamma \vdash M\colon \alpha]_{\mathbf{N}} \circ (\times_1^n h_{\alpha_i})$. We show this by induction on the derivation of $Sg \; \triangleright \; \Gamma \vdash M\colon \alpha$.

(*Case* $\Gamma \vdash M : \alpha$ *is* $\Gamma, x : \alpha, \Gamma' \vdash x : \alpha$):   We have

$$
\begin{aligned}
h_\alpha \circ \pi_{[\alpha]_{\mathbf{M}}} &= \pi_{[\alpha]_{\mathbf{N}}} \circ \langle (\times_1^n h_{\alpha_i}) \pi_{[\Gamma]_{\mathbf{M}}}, h_\alpha \circ \pi_{[\alpha]_{\mathbf{M}}}, (\times_1^m h_{\alpha'_j}) \pi_{[\Gamma']_{\mathbf{M}}} \rangle \\
&= \pi_{[\alpha]_{\mathbf{N}}} \circ (\times_1^n h_{\alpha_i}) \times h_\alpha \times (\times_1^m h_{\alpha'_j}).
\end{aligned}
$$

(*Case* $\Gamma \vdash M : \alpha$ *is* $\Gamma \vdash f(\vec{M}) : \alpha$):   Suppose that the context Γ is given by $[x_1 : \alpha'_1, \ldots, x_m : \alpha'_m]$, and that we have proved terms $\Gamma \vdash M_i : \alpha_i$. Then we have

$$
\begin{aligned}
h_\beta \circ [\![\Gamma \vdash f(M_1, \ldots, M_n) : \alpha]\!]_{\mathbf{M}} && \\
&= h_\beta \circ [\![f]\!]_{\mathbf{M}} \circ \langle [\![\Gamma \vdash M_1 : \alpha_1]\!]_{\mathbf{M}}, \ldots, [\![\Gamma \vdash M_n : \alpha_n]\!]_{\mathbf{M}} \rangle \\
&= [\![f]\!]_{\mathbf{N}} \circ (\times_1^n h_{\alpha_i}) \circ \langle [\![\Gamma \vdash M_1 : \alpha_1]\!]_{\mathbf{M}}, \ldots, [\![\Gamma \vdash M_n : \alpha_n]\!]_{\mathbf{M}} \rangle \\
\text{by induction} &= [\![f]\!]_{\mathbf{N}} \circ \langle [\![\Gamma \vdash M_1]\!]_{\mathbf{N}} \circ (\times_1^m h_{\alpha'_j}), \ldots, [\![\Gamma \vdash M_n]\!]_{\mathbf{N}} \circ (\times_1^m h_{\alpha'_j}) \rangle \\
&= [\![f]\!]_{\mathbf{N}} \circ \langle [\![\Gamma \vdash M_1]\!]_{\mathbf{N}}, \ldots, [\![\Gamma \vdash M_n]\!]_{\mathbf{N}} \rangle \circ (\times_1^m h_{\alpha'_j}) \\
&= [\![\Gamma \vdash f(M_1, \ldots, M_n)]\!]_{\mathbf{N}} \circ (\times_1^m h_{\alpha'_j}).
\end{aligned}
$$

Hence we see that $Ap_{\mathbf{G}}^{-1}$ is well defined.

Now we need to define natural isomorphisms

$$
\epsilon : Ap_{\mathbf{G}} Ap_{\mathbf{G}}^{-1} \cong id_{\mathcal{M}od(Th, \mathcal{D})} \quad \text{and} \quad \eta : id_{\mathcal{FP}(Cl(Th), \mathcal{D})} \cong Ap_{\mathbf{G}}^{-1} Ap_{\mathbf{G}}.
$$

To define ϵ, we need to define homomorphisms $\epsilon_{\mathbf{M}} : Ap_{\mathbf{G}}(Ap_{\mathbf{G}}^{-1}\mathbf{M}) \to \mathbf{M}$ which are isomorphisms in $\mathcal{M}od(Th, \mathcal{D})$ for each model $\mathbf{M}$ of Th in $\mathcal{D}$. But to define such a homomorphism, we have to give its components at a type α of Th. Now,

$$
Ap_{\mathbf{G}}(Ap_{\mathbf{G}}^{-1}\mathbf{M})(\alpha) = Ap_{\mathbf{G}}^{-1}([\alpha]_{\mathbf{G}}) = [\alpha]_{\mathbf{M}},
$$

and so we can define

$$
(\epsilon_{\mathbf{M}})_\alpha \stackrel{\text{def}}{=} id_{[\alpha]_{\mathbf{M}}} : [\alpha]_{\mathbf{M}} \to [\alpha]_{\mathbf{M}}.
$$

In order to define η, we have to give components

$$
\eta_F : F \to Ap_{\mathbf{G}}^{-1}(Ap_{\mathbf{G}}(F))
$$

in $\mathcal{FP}(Cl(Th), \mathcal{D})$ for each finite product preserving functor $F : Cl(Th) \to \mathcal{D}$, and then give the components of this natural transformation at an object $\vec{\alpha}$ of $Cl(Th)$. But we have

$$
Ap_{\mathbf{G}}^{-1}(Ap_{\mathbf{G}}(F))(\vec{\alpha}) = Ap_{\mathbf{G}}^{-1}(F_*\mathbf{G})(\vec{\alpha}) = \Pi_1^n F[\alpha_i]_{\mathbf{G}} = \Pi_1^n F[\alpha_i]
$$

and so we can define $(\eta_F)_{\vec{\alpha}} : F(\vec{\alpha}) \to \Pi_1^n F[\alpha_i]$ to be the canonical isomorphism arising from the fact that F is a finite product preserving functor. Certainly ϵ and η are natural. $\square$

DISCUSSION 3.8.7   The definition of classifying category that we have given
is a very general one, and we have seen that such a category is unique up
to equivalence. In fact the *canonical* classifying category $Cl(Th)$ given in
Theorem 3.8.6 satisfies an even stronger universal property than that stated
in Corollary 3.8.3, namely that the diagram in that corollary commutes up to
strict equality and not just isomorphism. This is stated formally as a corollary
to Theorem 3.8.6.

COROLLARY 3.8.8   Given any algebraic theory Th and a model $\mathbf{M}$ of Th in
a category $\mathcal{D}$ with finite products, there is (up to canonical isomorphism) a
unique finite product preserving functor $F\colon Cl(Th) \to \mathcal{D}$ for which $F_* \mathbf{G} = \mathbf{M}$,
where $Cl(Th)$ is the canonical classifying category of Th.

PROOF   The existence of F follows from the proof of Theorem 3.8.6; we
define $F \stackrel{\text{def}}{=} Ap_{\mathbf{G}}^{-1}\mathbf{M}$—see page 143. We could say informally that F is given
by "applying the structure $[\![-]\!]_{\mathbf{M}}$." All that remains is to check that the
structures $F_* \mathbf{G}$ and $\mathbf{M}$ are identical. If α is a type of Th we have

$$[\![\alpha]\!]_{F_* \mathbf{G}} \stackrel{\text{def}}{=} F([\![\alpha]\!]_{\mathbf{G}}) = F([\alpha]) \stackrel{\text{def}}{=} [\![\alpha]\!]_{\mathbf{M}}.$$

If $f\colon \alpha_1, \ldots, \alpha_n \to \beta$ is a function symbol of Th we have

$$
\begin{aligned}
[\![f]\!]_{F_* \mathbf{G}} &\stackrel{\text{def}}{=} F(\Gamma \mid f(\vec{x})) \\
&= [\![\Gamma \vdash f(\vec{x})\colon \beta]\!]_{\mathbf{M}} \\
&= [\![f]\!]_{\mathbf{M}} \circ \langle [\![\Gamma \vdash x_1\colon \alpha_1]\!]_{\mathbf{M}}, \ldots, [\![\Gamma \vdash x_n\colon \alpha_n]\!]_{\mathbf{M}} \rangle \\
&= [\![f]\!]_{\mathbf{M}} \circ \langle \pi_1, \ldots, \pi_n \rangle \\
&= [\![f]\!]_{\mathbf{M}}
\end{aligned}
$$

where $\Gamma = [x_1\colon \alpha_1, \ldots, x_n\colon \alpha_n]$.

Suppose also that $F'\colon Cl(Th) \to \mathcal{D}$ preserves finite products and that
$F'_* \mathbf{G} = \mathbf{M}$. If $\vec{\alpha}$ is any object of $Cl(Th)$, then there is a morphism (in fact a
canonical isomorphism) $\Phi_{\vec{\alpha}}\colon F\vec{\alpha} \to F'\vec{\alpha}$ given by

$$F\vec{\alpha} \stackrel{\text{def}}{=} \Pi_1^n [\![\alpha_i]\!]_{\mathbf{M}} = \Pi_1^n [\![\alpha_i]\!]_{F'_* \mathbf{G}} = \Pi_1^n F'[\alpha_i] \cong F'\vec{\alpha}.$$

It is an exercise to verify that such isomorphisms $\Phi_{\vec{\alpha}}\colon F\vec{\alpha} \cong F'\vec{\alpha}$ give rise to a
natural isomorphism $F \cong F'$ (in the functor category $[Cl(Th), \mathcal{D}]$) as asserted.
$\square$

3.9 The Categorical Type Theory Correspondence

DISCUSSION 3.9.1   In this section we shall show that algebraic theories and categories with finite products can be seen as essentially similar concepts. First, let us see that every category with finite products gives rise to an algebraic theory, and that this process is, in a sense to be made precise, mutually inverse to that of constructing a classifying category.

THEOREM 3.9.2   For any category $\mathcal{C}$ with finite products, we can associate a particular algebraic theory, $Th(\mathcal{C}) = (Sg(\mathcal{C}), Ax(\mathcal{C}))$. Moreover, there is a canonical model of $Th(\mathcal{C})$ in $\mathcal{C}$.

PROOF   The algebraic signature $Sg(\mathcal{C})$ has (essentially) types which are copies of the objects of $\mathcal{C}$ and function symbols which are copies of the morphisms of $\mathcal{C}$. More precisely, there is a type A for each object A of $\mathcal{C}$, a constant function symbol $k: A$ for each morphism $k: 1 \to A$ of $\mathcal{C}$, and there is a function symbol $f: A_1, \ldots, A_n \to B$ for each morphism $f: A_1 \times \ldots \times A_n \to B$ of $\mathcal{C}$.

Note: Each morphism of $\mathcal{C}$ gives rise to a number of function symbols. For example, if $f: A \times B \to C$ is a morphism of $\mathcal{C}$, then there are function symbols $f: A \times B \to C$ ($n = 1$ and $A_1 = A \times B$ above) and $f: A, B \to C$ ($n = 2$ and $A_1 = A$ and $A_2 = B$ above) in $Sg(\mathcal{C})$. We ought to decorate these function symbols with (say) subscripts, in order to distinguish them, but we will not do this—with a little common sense we will not run into problems.

With this definition there is an obvious canonical structure **M** for $Sg(\mathcal{C})$ in $\mathcal{C}$ given by setting $[A] \stackrel{\text{def}}{=} A$, $[k] \stackrel{\text{def}}{=} k$ and $[f] \stackrel{\text{def}}{=} f$. The collection $Ax(\mathcal{C})$ consists of those equations-in-context over $Sg(\mathcal{C})$ which are satisfied by **M**. It is thus immediate that **M** is a model of $Th(\mathcal{C})$.   □

THEOREM 3.9.3   There is an equivalence $Eq : Cl(Th(\mathcal{C})) \simeq \mathcal{C} : Eq^{-1}$ for each category $\mathcal{C}$ with finite products, where Eq is the functor arising from the universal property of $Cl(Th(\mathcal{C}))$ applied to the canonical model **M** of $Th(\mathcal{C})$ in $\mathcal{C}$.

PROOF   Write $\mathcal{D}$ for $Cl(Th(\mathcal{C}))$. Let us recall the definition of the functor $Eq: \mathcal{D} \to \mathcal{C}$, namely

$$(\Gamma \mid \vec{M}): \vec{\alpha} \longrightarrow \vec{\beta} \longmapsto$$

$$\begin{cases} \langle [\![\Gamma \vdash M_1: \beta_1]\!]_{\mathbf{M}}, \ldots, [\![\Gamma \vdash M_m: \beta_m]\!]_{\mathbf{M}} \rangle : \Pi_1^n [\![\alpha_i]\!]_{\mathbf{M}} \longrightarrow \Pi_1^m [\![\beta_j]\!]_{\mathbf{M}} \\ \text{if } \vec{\beta} \text{ is non-empty} \\ \; ! : \Pi_1^n [\![\alpha_i]\!]_{\mathbf{M}} \to 1 \quad \text{otherwise.} \end{cases}$$

Let $f: A \to B$ be any morphism of $\mathcal{C}$. We define a functor $Eq^{-1}: \mathcal{C} \to \mathcal{D}$ by setting $Eq^{-1}(A) \overset{\text{def}}{=} [A]$ and $Eq^{-1}(f) \overset{\text{def}}{=} ([x:A] \mid f(x))$. To prove the equivalence, we must show that there are natural isomorphisms $Eq \circ Eq^{-1} \cong id_{\mathcal{C}}$ and $Eq^{-1} \circ Eq \cong id_{\mathcal{D}}$. The first isomorphism is trivial to see: the components are identities on objects of $\mathcal{C}$. For the second isomorphism, we define a natural transformation $\mu: Eq^{-1} \circ Eq \to id_{\mathcal{D}}$ which has a component

$$[(x:\Pi_1^n A_i \mid \pi_1(x)), \ldots, (x:\Pi_1^n A_i \mid \pi_n(x))] : [\Pi_1^n A_i] \to [A_1, \ldots, A_n]$$

at any object $\vec{\alpha} = [A_1, \ldots, A_n]$ of $\mathcal{D}$, where $\pi_i: \Pi_1^n A_i \to A_i$ are product projections (the reader can consider for himself what happens if $\vec{\alpha}$ is the empty list). We define a natural transformation $\eta: id_{\mathcal{D}} \to Eq^{-1} \circ Eq$ by setting its component at $\vec{\alpha}$ to be

$$[(x_1:A_1, \ldots, x_n:A_n \mid id_{\Pi_1^n A_i}(x_1, \ldots, x_n))] : [A_1, \ldots, A_n] \to [\Pi_1^n A_i]$$

where the identity morphism $id_{\Pi_1^n A_i}: \Pi_1^n A_i \to \Pi_1^n A_i$ gives rise to a function symbol $id_{\Pi_1^n A_i}: A_1, \ldots, A_n \to \Pi_1^n A_i$. Appealing to Lemma 2.5.3, we need to prove that one of μ and η is a natural transformation, and that their components are isomorphisms in $\mathcal{D}$. We omit the routine details, except for one part of the verification, namely that

$$\eta_{\vec{\alpha}} \circ \mu_{\vec{\alpha}} = id_{(Eq^{-1} \circ Eq)\vec{\alpha}}.$$

We have

$$\eta_{\vec{\alpha}} \circ \mu_{\vec{\alpha}} = [(x:\Pi_1^n A_i \mid id_{\Pi_1^n A_i}(\pi_1(x), \ldots, \pi_n(x)))].$$

From the definition of a morphism in $\mathcal{D}$, we wish to show that

$$Th \;\rhd\; x:\Pi_1^n A_i \vdash id_{\Pi_1^n}(\pi_1(x), \ldots, \pi_n(x)) = x:\Pi_1^n A_i.$$

In fact the above equation-in-context is an axiom of $Th(\mathcal{C})$, because

$$
\begin{aligned}
[\![x:\Pi_1^n A_i \vdash id_{\Pi_1^n A_i}(\pi_1(x), \ldots, \pi_n(x))]\!] &= id_{\Pi_1^n A_i} \circ \langle \pi_1, \ldots, \pi_n \rangle \\
&= id_{\Pi_1^n A_i} \\
&= [\![x:\Pi_1^n A_i \vdash x:\Pi_1^n A_i]\!]
\end{aligned}
$$

where of course $[\![-]\!]$ refers to the canonical structure $\mathbf{M}$ for $Sg(\mathcal{C})$ in $\mathcal{C}$. □

We can summarise Theorem 3.9.3 with the following slogan:

── **Categorical Type Theory Correspondence** ────────────

Categories with finite products yield a representation of the notion of algebraic theory which is syntax independent.

DISCUSSION 3.9.4   Given any category $\mathcal{C}$ with finite products, the algebraic theory $Th(\mathcal{C})$ is called the *internal language* of $\mathcal{C}$. This language is extremely useful because it allows us to reason about the category $\mathcal{C}$ as though it were the category *Set* of sets and functions. For example, if $f: A \to B$ is a morphism of $\mathcal{C}$, then there is a proved term $x: A \vdash f(x): B$ in $Th(\mathcal{C})$. We can think of x as an "element" of the set A and $f(x)$ as the action of the "function" f on x. The soundness theorem allows us to prove facts about $\mathcal{C}$ using the internal language. For example, if we wish to prove that $h = gf$ in $\mathcal{C}$ it is enough to show that $x: A \vdash g(f(x)) = h(x): B$ in Th, because the soundness theorem gives

$$h = [\![x: A \vdash h(x): B]\!]_{\mathbf{G}} = [\![x: A \vdash g(f(x)): B]\!]_{\mathbf{G}} = gf.$$

It will often be easier to perform calculations in the internal language than argue category-theoretically. Note also that there is a derived syntax in $Th(\mathcal{C})$ for "binary products." The theory Th contains function symbols

$$\mathsf{Fst} \ \overset{\text{def}}{=}\ \pi: A \times B \to A$$

$$\mathsf{Snd} \ \overset{\text{def}}{=}\ \pi': A \times B \to B$$

$$\langle -, + \rangle \ \overset{\text{def}}{=}\ id_{A \times B}: A, B \to A \times B$$

and axioms

$$x: A, y: B \ \vdash\ \mathsf{Fst}(\langle x, y \rangle) = x: A$$

$$x: A, y: B \ \vdash\ \mathsf{Snd}(\langle x, y \rangle) = y: B$$

$$z: A \times B \ \vdash\ \langle \mathsf{Fst}(z), \mathsf{Snd}(z) \rangle = z: A \times B.$$

So we can say that in the internal language of $\mathcal{C}$, the "elements" of $A \times B$ are provably equal to pairs of "elements" of A and B.

DISCUSSION 3.9.5   An important question which remains thus far unanswered is "what might a notion of translation of algebraic theory be?" Another way of asking this question might be to inquire how we may interpret one theory in another theory. It turns out that our categorical machinery can be used to give a very general notion of translation using the concept of classifying category. In fact we shall define a *translation*, $T: Th \to Th'$, to be given by a finite product preserving functor $T: Cl(Th) \to Cl(Th')$. Using the equivalence

$$Ap_{\mathbf{G}} : \mathcal{FP}(Cl(Th), Cl(Th')) \simeq \mathcal{M}od(Th, Cl(Th'))$$

we see that to specify T amounts to giving a model $\mathbf{T}: Th \to Cl(Th')$. We look at what data are needed to give such a model and then summarise our conclusions. For each type α of Th we have to give an object of $Cl(Th')$, which

is a list $[\![\alpha]\!]_{\mathbf{T}} \stackrel{\text{def}}{=} \vec{\alpha}'$ of types of Th'. For each function symbol $f \colon \alpha_1, \ldots, \alpha_n \to \beta$
of Th, we have to give a morphism $[\![f]\!]_{\mathbf{T}} \colon [\![\alpha_1]\!]_{\mathbf{T}} \times \ldots \times [\![\alpha_n]\!]_{\mathbf{T}} \to [\![\beta]\!]_{\mathbf{T}}$. If
the source of this morphism is given by $[\vec{\alpha_1'}, \ldots, \vec{\alpha_n'}]$ and the target by $\vec{\beta}$,
then writing $\Gamma' \stackrel{\text{def}}{=} [\vec{x_1} \colon \vec{\alpha_1'}, \ldots, \vec{x_n} \colon \vec{\alpha_n'}]$ the morphism $[\![f]\!]_{\mathbf{T}} = (\Gamma' \mid \vec{N})$ will
be specified by a list of proved terms, say $Sg' \;\; \triangleright \;\; \Gamma' \vdash N_j \colon \beta_j$. In order
that these data define a model $\mathbf{T}$, the axioms of Th must be satisfied. If
$Ax \;\; \triangleright \;\; \Gamma \vdash M = M' \colon \alpha$ (where $Th = (Sg, Ax)$) then we must ask that there
is an equality $[\![\Gamma \vdash M \colon \alpha]\!]_{\mathbf{T}} = [\![\Gamma \vdash M' \colon \alpha]\!]_{\mathbf{T}}$ of morphisms in the category
$Cl(Th')$. Let us write $[\![\Gamma]\!]_{\mathbf{T}} = [\vec{\gamma_1}, \ldots, \vec{\gamma_n}]$ where of course each $\vec{\gamma_i}$ is a list of
types from Sg', and also $[\![\alpha]\!]_{\mathbf{T}} = \vec{\delta}$. Writing $\Gamma' \stackrel{\text{def}}{=} [\vec{x_1} \colon \vec{\gamma_1}, \ldots, \vec{x_n} \colon \vec{\gamma_n}]$ we will
have

$$[\![\Gamma \vdash M \colon \alpha]\!]_{\mathbf{T}} = [(\Gamma' \mid N_1), \ldots, (\Gamma' \mid N_m)]$$

$$[\![\Gamma \vdash M' \colon \alpha]\!]_{\mathbf{T}} = [(\Gamma' \mid N_1'), \ldots, (\Gamma' \mid N_m')]$$

for some raw terms N_j and N_j' such that $Sg' \;\; \triangleright \;\; \Gamma' \vdash N_j \colon \delta_j$ for each $1 \le j \le m$
(and similarly for the N_j'). From the definition of morphism in $Cl(Th')$, we
must have $Th' \;\; \triangleright \;\; \Gamma' \vdash N_j = N_j' \colon \delta_j$ for each j. So each axiom of Th is
translated into a finite set of theorems in Th'.

In summary, a translation $T \colon Th \to Th'$ is specified by giving a list of types
of Th' for each type of Th, and a list of proved terms of Th' for each function
symbol of Th, in such a way that the induced structure $[\![-]\!]_{\mathbf{T}}$ (as defined above)
transports each axiom of Th to a finite set of theorems of Th'.

We shall say that the theories Th and Th' are *equivalent*, denoted by $Th \simeq$
Th', if there is an equivalence of classifying categories $Cl(Th) \simeq Cl(Th')$. Note
that each of the functors giving rise to the equivalence is automatically finite
product preserving. In fact:

THEOREM 3.9.6   For every algebraic theory Th we have $Th \simeq Th(Cl(Th))$.

PROOF   A routine verification using the definitions.   □

DISCUSSION 3.9.7   We have seen that the categorical semantics given to
algebraic theories is sound, meaning that any theorem of a theory is satisfied by
a categorical model. The converse notion to soundness is called completeness.
The categorical semantics for an algebraic theory Th is said to be *complete*
if an equation-in-context E of Th is a theorem whenever for *all* categories $\mathcal{C}$
with finite products, E is satisfied by *all* models $\mathbf{M}$ in $\mathcal{C}$.

THEOREM 3.9.8   The categorical semantics of algebraic theories in categories
with finite products is both sound and complete.

PROOF   Soundness was proved in Theorem 3.6.4. Conversely, let $\Gamma \vdash M = M' : \alpha$ be an equation-in-context of an algebraic theory Th. If it is satisfied by all models, in particular it is satisfied by the generic model of Th in $Cl(Th)$. One can check by induction on the derivation of proved terms that $\llbracket \Gamma \vdash M : \alpha \rrbracket_{\mathbf{G}} = (\Gamma \mid M)$ for any proved term $Sg \; \triangleright \; \Gamma \vdash M : \alpha$, and so we have $(\Gamma \mid M) = (\Gamma \mid M')$. Hence $Th \; \triangleright \; \Gamma \vdash M = M' : \alpha$ as required. $\square$

3.10   Further Exercises

(1) Suppose that Th is any algebraic theory. Consider also a theory Th' which is identical to Th, but in which the rule

$$\left\{ \begin{array}{c} Th \; \triangleright \; x_1 : \alpha_1, \ldots, x_n : \alpha_n \vdash N = N' : \beta \\[4pt] Th \; \triangleright \; \Gamma \vdash M_1 = M_1' : \alpha_1 \quad \ldots \quad Th \; \triangleright \; \Gamma \vdash M_n = M_n' : \alpha_n \end{array} \right.$$
$$\overline{\rule{0pt}{12pt} Th \; \triangleright \; \Gamma \vdash N[\vec{M}/\vec{x}] = N'[\vec{M'}/\vec{x}] : \beta}$$

replaces the rule **Substitution** in Figure 3.2. Prove that the theorems generated by Th and Th' are the same. Warning: this will need a little care.

(2) Produce an algebraic theory, Th say, which has types α, β, ρ, τ for which given any model $\mathbf{M}$ of Th in a category $\mathcal{C}$ with finite products, $\llbracket \tau \rrbracket_{\mathbf{M}}$ is a terminal object in $\mathcal{C}$ and $\llbracket \alpha \rrbracket_{\mathbf{M}} \times \llbracket \beta \rrbracket_{\mathbf{M}}$ is isomorphic to $\llbracket \rho \rrbracket_{\mathbf{M}}$. Check that the theory Th does indeed satisfy these properties.

(3) Let Th be the theory of commutative monoids (see page 134) and Th' be the theory of monoids; so Th' is identical to Th but does not have the axiom $x : \alpha, y : \alpha \vdash x + y = y + x : \alpha$. Show that the category $\mathcal{M}od(Th', Set)$ has finite products, and that there is an isomorphism

$$\mathcal{M}od(Th', \mathcal{M}od(Th', Set)) \cong \mathcal{M}od(Th, Set).$$

(4) Let $\mathcal{FSMR}$ be the category of finite sets and multirelations and Th the theory of commutative monoids. Let $\mathbf{M}$ be a model of Th in Set, say $(M, +, e)$, and write $(M_{gen}, +_{gen}, e_{gen})$ for the generic model of Th in $\mathcal{FSMR}$—see Example 3.8.4.

(a) Show that there is a functor $F : \mathcal{FSMR} \to Set$ which takes an object X of $\mathcal{FSMR}$ to $X \Rightarrow M$, the set of functions from X to (the underlying set of) M, and which takes a morphism $R : X \to Y$ of $\mathcal{FSMR}$ to the function $FR : (X \Rightarrow M) \to (Y \Rightarrow M)$ defined by

$$FR(f)(y) \stackrel{\text{def}}{=} \Sigma_{x \in X} R(x, y) \, f(x)$$

where $\Sigma_{x \in X}$ indicates a finite sum of the elements $R(x,y) f(x)$ in M and $R(x,y) f(x)$ is the sum of $f(x)$ (in M) $R(x,y)$ times.

(b) Prove that F preserves finite products.

(c) Show that $F(M_{gen}) \cong M$ in *Set*.

(d) Prove that

$$
\begin{array}{ccccc}
F(M_{gen} \times M_{gen}) & \xrightarrow{\;\cong\;} & F(M_{gen}) \times F(M_{gen}) & \xrightarrow{\;\cong\;} & M \times M \\
{\scriptstyle F(+_{gen})}\Big\downarrow & & & & \Big\downarrow{\scriptstyle +} \\
F(M_{gen}) & & \xrightarrow[\;\cong\;]{\hspace{4cm}} & & M
\end{array}
$$

and

$$
\begin{array}{ccc}
F(\varnothing) & \xrightarrow{\;\cong\;} & 1 \\
{\scriptstyle F(e_{gen})}\Big\downarrow & & \Big\downarrow{\scriptstyle e} \\
F(M_{gen}) & \xrightarrow[\;\cong\;]{} & M
\end{array}
$$

are commutative diagrams in *Set*. Thus F transports the generic model **G** of *Th* in $\mathcal{FSMR}$ to the model **M** of *Th* in *Set*—see Corollary 3.8.3.

(5) Complete the proof of Theorem 3.9.3. In particular verify that μ and η are natural transformations.

3.11 Pointers to the Literature

Some of the early background ideas behind the kind of type theory presented in "Categories for Types" can be found in [Chu40]. The concepts of arity and sorting certainly go back to Frege [Fre67]. For an up-to-date textbook which gives a general account of both proof theory and type theory, see [Gir89]. A good introduction to set theory and logic, which gives background information about formal logic and (set-theoretic) models is [Joh87]—the idea of a single sorted equational theory is discussed in the first chapter. The first account of the connections between the notions of a syntactical theory and appropriate categorical structure appears in [Law63]. An account of algebraic theories from a slightly more "mathematical" rather than "logical" viewpoint can be found in [Man76]. The use of type theory as a programming formalism is due in the main to Per Martin-Löf—see the papers [ML71], [ML72], [ML] and [ML84]. Although none of these papers contain information about model theory, they do cover many more type-theoretical constructions than are presented in "Categories for Types." An excellent textbook reference for type theory is [NPS90]. This book is in part a polished account of the many works of Martin-Löf (amongst others). A nice account of propositional and predicate logic can be found in [vD89]. While not of direct relevance to type theory, predicate logic soon appears in more advanced work which involves type theory.

4 Functional Type Theory

4.1 Introduction

DISCUSSION 4.1.1 Our task now is to develop a categorical type theory correspondence for an equational type theory based on the "simply typed λ-calculus." It will be helpful if the reader has a nodding acquaintance with simply typed λ-calculus, but this is not crucial. Let us review in an informal fashion the basic principles involved. Originally, the λ-calculus developed from attempts to produce a notation for representing and calculating with functions. (Strictly speaking, the original work in this area was concerned with (a primitive form of) a system now known as the untyped λ-calculus, but we shall not worry about such details in this very superficial discussion). Consider an expression such as $x + y$. We might think of this as being a definition of a function f given by $x \mapsto x + y$ (where the value of y is constant), or as a function g defined by $y \mapsto x + y$ (where the value of x is held constant). In day to day working life, mathematicians deal with such niceties simply by using ad hoc notations, and letting a context of discussion allow an intelligent reader to deduce precisely what the author means by his ad hoc notation. However, present day computers are not quite as intelligent as the typical reader, and it is essential to develop precise notations and syntax in order to program up mathematical functions. The λ-calculus is a formalism for dealing with these problems. In the λ-calculus, the functions f and g would be denoted by

$$f = \lambda x.x + y \qquad \text{and} \qquad g = \lambda y.x + y.$$

The symbol which appears after the λ and before the dot, called the *binding* symbol, indicates that occurrences of the symbol after the dot are to be thought of as "slots" into which values can be plugged. Thus "λ-expressions" such as f and g can be thought of as functions which take an input, pop the input into occurrences of the slot, and produce a result; the binding symbol is said to be *bound* and occurrences of the binding symbol after the dot are also said to be bound. We refer to the syntactic expression λx as an *abstraction* and say that occurrences of the binding symbol after the dot are *captured* by the abstraction λx. So, if the function f is given an input 3, we write $(\lambda x.x + y)(3) = 3 + y$ to indicate this procedure. What about substitution? With the intended meaning of a λ-expression borne in mind, we would expect to define (for example) $(\lambda x.x + y)[4/y] \stackrel{\text{def}}{=} \lambda x.x + 4$. Now let us think about

$h \stackrel{\text{def}}{=} (\lambda x.x + y)[x + 4/y]$. The intended meaning of $\lambda x.x + y$ is "it is a function which adds y to its input;" so we would hope that h "is a function which adds $x + 4$ to its input." Yet if we put $(\lambda x.x + y)[x + 4/y] \stackrel{\text{def}}{=} \lambda x.x + (x + 4)$ we get a function which "doubles its input and adds 4." The problem arises because the symbol x appears in the expression which is being substituted; the symbol x in $x + 4$ has been captured by the abstraction λx, meaning that the symbol x in $x + 4$ has become bound (in the expression $\lambda x.x + (x + 4)$). The solution in such cases is to change the binding symbol to one which does not appear in the substituted expression. This makes sense, because such a binding symbol is just denoting some "slots" and clearly the *positions* of the same slots can be indicated by a different symbol. Thus

$$(\lambda x.x + y)[x + 4/y] \stackrel{\text{def}}{=} (\lambda z.z + y)[x + 4/y] \stackrel{\text{def}}{=} \lambda z.z + (x + 4)$$

where z is chosen not to appear in $x + 4$. Perhaps surprisingly, these ideas are more or less the complete essence of the λ-calculus; we have a basic syntax in which to write expressions, some of which we may want to denote functions, and then use the formal symbol λ to indicate which parts of an expression are to be regarded as inputs, thus giving rise to a function. This completes our informal review of the λ-calculus and now we shall give a summary of the contents of Chapter 4.

We begin by defining a formal syntax for a functional type theory based on the ideas given above. The word functional just indicates that there is a formal syntax for defining expressions which can be thought of as functions, and such type theories will subsume algebraic type theories. The types will be built from a given collection of basic types, and will include a type of "pairs of values" as well as a type of "functions from one type to another type." This is followed by the definition of an equational theory, which we shall call a $\lambda\times$-theory. This is much the same as an algebraic theory, but now we are dealing with a richer class of terms (or programs). Next, we show how to derive a categorical semantics for $\lambda\times$-theories, subject to certain basic assumptions over the way the syntax is interpreted. As for algebraic theories, types are modelled by objects in a category, and terms as morphisms. The most fundamental assumption about the model will be that substitution of one term in another term in the syntax is interpreted as a composition in the category of the interpretations of the two terms—recall Section 3.4. We can use this assumption to write down equations which must hold in the categorical model if the syntax and equations of our functional type theory are to be modelled soundly; and these equations will determine a minimal kind of category theory in which the syntax of a functional type theory can be interpreted in a sound way. In fact it turns out that we can interpret functional type theories in a cartesian closed category. With the basic definitions of $\lambda\times$-theory and a model of such a theory in a cartesian closed category, we move on to prove a categorical type theory correspondence for functional type theories. Just as for algebraic theories, we now show that we can construct a cartesian closed category $Cl(Th)$ from a $\lambda\times$-theory Th and a $\lambda\times$-theory $Th(\mathcal{C})$ from a cartesian closed category $\mathcal{C}$, and that these constructions are mutually inverse in a precise way. We shall see that the category $Cl(Th)$ contains a model of Th, and from this it will follow that our categorical semantics is both sound and complete. The chapter finishes with an application of the categorical semantics. If we are given an algebraic theory, we can consider the $\lambda\times$-theory which uses the types and function symbols of the algebraic theory as its own types and function symbols, and has the axioms of the algebraic theory as its own axioms. Then there is an important question, namely *is a given term of the $\lambda\times$-theory provably equal to a term of the algebraic theory?* We shall see that this question can be translated into a problem about category theory, using the categorical type theory correspondence, and that a proof of the categorical problem (which we give) amounts to a proof of the original question.

4.2   Definition of the Syntax

DISCUSSION 4.2.1   We shall define the notion of a signature for a functional type theory, which consists of basic data from which to build types and terms.

A $\lambda\times$-*signature*, Sg, is given by the following data:

• A collection of *ground types*. The collection of *types* is generated by the BNF grammar

$$\alpha ::= unit \mid \gamma \mid \alpha \times \alpha \mid \alpha \Rightarrow \alpha,$$

where γ is any ground type. We call $\alpha \times \beta$ a *binary product type* and $\alpha \Rightarrow \beta$ a *function type*.

• A collection of *function symbols* each of which has an *arity* which is a natural number (possibly 0).

• A *sorting* for each function symbol f, which is a non-empty list $[\alpha_1, \ldots, \alpha_a, \alpha]$ of $a + 1$ types, where a is the arity of f. We shall write $f : \alpha_1 \ldots \alpha_a \to \alpha$ to denote the sorting of f. In the case that k is a function symbol of arity 0 we shall denote the sorting by $k : \alpha$ and the function symbol k will be referred to as a *constant* of type α.

We can now define the *raw terms* generated by a $\lambda\times$-signature Sg, and these are given by the following BNF grammar, where we assume that we are given a countably infinite stock of *variables*, say $Var = \{x, y, \ldots\}$:

$$M ::= x \mid k \mid f(\underbrace{M, \ldots, M}_{\text{length } a}) \mid \langle\rangle \mid \langle M, M \rangle \mid \mathsf{Fst}(M) \mid \mathsf{Snd}(M) \mid \lambda x \colon \alpha.M \mid M\,M$$

Here, x is any variable, k is any constant and f is any function symbol of non-zero arity a. Informally, think of the raw terms in the following ways:

- For x, k and f see Chapter 3;

- $\langle\rangle$ can be thought of as "a unique element of a one point set;"

- $\langle -, - \rangle$ takes a pair of arguments M and N and returns the pair $\langle M, N \rangle$;

- Fst takes a pair P and returns the first argument $\mathsf{Fst}(P)$ and similarly Snd takes a pair P and returns the second argument $\mathsf{Snd}(P)$;

- $\lambda x \colon \alpha.M$ is a function whose value at an argument N is M with occurrences of the variable x in M replaced by N; and

- $F\,M$ is the result of the application of a function F to an argument M.

REMARK 4.2.2   We shall often write syntax in an *informal* fashion. When expressions are complicated, we might also write $M(N)$, $(M)(N)$ or $(M)N$ for MN. We will use brackets "(" and ")" in an informal fashion to indicate the structure of formal syntax. We shall also write $MNPQ$ for $((MN)P)Q$ so that "application associates from the left."

DISCUSSION 4.2.3   As discussed in Section 4.1, we will need to define the concept of free and bound variables of raw terms. In order to do this we shall need some auxiliary definitions. We define the relation R is a *raw subterm* of M, written $R \subset M$, through the following clauses:

- $M \subset M$,

- given M_i for $1 \leq i \leq n$, if $R \subset M_i$ for at least one i then $R \subset f(M_1, \ldots, M_n)$,

- if $R \subset M$ or $R \subset N$ then $R \subset \langle M, N \rangle$,

- if $R \subset P$ then $R \subset \mathsf{Fst}(P)$,

- if $R \subset P$ then $R \subset \mathsf{Snd}(P)$,

- if $R = x$ or $R \subset M$ then $R \subset \lambda x \colon \alpha.M$, and

- if $R \subset M$ or $R \subset N$ then $R \subset MN$.

An expression of the form $\lambda x\colon \alpha$ is called an *abstraction*. If $\lambda x\colon \alpha.N$ is a raw subterm of a raw term M, we say that N is the *scope* of the occurrence of the abstraction $\lambda x\colon \alpha$. If the variable x occurs in a raw term M, then x is *bound* if it occurs in a subterm of M of the form $\lambda x\colon \alpha.N$. We say that occurrences of x in N are *captured* by the abstraction $\lambda x\colon \alpha$. If the variable x occurs in M and is not bound, it is said to be *free*. If the variable x has at least one free occurrence in the raw term M, then x is said to be a *free variable* of M. In fact it will be convenient to give an inductive definition of the set $fv(M)$ of free variables of a raw term M:

- For the raw terms x, k, $f(M_1, \ldots, M_a)$ see page 123,
- $fv(\langle\rangle) \stackrel{\text{def}}{=} \varnothing$,
- $fv(\langle M, N\rangle) \stackrel{\text{def}}{=} fv(M) \cup fv(N)$,
- $fv(\mathsf{Fst}(P)) \stackrel{\text{def}}{=} fv(P)$ and $fv(\mathsf{Snd}(P)) \stackrel{\text{def}}{=} fv(P)$,
- $fv(\lambda x\colon \alpha.M) \stackrel{\text{def}}{=} fv(M) \setminus \{x\}$, and
- $fv(MN) \stackrel{\text{def}}{=} fv(M) \cup fv(N)$.

EXAMPLE 4.2.4   Consider the raw term

$$M \stackrel{\text{def}}{=} \lambda x\colon \alpha.yx(\lambda x\colon \beta.y(\lambda y\colon \delta.z)x).$$

The scope of the abstraction $\lambda x\colon \alpha$ is $yx(\lambda x\colon \beta.y(\lambda y\colon \delta.z)x)$. The scope of the abstraction $\lambda x\colon \beta$ is given by $y(\lambda y\colon \delta.z)x$. The scope of the abstraction $\lambda y\colon \delta$ is just z. The first and second occurrences of y in M, from the left hand side, are free, but the rightmost y is bound. All occurrences of x are bound. It is very important to note that variables can be both free and bound.

DISCUSSION 4.2.5   We shall say that a raw term M is *α-equivalent* to M' if they differ only in their bound variables. For example, the raw terms $\lambda x\colon \alpha.\langle x, y\rangle$ and $\lambda z\colon \alpha.\langle z, y\rangle$ are α-equivalent. Also, the raw term

$$\lambda v\colon \alpha.yv(\lambda v\colon \beta.y(\lambda u\colon \delta.z)v)$$

is α-equivalent to the raw term M of Example 4.2.4. Note that in the raw term $L \stackrel{\text{def}}{=} (\lambda x\colon \alpha.x)x$ the variable x is *both free and bound*; L is α-equivalent to (for example) $(\lambda y\colon \alpha.y)x$. Any raw term M clearly determines an α-equivalence class for which M is a representative. We shall also refer to such an equivalence class as a raw term. From now on, "the raw term M" will mean the α-equivalence class determined by M. Note that we could refer to the notion of α-equivalence as "the renaming of bound variables." The reason for this odd technicality is not a perversity on the part of the author to confuse the reader, but to provide a framework in which substitution of raw terms for variables is well defined. The definition of *substitution* of the raw term N for the variable x in the raw term M is defined by structural induction on M, through the following clauses:

- When M is x, k, or $f(M_1, \ldots, M_a)$ see page 123.
- $\langle\rangle[N/x] \overset{\text{def}}{=} \langle\rangle$.
- $\langle M, M'\rangle[N/x] \overset{\text{def}}{=} \langle M[N/x], M'[N/x]\rangle$.
- $\mathsf{Fst}(M)[N/x] \overset{\text{def}}{=} \mathsf{Fst}(M[N/x])$ and $\mathsf{Snd}(M)[N/x] \overset{\text{def}}{=} \mathsf{Snd}(M[N/x])$.
- $\begin{cases} \text{(i)} & (\lambda x\colon \alpha.M)[N/x] \overset{\text{def}}{=} \lambda x\colon \alpha.M. \\ \text{(ii)} & (\lambda y\colon \alpha.M)[N/x] \overset{\text{def}}{=} \lambda z\colon \alpha.(M[z/y][N/x]) \text{ where } z \notin fv(M) \cup fv(N) \\ & \text{and } z \text{ is different from } x \text{ and } y. \end{cases}$
- $(MM')[N/x] \overset{\text{def}}{=} (M[N/x])(M'[N/x])$.

Note that clause (ii) amounts to a simple renaming of the variable y to ensure that occurrences of y in N are not captured by the abstraction $\lambda y\colon \alpha$ when N is substituted for x. It is due to this renaming that substitution is only well defined up to α-equivalence, that is up to renaming of bound variables.

EXERCISE 4.2.6   Work carefully through the definition of a raw term as an α-equivalence class. Also make sure that you understand why substitution is well defined only up to α-equivalence. Think about which of the brackets in the definition of substitution are informal, and which are part of the formal syntax.

DISCUSSION 4.2.7   A *context* is a finite list of (variable, type) pairs, usually written as $\Gamma = [x_1\colon \alpha_1, \ldots, x_n\colon \alpha_n]$, where the variables are required to be distinct. A *term-in-context* is a judgement of the form $\Gamma \vdash M\colon \alpha$ where Γ is a context, M is a raw term and α a type. We shall now define a certain class of judgements of the form $Sg \,\triangleright\, \Gamma \vdash M\colon \alpha$ where $\Gamma \vdash M\colon \alpha$ is a term-in-context; we refer to $Sg \,\triangleright\, \Gamma \vdash M\colon \alpha$ as a proved term. Formally, the *proved terms* are generated by the rules in Figure 4.1.

REMARK 4.2.8

(1) It is assumed that both the hypothesis and conclusion of each of these rules are well formed. For example, in the rule which introduces a function type, it is implicit that x does not appear in Γ, because Γ is a well formed context in both the hypothesis and conclusion of the rule.

Variables ───

$$\overline{Sg \;\; \triangleright \;\; \Gamma, x{:}\,\alpha, \Gamma' \vdash x{:}\,\alpha}$$

Unit Term ───

$$\overline{Sg \;\; \triangleright \;\; \Gamma \vdash \langle\rangle{:}\,unit}$$

Function Symbols ──────────────────────────────────

$$\frac{}{Sg \;\; \triangleright \;\; \Gamma \vdash k{:}\,\alpha} \quad (k{:}\,\alpha)$$

$$\frac{Sg \;\; \triangleright \;\; \Gamma \vdash M_1{:}\,\alpha_1 \quad \ldots \quad Sg \;\; \triangleright \;\; \Gamma \vdash M_a{:}\,\alpha_a}{Sg \;\; \triangleright \;\; \Gamma \vdash f(M_1, \ldots, M_a){:}\,\beta} \quad (f{:}\,\alpha_1, \ldots, \alpha_a \to \beta)$$

Binary Product Terms ──────────────────────────────

$$\frac{Sg \;\; \triangleright \;\; \Gamma \vdash M{:}\,\alpha \quad Sg \;\; \triangleright \;\; \Gamma \vdash N{:}\,\beta}{Sg \;\; \triangleright \;\; \Gamma \vdash \langle M, N \rangle{:}\,\alpha \times \beta}$$

$$\frac{Sg \;\; \triangleright \;\; \Gamma \vdash P{:}\,\alpha \times \beta}{Sg \;\; \triangleright \;\; \Gamma \vdash \mathsf{Fst}(P){:}\,\alpha} \qquad \frac{Sg \;\; \triangleright \;\; \Gamma \vdash P{:}\,\alpha \times \beta}{Sg \;\; \triangleright \;\; \Gamma \vdash \mathsf{Snd}(P){:}\,\beta}$$

Function Terms ────────────────────────────────────

$$\frac{Sg \;\; \triangleright \;\; \Gamma, x{:}\,\alpha \vdash F{:}\,\beta}{Sg \;\; \triangleright \;\; \Gamma \vdash \lambda x{:}\,\alpha.F{:}\,\alpha \Rightarrow \beta} \qquad \frac{Sg \;\; \triangleright \;\; \Gamma \vdash M{:}\,\alpha \Rightarrow \beta \quad Sg \;\; \triangleright \;\; \Gamma \vdash N{:}\,\alpha}{Sg \;\; \triangleright \;\; \Gamma \vdash MN{:}\,\beta}$$

Figure 4.1: Proved Terms Generated from a $\lambda\times$-Signature.

(2) The terms-in-context which appear as part of the judgements $Sg \vartriangleright \Gamma \vdash M : \alpha$ form a sub-class of all of the terms-in-context; the formal symbol $Sg \vartriangleright$ is indicating that $\Gamma \vdash M : \alpha$ is in this sub-class, and reminds us that we are working with respect to the signature Sg. In practise, we shall just refer to a proved term $\Gamma \vdash M : \alpha$, when it is clear to which signature we are referring.

LEMMA 4.2.9   The Lemmas 3.2.10, 3.2.11 and 3.2.12, and Proposition 3.2.13 for algebraic theories are still valid for the proved terms of λ×-theories.

PROOF   Essentially the same as for algebraic type theory.   □

EXERCISE 4.2.10   Work through the details of the proof of Lemma 4.2.9.

4.3   λ×-Theories

DISCUSSION 4.3.1   A *λ×-theory*, *Th*, is a pair (Sg, Ax) where Sg is a λ×-signature and Ax is a collection of equations-in-context. An *equation-in-context* is a judgement of the form $\Gamma \vdash M = M' : \alpha$ where $\Gamma \vdash M : \alpha$ and $\Gamma \vdash M' : \alpha$ are proved terms. The equations-in-context in Ax are called the *axioms* of the theory. We indicate this by writing $Ax \vartriangleright \Gamma \vdash M = M' : \alpha$. The *theorems* of *Th* consist of the judgements of the form $Th \vartriangleright \Gamma \vdash M = M' : \alpha$ (where $Sg \vartriangleright \Gamma \vdash M : \alpha$ and $Sg \vartriangleright \Gamma \vdash M' : \alpha$) generated by the rules in Figure 4.2.

EXAMPLE 4.3.2   We now give an example of a λ×-theory. Consider the λ×-signature Sg which has ground types *nat* and *bool*, and has function symbols:

- tt: *bool*,

- ff: *bool*,

- C: *bool*, *nat*, *nat* → *nat*,

- k_n: *nat* for each $n \in \mathbb{N}$,

- S: *nat* → *nat*,

- P: *nat* → *nat*,

- Z: *nat* → *bool*, and

- $Y^\alpha : (\alpha \Rightarrow \alpha) \to \alpha$ for each type α.

We then set Ax to consist of the following equations-in-context:

- $x : nat, x' : nat \vdash C(tt, x, x') = x$,

Axioms

$$Ax \quad \triangleright \quad \Gamma \vdash M = M' \colon \alpha$$
$$\overline{Th \quad \triangleright \quad \Gamma \vdash M = M' \colon \alpha}$$

Unit Equations

$$Sg \quad \triangleright \quad \Gamma \vdash M \colon unit$$
$$\overline{Th \quad \triangleright \quad \Gamma \vdash M = \langle \rangle \colon unit}$$

Binary Product Equations

$$\frac{Sg \ \triangleright \ \Gamma \vdash M \colon \alpha \quad Sg \ \triangleright \ \Gamma \vdash N \colon \beta}{Th \ \triangleright \ \Gamma \vdash \mathsf{Fst}(\langle M, N \rangle) = M \colon \alpha} \qquad \frac{Sg \ \triangleright \ \Gamma \vdash M \colon \alpha \quad Sg \ \triangleright \ \Gamma \vdash N \colon \beta}{Th \ \triangleright \ \Gamma \vdash \mathsf{Snd}(\langle M, N \rangle) = N \colon \beta}$$

$$\frac{Sg \ \triangleright \ \Gamma \vdash P \colon \alpha \times \beta}{Th \ \triangleright \ \Gamma \vdash \langle \mathsf{Fst}(P), \mathsf{Snd}(P) \rangle = P \colon \alpha \times \beta}$$

Function Equations

$$\frac{Sg \ \triangleright \ \Gamma, x \colon \alpha \vdash F \colon \beta \quad Sg \ \triangleright \ \Gamma \vdash M \colon \alpha}{Th \ \triangleright \ \Gamma \vdash (\lambda x \colon \alpha . F) \, M = F[M/x] \colon \beta}$$

$$\frac{Sg \ \triangleright \ \Gamma \vdash M \colon \alpha \Rightarrow \beta}{Th \ \triangleright \ \Gamma \vdash \lambda x \colon \alpha . (Mx) = M \colon \alpha \Rightarrow \beta} \quad \text{(provided } x \notin fv(M))$$

$$\frac{Th \ \triangleright \ \Gamma, x \colon \alpha \vdash F = F' \colon \beta}{Th \ \triangleright \ \Gamma \vdash \lambda x \colon \alpha . F = \lambda x \colon \alpha . F' \colon \alpha \Rightarrow \beta}$$

Together with the rules for **Equational Reasoning, Permutation, Weakening** and **Substitution** as found on page 128.

Figure 4.2: Theorems Generated from a $\lambda \times$-Theory.

- $x\colon nat, x'\colon nat \vdash \mathtt{C}(\mathtt{ff}, x, x') = x'$,
- $\vdash \mathtt{S}(\mathtt{k}_n) = \mathtt{k}_{n+1}$,
- $\vdash \mathtt{P}(\mathtt{k}_0) = \mathtt{k}_0$,
- $\vdash \mathtt{P}(\mathtt{k}_{n+1}) = \mathtt{k}_n$,
- $\vdash \mathtt{Z}(\mathtt{k}_0) = \mathtt{tt}$,
- $\vdash \mathtt{Z}(\mathtt{k}_{n+1}) = \mathtt{ff}$, and
- $x\colon \alpha \Rightarrow \alpha \vdash \mathtt{Y}_\alpha(x) = x(\mathtt{Y}_\alpha(x))$.

One should think of this theory as having ground types the natural numbers and the booleans (where the latter is a two point set which indicates truth or falsity). The function symbols are to be thought of as truth, falsity, a conditional test for two terms, numerals, a successor operation on the natural numbers, a predecessor on the natural numbers, a test for zero, and a fixpoint operator. We shall see how to give a semantics to this theory later on.

4.4 Deriving a Categorical Semantics

DISCUSSION 4.4.1   The categorical semantics which we gave to algebraic theories in Chapter 3 was strongly motivated by traditional set-theoretic semantics. In this chapter we give a semantics to $\lambda\times$-theories. Some readers will know that this syntax can be modelled in cartesian closed categories. However, we shall present a uniform analysis of the syntax and rules of $\lambda\times$-theories to discover what, in categorical terms, is the most general interpretation. As discussed in Chapter 3, types will be modelled by objects in a category. In a $\lambda\times$-theory, the types are specified by giving a collection of ground types, and then constructing further types from the ground types using the type constructors $\times$ and $\Rightarrow$. The interpretation of a type $\alpha \times \beta$ will depend on the interpretations of α and β, and similarly for the function type constructor. The proved terms will be interpreted by morphisms in a category, and the assumption that the theorems are soundly interpreted will then determine equations which hold between morphisms. In the cases of binary product types and function types, we shall see that the equations between morphisms will determine the objects which model the types up to isomorphism. Finally, recall the basic assumption that all of our syntax is interpreted in a category with (at least) finite products: products are used to model the list of types which appear in contexts.

Let us suppose that we are given a $\lambda\times$-theory $Th = (Sg, Ax)$ and that $\mathcal{C}$ is a (locally small) category with finite products. First we consider the types of

Sg. We have to give an object $[\![\gamma]\!]$ of $\mathcal{C}$ to interpret each of the ground types γ, and an object $[\![unit]\!]$ to interpret *unit*—for the moment we cannot say anything more specific about $[\![unit]\!]$. We will assume that the interpretations of binary product types $\alpha \times \beta$ and function types $\alpha \Rightarrow \beta$ depend on the interpretations of α and β. So there should be operations in $\mathcal{C}$ which give objects $A \square B$ and $A \Diamond B$ for all objects A and B so that we can define $[\![\alpha \times \beta]\!] \overset{\text{def}}{=} [\![\alpha]\!] \square [\![\beta]\!]$ and $[\![\alpha \Rightarrow \beta]\!] \overset{\text{def}}{=} [\![\alpha]\!] \Diamond [\![\beta]\!]$. Having done this, we can now choose a morphism $[\![f]\!]: [\![\alpha_1]\!] \times \ldots \times [\![\alpha_n]\!] \to [\![\beta]\!]$ in $\mathcal{C}$ for each function symbol $f: \alpha_1 \ldots \alpha_n \to \beta$ of *Sg*. Now recall that the interpretation of a proved term $\Gamma \vdash M: \alpha$ is given by a morphism $[\![\Gamma \vdash M: \alpha]\!]: [\![\Gamma]\!] \to [\![\alpha]\!]$ in $\mathcal{C}$; see page 133. At the moment we do not know how to define such an interpretation, but by looking at how to soundly interpret the terms and equations of *Th* we will deduce how to do this.

Let us think about the rules of formation of proved terms in general, assuming just one hypothesis. A typical rule looks like

$$\frac{Sg \; \rhd \; \Gamma \vdash M: \alpha}{Sg \; \rhd \; \Gamma \vdash R(M): \beta} \quad \text{(R)}$$

where $R(M)$ is a new raw term depending on M (think of R as Fst, for example). Now suppose that $m \overset{\text{def}}{=} [\![\Gamma \vdash M: \alpha]\!]$ which is an element of $\mathcal{C}([\![\Gamma]\!], [\![\alpha]\!])$. How do we model $[\![\Gamma \vdash R(M): \beta]\!] \in \mathcal{C}([\![\Gamma]\!], [\![\beta]\!])$? All we can say at the moment is that this latter morphism will depend on m, and we can model this idea by having a function

$$\Phi_{[\![\alpha]\!],[\![\beta]\!],[\![\Gamma]\!]} : \mathcal{C}([\![\Gamma]\!], [\![\alpha]\!]) \longrightarrow \mathcal{C}([\![\Gamma]\!], [\![\beta]\!])$$

and setting $[\![\Gamma \vdash R(M): \beta]\!] \overset{\text{def}}{=} \Phi_{[\![\alpha]\!],[\![\beta]\!],[\![\Gamma]\!]}(m)$. Now think about how the raw terms are formed. The crucial point is that new raw terms are formed from old raw terms by substitution; and we can easily see that a derived rule for any $\lambda\times$-theory is

$$\frac{Sg \; \rhd \; x:\gamma \vdash M: \alpha \quad Sg \; \rhd \; y:\gamma' \vdash N:\gamma}{Sg \; \rhd \; y:\gamma' \vdash M[N/x]: \alpha} \quad \text{(Sub)}.$$

Suppose that $x:\gamma \vdash M: \alpha$ and $y:\gamma' \vdash N:\gamma$ are any two given proved terms. Using our basic assumption that substitution is modelled by composition of morphisms, if $m \overset{\text{def}}{=} [\![x:\gamma \vdash M:\alpha]\!]$ and $n \overset{\text{def}}{=} [\![y:\gamma' \vdash N:\gamma]\!]$ then we will *assert* that $[\![y:\gamma' \vdash M[N/x]:\alpha]\!] = m \circ n$. Applying each of (Sub) and (R) in turn, we deduce that there are proved terms

$$y:\gamma' \vdash R(M)[N/x]: \beta \qquad \text{and} \qquad y:\gamma' \vdash R(M[N/x]):\beta.$$

However, both of the above raw terms should be syntactically identical (by the definition of substitution), and therefore the categorical interpretations should be the same, that is

$$\Phi_{[\alpha],[\beta],[\gamma]}(m) \circ n = \Phi_{[\alpha],[\beta],[\gamma']}(m \circ n). \qquad (*)$$

The astute reader will notice that $(*)$ looks similar to a naturality condition; in fact we can be certain that it will hold if we demand the following. For every object A and B of $\mathcal{C}$ there is a natural transformation

$$\Phi_{A,B} : \mathcal{C}(-,A) \longrightarrow \mathcal{C}(-,B) : \mathcal{C} \longrightarrow Set.$$

We can summarise these thoughts in the slogan:

Categorical Modelling of Term Formation

The sound categorical interpretation of the notion of term formation amounts to requiring that certain naturality conditions hold in the categorical model.

Let us now think about specific types and terms.

First we deal with the type *unit*. There must always be a morphism $u_0 \stackrel{\text{def}}{=} [\Gamma \vdash \langle\rangle : unit] : [\Gamma] \to [unit]$. Looking at the **Unit Equations**, *if* this is to be soundly interpreted, then whenever there is a morphism $m \stackrel{\text{def}}{=} [\Gamma \vdash M : \alpha]$ in $\mathcal{C}$, we must have $m = u_0$. All this amounts to saying that for every object A of $\mathcal{C}$, there must exist a unique morphism $! : A \to [unit]$, that is *up to isomorphism* $[unit]$ *is a terminal object* 1 *of* $\mathcal{C}$.

Recall that the rule for introducing product terms is

$$\frac{\Gamma \vdash M : \alpha \quad \Gamma \vdash N : \beta}{\Gamma \vdash \langle M, N \rangle : \alpha \times \beta}$$

In order to soundly interpret this rule we shall need a natural transformation

$$\Phi_{A,B} : \mathcal{C}(-,A) \times \mathcal{C}(-,B) \longrightarrow \mathcal{C}(-,A \,\square\, B)$$

for all objects A and B of $\mathcal{C}$. Now let $m : C \to A$ and $n : C \to B$ be morphisms of $\mathcal{C}$. Applying naturality in C at the morphism $\langle m, n \rangle : C \to A \times B$ we deduce

$$(\Phi_{A,B})_C(\pi_A\langle m,n\rangle, \pi_B\langle m,n\rangle) = (\Phi_{A,B})_{A\square B}(\pi_A, \pi_B) \circ \langle m,n\rangle,$$

that is $(\Phi_{A,B})_C(m,n) = (\Phi_{A,B})_{A\square B}(\pi_A, \pi_B) \circ \langle m,n\rangle$. Now let us define the morphism $q_{A,B} : A \times B \to A \,\square\, B$ to be $(\Phi_{A,B})_{A\times B}(\pi_A, \pi_B)$. Then we can make the definition

$$[\![\Gamma \vdash \langle M, N \rangle \colon A \,\square\, B]\!] \overset{\text{def}}{=}$$

$$[\![\Gamma]\!] \xrightarrow{\langle [\![\Gamma \vdash M \colon \alpha]\!], [\![\Gamma \vdash N \colon \beta]\!] \rangle} [\![\alpha]\!] \times [\![\beta]\!] \xrightarrow{q_{[\![\alpha]\!],[\![\beta]\!]}} [\![\alpha]\!] \,\square\, [\![\beta]\!].$$

Recall one of the rules for eliminating product types

$$\frac{\Gamma \vdash P \colon \alpha \times \beta}{\Gamma \vdash \mathsf{Fst}(P) \colon \alpha}$$

Arguing as above, to model this rule we shall need (for each A and B) a natural transformation $\Phi_{A,B} \colon \mathcal{C}(-, A \,\square\, B) \longrightarrow \mathcal{C}(-, A)$. Recall the Yoneda lemma, namely Lemma 2.7.4. With this, we may deduce that

$$[\mathcal{C}^{op}, \mathcal{S}et](H_{A\square B}, H_A) \cong \mathcal{C}(A \,\square\, B, A)$$

which is to say that each natural transformation $\Phi_{A,B}$ corresponds to a unique morphism $p_{A,B} \colon A \,\square\, B \to A$. Moreover, the Yoneda Lemma says that the components of $\Phi_{A,B}$ are given by $(\Phi_{A,B})_C = \mathcal{C}(C, p_{A,B})$. So now we can define

$$[\![\Gamma \vdash \mathsf{Fst}(P) \colon \alpha]\!] \overset{\text{def}}{=} [\![\Gamma]\!] \xrightarrow{[\![\Gamma \vdash P \colon \alpha \times \beta]\!]} [\![\alpha]\!] \,\square\, [\![\beta]\!] \xrightarrow{p_{[\![\alpha]\!],[\![\beta]\!]}} [\![\alpha]\!].$$

Of course we can deduce a semantics for proved terms of the form $\Gamma \vdash \mathsf{Snd}(P) \colon \beta$ in much the same way, involving a morphism $p'_{A,B} \colon A \,\square\, B \to B$. Our last task is to see what information we obtain by soundly interpreting the equations-in-context for product types. These are

$$\frac{\Gamma \vdash M \colon \alpha \quad \Gamma \vdash N \colon \beta}{\Gamma \vdash \mathsf{Fst}(\langle M, N \rangle) = M \colon \alpha} \quad (1) \qquad \frac{\Gamma \vdash M \colon \alpha \quad \Gamma \vdash N \colon \beta}{\Gamma \vdash \mathsf{Snd}(\langle M, N \rangle) = N \colon \beta} \quad (2)$$

$$\frac{\Gamma \vdash P \colon \alpha \times \beta}{\Gamma \vdash \langle \mathsf{Fst}(P), \mathsf{Snd}(P) \rangle = P \colon \alpha \times \beta} \quad (3)$$

If we put $h \overset{\text{def}}{=} [\![\Gamma \vdash P \colon \alpha \times \beta]\!] \colon C \to A \,\square\, B$, $m \overset{\text{def}}{=} [\![\Gamma \vdash M \colon \alpha]\!] \colon C \to A$ and $n \overset{\text{def}}{=} [\![\Gamma \vdash N \colon \beta]\!] \colon C \to B$, and demand that our categorical interpretation satisfies the equations-in-context, this forces

$$p_{A,B} \circ q_{A,B} \circ \langle m, n \rangle = m \qquad (1)$$

$$p'_{A,B} \circ q_{A,B} \circ \langle m, n \rangle = n \qquad (2)$$

$$q_{A,B} \circ \langle p_{A,B} \circ h, p'_{A,B} \circ h \rangle = h \qquad (3)$$

At last we are done, because these equations imply that, up to isomorphism, $A \Box B$ and $A \times B$ are the same. Thus we may *soundly interpret binary product types by binary categorical product.*

Now we shall resume the investigation of the semantics of function types. To soundly interpret the introduction rule

$$\frac{\Gamma, x: \alpha \vdash F: \beta}{\Gamma \vdash \lambda x: \alpha.F: \alpha \Rightarrow \beta}$$

we shall need (for every object A and B) a natural transformation

$$\Phi_{A,B}: \mathcal{C}(- \times A, B) \longrightarrow \mathcal{C}(-, A \Diamond B),$$

and we can then define

$$[\![\Gamma \vdash \lambda x: \alpha.F: \alpha \Rightarrow \beta]\!] \stackrel{\text{def}}{=} (\Phi_{[\![\alpha]\!],[\![\beta]\!]})_{[\![\Gamma]\!]}([\![\Gamma, x: \alpha \vdash F: \beta]\!]): [\![\Gamma]\!] \to ([\![\alpha]\!] \Diamond [\![\beta]\!]).$$

To soundly interpret the elimination rule

$$\frac{\Gamma \vdash M: \alpha \Rightarrow \beta \quad \Gamma \vdash N: \alpha}{\Gamma \vdash MN: \beta}$$

we shall need a natural transformation

$$\Psi_{A,B}: \mathcal{C}(-, A \Diamond B) \times \mathcal{C}(-, A) \longrightarrow \mathcal{C}(-, B)$$

for all objects A and B of $\mathcal{C}$. Given any two morphisms $m: C \to A \Diamond B$ and $n: C \to A$ and applying naturality, we have

$$(\Psi_{A,B})_C(m, n) = (\Psi_{A,B})_{(A \Diamond B) \times A}(\pi, \pi') \circ \langle m, n \rangle$$

where $\pi: (A \Diamond B) \times A \to A \Diamond B$ and $\pi': (A \Diamond B) \times A \to A$. So if we define the morphism $ev_{A,B} \stackrel{\text{def}}{=} (\Psi_{A,B})_{(A \Diamond B) \times A}(\pi, \pi')$, we can make the definition

$$[\![\Gamma \vdash MN: \beta]\!] \stackrel{\text{def}}{=}$$

$$[\![\Gamma]\!] \xrightarrow{\langle [\![\Gamma \vdash M: \alpha \Rightarrow \beta]\!], [\![\Gamma \vdash N: \alpha]\!] \rangle} ([\![\alpha]\!] \Diamond [\![\beta]\!]) \times [\![\alpha]\!] \xrightarrow{ev_{[\![\alpha]\!],[\![\beta]\!]}} [\![\beta]\!].$$

The equations-in-context for the function type are

$$\frac{\Gamma, x: \alpha \vdash F: \beta \quad \Gamma \vdash M: \alpha}{\Gamma \vdash (\lambda x: \alpha.F) \, M = F[M/x]: \beta} \quad (4) \qquad \frac{\Gamma \vdash M: \alpha \Rightarrow \beta}{\Gamma \vdash \lambda x: \alpha.(Mx) = M: \alpha \Rightarrow \beta} \quad (5)$$

If our categorical interpretation is to satisfy the equation-in-context (4), then we must have $ev_{A,B} \langle (\Phi_{A,B})_C(f), m \rangle = f \langle id, m \rangle$ for all morphisms $f: C \times A \to B$

and $m: C \to A$. Using the naturality of $\Phi_{A,B}$ we can show that this equation holds just in case

$$ev_{A,B}((\Phi_{A,B})_C(f) \times id) = f. \qquad (*)$$

Satisfaction of (5) requires that $(\Phi_{A,B})_C(ev_{A,B}(m \times id_A)) = m$ for every morphism $m: C \to A \lozenge B$ and from the naturality of $\Phi_{A,B}$ this holds just in case

$$(\Phi_{A,B})_{A \lozenge B}(ev_{A,B}) = id. \qquad (\dagger)$$

Now we come to the crucial point. If we define a natural transformation $\theta: \mathcal{C}(- \times A, B) \longrightarrow \mathcal{C}(-, A \lozenge B)$ by setting $\theta_C(f) \stackrel{\text{def}}{=} ev_{A,B} \circ (f \times id)$ the equations $(*)$ and $(\dagger)$ imply that θ is a natural bijection. *Thus, up to isomorphism in the category $\mathcal{C}$, the object $A \lozenge B$ is exactly the exponential $A \Rightarrow B$ and of course $ev_{A,B}: (A \lozenge B) \times A \to B$ is the evaluation morphism, and such categorical structure will soundly interpret function types.*

REMARK 4.4.2   Recall that in Section 4.4 we assumed for convenience that $\mathcal{C}$ was locally small. In fact it is possible to apply very similar arguments when $\mathcal{C}$ is not locally small by considering a suitable system of set theory with universes, and modifying the Yoneda Lemma appropriately. We could also replace each of the natural transformations between functors of the form $\mathcal{C} \to Set$ (that is functors with *target Set*) with an indexed collection of class functions $\alpha_C: FC \to GC$ which are "natural in C" meaning that an obvious elementary naturality equation holds for each component α_C.

EXERCISES 4.4.3   With reference to Section 4.4:

(1) Work through the details of the derivation of the semantics of binary product types. Be careful to understand the crucial fact that because the procedures of deriving proved terms and performing substitutions *commute*, the procedures of deriving a proved term can be modelled in an appropriate categorical structure by operations which are *natural* in their arguments.

(2) Work through the details of the derivation of the semantics of function types. In particular, prove the equations $(*)$ and $(\dagger)$ hold using naturality of $\Phi_{A,B}$.

4.5   Categorical Semantics

DISCUSSION 4.5.1   We formalise the discussion of Section 4.4. Let $\mathcal{C}$ be a cartesian closed category and let Sg be a $\lambda\times$-signature. Then a *structure*, **M**, for Sg in $\mathcal{C}$ is specified by giving:

• For every ground type γ of Sg an object $[\![\gamma]\!]$ of $\mathcal{C}$,

• for every constant function symbol $k\colon\alpha$, a global element $[\![k]\!]$ of $[\![\alpha]\!]$ (where $[\![\alpha]\!]$ is defined below), and

• for every function symbol $f\colon\alpha_1\ldots\alpha_n\to\beta$ of Sg with non-zero arity, a morphism

$$[\![f]\!]\colon[\![\alpha_1]\!]\times\ldots\times[\![\alpha_n]\!]\to[\![\beta]\!],$$

where we define $[\![\alpha]\!]$ for an arbitrary type α via structural induction, setting $[\![unit]\!]\overset{\text{def}}{=}1$, $[\![\alpha\times\beta]\!]\overset{\text{def}}{=}[\![\alpha]\!]\times[\![\beta]\!]$ and $[\![\alpha\Rightarrow\beta]\!]\overset{\text{def}}{=}[\![\alpha]\!]\Rightarrow[\![\beta]\!]$ (and of course $[\![\gamma]\!]$ is given).

Given a context $\Gamma=[x_1\colon\alpha_1,\ldots,x_n\colon\alpha_n]$ we set $[\![\Gamma]\!]\overset{\text{def}}{=}[\![\alpha_1]\!]\times\ldots\times[\![\alpha_n]\!]$. Then for every proved term $\Gamma\vdash M\colon\alpha$ we shall use the structure $\mathbf{M}$ to specify a morphism

$$[\![\Gamma\vdash M\colon\alpha]\!]\colon[\![\Gamma]\!]\to[\![\alpha]\!]$$

in $\mathcal{C}$. The semantics of proved terms is specified inductively using the rules for introducing proved terms and the definition is given in Figures 4.3 and 4.4. It is easy to see that substitution of terms is modelled by categorical composition of morphisms. We have

LEMMA 4.5.2   Let $\Gamma'\vdash N\colon\beta$ be a proved term where $\Gamma'=[x_1\colon\alpha_1,\ldots,x_n\colon\alpha_n]$ and let $\Gamma\vdash M_i\colon\alpha_i$ be proved terms for $i=1$ to n. Then one can show that $\Gamma\vdash N[\vec{M}/\vec{x}]\colon\beta$ is a proved term and further that

$$[\![\Gamma\vdash N[\vec{M}/\vec{x}]\colon\beta]\!]=[\![\Gamma'\vdash N\colon\beta]\!]\circ\langle[\![\Gamma\vdash M_1\colon\alpha_1]\!],\ldots,[\![\Gamma\vdash M_n\colon\alpha_n]\!]\rangle$$

where $N[\vec{M}/\vec{x}]$ denotes simultaneous substitution.

PROOF   By induction on the derivation of the judgement $\Gamma'\vdash N\colon\beta$.   □

EXERCISES 4.5.3

(1) Look at the details of the categorical semantics of $\lambda\times$-theories and understand the ideas of such a model.

(2) Work through the details of the proof of Lemma 4.5.2.

Variables

$$\llbracket \Gamma, x\colon \alpha, \Gamma' \vdash x\colon \alpha \rrbracket \overset{\text{def}}{=} \pi\colon \llbracket \Gamma \rrbracket \times \llbracket \alpha \rrbracket \times \llbracket \Gamma' \rrbracket \to \llbracket \alpha \rrbracket$$

Unit Term

$$\llbracket \Gamma \vdash \langle\rangle\colon unit \rrbracket \overset{\text{def}}{=} !\colon \llbracket \Gamma \rrbracket \to 1 \qquad \text{(where 1 is the terminal object of } \mathcal{C}\text{)}$$

Function Symbols

$$\llbracket \Gamma \vdash k\colon \alpha \rrbracket \overset{\text{def}}{=} \llbracket k \rrbracket \circ !\colon \llbracket \Gamma \rrbracket \to 1 \to \llbracket \alpha \rrbracket \qquad (k\colon \alpha)$$

$$\frac{\llbracket \Gamma \vdash M_1\colon \alpha_1 \rrbracket = m_1\colon \llbracket \Gamma \rrbracket \to \llbracket \alpha_1 \rrbracket \quad \dots \quad \llbracket \Gamma \vdash M_n\colon \alpha_n \rrbracket = m_n\colon \llbracket \Gamma \rrbracket \to \llbracket \alpha_n \rrbracket}{\llbracket \Gamma \vdash f(\vec{M})\colon \beta \rrbracket = \llbracket f \rrbracket \circ \langle m_1, \dots, m_n \rangle\colon \llbracket \Gamma \rrbracket \to (\llbracket \alpha_1 \rrbracket \times \dots \times \llbracket \alpha_n \rrbracket) \to \llbracket \beta \rrbracket}$$

$$(f\colon \alpha_1, \dots, \alpha_n \to \beta)$$

Binary Product Terms

$$\frac{\llbracket \Gamma \vdash M\colon \alpha \rrbracket = m\colon \llbracket \Gamma \rrbracket \to \llbracket \alpha \rrbracket \quad \llbracket \Gamma \vdash N\colon \beta \rrbracket = n\colon \llbracket \Gamma \rrbracket \to \llbracket \beta \rrbracket}{\llbracket \Gamma \vdash \langle M, N \rangle\colon \alpha \times \beta \rrbracket = \langle m, n \rangle\colon \llbracket \Gamma \rrbracket \to (\llbracket \alpha \rrbracket \times \llbracket \beta \rrbracket)}$$

$$\frac{\llbracket \Gamma \vdash P\colon \alpha \times \beta \rrbracket = p\colon \llbracket \Gamma \rrbracket \to (\llbracket \alpha \rrbracket \times \llbracket \beta \rrbracket)}{\llbracket \Gamma \vdash \mathsf{Fst}(P)\colon \alpha \rrbracket = \pi_1 \circ p\colon \llbracket \Gamma \rrbracket \to (\llbracket \alpha \rrbracket \times \llbracket \beta \rrbracket) \to \llbracket \alpha \rrbracket}$$

$$\frac{\llbracket \Gamma \vdash P\colon \alpha \times \beta \rrbracket = p\colon \llbracket \Gamma \rrbracket \to (\llbracket \alpha \rrbracket \times \llbracket \beta \rrbracket)}{\llbracket \Gamma \vdash \mathsf{Snd}(P)\colon \beta \rrbracket = \pi_2 \circ p\colon \llbracket \Gamma \rrbracket \to (\llbracket \alpha \rrbracket \times \llbracket \beta \rrbracket) \to \llbracket \beta \rrbracket}$$

Figure 4.3: Categorical Semantics of Proved Terms Generated from a $\lambda\times$-Signature.

Function Terms

$$\frac{[\![\Gamma, x\colon\alpha \vdash F\colon\beta]\!] = f\colon [\![\Gamma]\!] \times [\![\alpha]\!] \to [\![\beta]\!]}{[\![\Gamma \vdash \lambda x\colon\alpha.F\colon\alpha \Rightarrow \beta]\!] = \lambda(f)\colon [\![\Gamma]\!] \to ([\![\alpha]\!] \Rightarrow [\![\beta]\!])}$$

$$\frac{[\![\Gamma \vdash M\colon\alpha \Rightarrow \beta]\!] = m\colon [\![\Gamma]\!] \to ([\![\alpha]\!] \Rightarrow [\![\beta]\!]) \quad [\![\Gamma \vdash N\colon\alpha]\!] = n\colon [\![\Gamma]\!] \to [\![\alpha]\!]}{[\![\Gamma \vdash MN\colon\beta]\!] \stackrel{\text{def}}{=} ev \circ \langle m, n\rangle\colon [\![\Gamma]\!] \to ([\![\alpha]\!] \Rightarrow [\![\beta]\!]) \times [\![\alpha]\!] \to [\![\beta]\!]}$$

Figure 4.4: Categorical Semantics of Proved Terms Generated from a $\lambda\times$-Signature, Continued.

4.6 Categorical Models and the Soundness Theorem

DISCUSSION 4.6.1 Let **M** be a structure for a $\lambda\times$-signature in a cartesian closed category $\mathcal{C}$. Given an equation-in-context $\Gamma \vdash M = M'\colon\alpha$ we say that **M** *satisfies* the equation-in-context if $[\![\Gamma \vdash M\colon\alpha]\!]$ and $[\![\Gamma \vdash M'\colon\alpha]\!]$ are equal morphisms in $\mathcal{C}$. We say that **M** is a *model* of a $\lambda\times$-theory $Th = (Sg, Ax)$ if **M** satisfies all of the equations-in-context in Ax. We shall also speak of **M** satisfying axioms and theorems. We will prove a soundness theorem for $\lambda\times$-theories after the following example:

EXAMPLE 4.6.2 We shall give a model for the $\lambda\times$-theory Th given on page 161. Consider the category $\omega\mathcal{CPO}_\perp$, which is a full subcategory of $\omega\mathcal{CPO}$, and whose objects are those ωcpos which have a bottom element. It is an easy exercise to check that $\omega\mathcal{CPO}_\perp$ is a cartesian closed category. We give a structure **M** in $\omega\mathcal{CPO}$ by setting $[\![bool]\!] \stackrel{\text{def}}{=} \Omega$ where Ω is the Sierpiński poset $\{t, f\}$ with $f \leq t$, and $[\![nat]\!] \stackrel{\text{def}}{=} \{\perp, 0, 1, 2, 3 \ldots\}$ with order $\perp \leq n$ and $n \leq n$ for each $n \in \mathbb{N}$, where $n \in \mathbb{N}$ and $m \in \mathbb{N}$ are incomparable if $m \neq n$. We call this ωcpo the *flat* natural numbers. Let us write B and N for these ωcpos, and $\{*\}$ for the terminal ωcpo. We then give the following interpretations to the function symbols:

- $[\![\mathtt{tt}]\!]\colon \{*\} \to B$ is the continuous function sending $*$ to t.
- $[\![\mathtt{ff}]\!]\colon \{*\} \to B$ is the continuous function sending $*$ to f.
- $[\![\mathtt{C}]\!]\colon B \times N \times N \to N$ is the continuous function which for all $m, n \in N$ sends (t, m, n) to m and (f, m, n) to n.
- $[\![\mathtt{k}_n]\!]\colon \{*\} \to N$ is the continuous function sending $*$ to n.
- $[\![\mathtt{S}]\!]\colon N \to N$ is the continuous function sending n to $n+1$.

- $[\![\mathrm{P}]\!]: N \to N$ is the continuous function sending $n+1$ to n and 0 to 0.

- $[\![\mathrm{Z}]\!]: N \to B$ is the continuous function sending 0 to t and $n+1$ to f.

- $[\![\mathrm{Y}_\alpha]\!]: ([\![\alpha]\!] \Rightarrow [\![\alpha]\!]) \to [\![\alpha]\!]$ is the continuous function sending a continuous function $f: [\![\alpha]\!] \to [\![\alpha]\!]$ to $\bigvee_{n \in \mathbb{N}} f^n(\bot)$ where α is any type of *Th* and $\bot \in [\![\alpha]\!]$ is the bottom element of $[\![\alpha]\!]$.

EXERCISE 4.6.3   It is essentially immediate from the definition of the structure **M** that it is a model of *Th*. Verify this fact.

THEOREM 4.6.4   Let $\mathcal{C}$ be a cartesian closed category, *Th* a $\lambda\times$-theory and **M** a model of *Th* in $\mathcal{C}$. Then **M** satisfies any equation-in-context which is a theorem of *Th*.

PROOF   We need to see that if $\Gamma \vdash M = M' : \alpha$ is a theorem of *Th*, then $[\![\Gamma \vdash M : \alpha]\!]$ and $[\![\Gamma \vdash M' : \alpha]\!]$ are equal morphisms in $\mathcal{C}$. This can be shown by demonstrating that **M** satisfies the conclusion of any of the rules given on page 162 if **M** satisfies any theorem which appears in the hypothesis of the rule. We give one example of this. Let $f \overset{\text{def}}{=} [\![\Gamma, x : \alpha \vdash F : \beta]\!] : [\![\Gamma]\!] \times [\![\alpha]\!] \to [\![\beta]\!]$ and $m \overset{\text{def}}{=} [\![\Gamma \vdash M : \alpha]\!] : [\![\Gamma]\!] \to [\![\alpha]\!]$. Then we have

(*Case* **Function Equations**):

$$
\begin{aligned}
[\![\Gamma \vdash (\lambda x : \alpha . F)\, M : \beta]\!] &= ev\langle [\![\Gamma \vdash \lambda x : \alpha . F : \beta]\!], [\![\Gamma \vdash M : \alpha]\!] \rangle \\
&= ev\langle \lambda(f), m \rangle \\
&= ev(\lambda(f) \times id)\langle id, m \rangle \\
&= f\langle id, m \rangle \\
&= [\![\Gamma \vdash F[M/x] : \beta]\!]
\end{aligned}
$$

where the last step follows by an application of Lemma 4.5.2.   □

EXERCISE 4.6.5   Work through the remaining details of the proof of Theorem 4.6.4.

4.7 Categories of Models

DISCUSSION 4.7.1   Recall the discussion in Section 3.7 in which we defined the category of models of an algebraic theory in a category with finite products, namely $\mathcal{M}od(Th, \mathcal{C})$, and the category of finite product preserving functors between categories with finite products, namely $\mathcal{FP}(\mathcal{C}, \mathcal{D})$. Let us consider a similar story in the case of functional type theories.

We describe an approach which mimics Section 3.7. Given that both $\mathcal{C}$ and $\mathcal{D}$ are cartesian closed categories, we define the category $\mathcal{CCat}(\mathcal{C}, \mathcal{D})$ to have objects which are cartesian closed functors, and morphisms which are natural transformations. It easy to check that this definition makes good sense. We shall now give one possible definition of homomorphism of models $\mathbf{M}$ and $\mathbf{N}$ of $\lambda\times$-theories (in a cartesian closed category $\mathcal{C}$, say). A homomorphism $h\colon \mathbf{M} \to \mathbf{N}$ is specified by giving a collection of morphisms $h_\alpha\colon [\![\alpha]\!]_\mathbf{M} \to [\![\alpha]\!]_\mathbf{N}$ for each type α, called the components of h, which commute with the interpretations of the function symbols (just as for algebraic theories—see page 137), and in addition the components of h commute with the interpretations of the syntax for binary product and function types, by which we mean the diagrams

$$
\begin{array}{ccc}
[\![\alpha]\!]_\mathbf{M} \times [\![\beta]\!]_\mathbf{M} & \xrightarrow{h_{\alpha\times\beta}} & [\![\alpha]\!]_\mathbf{N} \times [\![\beta]\!]_\mathbf{N} \\
{\scriptstyle\pi}\downarrow & & \downarrow{\scriptstyle\pi} \\
[\![\alpha]\!]_\mathbf{M} & \xrightarrow{h_\alpha} & [\![\alpha]\!]_\mathbf{N}
\end{array}
\qquad
\begin{array}{ccc}
\Pi_1^n[\![\gamma_i]\!]_\mathbf{M} & \xrightarrow{h_{\Pi_1^n\gamma_i}} & \Pi_1^n[\![\gamma_i]\!]_\mathbf{N} \\
{\scriptstyle\langle m, n\rangle}\downarrow & & \downarrow{\scriptstyle\langle m', n'\rangle} \\
[\![\alpha]\!]_\mathbf{M} \times [\![\beta]\!]_\mathbf{M} & \xrightarrow{h_{\alpha\times\beta}} & [\![\alpha]\!]_\mathbf{N} \times [\![\beta]\!]_\mathbf{N}
\end{array}
$$

$$
\begin{array}{ccc}
([\![\alpha]\!]_\mathbf{M} \Rightarrow [\![\beta]\!]_\mathbf{M}) \times [\![\alpha]\!]_\mathbf{M} & \xrightarrow{h_{(\alpha\Rightarrow\beta)\times\alpha}} & ([\![\alpha]\!]_\mathbf{N} \Rightarrow [\![\beta]\!]_\mathbf{N}) \times [\![\alpha]\!]_\mathbf{N} \\
{\scriptstyle ev}\downarrow & & \downarrow{\scriptstyle ev} \\
[\![\beta]\!]_\mathbf{M} & \xrightarrow{h_\beta} & [\![\beta]\!]_\mathbf{N}
\end{array}
$$

$$
\begin{array}{ccc}
\Pi_1^n[\![\gamma_i]\!]_\mathbf{M} & \xrightarrow{h_{\Pi_1^n\gamma_i}} & \Pi_1^n[\![\gamma_i]\!]_\mathbf{N} \\
{\scriptstyle\lambda(f)}\downarrow & & \downarrow{\scriptstyle\lambda(f)} \\
[\![\alpha]\!]_\mathbf{M} \Rightarrow [\![\beta]\!]_\mathbf{M} & \xrightarrow{h_{\alpha\Rightarrow\beta}} & [\![\alpha]\!]_\mathbf{N} \Rightarrow [\![\beta]\!]_\mathbf{N}
\end{array}
$$

commute for all morphisms m, n and f. Then the category of models of Th in $\mathcal{C}$, $\mathcal{M}od(Th, \mathcal{C})$, has objects which are models $\mathbf{M}$, and morphisms $h\colon \mathbf{M} \to \mathbf{N}$ are model homomorphisms. We would like to be able to show that for a given $\lambda\times$-theory Th, we can find a category $Cl(Th)$ such that for all cartesian closed categories $\mathcal{D}$ there is a natural equivalence

$$
Ap_\mathbf{G} : \mathcal{CCat}(Cl(Th), \mathcal{D}) \simeq \mathcal{M}od(Th, \mathcal{D})
$$

given by a modelling functor $Ap_\mathbf{G}$ similar to that defined for algebraic theories. Under such an equivalence, a homomorphism $h\colon \mathbf{M} \to \mathbf{N}$ of Th in $\mathcal{D}$ should be sent to a natural transformation $\phi: M \to N: Cl(Th) \to \mathcal{D}$ where $M(\alpha) \stackrel{\text{def}}{=} [\![\alpha]\!]_{\mathbf{M}}$ for each object α of $Cl(Th)$, and $\phi_\alpha \stackrel{\text{def}}{=} h_\alpha$. But there is a problem with this. One can check that ϕ is *not* (necessarily) a natural transformation.

EXERCISE 4.7.2   Prove that ϕ is not a natural transformation. *Hint: consider the naturality of ϕ in an object γ of $Cl(Th)$ at a morphism*

$$(z:\gamma \mid \lambda x: \alpha.M): \gamma \to (\alpha \Rightarrow \beta).$$

Try to think of a simple example of a $\lambda\times$-theory Th, a category with finite products $\mathcal{D}$ and a homomorphism $h: \mathbf{M} \to \mathbf{N}$ of models $\mathbf{M}$ and $\mathbf{N}$ of Th in $\mathcal{D}$. Do you think the components of the homomorphism h should be determined by those at ground type?

DISCUSSION 4.7.3   We can deal with the above problem of Discussion 4.7.1 by giving a slightly more restricted notion of homomorphism of models of $\lambda\times$-theories. This will still enable us to give a very general definition of classifying category, and will mean that the components of homomorphisms are determined by those at ground type. Let Th be a $\lambda\times$-theory, $\mathcal{C}$ a cartesian closed category, and $\mathbf{M}$ and $\mathbf{N}$ models of Th in $\mathcal{C}$. A *homomorphism* $h: \mathbf{M} \to \mathbf{N}$ of models of Th in $\mathcal{C}$ is given by

• a collection $h_\gamma: [\![\gamma]\!]_{\mathbf{M}} \to [\![\gamma]\!]_{\mathbf{N}}$ of *isomorphisms* in $\mathcal{C}$ for each ground type of Th, such that

• the *component* of h at a ground type γ of Th is h_γ, and at product and function types the components are given by $h_{\alpha\times\beta} \stackrel{\text{def}}{=} h_\alpha \times h_\beta$ and $h_{\alpha\Rightarrow\beta} \stackrel{\text{def}}{=} h_\alpha^{-1} \Rightarrow h_\beta$, and the components of h are required to commute with the function symbols of Th.

With this, we define the *category of models* $Mod_{\cong}(Th, \mathcal{C})$ to have objects the models of the $\lambda\times$-theory Th in $\mathcal{C}$, and morphisms homomorphisms of models. Also, let $\mathcal{C}$ and $\mathcal{D}$ be cartesian closed categories and write $\mathcal{CC}at_{\cong}(\mathcal{C}, \mathcal{D})$ for the category with objects which are cartesian closed functors $\mathcal{C} \to \mathcal{D}$, and morphisms natural *isomorphisms*. We now need a little more machinery to set up a natural equivalence between these two categories.

Suppose that we are given a morphism of cartesian closed categories $F: \mathcal{C} \to \mathcal{D}$. We shall define a functor

$$F_* : Mod_{\cong}(Th, \mathcal{C}) \longrightarrow Mod_{\cong}(Th, \mathcal{D}).$$

Let $\mathbf{M}$ be a model of Th in $\mathcal{C}$. If we define $[\![\gamma]\!]_{F.\mathbf{M}} \stackrel{\text{def}}{=} F[\![\gamma]\!]_{\mathbf{M}}$ where γ is a ground type of Th, then we can show that there is a canonical isomorphism

$[\alpha]_{F_*\mathbf{M}} \cong F[\alpha]_\mathbf{M}$ where α is any type of Th. Then the model $F_*\mathbf{M}$ is given by $[\gamma]_{F_*\mathbf{M}} \overset{\text{def}}{=} F[\gamma]_\mathbf{M}$ on ground types and $[f]_{F_*\mathbf{M}}$ is given by the composition

$$[\alpha_1]_{F_*\mathbf{M}} \times \ldots \times [\alpha_n]_{F_*\mathbf{M}} \cong F[\alpha_1]_\mathbf{M} \times \ldots \times F[\alpha_n]_\mathbf{M} \cong'$$

$$F([\alpha_1]_\mathbf{M} \times \ldots \times [\alpha_n]_\mathbf{M}) \overset{F[f]_\mathbf{M}}{\longrightarrow} F[\beta]_\mathbf{M} \cong [\beta]_{F_*\mathbf{M}}$$

where $f: \alpha_1, \ldots, \alpha_n \to \beta$ is a function symbol of Th and $\cong'$ arises from F preserving finite products. The homomorphism F_*h has components at ground type γ given by $(F_*h)_\gamma \overset{\text{def}}{=} F(h_\gamma)$. We need one more piece of machinery to set up our equivalence. Let $\phi: F \to G$ be a natural isomorphism between cartesian closed functors. We can define a homomorphism $\phi_*\mathbf{M}: F_*\mathbf{M} \to G_*\mathbf{M}$ of models of Th in $\mathcal{C}$ by setting $(\phi_*\mathbf{M})_\gamma \overset{\text{def}}{=} \phi_{[\gamma]_\mathbf{M}}: F[\gamma]_\mathbf{M} \to G[\gamma]_\mathbf{M}$, where here γ is any ground type of Th.

EXERCISE 4.7.4   Write out a proof which shows that $F_*\mathbf{M}$ really is a well defined model of Th in $\mathcal{D}$ and that F_*h really is a homomorphy of models. Verify that $\phi_*\mathbf{M}$ is a homomorphism.

DISCUSSION 4.7.5   Let $\mathcal{C}$ and $\mathcal{D}$ be fixed cartesian closed categories, and let $\mathbf{M}$ be any model of a fixed λ×-theory Th in $\mathcal{C}$. We define a family of *modelling functors*

$$Ap_\mathbf{M}: \mathcal{CCat}_\cong(\mathcal{C}, \mathcal{D}) \to \mathcal{Mod}_\cong(Th, \mathcal{D})$$

by setting $Ap_\mathbf{M}(F) \overset{\text{def}}{=} F_*\mathbf{M}$ and $Ap_\mathbf{M}(\phi) \overset{\text{def}}{=} \phi_*\mathbf{M}$, where $\phi: F \to G$ is any natural isomorphism between cartesian closed functors. It is the notion of modelling functor which we shall use in the next section to set up an equivalence between categories of models and categories of cartesian closed functors.

4.8   *Classifying Category of a* λ×-*Theory*

DISCUSSION 4.8.1   A classifying category for a λ×-theory can be thought of as a cartesian closed category which is in some sense the smallest such category in which Th can be modelled soundly. We shall see later that the classifying category arises through a formal construction using the syntax of the theory Th. The reader should compare this section with the idea of a freely generated vector space or group on a given set—compare the set to the λ×-theory Th and the freely generated gadgets to the classifying category—in just the same way as for algebraic theories.

Let Th be a λ×-theory. A cartesian closed category $Cl(Th)$ is called the *classifying* category of Th if there is a model $\mathbf{G}$ of Th in $Cl(Th)$ for which given any category $\mathcal{D}$ with finite products, the functor

$$Ap_{\mathbf{G}} \colon \mathcal{CCat}_{\cong}(Cl(Th), \mathcal{D}) \longrightarrow \mathcal{Mod}_{\cong}(Th, \mathcal{D})$$

is an equivalence. Such a model $\mathbf{G}$ will be called *generic* and its correspond-ing modelling functor the *generic* modelling functor. We shall see that such classifying categories are unique up to equivalence and that they play the role described at the start of Discussion 4.8.1. The following result is proved in the same way as for the corresponding results in Discussion 3.8.1.

PROPOSITION 4.8.2   Let Th be an $\lambda\times$-theory and $Cl(Th)$ a cartesian closed category for which there is a model $\mathbf{G}$ of Th in $Cl(Th)$. Suppose that given any cartesian closed category $\mathcal{D}$ there is an equivalence

$$Ap_{\mathbf{G}} \colon \mathcal{CCat}_{\cong}(Cl(Th), \mathcal{D}) \longrightarrow \mathcal{Mod}_{\cong}(Th, \mathcal{D}).$$

Then it is the case that whenever $Cl(Th)'$ and $\mathbf{G}'$ also have the above property there is an equivalence $Eq \colon Cl(Th) \simeq Cl(Th)'$ for which $Eq_*\mathbf{G} \cong \mathbf{G}'$.

It follows that for any model $\mathbf{M}$ of Th in a cartesian closed category $\mathcal{C}$, there is a cartesian closed functor $F \colon Cl(Th) \to \mathcal{C}$ for which the composition of the semantics of Th given by the generic model $\mathbf{G}$ in $Cl(Th)$ with the functor F yields the semantics given to Th by the model $\mathbf{M}$, up to isomorphism. This may be seen pictorially as

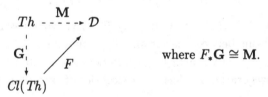

where $F_*\mathbf{G} \cong \mathbf{M}$.

Moreover, any two such functors F are naturally isomorphic.

PROOF   The proof is essentially the same as for Proposition 3.8.2 and Corol-lary 3.8.3.   □

DISCUSSION 4.8.3   The fundamental idea of the categorical type theory cor-respondence is the same as that for Chapter 3. However, because we model syntactical contexts by finite products, when we constructed the classifying category of an algebraic theory we had to construct finite products directly (by showing that juxtaposition of contexts gives rise to binary products and the empty context to a terminal object). In the case of $\lambda\times$-theories the presence of binary product types and a unit type makes the construction of a classifying category with finite products a little simpler. We have the following theorem:

THEOREM 4.8.4   Every λ×-theory *Th* has a classifying category *Cl(Th)*. We can construct a *canonical* classifying category using the syntax of *Th*.

PROOF   The construction of *Cl(Th)* can be simplified in some respects from the construction given for the classifying category of an algebraic theory. We had to define finite products in the classifying category of an algebraic theory by using concatenations of finite lists of types. Our syntax now has binary product types and a unit type and we can use this fact to define finite products in the classifying categories of λ×-theories.

The objects of *Cl(Th)* are exactly the types of the λ×-signature of *Th*. The morphisms of *Cl(Th)* are, roughly speaking, equivalence classes of raw terms with at most one free variable where the equivalence relation is given by provable equality in *Th*. More precisely, a morphism $\alpha \to \beta$ is an equivalence class $(x : \alpha \mid M)$ of pairs of the form $(x : \alpha, M)$ where x is a variable and M a raw term for which $Sg \;\rhd\; x : \alpha \vdash M : \beta$, with equivalence relation

$$(x : \alpha, M) \sim (x' : \alpha, M') \qquad \text{iff} \qquad Th \;\rhd\; x : \alpha \vdash M = M'[x/x'] : \beta.$$

Composition of morphisms is given by raw term substitution (as for the classifying category of an algebraic theory) and the identity on α is given by $(x : \alpha \mid x)$.

Given two objects α and β, the binary product consists of the object $\alpha \times \beta$ together with suitable projections. The projection $\pi_\alpha : \alpha \times \beta \to \alpha$ is given by $(z : \alpha \times \beta \mid \mathsf{Fst}(z))$ and the projection π_β is defined likewise from Snd. If we are given a pair of morphisms $(x : \gamma \mid M) : \gamma \to \alpha$ and $(y : \gamma \mid N) : \gamma \to \beta$, then the mediating morphism is given by

$$(z : \gamma \mid \langle M[z/x], N[z/y] \rangle) : \gamma \to \alpha \times \beta.$$

We leave the reader to check that we *have* defined a binary product, and that $(x : \alpha \mid \langle \rangle)$ is the unique morphism $\alpha \to unit$ so that $unit$ is a terminal object for *Cl(Th)*.

Now we move to the cartesian closed structure. The exponential of objects β and γ is given by $\beta \Rightarrow \gamma$. Given a morphism $(z : \alpha \times \beta \mid M) : \alpha \times \beta \to \gamma$ the exponential mate $\lambda(z : \alpha \times \beta \mid M) : \alpha \to (\beta \Rightarrow \gamma)$ is given by

$$(x : \alpha \mid \lambda y : \beta . M[\langle x, y \rangle / z])$$

(for which we can show that $Sg \;\rhd\; x : \alpha \vdash \lambda y : \beta . M[\langle x, y \rangle / z] : \beta \Rightarrow \gamma$ is a proved term). We leave the reader to check that we have specified a cartesian closed structure for *Cl(Th)*.

The generic model $\mathbf{G}$ of $Th \overset{\text{def}}{=} (Sg, Ax)$ in $Cl(Th)$ is given by defining $[\![\gamma]\!] \overset{\text{def}}{=} \gamma$ where γ is any ground type of Sg (and hence it follows that $[\![\alpha]\!] = \alpha$ for any type α). If $f: \alpha_1, \ldots, \alpha_n \to \beta$ is a function symbol of Sg with non-zero arity n then

$$[\![f]\!] \overset{\text{def}}{=} (z \colon \Pi_1^n \alpha_i \mid f(\mathsf{Proj}_1(z), \ldots, \mathsf{Proj}_n(z)))$$

where $\Pi_1^n \alpha_i \overset{\text{def}}{=} (\ldots((\alpha_1 \times \alpha_2) \times \alpha_3) \times \ldots) \times \alpha_n$ and where $\mathsf{Proj}_n(z) \overset{\text{def}}{=} \mathsf{Snd}(z)$, $\mathsf{Proj}_{n-1}(z) \overset{\text{def}}{=} \mathsf{Snd}(\mathsf{Fst}(z))$ and so on. Certainly we have

$$Sg \; \rhd \; z \colon \Pi_1^n \alpha_i \vdash f(\mathsf{Proj}_1(z), \ldots, \mathsf{Proj}_n(z)) \colon \beta.$$

Finally, if $k \colon \alpha$ then $[\![k]\!] \overset{\text{def}}{=} (x \colon \mathit{unit} \mid k)$.

To complete the proof we need to show that the modelling functor

$$Ap_{\mathbf{G}} : \mathcal{CCat}_{\cong}(Cl(Th), \mathcal{D}) \longrightarrow \mathcal{M}od_{\cong}(Th, \mathcal{D}),$$

$$\phi \colon F \longrightarrow F' \quad \mapsto \quad \phi_* \mathbf{G} \colon F_* \mathbf{G} \longrightarrow F'_* \mathbf{G}$$

is an equivalence for any cartesian closed category $\mathcal{D}$, where $\mathbf{G}$ is the generic model of Th in $Cl(Th)$. Let us define the functor $Ap_{\mathbf{G}}^{-1}$ as follows. Take an object $\mathbf{M}$ in $\mathcal{M}od_{\cong}(Th, \mathcal{D})$. We define $Ap_{\mathbf{G}}^{-1}\mathbf{M} \colon Cl(Th) \to \mathcal{D}$ by

$$(x \colon \alpha \mid M) : \alpha \longrightarrow \beta \quad \longmapsto \quad [\![x \colon \alpha \vdash M \colon \beta]\!]_{\mathbf{M}} : [\![\alpha]\!]_{\mathbf{M}} \longrightarrow [\![\beta]\!]_{\mathbf{M}}.$$

The soundness theorem says that the definition makes sense and it is easy to see that $Ap_{\mathbf{G}}^{-1}\mathbf{M}$ is a cartesian closed functor. Let $h \colon \mathbf{M} \to \mathbf{N}$ be a morphism of $\mathcal{M}od_{\cong}(Th, \mathcal{D})$. We can now define the natural isomorphism $Ap_{\mathbf{G}}^{-1}h \colon Ap_{\mathbf{G}}^{-1}\mathbf{M} \to Ap_{\mathbf{G}}^{-1}\mathbf{N}$ by setting the components at an object α of $Cl(Th)$ to be given by $(Ap_{\mathbf{G}}^{-1}h)_\alpha \overset{\text{def}}{=} h_\alpha \colon [\![\alpha]\!]_{\mathbf{M}} \to [\![\alpha]\!]_{\mathbf{N}}$. We have to see that this does indeed define a natural transformation, that is for each morphism $(x \colon \alpha \mid M) \colon \alpha \to \beta$ in $Cl(Th)$ the diagram

$$
\begin{array}{ccc}
[\![\alpha]\!]_{\mathbf{M}} & \xrightarrow{\quad h_\alpha \quad} & [\![\alpha]\!]_{\mathbf{N}} \\[4pt]
{\scriptstyle [\![x \colon \alpha \vdash M \colon \beta]\!]_{\mathbf{M}}}\Big\downarrow & & \Big\downarrow{\scriptstyle [\![x \colon \alpha \vdash M \colon \beta]\!]_{\mathbf{N}}} \\[4pt]
[\![\beta]\!]_{\mathbf{M}} & \xrightarrow[\quad h_\beta \quad]{} & [\![\beta]\!]_{\mathbf{N}}
\end{array}
$$

commutes. We can do this by showing that

$$[\![\Gamma \vdash M \colon \beta]\!]_{\mathbf{N}} \circ h_\Gamma = h_\beta \circ [\![\Gamma \vdash M \colon \beta]\!]_{\mathbf{M}}$$

for all proved terms $\Gamma \vdash M \colon \beta$, where $h_\Gamma \overset{\text{def}}{=} \times_1^n h_{\alpha_i}$ and the types α_i appear in Γ. We shall give just one case.

(Case $\Gamma \vdash M:\beta$ *is* $\Gamma \vdash \lambda y:\beta.M:\beta \Rightarrow \gamma$*):*   If $\Gamma \vdash \lambda y:\beta.M:\beta \Rightarrow \gamma$ is a proved term, then so is $\Gamma, y:\beta \vdash M:\gamma$. By the induction hypothesis, we have the following commutative diagram

$$
\begin{array}{ccc}
[\![\Gamma]\!]_{\mathbf{M}} \times [\![\beta]\!]_{\mathbf{M}} & \xrightarrow{\ h_\Gamma \times h_\beta\ } & [\![\Gamma]\!]_{\mathbf{N}} \times [\![\beta]\!]_{\mathbf{N}} \\
m \stackrel{\mathrm{def}}{=}\ \Big\downarrow & & \Big\downarrow\ m' \stackrel{\mathrm{def}}{=} \\
[\![\Gamma, y:\beta \vdash M:\gamma]\!]_{\mathbf{M}} & & [\![\Gamma, y:\beta \vdash M:\gamma]\!]_{\mathbf{N}} \\
[\![\gamma]\!]_{\mathbf{M}} & \xrightarrow[\ h_\gamma\ ]{} & [\![\gamma]\!]_{\mathbf{N}}
\end{array}
$$

in the category $\mathcal{D}$, that is $h_\gamma \circ m = m' \circ (h_\Gamma \times h_\beta)$, or equivalently

$$h_\gamma \circ m \circ (id \times h_\beta^{-1}) = m' \circ (h_\Gamma \times id). \tag{1}$$

Our aim is to prove that $(h_\beta^{-1} \Rightarrow h_\gamma) \circ \lambda(m) = \lambda(m') \circ h_\Gamma$, which by definition is

$$\underbrace{\lambda(h_\gamma \circ ev \circ (id \times h_\beta^{-1})) \circ \lambda(m)}_{l} = \underbrace{\lambda(m') \circ h_\Gamma}_{r}. \tag{2}$$

We shall prove (2) by showing that both l and r are equal to a certain derived exponential mate. We have

$$ev \circ ((\lambda(m') \circ h_\Gamma) \times id) = ev \circ (\lambda(m') \times id) \circ (h_\Gamma \times id) = m' \circ (h_\Gamma \times id)$$

implying that $\lambda(m' \circ (h_\Gamma \times id)) = \lambda(m') \circ h_\Gamma = r$, and we have

$$ev \circ ([\lambda(h_\gamma \circ ev \circ (id \times h_\beta^{-1})) \circ \lambda(m)] \times id)$$
$$= h_\gamma \circ ev \circ (id \times h_\beta^{-1}) \circ (\lambda(m) \times id)$$
$$= h_\gamma \circ m \circ (id \times h_\beta^{-1})$$

implying that

$$\lambda(h_\gamma \circ m \circ (id \times h_\beta^{-1})) = \lambda(h_\gamma \circ ev \circ (id \times h_\beta^{-1})) \circ \lambda(m) = l.$$

It follows from (1) that $l = r$. The other inductive cases proceed similarly.

To complete the proof we need we need to define natural isomorphisms

$$\epsilon : Ap_{\mathbf{G}} Ap_{\mathbf{G}}^{-1} \cong id_{\mathcal{M}od \simeq (Th, \mathcal{D})} \quad \text{and} \quad \eta : id_{\mathcal{C}\mathcal{C}at \simeq (Cl(Th), \mathcal{D})} \cong Ap_{\mathbf{G}}^{-1} Ap_{\mathbf{G}}.$$

We define ϵ by taking a model $\mathbf{M}$ of Th in $\mathcal{D}$ and giving the component $\epsilon_{\mathbf{M}} : Ap_{\mathbf{G}}(Ap_{\mathbf{G}}^{-1}\mathbf{M}) \to \mathbf{M}$, and we can define this homomorphism by giving its components at a ground type γ of Th. Working the details we see that $(\epsilon_{\mathbf{M}})_\gamma : [\![\gamma]\!]_{\mathbf{M}} \to [\![\gamma]\!]_{\mathbf{M}}$, and we take this to be $id_{[\![\gamma]\!]_{\mathbf{M}}}$, certainly an isomorphism. Similarly, given a cartesian closed functor $F: Cl(Th) \to \mathcal{D}$, and noting that $Ap_{\mathbf{G}}^{-1}(Ap_{\mathbf{G}}F)(\alpha) = F([\![\alpha]\!]_{\mathbf{G}}) = F\alpha$, we define $(\eta_F)_\alpha \stackrel{\mathrm{def}}{=} id : F\alpha \to F\alpha$. This completes the proof. $\qquad\square$

EXERCISES 4.8.5

(1) Why is the soundness theorem crucial to the definition of Ap_G^{-1}?

(2) Verify some of the cases which occur in the inductive proof that $Ap_G^{-1}h$ is a natural isomorphism.

(3) Verify that $\epsilon_M : Ap_G(Ap_G^{-1}M) \to M$ is a homomorphism of models—take care with this.

COROLLARY 4.8.6   The canonical classifying category satisfies the universal property of Proposition 4.8.2 in a strong way. Given a cartesian closed category C and a model M of a $\lambda\times$-theory Th in C, there is (up to canonical isomorphism) a unique cartesian closed functor $F : Cl(Th) \to C$ for which $F_*G = M$.

PROOF   Define $F \stackrel{\text{def}}{=} Ap_G^{-1}M$—see page 178. It is routine to verify that $F_*G = M$. The action of F is essentially to apply the structure $[\![-]\!]_M$. For example, consider a function symbol $f : \alpha_1, \alpha_2 \to \beta$. Then

$$
\begin{aligned}
[\![f]\!]_{F_*G} &= F(z : \alpha_1 \times \alpha_2 \mid f(\mathsf{Proj}_1(z), \mathsf{Proj}_2(z))) \\
&= [\![z : \alpha_1 \times \alpha_2 \vdash f(\mathsf{Proj}_1(z), \mathsf{Proj}_2(z)) : \beta]\!]_M \\
&= [\![f]\!]_M \circ \langle [\![z : \alpha_1 \times \alpha_2 \vdash \mathsf{Fst}(z) : \alpha_1]\!]_M, [\![z : \alpha_1 \times \alpha_2 \vdash \mathsf{Snd}(z) : \alpha_2]\!]_M \rangle \\
&= [\![f]\!]_M \circ \langle \pi, \pi' \rangle \\
&= [\![f]\!]_M.
\end{aligned}
$$

Suppose that there is another cartesian closed functor $F' : Cl(Th) \to C$ for which $F'_*G = M$. If α is an object of $Cl(Th)$ then

$$
F\alpha \stackrel{\text{def}}{=} [\![\alpha]\!]_M = [\![\alpha]\!]_{F_*G} \cong F'[\![\alpha]\!]_G = F'\alpha
$$

because F' preserves finite products and exponentials, and this gives rise to a natural isomorphism $F \cong F'$.   □

EXERCISE 4.8.7   Prove that $F \cong F'$ in Corollary 4.8.6.

4.9   The Categorical Type Theory Correspondence

DISCUSSION 4.9.1   We aim to show that, in a sense to be made precise, $\lambda\times$-theories and cartesian closed categories are essentially the same. First we show that any cartesian closed category C gives rise to a $\lambda\times$-theory $Th(C)$ in a very simple way, and then show that this process is mutually inverse to that of constructing a classifying category of such a theory.

THEOREM 4.9.2   For every cartesian closed category $\mathcal{C}$ we can associate a particular $\lambda\times$-theory, $Th(\mathcal{C}) \overset{\text{def}}{=} (Sg(\mathcal{C}), Ax(\mathcal{C}))$. There is a canonical model of the $\lambda\times$-theory $Th(\mathcal{C})$ in $\mathcal{C}$.

PROOF   The $\lambda\times$-signature $Sg(\mathcal{C})$ has ground types which are copies of the objects of $\mathcal{C}$ and function symbols which are copies of the morphisms of $\mathcal{C}$, together with some distinguished function symbols which will witness certain isomorphisms. More precisely, for each object A of $\mathcal{C}$ there is a ground type A. The types of $Sg(\mathcal{C})$ are therefore given by a grammar

$$\alpha ::= unit \mid A \mid \alpha \,^{\ulcorner}\times^{\urcorner}\, \alpha \mid \alpha \,^{\ulcorner}\Rightarrow^{\urcorner}\, \alpha$$

where A is any object of $\mathcal{C}$, and the notation $^{\ulcorner}\times^{\urcorner}$ simply distinguishes formal binary products of $Sg(\mathcal{C})$ from binary products $\times$ in $\mathcal{C}$ (and similarly for $\Rightarrow$). For each morphism of the form $k\colon 1 \to A$ in $\mathcal{C}$ there is a constant function symbol $k\colon A$, and for each morphism of the form $f\colon A_1 \times \ldots \times A_n \to B$ in $\mathcal{C}$ there is a function symbol $f\colon A_1, \ldots, A_n \to B$. There are also function symbols, each of arity 1, with the following sortings:

- $I_\alpha\colon [\![\alpha]\!] \to \alpha$, and

- $J_\alpha\colon \alpha \to [\![\alpha]\!]$ where $[\![\alpha]\!]$ is defined below. (Here, α runs over all types of $Sg(\mathcal{C})$).

The canonical structure $\mathbf{M}$ for $Sg(\mathcal{C})$ in $\mathcal{C}$ is defined by setting $[\![A]\!] \overset{\text{def}}{=} A$ for each ground type of $Sg(\mathcal{C})$, $[\![k]\!] = k$, $[\![f]\!] \overset{\text{def}}{=} f$ and $[\![I_\alpha]\!] = [\![J_\alpha]\!] \overset{\text{def}}{=} id_{[\![\alpha]\!]}$. (Note that *by definition* we have $[\![\alpha \,^{\ulcorner}\times^{\urcorner}\, \beta]\!] \overset{\text{def}}{=} [\![\alpha]\!] \times [\![\beta]\!]$ and $[\![\alpha \,^{\ulcorner}\Rightarrow^{\urcorner}\, \beta]\!] \overset{\text{def}}{=} [\![\alpha]\!] \Rightarrow [\![\beta]\!]$— see Discussion 4.5.1).

The collection of axioms $Ax(\mathcal{C})$ consists of those equations-in-context generated from $Sg(\mathcal{C})$ which are satisfied by $\mathbf{M}$. This means that $\mathbf{M}$ is indeed a model of $Th(\mathcal{C})$ in $\mathcal{C}$.   ☐

THEOREM 4.9.3   There is an equivalence of categories $Eq\colon Cl(Th(\mathcal{C})) \to \mathcal{C}$ for each cartesian closed category $\mathcal{C}$, where Eq is the functor arising from the universal property of $Cl(Th)$ applied to the canonical model $\mathbf{M}$ of $Th(\mathcal{C})$ in $\mathcal{C}$.

PROOF   We write $[\![-]\!]$ for the model $\mathbf{M}$ of $Th(\mathcal{C})$ in $\mathcal{C}$, and $\mathcal{D}$ for $Cl(Th(\mathcal{C}))$. Recall that the functor $Eq\colon \mathcal{D} \to \mathcal{C}$ is defined by $Eq(\alpha) \overset{\text{def}}{=} [\![\alpha]\!]$ on objects and

$$Eq(x\colon \alpha \mid M) \overset{\text{def}}{=} [\![x\colon \alpha \vdash M\colon \beta]\!]$$

on morphisms. We define $Eq^{-1}\colon \mathcal{C} \to \mathcal{D}$ by setting $Eq^{-1}(A) \overset{\text{def}}{=} A$ at any object A of $\mathcal{C}$ and $Eq^{-1}(f) \overset{\text{def}}{=} (x\colon A \mid f(x))$ at any morphism $f\colon A \to B$ of $\mathcal{C}$.

First we show that $Eq \circ Eq^{-1} \cong id_{\mathcal{C}}$. Let us define natural transformations $\epsilon\colon Eq \circ Eq^{-1} \to id_{\mathcal{C}}$ and $\nu\colon id_{\mathcal{C}} \to Eq \circ Eq^{-1}$ by setting

$$\epsilon_A \overset{\text{def}}{=} id_A\colon A \to A$$

$$\nu_A \overset{\text{def}}{=} id_A\colon A \to A.$$

It is trivial to see that $\epsilon\nu = id_{id_{\mathcal{C}}}$ and that $\nu\epsilon = id_{Eq \circ Eq^{-1}}$, and that ϵ and ν are indeed natural transformations.

Second we show that $Eq^{-1} \circ Eq \cong id_{\mathcal{D}}$. Let us define natural transformations $\mu\colon Eq^{-1} \circ Eq \to id_{\mathcal{D}}$ and $\eta\colon id_{\mathcal{D}} \to Eq^{-1} \circ Eq$ by setting

- $\mu_\alpha \overset{\text{def}}{=} (x\colon \llbracket \alpha \rrbracket \mid I_\alpha(x))$, and

- $\eta_\alpha \overset{\text{def}}{=} (x\colon \alpha \mid J_\alpha(x))$.

Appealing to Lemma 2.5.3, we need to show that one of μ and η is a natural transformation and that their components witness isomorphisms in $\mathcal{D}$. These calculations are tedious but trivial. We show that μ is natural. Take any morphism $(x\colon \alpha \mid M)\colon \alpha \to \beta$ of $\mathcal{D}$. We need to show that the diagram

$$
\begin{array}{ccc}
\llbracket \alpha \rrbracket & \overset{\mu_\alpha}{\longrightarrow} & \alpha \\
{\scriptstyle (z\colon \llbracket \alpha \rrbracket \mid m(z))} \downarrow & & \downarrow {\scriptstyle (x\colon \alpha \mid M)} \\
\llbracket \beta \rrbracket & \underset{\mu_\beta}{\longrightarrow} & \beta
\end{array}
$$

commutes, where $m \overset{\text{def}}{=} \llbracket x\colon \alpha \vdash M\colon \beta \rrbracket$, that is we wish to prove

$$(z\colon \llbracket \alpha \rrbracket \mid I_\beta(m(z))) = (z\colon \llbracket \alpha \rrbracket \mid M[I_\alpha(z)/x])$$

in $\mathcal{D}$. But this is the case, for in the canonical model **M** we have

$$\llbracket z\colon \llbracket \alpha \rrbracket \vdash I_\beta(m(z))\colon \beta \rrbracket = id_{\llbracket \beta \rrbracket} \circ m = m \circ id_{\llbracket \alpha \rrbracket} = \llbracket z\colon \llbracket \alpha \rrbracket \vdash M[I_\alpha(z)/x]\colon \beta \rrbracket.$$

$\square$

EXERCISE 4.9.4   Work through the details of the proof of Theorem 4.9.3, especially the verification that μ and η make up a natural isomorphism in the final paragraph. Note that the function symbols I and J are saying *in essence* that if A and B are objects of $\mathcal{C}$, then the objects $A \ulcorner \times \urcorner B$ and $A \times B$ of $Cl(Th(\mathcal{C}))$ *are isomorphic*—and similarly for $\Rightarrow$.

We can summarise our recent deductions in the following slogan:

— Categorical Type Theory Correspondence ——————

Theorem 4.9.3 is the basis of the slogan that cartesian closed categories give a notion of $\lambda\times$-theory which is syntax independent.

DISCUSSION 4.9.5   The *internal language* of a cartesian closed category $\mathcal{C}$ is the theory $Th(\mathcal{C})$. We can use the internal language to reason about the category $\mathcal{C}$. Let us give an example. Suppose we wish to prove that for any morphisms $f: A \times B \to C$ and $g: C \to D$ in $\mathcal{C}$ that $\lambda(gf) = \lambda(g \circ ev)\lambda(f)$. We can prove this directly using the universal property of exponentials. We have

$$
\begin{aligned}
ev \circ (\lambda(g \circ ev)\lambda(f) \times id) &= ev \circ (\lambda(g \circ ev) \times id) \circ (\lambda(f) \times id) \\
&= g \circ ev \circ (\lambda(f) \times id) \\
&= gf
\end{aligned}
$$

and hence the required equality follows from the said universal property.

However, we can proceed more directly using the internal language. We write down proved terms of $Th(\mathcal{C})$ which make use of the *function symbols* $f: A, B \to C$ and $g: C \to D$, namely

$$
Sg \;\rhd\; x{:}A \;\vdash\; \lambda y{:}B.f(x,y){:}B \Rightarrow C
$$
$$
Sg \;\rhd\; z{:}B \Rightarrow C \;\vdash\; \lambda w{:}B.g(zw){:}B \Rightarrow D
$$

and so $Sg \;\rhd\; x{:}A \vdash \lambda w{:}B.g((\lambda y{:}B.f(x,y))\,w){:}B \Rightarrow D$. This latter proved term "corresponds" to the composition of $\lambda(g \circ ev)$ and $\lambda(f)$. But

$$
Th \;\rhd\; x{:}A \vdash \lambda w{:}B.g(\lambda y{:}B.f(x,y)\,w) = \lambda w{:}B.g(f(x,w)){:}B \Rightarrow D
$$

and so writing $[\![-]\!]$ for the canonical model of $Th(\mathcal{C})$ in $\mathcal{C}$ we have

$$
\begin{aligned}
\lambda(gf) &= [\![x{:}A \vdash \lambda w{:}B.g(f(x,w)){:}B \Rightarrow D]\!] \\
&= [\![x{:}A \vdash \lambda w{:}B.g((\lambda y{:}B.f(x,y))\,w){:}B \Rightarrow D]\!] \\
&= \lambda(g \circ ev)\lambda(f).
\end{aligned}
$$

With a little practice, it becomes very easy to write down proved terms of an internal language which correspond to given morphisms, and to then prove statements about the morphisms by using rules for deducing theorems in the internal language. Note that the *crucial* step in the above proof using the internal language is the *derivation* of the given theorem *from* the proved terms, which is easier than the corresponding calculations involving the category morphisms f and g.

DISCUSSION 4.9.6   The notion of a translation of one $\lambda\times$-theory into another is similar to that for algebraic theories. However, the presence of a syntax for binary products in a $\lambda\times$-theory makes the definition of such a translation a little simpler than that for algebraic theories, as we shall see. Let us suppose that Th and Th' are $\lambda\times$-theories. Then we define a *translation* of the theory Th in the theory Th', written $T: Th \to Th'$, to be given by a cartesian closed functor $Cl(Th) \to Cl(Th')$. Using the equivalence

$$Ap_{\mathbf{G}} : \mathcal{CCat}_{\cong}(Cl(Th), Cl(Th')) \simeq \mathcal{Mod}_{\cong}(Th, Cl(Th'))$$

we can see that to specify T amounts to giving a model $\mathbf{T}: Th \to Cl(Th')$. Let us look at the data needed to specify such a model. Our task is to define a structure for the theory Th in the cartesian closed category $Cl(Th')$. First, for each of the ground types γ of Th, we will have to give an object $[\![\gamma]\!]_{\mathbf{T}}$ of $Cl(Th')$, that is a type α' of Th'. Second, for each basic function symbol $f: \alpha_1, \ldots, \alpha_n \to \beta$ of Th, we have to specify a morphism $[\![f]\!]_{\mathbf{T}}: [\![\alpha_1]\!]_{\mathbf{T}} \times \ldots \times [\![\alpha_n]\!]_{\mathbf{T}} \to [\![\beta]\!]_{\mathbf{T}}$ in $Cl(Th')$. If we suppose that the source of this morphism is $\alpha'_1 \times \ldots \times \alpha'_n$ and the target β' then the morphism $[\![f]\!]_{\mathbf{T}} = (z: \Pi_1^n \alpha'_i \mid N)$ will be given by a proved term $Sg' \;\triangleright\; z: \Pi_1^n \alpha'_i \vdash N: \beta'$. This gives us a structure for Th in $Cl(Th')$. For this structure to be a model, the axioms of Th must be satisfied by the structure. If we work through the details, we see that this will be the case if for every axiom $Ax \;\triangleright\; \Gamma \vdash M = M': \alpha$ of Th for which

$$[\![\Gamma \vdash M: \alpha]\!]_{\mathbf{T}} \;=\; (z: [\![\Gamma]\!]_{\mathbf{T}} \mid N) : [\![\Gamma]\!]_{\mathbf{T}} \to [\![\alpha]\!]_{\mathbf{T}}$$
$$[\![\Gamma \vdash M': \alpha]\!]_{\mathbf{T}} \;=\; (z: [\![\Gamma]\!]_{\mathbf{T}} \mid N') : [\![\Gamma]\!]_{\mathbf{T}} \to [\![\alpha]\!]_{\mathbf{T}}$$

for some raw terms N and N' of Th', then $Th' \;\triangleright\; z: [\![\Gamma]\!]_{\mathbf{T}} \vdash N = N': [\![\alpha]\!]_{\mathbf{T}}$. We can summarise this as follows. A translation $Th \to Th'$ between $\lambda\times$-theories amounts to giving a type of Th' for each ground type of Th and a proved term of Th' for each function symbol of Th, such that the induced translation of proved terms of Th into proved terms of Th' (via the structure $[\![-]\!]_{\mathbf{T}}$) carries axioms of Th into theorems of Th'.

We can say that Th and Th' are *equivalent*, $Th \simeq Th'$, if the corresponding classifying categories are equivalent. One can then show

THEOREM 4.9.7   For any $\lambda\times$-theory we have $Th \simeq Th(Cl(Th))$.

PROOF   Routine manipulations of the definitions. $\square$

4.10   Categorical Gluing

DISCUSSION 4.10.1   In this section, we shall apply techniques of category theory and categorical semantics to prove a result about $\lambda\times$-theories which have been generated from algebraic theories. By the $\lambda\times$-theory generated from a given algebraic theory, we mean the $\lambda\times$-theory which takes the types and function symbols of the algebraic signature as the ground types and function symbols of its $\lambda\times$-signature, and the axioms of the algebraic theory as its axioms. The result we are going to prove (stated formally in Theorem 4.10.7) says that any raw term of the $\lambda\times$-theory which has ground type is provably equal in the $\lambda\times$-theory to a raw term of the algebraic theory. We might interpret this informally by saying that if we enrich an algebraic theory with the syntax of functional type theory we will arrive at a "better" programming language which has "the same power" as the original.

In order to prove this result, we shall set up a little more category-theoretic machinery. Suppose that $\mathcal{C}$ is a category with finite products. Then a category $\mathcal{FC}$ is the *relatively free* cartesian closed category generated by $\mathcal{C}$ if there is a functor $I: \mathcal{C} \to \mathcal{FC}$ which satisfies the following two properties:

(i) Suppose that $F: \mathcal{C} \to \mathcal{D}$ is a finite product preserving functor and $\mathcal{D}$ is a cartesian closed category. Then there is a functor $\overline{F}: \mathcal{FC} \to \mathcal{D}$ which preserves finite products and exponentials, and for which the following diagram commutes up to natural isomorphism:

We shall write $\phi: \overline{F}I \cong F$ for this.

(ii) If also $\overline{\overline{F}}$ and $\overline{\phi}$ have the same properties as $\overline{F}$ and ϕ, then there is a unique natural isomorphism $\psi: \overline{F} \to \overline{\overline{F}}$ for which the following diagram commutes:

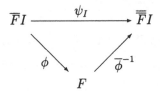

Let $Th = (Sg, Ax)$ be an algebraic theory. Let $Th' = (Sg', Ax')$ be the $\lambda\times$-theory for which the ground types of Sg' are the types of Sg, the function symbols of Sg' are the function symbols of Sg, and $Ax' \stackrel{\text{def}}{=} Ax$. We shall write $\mathcal{E}$ for the classifying category $Cl(Th)$ and $\mathcal{E}'$ for $Cl(Th')$. We shall now define a functor $I: \mathcal{E} \to \mathcal{E}'$. On an object $\vec{\gamma}$ of $\mathcal{E}$ set

$$I(\vec{\gamma}) \stackrel{\text{def}}{=} (\ldots (\gamma_1 \times \gamma_2) \times \ldots) \times \gamma_n$$

and given a morphism $(\Gamma \mid \vec{M})_{Th} \colon \vec{\gamma} \to \vec{\gamma'}$ (where the subscript Th denotes equivalence up to provable equality in Th), then we set

$$I(\Gamma \mid \vec{M})_{Th} \stackrel{\text{def}}{=} (z \colon \Pi \gamma_i \mid \langle \ldots \langle M_1', M_2' \rangle, \ldots, M_m' \rangle)_{Th'}$$

in which we have written $\Pi \gamma_i$ for $(\ldots (\gamma_1 \times \gamma_2) \times \ldots) \times \gamma_n$ and also

$$M_j' \stackrel{\text{def}}{=} M_j[\mathsf{Proj}_1(z)/x_1, \ldots, \mathsf{Proj}_j(z)/x_j, \ldots \mathsf{Proj}_n(z)/x_n]$$

where $\mathsf{Proj}_j(z)$ is defined on page 178.

Our programme for the rest of this section is as follows. First we prove Proposition 4.10.2 which shows that a certain classifying category plays the role of a relatively free cartesian closed category. Second, we prove a purely categorical result called the gluing lemma, which is Lemma 4.10.3. Third, we set up a final piece of notation in Discussion 4.10.5 and then prove Theorem 4.10.7.

PROPOSITION 4.10.2   The functor $I: \mathcal{E} \to \mathcal{E}'$ presents $\mathcal{E}'$ as the relatively free cartesian closed category generated by $\mathcal{E}$.

PROOF   Let $F: \mathcal{E} \to \mathcal{C}$ be a functor which preserves finite products where $\mathcal{C}$ is a cartesian closed category. We shall define a functor $\overline{F}: \mathcal{E}' \to \mathcal{C}$ (using the syntactic structure of the category $\mathcal{E}'$) through the following clauses. On objects we set

- $\overline{F}(unit) \stackrel{\text{def}}{=} 1_\mathcal{C}$, the terminal object of $\mathcal{C}$,
- $\overline{F}\gamma \stackrel{\text{def}}{=} F[\gamma]$ where γ is a ground type of Sg',
- $\overline{F}(\alpha \times \beta) \stackrel{\text{def}}{=} \overline{F}\alpha \times \overline{F}\beta$, and
- $\overline{F}(\alpha \Rightarrow \beta) \stackrel{\text{def}}{=} \overline{F}\alpha \Rightarrow \overline{F}\beta$.

On morphisms $(z \colon \delta \mid M)$ of $\mathcal{E}'$ we put

- $\overline{F}(z \colon \delta \mid \langle \rangle) \stackrel{\text{def}}{=} \, ! \colon \overline{F}\delta \to 1_\mathcal{C}$,
- $\overline{F}(z \colon \delta \mid z \colon \delta) \stackrel{\text{def}}{=} id_{\overline{F}\delta}$,
- $\overline{F}(z \colon \delta \mid f(\vec{M})) \stackrel{\text{def}}{=} F([x_1 \colon \gamma_1, \ldots, x_n \colon \gamma_n] \mid f(x_1, \ldots, x_n)) \circ$
$$\langle \overline{F}(z \colon \delta \mid M_1), \ldots, \overline{F}(z \colon \delta \mid M_n) \rangle,$$

- $\overline{F}(z\colon\delta \mid \mathsf{Fst}(P)) \overset{\text{def}}{=} \pi_1 \overline{F}(z\colon\delta \mid P)$ where $\pi_1\colon \overline{F}\alpha \times \overline{F}\beta \to \overline{F}\alpha$,

- $\overline{F}(z\colon\delta \mid \mathsf{Snd}(P)) \overset{\text{def}}{=} \pi_2 \overline{F}(z\colon\delta \mid P)$ where $\pi_2\colon \overline{F}\alpha \times \overline{F}\beta \to \overline{F}\beta$,

- $\overline{F}(z\colon\delta \mid \langle M, M'\rangle) \overset{\text{def}}{=} \langle \overline{F}(z\colon\delta \mid M), \overline{F}(z\colon\delta \mid M')\rangle$,

- $\overline{F}(z\colon\delta \mid MN) \overset{\text{def}}{=} ev\langle \overline{F}(z\colon\delta \mid M), \overline{F}(z\colon\delta \mid N)\rangle$,

- $\overline{F}(z\colon\delta \mid \lambda x\colon\alpha.M) \overset{\text{def}}{=} \lambda(\overline{F}(y\colon\delta \times \alpha \mid M[\mathsf{Fst}(y)/z]))$.

Note that $\overline{F}$ essentially preserves all of the structure of $\mathcal{E}'$ on the nose. It follows from this that $\overline{F}$ does indeed preserve finite products and exponentials, and that is $\overline{F}$ is a cartesian closed functor.

Now we shall define a natural isomorphism $\phi\colon \overline{F}I \cong F$. It follows from the definitions that given an object $\vec{\gamma}$ of $\mathcal{E}$, we have $\overline{F}I(\vec{\gamma}) = \Pi_1^n F[\gamma_i]$, and as F is finite product preserving we can set

$$\phi_{\vec{\gamma}} \overset{\text{def}}{=} \langle F\pi_1, \ldots, F\pi_n\rangle^{-1} : \Pi_1^n F[\gamma_i] \longrightarrow F(\vec{\gamma})$$

where $\pi_i\colon \vec{\gamma} \to [\gamma_i]$ in $\mathcal{E}$. Of course we have to check that ϕ is a natural transformation. The details are omitted, but the following fact will be needed. Suppose that $m\colon \vec{\gamma} \to \vec{\gamma}'$ is a morphism of $\mathcal{E}$. Then we have $\overline{F}I(m) = Fm$. This fact follows from the structural definition of the functor $\overline{F}$.

Suppose now that $\overline{\overline{F}}$ and $\overline{\phi}$ also satisfy the roles of $\overline{F}$ and ϕ. We shall define a natural isomorphism $\psi\colon \overline{F} \to \overline{\overline{F}}$ through the following clauses:

- $\psi_\gamma \overset{\text{def}}{=} \overline{\phi}_{[\gamma]}^{-1}\colon \overline{F}\gamma \to \overline{\overline{F}}\gamma$, where we note that $\overline{F}\gamma = F[\gamma]$ and $\overline{\overline{F}}\gamma = \overline{\overline{F}}I[\gamma]$,

- $\psi_{\alpha\times\beta} \overset{\text{def}}{=} \cong \circ \psi_\alpha \times \psi_\beta\colon (\overline{F}\alpha \times \overline{F}\beta) \to (\overline{\overline{F}}\alpha \times \overline{\overline{F}}\beta) \to \overline{\overline{F}}(\alpha \times \beta)$, and

- $\psi_{\alpha\Rightarrow\beta} \overset{\text{def}}{=} \cong \circ \psi_\alpha^{-1} \Rightarrow \psi_\beta\colon (\overline{F}\alpha \Rightarrow \overline{F}\beta) \to (\overline{\overline{F}}\alpha \Rightarrow \overline{\overline{F}}\beta) \to \overline{\overline{F}}(\alpha \Rightarrow \beta)$,

in which the isomorphisms are the canonical ones. It is clear from the definition that the morphisms ψ_α are always isomorphisms. It remains to see that ψ is a natural transformation. Suppose that $m\colon \alpha \to \beta$ is a morphism in $\mathcal{E}'$. Then we need to check that the diagram

$$
\begin{array}{ccc}
\overline{F}\alpha & \xrightarrow{\;\psi_\alpha\;} & \overline{\overline{F}}\alpha \\
{\scriptstyle \overline{F}m}\big\downarrow & (*) & \big\downarrow{\scriptstyle \overline{\overline{F}}m} \\
\overline{F}\alpha & \xrightarrow[\;\psi_\beta\;]{} & \overline{\overline{F}}\beta
\end{array}
$$

commutes. Any such morphism m is of the form $(x\colon\alpha \mid M)$; we prove that the diagram $(*)$ commutes by structural induction on the raw term M. We shall give an example of just one case, namely $m \stackrel{\text{def}}{=} (z\colon\delta \mid \lambda x\colon\alpha.M)\colon \delta \to \alpha \Rightarrow \beta$. So it remains to check the commutativity of the diagram

$$
\begin{array}{ccc}
\overline{F}\delta & \xrightarrow{\;\;\psi_\delta\;\;} & \overline{\overline{F}}\delta \\[4pt]
{\scriptstyle\overline{F}(z\colon\delta\,\mid\,\lambda x\colon\alpha.M)}\big\downarrow & & \big\downarrow{\scriptstyle\overline{\overline{F}}(z\colon\delta\,\mid\,\lambda x\colon\alpha.M)} \\[4pt]
\overline{F}\alpha \Rightarrow \overline{F}\beta & \xrightarrow[{\psi_\alpha^{-1} \Rightarrow \psi_\beta}]{} & \overline{\overline{F}}\alpha \Rightarrow \overline{\overline{F}}\beta \;\cong\; \overline{\overline{F}}(\alpha \Rightarrow \beta)
\end{array}
$$

Now, of course $\overline{\overline{F}}$ preserves binary products, and so our task is equivalently to see that the diagram

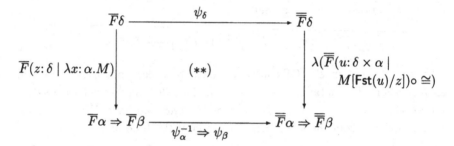

$$
\begin{array}{ccc}
\overline{F}\delta & \xrightarrow{\;\;\psi_\delta\;\;} & \overline{\overline{F}}\delta \\[4pt]
{\scriptstyle\overline{F}(z\colon\delta\,\mid\,\lambda x\colon\alpha.M)}\big\downarrow & (**) & \big\downarrow{\scriptstyle\lambda(\overline{\overline{F}}(u\colon\delta\times\alpha\mid M[\mathsf{Fst}(u)/z])\circ\,\cong)} \\[4pt]
\overline{F}\alpha \Rightarrow \overline{F}\beta & \xrightarrow[{\psi_\alpha^{-1} \Rightarrow \psi_\beta}]{} & \overline{\overline{F}}\alpha \Rightarrow \overline{\overline{F}}\beta
\end{array}
$$

commutes, where $\overline{\overline{F}}\delta \times \overline{\overline{F}}\alpha \cong \overline{\overline{F}}(\delta \times \alpha)$. Now, by induction, the following diagram commutes:

$$
\begin{array}{ccc}
\overline{F}(\delta \times \alpha) & \xrightarrow{\;\;\psi_{\delta\times\alpha}\;\;} & \overline{\overline{F}}(\delta \times \alpha) \\[4pt]
{\scriptstyle\overline{F}(u\colon\delta\times\alpha\,\mid\,M[\mathsf{Fst}(u)/z])}\big\downarrow & & \big\downarrow{\scriptstyle\overline{\overline{F}}(u\colon\delta\times\alpha\,\mid\,M[\mathsf{Fst}(u)/z])} \\[4pt]
\overline{F}\beta & \xrightarrow[{\psi_\beta}]{} & \overline{\overline{F}}\beta
\end{array}
$$

and so we have

$$
f \stackrel{\text{def}}{=} \overline{\overline{F}}(u\colon\delta\times\alpha \mid M[\mathsf{Fst}(u)/z]) \circ \psi_{\delta\times\alpha} \circ (id_{\overline{F}\delta} \times \psi_\alpha^{-1})
$$

$$
= \psi_\beta \circ \overline{F}(u\colon\delta\times\alpha \mid M[\mathsf{Fst}(u)/z]) \circ (id_{\overline{F}\delta} \times \psi_\alpha^{-1})\colon \overline{F}\delta \times \overline{\overline{F}}\alpha \to \overline{\overline{F}}\beta.
$$

We show that of each of the paths of $(**)$ is the exponential mate of f, implying that $(**)$ commutes via the universal property of exponentials. So,

$$ev \circ ([(\psi_\alpha^{-1} \Rightarrow \psi_\beta) \circ \overline{F}(z\!:\!\delta \mid \lambda x\!:\!\alpha.M)] \times id_{\overline{\overline{F}}\alpha})$$

$$= \psi_\beta \circ ev \circ (id_{\overline{\overline{F}}\alpha \Rightarrow \overline{\overline{F}}\beta} \times \psi_\alpha^{-1}) \circ (\overline{F}(z\!:\!\delta \mid \lambda x\!:\!\alpha.M) \times id_{\overline{\overline{F}}\alpha})$$

$$= \psi_\beta \circ ev \circ (\lambda(\overline{F}(u\!:\!\delta \times \alpha \mid M[\mathsf{Fst}(u)/z])) \times id_{\overline{F}\alpha}) \circ (id_{\overline{F}\delta} \times \psi_\alpha^{-1})$$

$$= \psi_\beta \circ \overline{F}(u\!:\!\delta \times \alpha \mid M[\mathsf{Fst}(u)/z]) \circ (id_{\overline{F}\delta} \times \psi_\alpha^{-1})$$

$$= f,$$

and also

$$ev \circ ([\lambda(\overline{\overline{F}}(u\!:\!\delta \times \alpha \mid M[\mathsf{Fst}(u)/z]) \circ \cong) \circ \psi_\delta] \times id_{\overline{\overline{F}}\alpha})$$

$$= \overline{\overline{F}}(u\!:\!\delta \times \alpha \mid M[\mathsf{Fst}(u)/z]) \circ \cong \circ (\psi_\delta \times id_{\overline{\overline{F}}\alpha})$$

$$= \overline{\overline{F}}(u\!:\!\delta \times \alpha \mid M[\mathsf{Fst}(u)/z]) \circ \cong \circ (\psi_\delta \times \psi_\alpha)(id_{\overline{F}\delta} \times \psi_\alpha^{-1})$$

$$= f$$

as required. The other inductive cases are similar; we deduce that ψ is indeed a natural transformation.

The final task is to verify that $\psi_I = \overline{\phi}^{-1}\phi\!:\!FI \to \overline{\overline{F}}I$. The details are omitted, but we remark that the equality follows essentially from the naturality of $\overline{\phi}^{-1}\!:\!F \to \overline{\overline{F}}I$ in $\vec{\gamma}$ at morphisms of the form $\pi_i\!:\!\vec{\gamma} \to [\gamma_i]$. This completes the proof. □

LEMMA 4.10.3   Suppose that $\mathcal{C}$ and $\mathcal{D}$ are cartesian closed categories and that $\Gamma\!:\!\mathcal{C} \to \mathcal{D}$ is a functor which preserves finite products. Suppose also that $\mathcal{D}$ has all pullbacks. Then the comma category $\mathcal{G}l(\Gamma) \stackrel{\mathrm{def}}{=} (id_\mathcal{D} \downarrow \Gamma)$ is also a cartesian closed category and the projection functor $P_2\!:\!\mathcal{G}l(\Gamma) \to \mathcal{C}$ defined by

$$(d,c)\!:\!(D,f,C) \to (D',f',C') \longmapsto c\!:\!C \to C'$$

(where of course $(d,c)\!:\!(D,f,C) \to (D',f',C')$ is any morphism of $\mathcal{G}l(\Gamma)$) is a cartesian closed functor. $\mathcal{G}l(\Gamma)$ is called a *glued* category. We say that $\mathcal{C}$ has been glued to $\mathcal{D}$ along the functor Γ.

PROOF   Let (D,f,C) and (D',f',C') be objects of $\mathcal{G}l(\Gamma)$. Then the object part of the definition of binary product is given by

$$(D,f,C) \times (D',f',C') \stackrel{\mathrm{def}}{=} (D \times D', \cong \circ (f \times f'), C \times C')$$

where $\cong\!:\!\Gamma C \times \Gamma C' \to \Gamma(C \times C')$ arises from the fact that Γ preserves finite products; and exponentials are defined by

$$(D,f,C) \Rightarrow (D',f',C') \stackrel{\mathrm{def}}{=} ((D \Rightarrow D') \times \Gamma(C \Rightarrow C'), \pi_2, C \Rightarrow C')$$

where π_2 is given by the pullback

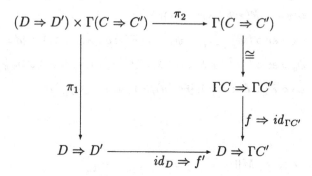

$$(D \Rightarrow D') \times \Gamma(C \Rightarrow C') \xrightarrow{\quad \pi_2 \quad} \Gamma(C \Rightarrow C')$$

EXERCISE 4.10.4   Complete the proof of Lemma 4.10.3. Now let $\mathcal{C}$ be any category. Prove that the Yoneda embedding $H \colon \mathcal{C} \to [\mathcal{C}^{op}, Set]$ preserves any finite product which exists in $\mathcal{C}$.

DISCUSSION 4.10.5   Define the functor $I^* \colon [\mathcal{FC}^{op}, Set] \to [\mathcal{C}^{op}, Set]$ (where $I \colon \mathcal{C} \to \mathcal{FC}$ is realising $\mathcal{FC}$ as the relatively free cartesian closed category generated by $\mathcal{C}$) by taking the morphism $\alpha \colon F \to G$ to the morphism $\alpha_I \colon FI \to GI$. Now set Γ to be the functor which is given by the composition

$$I^* \circ H : \mathcal{FC} \longrightarrow [\mathcal{FC}^{op}, Set] \longrightarrow [\mathcal{C}^{op}, Set],$$

where H is the Yoneda embedding. By definition, $\mathcal{FC}$ is a cartesian closed category, and the category of presheaves on $\mathcal{C}$ is also cartesian closed and has pullbacks; see page 114. Further, Γ preserves finite products, and so we can apply the gluing lemma (Lemma 4.10.3) to deduce that the comma category $\mathcal{Gl}(\Gamma) \stackrel{\text{def}}{=} (id_{[\mathcal{C}^{op}, Set]} \downarrow \Gamma)$ is a cartesian closed category and the functor $P_2 \colon \mathcal{Gl}(\Gamma) \to \mathcal{FC}$, which takes a morphism $(\alpha, h) \colon (F, \beta, D) \to (G, \beta', E)$ to $h \colon D \to E$, preserves finite products and exponentials.

We shall also define a functor $J \colon \mathcal{C} \to \mathcal{Gl}(\Gamma)$ by sending the morphism $f \colon A \to B$ of $\mathcal{C}$ to

$$(H_f, If) \colon (H_A, I_A, IA) \to (H_B, I_B, IB)$$

where the natural transformation $I_A \colon H_A \to \Gamma IA$ has component

$$(I_A)_C \colon \mathcal{C}(C, A) \to \mathcal{FC}(IC, IA)$$

at the object C of $\mathcal{C}^{op}$ which sends a morphism $g \colon C \to A$ of $\mathcal{C}$ to $Ig \colon IC \to IA$. Note that J preserves finite products because H and I do, and that J is full and faithful because H is. After the next exercise we can state and prove the main result of this section.

EXERCISE 4.10.6   Prove that the functor $J: \mathcal{C} \to \mathcal{G}l(\Gamma)$ of Discussion 4.10.5 is full, faithful and preserves finite products.

THEOREM 4.10.7   Let $Th = (Sg, Ax)$ be an algebraic theory. Let $Th' = (Sg', Ax')$ be the $\lambda\times$-theory for which the ground types of Sg' are the types of Sg, the function symbols of Sg' are the function symbols of Sg, and $Ax' \overset{\text{def}}{=} Ax$. Suppose that

$$Sg \;\rhd\; x_1{:}\gamma_1, \ldots, x_n{:}\gamma_n \vdash E{:}\gamma$$

is a proved term generated from the $\lambda\times$-signature Sg', where the types γ_i appearing in the context and the type γ are ground types of Sg', that is, types of Sg. Let us write $\Gamma \overset{\text{def}}{=} [x_1{:}\gamma_1, \ldots, x_n{:}\gamma_n]$. Then there is a raw term M for which

$$Sg \;\rhd\; \Gamma \vdash M{:}\gamma \quad \text{and} \quad Th' \;\rhd\; \Gamma \vdash E = M{:}\gamma.$$

Moreover, if there is another raw term M' for which $Sg \;\rhd\; \Gamma \vdash M'{:}\gamma$ and also $Th' \;\rhd\; \Gamma \vdash E = M'{:}\gamma$ then we have $Th \;\rhd\; \Gamma \vdash M = M'{:}\gamma$.

PROOF   Consider the following diagram

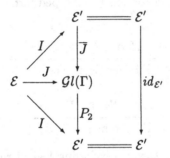

Using Proposition 4.10.2, the functor $\overline{J}$ exists and $\overline{J}I \cong J$ naturally. By definition, $P_2 J = I$. It follows that $P_2 \circ \overline{J} \circ I \cong I$ naturally, that is $(P_2 \circ \overline{J}) \circ I \cong I$, and as $id_{\mathcal{E}'} \circ I \cong I$ (trivially!) it follows from the defining property of relatively free cartesian closed category and Proposition 4.10.2 that $id_{\mathcal{E}'} \cong P_2 \overline{J}$ naturally. This latter isomorphism implies that $\overline{J}$ is faithful. This fact, together with J full and faithful by construction and $\overline{J}I \cong J$ implies that I is full and faithful. The fact that I is full and faithful proves the theorem: we expand on the details for the existence part of the theorem. Suppose that $Sg' \;\rhd\; x_1{:}\gamma_1, \ldots, x_n{:}\gamma_n \vdash E{:}\gamma$. We shall write

$$\widehat{E} \overset{\text{def}}{=} E[\mathsf{Proj}_1(z)/x_1, \ldots, \mathsf{Proj}_j(z)/x_j, \ldots, \mathsf{Proj}_n(z)/x_n]$$

and

$$\Pi\vec{\gamma} \overset{\text{def}}{=} (\ldots (\gamma_1 \times \gamma_2) \times \ldots) \times \gamma_n.$$

Then we certainly have $e \overset{\text{def}}{=} (z \colon \Pi\vec{\gamma} \mid \widehat{E})_{Th'} \colon I\vec{\gamma} \to I[\gamma]$ in $\mathcal{E}'$. Using the fullness of I, there is a morphism $([x_1 \colon \gamma_1, \dots, x_n \colon \gamma_n] \mid M)_{Th} \colon \vec{\gamma} \to [\gamma]$ which is taken to e by I. But this implies that $Th' \rhd z \colon \Pi\vec{\gamma} \vdash \widehat{M} = \widehat{E} \colon \gamma$ (using an obvious notation for $\widehat{M}$) that is $Th' \rhd x_1 \colon \gamma_1, \dots, x_n \colon \gamma_n \vdash M = E \colon \gamma$. The uniqueness part of the theorem follows from I's faithfulness in a similar fashion. $\square$

4.11   Further Exercises

(1) State a completeness result for $\lambda\times$-theories and prove it.

(2) In this exercise we derive a categorical semantics for a very small type theory in a (for convenience locally small) category $\mathcal{C}$ with finite products. The types are given by the grammar $\alpha ::= \gamma \mid \alpha \square \alpha$ where γ is any given ground type. The raw terms are given by

$$M ::= x \mid \mathsf{Vec}(M, M) \mid \mathsf{Atom}(M, x.y.M)$$

where x is a variable. In any raw term $\mathsf{Atom}(P, x.y.E)$, variables x and y are bound in E. The rules for introducing well typed terms-in-context (the proved terms) are

$$\frac{Sg \ \rhd \ \Gamma \vdash M \colon \alpha \quad Sg \ \rhd \ \Gamma \vdash N \colon \beta}{Sg \ \rhd \ \Gamma \vdash \mathsf{Vec}(M, N) \colon \alpha \square \beta} \quad (1)$$

$$\frac{Sg \ \rhd \ \Gamma \vdash P \colon \alpha \square \beta \quad Sg \ \rhd \ \Gamma, x \colon \alpha, y \colon \beta \vdash E \colon \delta}{Sg \ \rhd \ \Gamma \vdash \mathsf{Atom}(P, x.y.E) \colon \delta} \quad (2)$$

The pure equations of the theory (excluding logical rules such as equational reasoning, weakening of contexts etc) are

$$\frac{Sg \ \rhd \ \Gamma \vdash M \colon \alpha \quad Sg \ \rhd \ \Gamma \vdash N \colon \beta \quad Sg \ \rhd \ \Gamma, x \colon \alpha, y \colon \beta \vdash E \colon \delta}{Th \ \rhd \ \Gamma \vdash \mathsf{Atom}(\mathsf{Vec}(M, N), x.y.E) = E[M/x, N/y] \colon \delta} \quad (3)$$

$$\frac{Sg \ \rhd \ \Gamma \vdash P \colon \alpha \square \beta \quad Sg \ \rhd \ \Gamma, z \colon \alpha \square \beta \vdash F \colon \delta}{Th \ \rhd \ \Gamma \vdash \mathsf{Atom}(P, x.y.F[\mathsf{Vec}(x, y)/z]) = F[P/z] \colon \delta} \quad (4)$$

(a) Write down the "expected" definition of substitution of a raw term for a variable in a raw term—note the variable binding.

(b) To model the types we shall require an object $A \square B$ for all objects A and B of $\mathcal{C}$. Deduce that to soundly interpret (1) we need a function

$$\Phi_C : \mathcal{C}(C, A) \times \mathcal{C}(C, B) \longrightarrow \mathcal{C}(C, A \square B)$$

for all objects A, B and C of $\mathcal{C}$ which is natural in C. By considering naturality in C at $\langle m, n \rangle: C \to A \times B$ where $m: C \to A$ and $n: C \to B$ are any morphisms of $\mathcal{C}$, show that Φ_C is determined by a morphism $v_1: A \times B \to A \,\square\, B$ where

$$\Phi_C(m, n) = v_1 \circ \langle m, n \rangle. \tag{1'}$$

(c) Show that to soundly interpret (2) we shall require a function

$$\Psi_C : \mathcal{C}(C, A \,\square\, B) \times \mathcal{C}(C \times A \times B, D) \longrightarrow \mathcal{C}(C, D)$$

natural in C. By considering naturality in C at $\langle id_C, p \rangle: C \to C \times (A \,\square\, B)$ deduce that Ψ_C is in fact determined by giving for each object C of $\mathcal{C}$ a function

$$\Theta_C : \mathcal{C}(C \times A \times B, D) \longrightarrow \mathcal{C}(C \times (A \,\square\, B), D)$$

natural in C, where
$$\Psi_C(p, e) = \Theta_C(e) \circ \langle id_C, p \rangle. \tag{2'}$$

(d) Hence show that to satisfy equation (3) we need

$$\Theta_C(e) \circ \langle id_C, v_1 \langle m, n \rangle \rangle = e \circ \langle id_C, m, n \rangle \tag{3'}$$

for all morphisms $m: C \to A$, $n: C \to B$ and $e: C \times A \times B \to D$ in $\mathcal{C}$, and to satisfy (4) we need

$$\Theta_C(f \circ (id_C \times v_1)) \circ \langle id_C, p \rangle = f \circ \langle id_C, p \rangle \tag{4'}$$

for all morphisms $p: C \to A \,\square\, B$ and $f: C \times (A \,\square\, B) \to D$ in $\mathcal{C}$.

(e) By thinking about the three projections from $C \times A \times B$ to each of A, B and C, and using an instance of (3'), deduce that (3') holds just in case

$$\Theta_C(e) \circ (id \times v_1) = e, \tag{5}$$

and show similarly that (4') holds just in case

$$\Theta_C(f \circ (id \times v_1)) = f, \tag{6}$$

where (5) and (6) hold for all e and f as above.

(f) Show that (5) and (6) imply that there is a natural isomorphism

$$\Theta_C : \mathcal{C}(C \times A \times B, D) \cong \mathcal{C}(C \times (A \,\square\, B), D) : \mathcal{C}(id_C \times v_1, id_D)$$

and by taking C to be 1 deduce that the function

$$\mathcal{C}(v_1, id_D) : \mathcal{C}(A \,\square\, B, D) \cong \mathcal{C}(A \times B, D) \qquad f \mapsto f \circ v_1$$

is an isomorphism (bijection). The functions $\mathcal{C}(v_1, id_D)$ define a natural transformation $H^{A\Box B} \to H^{A\times B}$ (as D runs over the objects of $\mathcal{C}$) with components given by "pre-composition with v_1." Use the Yoneda lemma to deduce that $A \Box B \cong A \times B$. Hence write down a sound categorical semantics of our type theory in a category with finite products.

(3) In this exercise we derive a categorical semantics for a type theory in which there is a type of booleans and a syntax for conditional expressions. We omit a formal definition of raw types and terms, for which the reader ought to be able to provide a definition if desired. There is no variable binding in this syntax. The proved terms are given by

$$\overline{Sg \;\rhd\; \Gamma \vdash \textsf{true}: bool} \qquad\qquad \overline{Sg \;\rhd\; \Gamma \vdash \textsf{false}: bool}$$

$$\frac{Sg \;\rhd\; \Gamma \vdash B: bool \quad Sg \;\rhd\; \Gamma \vdash M: \alpha \quad Sg \;\rhd\; \Gamma \vdash N: \alpha}{Sg \;\rhd\; \Gamma \vdash \textsf{Cond}(B, M, N): \alpha} \tag{1}$$

$$\frac{Sg \;\rhd\; \Gamma \vdash M: \alpha \quad Sg \;\rhd\; \Gamma \vdash N: \alpha}{Th \;\rhd\; \Gamma \vdash \textsf{Cond}(\textsf{true}, M, N) = M: \alpha} \tag{2}$$

$$\frac{Sg \;\rhd\; \Gamma \vdash M: \alpha \quad Sg \;\rhd\; \Gamma \vdash N: \alpha}{Th \;\rhd\; \Gamma \vdash \textsf{Cond}(\textsf{false}, M, N) = N: \alpha} \tag{2'}$$

$$\frac{Sg \;\rhd\; \Gamma \vdash B: bool \quad Sg \;\rhd\; \Gamma, x: bool \vdash E: \alpha}{Th \;\rhd\; \Gamma \vdash \textsf{Cond}(B, E[\textsf{true}/x], E[\textsf{false}/x]) = E[B/x]: \alpha} \tag{3}$$

(a) The (raw) terms $\textsf{true}$ and $\textsf{false}$ are thought of as elements of the type $bool$. To interpret the rules introducing them we need an object Ω of a (locally small) category $\mathcal{C}$ with finite products, along with morphisms $t: 1 \to \Omega$ and $f: 1 \to \Omega$, so we can define

$$[\![\Gamma \vdash \textsf{true}: bool]\!] \overset{\text{def}}{=} t \circ !: [\![\Gamma]\!] \to 1 \to \Omega$$

$$[\![\Gamma \vdash \textsf{false}: bool]\!] \overset{\text{def}}{=} f \circ !: [\![\Gamma]\!] \to 1 \to \Omega$$

where $[\![\Gamma]\!]$ is of course the finite product of the interpretations of the types appearing in Γ. Write down a function on morphism sets which can be used to interpret (1). Show how your function is more simply determined by functions

$$\Phi_C : \mathcal{C}(C, A) \times \mathcal{C}(C, A) \longrightarrow \mathcal{C}(C \times \Omega, A)$$

which are natural in C.

(b) Write down the interpretation of the proved term $\Gamma \vdash \mathsf{Cond}(B, M, N)\colon \alpha$ in terms of Φ_C. Use this to write down equations which must hold for morphisms of C in order that the equations-in-context of (2), (2') and (3) are satisfied by the proposed categorical model.

(c) Use the equations of (b) to deduce that each function Φ_C is an isomorphism (bijection). By taking C to be 1, deduce that Ω is determined up to isomorphism in C. What is Ω?

(d) Now let C have at least binary coproducts. By considering the bijection

$$C((C \times 1) + (C \times 1), A) \cong C(C \times 1, A) \times C(C \times 1, A),$$

the isomorphism $\pi_C\colon C \times 1 \cong C$ and your deductions in (c), use the Yoneda lemma to deduce what property Ω must have in order to soundly interpret the syntax of conditional expressions. *Hint: think about the morphisms*

$$id_C \times t : C \times 1 \longrightarrow C \times \Omega \longleftarrow C \times 1 : id_C \times f.$$

(4) We shall deduce a categorical semantics for an equational type theory based around the "case" construct found in programming languages. The types are given by the grammar $\alpha ::= \gamma \mid \alpha + \alpha$ where γ is any given ground type, and raw terms by

$$M ::= x \mid \mathsf{Inl}_\beta(M) \mid \mathsf{Inr}_\alpha(M) \mid \mathsf{Case}(M, x.M \mid y.M).$$

In the raw term $\mathsf{Case}(C, x.E \mid y.F)$ the variable x is bound in E and the variable y is bound in F. The type theory is presented through the following rules:

$$\frac{Sg \; \triangleright \; \Gamma \vdash M\colon \alpha}{Sg \; \triangleright \; \Gamma \vdash \mathsf{Inl}_\beta(M)\colon \alpha + \beta} \quad (1) \qquad \frac{Sg \; \triangleright \; \Gamma \vdash N\colon \beta}{Sg \; \triangleright \; \Gamma \vdash \mathsf{Inr}_\alpha(N)\colon \alpha + \beta} \quad (2)$$

$$\frac{Sg \; \triangleright \; \Gamma \vdash C\colon \alpha + \beta \quad Sg \; \triangleright \; \Gamma, x\colon \alpha \vdash E\colon \delta \quad Sg \; \triangleright \; \Gamma, y\colon \beta \vdash F\colon \delta}{Sg \; \triangleright \; \Gamma \vdash \mathsf{Case}(C, x.E \mid y.F)\colon \delta} \quad (3)$$

$$\frac{Sg \; \triangleright \; \Gamma \vdash M\colon \alpha \quad Sg \; \triangleright \; \Gamma, x\colon \alpha \vdash E\colon \delta \quad Sg \; \triangleright \; \Gamma, y\colon \beta \vdash F\colon \delta}{Th \; \triangleright \; \Gamma \vdash \mathsf{Case}(\mathsf{Inl}_\beta(M), x.E \mid y.F) = E[M/x]\colon \delta} \quad (4)$$

$$\frac{Sg \; \triangleright \; \Gamma \vdash M\colon \alpha \quad Sg \; \triangleright \; \Gamma, x\colon \alpha \vdash E\colon \delta \quad Sg \; \triangleright \; \Gamma, y\colon \beta \vdash F\colon \delta}{Th \; \triangleright \; \Gamma \vdash \mathsf{Case}(\mathsf{Inr}_\alpha(N), x.E \mid y.F) = F[N/x]\colon \delta} \quad (5)$$

$$\frac{Sg \;\triangleright\; \Gamma \vdash C\colon \alpha + \beta \quad Sg \;\triangleright\; \Gamma, z\colon \alpha + \beta \vdash L\colon \delta}{Th \;\triangleright\; \Gamma \vdash \mathsf{Case}(C,\ x.L[\mathsf{Inl}_\beta(x)/z] \mid y.L[\mathsf{Inr}_\alpha(y)/z]) = L[C/z]\colon \delta} \quad (6)$$

The idea of the case syntax is that the type $\alpha + \beta$ is a "disjoint union" of the types α and β, that $\mathsf{Inl}_\beta(M)$ is an inclusion of M in a disjoint union, and that the raw term $\mathsf{Case}(C,\ x.M \mid y.N)$ represents $M[C/x]$ if it is the *case* that the term C is "of type α," and represents $N[C/y]$ if it is the case that C is "of type β." One might expect to be able to model the type $\alpha + \beta$ by a coproduct in a category, mimicking the intended meaning of the syntax. We shall show that this is about three quarters of the true story. We suppose that there is an object $A + B$ of $\mathcal{C}$ for all objects A and B which we expect to prove is binary coproduct, but we do not assume this.

(a) Use the Yoneda lemma to deduce that to soundly interpret rules (1) and (2) it is necessary and sufficient to give morphisms $i\colon A \to A+B$ and $j\colon B \to A+B$ of $\mathcal{C}$ for all objects A and B, where we may define

$$[\![\Gamma \vdash \mathsf{Inl}_\beta(M)\colon \alpha + \beta]\!] \overset{\text{def}}{=} i \circ [\![\Gamma \vdash M\colon \alpha]\!]$$

$$[\![\Gamma \vdash \mathsf{Inr}_\alpha(N)\colon \alpha + \beta]\!] \overset{\text{def}}{=} j \circ [\![\Gamma \vdash N\colon \beta]\!].$$

(b) By writing down an appropriate family of functions on morphism sets which will give a sound interpretation to (3), and considering naturality conditions, prove that your functions may be specified in terms of a family of functions

$$\Phi_C : \mathcal{C}(C \times A, D) \times \mathcal{C}(C \times B, D) \longrightarrow \mathcal{C}(C \times (A + B), D)$$

which are natural in C. We can then define

$$[\![\Gamma \vdash \mathsf{Case}(C,\ x.E \mid y.F)\colon \delta]\!] \overset{\text{def}}{=}$$

$$\Phi_{[\![\Gamma]\!]}([\![\Gamma, x\colon \alpha \vdash E\colon \delta]\!], [\![\Gamma, y\colon \beta \vdash F\colon \delta]\!]) \circ \langle id_{[\![\Gamma]\!]}, [\![\Gamma \vdash C\colon \alpha + \beta]\!]\rangle.$$

(c) Using the semantics assigned to proved terms in (a) and (b), write down the equations which must hold between morphisms of $\mathcal{C}$ in order that the equations-in-context (4), (5) and (6) are always satisfied. Deduce that the function

$$\mathcal{C}(C \times (A + B), D) \longrightarrow \mathcal{C}(C \times A, D) \times \mathcal{C}(C \times B, D)$$

given by $f \mapsto (f \circ (id_C \times i), f \circ (id_C \times j))$ is a bijection. Hence show that the object $A + B$ is indeed the binary coproduct of A and B.

(d) By considering the bijection

$$\mathcal{C}(C \times A, D) \times \mathcal{C}(C \times B, D) \cong \mathcal{C}((C \times A) + (C \times B), D),$$

use the Yoneda lemma to prove that the binary products of $\mathcal{C}$ must *distribute* over binary coproducts, that is for all objects A, B and C of $\mathcal{C}$ we have

$$C \times (A + B) \cong (C \times A) + (C \times B).$$

Thus to interpret the case syntax soundly we require a category with finite products and binary coproducts, for which binary products distribute over binary coproducts.

(5) For this exercise we shall need a few preliminary definitions. A *natural numbers object* in a category $\mathcal{C}$ with finite products is specified by an object N of $\mathcal{C}$ with morphisms $0: 1 \to N$ and $s: N \to N$ which enjoy the following universal property: given any morphisms $m: C \to A$ and $f: C \times A \to A$ in $\mathcal{C}$, there is a unique morphism $rec(f): C \times N \to A$ for which the following diagram commutes:

Now we give the notion of a nat-theory. This is similar to a $\lambda\times$-theory, but has a syntax for natural numbers. A nat-signature is specified by giving a signature Sg of ground types and function symbols just as in a $\lambda\times$-signature, and the raw terms are now given by a grammar of the form

$$M ::= x \mid k \mid f(\underbrace{M, \ldots, M}_{length\ a}) \mid \langle\rangle \mid \langle M, M \rangle \mid \mathsf{Fst}(M) \mid \mathsf{Snd}(M) \mid \lambda x{:}\,\alpha.M \mid$$
$$M\,M \mid \mathsf{O} \mid \mathsf{Suc}(M) \mid (x.M)^M(M)$$

where occurrences of the variable x in $x.M$ are bound. The rules for forming proved terms are those for a $\lambda\times$-signature augmented by

$$\frac{}{Sg \ \triangleright \ \Gamma \vdash \mathsf{O}{:}\,nat} \qquad \frac{Sg \ \triangleright \ \Gamma \vdash N{:}\,nat}{Sg \ \triangleright \ \Gamma \vdash \mathsf{Suc}(N){:}\,nat}$$

$$\frac{Sg \ \triangleright \ \Gamma, x{:}\,\alpha \vdash F{:}\,\alpha \quad Sg \ \triangleright \ \Gamma \vdash M{:}\,\alpha \quad Sg \ \triangleright \ \Gamma \vdash N{:}\,nat}{Sg \ \triangleright \ \Gamma \vdash (x.F)^N(M){:}\,\alpha}$$

A nat-theory $Th = (Sg, Ax)$ is given by such a signature Sg together with a collection of equations-in-context which are deemed the axioms of the nat-theory. The theorems are generated by the rules for $\lambda\times$-theories, augmented by the rules

$$\frac{Sg \;\rhd\; \Gamma, x{:}\,\alpha \vdash F{:}\,\alpha \quad Sg \;\rhd\; \Gamma \vdash M{:}\,\alpha}{Th \;\rhd\; \Gamma \vdash (x.F)^{\mathrm{O}}(M) = M{:}\,\alpha}$$

$$\frac{Sg \;\rhd\; \Gamma, x{:}\,\alpha \vdash F{:}\,\alpha \quad Sg \;\rhd\; \Gamma \vdash M{:}\,\alpha}{Th \;\rhd\; \Gamma \vdash (x.F)^{\mathsf{Suc}(N)}(M) = F[(x.F)^{N}(M)/x]{:}\,\alpha}$$

$$\frac{\left\{\begin{array}{lll} Sg & \rhd & \Gamma \vdash N{:}\,nat \\ Sg & \rhd & \Gamma, n{:}\,nat \vdash G{:}\,\alpha \\ Sg & \rhd & \Gamma, x{:}\,\alpha \vdash F{:}\,\alpha \\ Th & \rhd & \Gamma \vdash G[\mathrm{O}/n] = M{:}\,\alpha \\ Th & \rhd & \Gamma, n{:}\,nat \vdash G[\mathsf{Suc}(n)/n] = F[G/x]{:}\,nat \end{array}\right.}{Th \;\rhd\; \Gamma \vdash G[N/n] = (x.F)^{N}(M){:}\,\alpha}$$

(a) Show how to give a semantics to a nat-theory in a cartesian closed category with a natural numbers object. For example, we would have $[\![nat]\!] \stackrel{\mathrm{def}}{=} N$ and $[\![\Gamma \vdash \mathrm{O}{:}\,nat]\!] \stackrel{\mathrm{def}}{=} \mathrm{O}o!{:}\,[\![\Gamma]\!] \to 1 \to N$.

(b) Prove that the discrete natural numbers $\mathbb{N}$ gives a natural numbers object in the category $\omega\mathcal{CPO}$ of ωcpos.

(c) Given a nat-theory Th show how to construct a canonical classifying category $Cl(Th)$. Prove that $Cl(Th)$ has a natural numbers object and that it satisfies the expected universal property: given any other cartesian closed category $\mathcal{D}$ with a natural numbers object, there is a unique cartesian closed functor $H{:}\,Cl(Th) \to \mathcal{D}$ which preserves natural numbers objects.

(d) Consider the following category, $\mathcal{G}l$, constructed using a given nat-theory Th. Let $Gbl(\alpha)$ be the set of global elements of α in the category $Cl(Th)$. If $[([\,]\mid M){:}\,unit \to \alpha] \in Gbl(\alpha)$ then we shall write just M for $([\,]\mid M)$. Regard $Gbl(\alpha)$ as a discrete ωcpo. The objects are triples $(D, \lhd, \alpha)$ where D is an ω-cpo, α is an object of $Cl(Th)$, and $\lhd \subseteq D \times Gbl(\alpha)$ is an inductive subset of the product ωcpo. A morphism

$$(f, F) : (D, \lhd, \alpha) \longrightarrow (D', \lhd', \alpha')$$

is given by an ω-continuous function $f{:}\,D \to D'$ and morphism $F{:}\,\alpha \to \alpha'$ of $Cl(Th)$ for which if $d \lhd M$ then $f(d) \lhd' F \circ M$ where $\circ$ is composition in $Cl(Th)$. Prove that $\mathcal{G}l$ is indeed a category. Prove further that $\mathcal{G}l$ is a cartesian closed category with a natural numbers object. *Hint: The cartesian closed structure of $\mathcal{G}l$ is given coordinatewise. For example, the binary product of $(D, \lhd, \alpha)$ and $(D', \lhd', \alpha')$ is the object $(D \times D', \lhd'', \alpha \times \alpha')$ where $(d, d')\, \lhd''\, P$ just in case $d \lhd \mathsf{Fst}(P)$ and $d' \lhd' \mathsf{Snd}(P)$. The natural numbers object is $(\mathbb{N}, \lhd_{nat}, nat)$ where $n \lhd_{nat} N$ just in case $Th \rhd \vdash N = \mathsf{Suc}^n(\mathsf{O}): nat$ where $\mathsf{Suc}^n(\mathsf{O})$ indicates*

$$\underbrace{\mathsf{Suc}(\mathsf{Suc}(\ldots \mathsf{Suc}(\mathsf{O})\ldots))}_{length\ n}\,.$$

(e) Use the category $\mathcal{G}l$ to prove that all closed terms of Th of type nat are provably equal to standard natural numbers, that is if $Sg \rhd \vdash N: nat$ then $Th \rhd \vdash N = \mathsf{Suc}^n(\mathsf{O}): nat$. *Hint: Use the universal property (see (c)) of the classifier $Cl(Th)$: show that there is a commutative diagram of functors*

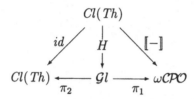

because both ωCPO and $\mathcal{G}l$ are cartesian closed categories with natural numbers objects. Here, $[\![-]\!]$ indicates the obvious functor derived from the semantics of Th in ωCPO. If $Sg \rhd \vdash N: nat$ then there is a morphism $N: unit \to nat$ in $Cl(Th)$. Complete your proof by thinking about the image of this morphism in $\mathcal{G}l$ by applying H.

(f) How does the category $\mathcal{G}l$ relate to the glued category of Section 4.10?

4.12   Pointers to the Literature

One can find a fairly detailed exposition of much of our Chapter 4 in [AL91]. The treatment in that textbook does not discuss categories of models, and the equational syntax of functional type theory is presented less formally than in "Categories for Types." A comprehensive discussion of many aspects of λ-calculus is given in [Bar84]. This book covers much of the syntactic and computational details of λ-calculus which are only just touched on in "Categories for Types." The textbook [BW90] contains a very brief discussion of the correspondence between functional type theory and cartesian closed categories. The first account of the connections between λ-calculus (functional type theory) and cartesian closed categories appears in [Lam80]. A rapid exposition of the correspondence between functional type theory and cartesian closed categories can be found in [LS80]. This book covers most of our Chapter 4 excluding a discussion of categories of models. The description of the internal language of cartesian closed categories is described through an approach making use of polynomial categories. A brief description of models of functional type theory appears in [Pie91] which is written for an audience of computer scientists.

5 Polymorphic Functional Type Theory

5.1 Introduction

DISCUSSION 5.1.1   Let us begin this chapter by taking a look at the basic form of "programming" judgement that has so far appeared, namely:

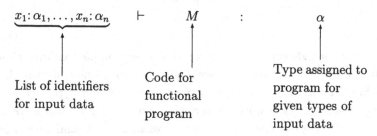

M is the code for a program. The list of (variable, type) pairs $x_1\colon\alpha_1,\ldots,x_n\colon\alpha_n$ gives the working environment for the program, giving a list of the identifiers (or variables) appearing in the body of the program, and shows the types for the input data. The type α gives the overall type assigned to the program M when it is fed with input data whose types match those appearing in the environment.

While this book is mainly concerned with giving an account of the formal syntax (and its semantics) which forms the background to modern typed (functional) programming, we shall pause here to consider, in broad terms, some of the underlying programming and implementation issues. First of all, think about the uses to which types are put. There are (at least) two different roles played by type information. On the one hand, it is used by the programmer to organise data and to make the task of designing programs easier. On the other hand, types are used by an implementor to organise storage space within the computer. A compiler needs information about the amount of storage space it should allocate, in order to work on a given data item. In most untyped languages, the computer will produce a package consisting of the data itself, information about the type of the data, and possibly information about the overall size of the entire package. The disadvantage here is that all of this information has to be checked at run time. In a typed language, checks on the type of data, storage allocations and so on can be performed at compile time, and the machine need only store the core program data. However, typing can lead quickly to certain disadvantages.

Consider the following procedure which performs the swapping of the values
of two variables:

```
Proc Swapint (var n,m :  Int);
       var t :  Int;
       Begin
            t := m;
            m := n;
            n := t
       end;
```

This piece of code contains the essence of a very simple "algorithm" for swapping the contents of two variables, but it has an obvious drawback. On the
machine, it will only perform this swap for variables of type integer. Yet the
same "algorithm" will work for variables of any type. We can solve this problem by allowing our code to contain a "variable type" and such a procedure
for doing variable swaps might then look like

```
Proc Anyswap ( type X; var n,m :  X);
       var t :  X;
       Begin
            t := m;
            m := n;
            n := t
       end;
```

where the type variable X would be assigned a value at each call of the above
procedure.

A second order functional type theory is a formal system which embodies
the principle of variable types as well as providing a formal syntax for writing
down functional expressions. We shall now give an informal example of a term
(program) of a second order functional type theory. Let us think about the
identity function as written in functional type theory, namely $\lambda x: \alpha.x$. This
program has the same disadvantage as the procedure for swapping two integers;
it is the identity function at the type α, yet has the same "form" whatever α
actually is. Consider the expression $\Lambda X.\lambda x: X.x$. Here, one should think of x
as a program or term variable, and X as a type variable. The idea is that the
ΛX performs the same role for type variables as λx does for term variables
and marks the variable X as a "hole" in which we can plug any type. So, if

we want to produce the identity function on integers, we apply our expression to the type *int* and "slot *int* into the 'hole' X:"

$$(\Lambda X.\lambda x{:}\,X.x)(int) = (\lambda x{:}\,X.x)[int/X] = \lambda x{:}\,int.x.$$

What about the type of the expression $\Lambda X.\lambda x{:}\,X.x$? The type of $\lambda x{:}\,X.x$ is $X \Rightarrow X$. We would like to formalise the idea that the expression $e \stackrel{\text{def}}{=} \Lambda X.\lambda x{:}\,X.x$ is the identity function *for all types* X, and that at a particular type α the type of e is $\alpha \Rightarrow \alpha$. In fact the type of e will be written $\forall X.X \Rightarrow X$, where $\forall$ should be read as "for all" and the symbol X is bound in $\forall X.X \Rightarrow X$, indicating that occurrences of the X after the . are "slots" to be filled by other types.

These simple ideas are the basis of a second order polymorphic (functional) type theory. Of course there are many points to be clarified; our aim here is to simply give the reader a feeling for the ideas of second order polymorphic type theory.

We can now give a summary of the contents of this chapter. We begin with a definition of the formal syntax of the so-called second order polymorphic functional type theory with finite products. We shall discuss the idea of a 2λ×-theory, which is a formal equational system much like a λ×-theory, except that we may now perform abstractions over type variables. Next a categorical semantics is derived, using the same principles as in previous chapters, namely that substitution in syntax is interpreted in a categorical structure by composition of morphisms. With this, we can give a formal definition of the semantics of a 2λ×-theory in a categorical structure known as a 2λ×-hyperdoctrine, which is a particular kind of indexed category. We give the details of both a recursion-theoretic and a domain-theoretic model of polymorphism, by giving an instance of a 2λ×-hyperdoctrine based on partial equivalence relations and domain constructions respectively. We prove that our semantics is sound, and then show that there is a categorical type theory correspondence between this kind of syntactical theory and its categorical semantics; the essence of these ideas is much the same as in Chapters 3 and 4, but the technical details are more complex (see Figure 5.1). This correspondence also shows that the semantics is complete.

5.2 *The Syntax and Equations of* 2λ×-*Theories*

DISCUSSION 5.2.1 A 2λ×-*signature* is a pair $Sg \stackrel{\text{def}}{=} (Sg^{ty}, Sg^{tm})$ where Sg^{ty} is a 2λ×-type signature and Sg^{tm} is a 2λ×-term signature. The specification

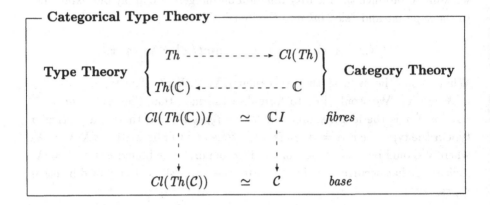

Figure 5.1: A Hyperdoctrinal Category Theory / Type Theory Correspondence.

of Sg^{tm} depends on the specification of Sg^{ty}. A $2\lambda\times$-*type signature* Sg^{ty} is specified by the following data:

- A collection of *type symbols*.

- An *arity* for each type symbol which is given by a natural number (possibly 0). A type symbol K with arity 0 is called a *constant*.

Let us define the so-called raw types. These play a similar role to raw terms. We assume that we are given a countably infinite set $Var^{ty} = \{X, Y, Z, \ldots\}$ of *type variables*. The *raw types* are generated by the BNF grammar

$$\Phi ::= X \mid K \mid F(\underbrace{\Phi, \ldots, \Phi}_{length\ a}) \mid unit \mid \Phi \times \Phi \mid \Phi \Rightarrow \Phi \mid \forall X.\Phi$$

where X is any type variable, K is any constant type, F is any type symbol of non-zero arity a and *unit* is a distinguished (constant) raw type.

In order to be able to discuss the idea of substitution of raw types for type variables, we will need notions of free and bound type variables (recall from Discussion 5.1.1 that the type variable X in $\forall X.\Phi$ is bound). In order to define such notions, we will require a definition of the relation Φ' is a *raw subtype* of Φ. We leave it as an exercise for the reader to give the formal definition, which should be intuitively clear; it may be helpful to read Discussion 4.2.3. We call an expression of the form $\forall X$ an *abstraction*. If the raw type $\forall X.\Psi$ is a raw subtype of Φ, then Ψ is the *scope* of the occurrence of the abstraction $\forall X$. If the type variable X occurs in the raw term Φ, then X is *bound* if it occurs in a raw subtype of the form $\forall X.\Psi$. We say that occurrences of X in the raw subtype $\forall X.\Psi$ are *captured* by the abstraction $\forall X$. If X occurs in Φ and is not bound, then it is said to be *free*. If X has at least one free occurrence in Φ it is called a *free variable*. In fact the set of free type variables of a raw type Φ is defined inductively by the following clauses:

- $ftyv(X) \stackrel{\text{def}}{=} \{X\}$,

- $ftyv(K) \stackrel{\text{def}}{=} \varnothing$,

- $ftyv(F(\Phi_1, \ldots, \Phi_a)) \stackrel{\text{def}}{=} ftyv(\Phi_1) \cup \ldots \cup ftyv(\Phi_a)$,

- $ftyv(unit) \stackrel{\text{def}}{=} \varnothing$,

- $ftyv(\Phi \times \Psi) \stackrel{\text{def}}{=} ftyv(\Phi) \cup ftyv(\Psi)$,

- $ftyv(\Phi \Rightarrow \Psi) \stackrel{\text{def}}{=} ftyv(\Phi) \cup ftyv(\Psi)$,

- $ftyv(\forall X.\Phi) \stackrel{\text{def}}{=} ftyv(\Phi) \setminus \{X\}$.

The raw type Φ is said to be α-equivalent to the raw type Ψ if Φ and Ψ differ only in their bound variables. The notion of α-equivalence is an equivalence relation, and we shall now regard a raw type Φ as the α-equivalence class which it determines. This is because the notion of substitution of raw types is only well defined up to α-equivalence—see page 158. Think of α-equivalence as "being the same up to a change of bound variables." Let us define the *substitution* of the raw type Ψ for occurrences of the type variable X in the raw type Φ, written $\Phi[\Psi/X]$, to be the raw term formed by replacing all occurrences of the type variable X in Φ with the raw type Ψ, changing bound variables to avoid capture. Formally we have:

- $X[\Psi/X] \stackrel{\text{def}}{=} \Psi$, and $Y[\Psi/X] \stackrel{\text{def}}{=} Y$ if Y is different from X,

- $K[\Psi/X] \stackrel{\text{def}}{=} K$ for a constant type K,

- $F(\Phi_1, \ldots, \Phi_n)[\Psi/X] \stackrel{\text{def}}{=} F(\Phi_1[\Psi/X], \ldots, \Phi_n[\Psi/X])$ for a type symbol F of non-zero arity n,

- $unit[\Psi/X] \stackrel{\text{def}}{=} unit$,

- $(\Phi \times \Phi')[\Psi/X] \stackrel{\text{def}}{=} (\Phi[\Psi/X]) \times (\Phi'[\Psi/X])$,

- $(\Phi \Rightarrow \Phi')[\Psi/X] \stackrel{\text{def}}{=} (\Phi[\Psi/X]) \Rightarrow (\Phi'[\Psi/X])$, and

- $\begin{cases} \text{(i)} & (\forall X.\Phi)[\Psi/X] \stackrel{\text{def}}{=} \forall X.\Phi, \\ \text{(ii)} & (\forall X.\Phi)[\Psi/Y] \stackrel{\text{def}}{=} \forall Z.(\Phi[Z/X][\Psi/Y]) \text{ where } Z \notin ftyv(\Phi) \cup ftyv(\Psi), \\ & \text{and } Z \text{ is chosen to be different from } X \text{ and } Y. \end{cases}$

EXAMPLES 5.2.2 The brackets "(" and ")" are used to indicate informally the structure of syntactical terms.

(1) $((X \Rightarrow Y) \times Z)[\Phi/X] \stackrel{\text{def}}{=} (\Phi \Rightarrow Y) \Rightarrow Z$.

(2) $(\forall Z.(X \Rightarrow Y) \times Z)[U \times Z/X] \stackrel{\text{def}}{=} \forall Z.((U \times Z) \Rightarrow Y) \times Z$ is *not* correct. The variable Z in the substituted raw term $U \times Z$ becomes bound, that is, it is captured by the abstraction $\forall Z$. We should have

$$(\forall Z.(X \Rightarrow Y) \times Z)[U \times Z/X] \stackrel{\text{def}}{=} \forall V.(((X \Rightarrow Y) \times Z)[V/Z][U \times Z/X])$$
$$\stackrel{\text{def}}{=} \forall V.(((X \Rightarrow Y) \times V)[U \times Z/X])$$
$$\stackrel{\text{def}}{=} \forall V.((U \times Z) \Rightarrow Y) \times V$$

where we change the bound type variable Z to a type variable V different from Z and X and such that

$$V \notin ftyv((X \Rightarrow Y) \times Z) \cup ftyv(U \times Z) = \{X, Y, Z, U\}.$$

DISCUSSION 5.2.3   We shall now give some rules which generate the syntax of the "well formed types," using the $2\lambda\times$-type signature Sg^{ty}. First we give a couple more definitions. A *type context* is a list of distinct type variables $\Delta \stackrel{\text{def}}{=} [X_1, \ldots, X_n]$. A *type-in-context* is a judgement of the form $\Delta \vdash \Phi$ where Φ is a raw type and Δ is a type context. We shall now define a class of judgements of the form $Sg^{ty} \rhd \Delta \vdash \Phi$ where $\Delta \vdash \Phi$ is a type-in-context. The judgement $Sg^{ty} \rhd \Delta \vdash \Phi$ is called a *proved type*, and the rules for introducing these judgements are given in Figure 5.2. One should think of the raw type Φ in a proved type $Sg^{ty} \rhd \Delta \vdash \Phi$ as being "well formed" or "well typed."

REMARK 5.2.4   Note that all rules for introducing syntax are assumed to be well formed. Thus in the rule for **Polymorphism Types**, because Δ, X is a well formed type context, X does not appear in Δ. Note also that if (for example) $\Delta = [X, Y]$ we may write $X, Y \vdash \Phi$ rather than $[X, Y] \vdash \Phi$.

PROPOSITION 5.2.5   We can derive rules for the permutation and weakening of type contexts, along with a rule of substitution, mimicking the rules found on page 125.

PROOF   Induction.   □

EXERCISE 5.2.6   Write down the rules of Proposition 5.2.5 and prove them.

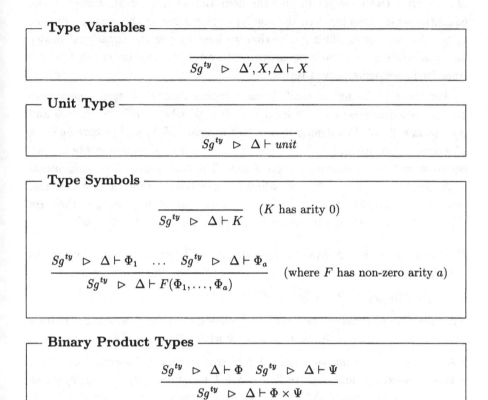

Type Variables
$$Sg^{ty} \; \triangleright \; \Delta', X, \Delta \vdash X$$

Unit Type
$$Sg^{ty} \; \triangleright \; \Delta \vdash unit$$

Type Symbols
$$\frac{}{Sg^{ty} \; \triangleright \; \Delta \vdash K} \quad (K \text{ has arity } 0)$$

$$\frac{Sg^{ty} \; \triangleright \; \Delta \vdash \Phi_1 \quad \dots \quad Sg^{ty} \; \triangleright \; \Delta \vdash \Phi_a}{Sg^{ty} \; \triangleright \; \Delta \vdash F(\Phi_1, \dots, \Phi_a)} \quad (\text{where } F \text{ has non-zero arity } a)$$

Binary Product Types
$$\frac{Sg^{ty} \; \triangleright \; \Delta \vdash \Phi \quad Sg^{ty} \; \triangleright \; \Delta \vdash \Psi}{Sg^{ty} \; \triangleright \; \Delta \vdash \Phi \times \Psi}$$

Function Types
$$\frac{Sg^{ty} \; \triangleright \; \Delta \vdash \Phi \quad Sg^{ty} \; \triangleright \; \Delta \vdash \Psi}{Sg^{ty} \; \triangleright \; \Delta \vdash \Phi \Rightarrow \Psi}$$

Polymorphism Types
$$\frac{Sg^{ty} \; \triangleright \; \Delta, X \vdash \Phi}{Sg^{ty} \; \triangleright \; \Delta \vdash \forall X.\Phi}$$

Figure 5.2: Proved Types Generated from a 2λ×-Signature.

DISCUSSION 5.2.7   We will see later on that a second order polymorphic theory will involve judgements asserting the equality of raw types and the equality
of raw terms (we have yet to give the definition of raw term). However, the
equalities which hold between the raw types play a role in the type assignment
system for raw terms. This means that we have to give the equational theory
of types *before* giving the type assignment system for raw terms, that is, the
rules for introducing proved terms.

For the time being we shall define a typing theory. A *type equation-in-
context* is a judgement of the form $\Delta \vdash \Phi = \Phi'$ where $Sg^{ty} \ \rhd \ \Delta \vdash \Phi$ and
$Sg^{ty} \ \rhd \ \Delta \vdash \Phi'$. A $2\lambda\times$-*typing theory* Th^{ty} is a pair (Sg^{ty}, Ax^{ty}) where Sg^{ty} is a
$2\lambda\times$-type signature and Ax^{ty} is a collection of type equations-in-context, each
equation-in-context known as a *type axiom*. The *type theorems* are judgements
of the form $Th^{ty} \ \rhd \ \Delta \vdash \Phi = \Phi'$, which are generated by the rules of algebraic
type theory (see page 128, where one needs to replace judgements of the form
$Th \ \rhd \ \Gamma \vdash M = M' \colon \alpha$ with those of the form $Th^{ty} \ \rhd \ \Delta \vdash \Phi = \Phi'$).

DISCUSSION 5.2.8   A $2\lambda\times$-*term signature* Sg^{tm} (which is defined using the
data from a $2\lambda\times$-type signature Sg^{ty}) is specified by the following data:

• A typing theory $Th^{ty} = (Sg^{ty}, Ax^{ty})$.

• A collection of *function symbols*, each having an *arity* a, which is a natural
number (possibly 0). A function symbol k with arity 0 is called a *constant*.

• A *sorting* for each function symbol f of arity a, which is specified by giving
a type context Δ^f and a finite list of $a + 1$ raw types $[\Phi_1, \ldots, \Phi_a, \Phi]$ (often
written suggestively as $f \colon \Delta^f; \Phi_1, \ldots, \Phi_a \to \Phi$), where we have $Sg^{ty} \ \rhd \ \Delta^f \vdash \Phi_i$
for each $1 \leq i \leq a$ and also $Sg^{ty} \ \rhd \ \Delta^f \vdash \Phi$. If k is a constant function symbol
then we write $k \colon \Delta^k; \Phi$.

Now we define the raw terms generated by a $2\lambda\times$-term signature Sg^{tm}. Let
us assume that we are given a countably infinite stock of *term variables*. The
raw terms are given by the (informal) BNF grammar

$M ::=$

$$x \mid k_{\Psi_1,\ldots,\Psi_n} \mid f_{\Psi_1,\ldots,\Psi_{n'}} \underbrace{(M, \ldots, M)}_{length\ a} \mid \langle\rangle \mid \langle M, M \rangle \mid \mathsf{Fst}(M) \mid \mathsf{Snd}(M) \mid$$
$$\lambda x \colon \Phi.M \mid M\,M \mid \Lambda X.M \mid M\,\Phi$$

where x is any term variable, k is any constant function symbol for which
$length(\Delta^k) = n$, f is any function symbol of non-zero arity a for which
$length(\Delta^f) = n'$ and the Ψ_i and Φ are any raw types. We shall often make use
of the self explanatory notation $k_{\vec{\Psi}}$ and $f_{\vec{\Psi}}(\vec{M})$.

The next task is to define the substitution of raw terms for term variables, and of raw types for type variables (which appear in raw terms). Such substitutions will be well defined up to α-equivalence or "change of bound variables." As these ideas should now be familiar, we give sketch definitions. First, it is an exercise for the reader to define the relation R is a *raw subterm* of the raw term M. Occurrences of the term variable x in subterms of the form $\lambda x\colon \Phi.N$ are *bound*. We say that x is *captured* by the abstraction $\lambda x\colon \Phi$. If the term variable x occurs in a raw term M and is not bound, then it is *free*. If x has at least one free occurrence in M then it is a *free term variable* of M. The set of free term variables of a raw term M, $ftmv(M)$, can be given explicitly by the following clauses:

- For the raw terms which "appear in" $\lambda\times$-theories, see page 158, replacing $fv(-)$ with $ftmv(-)$,

- $ftmv(k_{\vec{\Psi}}) \stackrel{\text{def}}{=} \varnothing$,

- $ftmv(f_{\vec{\Psi}}(\vec{M})) \stackrel{\text{def}}{=} \bigcup_1^a ftmv(M_j)$,

- $ftmv(\Lambda X.M) \stackrel{\text{def}}{=} ftmv(M)$, and

- $ftmv(M\Phi) \stackrel{\text{def}}{=} ftmv(M)$.

Occurrences of the type variable X in a subterm of the form $\Lambda X.M$ are *bound*, and said to be *captured* by the abstraction ΛX. Any type variable X which occurs in a raw term M and is not bound is said to be *free*. If X has at least one free occurrence in M then X is a *free type variable* of M. The set $ftyv(M)$ of free type variables of a raw term M is specified through the clauses:

- $ftyv(x) \stackrel{\text{def}}{=} \varnothing$,

- $ftyv(k_{\vec{\Psi}}) \stackrel{\text{def}}{=} \bigcup_1^n ftyv(\Psi_i)$ where k is a constant function symbol,

- $ftyv(f_{\vec{\Psi}}(\vec{M})) \stackrel{\text{def}}{=} \bigcup_1^n ftyv(\Psi_i) \cup \bigcup_1^a ftyv(M_j)$ where f is a function symbol of non-zero arity a,

- $ftyv(\langle\rangle) \stackrel{\text{def}}{=} \varnothing$,

- $ftyv(\langle M, N\rangle) \stackrel{\text{def}}{=} ftyv(M) \cup ftyv(N)$,

- $ftyv(\mathsf{Fst}(P)) \stackrel{\text{def}}{=} ftyv(P)$,

- $ftyv(\mathsf{Snd}(P)) \stackrel{\text{def}}{=} ftyv(P)$,

- $ftyv(\lambda x\colon \Phi.M) \stackrel{\text{def}}{=} ftyv(\Phi) \cup ftyv(M)$,

- $ftyv(MN) \stackrel{\text{def}}{=} ftyv(M) \cup ftyv(N)$,

- $ftyv(\Lambda X.M) \stackrel{\text{def}}{=} ftyv(M) \setminus \{X\}$, and

- $ftyv(M\Phi) \stackrel{\text{def}}{=} ftyv(\Phi) \cup ftyv(M)$.

We say that two raw terms are *α-equivalent* if they differ only in their bound type and term variables. This gives rise to an equivalence relation on raw terms, and we shall now refer to a "raw term" M to mean the α-equivalence class determined by M. The *substitution* of a raw term N for occurrences of a term variable x in a raw term M, $M[N/x]$, is defined by substituting the raw term N for free occurrences of x in M, changing bound term variables to avoid capture. More formally we have:

- If M "appears in" a $\lambda\times$-theory, see page 159,

- $k_{\vec{\Psi}}[N/x] \stackrel{\text{def}}{=} k_{\vec{\Psi}}$,

- $f_{\vec{\Psi}}(M_1, \ldots, M_a)[N/x] \stackrel{\text{def}}{=} f_{\vec{\Psi}}(M_1[N/x], \ldots, M_a[N/x])$,

- $(\Lambda X.M)[N/x] \stackrel{\text{def}}{=} \Lambda Y.(M[Y/X][N/x])$ where $Y \notin ftyv(M) \cup ftyv(N)$ and Y is different from X, and

- $(M\Phi)[N/x] \stackrel{\text{def}}{=} (M[N/x])\Phi$.

The *substitution* of a raw type Ψ for occurrences of a type variable X in a raw term M, $M[\Psi/X]$, is defined by the clauses

- $x[\Psi/X] \stackrel{\text{def}}{=} x$,

- $k_{\Psi_1, \ldots, \Psi_n}[\Psi/X] \stackrel{\text{def}}{=} k_{\Psi_1[\Psi/X], \ldots, \Psi_n[\Psi/X]}$,

- $f_{\Psi_1, \ldots, \Psi_n}(M_1, \ldots, M_a)[\Psi/X] \stackrel{\text{def}}{=} f_{\Psi_1[\Psi/X], \ldots, \Psi_n[\Psi/X]}(M_1[\Psi/X], \ldots, M_a[\Psi/X])$,

- $\langle\rangle[\Psi/X] \stackrel{\text{def}}{=} \langle\rangle$,

- $\langle M, N\rangle[\Psi/X] \stackrel{\text{def}}{=} \langle M[\Psi/X], N[\Psi/X]\rangle$,

- $\mathsf{Fst}(P)[\Psi/X] \stackrel{\text{def}}{=} \mathsf{Fst}(P[\Psi/X])$,

- $\mathsf{Snd}(P)[\Psi/X] \stackrel{\text{def}}{=} \mathsf{Snd}(P[\Psi/X])$,

- $(\lambda x\colon\Phi.M)[\Psi/X] \stackrel{\text{def}}{=} \lambda x\colon\Phi[\Psi/X].(M[\Psi/X])$,

- $(MN)[\Psi/X] \stackrel{\text{def}}{=} (M[\Psi/X])(N[\Psi/X])$,

- $\begin{cases} \text{(i) } (\Lambda X.M)[\Psi/X] \stackrel{\text{def}}{=} \Lambda X.M, \\ \text{(ii) } (\Lambda Y.M)[\Psi/X] \stackrel{\text{def}}{=} \Lambda Z.(M[Z/Y][\Psi/X]) \text{ where } Z \notin ftyv(M) \cup ftyv(\Psi), \\ \quad\text{ and } Z \text{ is chosen to be different from both } X \text{ and } Y, \end{cases}$

- $(M\Phi)[\Psi/X] \stackrel{\text{def}}{=} (M[\Psi/X])(\Phi[\Psi/X])$.

EXERCISE 5.2.9   Make sure you understand the definition of substitution. Note that the definition of $(\lambda y\colon\Phi.M)[N/x]$ requires a renaming of a bound term variable and that $(\Lambda X.M)[N/x]$ and $(\Lambda Y.M)[\Phi/X]$ require a renaming of bound type variables.

DISCUSSION 5.2.10   We now give a collection of rules for generating the
"well formed" terms using a $2\lambda\times$-term signature. Of course, the situation
is somewhat more complex than was the case for algebraic theories and $\lambda\times$-
theories, and we shall need a few more auxiliary definitions before we can give
rules for generating the well formed terms-in-context. A *term context*,

$$\Gamma \stackrel{\text{def}}{=} [x_1 \colon \Phi_1, \ldots, x_n \colon \Phi_n],$$

is a list of (term variable, raw type) pairs, where the variables are assumed to
be distinct. We shall write $\Delta \vdash \Gamma$ to mean $\Delta \vdash \Phi_i$ for each Φ_i which appears
in Γ. We shall also write $Sg^{ty} \;\triangleright\; \Delta \vdash \Gamma$ to mean that $Sg^{ty} \;\triangleright\; \Delta \vdash \Phi_i$ for
each Φ_i which appears in Γ, and if Γ is empty then $\Delta \vdash \Gamma$ will just say that
Δ is a type context. If we are given a type context $\Delta = [X_1, \ldots, X_n]$, and raw
types Φ and Ψ_i, then we shall sometimes write $\Phi[\vec{\Psi}/\Delta]$ for $\Phi[\vec{\Psi}/\vec{X}]$ and we
leave the reader to define the (obvious) notion of simultaneous substitution.
A *term-in-context* is a judgement of the form $\Delta \,|\, \Gamma \vdash M \colon \Phi$ where M is a raw
term and Φ is a raw type. A judgement of the form $Sg^{tm} \;\triangleright\; \Delta \,|\, \Gamma \vdash M \colon \Phi$,
where $\Delta \,|\, \Gamma \vdash M \colon \Phi$ is a term-in-context, is called a *proved term*. The rules for
generating these judgements are given by the rules in Figures 5.3 and 5.4.

EXERCISES 5.2.11

(1) Prove that in a judgement of the form $Sg^{ty} \;\triangleright\; \Delta \vdash \Phi$ any free type
variable of Φ appears in Δ. Prove also that in any judgement of the form
$Sg^{tm} \;\triangleright\; \Delta \,|\, \Gamma \vdash M \colon \Phi$, any free type variable in the set

$$ftyv(M) \cup \left(\bigcup_{1}^{m} ftyv(\Phi_j)\right) \cup ftyv(\Phi)$$

appears in Δ (where the Φ_j appear in Γ), and any free term variable in $ftmv(M)$
appears in Γ.

(2) Look at the rule **Polymorphism Terms** introducing $\Lambda X.F$. The hypothesis and conclusion are assumed to be well formed. This means that
$X \notin \bigcup_1^m ftyv(\Phi_j)$ where the Φ_j appear in Γ. Why is this restriction (very)
sensible?

PROPOSITION 5.2.12   We can derive rules for the permutation and weakening of type and term contexts, along with a rule of substitution, mimicking the
rules found on page 125. For example, the rule of substitution is

$$\frac{Sg^{tm} \;\triangleright\; \Delta, X \,|\, \Gamma, x \colon \Phi \vdash M \colon \Psi \quad Sg^{tm} \;\triangleright\; \Delta \,|\, \Gamma \vdash N \colon \Phi \quad Sg^{ty} \;\triangleright\; \Delta \vdash \Theta}{Sg^{tm} \;\triangleright\; \Delta \,|\, \Gamma[\Theta/X] \vdash M[N/x][\Theta/X] \colon \Psi[\Theta/X]}$$

where $\Gamma[\Theta/X]$ means substitute Θ for X in all raw types appearing in Γ.

Term Variables

$$\frac{Sg^{ty} \;\triangleright\; \Delta \vdash \Gamma' \quad Sg^{ty} \;\triangleright\; \Delta \vdash \Phi \quad Sg^{ty} \;\triangleright\; \Delta \vdash \Gamma}{Sg^{tm} \;\triangleright\; \Delta \,|\, \Gamma', x\!:\!\Phi, \Gamma \vdash x\!:\!\Phi}$$

Unit Term

$$\frac{Sg^{ty} \;\triangleright\; \Delta \vdash \Gamma}{Sg^{tm} \;\triangleright\; \Delta \,|\, \Gamma \vdash \langle\rangle\!:\! unit}$$

Function Symbols

$$\frac{Sg^{ty} \;\triangleright\; \Delta \vdash \Gamma \quad Sg^{ty} \;\triangleright\; \Delta \vdash \Psi_1 \quad \ldots \quad Sg^{ty} \;\triangleright\; \Delta \vdash \Psi_n}{Sg^{tm} \;\triangleright\; \Delta \,|\, \Gamma \vdash k_{\vec{\Psi}}\!:\! \Phi[\vec{\Psi}/\Delta^k]} \qquad (k\!:\!\Delta^k; \Phi)$$

$$\left\{ \begin{array}{l} Sg^{ty} \;\triangleright\; \Delta \vdash \Psi_1 \quad \ldots \quad Sg^{ty} \;\triangleright\; \Delta \vdash \Psi_n \\ Sg^{tm} \;\triangleright\; \Delta \,|\, \Gamma \vdash M_1\!:\! \Phi_1[\vec{\Psi}/\Delta^f] \quad \ldots \quad Sg^{tm} \;\triangleright\; \Delta \,|\, \Gamma \vdash M_a\!:\! \Phi_a[\vec{\Psi}/\Delta^f] \end{array} \right.$$
$$\overline{\qquad Sg^{tm} \;\triangleright\; \Delta \,|\, \Gamma \vdash f_{\vec{\Psi}}(M_1, \ldots, M_a)\!:\! \Phi[\vec{\Psi}/\Delta^f] \qquad}$$

$$(f\!:\!\Delta^f; \Phi_1, \ldots, \Phi_a \to \Phi)$$

Binary Product Terms

$$\frac{Sg^{tm} \;\triangleright\; \Delta \,|\, \Gamma \vdash M\!:\!\Phi \quad Sg^{tm} \;\triangleright\; \Delta \,|\, \Gamma \vdash N\!:\!\Psi}{Sg^{tm} \;\triangleright\; \Delta \,|\, \Gamma \vdash \langle M, N\rangle\!:\!\Phi \times \Psi}$$

$$\frac{Sg^{tm} \;\triangleright\; \Delta \,|\, \Gamma \vdash P\!:\!\Phi \times \Psi}{Sg^{tm} \;\triangleright\; \Delta \,|\, \Gamma \vdash \mathsf{Fst}(P)\!:\!\Phi} \qquad \frac{Sg^{tm} \;\triangleright\; \Delta \,|\, \Gamma \vdash P\!:\!\Phi \times \Psi}{Sg^{tm} \;\triangleright\; \Delta \,|\, \Gamma \vdash \mathsf{Snd}(P)\!:\!\Psi}$$

Figure 5.3: Proved Terms Generated from a $2\lambda\times$-Signature.

Function Terms

$$\frac{Sg^{tm} \;\triangleright\; \Delta\,|\,\Gamma, x\!:\!\Phi \vdash F\!:\!\Psi}{Sg^{tm} \;\triangleright\; \Delta\,|\,\Gamma \vdash \lambda x\!:\!\Phi.F\!:\!\Phi \Rightarrow \Psi}$$

$$\frac{Sg^{tm} \;\triangleright\; \Delta\,|\,\Gamma \vdash M\!:\!\Phi \Rightarrow \Psi \quad Sg^{tm} \;\triangleright\; \Delta\,|\,\Gamma \vdash N\!:\!\Phi}{Sg^{tm} \;\triangleright\; \Delta\,|\,\Gamma \vdash MN\!:\!\Psi}$$

Polymorphism Terms

$$\frac{Sg^{tm} \;\triangleright\; \Delta, X\,|\,\Gamma \vdash F\!:\!\Phi}{Sg^{tm} \;\triangleright\; \Delta\,|\,\Gamma \vdash \Lambda X.F\!:\!\forall X.\Phi}$$

$$\frac{Sg^{tm} \;\triangleright\; \Delta\,|\,\Gamma \vdash M\!:\!\forall X.\Phi \quad Sg^{tm} \;\triangleright\; \Delta \vdash \Psi}{Sg^{tm} \;\triangleright\; \Delta\,|\,\Gamma \vdash M\Psi\!:\!\Phi[\Psi/X]}$$

Term Typing

$$\frac{Sg^{tm} \;\triangleright\; \Delta\,|\,\Gamma \vdash M\!:\!\Phi \quad Th^{op} \;\triangleright\; \Delta \vdash \Phi = \Phi'}{Sg^{tm} \;\triangleright\; \Delta\,|\,\Gamma \vdash M\!:\!\Phi'}$$

Figure 5.4: Proved Terms Generated from a $2\lambda\times$-Signature, Continued.

PROOF   We use induction on the derivation of $Sg \; \rhd \; \Delta, X \mid \Gamma, x{:}\, \Phi \vdash M{:}\, \Psi$. Note that care is needed when dealing with the rule **Function Symbols**, where one needs the general result that if $ftyv(\Phi) \subseteq \{X_1, \ldots, X_n\}$ then

$$\Phi[\vec{\Psi}/\vec{X}][\vec{\Theta}/\vec{Y}] = \Phi[\Psi_1[\vec{\Theta}/\vec{Y}], \ldots, \Psi_n[\vec{\Theta}/\vec{Y}]]$$

where the equality symbol denotes α-equivalence of raw types. $\square$

DISCUSSION 5.2.13   A *term equation-in-context* is a judgement of the form

$$\Delta \mid \Gamma \vdash M = M'{:}\, \Phi$$

where $\Delta \mid \Gamma \vdash M{:}\, \Phi$ and $\Delta \mid \Gamma \vdash M'{:}\, \Phi$ are proved terms. We can now define the notion of a theory in second order polymorphic functional type theory.

A $2\lambda\times$-term theory Th^{tm} is a pair (Sg^{tm}, Ax^{tm}) where Sg^{tm} is a $2\lambda\times$-term signature and Ax^{tm} is a collection of term equations-in-context, each equation-in-context known as a *term axiom*. A *term theorem* is a judgement of the form $Th^{tm} \; \rhd \; \Delta \mid \Gamma \vdash M = M'{:}\, \Phi$. The term theorems are generated from the rules given in Figures 5.5, 5.6 and 5.7. We can then define a $2\lambda\times$-*theory* Th to be a pair (Th^{ty}, Th^{tm}) where the $2\lambda\times$-term signature of Th^{tm} depends on the typing theory Th^{ty}. A *theorem* of Th will then be any type theorem or any term theorem. Note that we will sometimes refer to a $2\lambda\times$-theory $Th = (Sg, Ax)$ where $Sg = (Sg^{ty}, Sg^{tm})$ and $Ax = (Ax^{ty}, Ax^{tm})$.

REMARK 5.2.14   From now on, we shall always be working with a given $2\lambda\times$-theory Th given by $((Sg^{ty}, Ax^{ty}), (Sg^{tm}, Ax^{tm}))$. We will usually omit superscripts from such expressions, providing the meaning is clear. So, for example, we will just write $Sg \; \rhd \; \Delta \vdash \Phi{:}\, K$ to mean $Sg^{ty} \; \rhd \; \Delta \vdash \Phi{:}\, K$. This overloading of notation should in fact aid clarity.

5.3   Deriving a Categorical Semantics

DISCUSSION 5.3.1   Some of the forms of judgement which arise in a $2\lambda\times$-theory are

(a) $Sg \; \rhd \; \Delta \vdash \Phi$ where $\Delta \stackrel{\text{def}}{=} [X_1, \ldots, X_n]$, and

(b) $Sg \; \rhd \; \Delta \mid \Gamma \vdash M{:}\, \Phi$ where $\Gamma \stackrel{\text{def}}{=} [x_1{:}\, \Phi_1, \ldots, x_m{:}\, \Phi_m]$.

```
┌─ Axioms ─────────────────────────────────────────────────────────────┐
│                                                                        │
│                    Ax^{tm}  ▷  Δ | Γ ⊢ M = M' : Φ                      │
│                    ─────────────────────────────────                   │
│                    Th^{tm}  ▷  Δ | Γ ⊢ M = M' : Φ                      │
│                                                                        │
└────────────────────────────────────────────────────────────────────────┘
```

```
┌─ Weakening ──────────────────────────────────────────────────────────┐
│                                                                        │
│              Th^{tm}  ▷  Δ | Γ ⊢ M = M' : Φ                            │
│              ─────────────────────────────────   (where Δ ⊆ Δ' and Γ ⊆ Γ')│
│              Th^{tm}  ▷  Δ' | Γ' ⊢ M = M' : Φ                          │
│                                                                        │
└────────────────────────────────────────────────────────────────────────┘
```

$$Ax^{tm} \;\triangleright\; \Delta \,|\, \Gamma \vdash M = M' : \Phi$$
$$\overline{Th^{tm} \;\triangleright\; \Delta \,|\, \Gamma \vdash M = M' : \Phi}$$

Weakening

$$\frac{Th^{tm} \;\triangleright\; \Delta \,|\, \Gamma \vdash M = M' : \Phi}{Th^{tm} \;\triangleright\; \Delta' \,|\, \Gamma' \vdash M = M' : \Phi} \quad \text{(where } \Delta \subseteq \Delta' \text{ and } \Gamma \subseteq \Gamma')$$

Permutation

$$\frac{Th^{tm} \;\triangleright\; \Delta \,|\, \Gamma \vdash M = M' : \Phi}{Th^{tm} \;\triangleright\; \pi\Delta \,|\, \pi'\Gamma \vdash M = M' : \Phi} \quad \text{(where } \pi \text{ and } \pi' \text{ are permutations)}$$

Substitution

$$\frac{\left\{ \begin{array}{l} Th^{ty} \;\triangleright\; \Delta \vdash \Theta = \Theta' \\ Th^{tm} \;\triangleright\; \Delta, X \,|\, \Gamma, x{:}\Phi \vdash M = M' : \Psi \quad Th^{tm} \;\triangleright\; \Delta \,|\, \Gamma \vdash N = N' : \Phi \end{array} \right.}{Th^{tm} \;\triangleright\; \Delta \,|\, \Gamma[\Theta/X] \vdash M[N/x][\Theta/X] = M'[N'/x][\Theta'/X] : \Psi[\Theta'/X]}$$

Equational Reasoning

$$\frac{Sg^{tm} \;\triangleright\; \Delta \,|\, \Gamma \vdash M : \Phi}{Th^{tm} \;\triangleright\; \Delta \,|\, \Gamma \vdash M = M : \Phi} \qquad \frac{Th^{tm} \;\triangleright\; \Delta \,|\, \Gamma \vdash M = M' : \Phi}{Th^{tm} \;\triangleright\; \Delta \,|\, \Gamma \vdash M' = M : \Phi}$$

$$\frac{Th^{tm} \;\triangleright\; \Delta \,|\, \Gamma \vdash M = M' : \Phi \quad Th^{tm} \;\triangleright\; \Delta \,|\, \Gamma \vdash M' = M'' : \Phi}{Th^{tm} \;\triangleright\; \Delta \,|\, \Gamma \vdash M = M'' : \Phi}$$

Unit Equations

$$\frac{Sg^{tm} \;\triangleright\; \Delta \,|\, \Gamma \vdash M : unit}{Th^{tm} \;\triangleright\; \Delta \,|\, \Gamma \vdash \langle\rangle = M : unit}$$

Figure 5.5: Term Theorems Generated from a $2\lambda\times$-Term Theory.

— Binary Product Equations —

$$\frac{Sg^{tm} \ \triangleright \ \Delta\,|\,\Gamma \vdash M\colon \Phi \quad Sg^{tm} \ \triangleright \ \Delta\,|\,\Gamma \vdash N\colon \Psi}{Th^{tm} \ \triangleright \ \Delta\,|\,\Gamma \vdash \mathsf{Fst}(\langle M, N\rangle) = M\colon \Phi}$$

$$\frac{Sg^{tm} \ \triangleright \ \Delta\,|\,\Gamma \vdash M\colon \Phi \quad Sg^{tm} \ \triangleright \ \Delta\,|\,\Gamma \vdash N\colon \Psi}{Th^{tm} \ \triangleright \ \Delta\,|\,\Gamma \vdash \mathsf{Snd}(\langle M, N\rangle) = N\colon \Psi}$$

$$\frac{Sg^{tm} \ \triangleright \ \Delta\,|\,\Gamma \vdash P\colon \Phi \times \Psi}{Th^{tm} \ \triangleright \ \Delta\,|\,\Gamma \vdash \langle \mathsf{Fst}(P), \mathsf{Snd}(P)\rangle = P\colon \Phi \times \Psi}$$

— Function Equations —

$$\frac{Sg^{tm} \ \triangleright \ \Delta\,|\,\Gamma, x\colon \Phi \vdash F\colon \Psi \quad Sg^{tm} \ \triangleright \ \Delta\,|\,\Gamma \vdash M\colon \Phi}{Th^{tm} \ \triangleright \ \Delta\,|\,\Gamma \vdash (\lambda x\colon \Phi.F)\,M = F[M/x]\colon \Psi}$$

$$\frac{Sg^{tm} \ \triangleright \ \Delta\,|\,\Gamma \vdash M\colon \Phi \Rightarrow \Psi}{Th^{tm} \ \triangleright \ \Delta\,|\,\Gamma \vdash \lambda x\colon \Phi.(Mx) = M\colon \Phi \Rightarrow \Psi} \quad \text{(where } x \notin \mathit{ftmv}(M)\text{)}$$

$$\frac{Th^{tm} \ \triangleright \ \Delta\,|\,\Gamma, x\colon \Phi \vdash F = F'\colon \Psi}{Th^{tm} \ \triangleright \ \Delta\,|\,\Gamma \vdash \lambda x\colon \Phi.F = \lambda x\colon \Phi.F'\colon \Phi \Rightarrow \Psi}$$

Figure 5.6: Term Theorems Generated from a $2\lambda\times$-Term Theory, Continued.

Polymorphism Equations ─────────────────────────────

$$\frac{Sg^{tm} \;\triangleright\; \Delta, X \,|\, \Gamma \vdash F : \Phi \quad Sg^{ty} \;\triangleright\; \Delta \vdash \Psi}{Th^{tm} \;\triangleright\; \Delta \,|\, \Gamma \vdash (\Lambda X.F)\,\Psi = F[\Psi/X] : \Phi[\Psi/X]}$$

$$\frac{Sg^{tm} \;\triangleright\; \Delta \,|\, \Gamma \vdash M : \forall X.\Phi}{Th^{tm} \;\triangleright\; \Delta \,|\, \Gamma \vdash \Lambda X.(MX) = M : \forall X.\Phi} \quad \text{(where } X \notin ftyv(M))$$

$$\frac{Th^{tm} \;\triangleright\; \Delta, X \,|\, \Gamma \vdash F = F' : \Phi}{Th^{tm} \;\triangleright\; \Delta \,|\, \Gamma \vdash \Lambda X.F = \Lambda X.F' : \forall X.\Phi}$$

Term Typing ─────────────────────────────────────

$$\frac{Th^{tm} \;\triangleright\; \Delta \,|\, \Gamma \vdash M = M' : \Phi \quad Th^{ty} \;\triangleright\; \Delta \vdash \Phi = \Phi'}{Th^{tm} \;\triangleright\; \Delta \,|\, \Gamma \vdash M = M' : \Phi'}$$

Figure 5.7: Term Theorems Generated from a $2\lambda\times$-Term Theory, Continued.

The discussion begins with the semantics for proved types. Suppose that we are given a $2\lambda\times$-theory $Th = (Sg, Ax)$. Let us begin by recalling the idea of a type α in an *algebraic* theory. We think of α, very roughly, as a collection of items (terms) all of which have a similar property. In particular, a judgement of the form

$$x_1 : \alpha, \ldots, x_n : \alpha \vdash M : \alpha$$

says that if $x_1, \ldots, x_n$ all have the same property ("have type α") then M has the same property. Now think about a type-in-context $X_1, \ldots, X_n \vdash \Phi$. One thinks of this as saying that if each X_i "is a type" then so too is Φ. If we regard the notion of "being a type" as a property, then we might try to consider the collection of all items having this property. By analogy with the algebraic case discussed above, this collection (written Type) could be thought of as a type:

$$X_1 : \text{Type}, \ldots, X_n : \text{Type} \vdash \Phi : \text{Type}.$$

To avoid confusion, in this new setting we replace the word referring to a collection (type) with *kind*. Thus Type is the kind of all types. Sometimes Type is called the "type of all types." We now have a setting very much like an algebraic theory in which

• there is one type (cf. kind), denoted by Type,

- there are function symbols (cf. type symbols) with sorting

$$F: \underbrace{\text{Type}, \ldots, \text{Type}}_{\text{length } a} \to \text{Type}$$

where F has arity a (cf. arity a).

Following an argument similar to that in Section 3.4, we see that the kind Type must be interpreted by an object in some category $\mathcal{C}$, which will have finite products in order to interpret type contexts. Let us put $[\![\text{Type}]\!] \stackrel{\text{def}}{=} U$ where U is an object of $\mathcal{C}$. Let $\Delta \stackrel{\text{def}}{=} [X_1, \ldots, X_n]$. With this, a proved type of the form $\Delta \vdash \Phi$ will be modelled by a morphism $[\![\Delta \vdash \Phi]\!] \colon [\![\Delta]\!] \to U$ of $\mathcal{C}$, where $[\![\Delta]\!] \stackrel{\text{def}}{=} \Pi_1^n U$. In fact we can achieve all this if the objects of $\mathcal{C}$ are simply finite products of the (distinguished) object U. We shall write U^n, where $n \in \mathbb{N}$, to denote a product of n copies of U, where $U^0 \stackrel{\text{def}}{=} 1$.

It is clear that the intended meaning of $Sg \rhd \Delta \vdash X$, where X appears in Δ, will be interpreted by a projection morphism $\pi \colon \Pi_1^n U \to U$. The idea of a type symbol F of (non-zero) arity a is that it takes a input types, and returns a new type for which we *have* an intended meaning. So for every such symbol we *specify* a morphism $[\![F]\!] \colon \Pi_1^a U \to U$ in $\mathcal{C}$ and then define

$$[\![\Delta \vdash F(\Phi_1, \ldots, \Phi_a)]\!] \stackrel{\text{def}}{=} [\![F]\!] \circ \langle [\![\Delta \vdash \Phi_1]\!], \ldots, [\![\Delta \vdash \Phi_a]\!] \rangle$$

where we are following the paradigm that substitution of raw types for type variables will be modelled by composition of morphisms in $\mathcal{C}$. Now let us think about how to interpret the remaining forms of proved type. We recommend the reader to review Discussion 4.4.1. We shall need:

- For **Unit Type**, a morphism $U^n \to U$ for each $n \in \mathbb{N}$.

- For **Binary Product Types**, an operation

$$\Box_{U^n} \colon \mathcal{C}(U^n, U) \times \mathcal{C}(U^n, U) \to \mathcal{C}(U^n, U)$$

for each object U^n of $\mathcal{C}$ which is natural in U^n. This means that if $\theta \colon U^m \to U^n$, then

$$\Box_{U^n}(\phi, \psi) \circ \theta = \Box_{U^m}(\phi \circ \theta, \psi \circ \theta).$$

Note that we are writing $\mathcal{C}(U^n, U)$ for the collection of morphisms $U^n \to U$ in $\mathcal{C}$—this is not necessarily assumed to form a set.

- For **Function Types**, an operation

$$\Diamond_{U^n} \colon \mathcal{C}(U^n, U) \times \mathcal{C}(U^n, U) \to \mathcal{C}(U^n, U)$$

natural in U^n. So for any $\theta \colon U^m \to U^n$ we have

$$\Diamond_{U^n}(\phi, \psi) \circ \theta = \Diamond_{U^m}(\phi \circ \theta, \psi \circ \theta).$$

• For **Polymorphism Types,** an operation

$$\forall_{U^n} : \mathcal{C}(U^n \times U, U) \to \mathcal{C}(U^n, U)$$

natural in U^n. So for any $\theta : U^m \to U^n$ we have

$$\forall_{U^n}(\phi) \circ \theta = \forall_{U^m}(\phi \circ (\theta \times id_U)).$$

So, for example, we would put $[\![\Delta \vdash \Phi \times \Psi]\!] \stackrel{\text{def}}{=} \square_{[\![\Delta]\!]}([\![\Delta \vdash \Phi]\!], [\![\Delta \vdash \Psi]\!])$. With these definitions, it is possible to show that if $\Delta \vdash \Phi$ (where Δ has length n) and $\Delta' \vdash \Psi_i$ for $1 \leq i \leq n$ are proved types, then

$$[\![\Delta' \vdash \Phi[\vec{\Psi}/\Delta]]\!] = [\![\Delta \vdash \Phi]\!] \circ \langle [\![\Delta' \vdash \Psi_1]\!], \ldots, [\![\Delta' \vdash \Psi_n]\!] \rangle \qquad (1)$$

where $[\vec{\Psi}/\Delta]$ denotes the expected simultaneous substitution.

Before we can say any more about these operations, we consider how to model proved terms. In the judgement (b) (page 214), we have $Sg \,\triangleright\, \Delta \vdash \Phi_j$ for $j = 1$ to m and $Sg \,\triangleright\, \Delta \vdash \Phi$. Let us write I for U^n in $\mathcal{C}$. We also write $\phi_j \stackrel{\text{def}}{=} [\![\Delta \vdash \Phi_j]\!]$ and $\phi \stackrel{\text{def}}{=} [\![\Delta \vdash \Phi]\!]$, thus we have $\phi_j, \phi : I \to U$ in $\mathcal{C}$. Using an argument similar to the one for deciding how to interpret proved terms of equational type theory (see Section 3.4), we see that we would like to interpret the proved term (b) by a "morphism of the form"

$$[\![\Delta \,|\, \Gamma \vdash M : \Phi]\!] : \phi_1 \times \ldots \times \phi_m \longrightarrow \phi,$$

where $\times$ denotes a binary product and ϕ_j and ϕ are objects of a category. How can we make sense of this? Well, we can demand that each of the collections of morphisms $I \to U$ index the collection of objects of a category which has finite products! We shall write $\mathcal{C}(I, U)$ for this category. This gives a framework for giving a categorical semantics to judgements of the form (a) and (b):

— Properties of a Framework for Interpreting *Th* —————

We need a category with finite products $\mathcal{C}$ whose objects are all finite products of an object U. Proved types are interpreted as morphisms in $\mathcal{C}$. The collection of morphisms $U^n \to U$ in $\mathcal{C}$ are the objects of a category with finite products, written $\mathcal{C}(U^n, U)$, and proved terms are interpreted as morphisms of $\mathcal{C}(U^n, U)$.

Now we deduce some more facts about our proposed categorical model of *Th*. We begin with a discussion of how to model the substitution of raw types for type variables which appear in raw terms. Suppose that J is a proved term of the form $\Delta \mid \Gamma \vdash M \colon \Phi$ and that $J_1, \ldots, J_n$ are proved types of the form $\Delta' \vdash \Psi_i$ for $i = 1$ to n. We shall write $\psi_i \stackrel{\text{def}}{=} [\![\Delta' \vdash \Psi_i]\!]$, $\phi_j \stackrel{\text{def}}{=} [\![\Delta \vdash \Phi_j]\!]$, $\phi \stackrel{\text{def}}{=} [\![\Delta \vdash \Phi]\!]$, $I \stackrel{\text{def}}{=} [\![\Delta]\!]$, $I' \stackrel{\text{def}}{=} [\![\Delta']\!]$ and

$$m \stackrel{\text{def}}{=} [\![\Delta \mid \Gamma \vdash M \colon \Phi]\!] \colon \phi_1 \times \ldots \times \phi_m \longrightarrow \phi.$$

Our aim is to see how we should interpret the proved term

$$J' \stackrel{\text{def}}{=} \Delta' \mid x_1 \colon \Phi_1[\vec{\Psi}/\vec{X}], \ldots, x_m \colon \Phi_m[\vec{\Psi}/\vec{X}] \vdash M[\vec{\Psi}/\vec{X}] \colon \Phi[\vec{\Psi}/\vec{X}]$$

whose interpretation ought to be a morphism in $\mathcal{C}(I', U)$. Clearly, the required morphism depends on the ψ_i, which are objects in $\mathcal{C}(I', U)$, and on m which is a morphism of $\mathcal{C}(I, U)$. So we need an operation

$$ob\,\mathcal{C}(I', U) \times \ldots \times ob\,\mathcal{C}(I', U) \times mor\,\mathcal{C}(I, U) \longrightarrow mor\,\mathcal{C}(I', U).$$

Note that $\mathcal{C}$ has finite products, and so equivalently we need an operation

$$F \colon \mathcal{C}(I', I) \times mor\,\mathcal{C}(I, U) \longrightarrow mor\,\mathcal{C}(I', U).$$

Given such an operation F, we can set

$$[\![J']\!] \stackrel{\text{def}}{=} F(\langle \vec{\psi} \rangle, m) : \phi_1 \langle \vec{\psi} \rangle \times \ldots \times \phi_m \langle \vec{\psi} \rangle \longrightarrow \phi \langle \vec{\psi} \rangle$$

where $\langle \vec{\psi} \rangle \stackrel{\text{def}}{=} \langle \psi_1, \ldots, \psi_n \rangle$, and we have used equation (1) to compute the source and target. This gives us a general framework for interpreting the behaviour of substitution of raw types for type variables which appear in raw terms. It remains to see what properties F must enjoy. First consider the instance $\Delta \mid x \colon \Phi \vdash x \colon \Phi$ of J. We certainly want

$$[\![J']\!] = id_{\phi \langle \vec{\psi} \rangle} \quad \text{in} \quad \mathcal{C}(I', U)$$

and so we shall require

$$F(\langle \vec{\psi} \rangle, id_\phi) \stackrel{\text{def}}{=} id_{\phi \langle \vec{\psi} \rangle}. \tag{2}$$

Second, consider two more instances of J, namely $\Delta \mid x_1 \colon \Phi_1 \vdash M \colon \Phi$ and $\Delta \mid y_1 \colon \Phi_1' \vdash N \colon \Phi_1$ and consider the proved terms

$$\Delta' \mid y_1 \colon \Phi_1'[\vec{\Psi}/\vec{X}] \;\vdash\; M[N/x_1][\vec{\Psi}/\vec{X}] \colon \Phi[\vec{\Psi}/\vec{X}]$$
$$\Delta' \mid y_1 \colon \Phi_1'[\vec{\Psi}/\vec{X}] \;\vdash\; M[\vec{\Psi}/\vec{X}][N[\vec{\Psi}/\vec{X}]/x_1] \colon \Phi[\vec{\Psi}/\vec{X}].$$

These two proved terms are identical by definition, and thus we must have

$$F(\langle \vec{\psi} \rangle, m \circ n) = F(\langle \vec{\psi} \rangle, m) \circ F(\langle \vec{\psi} \rangle, n). \tag{3}$$

Let us summarise our deductions. Suppose that $\psi \overset{\text{def}}{=} \langle \vec{\psi} \rangle : I' \to I$ is any morphism in $\mathcal{C}$. If we write $F(\psi, \phi) \overset{\text{def}}{=} \phi\psi$ where $\phi : I \to U$ is an object of $\mathcal{C}(I, U)$, then equations (2) and (3) say that for each morphism $\psi : I' \to I$ in $\mathcal{C}$, we must have a functor $F(\psi, -) : \mathcal{C}(I, U) \longrightarrow \mathcal{C}(I', U)$. Now consider instances of the judgements J_i being $\Delta \vdash X_i$ for $i = 1$ to n, so that there are projections $\pi_i \overset{\text{def}}{=} [\![\Delta \vdash X_i]\!] : I \to U$. In this case, the instance of the judgement J' is precisely J, and so we must have

$$m = [\![J]\!] = [\![J']\!] \overset{\text{def}}{=} F(\langle \vec{\pi} \rangle, m)$$

that is

$$F(id_I, m) \overset{\text{def}}{=} m. \tag{4}$$

Finally consider the case when J is of the form $X \mid \Gamma \vdash M : \Phi$ (so $n = 1$ here), and two instances of J_1 namely $\Delta' \vdash \Psi'$ and $Y \vdash \Psi$. It is easy to see that we shall require

$$F(\psi \circ \psi', m) = F(\psi', F(\psi, m)), \tag{5}$$

by considering the order of substitution of Ψ and Ψ'. Let us summarise again. Recall the definition of a $\mathcal{C}$-indexed category and of reindexing functor. With this in mind, and writing $\psi^*(-)$ for $F(\psi, -)$, equations (4) and (5) (together with the definition $\psi^*(\phi) \overset{\text{def}}{=} \phi\psi$ given above) say that $id_I^* = id_{\mathcal{C}(I,U)}$ and $(\psi'\psi)^* = \psi^* \circ \psi'^*$. Thus:

Properties of a Framework for Interpreting *Th*

We need a category $\mathcal{C}$ with finite products whose objects are all of the form U^n, together with a $\mathcal{C}$-indexed category $\mathbb{C} : \mathcal{C}^{op} \to \mathbf{Cat}$. If $\psi : I' \to I$ is a morphism of $\mathcal{C}$, then the objects of the category $\mathbb{C}(I)$ are morphisms $I \to U$ in $\mathcal{C}$, and the reindexing functors $\psi^* : \mathbb{C}(I) \to \mathbb{C}(I')$ send an object $\phi : I \to U$ to $\phi \circ \psi : I' \to I \to U$. We will usually write $\mathcal{C}(I, U)$ for the fibre $\mathbb{C}(I)$.

Let us assume that we are given such a $\mathcal{C}$-indexed category. Now we can say more about the natural operations $\square_I$ and $\Diamond_I$. If we apply a procedure identical to that of Discussion 4.4.1 to **Binary Product Equations** and **Function Equations** we will deduce that each category $\mathcal{C}(I, U)$ is in fact *cartesian closed* and that each of $\square_I$ and $\Diamond_I$ may be soundly interpreted by $\times$ and $\Rightarrow$. The naturality of these operations (recall page 218) amounts to requiring that the reindexing functors are *strict* cartesian closed functors.

To complete our analysis of the semantics of $2\lambda\times$-theories, we deduce the properties of the categorical model which will provide a sound interpretation of the rules for **Polymorphism Equations**. As we saw on page 218, there must be an operation on objects $\forall_I : \mathcal{C}(I \times U, U) \to \mathcal{C}(I, U)$ which is natural in the object I of $\mathcal{C}$. If $\phi, \psi : I \to U$ are objects of $\mathcal{C}(I, U)$, we shall write $\mathcal{C}(I, U)(\phi, \psi)$ for the collection of morphisms $\phi \to \psi$ in $\mathcal{C}(I, U)$, which is not necessarily assumed to form a set. In order to interpret the rules **Polymorphism Terms** we shall need an operation

$$\overline{(-)} : \mathcal{C}(I \times U, U)(\pi_1^*(\psi), \phi) \longrightarrow \mathcal{C}(I, U)(\psi, \forall_I(\phi))$$

(where $\pi_1 : I \times U \to I$) which is natural in I and ψ, and an operation

$$\nabla(\rho) : \mathcal{C}(I, U)(\psi, \forall_I(\phi)) \longrightarrow \mathcal{C}(I, U)(\psi, \phi\langle id_I, \rho \rangle)$$

for each object ρ of $\mathcal{C}(I, U)$, such that each $\nabla(\rho)$ is natural in I and ψ. We write out the formal naturality equations. Take morphisms $f : \pi_1^*(\psi) \to \phi$ in $\mathcal{C}(I \times U, U)$; $n : \psi' \to \psi$ and $m : \psi \to \forall_I(\phi)$ in $\mathcal{C}(I, U)$; and $\theta : I' \to I$, $\pi_1' : I' \times U \to I'$, and $\rho : I \to U$ in $\mathcal{C}$; then naturality says that

$$\overline{f \circ \pi_1^*(n)} \;=\; \overline{f} \circ n \tag{6}$$

$$\overline{(\theta \times id_U)^*(f)} \;=\; \theta^*(\overline{f}) \tag{7}$$

$$\theta^*(\nabla(\rho)(m)) \;=\; \nabla(\theta^*(\rho))(\theta^*(m)) \tag{8}$$

$$\nabla(\rho)(m)n \;=\; \nabla(\rho)(mn). \tag{9}$$

For our categorical structure to satisfy the **Polymorphism Equations**, we require

$$\nabla(\rho)(\overline{f}) \;=\; \langle id_I, \rho \rangle^*(f) \tag{10}$$

$$\overline{\nabla(\pi_2)(\pi_1^*(m))} \;=\; m \tag{11}$$

where $\pi_2 : I \times U \to U$ is projection. These equations force the operation $\overline{(-)}$ to be a bijection. To see this, define an operation

$$\widehat{(-)} : \mathcal{C}(I, U)(\psi, \forall_I(\phi)) \longrightarrow \mathcal{C}(I \times U, U)(\pi_1^*(\psi), \phi)$$

by $\widehat{m} \stackrel{\text{def}}{=} \nabla(\pi_2)(\pi_1^*(m))$ with π_1 and π_2 as above. Then clearly $\overline{\widehat{m}} = m$ using (11), and

$$
\begin{aligned}
\widehat{\overline{f}} \;&=\; \nabla(\pi_2)(\overline{(\pi_1 \times id)^*(f)}) && \textit{using (7)} \\
&=\; \langle id, \pi_2 \rangle^*((\pi_1 \times id)^*(f)) && \textit{using (10)} \\
&=\; \langle \pi_1, \pi_2 \rangle^*(f) && \textit{for } (-)^* \textit{ is functorial} \\
&=\; f.
\end{aligned}
$$

In fact it is not only *necessary* that we have an operation $\forall_I$ on objects which is natural in I, for which there is a bijection

$$\overline{(-)} : \mathcal{C}(I \times U, U)(\pi_1^*(\psi), \phi) \rightleftharpoons \mathcal{C}(I, U)(\psi, \forall_I(\phi)) : \widehat{(-)} \qquad (*)$$

which is natural in I and ψ, but also *sufficient*. For given such data, we can define $\nabla(\rho)(m) \stackrel{\text{def}}{=} \langle id, \rho \rangle^*(\widehat{m})$, and then check that the equations (6) to (11) do indeed hold. Let us refer to these necessary and sufficient conditions for modelling the **Polymorphism Equations** by NS$\forall$.

The reader will secretly suspect that the operation $\forall_I$ may lift to a functor on the category $\mathcal{C}(I \times U, U)$, and that the bijection arises because the functor π_1^* has a right adjoint $\forall_I$, for each I. In fact this is the case, as we now show. Suppose that $l: \phi \to \phi'$ is a morphism in $\mathcal{C}(I \times U, U)$, and we are given the operation $\forall_I$ on objects along with the bijection natural in I and ψ. We can lift $\forall_I$ to a functor $\forall_I: \mathcal{C}(I \times U, U) \to \mathcal{C}(I, U)$ by setting $\forall_I(l) \stackrel{\text{def}}{=} \overline{l \circ id_{\forall_I(\phi)}}$. With this definition, it now makes sense to consider the naturality of the bijection $(*)$ in ϕ, which would state that $\forall_I(l) \circ \overline{f} = \overline{lf}$ and $l \circ \widehat{m} = [\forall_I(l) \circ m]^\wedge$. These equations do hold, for example,

$$\forall_I(l) \circ \overline{f} = \overline{l \circ id_{\forall_I(\phi)}} \circ \overline{f} =_{(6)} \overline{l \circ \widehat{id_{\forall_I(\phi)}} \circ \pi_1^*(\overline{f})} =_{(\dagger)} \overline{l \circ [id_{\forall_I(\phi)} \circ \overline{f}]^\wedge} = \overline{lf}$$

where $(\dagger)$ follows from naturality in ψ. Of course, the existence of such a bijection which is natural in both ϕ and ψ implies that we do indeed have $(\pi_1^* \vdash \forall_I)$. In fact, specifying

(i) an adjunction $(\pi_1^* \vdash \forall_I)$,

(ii) together with the requirement that the canonical natural transformation

$$\alpha : \theta^* \circ \forall_I \longrightarrow \forall_{I'} \circ (\theta \times id_U)^*$$

is an identity, where $\theta: I' \to I$ in $\mathcal{C}$,

is *equivalent* to specifying conditions NS$\forall$. Let us refer to conditions (i) and (ii) by NS$\dashv$. Note that part of the force of (ii) is that $\theta^* \circ \forall_I = \forall_{I'} \circ (\theta \times id_U)^*$. By canonical natural transformation, we mean that the component of α at $\phi: I \times U \to U$ is given by

$$\alpha_\phi \stackrel{\text{def}}{=} \overline{(\theta \times id_U)^*(\widehat{id_{\forall_I(\phi)}})} : \theta^*(\forall_I(\phi)) \longrightarrow \forall_{I'}((\theta \times id_U)^*(\phi)).$$

All of the deductions of this section are put together at the start of Section 5.4, where we give a formal definition of a $2\lambda\times$-hyperdoctrine, which is an indexed category in which we may soundly interpret a $2\lambda\times$-theory. First, some exercises.

EXERCISES 5.3.2   Refer to Discussion 5.3.1:

(1) Make sure you understand the notion of a kind of types.

(2) Work through the details accompanying equations (2) to (4).

(3) Verify why we need the operations $\overline{(-)}$ and $\nabla(\rho)$ and check that they are well defined. Derive some of equations (6) to (9), ensuring that you understand in each case how the associated naturality conditions are modelling substitution in the syntax.

(4) Derive equations (10) and (11).

(5) Prove that a categorical structure satisfying NS∀ is indeed necessary and sufficient to model the **Polymorphism Equations**.

(6) Prove that the conditions NS∀ are equivalent to NS⊣.

5.4   *Categorical Semantics and Soundness Theorems*

DISCUSSION 5.4.1   A $2\lambda\times$-*hyperdoctrine* is specified by the following data:

(i) A category $\mathcal{C}$ with finite products, which consists of a distinguished object U which generates all other objects using the operation of forming finite products, which is to say that all objects in $\mathcal{C}$ are of the form U^n with $n \in \mathbb{N}$ where U^0 is a terminal object and U^n (for n positive) is the product of n copies of U. We shall refer to $\mathcal{C}$ as the *base* category of the hyperdoctrine.

(ii) A $\mathcal{C}$-indexed cartesian closed category, $\mathcal{C}(-,U)\colon \mathcal{C}^{op} \to \mathcal{CC}at$, where $\mathcal{CC}at$ is the category of cartesian closed categories and *strict* cartesian closed functors. Given an object I in $\mathcal{C}$, the underlying collection of objects of the cartesian closed category $\mathcal{C}(I,U)$ is indexed by the collection of morphisms $I \to U$ in $\mathcal{C}$, and $\mathcal{C}(I,U)$ is called the *fibre* over the object I. Given a morphism $f\colon I \to I'$ in $\mathcal{C}$, we shall write $f^* \overset{\text{def}}{=} \mathcal{C}(f,U)\colon \mathcal{C}(I',U) \to \mathcal{C}(I,U)$ for the cartesian closed functor assigned to f by the functor $\mathcal{C}(-,U)$.

(iii) For each object I of $\mathcal{C}$ we are given a functor $\forall_I\colon \mathcal{C}(I \times U, U) \to \mathcal{C}(I,U)$ which is right adjoint to the functor $\pi_I^*\colon \mathcal{C}(I,U) \to \mathcal{C}(I \times U, U)$. Moreover, given any morphism $f\colon J \to I$ in $\mathcal{C}$, the diagram of functors

$$
\begin{array}{ccc}
\mathcal{C}(I \times U, U) & \xrightarrow{\;\forall_I\;} & \mathcal{C}(I,U) \\[2pt]
{\scriptstyle (f \times id_U)^*}\Big\downarrow & & \Big\downarrow{\scriptstyle f^*} \\[2pt]
\mathcal{C}(J \times U, U) & \xrightarrow[\;\forall_J\;]{} & \mathcal{C}(J,U)
\end{array}
$$

commutes, and the canonical natural transformation $\theta^* \circ \forall_I \longrightarrow \forall_J \circ (\theta \times id_U)^*$ is an identity. We call the commutation of this diagram and the specification on the canonical natural transformation, the *Beck-Chevalley condition* for $2\lambda\times$-hyperdoctrines.

Let $\mathbb{C}: \mathcal{C}^{op} \to \mathcal{CCat}$ be a $2\lambda\times$-hyperdoctrine. A *type structure* $\mathbf{M}^{ty}$ for a $2\lambda\times$-type structure Sg^{ty} is specified by giving a morphism $[\![F]\!]: U^n \to U$ in $\mathcal{C}$ (equivalently an object $[\![F]\!]$ in $\mathcal{C}(U^n, U)$) for each type symbol F of Sg^{ty}, where n is the arity of F. Using these data we can now give the semantics of proved types. If Δ is a type context which has length n, then we define $[\![\Delta]\!] \stackrel{\text{def}}{=} U^n$. For each judgement of the form $Sg \rhd \Delta \vdash \Phi$ we specify an object $[\![\Delta \vdash \Phi]\!]$ of the category $\mathcal{C}(U^n, U)$ using the rules given in Figure 5.8. We have the following lemma which embodies the slogan that substitution of raw types is modelled by composition of morphisms:

LEMMA 5.4.2   Let $\Delta' \vdash \Psi$ be a proved type where $\Delta' \stackrel{\text{def}}{=} [X_1, \ldots, X_n]$ and let $\Delta \vdash \Phi_i$ be proved types for $i = 1, \ldots, n$. Then $Sg \rhd \Delta \vdash \Psi[\vec{\Phi}/\vec{X}]$ and

$$[\![\Delta \vdash \Psi[\vec{\Phi}/\vec{X}]]\!] \stackrel{\text{def}}{=} [\![\Delta' \vdash \Psi]\!] \circ \langle [\![\Delta \vdash \Phi_1]\!], \ldots, [\![\Delta \vdash \Phi_n]\!] \rangle$$

PROOF   Induct on the derivation of the proved type $Sg \rhd \Delta' \vdash \Psi$.   □

COROLLARY 5.4.3   Suppose that $Sg \rhd \Delta \vdash \Phi$ and $\Delta \subseteq \Delta'$. Then it is the case that $[\![\Delta' \vdash \Phi]\!] = [\![\Delta \vdash \Phi]\!] \circ \pi$ where $\pi: [\![\Delta']\!] \to [\![\Delta]\!]$ is formed from product projections.

PROOF   Immediate from Lemma 5.4.2.   □

DISCUSSION 5.4.4   Suppose that Sg^{ty} is a $2\lambda\times$-type signature. If $\Delta \vdash \Phi = \Phi'$ is any type equation-in-context, we shall say that $\mathbf{M}^{ty}$ *satisfies* the type equation-in-context if $[\![\Delta \vdash \Phi]\!]$ and $[\![\Delta \vdash \Phi']\!]$ are equal morphisms in $\mathcal{C}$. Given a typing theory $Th^{ty} = (Sg^{ty}, Ax^{ty})$ we say that $\mathbf{M}^{ty}$ is a *model* of Th^{ty} if $\mathbf{M}^{ty}$ satisfies the type axioms, that is

$$Ax \rhd \Delta \vdash \Phi = \Phi' \quad \text{implies} \quad [\![\Delta \vdash \Phi]\!] = [\![\Delta \vdash \Phi']\!].$$

We have a soundness theorem, namely

THEOREM 5.4.5   Let $\mathbf{M}^{ty}$ be a model of a typing theory $Th^{ty} = (Sg^{ty}, Ax^{ty})$. Then $\mathbf{M}^{ty}$ satisfies all the type theorems of Th^{ty}.

Type Variables ───────────────────────────────────

$$\frac{}{[\![\Delta', X, \Delta \vdash X]\!] \stackrel{\text{def}}{=} \pi \colon [\![\Delta]\!] \times U \times [\![\Delta]\!] \to U}$$

Unit Type ───────────────────────────────────

$$\frac{}{[\![\Delta \vdash \mathit{unit}]\!] \stackrel{\text{def}}{=} 1 \colon [\![\Delta]\!] \to U}$$

(where 1 is the terminal object of the cartesian closed category $\mathcal{C}([\![\Delta]\!], U)$)

Type Symbols ───────────────────────────────────

$$\frac{}{[\![\Delta \vdash K]\!] \stackrel{\text{def}}{=} [\![K]\!] \circ \,! \colon [\![\Delta]\!] \to 1 \to U} \qquad \text{(where } K \text{ has arity 0)}$$

$$\frac{[\![\Delta \vdash \Phi_1]\!] = \phi_1 \colon [\![\Delta]\!] \to U \quad \dots \quad [\![\Delta \vdash \Phi_n]\!] = \phi_n \colon [\![\Delta]\!] \to U}{[\![\Delta \vdash F(\Phi_1, \dots, \Phi_n)]\!] \stackrel{\text{def}}{=} [\![F]\!] \circ \langle \phi_1, \dots, \phi_n \rangle \colon [\![\Delta]\!] \to U^n \to U}$$

(where F has non-zero arity n)

Binary Product Type ───────────────────────────────────

$$\frac{[\![\Delta \vdash \Phi]\!] = \phi \colon [\![\Delta]\!] \to U \qquad [\![\Delta \vdash \Psi]\!] = \psi \colon [\![\Delta]\!] \to U}{[\![\Delta \vdash \Phi \times \Psi]\!] \stackrel{\text{def}}{=} \phi \times \psi \colon [\![\Delta]\!] \to U}$$

Function Type ───────────────────────────────────

$$\frac{[\![\Delta \vdash \Phi]\!] = \phi \colon [\![\Delta]\!] \to U \qquad [\![\Delta \vdash \Psi]\!] = \psi \colon [\![\Delta]\!] \to U}{[\![\Delta \vdash \Phi \Rightarrow \Psi]\!] \stackrel{\text{def}}{=} \phi \Rightarrow \psi \colon [\![\Delta]\!] \to U}$$

Polymorphism Types ───────────────────────────────────

$$\frac{[\![\Delta, X \vdash \Phi]\!] = \phi \colon [\![\Delta]\!] \times U \to U}{[\![\Delta \vdash \forall X.\Phi]\!] \stackrel{\text{def}}{=} \forall_{[\![\Delta]\!]}(\phi) \colon [\![\Delta]\!] \to U}$$

Figure 5.8: Categorical Semantics of Proved Types Generated from a $2\lambda\times$-Signature.

PROOF   The proof is a routine verification of the closure of the semantics with respect to the rules given on page 208 for deriving type theorems.   □

DISCUSSION 5.4.6   We need a little more notation. Suppose that we are given a $2\lambda\times$-term signature $Sg^{tm}(Th^{ty})$. Then a *term structure* $\mathbf{M^{tm}}$ is specified by giving a model $\mathbf{M^{ty}}$ of Th^{ty}, together with a morphism of the form

$$[\![f]\!]: [\![\Delta \vdash \Phi_1]\!] \times \ldots \times [\![\Delta \vdash \Phi_n]\!] \to [\![\Delta \vdash \Phi]\!]$$

where f is a function symbol with sorting $f: \Delta; \Phi_1, \ldots, \Phi_n \to \Phi$, and a global element $[\![k]\!]$ of $[\![\Delta \vdash \Phi]\!]$ for a constant $k: \Delta; \Phi$. Given a type context Δ, if $Sg \;\triangleright\; \Delta \vdash \Gamma$ for some term context $\Gamma = [x_1: \Phi_1, \ldots, x_m: \Phi_m]$, then we shall define $[\![\Delta \vdash \Gamma]\!] \overset{\text{def}}{=} \Pi_1^m [\![\Delta \vdash \Phi_i]\!]$; and we define $[\![\Delta \vdash \Gamma]\!] \overset{\text{def}}{=} 1$ if Γ is the empty list. Then for every judgement $Sg^{tm} \;\triangleright\; \Delta \,|\, \Gamma \vdash M: \Phi$, we specify a morphism

$$[\![\Delta \,|\, \Gamma \vdash M: \Phi]\!]: [\![\Delta \vdash \Gamma]\!] \to [\![\Delta \vdash \Phi]\!]$$

in $\mathcal{C}([\![\Delta]\!], U)$ by the clauses given in Figures 5.9, 5.10 and 5.11. The remaining results of this section show how various kinds of syntactical substitutions are modelled and include a soundness theorem for term theories.

LEMMA 5.4.7   Let $\Delta \,|\, \Gamma' \vdash N: \Psi$ be a proved term, $\Gamma' = [x_1: \Phi_1, \ldots, x_m: \Phi_m]$ and let $\Delta \,|\, \Gamma \vdash M_j: \Phi_j$ be proved terms for $j = 1, \ldots, m$. Then it is the case that $\Delta \,|\, \Gamma \vdash N[\vec{M}/\vec{x}]: \Psi$ is a proved term, and that its categorical semantics is given by

$$[\![\Delta \,|\, \Gamma \vdash N[\vec{M}/\vec{x}]: \Psi]\!] =$$
$$[\![\Delta \,|\, \Gamma' \vdash N: \Psi]\!] \circ \langle [\![\Delta \,|\, \Gamma \vdash M_1: \Phi_1]\!], \ldots, [\![\Delta \,|\, \Gamma \vdash M_m: \Phi_m]\!] \rangle.$$

PROOF   Induct on the derivation of the judgement $Sg \;\triangleright\; \Delta \,|\, \Gamma' \vdash N: \Psi$.   □

COROLLARY 5.4.8   Let $Sg \;\triangleright\; \Delta \,|\, \Gamma \vdash M: \Phi$, and $\Gamma \subseteq \Gamma'$ where $\Gamma' = [y_1: \Phi'_1, \ldots y_{m'}: \Phi'_{m'}]$ such that $Sg \;\triangleright\; \Delta \vdash \Phi'_j$ where $1 \leq j \leq m'$. Let us write $\Gamma = [x_1: \Phi_1, \ldots, x_m: \Phi_m]$ where $1 \leq i \leq m$, for the sublist Γ of Γ' (and so each Φ_i is a Φ'_j, and each x_i is a y_j). Then it is the case that $Sg \;\triangleright\; \Delta \,|\, \Gamma' \vdash M: \Phi$ and

$$[\![\Delta \,|\, \Gamma' \vdash M: \Phi]\!] = [\![\Delta \,|\, \Gamma \vdash M: \Phi]\!] \circ \pi$$

where $\pi: \Pi_1^{m'}[\![\Delta \vdash \Phi'_j]\!] \to \Pi_1^m[\![\Delta \vdash \Phi_i]\!]$ is formed from product projections.

PROOF   Follows from Lemma 5.4.7.   □

Term Variables ───────────────────────────────────

$$[\![\Delta \mid \Gamma', x{:}\,\Phi, \Gamma \vdash x{:}\,\Phi]\!] = \pi{:}\,[\![\Delta \vdash \Gamma']\!] \times [\![\Delta \vdash \Phi]\!] \times [\![\Delta \vdash \Gamma]\!] \to [\![\Delta \vdash \Phi]\!]$$

Unit Term ───────────────────────────────────

$$[\![\Delta \mid \Gamma \vdash \langle\rangle{:}\,unit]\!] =\,!{:}\,[\![\Delta \vdash \Gamma]\!] \to 1$$

(where 1 is the terminal object of the cartesian closed category $\mathcal{C}([\![\Delta]\!], U)$)

Function Symbols ───────────────────────────────────

$$\frac{[\![\Delta \vdash \Psi_1]\!] = \psi_1{:}\,[\![\Delta]\!] \to U \quad \ldots \quad [\![\Delta \vdash \Psi_n]\!] = \psi_n{:}\,[\![\Delta]\!] \to U}{[\![\Delta \mid \Gamma \vdash k_{\vec{\Psi}}{:}\,\Phi[\vec{\Psi}/\Delta^k]]\!] \overset{\text{def}}{=} \langle\vec{\psi}\rangle^*([\![k]\!]) \circ\, !{:}\,[\![\Delta \vdash \Gamma]\!] \to 1 \to [\![\Delta \vdash \Phi]\!] \circ \langle\vec{\psi}\rangle} \quad (k{:}\,\Delta^k; \Phi)$$

$$\frac{\left\{ \begin{array}{l} [\![\Delta \vdash \Psi_1]\!] = \psi_1{:}\,[\![\Delta]\!] \to U \quad \ldots \quad [\![\Delta \vdash \Psi_n]\!] = \psi_n{:}\,[\![\Delta]\!] \to U \\[4pt] [\![\Delta \mid \Gamma \vdash M_1{:}\,\Phi_1[\vec{\Psi}/\Delta^f]]\!] = m_1{:}\,[\![\Delta \vdash \Gamma]\!] \to [\![\Delta \vdash \Phi_1]\!] \circ \langle\vec{\psi}\rangle \\[4pt] \ldots \\[4pt] [\![\Delta \mid \Gamma \vdash M_a{:}\,\Phi_a[\vec{\Psi}/\Delta^f]]\!] = m_a{:}\,[\![\Delta \vdash \Gamma]\!] \to [\![\Delta \vdash \Phi_a]\!] \circ \langle\vec{\psi}\rangle \end{array} \right.}{\begin{array}{c} [\![\Delta \mid \Gamma \vdash f_{\vec{\Psi}}(\vec{M}){:}\,\Phi[\vec{\Psi}/\Delta^f]]\!] = \langle\vec{\psi}\rangle^*([\![f]\!]) \circ \langle m_1, \ldots, m_a\rangle{:} \\[4pt] [\![\Delta \vdash \Gamma]\!] \to (\Pi_1^a[\![\Delta \vdash \Phi_i]\!]) \circ \langle\vec{\psi}\rangle \to [\![\Delta \vdash \Phi]\!] \circ \langle\vec{\psi}\rangle \\[4pt] (\,f{:}\,\Delta^f; \Phi_1, \ldots, \Phi_a \to \Phi) \end{array}}$$

Figure 5.9: Categorical Semantics of Proved Terms Generated from a $2\lambda\times$-Signature.

Binary Product Terms

$$\begin{cases} [\![\Delta \mid \Gamma \vdash M : \Phi]\!] = m : [\![\Delta \vdash \Gamma]\!] \to [\![\Delta \vdash \Phi]\!] \\ [\![\Delta \mid \Gamma \vdash N : \Psi]\!] = n : [\![\Delta \vdash \Gamma]\!] \to [\![\Delta \vdash \Psi]\!] \end{cases}$$

$$[\![\Delta \mid \Gamma \vdash \langle M, N \rangle : \Phi \times \Psi]\!] = \langle m, n \rangle : [\![\Delta \vdash \Gamma]\!] \to ([\![\Delta \vdash \Phi]\!] \times [\![\Delta \vdash \Psi]\!])$$

$$[\![\Delta \mid \Gamma \vdash P : \Phi \times \Psi]\!] = p : [\![\Delta \vdash \Gamma]\!] \to ([\![\Delta \vdash \Phi]\!] \times [\![\Delta \vdash \Psi]\!])$$

$$[\![\Delta \mid \Gamma \vdash \mathsf{Fst}(P) : \Phi]\!] = \pi \circ p : [\![\Delta \vdash \Gamma]\!] \to ([\![\Delta \vdash \Phi]\!] \times [\![\Delta \vdash \Psi]\!]) \to [\![\Delta \vdash \Phi]\!]$$

$$[\![\Delta \mid \Gamma \vdash P : \Phi \times \Psi]\!] = p : [\![\Delta \vdash \Gamma]\!] \to ([\![\Delta \vdash \Phi]\!] \times [\![\Delta \vdash \Psi]\!])$$

$$[\![\Delta \mid \Gamma \vdash \mathsf{Snd}(P) : \Phi]\!] = \pi' \circ p : [\![\Delta \vdash \Gamma]\!] \to ([\![\Delta \vdash \Phi]\!] \times [\![\Delta \vdash \Psi]\!]) \to [\![\Delta \vdash \Psi]\!]$$

Function Terms

$$[\![\Delta \mid \Gamma, x : \Phi \vdash F : \Psi]\!] = f : ([\![\Delta \vdash \Gamma]\!] \times [\![\Delta \vdash \Phi]\!]) \to [\![\Delta \vdash \Psi]\!]$$

$$[\![\Delta \mid \Gamma \vdash \lambda x : \Phi. F : \Phi \Rightarrow \Psi]\!] = \lambda(f) : [\![\Delta \vdash \Gamma]\!] \to ([\![\Delta \vdash \Phi]\!] \Rightarrow [\![\Delta \vdash \Psi]\!])$$

$$\begin{cases} [\![\Delta \mid \Gamma \vdash M : \Phi \Rightarrow \Psi]\!] = m : [\![\Delta \vdash \Gamma]\!] \to ([\![\Delta \vdash \Phi]\!] \Rightarrow [\![\Delta \vdash \Psi]\!]) \\ [\![\Delta \mid \Gamma \vdash N : \Phi]\!] = n : [\![\Delta \vdash \Gamma]\!] \to [\![\Delta \vdash \Phi]\!] \end{cases}$$

$$[\![\Delta \mid \Gamma \vdash MN : \Psi]\!] = ev \circ \langle m, n \rangle :$$
$$[\![\Delta \vdash \Gamma]\!] \to (([\![\Delta \vdash \Phi]\!] \Rightarrow [\![\Delta \vdash \Psi]\!]) \times [\![\Delta \vdash \Phi]\!]) \to [\![\Delta \vdash \Psi]\!]$$

Polymorphism Terms

$$[\![\Delta, X \mid \Gamma \vdash F : \Phi]\!] = f : [\![\Delta, X \vdash \Gamma]\!] \to [\![\Delta, X \vdash \Phi]\!]$$

$$[\![\Delta \mid \Gamma \vdash \Lambda X. F : \forall X. \Phi]\!] = \overline{f} : [\![\Delta \vdash \Gamma]\!] \to \forall_{[\![\Delta]\!]}([\![\Delta, X \vdash \Phi]\!])$$

$$[\![\Delta \mid \Gamma \vdash M : \forall X. \Phi]\!] = m : [\![\Delta \vdash \Gamma]\!] \to [\![\Delta \vdash \forall X. \Phi]\!]$$

$$[\![\Delta \mid \Gamma \vdash M\Psi : \Phi[\Psi/X]]\!] = \langle id_{[\![\Delta]\!]}, [\![\Delta \vdash \Psi]\!] \rangle^* ([id_{\forall([\![\Delta, Y \vdash \Phi[Y/X]]\!])}]^{\wedge}) \circ m :$$
$$[\![\Delta \vdash \Gamma]\!] \to [\![\Delta \vdash \forall X. \Phi]\!] \to [\![\Delta \vdash \Phi[\Psi/X]]\!]$$

(where Y does not appear in Δ)

Figure 5.10: Categorical Semantics of Proved Terms Generated from a $2\lambda\times$-Signature, Continued.

┌─ **Term Typing** ──┐

$$\dfrac{[\![\Delta \,|\, \Gamma \vdash M : \Phi]\!] = m : [\![\Delta \vdash \Gamma]\!] \to [\![\Delta \vdash \Phi]\!] \quad Th^{ty} \;\rhd\; \Delta \vdash \Phi = \Phi'}{[\![\Delta \,|\, \Gamma \vdash M : \Phi']\!] = m : [\![\Delta \vdash \Gamma]\!] \to [\![\Delta \vdash \Phi]\!]}$$

└──┘

Figure 5.11: Categorical Semantics of Proved Terms Generated from a $2\lambda\times$-Signature, Continued.

LEMMA 5.4.9   Let $\Delta' \,|\, \Gamma \vdash N : \Psi$ be a proved term where $\Delta' = [X_1, \ldots, X_n]$ and let $\Delta \vdash \Phi_i$ be proved types for $i = 1, \ldots, n$. Then it is the case that $\Delta \,|\, \Gamma[\vec{\Phi}/\vec{X}] \vdash N[\vec{\Phi}/\vec{X}] : \Psi[\vec{\Phi}/\vec{X}]$ is a proved term and that its categorical semantics is given by

$$[\![\Delta \,|\, \Gamma[\vec{\Phi}/\vec{X}] \vdash N[\vec{\Phi}/\vec{X}] : \Psi[\vec{\Phi}/\vec{X}]]\!] =$$
$$\langle [\![\Delta \vdash \Phi_1]\!], \ldots, [\![\Delta \vdash \Phi_n]\!] \rangle^* ([\![\Delta' \,|\, \Gamma \vdash N : \Psi]\!]).$$

PROOF   The proof proceeds by induction on the derivation of $Sg \;\rhd\; \Delta' \,|\, \Gamma \vdash N : \Psi$. We shall give an example for the case where N is $\mathsf{Fst}(N)$. Let us take $Sg \;\rhd\; \Delta' \,|\, \Gamma \vdash \mathsf{Fst}(N) : \Psi$ where $Sg \;\rhd\; \Delta' \,|\, \Gamma \vdash N : \Psi \times \Psi'$. We have

$$[\![\Delta \,|\, \Gamma[\vec{\Phi}/\vec{X}] \vdash \mathsf{Fst}(N)[\vec{\Phi}/\vec{X}] : \Psi[\vec{\Phi}/\vec{X}]]\!]$$
$$= \; [\![\Delta \,|\, \Gamma[\vec{\Phi}/\vec{X}] \vdash \mathsf{Fst}(N[\vec{\Phi}/\vec{X}]) : \Psi[\vec{\Phi}/\vec{X}]]\!]$$
$$= \; \pi \circ [\![\Delta \,|\, \Gamma[\vec{\Phi}/\vec{X}] \vdash N[\vec{\Phi}/\vec{X}] : (\Psi \times \Psi')[\vec{\Phi}/\vec{X}]]\!]$$

by induction
$$= \; \pi \circ \langle [\![\Delta \vdash \Phi_1]\!], \ldots, [\![\Delta \vdash \Phi_n]\!] \rangle^* ([\![\Delta' \,|\, \Gamma \vdash N : \Psi \times \Psi']\!])$$
$$= \; \langle [\![\Delta \vdash \Phi_1]\!], \ldots, [\![\Delta \vdash \Phi_n]\!] \rangle^* (\pi) \circ$$
$$\qquad \langle [\![\Delta \vdash \Phi_1]\!], \ldots, [\![\Delta \vdash \Phi_n]\!] \rangle^* ([\![\Delta' \,|\, \Gamma \vdash N : \Psi \times \Psi']\!])$$
$$= \; \langle [\![\Delta \vdash \Phi_1]\!], \ldots, [\![\Delta \vdash \Phi_n]\!] \rangle^* (\pi \circ [\![\Delta' \,|\, \Gamma \vdash N : \Psi \times \Psi']\!])$$
$$= \; \langle [\![\Delta \vdash \Phi_1]\!], \ldots, [\![\Delta \vdash \Phi_n]\!] \rangle^* ([\![\Delta' \,|\, \Gamma \vdash \mathsf{Fst}(N) : \Psi]\!]).$$

Note that in the above calculation we have a projection

$$[\![\Delta' \vdash \Psi \times \Psi']\!] = [\![\Delta' \vdash \Psi]\!] \times [\![\Delta' \vdash \Psi']\!] \xrightarrow{\pi} [\![\Delta' \vdash \Psi]\!]$$

and a strict cartesian closed category morphism

$$\langle [\![\Delta \vdash \Phi_1]\!], \ldots, [\![\Delta \vdash \Phi_n]\!] \rangle^* : \mathcal{C}(U^m, U) \longrightarrow \mathcal{C}(U^n, U)$$

from which we can deduce that the morphism $\langle[\![\Delta \vdash \Phi_1]\!], \ldots, [\![\Delta \vdash \Phi_n]\!]\rangle^*(\overline{\pi})$ is exactly the projection

$$[\![\Delta \vdash (\Psi \times \Psi')[\vec{\Phi}/\vec{X}]]\!] = ([\![\Delta \vdash \Psi[\vec{\Phi}/\vec{X}]]\!] \times [\![\Delta \vdash \Psi'[\vec{\Phi}/\vec{X}]]\!]) \xrightarrow{\pi} [\![\Delta \vdash \Psi[\vec{\Phi}/\vec{X}]]\!].$$

by using Lemma 5.4.2.   □

COROLLARY 5.4.10   Suppose that $Sg \;\triangleright\; \Delta \,|\, \Gamma \vdash M : \Phi$ and $\Delta \subseteq \Delta'$. Then we can deduce that $Sg \;\triangleright\; \Delta' \,|\, \Gamma \vdash M : \Phi$, and

$$[\![\Delta' \,|\, \Gamma \vdash M : \Phi]\!] = \pi^*([\![\Delta \,|\, \Gamma \vdash M : \Phi]\!])$$

where $\pi : [\![\Delta']\!] \to [\![\Delta]\!]$ is formed from product projections.

PROOF   Immediate from Lemma 5.4.9.   □

DISCUSSION 5.4.11   We can now define the notion of a model of a $2\lambda\times$-theory. Once again, the idea is to give an interpretation of such a $2\lambda\times$-theory in a suitable categorical structure, such that the axioms of the theory are satisfied by the interpretation. Suppose that $\mathbf{M^{tm}}$ is a term structure for a $2\lambda\times$-term structure $Sg^{tm}(Th^{ty})$ in a $2\lambda\times$-hyperdoctrine $\mathbb{C} : \mathcal{C}^{op} \to \mathcal{CCat}$. If

$$\Delta \,|\, \Gamma \vdash M = M' : \Phi$$

is any term equation-in-context, we shall say that $\mathbf{M^{tm}}$ *satisfies* the term equation-in-context provided that $[\![\Delta \,|\, \Gamma \vdash M : \Phi]\!]$ and $[\![\Delta \,|\, \Gamma \vdash M' : \Phi]\!]$ are equal morphisms in the cartesian closed category $\mathbb{C}([\![\Delta]\!]) = \mathcal{C}([\![\Delta]\!], U)$. A *model* $\mathbf{M^{tm}}$ of a $2\lambda\times$-term theory $Th^{tm} = (Sg^{tm}, Ax^{tm})$ is a term structure $\mathbf{M^{tm}}$ for the term signature Sg^{tm} in a $2\lambda\times$-hyperdoctrine $\mathbb{C} : \mathcal{C}^{op} \to \mathcal{CCat}$, which satisfies each of the term axioms, that is

$$Ax \;\triangleright\; \Delta \,|\, \Gamma \vdash M = M' : \Phi \quad \text{implies} \quad [\![\Delta \,|\, \Gamma \vdash M : \Phi]\!] = [\![\Delta \,|\, \Gamma \vdash M' : \Phi]\!].$$

We can prove the following soundness theorem for the categorical semantics which we have assigned to $2\lambda\times$-term theories.

THEOREM 5.4.12   Let Th^{tm} be a $2\lambda\times$-term theory and $\mathbb{C} : \mathcal{C}^{op} \to \mathcal{CCat}$ a $2\lambda\times$-hyperdoctrine. If $\mathbf{M^{tm}}$ is a model of Th^{tm} in $\mathbb{C}$, then $\mathbf{M^{tm}}$ satisfies all of the term theorems of Th^{tm}.

PROOF   The proof is a routine verification of the closure of the semantics with respect to the rules given on page 215, page 216 and page 217 for deducing term theorems. We show that if $\mathbf{M^{tm}}$ satisfies any of the equations-in-context which appear in the hypotheses of the rules for generating the term theorems of Th^{tm}, then it satisfies the equation-in-context which is the conclusion of the rule. We shall give some example calculations:

(*Case* **Weakening**):   The assumption is that the theorem

$$Th \ \triangleright \ \Delta \,|\, \Gamma \vdash M = M' \colon \Phi$$

is satisfied by $\mathbf{M^{tm}}$. Let us write $\pi \colon [\![\Delta']\!] \to [\![\Delta]\!]$ and $\tilde{\pi} \colon [\![\Delta \vdash \Gamma']\!] \to [\![\Delta \vdash \Gamma]\!]$. Then we have

$$
\begin{aligned}
[\![\Delta' \,|\, \Gamma' \vdash M \colon \Phi]\!] &= \pi^*([\![\Delta \,|\, \Gamma' \vdash M \colon \Phi]\!]) && \textit{by Corollary 5.4.10} \\
&= \pi^*([\![\Delta \,|\, \Gamma \vdash M \colon \Phi]\!] \circ \tilde{\pi}) && \textit{by Corollary 5.4.8} \\
&= \pi^*([\![\Delta \,|\, \Gamma \vdash M' \colon \Phi]\!] \circ \tilde{\pi}) && \textit{by hypothesis} \\
&= [\![\Delta' \,|\, \Gamma' \vdash M' \colon \Phi]\!],
\end{aligned}
$$

which shows that $\mathbf{M^{tm}}$ satisfies the conclusion of the **Weakening** rule.

(*Case* **Function Equations**):   Let us put:

$$m \overset{\text{def}}{=} [\![\Delta \,|\, \Gamma \vdash M \colon \Phi]\!]$$

$$f \overset{\text{def}}{=} [\![\Delta \,|\, \Gamma, x \colon \Phi \vdash F \colon \Psi]\!].$$

Using the definition of the categorical semantics we have the following calculations:

$$
\begin{aligned}
[\![\Delta \,|\, \Gamma \vdash (\lambda x \colon \Phi.F)\,M \colon \Psi]\!] &= ev \circ \langle [\![\Delta \,|\, \Gamma \vdash \lambda x \colon \Phi.F \colon \Phi \Rightarrow \Psi]\!], [\![\Delta \,|\, \Gamma \vdash M \colon \Phi]\!] \rangle \\
&= ev \circ \langle \lambda(f), m \rangle \\
&= ev \circ (\lambda(f) \times id) \circ \langle id, m \rangle \\
&= f \circ \langle id, m \rangle \\
\textit{using Lemma 5.4.7} \quad &= [\![\Delta \,|\, \Gamma \vdash F[M/x] \colon \Psi]\!].
\end{aligned}
$$

(*Case* **Polymorphism Equations**):   Let us make the following definitions:

$$\psi \overset{\text{def}}{=} [\![\Delta \vdash \Psi]\!]$$

$$\phi \overset{\text{def}}{=} [\![\Delta, X \vdash \Phi]\!]$$

$$f \overset{\text{def}}{=} [\![\Delta, X \,|\, \Gamma \vdash F \colon \Phi]\!]$$

$$\pi \colon [\![\Delta, X]\!] \to [\![\Delta]\!] \ \overset{\text{def}}{=} \ \text{the obvious projection.}$$

Then we have

$$[\![\Delta\mid\Gamma\vdash(\Lambda X.F)\Psi\colon\Phi[\Psi/X]]\!] = \langle id_{[\Delta]},\psi\rangle^*(\widehat{id_{\forall(\phi)}})\circ[\![\Delta\mid\Gamma\vdash\Lambda X.F\colon\forall X.\Phi]\!]$$

$$= \langle id_{[\Delta]},\psi\rangle^*(\widehat{id_{\forall(\phi)}})\circ\overline{f}$$

$$= \langle id_{[\Delta]},\psi\rangle^*(\widehat{id_{\forall(\phi)}})\circ\langle id_{[\Delta]},\psi\rangle^*(\pi^*(\overline{f}))$$

$$= \langle id_{[\Delta]},\psi\rangle^*[(\widehat{id_{\forall(\phi)}})\circ\pi^*(\overline{f})]$$

$$because\ (\pi\dashv\forall) = \langle id_{[\Delta]},\psi\rangle^*(f)$$

$$using\ Lemma\ 5.4.9 = [\![\Delta\mid\Gamma\vdash F[\Psi/X]\colon\Phi[\Psi/X]]\!].$$

For the final example calculation, we shall use the following definitions:

$$\phi\ \stackrel{def}{=}\ [\![\Delta,X\vdash\Phi]\!]$$

$$m\ =\ [\![\Delta\mid\Gamma\vdash M\colon\forall X.\Phi]\!]$$

$$\pi_U\colon[\![\Delta]\!]\times U\to U\ \stackrel{def}{=}\ \text{the obvious projection.}$$

$$\pi_{[\Delta]}\colon[\![\Delta]\!]\times U\to[\![\Delta]\!]\ \stackrel{def}{=}\ \text{the obvious projection.}$$

Appealing to the definitions of the categorical semantics we have

$$[\![\Delta\mid\Gamma\vdash\Lambda X.(MX)\colon\forall X.\Phi]\!] = \overline{[\![\Delta,X\mid\Gamma\vdash MX\colon\Phi]\!]}$$

$$= \overline{\langle id_{[\Delta,X]},[\![\Delta,X\vdash X]\!]\rangle^*[(id_{\forall([\![\Delta,X,Y\vdash\Phi[Y/X]]\!])})^\wedge]\circ[\![\Delta,X\mid\Gamma\vdash M\colon\forall X.\Phi]\!]}$$

$$Cor's\ 5.4.3\ and\ 5.4.10 = \overline{\langle id,\pi_U\rangle^*[(id_{\forall_{[\Delta]\times U}((\pi_{[\Delta]}\times id_U)^*(\phi))})^\wedge]\circ\pi^*_{[\Delta]}(m)}$$

$$Beck\text{-}Chevalley = \overline{\langle id,\pi_U\rangle^*[(id_{\pi^*_{[\Delta]}(\forall_{[\Delta]}(\phi))})^\wedge]\circ\pi^*_{[\Delta]}(m)}$$

$$Beck\text{-}Chevalley = \overline{\langle id,\pi_U\rangle^*[(\pi_{[\Delta]}\times id_U)^*(\widehat{id_{\forall_{[\Delta]}(\phi)}})]\circ\pi^*_{[\Delta]}(m)}$$

$$= \overline{\langle\pi_{[\Delta]},\pi_U\rangle^*(\widehat{id_{\forall_{[\Delta]}(\phi)}})\circ\pi^*_{[\Delta]}(m)}$$

$$= \overline{\widehat{id_{\forall_{[\Delta]}(\phi)}}\circ\pi^*_{[\Delta]}(m)}$$

$$(\pi_{[\Delta]}\dashv\forall_{[\Delta]}) = \overline{\overline{m}}$$

$$= m,$$

where certain subscripts have been omitted to save space. □

EXERCISE 5.4.13 Make sure that you understand the role of the Beck-Chevalley conditions: the informal slogan is that "in a categorical model, the interpretations of $\forall X$ and ΛX abstractions commute with the interpretation of substitution."

DISCUSSION 5.4.14   Let us complete this section with the following defi-
nition. A *structure* **M** in a $2\lambda\times$-hyperdoctrine $\mathbb{C}:\mathcal{C}^{op} \rightarrow \mathcal{ACat}$ for a $2\lambda\times$-
signature $Sg = (Sg^{ty}, Sg^{tm}(Th^{ty}))$ is a pair $(\mathbf{M^{ty}}, \mathbf{M^{tm}})$ where $\mathbf{M^{ty}}$ is a model
of Th^{ty} and $\mathbf{M^{tm}}$ is a term structure. The specification of $\mathbf{M^{tm}}$ depends on
the specification of $\mathbf{M^{ty}}$. A *model* **M** of a $2\lambda\times$-theory $Th = (Th^{ty}, Th^{tm}) =$
(Sg, Ax) in a $2\lambda\times$-hyperdoctrine is specified by a structure $(\mathbf{M^{ty}}, \mathbf{M^{tm}})$ for Sg
where $\mathbf{M^{tm}}$ is a model of Th^{tm} (and $\mathbf{M^{ty}}$ is a model of Th^{ty}). We have

THEOREM 5.4.15   The categorical semantics of a $2\lambda\times$-theory Th in a $2\lambda\times$-
hyperdoctrine given by a model **M** is sound, that is, **M** satisfies all theorems
of Th.

PROOF   This is a restatement of Theorems 5.4.5 and 5.4.12.   □

5.5   A PER Model

DISCUSSION 5.5.1   In this section we shall present an example of a $2\lambda\times$-
hyperdoctrine. Before commencing with the technical details, we pause to
consider, in an informal fashion, the meaning of polymorphic types. Consider
judgements $Sg \triangleright X \vdash \Phi$ and $Sg \triangleright \vdash \forall X.\Phi$. We have seen that $\phi \stackrel{\text{def}}{=} [\![X \vdash \Phi]\!]$
should be interpreted as a morphism of the form $U \rightarrow U$ in a category $\mathcal{C}$, and
of course $[\![\vdash \forall X.\Phi]\!]:1 \rightarrow U$. Let us suppose that the object U is a "universe
of sets." Then the interpretation of any proved type $\vdash \Psi$ will be a set $[\![\vdash \Psi]\!]$
in U. Intuitively, $\forall X.\Phi$ is an expression which acts like Φ for all values of X.
Thus one might postulate that $x \in [\![\vdash \forall X.\Phi]\!]$ just in case $x \in [\![X \vdash \Phi]\!](\xi)$ for
all sets $\xi \in U$. Thus we might set

$$[\![\vdash \forall X.\Phi]\!] \stackrel{\text{def}}{=} \bigcap_{\xi \in U} [\![X \vdash \Phi]\!](\xi)$$

which will make sense provided the universe U is not too large. Let us continue
now with a formal presentation.

DISCUSSION 5.5.2   We shall describe a model of the pure $2\lambda\times$-theory, that is
to say the $2\lambda\times$-theory with empty $2\lambda\times$-signature and no axioms. This model
will be based on the notion of a partial equivalence relation, or a PER. A *PER*
on a given set X is a binary relation on X which is symmetric and transitive.
We shall just consider the case when X is the set $\mathbb{N}$ of natural numbers. So
now let A be a PER (on the set $\mathbb{N}$). We define the *domain* of A, $Dom(A)$, by
setting

$$Dom(A) \stackrel{\text{def}}{=} \{a \in \mathbb{N} \mid aAa\}.$$

It is easy to see that $A \subseteq Dom(A) \times Dom(A)$ is an equivalence relation on $Dom(A)$. Recall that we usually write

$$Dom(A)/A \stackrel{\text{def}}{=} \{[a] \mid a \in A\}$$

for the set of equivalence classes of A.

We shall also need to make use of the partial recursive functions $\mathbb{N} \to \mathbb{N}$. Suppose that $\{\nabla_e \mid e \in E \subseteq \mathbb{N}\}$ is a coding of such functions $\nabla_e \colon \mathbb{N} \to \mathbb{N}$ where ∇_e is the partial recursive function given by the code $e \in \mathbb{N}$. If $\lambda n.f(n) \colon \mathbb{N} \to \mathbb{N}$ is any partial recursive function then there is a code $e \in \mathbb{N}$ for which $\nabla_e = \lambda n.f(n)$. We shall write $\Lambda n.f(n)$ for such a code e, thus

$$\forall m \in \mathbb{N}. \quad \nabla_{\Lambda n.f(n)}(m) = f(m) \in \mathbb{N}.$$

(Note that this definition makes implicit use of the S-m-n theorem). If e and e' code the partial recursive functions ∇_e and $\nabla_{e'}$, then we shall write $e'.e$ for the code of the composition of ∇_e and $\nabla_{e'}$, that is $e'.e \stackrel{\text{def}}{=} \Lambda n.\nabla_{e'}(\nabla_e(n))$.

We can now define a new category $\mathcal{PER}$ whose objects are PERs (on the natural numbers). First a little notation. If $f \colon \mathbb{N} \to \mathbb{N}$ is *any* partial endofunction on $\mathbb{N}$, we shall say that f is *defined* on a subset $X \subseteq \mathbb{N}$ if $f(x)$ is defined for each $x \in \mathbb{N}$. If $f(x)$ is defined, we shall sometimes write $f(x){\downarrow}$ to indicate this. Let A and B be PERs. If $e \in \mathbb{N}$, we say that e *tracks* from A to B if ∇_e is defined on $Dom(A)$ and whenever aAa' then $\nabla_e(a)B\nabla_e(a')$. We write $Tr(A,B)$ for the set of those $e \in \mathbb{N}$ which track from A to B. We define an equivalence relation on $Tr(A,B)$ by setting $e \sim e'$ just in case $a \in Dom(A)$ implies that $\nabla_e(a)B\nabla_{e'}(a)$. With this, the collection of morphisms $A \to B$ in $\mathcal{PER}$ is given by

$$\mathcal{PER}(A,B) \stackrel{\text{def}}{=} Tr(A,B)/\sim.$$

(Note that strictly speaking, a morphism $A \to B$ is a triple $([e], A, B)$, but we shall not be fussy about this). If A is any PER, then the identity on A is $id_A \stackrel{\text{def}}{=} [\Lambda n.n]$. Composition in $\mathcal{PER}$ is given by taking the code of the composition of the corresponding partial recursive functions, that is if $[e] \colon A \to B$ and $[e'] \colon B \to C$ then $[e'] \circ [e] \stackrel{\text{def}}{=} [e'.e] \colon A \to C$.

EXERCISE 5.5.3   Verify that $\mathcal{PER}$ is a well defined category.

DISCUSSION 5.5.4   It will be useful to identify some elementary constructions on PERs. Let us recall how to encode the pairing of natural numbers via partial recursive functions. The partial recursive function

$$p \colon \mathbb{N} \times \mathbb{N} \to \mathbb{N} \qquad (n, n') \mapsto \langle n, n' \rangle \stackrel{\text{def}}{=} (n+1)(n'+n+1)$$

is a bijection of sets. If the inverse is denoted $p^{-1} \colon \mathbb{N} \to \mathbb{N} \times \mathbb{N}$, then we will write

$$\pi_1 \circ p^{-1} : \mathbb{N} \longrightarrow \mathbb{N} \qquad m \mapsto m_1 \overset{\text{def}}{=} \pi_1(p^{-1}(m))$$

$$\pi_2 \circ p^{-1} : \mathbb{N} \longrightarrow \mathbb{N} \qquad m \mapsto m_2 \overset{\text{def}}{=} \pi_2(p^{-1}(m))$$

where $\pi_1, \pi_2 \colon \mathbb{N} \times \mathbb{N} \to \mathbb{N}$ are coordinate projections. This will allow us to write $\Lambda m. m_i$ for the code of the partial recursive function $\pi_i \circ p^{-1} \colon \mathbb{N} \to \mathbb{N}$, and this will prove to be a convenient notation. We can now give our constructions.

(i) Given PERs A and B there is a PER $A \times B$ defined by $n(A \times B)m$ iff $n_1 A m_1$ and $n_2 B m_2$ (for any $n, m \in \mathbb{N}$).

(ii) Given PERs A and B there is a PER $A \Rightarrow B$ where $e(A \Rightarrow B)e'$ iff both ∇_e and $\nabla_{e'}$ are defined on $Dom(A)$ and also whenever aAa' then $\nabla_e(a)B\nabla_{e'}(a')$.

(iii) If $(A_i \mid i \in I)$ is a non-empty family of PERs, then there is a PER $\bigcap_{i \in I} A_i$ given by $n(\bigcap_{i \in I} A_i)m$ iff $nA_i m$ for each $i \in I$.

With this, we have the following crucial theorem:

THEOREM 5.5.5   The category $\mathcal{PER}$ is a cartesian closed category.

PROOF   Define a PER 1 by setting $n1m$ for every $n, m \in \mathbb{N}$. Then 1 is a terminal object, with a unique morphism $[\Lambda n.n] \colon A \to 1$ for any PER A. The binary product of A and B is $A \times B$ as defined in Discussion 5.5.4. The projection functions are

$$\pi_1 \overset{\text{def}}{=} [\Lambda n.n_1] : A \times B \to A \qquad \pi_2 \overset{\text{def}}{=} [\Lambda n.n_2] : A \times B \to B.$$

Given morphisms $[e] \colon C \to A$ and $[e'] \colon C \to B$, then it is easy to see that the unique mediating morphism for the binary product is

$$\langle [e], [e'] \rangle \overset{\text{def}}{=} [\Lambda n. \langle \nabla_e(n), \nabla_{e'}(n) \rangle] : C \to A \times B.$$

The exponential of A and B is $A \Rightarrow B$. The evaluation morphism is

$$ev \overset{\text{def}}{=} [\Lambda n. \nabla_{n_1}(n_2)] : (A \Rightarrow B) \times A \longrightarrow B.$$

If $f = [e] \colon A \times B \to C$ is any morphism of $\mathcal{PER}$ then the exponential mate of f is given by

$$\lambda(f) \overset{\text{def}}{=} [\Lambda n. \Lambda m. \nabla_e(\langle n, m \rangle)] : A \to (B \Rightarrow C).$$

Let us show the universal property of exponentials. First we show that the diagram

$$A \times B \xrightarrow{\ f\ } C$$

$$\lambda(f) \times id_B \Big\downarrow \qquad \nearrow ev$$

$$(B \Rightarrow C) \times B$$

commutes. We have

$$
\begin{aligned}
ev \circ (\lambda(f) \times id_B) &= [\Lambda n.\nabla_{n_1}(n_2)] \circ [\Lambda x.\langle \Lambda m.\nabla_e(\langle x_1, m \rangle), x_2 \rangle] \\
&= [\Lambda x.\nabla_{\Lambda m.\nabla_e(\langle x_1 m, \rangle)}(x_2)] \\
&= [\Lambda x.\nabla_e(\langle x_1, x_2 \rangle)] \\
&= [e].
\end{aligned}
$$

Next we show uniqueness of the mediating morphism; suppose also that $h = [\bar{e}] : A \to (B \Rightarrow C)$ and that $ev \circ (h \times id_B) = f$, that is

$$[e] = [\Lambda x.\nabla_{\nabla_{\bar{e}}(x_1)}(x_2)] \qquad (*)$$

in $\mathcal{PER}(A \times B, C)$. We wish to prove that $h = \lambda(f)$, that is

$$[\bar{e}] = [\Lambda n.\Lambda m.\nabla_e(\langle n, m \rangle)].$$

Let $a \in Dom(A)$; it remains to prove that $\nabla_{\bar{e}}(a)(B \Rightarrow C)\Lambda m.\nabla_e(\langle a, m \rangle)$. Recall the definition of $B \Rightarrow C$. Take $b \in Dom(B)$. As $h \in \mathcal{PER}(A, B \Rightarrow C)$ we have $\nabla_{\bar{e}}(a)\!\downarrow$ and $\nabla_{\bar{e}}(a)(B \Rightarrow C)\nabla_{\bar{e}}(a)$ implying that $\nabla_{\nabla_{\bar{e}}(a)}(b)\!\downarrow$. One can check similarly that $\nabla_{\Lambda m.\nabla_e(\langle a, m \rangle)}(b)\!\downarrow$. Finally take $b B b'$ for which it remains to show that $\nabla_{\nabla_{\bar{e}}(a)}(b) C \nabla_e(\langle a, b' \rangle)$. From $(*)$ and that $\langle a, b \rangle \in Dom(A \times B)$ we have $\nabla_{\nabla_{\bar{e}}(a)}(b) C \nabla_e(\langle a, b \rangle)$. Also, as e tracks from $A \times B$ to C we have $\nabla_e(\langle a, b \rangle) C \nabla_e(\langle a, b' \rangle)$. The result follows from transitivity of C. $\qquad \square$

EXERCISES 5.5.6

(1) Work through the proof of Theorem 5.5.5. Prove in *full detail* that $\mathcal{PER}$ has finite products—be careful to verify all the details. In particular, check that all morphisms you specify are well defined.

(2) Prove that $\mathcal{PER}$ has equalisers and binary coproducts. If you feel ambitious, try to prove that any slice of $\mathcal{PER}$ is cartesian closed.

DISCUSSION 5.5.7   Now we can present an example of a $2\lambda\times$-hyperdoctrine. In this discussion we shall give the details of the structure; the proof that we have indeed defined a $2\lambda\times$-hyperdoctrine $\mathbb{C}: \mathcal{C}^{op} \to \mathcal{CCat}$ will follow.

(i) The object U which generates the base category $\mathcal{C}$ is a set, defined by

$$U \overset{\text{def}}{=} \{A \subseteq \mathbb{N} \times \mathbb{N} \mid A \text{ is a PER on } \mathbb{N}\}.$$

Let U^n be the finite product of n copies of the set U, that is, a finite product in *Set*. Then the objects of $\mathcal{C}$ are of the form U^n by definition, and a morphism $U^n \to U^m$ is simply a set-theoretic function $f \colon U^n \to U^m$.

(ii) Let us write I for U^n. We define the fibre $\mathbb{C}I = \mathcal{C}(I, U)$. The objects of $\mathcal{C}(I, U)$ are (by definition of $2\lambda\times$-hyperdoctrine) set-theoretic functions $I \to U$. Let $x \in I$ be any element of the set I. If $F \colon I \to U$ and $G \colon I \to U$ are any two objects of the fibre over I, then Fx and Gx are PERs: here, Fx is the result of the function F applied to x. Hence there is a PER $R \overset{\text{def}}{=} \bigcap_{x \in I}(Fx \Rightarrow Gx)$. We shall define

$$\mathcal{C}(I, U)(F, G) \overset{\text{def}}{=} Dom(R)/R.$$

It will be helpful to introduce the following convention: if we talk of a morphism $[e] \colon F \to G$ then it will be *implicit that the equivalence class $[e]$ is taken with respect to the equivalence relation $\bigcap_{x \in I}(Fx \Rightarrow Gx)$ on the set $Dom(\bigcap_{x \in I}(Fx \Rightarrow Gx))$ and that for the morphism to be well defined, $e \in Dom(\bigcap_{x \in I}(Fx \Rightarrow Gx))$.*

The identity morphism $F \to F$ in $\mathcal{C}(I, U)$ is $[\Lambda n.n] \in \mathcal{C}(I, U)(F, F)$. Given morphisms $\phi = [e] \colon F \to G$ and $\psi = [e'] \colon G \to H$ in the fibre over I, then set $\psi \circ \phi \overset{\text{def}}{=} [e'.e] \colon F \to H$. *Recall the convention—$[e] \colon F \to G$ refers to an equivalence class in $\mathcal{C}(I, U)(F, G)$, $[e'] \colon G \to H$ to an equivalence class in $\mathcal{C}(I, U)(G, H)$, and $[e'.e] \colon F \to H$ to an equivalence class in $\mathcal{C}(I, U)(F, H)$. One needs to verify that these are good definitions.*

We define a functor $\mathcal{C}(-, U) \colon \mathcal{C}^{op} \to \mathcal{CCat}$ by the assignment

$$H \colon I' \to I \qquad \mapsto \qquad H^* \colon \mathcal{C}(I, U) \longrightarrow \mathcal{C}(I', U)$$

where H sends an object $F \colon I \to U$ of $\mathcal{C}(I, U)$ to the object $FH \colon I' \to U$ of $\mathcal{C}(I', U)$, and the morphism $\phi = [e] \colon F \to G$ of $\mathcal{C}(I, U)$ to the morphism $[e] \colon FH \to GH$ of $\mathcal{C}(I', U)$.

Let us postulate a specified cartesian closed structure for the fibre $\mathcal{C}(I, U)$. In fact, such a structure can be given "pointwise." The terminal object of $\mathcal{C}(I, U)$ is the function $1 \colon I \to U$ which sends each $x \in I$ to the PER $1 \in U$— see Discussion 5.5.4. If F and G are objects of $\mathcal{C}(I, U)$ then $F \times G \colon I \to U$ is the function defined by $(F \times G)x \overset{\text{def}}{=} Fx \times Gx$ for each $x \in I$. The projection morphisms are

$$\pi \overset{\text{def}}{=} [\Lambda n.n_1] \colon F \times G \to F \quad \text{and} \quad \pi' \overset{\text{def}}{=} [\Lambda n.n_2] \colon F \times G \to G.$$

The exponential $F \Rightarrow G\colon I \to U$ is defined by $(F \Rightarrow G)x \stackrel{\text{def}}{=} Fx \Rightarrow Gx$ for each $x \in I$ and $ev \stackrel{\text{def}}{=} [\Lambda n.\nabla_{n_1}(n_2)]\colon (F \Rightarrow G) \times F \to G$.

(iii) Finally, let us give a specified right adjoint to $\pi_I^*\colon \mathcal{C}(I, U) \to \mathcal{C}(I \times U, U)$, say

$$\forall_I : \mathcal{C}(I \times U, U) \longrightarrow \mathcal{C}(I, U).$$

If $F\colon I \times U \to U$ is an object of $\mathcal{C}(I \times U, U)$, then the function $\forall_I F\colon I \to U$ is defined by

$$\forall_I F(x) \stackrel{\text{def}}{=} \bigcap_{A \in U} F(x, A)$$

for each $x \in I$. If $\phi = [e]\colon F \to G$ is a morphism of $\mathcal{C}(I \times U, U)$ then $\forall_I \phi \stackrel{\text{def}}{=} [e]\colon \forall_I F \to \forall_I G$.

THEOREM 5.5.8 The structure defined in Discussion 5.5.7 is indeed a $2\lambda\times$-hyperdoctrine.

PROOF We check that the concrete structure described in Discussion 5.5.7 satisfies the criteria (i), (ii) and (iii) in the definition of $2\lambda\times$-hyperdoctrine given in Discussion 5.4.1.

(i) It is easy to see that $\mathcal{C}$ is the base of a $2\lambda\times$-hyperdoctrine.

(ii) It is easy to see that fibre identity morphisms are as stated. Let us see that composition of fibre morphisms is well defined. Using the notation of Discussions 5.5.7, we first need to verify that $e'.e \in Dom(\bigcap_{x \in I}(Fx \Rightarrow Hx))$. Let $x \in I$ be arbitrary, and let $n(Fx)n'$. Because $[e]\colon F \to G$, it follows that ∇_e is defined on $Dom(Fx)$ and $\nabla_e(n)(Gx)\nabla_e(n')$. Because $[e']\colon G \to H$, one can see that $\nabla_{e'.e} \stackrel{\text{def}}{=} \nabla_{e'} \circ \nabla_e$ is defined on $Dom(Fx)$ and that $\nabla_{e'}(\nabla_e(n))(Hx)\nabla_{e'}(\nabla_e(n'))$ and so we are done. We also need to check that if $[e] = [\bar{e}]\colon F \to G$ and $[e'] = [\bar{e}']\colon G \to H$, then $[e'.e] = [\bar{e}'.\bar{e}]\colon F \to H$ and this is left as an exercise. It is simple to check that composition is associative.

To verify that the functor $\mathcal{C}(-, U)$ is well defined, we need to see that if $[e]\colon F \to G$ then $[e]\colon FH \to GH$ and that if $[e] = [e']\colon F \to G$ then $[e] = [e']\colon FH \to GH$. First, if $e \in Dom(\bigcap_{x \in I}(Fx \Rightarrow Gx))$ then it is clear that $e \in Dom(\bigcap_{y \in I'}(FHy \Rightarrow GHy))$. Second, if $e(\bigcap_{x \in I}(Fx \Rightarrow Gx))e'$ then it follows routinely from the definitions that $e(\bigcap_{y \in I'}(FHy \Rightarrow GHy))e'$. It is immediate that $\mathcal{C}(-, U)$ *is* a functor.

The details which show that $\mathcal{C}(I, U)$ is a cartesian closed category for our specified structure are essentially the same as those which appear in the verification that $\mathcal{PER}$ is such a category, provided that we have given sensible definitions. For this reason, we shall only show that our definition of binary product projections is well defined, and leave all the remaining details as an exercise. To see that $\pi \stackrel{\text{def}}{=} [\Lambda n.n_1]: F \times G \to F$ we need

$$\Lambda n.n_1 \in Dom(\bigcap_{x\in I}((Fx \times Gx) \Rightarrow Fx)).$$

So for any $x \in I$ we need to show that

$$\Lambda n.n_1((Fx \times Gx) \Rightarrow Fx)\Lambda n.n_1.$$

Let $a(Fx \times Gx)a'$. Then certainly $\nabla_{\Lambda n.n_1}(a) = a_1$ is defined, and similarly for a'. Also $a_1(Fx)a'_1$, from the definition of $Fx \times Gx$, and we are done.

(iii) We shall check that $(\forall_I \dashv \pi_I)$. First we see that $\forall_I$ is well defined (on morphisms). If $\phi = [e]: F \to G$ in the fibre $\mathcal{C}(I \times U, U)$ we need to see that $\forall_I \phi \stackrel{\text{def}}{=} [e]: \forall_I F \to \forall_I G$. Let $x \in I$. We need to show that

$$e(\bigcap_{A\in U} F(x, A) \Rightarrow \bigcap_{A\in U} G(x, A))e.$$

Let $n \bigcap_{A\in U} F(x, A)n'$. Hence for any $A \in U$, $nF(x, A)n'$. Thus $\nabla_e(n)\downarrow$, $\nabla_e(n')\downarrow$ and $\nabla_e(n)G(x, A)\nabla_e(n')$ because $[e]: F \to G$ by hypothesis, and with this we are done. To complete the proof that $(\forall_I \dashv \pi_I)$ let us use the characterisation of adjunctions given by Proposition 2.10.24. We shall now omit all verifications that any morphisms we specify are well defined. We have to define a counit (natural transformation)

$$\epsilon : \pi_I^* \circ \forall_I \longrightarrow id : \mathcal{C}(I \times U, U) \longrightarrow \mathcal{C}(I \times U, U)$$

and we set $\epsilon_G \stackrel{\text{def}}{=} [\Lambda n.n]: \pi_I^*(\forall_I G) \to G$. It is simple to verify that ϵ *is* a natural transformation. If $\phi = [e]: \pi_I^* F \to G$ is a morphism in $\mathcal{C}(I \times U, U)$ we define its mate across the (asserted) adjunction to be $\bar{\phi} = [e]: F \to \forall_I G$ in $\mathcal{C}(I, U)$. We check that the diagram

$$
\begin{array}{ccc}
\pi_I^* F & \xrightarrow{\phi} & G \\
{\scriptstyle \pi_I^* \bar\phi} \downarrow & \nearrow & \\
& {\scriptstyle \epsilon_G} & \\
\pi_I^* \forall_I G & &
\end{array}
$$

commutes:

$$
\begin{aligned}
\epsilon_G \circ \pi_I^*(\bar\phi) &= [\Lambda n.n] \circ \pi_I^*([e]) \\
&= [\Lambda n.n] \circ [e] \\
&= [e].
\end{aligned}
$$

It is easy to see that $\overline{\phi}$ is the unique morphism making the above diagram commute, and so we have the required adjunction.

Finally we come to the Beck-Chevalley condition. It is a simple exercise to verify that if $H: J \to I$ in $\mathcal{C}$, then $H^* \circ \forall_I = \forall_J \circ (H \times id_U)^*$. We also need to verify that the canonical natural transformation

$$\alpha : H^* \circ \forall_I \longrightarrow \forall_J \circ (H \times id_U)^*$$

is the identity, and so we check that its components

$$\alpha_G \overset{\text{def}}{=} \overline{(H \times id_U)^* (\widetilde{id_{\forall_{I(G)}}})} : H^*(\forall_I(G)) \longrightarrow \forall_J((H \times id_U)^*(G))$$

are identity morphisms in $\mathcal{C}(J, U)$. We have

$$
\begin{aligned}
\overline{(H \times id_U)^*(\widehat{id_{\forall_I G}})} &= \overline{(H \times id_U)^*(\epsilon_G \circ \pi_I^*(id_{\forall_I G}))} \\
&= \overline{(H \times id_U)^*([\Lambda n.n])} \\
&= [\Lambda n.n]
\end{aligned}
$$

as required. $\qquad\qquad\qquad\qquad\qquad\qquad\qquad\qquad\qquad\qquad\qquad\qquad$ $\square$

EXERCISES 5.5.9   Refer to the proof of Theorem 5.5.8.

(1) Complete the verification that composition of fibre morphisms is well defined and associative.

(2) Verify in detail that each fibre $\mathcal{C}(I, U)$ is a cartesian closed category.

(3) Check that the counit for and mates across the adjunction $(\forall_I \dashv \pi_I)$ are well defined.

(4) Verify that $H^* \circ \forall_I = \forall_J \circ (H \times id_U)^*$.

5.6   A Domain Model

DISCUSSION 5.6.1   We shall give a domain-theoretic example of a model of the pure $2\lambda\times$-theory, that is to say the $2\lambda\times$-theory with empty $2\lambda\times$-signature and no axioms. In order to do this, we shall set up some domain-theoretic machinery which will use ideas from both Chapter 1 and Chapter 2. Before beginning, we give another informal discussion of possible interpretations of $Sg \vartriangleright \forall X.\Phi$. As in Discussion 5.5.1, let U be some kind of universe of "sets." Write $F \overset{\text{def}}{=} [\![X \vdash \Phi]\!]$. If we regard $[\![\vdash \forall X.\Phi]\!]$ as a uniform display of the interpretations $F(\xi)$ where $\xi \in U$ we might try to set $[\![\vdash \forall X.\Phi]\!] \overset{\text{def}}{=} \Pi_{\xi \in U} F(\xi)$. However, if U is too large, then the product will not be a member of U. A way around this is to find a subuniverse of U, say S_U, in which every set in U is represented as a "union" or "colimit" of sets in S_U, where S_U is small enough to make $\Pi_{\xi \in S_U} F(\xi) \in U$, and "$\Pi_{\xi \in S_U} F(\xi) \cong \Pi_{\xi \in U} F(\xi)$." In fact in our example, $\mathcal{U} \overset{\text{def}}{=} U$ will be a category of domains and $\mathbb{S} \overset{\text{def}}{=} S_U$ will be a *set* of domains for which any domain $D \in \mathcal{U}$ will be a colimit of domains from $\mathbb{S}$. Then $\Pi_{X \in \mathbb{S}} FX \in \mathcal{U}$ and such colimits $(\eta_X \colon X \to D \mid X \in \mathbb{S})$ can be used to induce an "isomorphism" $i \colon \Pi_{X \in \mathbb{S}} FX \cong \Pi_{D \in \mathcal{U}} FD$ where

$$(t_X \mid X \in \mathbb{S}) \overset{i}{\mapsto} (\bigvee \{F\eta_X(t_X) \mid \eta_X \in \mathcal{U}(X, D)\} \mid D \in \mathcal{U}).$$

We continue with the formal discussion.

DISCUSSION 5.6.2   Let D and D' be dcpos. Then an *embedding-projection pair* $(e, p) \colon D \to D'$ consists of two continuous functions $e \colon D \to D'$ and $p \colon D' \to D$ for which $pe = id_D$, and $ep \le id_{D'}$ (the latter inequality holding in the exponential dcpo $D' \Rightarrow D'$, an object of the cartesian closed category $\mathcal{DCPO}$). Such an e is called an *embedding* and such a p a *projection*. We will usually write just $f \colon D \to D'$ for such an embedding-projection pair, denoting the embedding by f^e and the projection by f^p, and will abbreviate embedding-projection pair to *e-p pair*. Note that e and p regarded as monotone functions between posets form an adjunction $(e \dashv p)$. It follows from Theorem 2.10.6 that if a pair (e, p) satisfies the definition of e-p pair except that e is only required to be monotone, then e is *automatically* continuous.

The category of *Scott domains and embedding-projection pairs*, $\mathcal{SDom}^{ep}$, has for objects the Scott domains, and a morphism $(e, p) \colon D \to D'$ between Scott domains D and D' is an e-p pair (where of course we note that any Scott domain is indeed a dcpo). The composition of $(e, p) \colon D \to D'$ and $(e', p') \colon D' \to D''$ is given by the e-p pair $(e' \circ e, p \circ p') \colon D \to D''$.

Before giving our domain-theoretic example of a $2\lambda\times$-hyperdoctrine, we need to state and prove a number of results. Here is a summary of our plan of action:

• We prove that $\mathcal{SDom}^{ep}$ has all directed colimits—$\mathcal{SDom}^{ep}$ plays the role of the distinguished object U. This is Theorem 5.6.3.

• We show that there is a set of domains $\mathbb{S}$ of which all other domains in $\mathcal{SDom}^{ep}$ are directed colimits—$\mathbb{S}$ is the set S_U described in Discussion 5.6.1. This is done in Lemma 5.6.5 and Theorem 5.6.6.

• Next we give some technical results, namely Lemmas 5.6.8, 5.6.9, 5.6.11 and 5.6.13. Note that Lemma 5.6.11 shows that $\mathcal{SDom}^{ep}$ is closed under products indexed by $\mathbb{S}$.

• Finally we show in Theorem 5.6.17 that the structure described in Discussion 5.6.15 is indeed a $2\lambda\times$-hyperdoctrine.

THEOREM 5.6.3   The category $\mathcal{SD}om^{ep}$ is directed cocomplete. Moreover, the directed cocompleteness is characterised by the following criterion. Given a directed poset I and a diagram $D: I \to \mathcal{SD}om^{ep}$, a cone $(k_i: D(i) \to C \mid i \in I)$ is a (directed) colimit in $\mathcal{SD}om^{ep}$ iff the set of continuous functions $\{k_i^e k_i^p \mid i \in I\}$ regarded as a subset of the Scott domain $C \Rightarrow C$ is directed and

$$id_C = \bigsqcup\{k_i^e k_i^p \mid i \in I\}.$$

PROOF   We shall give an explicit construction of directed colimits in $\mathcal{SD}om^{ep}$. Let I be a directed poset and $D: I \to \mathcal{SD}om^{ep}$ be a diagram on I. We shall write $f_{ij}: D(i) \to D(j)$ for the image of $i \leq j \in I$ under D. Let us define a cone under D, say $(\eta_i: D(i) \to \varinjlim D \mid i \in I)$, as follows. $\varinjlim D$ consists of families $(s_i \mid i \in I)$ for which $s_i \in D(i)$ and $f_{ij}^p(s_j) = s_i$ holds whenever $i \leq j$. The elements $(s_i \mid i \in I)$ of $\varinjlim D$ are ordered pointwise. The e-p pair $\eta_i: D(i) \to \varinjlim D$ is defined by setting the continuous function $\eta_i^e: D(i) \to \varinjlim D$ to have $\eta_i^e(d)_j \overset{\text{def}}{=} f_{jk}^p f_{ik}^e(d)$ where $i, j \in I$, $d \in D(i)$ and $k \in I$ is any element satisfying $\{i,j\} \leq k$. The continuous function $\eta_i^p: \varinjlim D \to D(i)$ is given by $\eta_i^p(s) \overset{\text{def}}{=} s_i$ where $s \in \varinjlim D$.

We claim that the cone $(\eta_i: D(i) \to \varinjlim D \mid i \in I)$ is in fact a colimit for the diagram D. Let us first check that such a family is well defined.

The poset $\varinjlim D$ is a bounded cocomplete dcpo. Directed joins and non-empty meets are given pointwise; we give the details for the latter. Let $\{(s_i^\alpha \mid i \in I) \mid \alpha \in A\}$ be a non-empty subset of $\varinjlim D$. If we set

$$s_i \overset{\text{def}}{=} \bigwedge\{s_i^\alpha \mid \alpha \in A\} \in D(i)$$

(which exists for $D(i)$ is a Scott domain) then provided $(s_i \mid i \in I) \in \varinjlim D$ it must be the required meet; but this is the case for

$$f_{ij}^p(s_j) = f_{ij}^p(\bigwedge\{s_j^\alpha \mid \alpha \in A\}) = \bigwedge\{f_{ij}^p(s_j^\alpha) \mid \alpha \in A\} = s_i$$

where f_{ij}^p preserves meets because it is a right adjoint. To see that $\varinjlim D$ is a Scott domain we need to prove that it is algebraic; this is done shortly.

We omit the easy details which show that η_i is indeed an e-p pair, except for the proof that the embedding function η_i^e is well defined. So suppose that

$\{i, j\} \leq \{k, k'\}$ in I (where at least one choice of k exists because I is directed) and that $\{k, k'\} \leq k''$ in I. Then we have for any $d \in D(i)$:

$$
\begin{aligned}
\eta_i^e(d)_j &= f_{jk}^p f_{ik}^e(d) \\
&= f_{jk}^p f_{kk''}^p f_{kk''}^e f_{ik}^e(d) \\
&= f_{jk}^p f_{kk''}^p f_{k'k''}^e f_{ik'}^e(d) \\
&= f_{jk'}^p f_{k'k''}^p f_{k'k''}^e f_{ik'}^e(d) \\
&= f_{jk'}^p f_{ik'}^e(d).
\end{aligned}
$$

Now that we have proved each $\eta_i \colon D(i) \to \varinjlim D$ is an e-p pair between dcpos, we can show that $\varinjlim D$ is algebraic. We shall need a little more machinery. Let us show that $\{\eta_i^e \eta_i^p \mid i \in I\}$ is directed in the dcpo $\varinjlim D \Rightarrow \varinjlim D$. Given i and j in I choose k such that $\{i, j\} \leq k$. Without loss of generality, it is enough to show $\eta_i^e \eta_i^p \leq \eta_k^e \eta_k^p$. So pick any $s \in \varinjlim D$ and show that for each $r \in I$ we have $\eta_i^e(s_i)_r \leq \eta_k^e(s_k)_r$. Choose r' and r'' in I for which $\{i, r\} \leq r'$ and $\{k, r'\} \leq r''$. Then

$$
\begin{aligned}
\eta_i^e(s_i)_r &= f_{rr''}^p f_{ir''}^e(s_i) \\
&= f_{rr''}^p f_{kr''}^e f_{ik}^e f_{ik}^p(s_k) \\
&\leq f_{rr''}^p f_{kr''}^e(s_k) \\
&= \eta_k^e(s_k)_r.
\end{aligned}
$$

In fact $id = \bigsqcup \{\eta_i^e \eta_i^p \mid i \in I\}$. The only thing to prove is $id \leq \bigsqcup \{\eta_i^e \eta_i^p \mid i \in I\}$. But given any $s \in \varinjlim D$ and $i \in I$ we have

$$
s_i = \eta_i^e \eta_i^p(s)_i \leq \bigsqcup \{\eta_j^e \eta_j^p(s)_i \mid j \in I\} = [(\bigsqcup \{\eta_j^e \eta_j^p \mid j \in I\})(s)]_i
$$

that is $id \leq \bigsqcup \{\eta_i^e \eta_i^p \mid i \in I\}$. Now we show that $\varinjlim D$ is algebraic using these results. Note that

$$
\{\eta_i^e(e) \mid i \in I, e \in D(i)^\circ, e \leq s_i\} \subseteq \{t \in (\varinjlim D)^\circ \mid t \leq s\}
$$

because embeddings preserve compact elements (why?), and $\eta_i^e(e) \leq s$ because

$$
\eta_i^e(e)_j \leq \eta_i^e(s_i)_j = f_{jk}^p f_{ik}^e(s_i) \leq s_j
$$

for some k satisfying $\{i, j\} \leq k$ in I. We will have shown algebraicity if $s = \bigsqcup \{\eta_i^e(e) \mid i \in I, e \in D(i)^\circ, e \leq s_i\}$. Now,

$$
s = id(s) = \bigsqcup \{\eta_i^e \eta_i^p(s) \mid i \in I\} = \bigsqcup \{\eta_i^e(s_i) \mid i \in I\}.
$$

But $s_i = \bigsqcup\{e \in D(i)^{\circ} \mid e \leq s_i\}$ for $D(i)$ is algebraic and so

$$s = \bigsqcup\{\bigsqcup\{\eta_i^e(e) \mid e \in D(i)^{\circ}, e \leq s_i\} \mid i \in I\},$$

and through a rearrangement of directed joins we are done.

Now that we know each η_i is a well defined e-p pair between Scott domains, it makes sense to verify that $(\eta_i: D(i) \to \varinjlim D \mid i \in I)$ is a cone; the details are omitted. Let us complete the details which show that the cone is a colimit. Suppose that $(h_i: D(i) \to E \mid i \in I)$ is a cone under the diagram D. Define a mediating e-p pair $h: \varinjlim D \to E$ by setting $h^e \overset{\text{def}}{=} \bigsqcup\{h_i^e \eta_i^p \mid i \in I\}$ and $h^p \overset{\text{def}}{=} \bigsqcup\{\eta_i^e h_i^p \mid i \in I\}$. We omit to check that this is a good definition of h, that is, h is well defined. Finally we need to see that for any $i \in I$ we have $h_i = h \circ \eta_i$ and that h is the unique such morphism; we just verify that $h^e \eta_i^e = h_i^e$:

$$
\begin{aligned}
h^e \eta_i^e &= (\bigsqcup\{h_j^e \eta_j^p \mid j \in I\})\eta_i^e \\
&= \bigsqcup\{h_j^e \eta_j^p \eta_i^e \mid j \in I\} \\
\text{as } I \text{ is directed} \quad &= \bigsqcup\{h_j^e \eta_j^p \eta_i^e \mid j \in I, j \geq i\} \\
&= \bigsqcup\{h_j^e \eta_j^p \eta_j^e f_{ij}^e \mid j \in I, j \geq i\} \\
&= \bigsqcup\{h_i^e \mid j \in I, j \geq i\} \\
&= h_i^e.
\end{aligned}
$$

Thus $\mathcal{S}Dom^{ep}$ is indeed directed cocomplete and the characterisation now follows easily:

($\Rightarrow$) Given a directed diagram $D: I \to \mathcal{S}Dom^{ep}$ and a cone

$$(k_i: D(i) \to C \mid i \in I)$$

for which $id_C = \bigsqcup\{k_i^e k_i^p \mid i \in I\}$ then the cone is a colimit because we can define a mediating e-p pair $k: C \to E$ for any other cone $(f_i: D(i) \to E \mid i \in I)$ using an identical construction to that in the last paragraph.

($\Leftarrow$) Conversely, given a colimit $(k_i: D(i) \to C \mid i \in I)$ there is an isomorphism $\theta: \varinjlim D \cong C$ and certainly $k_i = \theta\eta_i$; the result follows. $\square$

EXERCISES 5.6.4 With reference to the proof of Theorem 5.6.3.

(1) Prove that $\eta_i: D(i) \to \varinjlim D$ is an e-p pair for each $i \in I$, and that such a family forms a cone for the diagram $D: I \to \mathcal{S}Dom^{ep}$.

(2) Verify in detail the universal property of the (asserted) colimit $\eta_i: D(i) \to \varinjlim D$.

(3) Make sure you understand the implication ($\Rightarrow$) of the proof.

LEMMA 5.6.5   Let $f\colon X \to D$ and $g\colon Y \to D$ be e-p pairs between Scott domains where X and Y are finite. Then there is an e-p pair $(i,h)\colon Z \to D$ with Z a finite Scott domain for which $\{f^e f^p, g^e g^p\} \leq ih$ in $D \Rightarrow D$, and moreover there are e-p pairs $l \overset{\text{def}}{=} (hf^e, f^p i)\colon X \to Z$ and $m \overset{\text{def}}{=} (hg^e, g^p i)\colon Y \to Z$ where $f = (i,h) \circ l$ and $g = (i,h) \circ m$.

PROOF   The set $Z \overset{\text{def}}{=} \{f^e f^p(d) \vee g^e g^p(d) \mid d \in D\}$ is well defined because $f^e f^p \leq id$ and $g^e g^p \leq id$. The set Z is a poset with order induced from D and the inclusion $i\colon Z \to D$ is clearly monotone. Now consider a function $h\colon D \to Z$ defined by $h(d) \overset{\text{def}}{=} f^e f^p(d) \vee g^e g^p(d)$ for $d \in D$. By definition, $ih \leq id_D$. It is routine to verify that h is indeed continuous and that $hi = id_Z$; we just give some of the details for the latter equation. Suppose that $d \in D$ and that $f^e f^p(d) \vee g^e g^p(d)$ is a typical element of Z; it remains to prove that

$$f^e f^p(f^e f^p(d) \vee g^e g^p(d)) \vee g^e g^p(f^e f^p(d) \vee g^e g^p(d)) = f^e f^p(d) \vee g^e g^p(d).$$

This equality follows quite easily from the definition of binary join, together with the observation that $f^e f^p \leq f^e f^p \vee g^e g^p$ in the Scott domain $D \Rightarrow D$ implies

$$
\begin{aligned}
f^e f^p(d) \;&=\; f^e f^p(f^e f^p(d)) \\
&\leq\; f^e f^p(f^e f^p(d) \vee g^e g^p(d)) \\
&\leq\; f^e f^p(f^e f^p(d) \vee g^e g^p(d)) \vee g^e g^p(f^e f^p(d) \vee g^e g^p(d)).
\end{aligned}
$$

Z is a finite poset and is therefore an algebraic dcpo. Further, from the existence of the functions i and h, it is easy to see that Z is bounded cocomplete (that is it has non-empty meets) by defining $\bigwedge_Z Z' \overset{\text{def}}{=} h(\bigwedge_D i(Z'))$ for each non-empty subset Z' of Z. Thus $(i,h)\colon Z \to D$ is indeed an e-p pair in $\mathcal{SD}om^{ep}$ for which $\{f^e f^p, g^e g^p\} \leq ih$. It is routine calculation to show that l and m are e-p pairs. For example, to see that $l^p l^e = id$ we have

$$id = f^p(f^e f^p)f^e \leq f^p(ih)f^e \overset{\text{def}}{=} l^p l^e \leq id.$$

Finally, that $f = (i,h) \circ l$ and $g = (i,h) \circ m$ is just simple calculation from the definitions. $\square$

THEOREM 5.6.6   Let D be a Scott domain and write $\mathbb{S}$ for the *set* of Scott domains whose underlying sets have finite cardinality and are subsets of the natural numbers $\mathbb{N}$. The set

$$\{f^e f^p \mid S \in \mathbb{S}, f \in \mathcal{SD}om^{ep}(S,D)\}$$

is a directed subset of compact elements of the Scott domain $D \Rightarrow D$. Further,

$$id_D = \bigsqcup \{f^e f^p \mid S \in \mathbb{S}, f \in SDom^{ep}(S, D)\}.$$

Hence it follows that any Scott domain D is a directed colimit of finite domains in $\mathbb{S}$.

PROOF   Appealing to Lemma 5.6.5 we see that

$$\{f^e f^p \mid S \in \mathbb{S}, f \in SDom^{ep}(S, D)\}$$

is directed. Recall from page 68 the characterisation of compact elements in exponential Scott domains and the notation $[-, +]$. Considering the Scott domain $D \Rightarrow D$ and the simple fact that embeddings preserve compactness, it is clear that $F \overset{\text{def}}{=} \bigvee\{[f^e(x), f^e(x)] \mid x \in S\}$ is well defined and a compact element of $D \Rightarrow D$ whenever S is a finite Scott domain. This continuous function $F: D \to D$ equals $f^e f^p$. To see this, let $d \in D$ and set $x_0 \overset{\text{def}}{=} f^p(d) \in S$. Then

$$
\begin{aligned}
F(d) &= \bigvee\{[f^e(x), f^e(x)](d) \mid x \in S\} \\
&= \bigvee\{f^e(x) \mid x \in S, f^e(x) \le d\} \\
&= \bigvee\{f^e(x) \mid x \in S, x \le x_0\} \\
&= f^e(x_0) = f^e f^p(d)
\end{aligned}
$$

and so $f^e f^p$ is compact in $D \Rightarrow D$.

Finally, we wish to see that $id_D = \bigsqcup\{f^e f^p \mid S \in \mathbb{S}, f \in SDom^{ep}(S, D)\}$. As embeddings and projections are strict functions (why?), it is enough to prove that for any non-bottom $d \in D$ we have

$$d \le \bigsqcup\{f^e f^p(d) \mid S \in \mathbb{S}, f \in SDom^{ep}(S, D)\}.$$

Consider the function $\tilde{e}: \Omega \to D$ (where $\perp \neq e \le d, e \in D^\circ$, and Ω is a two point lattice in $\mathbb{N}$) defined by

$$\tilde{e}(x) \overset{\text{def}}{=} \begin{cases} e & \text{if } x = 1 \\ \perp & \text{otherwise} \end{cases}$$

and also the function $p: D \to \Omega$ defined by

$$p(l) \overset{\text{def}}{=} \begin{cases} 1 & \text{if } e \le l \\ 0 & \text{otherwise.} \end{cases}$$

Note of course that p depends on e, and for any given e, the pair $(\tilde{e}, p): \Omega \to D$ is an e-p pair. We now have

$$\bigsqcup\{f^e f^p(d) \mid S \in \mathbb{S}, f \in SDom^{ep}(S, D)\} \geq \bigsqcup\{\tilde{e}p(d) \mid e \in D^\circ, \bot \neq e \leq d\}$$
$$= \bigsqcup\{e \mid e \in D^\circ, \bot \neq e \leq d\}$$
$$= d.$$

To complete the theorem, set $I \overset{\text{def}}{=} \{f^e f^p \mid S \in \mathbb{S}, f \in SDom^{ep}(S, D)\}$, and define a (directed) diagram $F: I \to SDom^{ep}$ by sending $f^e f^p \leq g^e g^p$ to $(g^p f^e, f^p g^e): X \to Y$ (where $f: X \to D$ and $g: Y \to D$). Then we have a directed cone $(f: X \to D \mid f^e f^p \in I)$ and $D \cong \varinjlim F$ follows from appeal to Theorem 5.6.3.   □

EXERCISE 5.6.7   With reference to the proof of Theorem 5.6.6. Show that each $(\tilde{e}, p)$ is an e-p pair. Make sure you understand the final paragraph of the proof.

LEMMA 5.6.8   Let $D: I \to SDom^{ep}$ be a directed diagram and let

$$(\eta_i: D(i) \to \varinjlim D \mid i \in I)$$

be the colimiting cone under D. If $f: X \to \varinjlim D$ is an e-p pair with X finite, then there is some $i \in I$ and e-p pair $h: X \to D(i)$ such that $f = \eta_i \circ h$.

PROOF   Appealing to Theorem 5.6.3 and carefully rearranging indexing sets, we see that

$$f^e f^p = \bigsqcup\{\eta_i^e \eta_i^p f^e f^p \eta_i^e \eta_i^p \mid i \in I\} : \varinjlim D \to \varinjlim D$$

and hence there is $i \in I$ for which $f^e f^p \leq \eta_i^e \eta_i^p f^e f^p \eta_i^e \eta_i^p$ (call this inequality $(*)$) because Theorem 5.6.6 shows that $f^e f^p$ is a compact element. Let us put $h^e \overset{\text{def}}{=} \eta_i^p f^e$ and $h^p \overset{\text{def}}{=} f^p \eta_i^e$. We have to check that (h^e, h^p) is an e-p pair and that $f = \eta_i \circ h$; we just do the latter:

$$\begin{aligned} & & f^p &= f^p \circ f^e f^p \\ h^p \eta_i^p &= f^p \eta_i^e \eta_i^p & (*) &\leq f^p \eta_i^e \eta_i^p f^e f^p \eta_i^e \eta_i^p \\ &\leq f^p & &\leq f^p \eta_i^e \eta_i^p \\ & & &= h^p \eta_i^p \end{aligned}$$

$$f^e = f^e f^p \circ f^e$$

$$\eta_i^e h^e = \eta_i^e \eta_i^p f^e$$

$$(*) \leq \eta_i^e \eta_i^p f^e f^p \eta_i^e \eta_i^p f^e$$

$$\leq f^e$$

$$\leq \eta_i^e \eta_i^p f^e$$

$$= \eta_i^e h^e$$

$$\square$$

LEMMA 5.6.9 Let $D: I \to C$ be a directed diagram where C is any category with directed colimits, and $F: C \to SDom^{ep}$ any functor. Suppose that $(f_i: D(i) \to \varprojlim D \mid i \in I)$ is a colimit in C. Then F preserves such a colimit just in case

$$id_{F \varprojlim D} = \bigsqcup \{(F f_i)^e (F f_i)^p \mid i \in I\}.$$

PROOF

($\Rightarrow$) Let $D: I \to SDom^{ep}$ be a diagram on I with colimit

$$(f_i: D(i) \to \varprojlim D \mid i \in I).$$

Then by hypothesis $(F(f_i): FD(i) \to F(\varprojlim D) \mid i \in I)$ is a colimit and the result follows from Theorem 5.6.3.

($\Leftarrow$) Clear from Theorem 5.6.3. $\square$

DISCUSSION 5.6.10 Let $F: SDom^{ep} \to SDom^{ep}$ be a functor which preserves directed colimits. Recall that S is the (countable) set of finite Scott domains whose underlying sets are subsets of the natural numbers. We shall define an S-*section* of F to be a family $(t_S \mid S \in S)$ indexed by the set S, where

- each t_S is an element of FS, and
- if $f: S \to S'$ is any e-p pair where $S, S' \in S$, then $F(f)^e(t_S) \leq t_{S'}$.

The set of S-sections of F will be denoted $\forall_S(F)$.

LEMMA 5.6.11 The set $\forall_S(F)$ of such S-sections for a directed colimit preserving functor $F: SDom^{ep} \to SDom^{ep}$ is a Scott domain for the pointwise order.

PROOF It is easy to check that $\forall_S(F)$ is a bounded cocomplete dcpo: all constructions happen pointwise. We just check algebraicity. Suppose that t is any element of $\forall_S F$, that $X \in S$, and $x \in (FX)^\circ$ is such that $x \leq t_X$. We define an S-section $[X, x]$ by setting

$$[X, x]_S \overset{\text{def}}{=} \bigvee \{(F f)^e(x) \mid f \in SDom^{ep}(X, S)\}$$

where the join exists for each $(Ff)^e(x)$ is bounded by t_S. This definition is a good one. Let $g: S \to S'$ and we have

$$
\begin{aligned}
(Fg)^e([X,x]_S) &= (Fg)^e(\bigvee\{(Ff)^e(x) \mid f \in \mathcal{S}\mathcal{D}om^{ep}(X,S)\}) \\
\text{for } ((Fg)^e \dashv (Fg)^p) \quad &= \bigvee\{(Fg)^e(Ff)^e(x) \mid f \in \mathcal{S}\mathcal{D}om^{ep}(X,S)\} \\
&\leq \bigvee\{(Ff)^e(x) \mid f \in \mathcal{S}\mathcal{D}om^{ep}(X,S')\} \\
&= [X,x]_{S'}.
\end{aligned}
$$

Note that because X and S are finite, so too is the set of e-p pairs $X \to S$. As such, given that x is a compact element of FX, $[X,x]_S$ is a compact element of FS.

The collection of such $[X,x]$ forms a basis of compact elements of $\forall_S(F)$. Let us write $[X_i, x_i]$, where $i = 1, \dots, n$, for n elements of $\forall_S(F)$; we shall show that $\bigvee_1^n[X_i, x_i]$ is compact. Suppose that $\{t^\alpha \mid \alpha \in A\}$ is a directed subset of $\forall_S(F)$, and that $\bigvee_1^n[X_i, x_i] \leq \bigsqcup\{t^\alpha \mid \alpha \in A\}$. Then $\bigvee_1^n[X_i, x_i]_S \leq \bigsqcup\{t_S^\alpha \mid \alpha \in A\}$ in FS which implies $[X_i, x_i]_S \leq t_S^{\alpha(i)}$ for each i (as each $[X_i, x_i]_S$ is compact as noted above). From directedness it follows that there is some $\alpha \in A$ for which $[X_i, x_i]_S \leq t_S^\alpha$ holds for any i; hence $\bigvee_1^n[X_i, x_i] \leq t^\alpha$ as required. The proof is completed by showing that any S-section t satisfies

$$
t = \bigvee\{[X_1, x_1] \vee \dots \vee [X_n, x_n] \mid X_i \in \mathbb{S}, x_i \in (FX_i)^\circ, x_i \leq t_{X_i}\}.
$$

$\square$

EXERCISE 5.6.12   Complete the proof of Lemma 5.6.11; be careful to verify every step of your calculations.

LEMMA 5.6.13   Let $F, G: (\mathcal{S}\mathcal{D}om^{ep})^n \to \mathcal{S}\mathcal{D}om^{ep}$ be directed colimit preserving functors where $(\mathcal{S}\mathcal{D}om^{ep})^n$ is the product category formed from n copies of $\mathcal{S}\mathcal{D}om^{ep}$. Let $\pi_F: \mathbb{G}(F) \to \mathcal{S}\mathcal{D}om^{ep}$ and $\pi_G: \mathbb{G}(G) \to \mathcal{S}\mathcal{D}om^{ep}$ be the Grothendieck fibrations of F and G. (Recall that this means $\mathbb{G}(F)$ is the category with objects (X, t) where X is an object of $(\mathcal{S}\mathcal{D}om^{ep})^n$ and $t \in FX$, and morphisms $f: (X, t) \to (X', t')$ are $f: X \to X'$ in $(\mathcal{S}\mathcal{D}om^{ep})^n$ satisfying $(Ff)^e(t) \leq t'$). Then a functor $\mu: \mathbb{G}(F) \to \mathbb{G}(G)$ which preserves directed colimits and makes the diagram

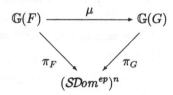

commute is exactly determined by a family $(\mu_X \mid X \in (\mathcal{SD}om^{ep})^n)$ where $\mu_X \colon FX \to GX$ is a continuous function satisfying the following conditions:

(i) If $f \colon X \to Y$ is a morphism in $(\mathcal{SD}om^{ep})^n$, then $(Gf)^e(\mu_X) \le \mu_Y(Ff)^e$, and

(ii) If $(\eta_i \colon X(i) \to \varinjlim X \mid i \in I)$ is a directed colimit for a diagram $X \colon I \to (\mathcal{SD}om^{ep})^n$, then

$$\mu_{\varinjlim X} = \bigsqcup\{(Gf_i)^e \mu_{X(i)}(Ff_i)^p \mid i \in I\}.$$

PROOF

($\Rightarrow$): Suppose that we are given a functor $\mu \colon \mathbb{G}(F) \to \mathbb{G}(G)$ which preserves directed colimits and for which $\pi_G \mu = \pi_F$. So μ defines an assignment

$$\underbrace{(X,t) \xrightarrow{f} (X',t')}_{\text{in } \mathbb{G}(F)} \quad \overset{\mu}{\mapsto} \quad \underbrace{(X,\mu_X(t)) \xrightarrow{f} (X',\mu_{X'}(t'))}_{\text{in } \mathbb{G}(G)} \qquad (\ast)$$

where of course $\mu(f) = f$ for $\pi_G \mu = \pi_F$. These data determine a function $\mu_X \colon FX \to GX$. Considering that $f = \mu(f)$ is a morphism in $\mathbb{G}(G)$, we see that $(\ast)$ yields

$$(Gf)^e(\mu_X(t)) \le \mu_{X'}(t')$$

which shows that (i) holds by taking $t' \overset{\text{def}}{=} (Ff)^e(t)$, and by taking $f = id_X$ (and thus $t \le t'$) we have $\mu_X(t) \le \mu_X(t')$ which is to say that the function μ_X is monotone. It remains to prove (ii) and that μ_X is a continuous function for each X. Suppose that $P \colon I \to \mathbb{G}(F)$ is a diagram where I is a directed poset. Then so too is $D \overset{\text{def}}{=} \pi_F \circ P \colon I \to \mathbb{G}(F) \to \mathcal{I}$, where we have written $\mathcal{I}$ for $(\mathcal{SD}om^{ep})^n$. It is an exercise to check that a colimit for the diagram P is given by the cone

$$(\eta_i \colon (D(i), t(i)) \to (\varinjlim D, t) \mid i \in I)$$

where $t \overset{\text{def}}{=} \bigsqcup\{(F\eta_i)^e(t(i)) \mid i \in I\}$, we have written $(D(i), t(i))$ for $P(i)$ and $(\eta_i \colon D(i) \to \varinjlim D \mid i \in I)$ is a directed colimit in $\mathcal{I}$ for the diagram D. By appeal to Lemma 5.6.9 and the fact that F preserves directed colimits, one sees that for any diagram $X \colon I \to \mathcal{I}$ and $t \in FX$, that

$$(\eta_i \colon (D(i), (F\eta_i)^p(t)) \to (\varinjlim D, t) \mid i \in I) \qquad (\dagger)$$

is a colimit for the particular diagram $P \colon I \to \mathbb{G}(F)$ where $i \le j$ is sent to

$$(D(i), (F\eta_i)^p(t)) \to (D(j), (F\eta_j)^p(t)).$$

Now, $\mu \colon \mathbb{G}(F) \to \mathbb{G}(G)$ is a functor preserving directed colimits (in particular $(\dagger)$), and so it follows that

$$\mu_{\varinjlim D}(t) = \bigsqcup\{(G\eta_i)^e(\mu_{D_i}((F\eta_i)^p(t))) \mid i \in I\}$$

which is exactly (ii).

We show that μ_X is continuous. Let X be an object of $\mathcal{I}$, take a directed subset $\{t_i \mid i \in I\}$ in FX (so here I is any indexing *set*), and put $t \stackrel{\text{def}}{=} \bigsqcup\{t_i \mid i \in I\}$. Then there is a colimit

$$(id_X\colon (X, t_i) \to (X, t) \mid i \in I)$$

in $\mathbb{G}(F)$ for the particular diagram $P\colon I \to \mathbb{G}(F)$, where I is viewed as a directed poset by requiring $i \leq j$ in I just in case $t_i \leq t_j$ in FX, and P sends $i \leq j$ to $id_X\colon (X, t_i) \to (X, t_j)$. Then we can deduce that

$$\mu_X(\bigsqcup\{t_i \mid i \in I\}) = \bigsqcup\{\mu_X(t_i) \mid i \in I\}$$

because μ preserves directed colimits and we have used an instance of (ii) which was proved above. Hence μ_X is continuous.

($\Leftarrow$): Conversely take a family $(\mu_X\colon FX \to GX \mid X \in \mathcal{I})$ of continuous functions for which the conditions (i) and (ii) hold. Let us define a functor $\mu\colon \mathbb{G}(F) \to \mathbb{G}(G)$ by the assignment

$$(X, t) \stackrel{f}{\longrightarrow} (X', t') \quad \longmapsto \quad (X, \mu_X(t)) \stackrel{f}{\longrightarrow} (X', \mu_{X'}(t'))$$

which is well defined because

$$(Gf)^e(\mu_X(t)) \leq \mu_{X'}((Ff)^e(t)) \leq \mu_{X'}(t')$$

where we have used (i) and the fact that $\mu_{X'}$ is a monotone function; it is easy to verify that μ is indeed a functor. We have to show that $\mu\colon \mathbb{G}(F) \to \mathbb{G}(G)$ preserves directed colimits. Suppose that $P\colon I \to \mathbb{G}(F)$ is a directed diagram with colimit

$$(\eta_i\colon (X(i), t(i)) \to (X, t) \mid i \in I)$$

where $(X(i), t(i)) \stackrel{\text{def}}{=} P(i)$. Thus $t = \bigsqcup\{(F\eta_i)^e(t(i)) \mid i \in I\}$. We are done if

$$\mu_X(t) = \bigsqcup\{(G\eta_i)^e(\mu_{X(i)}(t(i))) \mid i \in I\},$$

that is

$$\mu_X(\bigsqcup\{(F\eta_i)^e(t(i)) \mid i \in I\}) = \bigsqcup\{(G\eta_i)^e(\mu_{X(i)}(t(i))) \mid i \in I\}.$$

We have

$$\mu_X(\bigsqcup\{(F\eta_i)^e(t(i)) \mid i \in I\})$$

$$(1) \quad = \quad \bigsqcup\{\mu_X((F\eta_i)^e(t(i))) \mid i \in I\}$$

$$(2) \quad = \quad \bigsqcup\{\bigsqcup\{(G\eta_j)^e(\mu_{X(j)}((F\eta_j)^p((F\eta_i)^e(t(i))))) \mid j \in J\} \mid i \in I\}$$

$$(3) \quad = \quad \bigsqcup\{(G\eta_i)^e(\mu_{X(i)}(t(i))) \mid i \in I\}$$

where (1) uses the continuity of μ_X, (2) is an instance of (ii) and (3) is a rearrangement of directed joins. □

EXERCISE 5.6.14 Verify the characterisation of directed colimits $P: I \to \mathbb{G}(F)$ given in the proof of Lemma 5.6.13, on page 251.

DISCUSSION 5.6.15 We can now give a rather lengthy definition of a domain-theoretic example of a $2\lambda\times$-hyperdoctrine. We shall write $\mathcal{U}$ for $SDom^{ep}$ and $\mathcal{I}$ for $(SDom^{ep})^n$.

The object U which generates the base category by finite powers is $\mathcal{U}$. A morphism $F: \mathcal{U}^n \to \mathcal{U}^m$ is a functor between the product categories which preserves directed colimits. We shall write $\mathcal{C}(\mathcal{I},\mathcal{U})$ for the category which has objects the directed colimit preserving functors $F: \mathcal{I} \to \mathcal{U}$ and in which a morphism $\mu: F \to G$ is given by a functor $\mu: \mathbb{G}(F) \to \mathbb{G}(G)$ for which $\pi_F = \pi_G \circ \mu$, where $\pi_F: \mathbb{G}(F) \to \mathcal{I}$ and $\pi_G: \mathbb{G}(G) \to \mathcal{I}$ are the Grothendieck fibrations of F and G—see Remark 5.6.16.

We shall postulate a specified cartesian closed structure for the category $\mathcal{C}(\mathcal{I},\mathcal{U})$. $\mathcal{C}(\mathcal{I},\mathcal{U})$ has finite products. The terminal object is the functor $1: \mathcal{I} \to \mathcal{U}$ which sends a morphism $f: X \to Y$ in $\mathcal{I}$ to the morphism $id_{\{*\}}: \{*\} \to \{*\}$ in $\mathcal{U}$. $\mathcal{C}(\mathcal{I},\mathcal{U})$ has binary products: if F and G are objects of $\mathcal{C}(\mathcal{I},\mathcal{U})$, their binary product $F \times G$ is given pointwise. More explicitly, if $f: X \to X'$ in $\mathcal{I}$ then we define

$$(F \times G)(f): (F \times G)(X) \to (F \times G)(X')$$

to be

$$FX \times GX \xrightarrow[(Ff)^p \times (Gf)^p]{(Ff)^e \times (Gf)^e} FX' \times GX'.$$

The remaining easy details are omitted. It remains to define exponentials in $\mathcal{C}(\mathcal{I},\mathcal{U})$. Take objects G and H, let X be an object of $\mathcal{I}$ and $f: X \to X'$ a morphism of $\mathcal{I}$. We define the exponential $G \Rightarrow H: \mathcal{I} \to \mathcal{U}$ as follows: set $(G \Rightarrow H)(X) \stackrel{\text{def}}{=} GX \Rightarrow HX$ where $GX \Rightarrow HX$ is the set of continuous functions $GX \to HX$, and define

$$(G \Rightarrow H)(f): (GX \Rightarrow HX) \to (GX' \Rightarrow HX')$$

by setting

$$((G \Rightarrow H)f)^e(g) \stackrel{\text{def}}{=} (Hf)^e g (Gf)^p$$
$$((G \Rightarrow H)f)^p(g') \stackrel{\text{def}}{=} (Hf)^p g' (Gf)^e,$$

for any $g \in GX \Rightarrow HX$ and $g' \in GX' \Rightarrow HX'$. Recall Lemma 5.6.13. We define the evaluation morphism $ev \colon (G \Rightarrow H) \times G \to H$ by the family

$$(ev_X \colon (GX \Rightarrow HX) \times GX \longrightarrow HX \mid X \in \mathcal{I})$$

where if X is an object of $\mathcal{I}$, then $ev_X \colon (GX \Rightarrow HX) \times GX \longrightarrow HX$ is evaluation in the cartesian closed category $\mathcal{SD}om$. Given a morphism $\mu \colon (F \times G) \to H$ in $\mathcal{C}(\mathcal{I}, \mathcal{U})$, the morphism $\lambda(\mu) \colon F \to (G \Rightarrow H)$ is also defined pointwise; more precisely $\lambda(\mu)$ is given by the family $(\lambda(\mu_X) \mid X \in \mathcal{I})$ where each component of the family is the exponential mate of the continuous function $\mu_X \colon FX \times GX \to HX$ in $\mathcal{SD}om$. This completes the specification of the cartesian closed structure of $\mathcal{C}(\mathcal{I}, \mathcal{U})$.

Let us now define a C-indexed cartesian closed category $\mathcal{C}(-, \mathcal{U}) \colon \mathcal{C}^{op} \to \mathcal{C}\mathcal{C}at$ through the assignment

$$H : \mathcal{U}^m \longrightarrow \mathcal{U}^n \quad \overset{\mathcal{C}(-,\mathcal{U})}{\longmapsto} \quad H^* : \mathcal{C}(\mathcal{U}^n, \mathcal{U}) \longrightarrow \mathcal{C}(\mathcal{U}^m, \mathcal{U})$$

in which H^* is defined (with appeal to Lemma 5.6.13) by the assignment

$$(\mu_X \colon FX \to GX \mid X \in \mathcal{U}^n) \quad \overset{H^*}{\longmapsto} \quad (\mu_{HY} \colon FHY \to GHY \mid Y \in \mathcal{U}^m)$$

where $F, G \colon \mathcal{U}^n \to \mathcal{U}$, and $\mu \colon F \to G$ is any morphism of $\mathcal{C}(\mathcal{U}^n, \mathcal{U})$.

Let us now write $\pi_{\mathcal{I}} \colon \mathcal{I} \times \mathcal{U} \to \mathcal{I}$ and $\pi_{\mathcal{U}} \colon \mathcal{I} \times \mathcal{U} \to \mathcal{U}$ for the obvious projections. It remains to define an adjunction

$$\pi_{\mathcal{I}}^* : \mathcal{C}(\mathcal{I}, \mathcal{U}) \rightleftarrows \mathcal{C}(\mathcal{I} \times \mathcal{U}, \mathcal{U}) : \forall_{\mathcal{I}}.$$

Firstly we define $\forall_{\mathcal{I}}$ on objects. Take $F \colon \mathcal{I} \times \mathcal{U} \to \mathcal{U}$ an object in $\mathcal{C}(\mathcal{I} \times \mathcal{U}, \mathcal{U})$. Then we have to define the functor $\forall_{\mathcal{I}} F \colon \mathcal{I} \to \mathcal{U}$. If $f \colon X \to X'$ in $\mathcal{I}$ we define $\forall_{\mathcal{I}} F(X) \overset{\text{def}}{=} \forall_{\mathcal{S}}(F(X, -))$ (here we note that $F(X, -) \colon \mathcal{U} \to \mathcal{U}$ and appeal to Lemma 5.6.11) and

$$\forall_{\mathcal{I}} F(f) \colon \forall_{\mathcal{I}} F(X) \to \forall_{\mathcal{I}} F(X')$$

is defined by setting

$$\forall_{\mathcal{S}}(F(X, -)) \xrightarrow[\;\;(t_S \mid S \in \mathbb{S})\; \overset{(\forall_{\mathcal{I}} F(f))^e}{\longmapsto} \;((F(f, id_S))^e (t_S) \mid S \in \mathbb{S})\;]{} \forall_{\mathcal{S}}(F(X', -))$$

and

$$\forall_{\mathcal{S}}(F(X', -)) \xrightarrow[\;\;(t'_S \mid S \in \mathbb{S})\; \overset{(\forall_{\mathcal{I}} F(f))^p}{\longmapsto} \;((F(f, id_S))^p (t'_S) \mid S \in \mathbb{S})\;]{} \forall_{\mathcal{S}}(F(X, -))$$

where $t_S \in F(X, S)$ and $t'_S \in F(X', S)$. Now we have to define $\forall_{\mathcal{I}}$ on morphisms. Suppose that $\mu: F \to G$ is a morphism of $\mathcal{C}(\mathcal{I} \times \mathcal{U}, \mathcal{U})$. Then $\forall_{\mathcal{I}}\mu: \forall_{\mathcal{I}}F \to \forall_{\mathcal{I}}G$ is given by defining

$$(\forall_{\mathcal{I}}\mu)_X : \forall_{\mathbb{S}}(F(X, -)) \xrightarrow{\;(t_S \mid S \in \mathbb{S}) \mapsto (\mu_{(X,S)}(t_S) \mid S \in \mathbb{S})\;} \forall_{\mathbb{S}}(G(X, -))$$

for each object X of $\mathcal{I}$, where of course $t_S \in F(X, S)$ and $\mu_{(X,S)}: F(X, S) \to G(X, S)$. This completes the definition of our domain-theoretic model of second order polymorphism.

REMARK 5.6.16   Refer to Discussion 5.6.15. This remark may help to explain the definition of a morphism $\mu: F \to G$ in $\mathcal{C}(\mathcal{I}, \mathcal{U})$ as a (directed colimit) preserving functor $\mu: \mathbb{G}(F) \to \mathbb{G}(G)$. First, look at the definition of $\mathbb{G}(F)$ and work out why we can think of $\mathbb{G}(F)$ as the "disjoint union" of the Scott domains FX as X runs over $\mathcal{I}$. Now let $\Delta \mid x: \Phi \vdash M: \Psi$ be a proved term. Suppose that $[\![\Delta]\!] = X \in \mathcal{I}$, $F \stackrel{\text{def}}{=} [\![\Delta \vdash \Phi]\!]: \mathcal{I} \to \mathcal{U}$ and also that $G \stackrel{\text{def}}{=} [\![\Delta \vdash \Psi]\!]: \mathcal{I} \to \mathcal{U}$. Then FX is the meaning of $\Delta \vdash \Phi$ when Δ is interpreted by X, and $\mathbb{G}(F)$ is the union of all possible interpretations of $\Delta \vdash \Phi$—similarly for G. Now, the intended interpretation $\mu \stackrel{\text{def}}{=} [\![\Delta \mid x: \Phi \vdash M: \Psi]\!]: F \to G$ should be a uniform interpretation of $\Delta \mid x: \Phi \vdash M: \Psi$ over all possible interpretations of the type variables in Δ. If μ is given by a family $(\mu_X: FX \to GX \mid X \in \mathcal{I})$, we can think of μ_X as the meaning of $\Delta \mid x: \Phi \vdash M: \Psi$ when Δ is interpreted by X (and hence $\Delta \vdash \Phi$ and $\Delta \vdash \Psi$ are interpreted by FX and GX respectively). Draw some pictures of these ideas.

THEOREM 5.6.17   The structure defined in Discussion 5.6.15 is indeed a $2\lambda\times$-hyperdoctrine.

PROOF   We check that the concrete structure described in Discussion 5.6.15 satisfies the criteria (i), (ii) and (iii) in the definition of $2\lambda\times$-hyperdoctrine given in Discussion 5.4.1.

(i) It is very easy to check that the base category $\mathcal{C}$ with objects the finite powers of $\mathcal{U} \stackrel{\text{def}}{=} SDom^{ep}$ satisfies the structure described in (i) and the details are omitted.

(ii) There are a lot of details to check here. We will only give a small number of examples of the kind of calculations which have to be performed in order to completely verify (ii), but will point out explicitly which details are missing.

To begin, we leave all technicalities which show that $\mathcal{C}(\mathcal{I}, \mathcal{U})$ is a category with finite products to the reader; one needs to verify that given objects

$F, G: \mathcal{I} \to \mathcal{U}$ of $\mathcal{C}(\mathcal{I}, \mathcal{U})$, $F \times G: \mathcal{I} \to \mathcal{U}$ is well defined, that the projections (such as $\pi_F: F \times G \to F$) given by

$$((\pi_F)_X: FX \times GX \to FX \mid X \in \mathcal{I})$$

are well defined, and that these data do indeed yield products in $\mathcal{C}(\mathcal{I}, \mathcal{U})$.

Let us move on to the exponentials in $\mathcal{C}(\mathcal{I}, \mathcal{U})$. Suppose that $G, H: \mathcal{I} \to \mathcal{U}$ are objects of $\mathcal{C}(\mathcal{I}, \mathcal{U})$. We shall check that $G \Rightarrow H: \mathcal{I} \to \mathcal{U}$ is indeed an object of $\mathcal{C}(\mathcal{I}, \mathcal{U})$, that is, it (is a functor and) preserves directed colimits. Let us use Lemma 5.6.9. Suppose that $(f_i: X(i) \to X \mid i \in I)$ is a directed colimit for a diagram $X: I \to \mathcal{I}$. With appeal to Lemma 5.6.9 and noting the following calculation (in which $g: GX \to HX$ is a continuous function)

$$(\bigsqcup \{((G \Rightarrow H)(f_i))^e((G \Rightarrow H)(f_i))^p \mid i \in I\})(g)$$

$$= \bigsqcup \{((G \Rightarrow H)(f_i))^e[((G \Rightarrow H)(f_i))^p(g)] \mid i \in I\}$$

$$= \bigsqcup \{(Hf_i)^e(Hf_i)^p g(Gf_i)^e(Gf_i)^p \mid i \in I\}$$

$$(1) \quad = \bigsqcup \{(Hf_i)^e(Hf_i)^p \mid i \in I\} \circ g \circ \bigsqcup \{(Gf_i)^e(Gf_i)^p \mid i \in I\}$$

$$(2) \quad = g$$

we are done. Here, (1) is a rearrangement of directed joins and (2) follows because G and H preserve directed colimits. We omit the routine calculation showing that the action of $G \Rightarrow H$ on morphisms is well defined. Next we show $ev: (G \Rightarrow H) \times G \to H$ is well defined: the family $(ev_X \mid X \in \mathcal{I})$ should satisfy the criterion of Lemma 5.6.13. We just check that (ii) holds. Take a directed colimit $(\eta_i: X(i) \to X \mid i \in I)$ in $\mathcal{I}$ and $(g, t) \in (GX \Rightarrow HX) \times GX$ and calculate:

$$\bigsqcup \{(H\eta_i)^e ev_{X(i)}(((G \Rightarrow H) \times G)(\eta_i))^p(g, t) \mid i \in I\}$$

$$= \bigsqcup \{(H\eta_i)^e ev_{X(i)}[((G \Rightarrow H)\eta_i)^p \times (G\eta_i)^p](g, t) \mid i \in I\}$$

$$= \bigsqcup \{(H\eta_i)^e((H\eta_i)^p g(G\eta_i)^e[(G\eta_i)^p(t)]) \mid i \in I\}$$

$$(1) \quad = \bigsqcup \{g((G\eta_i)^e((G\eta_i)^p(t))) \mid i \in I\}$$

$$(2) \quad = g(\bigsqcup \{(G\eta_i)^e(G\eta_i)^p(t) \mid i \in I\})$$

$$(3) \quad = g(t)$$

$$= ev_X(g, t).$$

Here, (1) and (3) follow because H and G preserve directed colimits, and (2) because g is a continuous function. Given $\mu: F \times G \to H$ we just check that

$\lambda(\mu): F \to (G \Rightarrow H)$ satisfies criterion (ii) of Lemma 5.6.13:

$$\bigsqcup\{((G \Rightarrow H)\eta_i)^e \lambda(\mu_{X_i})(F\eta_i)^p(t) \mid i \in I\}$$

$$= \bigsqcup\{((G \Rightarrow H)\eta_i)^e(\mu_{X(i)}((F\eta_i)^p(t), -)) \mid i \in I\}$$

$$= \bigsqcup\{(H\eta_i)^e \mu_{X(i)}((F\eta_i)^p(t), -)(G\eta_i)^p \mid i \in I\}$$

$$= \bigsqcup\{[(H\eta_i)^e \mu_{X(i)}((F \times G)\eta_i)^p](t, -) \mid i \in I\}$$

using (ii) for μ $\quad = \mu_X(t)$

where $t \in FX$. (We have used the notation $\lambda(\mu_Y)(\xi) \overset{\text{def}}{=} \mu_Y(\xi, -): GY \to HY$ (where Y is some object of $\mathcal{I}$ and $\xi \in FY$) in the above calculation).

It remains to show that these data satisfy the correct properties to make $\mathcal{C}(\mathcal{I}, \mathcal{U})$ a cartesian closed category; everything follows immediately from the pointwise definitions and the fact that $\mathcal{SDom}$ is cartesian closed.

We require the reindexing functor H^* to be a strict morphism of cartesian closed categories for every morphism $H: \mathcal{I} \to \mathcal{I}'$ in $\mathcal{C}$. This is more or less immediate from the definition; we check preservation of binary products. Take $\pi: F \times G \to F$ and $\pi': F \times G \to G$ in $\mathcal{I}$. Then certainly $H^*(F \times G) = (H^*F) \times (H^*G)$ and if $X \in \mathcal{I}$ then

$$\langle H^*\pi, H^*\pi' \rangle_X = \langle (H^*\pi)_X, (H^*\pi')_X \rangle = \langle \pi_{HX}, \pi'_{HX} \rangle = (id_{H^*(F \times G)})_X.$$

(iii) Suppose that $F: \mathcal{I} \times \mathcal{U} \to \mathcal{U}$ is an object of $\mathcal{C}(\mathcal{I} \times \mathcal{U}, \mathcal{U})$ and $f: X \to X'$ is a morphism of $\mathcal{I}$. We omit the verification that $\forall_{\mathcal{I}} F$ is a directed colimit preserving functor. We know that $\forall_{\mathbb{S}}(F(X, -))$ is a Scott domain as this was proved separately in Lemma 5.6.11. The following computations show that $(\forall_{\mathcal{I}} F(f))^e$ and $(\forall_{\mathcal{I}} F(f))^p$ are well defined, that is, they map $\mathbb{S}$-sections to $\mathbb{S}$-sections:

$$F(id, g)^e(F(f, id)^e(t_S)) = F(f, id)^e(F(id, g)^e(t_S))$$
$$\leq F(f, id)^e(t_{S'})$$

for any e-p pair $g: S \to S'$ and $(t_S \mid S \in \mathbb{S}) \in \forall_{\mathbb{S}}(F(X, -))$, and

$$F(id, g)^e(F(f, id)^p(t_S)) \leq F(id, g)^e(F(f, id)^p F(id, g)^p(t_{S'}))$$
$$= F(id, g)^e F(id, g)^p(F(f, id)^p(t_{S'}))$$
$$\leq F(f, id)^p(t_{S'})$$

for any e-p pair $g: S \to S'$ and $(t_S \mid S \in \mathbb{S}) \in \forall_{\mathbb{S}}(F(X', -))$. Suppose that $\mu: F \to G$ is a morphism in $\mathcal{C}(\mathcal{I} \times \mathcal{U}, \mathcal{U})$. Again we omit most of the verifications that $\forall_{\mathcal{I}}(\mu)$ is well defined and that it satisfies the conditions of

Lemma 5.6.13, except for details of criterion (ii). Take a directed colimit $(\eta_i \colon X(i) \to X \mid i \in I)$ in $\mathcal{I}$ and $t \in \forall_{\mathcal{I}} F(X) = \forall_{\mathbb{S}}(F(X, -))$:

$$
\begin{aligned}
(\bigsqcup \{(\forall_{\mathcal{I}} G(\eta_i))^e \forall_{\mathcal{I}}(\mu)_{X(i)} (\forall_{\mathcal{I}} F(\eta_i))^p \mid i \in I\}](t))_S \\
= \bigsqcup \{G(\eta_i, id)^e \mu_{(X(i), S)} F(\eta_i, id)^p(t_S) \mid i \in I\} \\
\textit{using (ii) for } \mu \quad = \quad \mu_{(X, S)}(t_S) \\
= \quad (\forall_{\mathcal{I}}(\mu)_X(t))_S
\end{aligned}
$$

where we note that $((\eta_i, id_S) \colon (X(i), S) \to (X, S) \mid i \in I)$ is a directed colimit in $\mathcal{I} \times \mathcal{U}$ for every $S \in \mathbb{S}$, in order to apply (ii) of Lemma 5.6.13 to μ.

Our remaining task consists of showing that we have an adjunction $(\pi_{\mathcal{I}}^* \vdash \forall_{\mathcal{I}})$ satisfying the Beck-Chevalley condition. Let us use the characterisation of adjunctions given by Proposition 2.10.24. This means we have to define a counit (natural transformation)

$$
\epsilon \colon \pi_{\mathcal{I}}^* \forall_{\mathcal{I}} \longrightarrow id \colon \mathcal{C}(\mathcal{I} \times \mathcal{U}, \mathcal{U}) \longrightarrow \mathcal{C}(\mathcal{I} \times \mathcal{U}, \mathcal{U})
$$

such that if $\mu \colon \pi_{\mathcal{I}}^* F \to G$ (where F is an object of $\mathcal{C}(\mathcal{I}, \mathcal{U})$ and G is an object of $\mathcal{C}(\mathcal{I} \times \mathcal{U}, \mathcal{U})$) then there is a unique morphism $\bar{\mu} \colon F \to \forall_{\mathcal{I}} G$ in $\mathcal{C}(\mathcal{I}, \mathcal{U})$, for which the diagram

$$
\begin{array}{ccc}
\pi_{\mathcal{I}}^* F & \xrightarrow{\ \mu\ } & G \\
{\scriptstyle \pi_{\mathcal{I}}^* \bar{\mu}} \downarrow & \nearrow {\scriptstyle \epsilon_G} & \\
\pi_{\mathcal{I}}^* \forall_{\mathcal{I}} G & &
\end{array}
$$

commutes, where by definition

$$
\epsilon_G \colon \forall_{\mathcal{I}} G \circ \pi_{\mathcal{I}} \to G \colon \mathcal{I} \times \mathcal{U} \to \mathcal{U}.
$$

In order to define the natural transformation ϵ we have to give its components ϵ_G at each object G of $\mathcal{C}(\mathcal{I} \times \mathcal{U}, \mathcal{U})$. Each such component is a morphism in the category $\mathcal{C}(\mathcal{I} \times \mathcal{U}, \mathcal{U})$ and we appeal as ever to Lemma 5.6.13 and give a family of continuous functions

$$
((\epsilon_G)_{(X, D)} \colon \forall_{\mathbb{S}}(G(X, -)) \to G(X, D) \mid (X, D) \in \mathcal{I} \times \mathcal{U}).
$$

Each such continuous function $(\epsilon_G)_{(X, D)}$ is given by

$$
(t_S \mid S \in \mathbb{S}) \xmapsto{\ (\epsilon_G)_{(X, D)}\ } \bigsqcup \{G(id_X, f)^e(t_S) \mid S \in \mathbb{S}, f \in \mathcal{U}(S, D)\}
$$

wherein $t_S \in G(X, S)$ and $(t_S \mid S \in \mathbb{S}) \in \forall_{\mathbb{S}}(G(X, -))$. Let us see that $(\epsilon_G)_{(X,D)}$ is well defined. First we check that the set

$$\{G(id_X, f)^e(t_S) \mid S \in \mathbb{S}, f \in \mathcal{U}(S, D)\}$$

is indeed directed. Consider $G(id, f)^e(t_S)$ and $G(id, f')^e(t_{S'})$. By Lemma 5.6.5 there is a finite Scott domain S'' and e-p pairs $f'': S'' \to D$, $l: S \to S''$ and $m: S' \to S''$ for which $f = f''l$ and $f' = f''m$. Now

$$G(id, f)^e(t_S) = G(id, f'')^e G(id, l)^e(t_S) \le G(id, f'')^e(t_{S''})$$

because t is an $\mathbb{S}$-section; a similar argument applies for f', S', proving directedness. It is simple to verify that $(\epsilon_G)_{(X,D)}$ is monotone. To see continuity of $(\epsilon_G)_{(X,D)}$, take a directed subset

$$\{t^a \mid a \in A\} \subseteq \forall_{\mathbb{S}}(G(X, -))$$

and note that

$$
\begin{aligned}
(\epsilon_G)_{(X,D)}(\bigsqcup\{t^a \mid a \in A\}) \\
&= \bigsqcup\{G(id, f)^e(\bigsqcup\{t_S^a \mid a \in A\}) \mid S \in \mathbb{S}, f \in \mathcal{U}(S, D)\} \\
&= \bigsqcup\{\bigsqcup\{G(id, f)^e(t_S^a) \mid a \in A\} \mid S \in \mathbb{S}, f \in \mathcal{U}(S, D)\} \\
&= \bigsqcup\{\bigsqcup\{G(id, f)^e(t_S^a) \mid S \in \mathbb{S}, f \in \mathcal{U}(S, D)\} \mid a \in A\} \\
&= \bigsqcup\{(\epsilon_G)_{(X,D)}(t_S^a \mid S \in \mathbb{S}) \mid a \in A\} \\
&= \bigsqcup\{(\epsilon_G)_{(X,D)}(t^a) \mid a \in A\}.
\end{aligned}
$$

Next we show that $(\epsilon_G)_{(X,D)}$ satisfies (i) of Lemma 5.6.13. Take a morphism

$$(\bar{f}, f): (X, D) \to (X', D')$$

in $\mathcal{I} \times \mathcal{U}$ and an $\mathbb{S}$-section $t \in \forall_{\mathbb{S}}(G(X, -))$. Then

$$
\begin{aligned}
[G(\bar{f}, f)^e \circ (\epsilon_G)_{(X,D)}](t) &= G(\bar{f}, f)^e(\bigsqcup\{G(id, h)^e(t_S) \mid S \in \mathbb{S}, h \in \mathcal{U}(S, D)\}) \\
&= \bigsqcup\{G(\bar{f}, fh)^e(t_S) \mid S \in \mathbb{S}, h \in \mathcal{U}(S, D)\} \\
&\le \bigsqcup\{G(\bar{f}, k)^e(t_S) \mid S \in \mathbb{S}, k \in \mathcal{U}(S, D')\} \\
&= (\epsilon_G)_{(X',D')}(G(\bar{f}, id)^e(t_S) \mid S \in \mathbb{S}) \\
&= [(\epsilon_G)_{(X',D')} \circ (\forall_{\mathcal{I}} G(\bar{f}))^e](t) \\
&= [(\epsilon_G)_{(X',D')} \circ ((\forall_{\mathcal{I}} G \circ \pi_{\mathcal{I}})(\bar{f}, f))^e](t)
\end{aligned}
$$

which shows that (i) holds. To verify (ii), let

$$((\bar{\eta}_i, \eta_i) \colon (X(i), D(i)) \to (X, D) \mid i \in I)$$

be a directed colimit in $\mathcal{I} \times \mathcal{U}$. We need to show that

$$(\epsilon_G)_{(X,D)} = \bigsqcup \{G(\bar{\eta}_i, \eta_i)^e (\epsilon_G)_{(X(i),D(i))} (\forall_{\mathcal{I}} G(\bar{\eta}_i))^p \mid i \in I\}. \tag{1}$$

Suppose that $t = (t_S \mid S \in \mathbb{S}) \in \forall_{\mathbb{S}}(G(X, -))$ is any $\mathbb{S}$-section. To prove (1) it is sufficient to prove that for any $S \in \mathbb{S}$ and e-p pair $h \colon S \to D$

$$G(id_X, h)^e (t_S) \leq (\bigsqcup \{G(\bar{\eta}_i, \eta_i)^e (\epsilon_G)_{(X(i),D(i))} (\forall_{\mathcal{I}} G(\bar{\eta}_i))^p \mid i \in I\})(t).$$

Note that if $h \colon S \to D$ in $\mathcal{U}$ where $S \in \mathbb{S}$ then by Lemma 5.6.8 there is some $i \in I$ for which there is an e-p pair $\theta(h) \colon S \to D(i(h))$ satisfying $h = \eta_{i(h)} \circ \theta(h)$. A moment's thought reveals that the family

$$((\bar{\eta}_i, id_S) \colon (X(i), S) \to (X, S) \mid i \in I)$$

is a colimit in $\mathcal{I} \times \mathcal{U}$ for each $S \in \mathbb{S}$, and hence by Theorem 5.6.3 and the continuity of the functor G we have

$$id_{G(X,S)} = \bigsqcup \{G(\bar{\eta}_i, id_S)^e G(\bar{\eta}_i, id_S)^p \mid i \in I\}. \tag{2}$$

We have

$$\bigsqcup \{G(\bar{\eta}_i, \eta_i)^e (\epsilon_G)_{(X(i),D(i))} (\forall_{\mathcal{I}} G(\bar{\eta}_i))^p \mid i \in I\}(t)$$

$$= \bigsqcup \{G(\bar{\eta}_i, \eta_i)^e (\epsilon_G)_{(X(i),D(i))} (\forall_{\mathcal{I}} G(\bar{\eta}_i))^p (t) \mid i \in I\}$$

$$= \bigsqcup \{G(\bar{\eta}_i, \eta_i)^e [(\epsilon_G)_{(X(i),D(i))} (G(\bar{\eta}_i, id_S)^p (t_S) \mid S \in \mathbb{S})] \mid i \in I\}$$

$$= \bigsqcup \{G(\bar{\eta}_i, \eta_i)^e [\bigsqcup \{G(id_{X(i)}, \theta)^e G(\bar{\eta}_i, id_S)^p (t_S) \mid$$
$$S \in \mathbb{S}, \theta \in \mathcal{U}(S, D(i))\}] \mid i \in I\}$$

$$= \bigsqcup \{\bigsqcup \{G(id, \eta_i)^e G(id, \theta)^e G(\bar{\eta}_i, id)^e G(\bar{\eta}_i, id)^p (t_S) \mid$$
$$S \in \mathbb{S}, \theta \in \mathcal{U}(S, D(i))\} \mid i \in I\}$$

$$= \bigsqcup \{\{G(id, \eta_i)^e G(id, \theta)^e [\bigsqcup \{G(\bar{\eta}_j, id)^e G(\bar{\eta}_j, id)^p (t_S) \mid j \in J\}] \mid$$
$$S \in \mathbb{S}, \theta \in \mathcal{U}(S, D(i))\} \mid i \in I\}$$

$$\text{by (2)} \quad = \bigsqcup \{\{G(id, \eta_i)^e G(id, \theta)^e (t_S) \mid S \in \mathbb{S}, \theta \in \mathcal{U}(S, D(i))\} \mid i \in I\}$$

$$\geq G(id, \eta_{i(h)})^e G(id, \theta(h))^e (t_S)$$

$$= G(id, h)^e (t_S)$$

and so we are done. Now we define a mate across the adjunction for the counit ϵ. If $\mu\colon \pi_{\mathcal{I}}^* F \to G$ then $\bar{\mu}\colon F \to \forall_{\mathcal{I}} G$ is defined from the family

$$\bar{\mu}_X : FX \xrightarrow{\ x \mapsto (\mu_{(X,S)}(x) \mid S \in \mathbb{S})\ } \forall_{\mathbb{S}}(G(X,-))$$

of continuous functions, where X is an object of $\mathcal{I}$. If $\nu\colon F \to \forall_{\mathcal{I}} G$ then its mate $\hat{\nu}\colon \pi_{\mathcal{I}}^* F \to G$ is given by a family of functions

$$\hat{\nu}_X : FX \xrightarrow{\ x \mapsto \bigsqcup\{G(id_X,f)^e(\nu_X(x))_S \mid S \in \mathbb{S}, f \in \mathcal{U}(S,D)\}\ } G(X,D)$$

where (X,D) runs over the objects of $\mathcal{I}$. Once again there are a number of things to do to see that everything is well defined. All of the calculations are quite routine (and certainly should be now after the last few pages of examples!); let us simply verify that $\bar{\mu}$ satisfies criterion (ii) of Lemma 5.6.13. Take a colimit $(\eta_i\colon X(i) \to X \mid i \in I)$ in $\mathcal{I}$ and element $x \in FX$. Then

$$\bigsqcup\{(\forall_{\mathcal{I}} G(\eta_i))^e \circ (\bar{\mu})_{X(i)} \circ (F\eta_i)^p \mid i \in I\}(x)$$

$$= \bigsqcup\{(\forall_{\mathcal{I}} G(\eta_i))^e(\mu_{(X(i),S)}(F(\eta_i)^p(x)) \mid S \in \mathbb{S}) \mid i \in I\}$$

$$= (\bigsqcup\{G(\eta_i, id)^e \mu_{(X(i),S)} F(\eta_i)^p(x) \mid i \in I\} \mid S \in \mathbb{S})$$

using (ii) for $\mu \quad = \quad (\mu_{(X,S)}(x) \mid S \in \mathbb{S})$

$$= \bar{\mu}_X(x).$$

We have to show that the above data yield an adjunction $(\pi_{\mathcal{I}}^* \vdash \forall_{\mathcal{I}})$ which will be the case if

$$\epsilon_G \circ \pi_{\mathcal{I}}^* \bar{\mu} \ = \ \mu$$
$$\hat{\nu} \ = \ \epsilon_G \circ \pi_{\mathcal{I}}^* \nu.$$

Let us just verify the first equation; take $\mu_{(X,D)}\colon FX \to G(X,D)$ and $x \in FX$:

$$(\epsilon_G)_{(X,D)}((\pi_{\mathcal{I}}^* \bar{\mu})_{(X,D)}(x))$$

$$= \ (\epsilon_G)_{(X,D)}(\bar{\mu}_X(x))$$

$$= \ \bigsqcup\{G(id_X,f)^e \mu_{(X,S)}(x) \mid S \in \mathbb{S}, f \in \mathcal{U}(S,D)\}$$

$$= \ \bigsqcup\{G(id_X,f)^e \mu_{(X,S)}([(\pi_{\mathcal{I}}^* F)(id_X,f)]^p(x)) \mid S \in \mathbb{S}, f \in \mathcal{U}(S,D)\}$$

$$= \ \mu_{(X,D)}(x)$$

where the final step follows from the fact that Theorem 5.6.6 implies that

$$((id_X,f)\colon (X,S) \to (X,D) \mid f^e f^p \in \{f^e f^p \mid S \in \mathbb{S}, f \in \mathcal{U}(S,D)\})$$

is a colimit in $\mathcal{I} \times \mathcal{U}$, and once again we have applied (ii) of Lemma 5.6.13, in this case to the above colimit. The verification of Beck-Chevalley is omitted. $\square$

EXERCISE 5.6.18   Prove the Beck-Chevalley condition for the 2λ×-hyper-doctrine of Discussion 5.6.15.

5.7   Classifying Hyperdoctrine of a 2λ×-Theory

DISCUSSION 5.7.1   We begin by constructing the so-called classifying hyper-doctrine of a 2λ×-theory. This will be used to prove a correspondence between 2λ×-theories and 2λ×-hyperdoctrines, along the same lines as those category theory / type theory correspondences of Chapters 3 and 4. We shall use a notion of a "morphism" between 2λ×-hyperdoctrines, which is basically an indexed functor which preserves categorical structure. Let $\mathbb{C}: \mathcal{C}^{op} \to \mathcal{CCat}$ and $\mathbb{D}: \mathcal{D} \to \mathcal{CCat}$ be a pair of 2λ×-hyperdoctrines. A 2λ×-*functor* $(\alpha, F): \mathbb{C} \to \mathbb{D}$ is a morphism of indexed (cartesian closed) categories for which

• the functor $F: \mathcal{C} \to \mathcal{D}$ sends the distinguished object U of $\mathcal{C}$ to the V of $\mathcal{D}$, and preserves finite products;

• for every object I of $\mathcal{C}$, $\alpha_I: \mathbb{C}I \to \mathbb{D}FI$ is a strict cartesian closed functor which on objects agrees with F, and

• for each object I of $\mathcal{C}$, the diagram

$$
\begin{array}{ccc}
\mathbb{C}(I \times U) & \xrightarrow{\;\;\forall_I\;\;} & \mathbb{C}(I) \\
{\scriptstyle \alpha_{I \times U}}\downarrow & & \downarrow{\scriptstyle \alpha_I} \\
\mathbb{D}(F(I \times U)) \;\stackrel{\cong^*}{=}\; \mathbb{D}(FI \times V) & \xrightarrow[\forall_{FI}]{} & \mathbb{D}(FI)
\end{array}
$$

commutes, where $\cong: FI \times V \to F(I \times U)$ is the canonical isomorphism.

The definitions of classifying category given in Chapters 3 and 4 are very general, involving categories of models. Here we content ourselves with a more restricted notion which is analogous to the universal properties enjoyed by the *canonical* classifying categories of the last two chapters, but now we work with hyperdoctrines instead of categories. Before defining a classifying 2λ×-hyperdoctrine, we need some notation. Let $\mathbb{C}: \mathcal{C}^{op} \to \mathcal{CCat}$ and $\mathbb{D}: \mathcal{D}^{op} \to \mathcal{CCat}$ be 2λ×-hyperdoctrines, and let Th be a 2λ×-theory with model $\mathbf{M}$ in $\mathbb{C}$. Further, suppose that $(\alpha, F): \mathbb{C} \to \mathbb{D}$ is a 2λ×-functor. Then there is a model $(\alpha, F)_* \mathbf{M}$ of Th in $\mathbb{D}$ defined by the clauses

• $[\![T]\!]_{((\alpha, F)_* \mathbf{M})^{ty}} \stackrel{\text{def}}{=} F([\![T]\!]_{\mathbf{M}^{ty}}) \circ \cong\, : V^n \to F(U^n) \to V$ where U and V are the distinguished objects of $\mathbb{C}$ and $\mathbb{D}$, and T is any type symbol of Th with arity n, and

• $[\![f]\!]_{((\alpha,F)_*\mathbf{M})^{tm}} \overset{\text{def}}{=} \cong^* (\alpha_{U^n}([\![f]\!]_{\mathbf{M}^{tm}}))$ for any function symbol with sorting $f: \Delta; \Phi_1, \ldots, \Phi_a \to \Phi$ of Th, where Δ has length n and $V^n \cong F(U^n)$ as above.

EXERCISE 5.7.2   Prove that the structure $(\alpha, F)_*\mathbf{M}$ is indeed a model of Th.

DISCUSSION 5.7.3   Given a 2λ×-theory Th, suppose that $Cl(Th)$ is a 2λ×-hyperdoctrine in which there is a model $\mathbf{G}$. Then $Cl(Th)$ is said to be a *classifying* 2λ×-hyperdoctrine for Th, and the model $\mathbf{G}$ *generic*, if the following universal property holds: given any other 2λ×-hyperdoctrine $\mathbb{C}: \mathcal{C}^{op} \to \mathcal{CCat}$ and model $\mathbf{M}$ of Th in $\mathbb{C}$, there is (up to isomorphism in the category $[Cl(Th), \mathbb{C}]$—see page 109) a unique 2λ×-functor $(\alpha, F): Cl(Th) \to \mathbb{C}$ for which $(\alpha, F)_*\mathbf{G} = \mathbf{M}$. Note that this determines $Cl(Th)$ up to equivalence (of indexed categories). Let us now prove that such classifiers exist for all 2λ×-theories.

THEOREM 5.7.4   For any given 2λ×-theory Th there exists a classifying 2λ×-hyperdoctrine $Cl(Th)$ with a generic model $\mathbf{G}$ of Th in $Cl(Th)$.

PROOF   Suppose that $Th = (Sg, Ax)$. To keep the notation in this proof as clean as possible, let us write $\mathbb{C}: \mathcal{C}^{op} \to \mathcal{CCat}$ for the classifying hyperdoctrine. We begin by defining the base category $\mathcal{C}$. The objects of $\mathcal{C}$ are in bijection with the natural numbers, and will be written as $1, Type, Type^2, Type^3, \ldots$ In order to define the morphisms of $\mathcal{C}$, we will introduce a little more notation. Let n be a given fixed natural number. We shall write $(\Delta \mid \Phi)$ to denote an equivalence class of pairs of the form (Δ, Φ) where

• Δ is a type context of length n, and Φ is a raw type for which $Sg \,\triangleright\, \Delta \vdash \Phi$, and

• the equivalence relation is given by $(\Delta, \Phi) \sim (\Delta', \Phi')$ just in case we can derive the theorem $Th \,\triangleright\, \Delta \vdash \Phi = \Phi'[\Delta/\Delta']$ using an obvious notation for simultaneous substitution.

A morphism $Type^n \to Type^m$ in $\mathcal{C}$ is given by a list $[(\Delta \mid \Phi_1), \ldots, (\Delta \mid \Phi_m)]$ of m such equivalence classes, where the length of Δ is n. Composition of morphisms in $\mathcal{C}$ is given by substitution of types for type variables. More formally, if we are given morphisms

$$[(\Delta \mid \Phi_1), \ldots, (\Delta \mid \Phi_m)]: Type^n \to Type^m$$

and

$$[(\Delta' \mid \Phi_1'), \ldots, (\Delta' \mid \Phi_l')]: Type^m \to Type^l$$

then the composition is given by

$$[(\Delta \mid \Phi'_1[\vec{\Phi}/\Delta']), \ldots, (\Delta \mid \Phi'_l[\vec{\Phi}/\Delta'])] : Type^n \to Type^l.$$

We have to define a functor $\mathbb{C} : \mathcal{C}^{op} \to \mathcal{CCat}$. First we deal with the action of the functor $\mathbb{C}$ on objects of $\mathcal{C}$. The definition of $2\lambda\times$-hyperdoctrine says that at an object $Type^n$ of $\mathcal{C}$, we have to give a cartesian closed category $\mathbb{C}(Type^n)$ whose objects are morphisms $Type^n \to Type$ in the base category $\mathcal{C}$, and we shall write $\mathcal{C}(Type^n, Type)$ for this (cartesian closed) category. In order to define the morphisms of $\mathcal{C}(Type^n, Type)$, we shall once more introduce some notation. Note that because $(\Delta' \mid \Psi) = (\Delta \mid \Psi[\Delta/\Delta'])$, without loss of generality we may as well just consider morphisms $(\Delta \mid \Phi) \to (\Delta \mid \Psi)$ in the fibre $\mathcal{C}(Type^n, Type)$. Consider triples of the from $(\Delta_1, x_1 : \Phi_1, M_1)$ where Δ_1 is a type context of length n, x_1 is a term variable, Φ_1 is a raw type and M_1 is a raw term. Then we define an equivalence relation on such triples by setting

$$(\Delta_1, x_1 : \Phi_1, M_1) \sim (\Delta_2, x_2 : \Phi_2, M_2)$$

just in case we can derive the theorem

$$Th \quad \triangleright \quad \Delta_1 \mid x_1 : \Phi_1 \vdash M_1 = M_2[\Delta_1/\Delta_2][x_1/x_2] : \Psi_1$$

where $Sg \; \triangleright \; \Delta_1 \mid x_1 : \Phi_1 \vdash M_1 : \Psi_1$, and we shall denote the equivalence class of $(\Delta_1, x_1 : \Phi_1, M_1)$ by

$$(\Delta_1 \mid x_1 : \Phi_1 \mid M_1).$$

A morphism $(\Delta \mid \Phi) \to (\Delta \mid \Psi)$ in $\mathcal{C}(Type^n, Type)$ is given by an equivalence class $(\Delta_1 \mid x_1 : \Phi_1 \mid M_1)$ where (say) $Sg \; \triangleright \; \Delta_1 \mid x_1 : \Phi_1 \vdash M_1 : \Psi_1$ and also we can derive $Th \; \triangleright \; \Delta \vdash \Phi = \Phi_1[\Delta/\Delta_1]$ and $Th \; \triangleright \; \Delta \vdash \Psi = \Psi_1[\Delta/\Delta_1]$. Composition is given by the substitution of raw terms for term variables; more formally, if we are given morphisms

$$(\Delta \mid x : \Phi \mid M) : (\Delta \mid \Phi) \to (\Delta \mid \Psi)$$

and

$$(\Delta \mid y : \Psi \mid N) : (\Delta \mid \Psi) \to (\Delta \mid \Theta)$$

then the composition is given by

$$(\Delta \mid x : \Phi \mid N[M/y]) : (\Delta \mid \Phi) \to (\Delta \mid \Theta).$$

Now we define the action of the functor $\mathbb{C}$ on morphisms. Let us take a morphism $f \stackrel{\text{def}}{=} [(\Delta \mid \Phi_1), \ldots, (\Delta \mid \Phi_m)] : Type^n \to Type^m$ in the base category

C. Then the functor $\mathbb{C} f = f^* : \mathcal{C}(Type^m, Type) \to \mathcal{C}(Type^n, Type)$ is defined by the assignment

$$(\Delta' \mid x : \Phi \mid M) : (\Delta' \mid \Phi) \longrightarrow (\Delta' \mid \Psi) \qquad \mapsto$$

$$(\Delta \mid x : \Phi[\vec{\Phi}/\Delta'] \mid M[\vec{\Phi}/\Delta']) : (\Delta \mid \Phi[\vec{\Phi}/\Delta']) \longrightarrow (\Delta \mid \Psi[\vec{\Phi}/\Delta'])$$

where Δ and Δ' are type contexts of length n and m respectively, and $\vec{\Phi}$ denotes the raw types $\Phi_1, \ldots, \Phi_m$.

Next we show that $\mathcal{C}(Type^n, Type)$ is indeed a cartesian closed category. Let Δ be a type context of length n. The terminal object is $(\Delta \mid unit)$. The binary product of $(\Delta \mid \Phi)$ and $(\Delta \mid \Psi)$ is given by $(\Delta \mid \Phi \times \Psi)$, and the exponential is given by $(\Delta \mid \Phi \Rightarrow \Psi)$. It will be left to the reader to fill out the details here.

Our final task is to give the adjunction between the fibres which interprets abstraction of type variables. Let $\pi_{Type^n} : Type^n \times Type \to Type^n$ be a projection in the base category $\mathcal{C}$. Formally $\pi_{Type^n} \stackrel{\text{def}}{=} [(\Delta, X \mid X_1), \ldots, (\Delta, X \mid X_n)]$ where $\Delta \stackrel{\text{def}}{=} [X_1, \ldots, X_n]$. It is easy to see that the functor

$$\pi_{Type^n}^* : \mathcal{C}(Type^n, Type) \longrightarrow \mathcal{C}(Type^n \times Type, Type)$$

is given by the assignment

$$(\Delta \mid x : \Phi \mid M) : (\Delta \mid \Phi) \longrightarrow (\Delta \mid \Psi) \qquad \longmapsto$$

$$(\Delta, X \mid x : \Phi \mid M) : (\Delta, X \mid \Phi) \longrightarrow (\Delta, X \mid \Psi).$$

It is because of this fact that reindexing functors obtained from projections are often referred to as *weakening* functors. For each object $Type^n$ of $\mathcal{C}$ we define a functor

$$\forall_{Type^n} : \mathcal{C}(Type^n \times Type, Type) \longrightarrow \mathcal{C}(Type^n, Type)$$

by the assignment

$$(\Delta, X \mid x : \Phi \mid M) : (\Delta, X \mid \Phi) \longrightarrow (\Delta, X \mid \Psi) \qquad \mapsto$$

$$(\Delta \mid z : \forall X.\Phi \mid \Lambda X.M[zX/x]) : (\Delta \mid \forall X.\Phi) \longrightarrow (\Delta \mid \forall X.\Phi).$$

We now have to check that we have defined an adjunction $(\pi_{Type^n}^* \vdash \forall_{Type^n})$ for each object $Type^n$. We shall write

$$\phi \stackrel{\text{def}}{=} (\Delta, X \mid \Phi) : Type^n \times Type \to Type \quad \text{and} \quad \psi \stackrel{\text{def}}{=} (\Delta \mid \Psi) : Type^n \to Type.$$

We have to give a bijection between morphisms $\pi_{Type^n}^*(\psi) \to \phi$ in the category $\mathcal{C}(Type^n \times Type, Type)$ and morphisms $\psi \to \forall_{Type^n}(\phi)$ in the category

$C(Type^n, Type)$, which is natural in ϕ and ψ. Let us define the bijection by the rules

$$\frac{(\Delta, X \mid x\colon \Psi \mid F) \colon (\Delta, X \mid \Psi) \longrightarrow (\Delta, X \mid \Phi)}{(\Delta \mid x\colon \Psi \mid \Lambda X.F) \colon (\Delta \mid \Psi) \longrightarrow (\Delta \mid \forall X.\Phi)} \quad \overline{(-)}$$

and

$$\frac{(\Delta \mid x\colon \Psi \mid M) \colon (\Delta \mid \Psi) \longrightarrow (\Delta \mid \forall X.\Phi)}{(\Delta, X \mid x\colon \Psi \mid MX) \colon (\Delta, X \mid \Psi) \longrightarrow (\Delta, X \mid \Phi)} \quad \widehat{(-)}$$

Now it is immediate from the **Polymorphism Equations** that these rules define a bijection. It remains to verify that the bijection is natural in ϕ and ψ and we shall just give details for the case of the mapping $\overline{(-)}$. Let us write

$$m \stackrel{\mathrm{def}}{=} (\Delta, X \mid x\colon \Phi \mid M)\colon (\Delta, X \mid \Phi) \to (\Delta, X \mid \Phi'),$$

$$\phi' \stackrel{\mathrm{def}}{=} (\Delta, X \mid \Phi'),$$

$$n \stackrel{\mathrm{def}}{=} (\Delta \mid y\colon \Psi' \mid N)\colon (\Delta \mid \Psi') \to (\Delta \mid \Psi),$$

$$\psi' \stackrel{\mathrm{def}}{=} (\Delta \mid \Psi'),$$

$$f \stackrel{\mathrm{def}}{=} (\Delta, X \mid u\colon \Psi \mid F)\colon (\Delta, X \mid \Psi) \to (\Delta, X \mid \Phi).$$

Then we have to verify that the naturality equation given in the following picture commutes:

$$
\begin{array}{ccc}
f & \longmapsto & \overline{f} \\
\Big\downarrow & & \Big\downarrow \\
m \circ f \circ \pi^{*}_{Type^n}(n) & \longmapsto \underbrace{\overline{m \circ f \circ \pi^{*}_{Type^n}(n)}}_{L} & = \underbrace{\forall_{Type^n}(m) \circ \overline{f} \circ n}_{R}
\end{array}
$$

Then we have

$$
\begin{aligned}
R &= (\Delta \mid y\colon \Psi' \mid ((\Lambda X.M[zX/x])[\Lambda X.F/z])[N/u]) \\
&= (\Delta \mid y\colon \Psi' \mid (\Lambda X.M[(\Lambda X.F)X/x])[N/u]) \\
&= (\Delta \mid y\colon \Psi' \mid \Lambda X.M[F[N/u]/x]) \\
&= \overline{(\Delta, X \mid y\colon \Psi' \mid M[F[N/u]/x])} \\
&= L.
\end{aligned}
$$

It remains to verify the Beck-Chevalley conditions, and we omit the details.

Let us give the generic model **G** of $Th = (Th^{ty}, Th^{tm})$ in $Cl(Th)$. First we give a structure for **G** in the $2\lambda\times$-hyperdoctrine. If F is a type symbol of arity n in Sg, then we set

$$[\![F]\!]_{\mathbf{G}^{ty}} \stackrel{\mathrm{def}}{=} (\Delta \mid F(\vec{X}))\colon Type^n \longrightarrow Type,$$

giving a type structure $\mathbf{G^{ty}}$ in $Cl(Th)$—what if $n=0$? One can prove by induction that $\mathbf{G^{ty}}$ is in fact a model for Th^{ty} in $Cl(Th)$. If $f: \Delta; \Phi_1, \ldots, \Phi_m \to \Phi$ is a function symbol in Sg then we put

$$[\![f]\!]_{\mathbf{G^{tm}}} \stackrel{\text{def}}{=}$$

$$(\Delta \mid z: \Pi_1^m \Phi_i \mid f(\mathsf{Proj}_1(z), \ldots, \mathsf{Proj}_m(z))): (\Delta \mid \Pi_1^m \Phi_i) \to (\Delta \mid \Phi),$$

and if $k: \Delta; \Phi$ then $[\![k]\!]_{\mathbf{G^{tm}}} \stackrel{\text{def}}{=} (\Delta \mid x: unit \mid k)$ giving a term structure $\mathbf{G^{tm}}$. Again, it is an exercise to prove by induction that $\mathbf{G^{tm}}$ is a model of Th^{tm} in $Cl(Th)$.

Now let $\mathbb{D}: \mathcal{D}^{op} \to \mathcal{CCat}$ be a 2λ×-hyperdoctrine and $\mathbf{M}$ a model of Th in $\mathbb{D}$. We define $(\alpha, F): \mathbb{C} \to \mathbb{D}$ as follows: the finite product preserving functor $F: \mathcal{D} \to \mathcal{C}$ is defined by the assignment (where $[\![-]\!]$ refers to $\mathbf{M}$)

$$[(\Delta \mid \Phi_1), \ldots, (\Delta \mid \Phi_m)]: Type^n \to Type^m \qquad \mapsto$$

$$\langle [\![\Delta \vdash \Phi_1]\!], \ldots, [\![\Delta \vdash \Phi_m]\!] \rangle : U^n \to U^m.$$

The component of the $\mathcal{D}$-indexed functor $\alpha: \mathbb{D} \to \mathbb{C} F^{op}$ at an object $Type^n$ of $\mathcal{D}$ is a functor

$$\alpha_{Type^n} : \mathcal{D}(Type^n, Type) \longrightarrow \mathcal{C}(U^n, U)$$

which is defined by the assignment

$$(\Delta \mid x: \Phi \mid M) : (\Delta \mid \Phi) \longrightarrow (\Delta \mid \Psi) \qquad \mapsto$$

$$[\![\Delta \mid x: \Phi \vdash M: \Psi]\!] : [\![\Delta \vdash \Phi]\!] \longrightarrow [\![\Delta \vdash \Psi]\!].$$

It is a routine though lengthy exercise to verify that (α, F) is a 2λ×-functor determined up to isomorphism in $[\mathbb{C}, \mathbb{D}]$, and that $(\alpha, F)_* \mathbf{G} = \mathbf{M}$. $\square$

EXERCISES 5.7.5   Refer to the proof of Theorem 5.7.4.

(1) Verify that you understand the definition of composition in $\mathcal{C}$ and that the composition is well defined. Show that $\mathcal{C}$ has a terminal object and binary products, working out the details of a binary product of two objects in detail.

(2) Complete the details which verify that $\mathcal{C}(Type^n, Type)$ is indeed a cartesian closed category. You will, of course, have to define binary product projections and check the universal property of both the terminal object and the binary product, to see that the category has finite products. You will also need to define the evaluation morphisms and exponential mates to check the category is cartesian closed. Finally verify that $\mathbb{C}(-) \stackrel{\text{def}}{=} \mathcal{C}(-, Type)$ is indeed a functor $\mathcal{C}^{op} \to \mathcal{CCat}$ by checking that the reindexing functors are *strict* morphisms of cartesian closed categories.

(3) Write down the essence of the details of the proof of Theorem 5.7.4. Try to see that most of the details are routine verifications involving awkward manipulations of syntax, but that the basic ideas of the proof are quite simple. In particular, do make sure that you understand the definitions in the proof which involve a number of syntactic equivalence classes. Complete a verification of the Beck-Chevalley condition.

(4) Prove that $\mathbf{G}$ is indeed a model of Th. Verify that (α, F) is a $2\lambda\times$-functor and that $(\alpha, F)_*\mathbf{G} = \mathbf{M}$. Convince yourself that (α, F) is determined up to isomorphism.

5.8   *Categorical Type Theory Correspondence*

DISCUSSION 5.8.1   Let us first construct a $2\lambda\times$-theory from any $2\lambda\times$-hyperdoctrine, which is Theorem 5.8.2. We then show that any $2\lambda\times$-hyperdoctrine arises as the classifying category of such a $2\lambda\times$-theory in Theorem 5.8.3.

THEOREM 5.8.2   For any given $2\lambda\times$-hyperdoctrine $\mathbb{C}: \mathcal{C}^{op} \to \mathcal{C\!Cat}$, we can define a $2\lambda\times$-theory $Th(\mathbb{C})$ for which there is a canonical model $\mathbf{M}$ of $Th(\mathbb{C})$ in $\mathbb{C}$.

PROOF   For each morphism $\phi: U^n \to U$ in the base category $\mathcal{C}$, we take a type symbol ϕ of arity n (possibly $n = 0$). This gives us data for a $2\lambda\times$-type signature Sg^{ty}, and hence we can we can derive judgements of the form $Sg^{ty} \vartriangleright \Delta \vdash \Phi$ using the rules on page 207. We can define a type structure $\mathbf{M}^{ty}$ by setting $[\![\phi]\!] \overset{\text{def}}{=} \phi$. We can then use the rules on page 226 to define $[\![\Delta \vdash \Phi]\!]$ for each proved type $Sg^{ty} \vartriangleright \Delta \vdash \Phi$. From this we can define a collection of type axioms Ax^{ty} by requiring that a type axiom be any type equation-in-context $\Delta \vdash \Phi = \Phi'$ for which $[\![\Delta \vdash \Phi]\!] = [\![\Delta \vdash \Phi']\!]$. It is immediate that $\mathbf{M}^{ty}$ is a model of the typing theory $Th^{ty} = (Sg^{ty}, Ax^{ty})$.

Now we define a $2\lambda\times$-term signature Sg^{tm}. For the typing theory we take Th^{ty} as described above. For every morphism of the form $m: \phi_1 \times \ldots \times \phi_a \to \phi$ in the fibre $\mathcal{C}(U^n, U)$, we take a function symbol m which has sorting

$$m : \Delta; \phi_1(\vec{X}), \ldots, \phi_a(\vec{X}) \longrightarrow \phi(\vec{X})$$

where, say, $\Delta \overset{\text{def}}{=} [X_1, \ldots, X_n]$. (Recall that for this sorting to be a good definition, each of the raw types appearing in the sorting must be proved types in the context Δ, that is $Sg^{ty} \vartriangleright \Delta \vdash \phi_i(\vec{X})$ for each $1 \leq i \leq a$, and $Sg^{ty} \vartriangleright \Delta \vdash \phi(\vec{X})$. This is of course immediate because each ϕ_i and ϕ is a type symbol of arity n). For each morphism $m: 1 \to \phi$ in $\mathcal{C}(U^n, U)$ there is a constant function symbol $m: \Delta; \phi(\vec{X})$. In addition to these type and function symbols, for each type context Δ and raw type Φ for which $Sg^{ty} \,\triangleright\, \Delta \vdash \Phi$, there are function symbols $I^{\Delta,\Phi}$ and $J^{\Delta,\Phi}$ of arity 1 with sortings

- $I^{\Delta,\Phi}: \Delta; [\![\Delta \vdash \Phi]\!](\vec{X}) \to \Phi$, and
- $J^{\Delta,\Phi}: \Delta; \Phi \to [\![\Delta \vdash \Phi]\!](\vec{X})$.

Let us define a term structure $\mathbf{M^{tm}}$ for Sg^{tm}. The term structure $\mathbf{M^{tm}}$ depends on the model $\mathbf{M^{ty}}$ of Th^{ty} given above, and we set

$$[\![m]\!] \stackrel{\mathrm{def}}{=} m: [\![\Delta \vdash \phi_1(\vec{X})]\!] \times \ldots \times [\![\Delta \vdash \phi_a(\vec{X})]\!] \longrightarrow [\![\Delta \vdash \phi(\vec{X})]\!],$$

where $m: \phi_1 \times \ldots \times \phi_a \to \phi$. This makes sense, because certainly we have $[\![\Delta \vdash \phi_i(\vec{X})]\!] = \phi_i$ for each i, and of course $[\![\Delta \vdash \phi(\vec{X})]\!] = \phi$. We also set $[\![I^{\Delta,\Phi}]\!] = [\![J^{\Delta,\Phi}]\!] \stackrel{\mathrm{def}}{=} id_{[\![\Delta \vdash \Phi]\!]}$. Using the term structure $\mathbf{M^{tm}}$, we can then define $[\![\Delta \,|\, \Gamma \vdash M: \Phi]\!]$ for each proved term $Sg \,\triangleright\, \Delta \,|\, \Gamma \vdash M: \Phi$, using the rules on pages 228, 229 and 230. We can define a term theory $Th^{tm} = (Sg^{tm}, Ax^{tm})$ by demanding a term axiom to be any equation-in-context $\Delta \,|\, \Gamma \vdash M = M': \Phi$ for which $[\![\Delta \,|\, \Gamma \vdash M: \Phi]\!] = [\![\Delta \,|\, \Gamma \vdash M': \Phi]\!]$, and it is immediate that $\mathbf{M^{tm}}$ is a model of Th^{tm}.

We finally take $Th(\mathbb{C}) = (Th^{ty}, Th^{tm})$ for which there is a canonical model $\mathbf{M} = (\mathbf{M^{ty}}, \mathbf{M^{tm}})$. $\square$

THEOREM 5.8.3   Let $\mathbb{C}: \mathcal{C}^{op} \to \mathcal{ACat}$ be a $2\lambda\times$-hyperdoctrine. Then the $2\lambda\times$-functor $(\beta, G): Cl(Th(\mathbb{C})) \to \mathbb{C}$ which arises from the universal property of the classifying $2\lambda\times$-hyperdoctrine applied to the canonical model $\mathbf{M}$ of $Th(\mathbb{C})$ in $\mathbb{C}$ is one half of an equivalence $Cl(Th(\mathbb{C})) \simeq \mathbb{C}$ of indexed categories.

PROOF   To save on notation, we write $\mathcal{D}$ for the base category of $Cl(Th(\mathbb{C}))$ and $\mathbb{D}: \mathcal{D}^{op} \to \mathcal{ACat}$ for the functor giving rise to the $2\lambda\times$-hyperdoctrine $Cl(Th(\mathbb{C}))$. We have to show that there is a choice of equivalence, $\mathbb{D} \simeq \mathbb{C}$. First, we define a $2\lambda\times$-hyperdoctrine morphism $(\alpha, F): \mathbb{C} \to \mathbb{D}$; recall that (β, G) is defined in the proof of Theorem 5.7.4. Let us write U for the distinguished object of $\mathcal{C}$. The finite product preserving functor $F: \mathcal{C} \to \mathcal{D}$ is given by the assignment

$$\phi: U^n \to U^m \qquad \mapsto$$

$$[(\Delta \,|\, \pi_1\phi(\vec{X})), \ldots, (\Delta \,|\, \pi_m\phi(\vec{X}))] : Type^n \to Type^m$$

where Δ is a type context of length n and $\pi_i: U^m \to U$ is projection on the ith component for $1 \leq i \leq m$. The $\mathcal{C}$-indexed functor $\alpha: \mathbb{C} \to \mathbb{D}F^{op}$ is given by defining its components at an object U^n of $\mathcal{C}$. Such a component α_{U^n} is a functor $\alpha_{U^n} : \mathcal{C}(U^n, U) \longrightarrow \mathcal{D}(Type^n, Type)$ which we shall define by the assignment

$$m: \phi \to \phi' \qquad \longmapsto$$

$$(\Delta \,|\, x: \phi(\vec{X}) \,|\, m(x)) : (\Delta \,|\, \phi(\vec{X})) \longrightarrow (\Delta \,|\, \phi'(\vec{X})).$$

In order to show that $\mathbb{C} \simeq \mathbb{D}$, we shall define isomorphisms

$$(\beta, G)(\alpha, F) \cong id_{\mathbb{C}} \qquad \text{in} \qquad [\mathbb{C}, \mathbb{C}] \qquad (1)$$

$$(\alpha, F)(\beta, G) \cong id_{\mathbb{D}} \qquad \text{in} \qquad [\mathbb{D}, \mathbb{D}]. \qquad (2)$$

First we define the isomorphism (1) in $[\mathbb{C}, \mathbb{C}]$, by giving morphisms

$$(\rho, \eta) : (id_{\mathbb{C}}, id_{\mathcal{C}}) \longrightarrow (\beta_F \circ \alpha, GF)$$

and

$$(\delta, \eta^{-1}) : (\beta_F \circ \alpha, GF) \longrightarrow (id_{\mathbb{C}}, id_{\mathcal{C}}).$$

Let us define (ρ, η). The component of the natural transformation η at the object U^n of $\mathcal{C}$ is given by $\eta_{U^n} \stackrel{\text{def}}{=} id_{U^n} : U^n \to U^n$. The modification ρ is by definition a $\mathcal{C}$-indexed natural transformation of the form

$$\rho : id_{\mathbb{C}} \longrightarrow (\eta_{(-)})^* \circ \beta_F \circ \alpha : \mathbb{C} \longrightarrow \mathbb{C} : \mathcal{C}^{op} \longrightarrow \mathcal{CCat}$$

and specified by giving a natural transformation

$$\rho_{U^n} : id_{\mathcal{C}(U^n, U)} \longrightarrow (\eta_{U^n}^* \circ \beta_{Type^n} \circ \alpha_{U^n}) : \mathcal{C}(U^n, U) \longrightarrow \mathcal{C}(U^n, U)$$

for each object U^n of $\mathcal{C}$, whose component at the object ϕ of $\mathcal{C}(U^n, U)$ is given by

$$(\rho_{U^n})_\phi \stackrel{\text{def}}{=} id_\phi : id_{\mathcal{C}(U^n, U)}(\phi) = \phi \longrightarrow \phi = \eta_{U^n}^*(\beta_{Type^n}(\alpha_{U^n}(\phi))).$$

It is trivial to see that ρ_{U^n} is a natural transformation and that ρ satisfies the intreid condition. Next we define (δ, η^{-1}). The natural transformation η^{-1} has components at U^n of $\mathcal{C}$ given by $\eta_{U^n}^{-1} \stackrel{\text{def}}{=} id_{U^n} : U^n \to U^n$. The modification δ is defined by specifying a natural transformation

$$\delta_{U^n} : \beta_{Type^n} \circ \alpha_{U^n} \longrightarrow (\eta_{U^n}^{-1})^* : \mathcal{C}(U^n, U) \longrightarrow \mathcal{C}(U^n, U)$$

for each object U^n of $\mathcal{C}$, whose component at an object $\phi: U^n \to U$ of $\mathcal{C}(U^n, U)$ is given by $(\delta_{U^n})_\phi \stackrel{\text{def}}{=} id_\phi : \phi \to \phi$ where in order to see that this makes sense we note that

$$\beta_{Type^n}(\alpha_{U^n}(\phi)) = \beta_{Type^n}((\Delta \,|\, \phi(\vec{X}))) = [\![\Delta \vdash \phi(\vec{X})]\!]_{\mathbf{M}} = \phi$$

and $(\eta_{U^n}^{-1})^*(\phi) = id_{U^n}^*(\phi) = \phi$.

Now we turn to the isomorphism (2) in $[\mathbb{D}, \mathbb{D}]$. So let us define two mutually inverse morphisms

$$(\mu, \epsilon) : (\alpha_G \circ \beta, FG) \longrightarrow (id_{\mathbb{D}}, id_{\mathcal{D}})$$

and

$$(\nu, \epsilon^{-1}) : (id_{\mathbb{D}}, id_{\mathcal{D}}) \longrightarrow (\alpha_G \circ \beta, FG)$$

in the category $[\mathbb{D}, \mathbb{D}]$. The component of ϵ at $Type^n$ is

$$\epsilon_{Type^n} \overset{\text{def}}{=} id_{Type^n} : Type^n \to Type^n.$$

The modification μ is by definition a $\mathcal{D}$-indexed natural transformation of the form

$$\mu : \alpha_G \circ \beta \longrightarrow (\epsilon_{(-)})^* \circ id_{\mathbb{D}} : \mathbb{D} \longrightarrow \mathbb{D}\,FG : \mathcal{D}^{op} \longrightarrow \mathcal{CCat},$$

and is specified by giving for each object $Type^n$ of $\mathcal{D}$ a natural transformation

$$\mu_{Type^n} : \alpha_{U^n} \circ \beta_{Type^n} \longrightarrow \epsilon_{Type^n}^* : \mathcal{D}(Type^n, Type) \longrightarrow \mathcal{D}(Type^n, Type)$$

for which if $f \overset{\text{def}}{=} [(\Delta \mid \Phi_1), \dots, (\Delta \mid \Phi_m)] : Type^n \to Type^m$ is any morphism in $\mathcal{D}$, then the intreid condition holds, that is the following diagram commutes:

$$
\begin{array}{ccc}
\mathcal{D}(Type^m, Type) & \xrightarrow[\substack{\downarrow \mu_{Type^m} \\ id_{\mathcal{D}(Type^m, Type)}}]{\alpha_{U^m} \circ \beta_{Type^m}} & \mathcal{D}(Type^m, Type) \\
\Big\downarrow f^* & (*) & \Big\downarrow (FGf)^* \\
\mathcal{D}(Type^n, Type) & \xrightarrow[\substack{\downarrow \mu_{Type^n} \\ id_{\mathcal{D}(Type^n, Type)}}]{\alpha_{U^n} \circ \beta_{Type^n}} & \mathcal{D}(Type^n, Type)
\end{array}
$$

A component of μ_{Type^n} at an object $(\Delta \mid \Phi)$ of $\mathcal{D}(Type^n, Type)$ will be given by some morphism $(\mu_{Type^n})_{(\Delta \mid \Phi)} : (\Delta \mid [\![\Delta \vdash \Phi]\!](\vec{X})) \longrightarrow (\Delta \mid \Phi)$ and indeed we shall set

$$(\mu_{Type^n})_{(\Delta \mid \Phi)} \overset{\text{def}}{=} (\Delta \mid x : [\![\Delta \vdash \Phi]\!](\vec{X}) \mid I_{\vec{X}}^{\Delta, \Phi}(x)).$$

This completes the definition of the modification μ; let us check that the diagram $(*)$ commutes. Let $(\Delta' \mid \Phi)$ be any object of $\mathcal{D}(Type^m, Type)$, let f

be as above, and define $[\![\Delta' \vdash \Theta]\!] \overset{\text{def}}{=} \theta$ and $[\![\Delta \vdash \Phi_i]\!] \overset{\text{def}}{=} \phi_i$. Then we have

$$
\begin{aligned}
(\mu_{Type^n})_{f*(\Delta'|\Theta)} \\
&= (\mu_{Type^n})_{(\Delta|\Theta[\vec{\Phi}/\Delta'])} \\
&= (\Delta \mid x\colon\! \theta \circ \langle\vec{\phi}\rangle(\vec{X}) \mid I_{\vec{X}}(x)) \\
&= (\Delta \mid z\colon\! \theta(\phi_1(\vec{X}),\ldots,\phi_m(\vec{X})) \mid I_{\phi_1(\vec{X}),\ldots,\phi_m(\vec{X})}(z)) \\
&= [(\Delta \mid \phi_1(\vec{X})),\ldots,(\Delta \mid \phi_m(\vec{X}))]^*(\Delta' \mid z\colon\! \theta(\vec{X}') \mid I_{\vec{X}'}(z)) \\
&= (F(\langle\phi_1,\ldots,\phi_m\rangle))^*((\mu_{Type^m})_{(\Delta'|\Theta)}) \\
&= (FGf)^*((\mu_{Type^m})_{(\Delta'|\Theta)}),
\end{aligned}
$$

where the superscripts have been dropped from the I's. Now we turn to the definition of (ν, ϵ^{-1}). The component of the natural transformation ϵ^{-1} at $Type^n$ is defined to be $\epsilon^{-1}_{Type^n} \overset{\text{def}}{=} id_{Type^n}\colon Type^n \to FG(Type^n) = Type^n$. The component of the modification ν at an object $Type^n$ of $\mathcal{D}$ is a natural transformation

$$
\nu_{Type^n}\colon id_{\mathcal{D}(Type^n, Type)} \longrightarrow (\epsilon^{-1}_{Type^n})^* \circ \alpha_{U^n} \circ \beta_{Type^n}\colon
$$
$$
\mathcal{D}(Type^n, Type) \longrightarrow \mathcal{D}(Type^n, Type)
$$

and it is simple to check that the component of this natural transformation at an object $(\Delta \mid \Phi)$ of $\mathcal{D}(Type^n, Type)$ is precisely a morphism

$$
(\nu_{Type^n})_{(\Delta|\Phi)}\colon (\Delta \mid \Phi) \to (\Delta \mid [\![\Delta \vdash \Phi]\!](\vec{X})),
$$

and we shall set

$$
(\nu_{Type^n})_{(\Delta|\Phi)} \overset{\text{def}}{=} (\Delta \mid x\colon\! \Phi \mid J^{\Delta,\Phi}_{\vec{X}}(x)).
$$

To complete the proof of Theorem 5.8.3, we shall verify that the isomorphisms (1) and (2) on page 270 are witnessed by the morphisms (δ, η^{-1}), (ρ, η), and (μ, ϵ^{-1}), (ν, ϵ) respectively. In fact we shall just give two calculations which show how the verification goes. For the isomorphism (1) we shall show that

$$
(\delta, \eta^{-1})(\rho, \eta) \overset{\text{def}}{=} ((\eta_{(-)})^* \delta_{(-)} \circ \rho_{(-)}, \eta^{-1}\eta) = (id_{id_{\mathcal{C}_{(-)}}}, id_{id_{\mathcal{C}}}).
$$

At an object U^n of $\mathcal{C}$ we have $\eta^{-1}_{U^n}\eta_{U^n} = (id_{id_{\mathcal{C}}})_{U^n} = id_{U^n}$, as required. We also have to verify that $\eta^*_{U^n}\delta_{U^n} \circ \rho_{U^n} = id_{id_{\mathcal{C}(U^n, U)}}$, and we can see that this holds by taking a component at an object $\phi\colon U^n \to U$ as follows:

$$
\eta^*_{U^n}((\delta_{U^n})_\phi) \circ (\rho_{U^n})_\phi \overset{\text{def}}{=} id^*_{U^n}(id_\phi) \circ id_\phi = id_\phi = (id_{id_{\mathcal{C}(U^n, U)}})_\phi.
$$

For the isomorphism (2) we shall verify that

$$(\mu, \epsilon)(\nu, \epsilon^{-1}) \stackrel{\text{def}}{=} ((\epsilon_{(-)}^{-1})^* \mu_{(-)} \circ \nu_{(-)}, \epsilon\epsilon^{-1}) = (id_{id_{\mathcal{D}_{(-)}}}, id_{id_{\mathcal{D}}}).$$

It is easy to see that $\epsilon_{Type^n} \epsilon_{Type^n}^{-1} = (id_{id_{\mathcal{D}}})_{Type^n} = id_{Type^n}$. We also need to verify that if $(\Delta \mid \Phi)$ is an object of the fibre $\mathcal{D}(Type^n, Type)$, then we have

$$(\epsilon_{Type^n}^{-1})^* ((\mu_{Type^n})_{(\Delta|\Phi)}) \circ (\nu_{Type^n})_{(\Delta|\Phi)} = (id_{id_{\mathcal{D}(Type^n, Type)}})_{(\Delta|\Phi)} = id_{(\Delta|\Phi)}$$

which amounts to verifying $(\mu_{Type^n})_{(\Delta|\Phi)} \circ (\nu_{Type^n})_{(\Delta|\Phi)} = id_{(\Delta|\Phi)}$. This calculation is easy and is left as an exercise. □

DISCUSSION 5.8.4   We can summarise the thrust of Theorem 5.8.3 in the following slogan:

Categorical Type Theory Correspondence

A $2\lambda\times$-hyperdoctrine is a representation of the notion of a $2\lambda\times$-theory which is syntax independent.

The $2\lambda\times$-theory $Th(\mathbb{C})$ derived from a $2\lambda\times$-hyperdoctrine $\mathbb{C}$ is known as the *internal language* of the $2\lambda\times$-hyperdoctrine. We can use it to reason about the categorical structure in much the same way as illustrated for the internal language of cartesian closed categories.

DISCUSSION 5.8.5   We can show that the categorical semantics which we have presented for $2\lambda\times$-theories is complete. Such a semantics is *complete* for a $2\lambda\times$-theory Th if an equation-in-context of the theory is a theorem just in case it is satisfied by all models of Th. This follows more or less immediately from the existence of generic models in classifying categories.

THEOREM 5.8.6 $2\lambda\times$-hyperdoctrines yield a complete semantics for $2\lambda\times$-theories.

PROOF   Let Th be a $2\lambda\times$-theory. A theorem is satisfied in all models because a $2\lambda\times$-hyperdoctrine semantics is sound—see Theorem 5.4.15. Conversely, if an equation-in-context is satisfied by all models then it is satisfied by the generic model in $Cl(Th)$. It is a simple exercise to show that this implies the equation-in-context is in fact a theorem of Th. □

DISCUSSION 5.8.7   Let us end this chapter by remarking that one can give a definition of translation of $2\lambda\times$-theories $Th \to Th'$ as a $2\lambda\times$-functor $Cl(Th) \to Cl(Th')$. We leave it as an exercise to formulate this idea formally, and to prove an "equivalence" $Th \simeq Th(Cl(Th))$.

5.9   Pointers to the Literature

The book [AL91] by Asperti and Longo provides a detailed account of second
order polymorphism. However, the syntax of polymorphic theories is not presented quite as formally as in our Chapter 5 and the Scott domain model is
not discussed. Asperti and Longo do present categorical models which make
use of internal category theory, an important topic not covered in "Categories
for Types." For a discussion of polymorphism in real programming languages
see [Car86] and [Car89]. A full account of the Scott domain model of second
order polymorphism can be found in [CGW89]. This contains much of the
material of our Section 5.6, except that the domain model is not presented
as an instance of a $2\lambda\times$-hyperdoctrine. See also [CGW87]. A very general
account of polymorphism appears in [Gir86] which includes a discussion of
domain-theoretic semantics. This paper provides references to Girard's original work on this topic. A description of categorical semantics of second order
polymorphism appears in [Pit87], along with a full account of topos theoretic
models.

6 Higher Order Polymorphism

6.1 Introduction

DISCUSSION 6.1.1   Let us take stock of the type theories so far introduced in "Categories for Types." We began with algebraic type theory, which gave us a basic framework in which to write down syntactical theories involving equational reasoning. This was extended to functional type theory in which there is a formal syntax for the representation of functions. We then noted that it would be desirable to work with a syntax in which certain programs (terms) yielded instances of a uniform procedure at differing types, this feature being known as polymorphism. We now extend this latter kind of type theory to one in which there is a syntax for describing functions "at the level of types" as well as functions at the level of terms. In this new system, the syntax splits into two levels, let us say level 1 and level 2. At level 1 there are types and terms, and one thinks of the types as "collections" of terms with a similar property. Analogously at level 2 there are (so-called) kinds and operators, and one thinks of a kind as a "collection" of operators with similar properties. These two levels are connected by a distinguished kind, often denoted by *Type*, which is thought of as the collection of all types. This new formal system will be referred to as higher order polymorphic functional type theory. In the second order system we could quantify over type variables, for example $\forall X.\Phi$, which would be written here as $\forall X: Type.\Phi$. In the higher order system, *Type* is a ground kind from which we generate *higher order* function and product kinds (see page 276), and we may quantify over all kinds: $\forall X: K.\Phi$.

As an informal example, let us think about the datatype of lists. The operator list has kind $Type \Rightarrow Type$. When applied to a type X (so the kind of X is *Type*), it yields the operator list X which has kind *Type*, that is list X is the type of "lists of type X." The term rev has type $\forall X : Type.(\text{list } X \Rightarrow \text{list } X)$, so rev X is a term which may be applied to a list of terms of type X to produce a reversed list. All of these ideas are illustrated in Figure 6.1.

6.2   The Syntax and Equations of $\omega\lambda\times$-Theories

DISCUSSION 6.2.1   Bearing in mind the informal description of a higher order polymorphic functional type theory, we now give a formal definition of such a system which has "products" and "functions" at both level 1 and level 2.

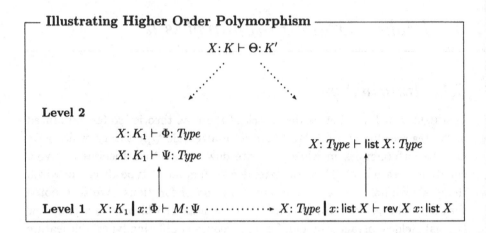

Figure 6.1: In this figure, Θ, Φ and Ψ are operators; K, K', K_1 and *Type* are kinds; and M is a term.

An $\omega\lambda\times$-*signature* is a pair $Sg \stackrel{\text{def}}{=} (Sg^{op}, Sg^{tm})$ where Sg^{op} is an $\omega\lambda\times$-operator signature and Sg^{tm} is an $\omega\lambda\times$-term signature. The specification of Sg^{tm} depends on the data which specify Sg^{op}. An $\omega\lambda\times$-*operator signature* Sg^{op} is specified by the following data:

• A collection of *ground kinds*. The collection of *kinds* is then given by the BNF grammar

$$K \ ::= \ G \mid Unit \mid Type \mid K \times K \mid K \Rightarrow K$$

where G is any ground kind.

• A collection of *operator symbols* each having an *arity* which is a natural number.

• A *sorting* for each operator symbol which is a list of $a + 1$ kinds for each operator of arity a. If the operator symbol F has non-zero arity a we write $F: K_1, \ldots, K_a \to K$ for this. An operator symbol C of arity 0 is called a *constant* operator symbol and we write $C: K$ for its sorting.

We can now give the *raw* operators generated from an $\omega\lambda\times$-operator signature and we assume that we are given a countably infinite stock of *operator variables*. The raw operators are specified by the (informal) BNF grammar:

$$\Phi \ ::= \ X \mid C \mid F(\underbrace{\Phi, \ldots, \Phi}_{length\ a}) \mid \langle\rangle \mid \langle\Phi, \Phi\rangle \mid \mathsf{Fst}(\Phi) \mid \mathsf{Snd}(\Phi) \mid \lambda X\!:\!K.\Phi \mid \Phi\,\Phi \mid$$
$$unit \mid \Phi \times \Phi \mid \Phi \Rightarrow \Phi \mid \forall X\!:\!K.\Phi$$

where X is any operator variable, C any constant kind and F any operator symbol of non-zero arity a.

We shall need the notion of substitution of a raw operator for an operator variable. The concept of substitution should by now be very familiar so the details are sketched. There is an obvious notion of a *raw suboperator* Ψ of a raw operator Φ. If the operator variable X occurs in the raw operator Φ then X is *bound* in any raw suboperator of Φ of the form $\lambda X\!:\!K.\Psi$ and $\forall X\!:\!K.\Psi$. For each raw operator Φ there is a finite set of operator variables $fopv(\Phi)$ known as the *free* operator variables. This set consists of all operator variables appearing in Φ which are not bound variables of Φ—do not forget that an operator variable may be both free and bound. Then the *substitution* of the raw operator Ψ for occurrences of the operator variable X in Φ, $\Phi[\Psi/X]$, is the raw term given by replacing each appearance of X in Φ with Ψ and changing bound variables so that no free variable of Ψ becomes bound when substituted into Φ. In order that substitution is well defined, we regard each raw term as defined up to α-equivalence, that is, up to a change of bound variables.

An *operator context* is a finite list of (operator variable, kind) pairs, usually written as $[X_1\!:\!K_1, \ldots, X_n\!:\!K_n]$, where the operator variables are required to be distinct. An *operator-in-context* is a judgement of the form $\Delta \vdash \Phi\!:\!K$ where Δ is an operator context, Φ is a raw operator and K is a kind. A proved operator is a judgement of the form $Sg^{op} \,\triangleright\, \Delta \vdash \Phi\!:\!K$, and one thinks of the raw operator Φ in such a proved operator as being "well formed." The rules for generating *proved operators* from an $\omega\lambda\times$-operator signature are given in Figures 6.2 and 6.3. An *operator equation-in-context* is a judgement of the form $\Delta \vdash \Phi = \Phi'\!:\!K$ where $Sg^{op} \,\triangleright\, \Delta \vdash \Phi\!:\!K$ and $Sg^{op} \,\triangleright\, \Delta \vdash \Phi'\!:\!K$. An $\omega\lambda\times$-*operator theory* Th^{op} is a pair (Sg^{op}, Ax^{op}) where Sg^{op} is an $\omega\lambda\times$-operator signature and Ax^{op} is a collection of operator equations-in-context, each equation-in-context known as an *operator axiom*. The *operator theorems* are judgements of the form $Th^{op} \,\triangleright\, \Delta \vdash \Phi = \Phi'\!:\!K$, which are generated by the rules in Figure 6.4.

DISCUSSION 6.2.2 An $\omega\lambda\times$-*term signature* Sg^{tm} is specified by the following data:

- An $\omega\lambda\times$-operator theory $Th^{op} = (Sg^{op}, Ax^{op})$.

- A collection of *function symbols* each having an *arity* which is a natural number.

- A *sorting* for each function symbol f, which is given by an operator context Δ^f and a list of $a+1$ raw operators (where a is the arity of f) usually written

---

Operator Variables

$$Sg^{op} \quad \triangleright \quad \Delta, X\colon K, \Delta' \vdash X\colon K$$

Unit Operator

$$Sg^{op} \quad \triangleright \quad \Delta \vdash \langle\rangle\colon Unit$$

Operator Symbols

$$\frac{}{Sg^{op} \quad \triangleright \quad \Delta \vdash C\colon K} \quad (C\colon K)$$

$$\frac{Sg^{op} \quad \triangleright \quad \Delta \vdash \Phi_1\colon K_1 \quad \ldots \quad Sg^{op} \quad \triangleright \quad \Delta \vdash \Phi_n\colon K_n}{Sg^{op} \quad \triangleright \quad \Delta \vdash F(\Phi_1, \ldots, \Phi_n)\colon K} \quad (F\colon K_1, \ldots, K_n \to K)$$

Binary Product Operators

$$\frac{Sg^{op} \quad \triangleright \quad \Delta \vdash \Phi\colon K \quad Sg^{op} \quad \triangleright \quad \Delta \vdash \Psi\colon L}{Sg^{op} \quad \triangleright \quad \Delta \vdash \langle\Phi, \Psi\rangle\colon K \times L}$$

$$\frac{Sg^{op} \quad \triangleright \quad \Delta \vdash \Theta\colon K \times L}{Sg^{op} \quad \triangleright \quad \Delta \vdash \mathsf{Fst}(\Theta)\colon K} \qquad \frac{Sg^{op} \quad \triangleright \quad \Delta \vdash \Theta\colon K \times L}{Sg^{op} \quad \triangleright \quad \Delta \vdash \mathsf{Snd}(\Theta)\colon L}$$

Function Operators

$$\frac{Sg^{op} \quad \triangleright \quad \Delta, X\colon K \vdash \Phi\colon L}{Sg^{op} \quad \triangleright \quad \Delta \vdash \lambda X\colon K.\Phi\colon K \Rightarrow L} \qquad \frac{Sg^{op} \quad \triangleright \quad \Delta \vdash \Phi\colon K \Rightarrow L \quad Sg^{op} \quad \triangleright \quad \Delta \vdash \Psi\colon K}{Sg^{op} \quad \triangleright \quad \Delta \vdash \Phi\,\Psi\colon L}$$

Figure 6.2: Proved Operators Generated from an $\omega\lambda\times$-Operator Signature.

Unit *Type* ─────────────────────────────────────

$$\overline{Sg^{op} \;\; \triangleright \;\; \Delta \vdash unit \colon Type}$$

Binary Product *Type* ─────────────────────────

$$\frac{Sg^{op} \;\; \triangleright \;\; \Delta \vdash \Phi \colon Type \quad Sg^{op} \;\; \triangleright \;\; \Delta \vdash \Psi \colon Type}{Sg^{op} \;\; \triangleright \;\; \Delta \vdash \Phi \times \Psi \colon Type}$$

Function *Type* ───────────────────────────────

$$\frac{Sg^{op} \;\; \triangleright \;\; \Delta \vdash \Phi \colon Type \quad Sg^{op} \;\; \triangleright \;\; \Delta \vdash \Psi \colon Type}{Sg^{op} \;\; \triangleright \;\; \Delta \vdash \Phi \Rightarrow \Psi \colon Type}$$

Kind Abstraction ──────────────────────────────

$$\frac{Sg^{op} \;\; \triangleright \;\; \Delta, X \colon K \vdash \Phi \colon Type}{Sg^{op} \;\; \triangleright \;\; \Delta \vdash \forall X \colon K.\Phi \colon Type}$$

Figure 6.3: Proved Operators Generated from an $\omega\lambda\times$-Operator Signature, Continued from Figure 6.2.

Axioms

$$\frac{Ax^{op} \;\; \rhd \;\; \Delta \vdash \Phi = \Phi' \colon K}{Th^{op} \;\; \rhd \;\; \Delta \vdash \Phi = \Phi' \colon K}$$

Operator Unit Equations

$$\frac{Sg^{op} \;\; \rhd \;\; \Delta \vdash \Phi \colon Unit}{Th^{op} \;\; \rhd \;\; \Delta \vdash \Phi = \langle\rangle \colon Unit}$$

Operator Binary Product Equations

$$\frac{Sg^{op} \;\; \rhd \;\; \Delta \vdash \Theta \colon K \times L}{Th^{op} \;\; \rhd \;\; \Delta \vdash \langle \mathsf{Fst}(\Theta), \mathsf{Snd}(\Theta) \rangle = \Theta \colon K \times L}$$

$$\frac{Sg^{op} \;\; \rhd \;\; \Delta \vdash \Phi \colon K \quad Sg^{op} \;\; \rhd \;\; \Delta \vdash \Psi \colon L}{Th^{op} \;\; \rhd \;\; \Delta \vdash \mathsf{Fst}(\langle \Phi, \Psi \rangle) = \Phi \colon K}$$

$$\frac{Sg^{op} \;\; \rhd \;\; \Delta \vdash \Phi \colon K \quad Sg^{op} \;\; \rhd \;\; \Delta \vdash \Psi \colon L}{Th^{op} \;\; \rhd \;\; \Delta \vdash \mathsf{Snd}(\langle \Phi, \Psi \rangle) = \Psi \colon L}$$

Operator Function Equations

$$\frac{Sg^{op} \;\; \rhd \;\; \Delta, X \colon K \vdash \Phi \colon L \quad Sg^{op} \;\; \rhd \;\; \Delta \vdash \Psi \colon K}{Th^{op} \;\; \rhd \;\; \Delta \vdash (\lambda X \colon K.\Phi)\,\Psi = \Phi[\Psi/X] \colon L}$$

$$\frac{Sg^{op} \;\; \rhd \;\; \Delta \vdash \Phi \colon K \Rightarrow L}{Th^{op} \;\; \rhd \;\; \Delta \vdash \lambda X \colon K.(\Phi X) = \Phi \colon K \Rightarrow L} \quad (X \notin fopv(\Phi))$$

$$\frac{Th^{op} \;\; \rhd \;\; \Delta, X \colon K \vdash \Phi = \Phi' \colon L}{Th^{op} \;\; \rhd \;\; \Delta \vdash \lambda X \colon K.\Phi = \lambda X \colon K.\Phi' \colon K \Rightarrow L}$$

Together with the expected rules for **Weakening, Permutation, Substitution** and **Equational Reasoning.**

Figure 6.4: Operator Theorems Generated from an $\omega\lambda\times$-Operator Theory.

$f: \Delta^f; \Phi_1, \ldots, \Phi_a \to \Phi$ if a is non-zero. These raw operators are required to satisfy $Sg^{op} \ \triangleright \ \Delta^f \vdash \Phi_i$: *Type* for $1 \le i \le a$ and $Sg^{op} \ \triangleright \ \Delta^f \vdash \Phi$: *Type*. In the case that a is zero we write $k: \Delta^k; \Phi$ and say that k is a *constant* function symbol, where we demand $Sg^{op} \ \triangleright \ \Delta^k \vdash \Phi$: *Type*.

The *raw* terms generated from an $\omega\lambda\times$-term signature Sg^{tm} are specified by the (informal) BNF grammar:

$$M ::=$$

$$x \mid k_{\Psi_1, \ldots, \Psi_n} \mid f_{\Psi_1, \ldots, \Psi_{n'}} \underbrace{(M, \ldots, M)}_{length\ a} \mid \langle\rangle \mid \langle M, M \rangle \mid \mathsf{Fst}(M) \mid \mathsf{Snd}(M) \mid$$

$$\lambda x: \Phi.M \mid M\,M \mid \Lambda X: K.M \mid M\,\Phi$$

where x is any *term variable* (we assume that there is an infinite stock of such term variables), k is any constant function symbol for which $length(\Delta^k) = n$, f is any function symbol of non-zero arity a for which $length(\Delta^f) = n'$ and the Ψ_i and Φ are any raw operators. We shall often make use of the self explanatory notation $k_{\vec{\Psi}}$ and $f_{\vec{\Psi}}(\vec{M})$.

The *abstractions* $\lambda x: \Phi$ and $\Lambda X: K$ bind occurrences of x and X respectively within their *scopes*. The reader is left to define the *free* term variables of a raw term, $ftmv(\Phi)$, the *bound* term variables of a raw term, the *free* operator variables of a raw term, $fopv(\Phi)$, and the *bound* operator variables of a raw term. We also omit the definition of the substitutions $M[N/x]$ and $M[\Phi/X]$, these being essentially the same in principle as for second order polymorphic functional type theory—see Discussion 5.2.8.

Let us now give the "well formed" raw terms generated from an $\omega\lambda\times$-term signature Sg^{tm}. We need the following definitions. A *term context* is a finite list of (term variable, raw operator) pairs, usually written $[x_1: \Phi_1, \ldots, x_m: \Phi_m]$, where the term variables are required to be distinct. A *term-in-context* is a judgement of the form $\Delta \mid \Gamma \vdash M: \Phi$ where Δ is an operator context, Γ is a term context, M is a raw term and Φ is a raw operator. A *proved term* is a judgement of the form $Sg^{tm} \ \triangleright \ \Delta \mid \Gamma \vdash M: \Phi$. Note that a consequence of the rules for generating such proved terms is that necessarily $Sg^{op} \ \triangleright \ \Delta \vdash \Phi_i$: *Type* for each Φ_i appearing in Γ, and $Sg^{op} \ \triangleright \ \Delta \vdash \Phi$: *Type*. We shall abbreviate $\Delta \vdash \Phi$: *Type* to $\Delta \vdash \Phi$ when no ambiguities are likely to arise, with a similar convention for $\Delta \vdash \Phi = \Phi'$. If Δ is an operator context and Γ a term context, then the judgement $\Delta \vdash \Gamma$ will simply be shorthand for $\Delta \vdash \Phi_i$ (each i) where the Φ_i appear in Γ. The proved terms are generated from the rules given in Figures 6.5 and 6.6.

Term Variables

$$\frac{Sg^{op} \ \triangleright \ \Delta \vdash \Gamma' \quad Sg^{op} \ \triangleright \ \Delta \vdash \Phi \quad Sg^{op} \ \triangleright \ \Delta \vdash \Gamma}{Sg^{tm} \ \triangleright \ \Delta \,|\, \Gamma', x \colon \Phi, \Gamma \vdash x \colon \Phi}$$

Unit Term

$$\frac{Sg^{op} \ \triangleright \ \Delta \vdash \Gamma}{Sg^{tm} \ \triangleright \ \Delta \,|\, \Gamma \vdash \langle \rangle \colon unit}$$

Function Symbols

$$\frac{Sg^{op} \ \triangleright \ \Delta \vdash \Gamma \quad Sg^{op} \ \triangleright \ \Delta \vdash \Psi_1 \quad \ldots \quad Sg^{op} \ \triangleright \ \Delta \vdash \Psi_n}{Sg^{tm} \ \triangleright \ \Delta \,|\, \Gamma \vdash k_{\vec{\Psi}} \colon \Phi[\vec{\Psi}/\Delta^k]} \quad (k \colon \Delta^k; \Phi)$$

$$\left\{ \begin{array}{c} Sg^{op} \ \triangleright \ \Delta \vdash \Psi_1 \quad \ldots \quad Sg^{op} \ \triangleright \ \Delta \vdash \Psi_n \\[2pt] \dfrac{Sg^{tm} \ \triangleright \ \Delta \,|\, \Gamma \vdash M_1 \colon \Phi_1[\vec{\Psi}/\Delta^f] \quad \ldots \quad Sg^{tm} \ \triangleright \ \Delta \,|\, \Gamma \vdash M_a \colon \Phi_a[\vec{\Psi}/\Delta^f]}{Sg^{tm} \ \triangleright \ \Delta \,|\, \Gamma \vdash f_{\vec{\Psi}}(M_1, \ldots, M_a) \colon \Phi[\vec{\Psi}/\Delta^f]} \end{array} \right.$$

$$(f \colon \Delta^f; \Phi_1, \ldots, \Phi_a \to \Phi)$$

Binary Product Terms

$$\frac{Sg^{tm} \ \triangleright \ \Delta \,|\, \Gamma \vdash M \colon \Phi \quad Sg^{tm} \ \triangleright \ \Delta \,|\, \Gamma \vdash N \colon \Psi}{Sg^{tm} \ \triangleright \ \Delta \,|\, \Gamma \vdash \langle M, N \rangle \colon \Phi \times \Psi}$$

$$\frac{Sg^{tm} \ \triangleright \ \Delta \,|\, \Gamma \vdash P \colon \Phi \times \Psi}{Sg^{tm} \ \triangleright \ \Delta \,|\, \Gamma \vdash \mathsf{Fst}(P) \colon \Phi} \qquad \frac{Sg^{tm} \ \triangleright \ \Delta \,|\, \Gamma \vdash P \colon \Phi \times \Psi}{Sg^{tm} \ \triangleright \ \Delta \,|\, \Gamma \vdash \mathsf{Snd}(P) \colon \Psi}$$

Figure 6.5: Proved Terms Generated from an $\omega\lambda\times$-Signature.

Function Terms ────────────────────────────────

$$\frac{Sg^{tm} \;\triangleright\; \Delta\,|\,\Gamma, x\!:\!\Phi \vdash F\!:\!\Psi}{Sg^{tm} \;\triangleright\; \Delta\,|\,\Gamma \vdash \lambda x\!:\!\Phi.F\!:\!\Phi \Rightarrow \Psi}$$

$$\frac{Sg^{tm} \;\triangleright\; \Delta\,|\,\Gamma \vdash M\!:\!\Phi \Rightarrow \Psi \quad Sg^{tm} \;\triangleright\; \Delta\,|\,\Gamma \vdash N\!:\!\Phi}{Sg^{tm} \;\triangleright\; \Delta\,|\,\Gamma \vdash MN\!:\!\Psi}$$

Polymorphism Terms ───────────────────────────

$$\frac{Sg^{tm} \;\triangleright\; \Delta, X\!:\!K\,|\,\Gamma \vdash F\!:\!\Phi}{Sg^{tm} \;\triangleright\; \Delta\,|\,\Gamma \vdash \Lambda X\!:\!K.F : \forall X\!:\!K.\Phi}$$

$$\frac{Sg^{tm} \;\triangleright\; \Delta\,|\,\Gamma \vdash M : \forall X\!:\!K.\Phi \quad Sg^{op} \;\triangleright\; \Delta \vdash \Psi\!:\!K}{Sg^{tm} \;\triangleright\; \Delta\,|\,\Gamma \vdash M\Psi\!:\!\Phi[\Psi/X]}$$

Term Typing ─────────────────────────────────

$$\frac{Sg^{tm} \;\triangleright\; \Delta\,|\,\Gamma \vdash M\!:\!\Phi \quad Th^{op} \;\triangleright\; \Delta \vdash \Phi = \Phi'}{Sg^{tm} \;\triangleright\; \Delta\,|\,\Gamma \vdash M\!:\!\Phi'}$$

Figure 6.6: Proved Terms Generated from an $\omega\lambda\times$-Term Signature, Continued from Figure 6.5.

Those rules which appear in Figures 5.5, 5.6 and 5.7 in Chapter 5, with the
rules **Polymorphism Equations** replaced by:

Polymorphism Equations

$$\frac{Sg^{tm} \;\; \triangleright \;\; \Delta, X\!:\!K \,|\, \Gamma \vdash F\!:\!\Phi \quad Sg^{op} \;\; \triangleright \;\; \Delta \vdash \Psi\!:\!K}{Th^{tm} \;\; \triangleright \;\; \Delta \,|\, \Gamma \vdash (\Lambda X\!:\!K.F)\,\Psi = F[\Psi/X]\!:\!\Phi[\Psi/X]}$$

$$\frac{Sg^{tm} \;\; \triangleright \;\; \Delta \,|\, \Gamma \vdash M : \forall X\!:\!K.\Phi}{Th^{tm} \;\; \triangleright \;\; \Delta \,|\, \Gamma \vdash \Lambda X\!:\!K.(MX) = M : \forall X\!:\!K.\Phi} \quad \text{(where } X \notin fopv(M))$$

$$\frac{Th^{tm} \;\; \triangleright \;\; \Delta, X\!:\!K \,|\, \Gamma \vdash F = F'\!:\!\Phi}{Th^{tm} \;\; \triangleright \;\; \Delta \,|\, \Gamma \vdash \Lambda X\!:\!K.F = \Lambda X\!:\!K.F' : \forall X\!:\!K.\Phi}$$

Figure 6.7: Term Theorems Generated from an $\omega\lambda\times$-Term Theory.

DISCUSSION 6.2.3   Let us begin with some definitions. Suppose that we are
given an $\omega\lambda\times$-term signature Sg^{tm}. A *term equation-in-context* is a judgement
of the form $\Delta \mid \Gamma \vdash M = M'\!:\!\Phi$ for which $Sg^{tm} \;\; \triangleright \;\; \Delta \mid \Gamma \vdash M\!:\!\Phi$ and
$Sg^{tm} \;\; \triangleright \;\; \Delta \mid \Gamma \vdash M'\!:\!\Phi$.

Now we can give the notion of a higher order polymorphic functional type
theory. We define an $\omega\lambda\times$-*term theory* Th^{tm} to be a pair (Sg^{tm}, Ax^{tm}) where
Sg^{tm} is an $\omega\lambda\times$-term signature and Ax^{tm} is a collection of term equations-in-
context, each equation-in-context known as a *term axiom*. A *term theorem* is
a judgement of the form

$$Th^{tm} \;\; \triangleright \;\; \Delta \mid \Gamma \vdash M = M'\!:\!\Phi.$$

The term theorems are generated by the rules in Figure 6.7. An $\omega\lambda\times$-*theory*,
Th, is then a pair (Th^{op}, Th^{tm}) where the $\omega\lambda\times$-term signature of Th^{tm} depends
on the operator theory Th^{op}. A *theorem* of Th will then be any operator
theorem or any term theorem. Sometimes we may refer to an $\omega\lambda\times$-theory
$Th = (Sg, Ax)$ in the obvious way.

REMARK 6.2.4   From now on, we shall always be working with a given $\omega\lambda\times$-
theory Th given by $((Sg^{op}, Ax^{op}), (Sg^{tm}, Ax^{tm}))$. We will usually omit superscripts from such expressions, providing the meaning is clear. So, for example,
we will just write $Sg \;\; \triangleright \;\; \Delta \vdash \Phi\!:\!K$ to mean $Sg^{op} \;\; \triangleright \;\; \Delta \vdash \Phi\!:\!K$. This
overloading of notation should in fact aid clarity.

6.3 Categorical Semantics and Soundness Theorems

DISCUSSION 6.3.1 An $\omega\lambda\times$-*hyperdoctrine* is specified by the following data:

(i) A category $\mathcal{C}$, called the *base*, which is a cartesian closed category containing a distinguished object U.

(ii) A functor $\mathcal{C}(-,U):\mathcal{C}^{op} \to \mathcal{CCat}$ where $\mathcal{CCat}$ is the category of cartesian closed categories and strict cartesian closed functors. For each object I of $\mathcal{C}$, the objects of $\mathcal{C}(I,U)$ are by definition the morphisms $I \to U$ in $\mathcal{C}$, and $\mathcal{C}(I,U)$ is the *fibre* of the $\omega\lambda\times$-hyperdoctrine at I. Given a morphism $f:I' \to I$ in $\mathcal{C}$, we shall write $f^* \overset{\text{def}}{=} \mathcal{C}(f,U):\mathcal{C}(I,U) \to \mathcal{C}(I',U)$ for the strict cartesian closed functor assigned to f by $\mathcal{C}(-,U)$; if $g:I \to U$ is an object of $\mathcal{C}(I,U)$, then by definition $f^*(g) \overset{\text{def}}{=} g \circ f$ where the composition $\circ$ is in $\mathcal{C}$.

(iii) For objects I and K of $\mathcal{C}$ we are given a functor $\forall_I^K:\mathcal{C}(I \times K,U) \to \mathcal{C}(I,U)$ which is right adjoint to the functor $(\pi_I^K)^*:\mathcal{C}(I,U) \to \mathcal{C}(I \times K,U)$ where $\pi_I^K:I \times K \to I$ is projection in $\mathcal{C}$. Moreover, given any morphism $f:J \to I$ in $\mathcal{C}$, the diagram

$$
\begin{array}{ccc}
\mathcal{C}(I \times K,U) & \overset{\forall_I^K}{\longrightarrow} & \mathcal{C}(I,U) \\
{\scriptstyle (f \times id_K)^*}\downarrow & & \downarrow{\scriptstyle f^*} \\
\mathcal{C}(J \times K,U) & \underset{\forall_J^K}{\longrightarrow} & \mathcal{C}(J,U)
\end{array}
$$

commutes and in fact the canonical natural transformation

$$\alpha: f^* \circ \forall_I^K \to \forall_J^K \circ (f \times id_K)^*$$

is the identity. We call these requirements on $\forall_I^K$ the *Beck-Chevalley condition* for $\omega\lambda\times$-theories.

We define a structure for an $\omega\lambda\times$-signature in an $\omega\lambda\times$-hyperdoctrine. As usual, the idea is to give an interpretation of the data of an $\omega\lambda\times$-signature in an appropriate categorical world; in this case a certain kind of indexed category with structure. More formally, suppose that we are given an $\omega\lambda\times$-hyperdoctrine $\mathbb{C}:\mathcal{C}^{op} \to \mathcal{CCat}$ and an $\omega\lambda\times$-operator signature Sg^{op}. An *operator structure* $\mathbf{M^{op}}$ is specified by giving an object $[G]$ of $\mathcal{C}$ for each ground kind G of Sg^{op}, a global element $[C]$ of $[K]$ in $\mathcal{C}$ for each constant operator $C:K$, and a morphism $[F]:[K_1] \times \ldots \times [K_n] \to [K]$ for each operator symbol $F:K_1,\ldots,K_n \to K$ of non-zero arity n. Here, for each kind K, we define $[K]$ inductively through the clauses

- $[Unit] \overset{\text{def}}{=} 1$,

- $[Type] \stackrel{\text{def}}{=} U$,

- $[K \times K'] \stackrel{\text{def}}{=} [K] \times [K']$, and

- $[K \Rightarrow K'] \stackrel{\text{def}}{=} [K] \Rightarrow [K']$

where $[G]$ has been given in $\mathbf{M}^{op}$. If $\Delta = [X_1 : K_1, \ldots, X_n : K_n]$ then we shall define $[\Delta] \stackrel{\text{def}}{=} \Pi_1^n [K_i]$ (and $[\Delta] \stackrel{\text{def}}{=} 1$ if Δ is the empty list). We now define for each proved operator $Sg^{op} \; \rhd \; \Delta \vdash \Phi : K$ a morphism in $\mathcal{C}$ of the form $[\Delta \vdash \Phi : K] : [\Delta] \to [K]$ using the rules given in Figures 6.8 and 6.9. We have the following lemma:

LEMMA 6.3.2   Suppose that we are given an $\omega \lambda \times$-operator signature Sg^{op}, that $Sg^{op} \; \rhd \; \Delta' \vdash \Psi : L$ where $\Delta' = [X_1 : K_1, \ldots, X_n : K_n]$, and that $Sg^{op} \; \rhd \; \Delta \vdash \Phi_i : K_i$ for $1 \leq i \leq n$. From this one may deduce $Sg^{op} \; \rhd \; \Delta \vdash \Psi[\vec{\Phi}/\Delta'] : L$. Further we can deduce that

$$[\Delta \vdash \Psi[\vec{\Phi}/\Delta'] : L] \;=\; [\Delta' \vdash \Psi : L] \circ \langle [\Delta \vdash \Phi_1 : K_1], \ldots, [\Delta \vdash \Phi_n : K_n] \rangle$$

$$\stackrel{\text{def}}{=} \; \langle [\Delta \vdash \Phi_1 : K_1], \ldots, [\Delta \vdash \Phi_n : K_n] \rangle^*([\Delta' \vdash \Psi : L]).$$

PROOF   Induction on the derivation of $Sg^{op} \; \rhd \; \Delta' \vdash \Psi : L$. $\square$

COROLLARY 6.3.3   Suppose that we have $Sg^{op} \; \rhd \; \Delta \vdash \Phi : K$ and $\Delta \subseteq \Delta'$. Then we can show that $Sg^{op} \; \rhd \; \Delta' \vdash \Phi : K$. Further, we can prove that

$$[\Delta' \vdash \Phi : K] = [\Delta \vdash \Phi : K] \circ \pi \stackrel{\text{def}}{=} \pi^*([\Delta \vdash \Phi : K])$$

where $\pi : [\Delta'] \to [\Delta]$ is defined from the obvious product projections.

PROOF   Follows from Lemma 6.3.2. $\square$

DISCUSSION 6.3.4   Suppose that Sg^{op} is an $\omega \lambda \times$-operator signature. Then if $\Delta \vdash \Phi = \Phi' : K$ is any operator equation-in-context we say that $\mathbf{M}^{op}$ *satisfies* the operator equation-in-context if $[\Delta \vdash \Phi : K]$ and $[\Delta \vdash \Phi' : K]$ are equal morphisms in $\mathcal{C}$. If $Th^{op} = (Sg^{op}, Ax^{op})$ is an $\omega \lambda \times$-operator theory, then $\mathbf{M}^{op}$ is a *model* of Th^{op} if it satisfies the operator axioms. As ever, we have:

THEOREM 6.3.5   Let $\mathbf{M}^{op}$ be a model of $Th^{op} = (Sg^{op}, Ax^{op})$. Then $\mathbf{M}^{op}$ satisfies the theorems of Th^{op}.

PROOF   A routine verification that the rules in Figure 6.4 for generating $\omega \lambda \times$-operator theorems are closed under satisfaction by $\mathbf{M}^{op}$. $\square$

Operator Variables ——————————————————————————————————

$$[\![\Delta, X\colon K, \Delta' \vdash X\colon K]\!] = \pi\colon [\![\Delta]\!] \times [\![K]\!] \times [\![\Delta']\!] \to [\![K]\!]$$

Unit Operator ——————————————————————————————————————

$$[\![\Delta \vdash \langle\rangle\colon \mathit{Unit}]\!] =\,!\colon [\![\Delta]\!] \to 1$$

Operator Symbols —————————————————————————————————

$$\frac{}{[\![\Delta \vdash C\colon K]\!] \overset{\text{def}}{=} [\![C]\!] \circ \,!\colon [\![\Delta]\!] \to 1 \to [\![K]\!]} \;\; (C\colon K)$$

$$\frac{[\![\Delta \vdash \Phi_1\colon K_1]\!] = \phi_1\colon [\![\Delta]\!] \to [\![K_1]\!] \quad \ldots \quad [\![\Delta \vdash \Phi_n\colon K_n]\!] = \phi_n\colon [\![\Delta]\!] \to [\![K_n]\!]}{[\![\Delta \vdash F(\vec{\Phi})\colon K]\!] = [\![F]\!] \circ \langle \phi_1, \ldots, \phi_n \rangle\colon [\![\Delta]\!] \to [\![K]\!]}$$

$$(F\colon K_1, \ldots, K_n \to K)$$

Binary Product Operators ——————————————————————————

$$\frac{[\![\Delta \vdash \Phi\colon K]\!] = \phi\colon [\![\Delta]\!] \to [\![K]\!] \quad [\![\Delta \vdash \Psi\colon L]\!] = \psi\colon [\![\Delta]\!] \to [\![L]\!]}{[\![\Delta \vdash \langle \Phi, \Psi \rangle\colon K \times L]\!] = \langle \phi, \psi \rangle\colon [\![\Delta]\!] \to [\![K]\!] \times [\![L]\!]}$$

$$\frac{[\![\Delta \vdash \Theta\colon K \times L]\!] = \theta\colon [\![\Delta]\!] \to [\![K]\!] \times [\![L]\!]}{[\![\Delta \vdash \mathsf{Fst}(\Theta)\colon K]\!] = \pi \circ \theta\colon [\![\Delta]\!] \to ([\![K]\!] \times [\![L]\!]) \to [\![K]\!]}$$

$$\frac{[\![\Delta \vdash \Theta\colon K \times L]\!] = \theta\colon [\![\Delta]\!] \to [\![K]\!] \times [\![L]\!]}{[\![\Delta \vdash \mathsf{Snd}(\Theta)\colon L]\!] = \pi' \circ \theta\colon [\![\Delta]\!] \to ([\![K]\!] \times [\![L]\!]) \to [\![L]\!]}$$

Figure 6.8: Categorical Semantics of Proved Operators Generated from an $\omega\lambda\times$-Operator Signature.

Function Operators ─────────────────────────────

$$[\![\Delta, X\colon K \vdash \Phi\colon L]\!] = \phi\colon ([\![\Delta]\!] \times [\![K]\!]) \to [\![L]\!]$$
$$\overline{[\![\Delta \vdash \lambda X\colon K.\Phi : K \Rightarrow L]\!] = \lambda(\phi)\colon [\![\Delta]\!] \to ([\![K]\!] \Rightarrow [\![L]\!])}$$

$$[\![\Delta \vdash \Phi\colon K \Rightarrow L]\!] = \phi\colon [\![\Delta]\!] \to ([\![K]\!] \Rightarrow [\![L]\!]) \quad [\![\Delta \vdash \Psi\colon K]\!] = \psi\colon [\![\Delta]\!] \to [\![K]\!]$$
$$\overline{[\![\Delta \vdash \Phi\Psi\colon L]\!] = ev \circ \langle\phi,\psi\rangle\colon [\![\Delta]\!] \to ([\![K]\!] \Rightarrow [\![L]\!]) \times [\![K]\!] \to [\![L]\!]}$$

Unit *Type* ─────────────────────────────

$$\overline{[\![\Delta \vdash unit\colon Type]\!] = 1\colon [\![\Delta]\!] \to U}$$

(where 1 is the terminal object of $\mathcal{C}([\![\Delta]\!], U)$)

Binary Product *Type* ─────────────────────────────

$$[\![\Delta \vdash \Phi\colon Type]\!] = \phi\colon [\![\Delta]\!] \to U \quad [\![\Delta \vdash \Psi\colon Type]\!] = \psi\colon [\![\Delta]\!] \to U$$
$$\overline{[\![\Delta \vdash \Phi \times \Psi\colon Type]\!] = \phi \times \psi\colon [\![\Delta]\!] \to U}$$

Function *Type* ─────────────────────────────

$$[\![\Delta \vdash \Phi\colon Type]\!] = \phi\colon [\![\Delta]\!] \to U \quad [\![\Delta \vdash \Psi\colon Type]\!] = \psi\colon [\![\Delta]\!] \to U$$
$$\overline{[\![\Delta \vdash \Phi \Rightarrow \Psi\colon Type]\!] = \phi \Rightarrow \psi\colon [\![\Delta]\!] \to U}$$

Kind Abstraction ─────────────────────────────

$$[\![\Delta, X\colon K \vdash \Phi\colon Type]\!] = \phi\colon [\![\Delta]\!] \times [\![K]\!] \to U$$
$$\overline{[\![\Delta \vdash \forall X\colon K.\Phi : Type]\!] = \forall^{[\![K]\!]}_{[\![\Delta]\!]}(\phi)\colon [\![\Delta]\!] \to U}$$

Figure 6.9: Categorical Semantics of Proved Operators Generated from an $\omega\lambda\times$-Operator Signature, Continued from Figure 6.8.

Instances of the rules appearing in Figures 5.9 and 5.10 of Chapter 5, with the rules for **Polymorphism Terms** replaced by

---

Polymorphism Terms ——————————————————

$$\frac{[\Delta, X\!:\!K \mid \Gamma \vdash F\!:\!\Phi] = f\!:\![\Delta, X\!:\!K \vdash \Gamma] \to [\Delta, X\!:\!K \vdash \Phi]}{[\Delta \mid \Gamma \vdash \Lambda X\!:\!K.F : \forall X\!:\!K.\Phi] = \bar{f}\!:\![\Delta \vdash \Gamma] \to \forall^{[K]}_{[\Delta]}([\Delta, X\!:\!K \vdash \Phi])}$$

$$[\Delta \mid \Gamma \vdash M : \forall X\!:\!K.\Phi] = m\!:\![\Delta \vdash \Gamma] \to [\Delta \vdash \forall X\!:\!K.\Phi]$$

$$[\Delta \mid \Gamma \vdash M\Psi\!:\!\Phi[\Psi/X]] = \langle id_{[\Delta]}, [\Delta \vdash \Psi\!:\!K]\rangle^*([id_{\forall([\Delta, Y\!:\!K \vdash \Phi[Y/X])})]^\wedge) \circ m\!:$$

$$[\Delta \vdash \Gamma] \to [\Delta \vdash \forall X\!:\!K.\Phi] \to [\Delta \vdash \Phi[\Psi/X]]$$

(where Y does not appear in Δ)

Figure 6.10: Categorical Semantics of Proved Terms Generated from an $\omega\lambda\times$-Term Signature.

DISCUSSION 6.3.6   Let $Sg^{tm}(Th^{op})$ be an $\omega\lambda\times$-term signature. A *term structure* $\mathbf{M^{tm}}$ is specified by giving a model $\mathbf{M^{op}}$ for Th^{op}, a morphism in $\mathcal{C}([\Delta], U)$ of the form

$$[f]\!:\![\Delta \vdash \Phi_1] \times \ldots \times [\Delta \vdash \Phi_n] \to [\Delta \vdash \Phi]$$

where f is a function symbol with sorting $f\!:\!\Delta; \Phi_1, \ldots, \Phi_n \to \Phi$, and a global element $[k]$ of $[\Delta \vdash \Phi]$ for a constant $k\!:\!\Delta; \Phi$. Given an operator context Δ, if $Sg^{op} \,\triangleright\, \Delta \vdash \Gamma$ for some term context $\Gamma = [x_1\!:\!\Phi_1, \ldots, x_m\!:\!\Phi_m]$, then we shall define $[\Delta \vdash \Gamma] \stackrel{\text{def}}{=} \Pi_1^m[\Delta \vdash \Phi_i]$; and we define $[\Delta \vdash \Gamma] \stackrel{\text{def}}{=} 1$ if Γ is the empty list. Then for every judgement $Sg^{tm} \,\triangleright\, \Delta \mid \Gamma \vdash M\!:\!\Phi$, we specify a morphism

$$[\Delta \mid \Gamma \vdash M\!:\!\Phi]\!:\![\Delta \vdash \Gamma] \to [\Delta \vdash \Phi]$$

in $\mathcal{C}([\Delta], U)$ by the clauses given in Figure 6.10.

LEMMA 6.3.7   Let $Sg^{tm} \,\triangleright\, \Delta' \mid \Gamma \vdash N\!:\!\Psi$ be a proved term and let $\Delta \vdash \Phi_i\!:\!K_i$ be proved operators, where $\Delta' = [X_1\!:\!K_1, \ldots, X_n\!:\!K_n]$. Then we have a proved term $Sg^{tm} \,\triangleright\, \Delta \mid \Gamma[\vec{\Phi}/\Delta'] \vdash N[\vec{\Phi}/\Delta']\!:\!\Psi[\vec{\Phi}/\Delta']$ and moreover its semantics is given by

$$[\Delta \mid \Gamma[\vec{\Phi}/\Delta'] \vdash N[\vec{\Phi}/\Delta']\!:\!\Psi[\vec{\Phi}/\Delta']] =$$

$$\langle[\Delta \vdash \Phi_1\!:\!K_1], \ldots, [\Delta \vdash \Phi_n\!:\!K_n]\rangle^*([\Delta' \mid \Gamma \vdash N\!:\!\Psi]).$$

PROOF   Induction on the derivation of $Sg^{tm} \,\triangleright\, \Delta' \mid \Gamma \vdash N\!:\!\Psi$.   □

LEMMA 6.3.8   Let $Sg^{tm} \; \triangleright \; \Delta \mid \Gamma' \vdash N : \Psi$ be a proved term and let $Sg^{tm} \; \triangleright \; \Delta \mid \Gamma \vdash M_j : \Phi_j$ be proved terms where the term context Γ' is $[x_1 : \Phi_1, \ldots, x_m : \Phi_m]$. Then there is a proved term $Sg^{tm} \; \triangleright \; \Delta \mid \Gamma \vdash N[\vec{M}/\Gamma'] : \Psi$ and moreover

$$[\![\Delta \mid \Gamma \vdash N[\vec{M}/\Gamma'] : \Psi]\!] =$$

$$[\![\Delta \mid \Gamma' \vdash N : \Psi]\!] \circ \langle [\![\Delta \mid \Gamma \vdash M_1 : \Phi_1]\!], \ldots, [\![\Delta \mid \Gamma \vdash M_m : \Phi_m]\!] \rangle.$$

PROOF   Induction on the derivation of $Sg^{tm} \; \triangleright \; \Delta \mid \Gamma' \vdash N : \Psi$.   □

COROLLARY 6.3.9   Let $Sg^{tm} \; \triangleright \; \Delta \mid \Gamma \vdash M : \Phi$ be a proved term, $\Delta \subseteq \Delta'$ and $\Gamma \subseteq \Gamma'$. Then certainly $Sg^{tm} \; \triangleright \; \Delta' \mid \Gamma' \vdash M : \Phi$, and moreover

$$[\![\Delta' \mid \Gamma' \vdash M : \Phi]\!] = \pi^*([\![\Delta \mid \Gamma \vdash M : \Phi]\!] \circ \pi')$$

where $\pi : [\![\Delta']\!] \to [\![\Delta]\!]$ and $\pi' : [\![\Delta \vdash \Gamma']\!] \to [\![\Delta \vdash \Gamma]\!]$ are formed from product projections.

PROOF   Follows from Lemmas 6.3.7 and 6.3.8.   □

DISCUSSION 6.3.10   Suppose that Sg^{tm} is an $\omega\lambda\times$-term signature and that $\mathbf{M^{tm}}$ is a term structure for Sg^{tm} in an $\omega\lambda\times$-hyperdoctrine $\mathbb{C} : \mathcal{C}^{op} \to \mathcal{CCat}$. If $\Delta \mid \Gamma \vdash M = M' : \Phi$ is any term equation-in-context, we shall say that $\mathbf{M^{tm}}$ *satisfies* the term equation-in-context provided the morphisms $[\![\Delta \mid \Gamma \vdash M : \Phi]\!]$ and $[\![\Delta \mid \Gamma \vdash M' : \Phi]\!]$ are equal in the cartesian closed category $\mathbb{C}([\![\Delta]\!]) \stackrel{\text{def}}{=} \mathcal{C}([\![\Delta]\!], U)$. A *model* $\mathbf{M^{tm}}$ of an $\omega\lambda\times$-term theory $Th^{tm} = (Sg^{tm}, Ax^{tm})$ is a structure $\mathbf{M^{tm}}$ for the signature Sg^{tm} in an $\omega\lambda\times$-hyperdoctrine $\mathbb{C} : \mathcal{C}^{op} \to \mathcal{CCat}$, which satisfies each of the term axioms of Ax^{tm}. We can now prove the soundness theorem for $\omega\lambda\times$-term theories.

THEOREM 6.3.11   Let Th^{tm} be an $\omega\lambda\times$-term theory and $\mathbb{C} : \mathcal{C}^{op} \to \mathcal{CCat}$ be an $\omega\lambda\times$-hyperdoctrine. If $\mathbf{M^{tm}}$ is a model of Th^{tm} in $\mathbb{C}$, then $\mathbf{M^{tm}}$ satisfies all of the term theorems of Th^{tm}.

PROOF   A routine verification that the rules in Figure 6.7 for generating $\omega\lambda\times$-term theorems are closed under satisfaction by the structure $\mathbf{M^{tm}}$.   □

EXERCISE 6.3.12   Complete some of the verifications of the proof of Theorem 6.3.11.

DISCUSSION 6.3.13   Let us complete this section with the following definition. A *structure* **M** in an $\omega\lambda\times$-hyperdoctrine $\mathbb{C}:\mathcal{C}^{op} \to \mathcal{ACat}$ for an $\omega\lambda\times$-signature $Sg = (Sg^{op}, Sg^{tm}(Th^{op}))$ is a pair $(\mathbf{M^{op}}, \mathbf{M^{tm}})$ where $\mathbf{M^{op}}$ is a model of Th^{op} and $\mathbf{M^{tm}}$ is a term structure. The specification of $\mathbf{M^{tm}}$ depends on the specification of $\mathbf{M^{op}}$. A *model* **M** of an $\omega\lambda\times$-theory $Th = (Th^{op}, Th^{tm}) = (Sg, Ax)$ in an $\omega\lambda\times$-hyperdoctrine is specified by a structure $(\mathbf{M^{op}}, \mathbf{M^{tm}})$ for Sg where $\mathbf{M^{tm}}$ is a model of Th^{tm} (and $\mathbf{M^{op}}$ is a model of Th^{ty}). We have

THEOREM 6.3.14   The categorical semantics of an $\omega\lambda\times$-theory Th in an $\omega\lambda\times$-hyperdoctrine given by a model **M** is sound, that is, **M** satisfies all theorems of Th.

PROOF   This is a restatement of Theorems 6.3.5 and 6.3.11.   □

6.4   A PER Model

DISCUSSION 6.4.1   Our first example of an $\omega\lambda\times$-hyperdoctrine is based on PERs.

(i) The base category is the category *Set* of sets and functions. The distinguished object U is the set of PERs on $\mathbb{N}$,

$$U \stackrel{\text{def}}{=} \{A \subseteq \mathbb{N} \times \mathbb{N} \mid A \text{ is a PER on } \mathbb{N}\}.$$

(ii) Let us write I for U^n. We define the fibre $\mathbb{C}I = \mathcal{C}(I, U)$. The objects of $\mathcal{C}(I, U)$ are (by definition of $\omega\lambda\times$-hyperdoctrine) set-theoretic functions $I \to U$. Let $x \in I$ be any element of the set I. If $F: I \to U$ and $G: I \to U$ are any two objects of the fibre over I, then Fx and Gx are PERs. Hence there is a PER $R \stackrel{\text{def}}{=} \bigcap_{x \in I} (Fx \Rightarrow Gx)$. We shall define

$$\mathcal{C}(I, U)(F, G) \stackrel{\text{def}}{=} Dom(R)/R.$$

Note that this definition is essentially the same as for the PER example of a $2\lambda\times$-hyperdoctrine; identities and composition are given in a similar manner too—see Discussion 5.5.7.

We define a functor $\mathcal{C}(-, U): \mathcal{C}^{op} \to \mathcal{ACat}$ by the assignment

$$H: I' \to I \qquad \mapsto \qquad H^*: \mathcal{C}(I, U) \longrightarrow \mathcal{C}(I', U)$$

where H sends an object $F: I \to U$ of $\mathcal{C}(I, U)$ to the object $FH: I' \to U$ of $\mathcal{C}(I', U)$, and the morphism $\phi = [e]: F \to G$ of $\mathcal{C}(I, U)$ to the morphism $[e]: FH \to GH$ of $\mathcal{C}(I', U)$.

(iii) We give a specified right adjoint to $(\pi_I^K)^*: C(I,U) \to C(I \times K, U)$, say

$$\forall_I^K : C(I \times K, U) \longrightarrow C(I,U).$$

If $F: I \times K \to U$ is an object of $C(I \times K, U)$, then the function $\forall_I^K F: I \to U$ is defined by

$$\forall_I^K F(x) \overset{\text{def}}{=} \bigcap_{k \in K} F(x,k)$$

for each $x \in I$. If $\phi = [e]: F \to G$ is a morphism of $C(I \times K, U)$ then $\forall_I^K \phi \overset{\text{def}}{=}$ $[e]: \forall_I^K F \to \forall_I^K G$.

EXERCISE 6.4.2   Verify that the indexed cartesian closed category described in Discussion 6.4.1 is an $\omega\lambda\times$-hyperdoctrine.

6.5   A Domain Model

DISCUSSION 6.5.1   We shall need some more definitions from category theory in order to present a concrete model of the pure $\omega\lambda\times$-theory.

Suppose that C is a locally small category. Then we shall say that an object S of C is *finitely presentable* if the representable functor $H^S: C \to Set$ preserves filtered colimits. To spell this definition out a little more, if $D: \mathbb{I} \to C$ is a filtered diagram where $\mathbb{I}$ is small, and has filtered colimit $(k_I: DI \to \varinjlim D \mid I \in \mathbb{I})$ in C then

$$(C(S, k_I): C(S, DI) \to \varinjlim C(S, D(-)) \mid I \in \mathbb{I})$$

is a filtered colimit in *Set*, where the functor $C(S, D(-)): \mathbb{I} \to Set$ is given by

$$\alpha: I \to J \quad \longmapsto \quad C(S, DI) \xrightarrow{f \mapsto D\alpha \circ f} C(S, DJ)$$

where $\alpha: I \to J$ is a morphism of $\mathbb{I}$ and $f: S \to DI$ in C.

A category C is called *locally finitely presentable* if

• C has all limits and all filtered colimits, and

• there is a *set* $\mathbb{S}$ of finitely presentable objects of C such that for any object C of C, there is a filtered diagram $D: \mathbb{I} \to C$ and colimit $(k_I: DI \to C \mid I \in \mathbb{I})$ for which each $DI \in \mathbb{S}$. $\mathbb{S}$ is called a set of *fp-generators* for C.

Informally, we could say that every object of C is a filtered colimit of finitely presentable objects. We shall talk of a locally finitely presentable category $(C, \mathbb{S})$.

We shall need the category of *algebraic complete lattices and l-r pairs*, $\mathcal{ACC}at^{lr}$, and the reader should compare this to the category $\mathcal{SDom}^{ep}$ of Scott domains and embedding-projection pairs.

Suppose that X and Y are algebraic complete lattices and that $l: X \to Y$ and $r: Y \to X$ are monotone functions. If $(l \dashv r)$ is a poset adjunction and also r is continuous (by which we shall just mean that r preserves directed joins) then we shall say that (l, r) is a *left-right-continuous pair* or just an *l-r pair*. So the objects of $\mathcal{ACC}at^{lr}$ are the algebraic complete lattices and the morphisms are the l-r pairs. If $f: X \to Y$ is an l-r pair then we write f^l for the left adjoint and f^r for the right adjoint. If $g: Y \to Z$ is another l-r pair then the composition $gf: X \to Z$ is defined by setting $(gf)^l \overset{\text{def}}{=} g^l f^l$ and $(gf)^r \overset{\text{def}}{=} f^r g^r$.

EXERCISE 6.5.2   Verify that $\mathcal{ACC}at^{lr}$ is a category; what are the identity morphisms?

DISCUSSION 6.5.3   With these definitions, we can consider a new category which will play a central role in our formulation of a concrete model of a higher order polymorphic theory. The category $\mathcal{LFP}$ has objects the locally finitely presentable categories and morphisms *isomorphism classes* of functors which preserve filtered colimits. Let us sketch our domain-theoretic example of an $\omega\lambda\times$-hyperdoctrine. In fact we shall see that $\mathcal{LFP}$ is a cartesian closed category and this will form the base category of an $\omega\lambda\times$-hyperdoctrine. We will show that the category $\mathcal{ACC}at^{lr}$ is in fact locally finitely presentable, and we will interpret the kind *Type* by $\mathcal{ACC}at^{lr}$. If $\mathcal{A}$ is a locally finitely presentable category, the fibre of the hyperdoctrine at $\mathcal{A}$ will be given by a certain category whose objects are isomorphism classes of filtered colimit preserving functors $\mathcal{A} \to \mathcal{ACC}at^{lr}$; we omit the precise definition of the morphisms at this point. The strategy for presenting this example of an $\omega\lambda\times$-hyperdoctrine is as follows:

• We state that $\mathcal{LFP}$ is a cartesian closed category; this is Theorem 6.5.4.

• We prove that $\mathcal{ACC}at^{lr}$ is a locally finitely presentable category. First, Lemmas 6.5.5, 6.5.6, 6.5.7, 6.5.8 and 6.5.9 provide some technical machinery, and are used in Theorem 6.5.11 which shows that $\mathcal{ACC}at^{lr}$ has filtered colimits, and in Theorem 6.5.13 which shows that $\mathcal{ACC}at^{lr}$ has all (small) limits. Propositions 6.5.14 and 6.5.15 show that $\mathcal{ACC}at^{lr}$ has a set of fp-generators. Theorem 6.5.16 concludes the result.

• We give a characterisation of the morphisms in the fibre $\mathcal{LFP}(\mathcal{A}, \mathcal{ACC}at^{lr})$ for each object $\mathcal{A}$ of $\mathcal{LFP}$. This is done in Lemmas 6.5.18, 6.5.19 and 6.5.20.

• Finally we state a theorem which says that there is an $\omega\lambda\times$-hyperdoctrine of the form $\mathcal{LFP}(-, \mathcal{ACCat}^{lr})\colon \mathcal{LFP} \to \mathcal{OCat}$, and sketch the proof. This is Theorem 6.5.21.

THEOREM 6.5.4   The category $\mathcal{LFP}$ is cartesian closed.

PROOF   The formal proof that $\mathcal{LFP}$ is cartesian closed is beyond the scope of this book, relying on some technical machinery known as Gabriel-Ulmer duality. It is clear that the one point category is a terminal object. Given locally finitely presentable categories $(\mathcal{A}, \mathbb{S}_\mathcal{A})$ and $(\mathcal{B}, \mathbb{S}_\mathcal{B})$, their binary product is given pointwise: a set of fp-generators for $\mathcal{A} \times \mathcal{B}$ is given by the set $\mathbb{S}_\mathcal{A} \times \mathbb{S}_\mathcal{B}$. The exponential is given by the functor category $[\mathbb{S}_\mathcal{A}, \mathcal{B}]$, where $\mathbb{S}_\mathcal{A}$ is regarded as a full subcategory of $\mathcal{A}$. This functor category has all filtered colimits and all (small) limits because $\mathcal{B}$ is locally finitely presentable and such (co)limits are computed pointwise. What is difficult to check is that $[\mathbb{S}_\mathcal{A}, \mathcal{B}]$ has a set of fp-generators and we omit the proof. *Provided* that $[\mathbb{S}_\mathcal{A}, \mathcal{B}]$ lives in $\mathcal{LFP}$ then $\mathcal{LFP}$ will be cartesian closed, because it is routine to verify that isomorphism classes of filtered colimit preserving functors $\mathcal{A} \times \mathcal{B} \to \mathcal{C}$ correspond bijectively to isomorphism classes of such functors $\mathcal{A} \to [\mathbb{S}_\mathcal{B}, \mathcal{C}]$.   □

LEMMA 6.5.5   Let $\mathbb{I}$ be a filtered category and suppose that we are given morphisms α and β as in the diagram:

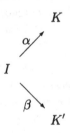

Then there are morphisms $\gamma\colon K \to K''$ and $\gamma'\colon K' \to K''$ for which $\gamma\alpha = \gamma'\beta$.

PROOF   It is a simple exercise to prove the lemma using the definition of filtered category.   □

LEMMA 6.5.6   Recall the category $\mathcal{JSLat}$ of join-semilattices whose morphisms are the (monotone) functions which preserve finite joins. This category has all small products and in particular the forgetful functor $U\colon \mathcal{JSLat} \to \mathcal{Set}$ creates them. Recall that $\overline{X}$ is the set of ideals of a join-semilattice X. If $\{X_\alpha \mid \alpha \in A\}$ is any set of join-semilattices, and if $M_\alpha \in \overline{X_\alpha}$ is a given ideal for each $\alpha \in A$, then $\Pi_{\alpha \in A} I_\alpha$ is an ideal in $\overline{\Pi_{\alpha \in A} X_\alpha}$, where we are taking the product of the underlying join-semilattices of the ideals I_α in the category *JSLat*.

PROOF   A routine verification. That the functor U creates products amounts to the statement that products in *JSLat* are given by pointwise order of the product of the underlying sets of the X_α in *Set*. That $\Pi_{\alpha \in A} I_\alpha$ is an ideal of $\Pi_{\alpha \in A} X_\alpha$ is immediate; all the properties are defined pointwise. $\square$

LEMMA 6.5.7   Let $f: X \to Y$ be a morphism in *JSLat*. Then the ideal lifting $\overline{f}: \overline{X} \to \overline{Y}$ is an l-r pair in *ACCat^{lr}*

PROOF   Use Lemma 1.5.14, Proposition 1.5.18 and Theorem 2.10.8. $\square$

LEMMA 6.5.8   The operation of taking ideal liftings is functorial. More precisely, if we have morphisms $X \xrightarrow{f} Y \xrightarrow{g} Z$ in *JSLat*, then $\overline{g \circ f} = \overline{g} \circ \overline{f}$ where of course $\overline{f}: \overline{X} \to \overline{Y}$ and $\overline{g}: \overline{Y} \to \overline{Z}$

PROOF   Suppose that $M \in \overline{X}$. We have to see that $\overline{gf}(M) = \overline{g}\overline{f}(M)$, that is

$$\bigcup \{gf(x)\!\downarrow \; | \; x \in M\} = \bigcup \{g(y)\!\downarrow \; | \; y \in \bigcup\{f(x)\!\downarrow \; | \; x \in M\}\}.$$

If $z \in \overline{g}\overline{f}(M)$, then $z \leq g(y_0)$ for some $y_0 \in Y$ where $y_0 \leq f(x_0)$ for some $x_0 \in X$. So $z \leq gf(x_0)$, implying that $z \in \overline{gf}(M)$. So we have $\overline{g}\overline{f}(M) \subseteq \overline{gf}(M)$ and the reverse inclusion is equally easy. $\square$

LEMMA 6.5.9   Suppose that $\mathbb{I}$ is a filtered category and we are given morphisms $\beta: I \to K'$, $\alpha': J \to K$, α and β' as pictured in the diagram below. Then there are morphisms θ and θ' for which $\theta\alpha = \theta'\beta$ and $\theta\alpha' = \theta'\beta'$.

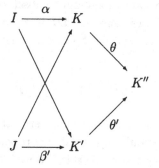

PROOF   We shall give an informal description of the proof, which is in principle quite easy, but tedious to describe. Appealing to Lemma 6.5.5, choose morphisms γ, γ' along with $\overline{\gamma}$ and $\overline{\gamma}'$ whose composites with α, β and α', β' are equal. By filteredness of $\mathbb{I}$, choose a pair of morphisms, one morphism with source equal to $tar(\gamma) = tar(\gamma')$ and the other morphism with source equal to $tar(\overline{\gamma}) = tar(\overline{\gamma}')$, and both morphisms having a common target. Call these δ and δ'. Again by filteredness, choose $\epsilon\colon tar(\delta) \to tar(\epsilon)$ which equalises $\delta\gamma'$ and $\delta'\overline{\gamma}'$, and $\epsilon'\colon tar(\delta) \to tar(\epsilon')$ which equalises $\delta\gamma$ and $\delta'\overline{\gamma}$. Finally, again appealing to Lemma 6.5.5, choose ρ and ρ' whose compositions with ϵ and ϵ' respectively are equal. Then the morphisms $\rho\epsilon\delta\gamma$ and $\rho'\epsilon'\delta'\overline{\gamma}'$ will do for θ and θ'.   □

EXERCISE 6.5.10   Verify the details of the proof of Lemma 6.5.9—draw a diagram!

THEOREM 6.5.11   The category $\mathcal{ACL}at^{lr}$ has (small) filtered colimits.

PROOF   Let $D\colon \mathbb{I} \to \mathcal{ACL}at^{lr}$ be a diagram where $\mathbb{I}$ is (small and) filtered. We define a cone

$$(\eta_I\colon DI \to \varinjlim D \mid I \in \mathbb{I})$$

as follows: Let $\varinjlim D$ be the object of $\mathcal{ACL}at^{lr}$ which consists of families of elements $(s_I \mid I \in \mathbb{I})$ where $s_I \in DI$ and $D(\alpha)^r(s_J) = s_I$ holds whenever $\alpha\colon I \to J$ in $\mathbb{I}$. The l-r pair η_I is defined by giving the function $\eta_I^r\colon \varinjlim D \to DI$ for which $(s_I \mid I \in \mathbb{I}) \mapsto s_I$, and also the function $\eta_I^l\colon DI \to \varinjlim D$ for which

$$d \mapsto (\bigsqcup\{D(\beta)^r D(\alpha)^l(d) \mid K \in \mathbb{I}, \alpha \in \mathbb{I}(I,K), \beta \in \mathbb{I}(J,K)\} \mid J \in \mathbb{I})$$

where $d \in DI$. We have a number of points to verify.

$\varinjlim D$ is a complete lattice (we prove that it is algebraic later on). Let $\{(s_I^a \mid I \in \mathbb{I}) \mid a \in A\}$ be any non-empty subset of $\varinjlim D$. Setting $s_I \stackrel{\text{def}}{=} \bigwedge\{s_I^a \mid a \in A\}$ (which makes sense for DI is a complete lattice) then provided $(s_I \mid I \in \mathbb{I}) \in \varinjlim D$ it must be the required meet. Taking $\alpha\colon I \to J$ in $\mathbb{I}$, we have

$$D(\alpha)^r(s_J) = D(\alpha)^r(\bigwedge\{s_J^a \mid a \in A\}) = \bigwedge\{D(\alpha)^r(s_J^a) \mid a \in A\} = s_I$$

where of course the right adjoints $D(\alpha)^r$ preserve all meets. $\varinjlim D$ has a top element given by the "constantly top" family; note that $D(\alpha)^r(\top) = \top$ because $\top$ is the meet of the empty subset, so this is a well defined family in $\varinjlim D$.

Now we verify that (η_I^l, η_I^r) form an l-r pair. We begin by checking that η_I^l is well defined. Let $d \in DI$; the component of $\eta_I^l(d)$ at $J \in \mathbb{I}$ is

$$\eta_I^l(d)_J \overset{\text{def}}{=} \bigsqcup \{D(\beta)^r D(\alpha)^l(d) \mid K \in \mathbb{I}, \alpha \in \mathbb{I}(I, K), \beta \in \mathbb{I}(J, K)\}.$$

To see this is a *directed* join take $D(\beta)^r D(\alpha)^l(d)$ and $D(\beta')^r D(\alpha')^l(d)$ in $\eta_I^l(d)_J$. Choose γ and γ' as per Lemma 6.5.9, and note that

$$D(\gamma\beta)^r D(\gamma\alpha)^l(d) = D(\beta)^r D(\gamma)^r D(\gamma)^l D(\alpha)^l(d) \geq D(\beta)^r D(\alpha)^l(d)$$

with a similar inequality for α' and β', proving directedness. We also need to check that if $\delta \colon J \to J'$ in $\mathbb{I}$, then $D(\delta)^r(\eta_I^l(d)_{J'}) = \eta_I^l(d)_J$. Using the continuity of $D(\delta)^r$, this amounts to proving

$$\underbrace{\bigsqcup \{D(\delta)^r D(\beta)^r D(\alpha)^l(d) \mid K \in \mathbb{I}, \alpha \in \mathbb{I}(I, K), \beta \in \mathbb{I}(J', K)\}}_{L}$$

$$= \underbrace{\bigsqcup \{D(\gamma)^r D(\alpha)^l(d) \mid K \in \mathbb{I}, \alpha \in \mathbb{I}(I, K), \gamma \in \mathbb{I}(J, K)\}}_{R}.$$

It is immediate that $L \subseteq R$, that is $\bigsqcup L \leq \bigsqcup R$. We shall show that for each element $\xi \in R$ there is an element of L which is greater than ξ, which will prove $\bigsqcup R \leq \bigsqcup L$. Consider the following diagram, where α and γ are given

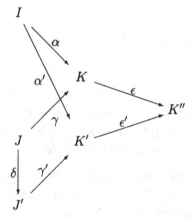

and we have defined α', γ' and K' from filteredness of $\mathbb{I}$, and ϵ and ϵ' by appeal to Lemma 6.5.9. We have

$$D(\delta)^r D(\epsilon'\gamma')^r D(\epsilon\alpha)^l(d) = D(\epsilon\gamma)^r D(\epsilon\alpha)^l(d) \geq D(\gamma)^r D(\alpha)^l(d)$$

where the left hand side is an element of L, and the right hand side is an element of R. Now let us see that $(\eta_I^l \dashv \eta_I^r)$. To show $\eta_I^r \eta_I^l \geq id_{DI}$, take $d \in DI$ and note that

$$\eta_I^r \eta_I^l(d) = \bigsqcup \{D(\beta)^r D(\alpha)^l(d) \mid K \in \mathbb{I}, \alpha \in \mathbb{I}(I, K), \beta \in \mathbb{I}(I, K)\}.$$

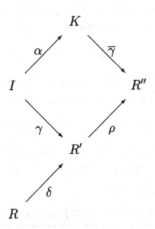

Figure 6.11: A Commutative Diagram.

To see that $\eta_I^l \eta_I^r \le id_{\varinjlim D}$, take $s \in \varinjlim D$; we need to show that for each $J \in \mathbb{I}$ we have $\eta_I^l(s_I)_J \le s_J$. It is clear that this happens just in case given $\alpha \colon I \to K$ and $\beta \colon J \to K$, we have $D(\beta)^r D(\alpha)^l(s_I) \le s_J$. But this latter inequality does indeed hold:

$$D(\beta)^r D(\alpha)^l(s_I) = D(\beta)^r D(\alpha)^l D(\alpha)^r(s_K) \le D(\beta)^r(s_K) = s_J.$$

To summarise, it is easy to see that η_I^l and η_I^r are both monotone functions, and the above calculations show that they form a poset adjunction. Finally, η_I^r is continuous, as is easily verified because directed joins in $\varinjlim D$ are given pointwise, that is, if $S \overset{\mathrm{def}}{=} \{s^a \mid a \in A\} \subseteq \varinjlim D$ and S is directed, then $(\bigsqcup S)_I = \bigsqcup\{s_I^a \mid a \in A\}$. So we do have an l-r pair.

Now we shall verify that the set $\{\eta_I^l \eta_I^r \mid I \in \mathbb{I}\}$ is directed. Given I and J in $\mathbb{I}$, pick $\alpha \colon I \to K$ and $\beta \colon J \to K$ by filteredness of $\mathbb{I}$. We claim that $\eta_I^l \eta_I^r \le \eta_K^l \eta_K^r$, and similarly for J. This amounts to proving that for any object R of $\mathbb{I}$

$$\left. \begin{aligned} &\bigsqcup\{D(\delta)^r D(\gamma)^l(s_I) \mid R' \in \mathbb{I}, \gamma \in \mathbb{I}(I, R'), \delta \in \mathbb{I}(R, R')\} \\ &\quad \le \bigsqcup\{D(\overline{\delta})^r D(\overline{\gamma})^l(s_K) \mid R'' \in \mathbb{I}, \overline{\gamma} \in \mathbb{I}(K, R''), \overline{\delta} \in \mathbb{I}(R, R'')\}. \end{aligned} \right\} \quad (*)$$

Consider the commutative diagram of Figure 6.11, in which we regard α, δ and γ as being given, and $\overline{\gamma}$ and ρ as being chosen according to Lemma 6.5.5. So we have $D(\delta)^r D(\gamma)^l(s_I)$ an element of the set on the left hand side of the inequality $(*)$; then we may deduce

$$
\begin{aligned}
D(\delta)^r D(\gamma)^l(s_I) &= D(\delta)^r D(\gamma)^l D(\alpha)^r(s_K) \\
&\leq D(\delta)^r D(\rho)^r D(\rho)^l D(\gamma)^l D(\alpha)^r(s_K) \\
&= D(\delta)^r D(\rho)^r D(\bar{\gamma})^l D(\alpha)^l D(\alpha)^r(s_K) \\
&= D(\delta)^r D(\rho)^r D(\bar{\gamma})^l D(\alpha)^l(s_I) \\
&\leq D(\delta)^r D(\rho)^r D(\bar{\gamma})^l(s_K) \\
&= D(\rho\delta)^r D(\bar{\gamma})^l(s_K)
\end{aligned}
$$

in which the final element appearing in the above inequality is in the right hand set of the inequality $(*)$. An analogous argument applies to J and this proves directedness.

Now we shall show that $id_{\varinjlim D} = \bigsqcup\{\eta_I^l \eta_I^r \mid I \in \mathbb{I}\}$. The only thing that is not clear is $\bigsqcup\{\eta_I^l \eta_I^r \mid I \in \mathbb{I}\} \geq id$. But if $s = (s_I \mid I \in \mathbb{I}) \in \varinjlim D$ we can calculate

$$
\begin{aligned}
s_I &= \eta_I^l(s_I)_I \\
&= \eta_I^r \eta_I^l \eta_I^r(s) \\
&\leq \bigsqcup\{\eta_I^r \eta_J^l \eta_J^r(s) \mid J \in \mathbb{I}\} \\
&= (\bigsqcup\{\eta_J^l \eta_J^r(s) \mid J \in \mathbb{I}\})_I
\end{aligned}
$$

and so we are done. To prove that $\varinjlim D$ is algebraic, let us take $t \in \varinjlim D$, and prove that

$$
S \stackrel{\text{def}}{=} \{\eta_I^l(d) \mid I \in \mathbb{I}, d \in DI^\circ, d \leq t_I\} \subseteq \{s \mid s \in (\varinjlim D)^\circ, s \leq t\}.
$$

First note that d is compact, and thus by Lemma 1.5.14 $\eta_I^l(d)$ is too, for η_I^l has a continuous right adjoint. Let $\alpha\colon I \to K$ and $\beta\colon J \to K$ be morphisms of $\mathbb{I}$. Then note that $d \leq t_I$ implies that $D(\alpha)^l(d) \leq D(\alpha)^l(t_I) \leq t_K$ and thus we have $D(\beta)^r D(\alpha)^l(d) \leq t_J$, implying that $\eta_I^l(d) \leq t$. This shows the above subset inclusion. Then algebraicity will follow if t is the join of the subset S, which is itself proved by using $id = \bigsqcup\{\eta_I^l \eta_I^r \mid I \in \mathbb{I}\}$.

It is easy to verify that the family $(\eta_I\colon DI \to \varinjlim D \mid i \in I)$ is a cone and so we are now in a position to see that $\mathcal{ACL}at^{lr}$ has all (small) filtered colimits. Take a cone $(h_I\colon DI \to E \mid I \in \mathbb{I})$ and define a morphism h where

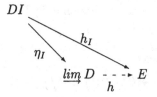

by setting $h^l \overset{\text{def}}{=} \bigsqcup\{h^l_I \eta^r_I \mid I \in \mathbb{I}\}$ and $h^r \overset{\text{def}}{=} \bigsqcup\{\eta^l_I h^r_I \mid I \in \mathbb{I}\}$. We have to check that h is a well defined l-r pair, that $h_I = h \circ \eta_I$ for each I in $\mathbb{I}$, and that h is the unique l-r pair for which such an equation holds. We omit all the details.

$\square$

EXERCISE 6.5.12   Work the details of the proof of Theorem 6.5.11, especially those concerning algebraicity of $\varprojlim D$, that $(\eta_I \colon DI \to \varprojlim D \mid i \in I)$ is a cone, and the (direct) verification that $\mathcal{ACL}at^{lr}$ has filtered colimits (omitted from the final paragraph of the proof).

THEOREM 6.5.13   The category $\mathcal{ACL}at^{lr}$ has all (small) limits.

PROOF   We shall prove this proposition by appealing to Theorem 2.11.8 and thus showing that $\mathcal{ACL}at^{lr}$ has equalisers and all small products. The idea of the proof uses the fact that the set of ideals $\overline{X}$ (see Discussion 1.5.17) of a join-semilattice is itself a complete algebraic lattice, together with Corollary 1.5.19. Thus constructing limits in a category of join-semilattices yields a construction of limits in $\mathcal{ACL}at^{lr}$.

We begin by showing that $\mathcal{ACL}at^{lr}$ has all small products. Let $D \colon \mathbb{I} \to \mathcal{ACL}at^{lr}$ be a diagram, where $\mathbb{I}$ is small and discrete. We shall define a limit for D, say

$$(\pi_I \colon \varprojlim D \to DI \mid I \in \mathbb{I})$$

as follows. We shall set $\varprojlim D \overset{\text{def}}{=} \overline{\Pi_{I \in \mathbb{I}}(DI)^\circ}$. This requires a few words of explanation. The set of compact elements $(DI)^\circ$ of each algebraic complete lattice DI is easily seen to be a join-semilattice. The category $\mathcal{JSL}at$ has all small products, created by the forgetful functor $U \colon \mathcal{JSL}at \to \mathcal{S}et$; thus $\Pi_{I \in \mathbb{I}}(DI)^\circ$ is a product in $\mathcal{JSL}at$. We have defined $\varprojlim D$ to be the set of ideals of this product. Note that Proposition 1.5.18 tells us that $\varprojlim D$ is an algebraic complete lattice. We shall define

$$\tilde{\pi}^l_I \overset{\text{def}}{=} \overline{p_I} \colon \overline{\Pi_{I \in \mathbb{I}}(DI)^\circ} \longrightarrow \overline{(DI)^\circ} \qquad\qquad M \mapsto \bigcup\{p_I(e){\downarrow} \mid e \in M\}$$

where $p_I \colon \Pi_{I \in \mathbb{I}}(DI)^\circ \to (DI)^\circ$ is product projection in the category $\mathcal{JSL}at$. Proposition 1.5.18 says that $\tilde{\pi}^l_I$ preserves all joins (and all joins exist) and thus it has a right adjoint. We wish to see that $\tilde{\pi}^l_I$ has a *continuous* right adjoint (say $\tilde{\pi}^r_I$); using Lemma 1.5.14 we shall verify that $\tilde{\pi}^l_I$ preserves compactness of elements. This will be the case if given any finite subset $F \subseteq^f \Pi_{I \in \mathbb{I}}(DI)^\circ$, we have

$$\tilde{\pi}^l_I((\textstyle\bigvee F){\downarrow}) = (\textstyle\bigvee p_I(F)){\downarrow} \tag{1}$$

where we note that $p_I(F) \subseteq^f (DI)^\circ$ and thus $(\bigvee p_I(F))\downarrow$ is a compact element of $\overline{(DI)^\circ}$. To show (1), we note that for any ideal $M \in \overline{\Pi_{I \in \mathbb{I}}(DI)^\circ}$, the underlying set of the ideal $\tilde{\pi}_I^l(M)$ is given by $p_I(M)$ where p_I acts on the underlying set of M, that is

$$\tilde{\pi}_I^l(M) \overset{\text{def}}{=} \bigcup\{p_I(e)\downarrow \mid e \in M\} = p_I(M) \tag{2}$$

and it is routine to verify this. We check one half of (1), namely that

$$(\bigvee p_I(F))\downarrow \subseteq p_I((\bigvee F)\downarrow).$$

Certainly p_I preserves finite joins, for they are calculated pointwise in products. Thus if $e \in (\bigvee p_I(F))\downarrow$, then $e \leq p_I(\bigvee F)$, and so $(\vec{\perp}, e) \leq \bigvee F \in \Pi_{I \in \mathbb{I}}(DI)^\circ$ where $\vec{\perp}$ denotes the bottom element of $\Pi_{J \in \mathbb{I}, J \neq I}(DI)^\circ$. Thus $(\vec{\perp}, e) \in (\bigvee F)\downarrow$ implying that $e \in p_I((\bigvee F)\downarrow)$. The reverse subset inclusion which we need for (1) is equally easy to show. This completes the verification that $\tilde{\pi}_I \overset{\text{def}}{=} (\tilde{\pi}_I^l, \tilde{\pi}_I^r)$ is an l-r pair. We can now define $\pi_I^l \overset{\text{def}}{=} \theta \circ \tilde{\pi}_I^l \colon \varprojlim D \to \overline{(DI)^\circ} \cong DI$, using Corollary 1.5.19.

Now suppose that $(f_I \colon E \to DI \mid I \in \mathbb{I})$ is a cone over D in $\mathcal{ACLat}^{lr}$. Then $f_I^l \colon E^\circ \to (DI)^\circ$ for each I in $\mathbb{I}$. Thus using the existence of products in $\mathcal{JSLat}$, we can form the ideal lifting $\overline{\langle f_I^l \mid I \in \mathbb{I}\rangle} \colon \overline{E^\circ} \to \overline{\Pi_{I \in \mathbb{I}}(DI)^\circ}$. Let us check that $\tilde{\pi}_I^l \circ \overline{\langle f_I^l \mid I \in \mathbb{I}\rangle} = \overline{f_I^l}$. Taking $M \in \overline{E^\circ}$, we have

$$
\begin{aligned}
\tilde{\pi}_I^l(\bigcup\{\langle f_I^l \mid I \in \mathbb{I}\rangle(m)\downarrow \mid m \in M\}) &= \tilde{\pi}_I^l(\bigcup\{\Pi_{I \in \mathbb{I}}[f_I^l(m)\downarrow] \mid m \in M\}) \\
&= \bigcup\{f_I^l(m)\downarrow \mid m \in M\} \\
&= \overline{f_I^l}(M).
\end{aligned}
$$

We can now define the mediating morphism $f \colon E \to \varprojlim D$ for the product of the diagram D by setting the left adjoint to be

$$f^l \overset{\text{def}}{=} \overline{\langle f_I^l \mid I \in \mathbb{I}\rangle} \circ \theta^{-1} \colon E \to \overline{E^\circ} \to \varprojlim D.$$

Note that f^l *is* a left adjoint, being the composition of two other left adjoints. We can see that $\pi_I^l \circ f^l = f_I^l$ for each I from the commutative diagram of Figure 6.12 where we are appealing to Corollary 1.5.19. It follows that the corresponding diagram of right adjoints commutes, by appealing to Corollary 2.10.22 (in the poset case). Thus $\pi_I \circ f = f_I$. The uniqueness of f is immediate.

Now we show that $\mathcal{ACLat}^{lr}$ has all equalisers. Let $f, f' \colon X \to Y$ be a parallel pair of morphisms in $\mathcal{ACLat}^{lr}$. Define a subset

$$E \overset{\text{def}}{=} \{e \in X^\circ \mid f^l(e) = f'^l(e)\} \subseteq X^\circ,$$

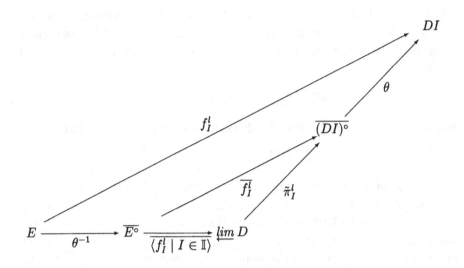

Figure 6.12: A Commutative Diagram.

where we note that E is non-empty for $\perp_X \in E$. Certainly each of f^l and f'^l preserves finite joins, and it follows that E is a sub-join-semilattice of X°. In particular, we can say that the inclusion $i\colon E \to X^\circ$ preserves finite joins, where we give the subset E the restriction ordering from X°. Hence Lemma 6.5.7 says we have an l-r pair $\bar{i}\colon \overline{E} \to \overline{X^\circ}$. Appealing to Lemma 6.5.8, we have

$$\overline{f^l} \circ \bar{i} = \overline{f^l \circ i} = \overline{f'^l \circ i} = \overline{f'^l} \circ \bar{i}.$$

It follows that the diagram

$$E \xrightarrow{\;\;i\;\;} X \underset{f'}{\overset{f}{\rightrightarrows}} Y$$

commutes by using Corollary 1.5.19. It is routine to verify that this is indeed an equaliser diagram.   □

PROPOSITION 6.5.14   Any finite algebraic complete lattice is a finitely presentable object of $\mathcal{ACL}at^{lr}$.

PROOF   Suppose that X is a finite algebraic complete lattice and that L is any other algebraic complete lattice. Given an l-r pair $f\colon X \to L$ it is clear that we have a continuous endofunction $f^l f^r\colon L \to L$. Then it is the case that $f^l f^r$ is a compact element in the poset $L \Rightarrow L$ of continuous functions $L \to L$ (where we take the pointwise order). Note that in fact any algebraic complete lattice L is a Scott domain, and thus in particular the poset $L \Rightarrow L$ is a Scott domain too. We can use the characterisation of compact elements in $L \Rightarrow L$ (see page 68) to show the compactness of $f^l f^r$. We claim that

$$f^l f^r = \underbrace{\bigvee \{[f^l(x), f^l(x)] \mid x \in X\}.}_{(*)}$$

It is easy to see that this join exists. Note also that as X is finite, any element $x \in X$ is compact and thus $f^l(x)$ is a compact element of L. Hence the join $(*)$ is a compact element of $L \Rightarrow L$. Let us prove our claim, thus showing $f^l f^r$ is compact. For any $d \in L$

$$\begin{aligned}
\bigvee \{[f^l(x), f^l(x)](d) \mid x \in X\} &= \bigvee \{f^l(x) \mid x \in X, f^l(x) \le d\} \\
&= \bigvee \{f^l(x) \mid x \in X, x \le f^r(d)\} \\
&= f^l f^r(d).
\end{aligned}$$

Take a colimit $(\eta_I : DI \to \varinjlim D \mid I \in \mathbb{I})$ in $\mathcal{ACL}at^{lr}$. We wish to prove that

$$\mathcal{ACL}at^{lr}(X, \varinjlim D) \cong \varinjlim \mathcal{ACL}at^{lr}(X, D(-)).$$

Recall (page 115) the construction of filtered colimits in the category *Set*. We have that

$$\varinjlim \mathcal{ACL}at^{lr}(X, D(-))$$

is the set of equivalence classes $\biguplus \{\mathcal{ACL}at^{lr}(X, DI) \mid I \in \mathbb{I}\}/ \sim$, where if $f : X \to DI$ and $g : X \to DJ$, then $f \sim g$ just in case there is some $K \in \mathbb{I}$ and morphisms $\alpha : I \to K$ and $\beta : J \to K$ for which $D\alpha \circ f = D\beta \circ g$. The proof is completed by using the above characterisation of compactness to induce the required bijection. $\qquad\square$

PROPOSITION 6.5.15 Let L be a fixed algebraic complete lattice, and let us write $L \Rightarrow L$ for the poset of continuous functions $L \to L$. Write $f : X \hookrightarrow Y$ to indicate that f is an l-r pair for which $f^r f^l = id_X$, that is, f is an e-p pair. Let $\mathbb{S}$ be the set of finite algebraic complete lattices whose underlying sets are subsets of $\mathbb{N}$. Then the *poset*

$$\mathbb{I} \stackrel{\text{def}}{=} \{f^l f^r \mid X \in \mathbb{S}, (f : X \hookrightarrow L) \in \mathcal{ACL}at^{lr}(X, L)\}$$

is directed (regarded as having the restriction order from $L \Rightarrow L$) and hence trivially a filtered category. There is a diagram $D : \mathbb{I} \to \mathcal{ACL}at^{lr}$ given by

$$f^l f^r \le g^l g^r \quad \longmapsto \quad (g^r f^l, f^r g^l) : X \hookrightarrow Y,$$

where we have written $X \stackrel{\text{def}}{=} D(f^l f^r)$ and $Y \stackrel{\text{def}}{=} D(g^l g^r)$, and a cone

$$(f: X \rightarrow L \mid f^l f^r \in \mathbb{I})$$

under D. In particular, it is the case that $id_L = \bigsqcup\{f^l f^r \mid f^l f^r \in \mathbb{I}\}$, and so we have that L is a filtered colimit for the diagram D.

PROOF   Let us write $L \Rightarrow L$ for the set of continuous functions $L \rightarrow L$. We begin by showing that the poset $\mathbb{I}$ is directed. Take $f^l f^r$ and $g^l g^r$ in $\mathbb{I}$, and define the set $X'' \subseteq L$ by

$$X'' \stackrel{\text{def}}{=} \{f^l f^r(d) \vee g^l g^r(d) \mid d \in L\}$$

which is finite. In fact, X'' is a complete sublattice of L: as X'' is finite it is sufficient to show that $\perp_L \in X''$, and that if $x, y \in X''$ then $x \vee_L y \in X''$. We have

$$\perp_L = f^l f^r(\perp_L) \vee g^l g^r(\perp_L) \in X''.$$

If we put $x \stackrel{\text{def}}{=} f^l f^r(d) \vee g^l g^r(d) \in X''$ and $y \stackrel{\text{def}}{=} f^l f^r(d') \vee g^l g^r(d') \in X''$, then if we can show that

$$\underbrace{(f^l f^r(d) \vee g^l g^r(d)) \vee (f^l f^r(d') \vee g^l g^r(d'))}_{A}$$
$$= \underbrace{f^l f^r(f^l f^r(d) \vee f^l f^r(d')) \vee g^l g^r(g^l g^r(d) \vee g^l g^r(d'))}_{B}$$

we will indeed have $x \vee_L y \in X''$. By definition we have $f^l f^r \leq id$, implying that $f^l f^r(f^l f^r(d) \vee f^l f^r(d')) \leq f^l f^r(d) \vee f^l f^r(d')$, and with a similar inequality for g it follows that $B \leq A$. Further, note that $id = f^r f^l$ implying that

$$f^l f^r(d) = f^l f^r f^l f^r(d) \leq f^l f^r(f^l f^r(d) \vee f^l f^r(d'))$$

and likewise $f^l f^r(d') \leq f^l f^r(f^l f^r(d) \vee f^l f^r(d'))$. Together with similar inequalities for g we have $A \leq B$. Regarding X'' as a poset with the restriction order from L, it is now clear that X'' is an algebraic complete lattice.

Consider the inclusion function $i: X'' \rightarrow L$ and the function $h: L \rightarrow X''$ defined by $h(d) \stackrel{\text{def}}{=} f^l f^r(d) \vee g^l g^r(d)$ for $d \in L$. In fact (i, h) is an e-p pair, which we now verify. It is clear that $ih \leq id_L$ because f and g are l-r pairs. In order to show that $hi = id_{X''}$, we shall take $d \in L$ and prove that

$$\underbrace{f^l f^r(f^l f^r(d) \vee g^l g^r(d)) \vee g^l g^r(f^l f^r(d) \vee g^l g^r(d))}_{L} = \underbrace{f^l f^r(d) \vee g^l g^r(d)}_{R}.$$

It is clear that $L \leq R$. Conversely, note that

$$f^l f^r(d) = f^l f^r f^l f^r(d) \leq f^l f^r(f^l f^r(d) \vee g^l g^r(d))$$

and together with a similar inequality for g we see that $R \leq L$. It is certainly the case that h is a continuous function, being the composition of continuous functions. Thus $(i, h): X'' \to L$ is an e-p pair, and $\{f^l f^r, g^l g^r\} \leq ih$ so $\mathbb{I}$ is directed.

It is easy to see that the diagram D is well defined, that is $(g^r f^l, f^r g^l): X \to Y$ is an embedding-projection pair whenever $f: X \to L$ and $g: Y \to L$ are. Moreover, to see that the family $(f: X \to L \mid f^l f^r \in \mathbb{I})$ is a cone under D, we have to check that the diagram

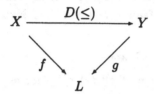

commutes, where $f^l f^r \leq g^l g^r$. This follows from a simple calculation with the definitions.

Finally, we wish to see that $id_{\varinjlim D} = \bigsqcup \{f^l f^r \mid f^l f^r \in \mathbb{I}\}$. It is enough to prove that for any $d \in L$ we have

$$d \leq \bigsqcup \{f^l f^r(d) \mid f^l f^r \in \mathbb{I}\}.$$

If $d = \bot_L$ we are okay. Otherwise, consider the function $\tilde{e}: \Omega \to L$ (where $\bot_L \neq e \leq d$, $e \in L^\circ$, and $\Omega \in \mathbb{S}$ is the two point lattice with underlying set $\{0, 1\} \subseteq \mathbb{N}$) defined by

$$\tilde{e}(x) \stackrel{\text{def}}{=} \begin{cases} e \text{ if } x = 1 \\ \bot \text{ otherwise} \end{cases}$$

and also the function $p: L \to \Omega$ defined by

$$p(l) \stackrel{\text{def}}{=} \begin{cases} 1 \text{ if } e \leq l \\ 0 \text{ otherwise.} \end{cases}$$

Note that p depends on e, and that for any given e, the pair $(\tilde{e}, p): \Omega \hookrightarrow L$ is an e-p pair. We now have

$$\bigsqcup \{f^l f^r(d) \mid f^l f^r \in \mathbb{I}\} \geq \bigvee \{\tilde{e}p(d) \mid e \in L^\circ, \bot_L \neq e \leq d\}$$
$$= \bigvee \{e \mid e \in L^\circ, \bot_L \neq e \leq d\}$$
$$= d.$$

Appeal to Theorem 6.5.11 to deduce that the cone $(f: X \to L \mid f^l f^r \in \mathbb{I})$ is a filtered colimit. $\square$

THEOREM 6.5.16   The category $\mathcal{ALCat}^{lr}$ is locally finitely presentable, with a set S of fp-generators given by the finite algebraic complete lattices whose underlying sets are subsets of $\mathbb{N}$.

PROOF   Follows from Theorems 6.5.11 and 6.5.13, and Propositions 6.5.14 and 6.5.15. $\square$

DISCUSSION 6.5.17   Let $(\mathcal{C}, \mathbb{S})$ be a locally finitely presentable category and $F: \mathcal{C} \to \mathcal{ALCat}^{lr}$ be a functor which preserves filtered colimits. We shall define an S-*section* of F to be a family $(t_S \mid S \in \mathbb{S})$ indexed by the set of objects $\mathbb{S}$ where

- each t_S is an element of FS, and
- the t_S satisfy the condition $(Ff)^l(t_S) \leq t_{S'}$ for any morphism $f: S \to S'$ of $\mathcal{C}$, where $S, S' \in \mathbb{S}$.

We shall write $\forall_{\mathbb{S}} F$ for the set of S-sections of the functor F.

LEMMA 6.5.18   Let $(\mathcal{C}, \mathbb{S})$ be a locally finitely presentable category. We can regard the set $\forall_{\mathbb{S}} F$ of S-sections of a filtered colimit preserving functor $F: \mathcal{C} \to \mathcal{ALCat}^{lr}$ as a poset via the pointwise ordering, namely that if t and s are S-sections, then $t \leq s$ just in case $t_S \leq s_S$ for each $S \in \mathbb{S}$. Moreover, $\forall_{\mathbb{S}} F$ is an algebraic complete lattice.

PROOF   It is easy to check that $\forall_{\mathbb{S}} F$ is a complete lattice. The least element of $\forall_{\mathbb{S}} F$ is the family $(\bot_S \mid S \in \mathbb{S})$ of least elements of the complete lattices FS. Note that this family is certainly an S-section, because any (posetal) left adjoint preserves all joins. To see that non-empty joins exist in $\forall_{\mathbb{S}} F$, take a subset $U \overset{\text{def}}{=} \{t^a \mid a \in A\}$, and define an S-section t by setting

$$t_S \overset{\text{def}}{=} \bigvee \{t_S^a \mid a \in A\}.$$

If t is a well defined S-section, it is certainly the join of U. So let $f: S \to S'$ be a morphism of $\mathcal{C}$ with $S, S' \in \mathbb{S}$ and note

$$
\begin{aligned}
(Ff)^l(t_S) &= \bigvee \{(Ff)^l(t_S^a) \mid a \in A\} \\
&\leq \bigvee \{t_{S'}^a \mid a \in A\} \\
&= t_{S'}.
\end{aligned}
$$

Now we prove that $\forall_\mathbb{S} F$ is algebraic. Suppose that $X \in \mathbb{S}$ and $x \in (FX)^\circ$, and define

$$[X, x]_S \overset{\text{def}}{=} \bigvee \{(Ff)^l(x) \mid f \in \mathcal{ACL}\mathit{at}^{lr}(X, S)\}.$$

It is easy to check that $[X, x]_S$ is an $\mathbb{S}$-section; in fact the set of all such $\mathbb{S}$-sections forms a basis of compact elements of $\forall_\mathbb{S} F$. We shall write

$$\bigvee_1^n [X_i, x_i] \overset{\text{def}}{=} [X_1, x_1] \vee \ldots \vee [X_n, x_n],$$

and will say that part of the force of the notation $[X, x]$ is that $X \in \mathbb{S}$ and $x \in (FX)^\circ$. It is a simple exercise to verify that any $\bigvee_1^n [X_i, x_i]$ is a compact element of $\forall_\mathbb{S} F$. To prove that all compact elements arise in this way, we shall show that for any $u \in \forall_\mathbb{S} F$ it is the case that

$$u = \underbrace{\bigsqcup \{\bigvee_1^n [X_i, x_i] \mid X_i \in \mathbb{S}, x_i \in (FX_i)^\circ, x_i \leq u_{X_i}\}}_{r}. \qquad (*)$$

Too see that $r \leq u$, take $S \in \mathbb{S}$ and note that

$$\bigvee_1^n [X_i, x_i]_S = \bigvee_1^n \bigvee \{(Ff)^l(x_i) \mid f \in \mathcal{ACL}\mathit{at}^{lr}(X_i, S)\} \leq u_S$$

which follows because u is an $\mathbb{S}$-section. In order to verify that $u \leq r$, first note that

$$\bigvee \{[X, x] \mid X \in \mathbb{S}, x \in (FX)^\circ, x \leq u_X\} \leq r.$$

Also, for a fixed $S \in \mathbb{S}$, we have $u_S = \bigsqcup \{c \in (FS)^\circ \mid c \leq u_S\}$. Thus it is sufficient to prove that for any given $c \in (FS)^\circ$, we have $c \leq u_S$ implies $c \leq \bigvee \{[X, x]_S \mid X \in \mathbb{S}, x \in (FX)^\circ, x \leq u_X\}$; but this follows from

$$\begin{aligned} c &\leq \bigvee \{(Ff)^l(c) \mid f \in \mathcal{ACL}\mathit{at}^{lr}(S, S)\} \\ &= [S, c]_S \\ &\leq \bigvee \{[X, x]_S \mid X \in \mathbb{S}, x \in (FX)^\circ, x \leq u_X\}. \end{aligned}$$

We have proved the representation $(*)$ for any $\mathbb{S}$-section u, and so if u is compact, it must be of the form $\bigvee_1^n [X_i, x_i]$ as required. Algebraicity of $\forall_\mathbb{S} F$ follows immediately. $\qquad \square$

LEMMA 6.5.19   Let $\mathcal{A}$ be a locally finitely presentable category, and let $F: \mathcal{A} \to \mathcal{ACL}\mathit{at}^{lr}$ a functor; F preserves filtered colimits iff given any filtered colimit $(f_I: DI \to \varinjlim D \mid I \in \mathbb{I})$ for a diagram $D: \mathbb{I} \to \mathcal{ACL}\mathit{at}^{lr}$ we have

$$id_{F(\varinjlim D)} = \bigsqcup \{(Ff_I)^l (Ff_I)^r \mid I \in \mathbb{I}\}.$$

PROOF   Immediate from Theorem 6.5.11.   □

LEMMA 6.5.20   Let $\mathcal{A}$ be a locally finitely presentable category and let $F, G: \mathcal{A} \to \mathcal{ACL}at^{lr}$ be two functors which preserve filtered colimits. Applying the (covariant) Grothendieck construction to F, we have a functor $\pi_F: \mathbb{G}(F) \to \mathcal{A}$ (and similarly for G). Then a functor $\mu: \mathbb{G}(F) \to \mathbb{G}(G)$ which preserves filtered colimits and which makes the diagram

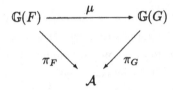

commute, is specified by giving a family $(\mu_A \mid A \in \mathcal{A})$ where each $\mu_A: FA \to GA$ is a continuous function between algebraic complete lattices which satisfies

(i) If $f: A \to B$ is a morphism of $\mathcal{A}$, then $(Gf)^l \circ \mu_A \leq \mu_B \circ (Ff)^l$, and

(ii) if we are given a filtered colimit $(\eta_I: DI \to \varinjlim D \mid I \in \mathbb{I})$ for a diagram $D: \mathbb{I} \to \mathcal{ACL}at^{lr}$, then

$$\mu_{\varinjlim D} = \bigsqcup \{(G\eta_I)^l \circ \mu_{DI} \circ (F\eta_I)^r \mid I \in \mathbb{I}\}.$$

PROOF   Note that any (small) filtered category $\mathbb{I}$ may certainly be considered as a directed set, and thus the result follows from Lemma 5.6.13.   □

THEOREM 6.5.21   The following data define an $\omega\lambda\times$-hyperdoctrine:

(i) The base category is $\mathcal{LFP}$. The distinguished object of $\mathcal{LFP}$ is the category $\mathcal{ACL}at^{lr}$. We shall write $\mathcal{U}$ for this category.

(ii) We give an $\mathcal{LFP}$-indexed category $\mathcal{LFP}(-,\mathcal{U}): \mathcal{LFP} \to \mathcal{CCat}$ as follows. The objects of the fibre $\mathcal{LFP}(\mathcal{A},\mathcal{U})$, where $\mathcal{A}$ is an object of $\mathcal{LFP}$, are isomorphism classes of filtered colimit preserving functors $\mathcal{A} \to \mathcal{U}$. Note that this notation does not imply that the collection of such functors forms a set. Suppose that $[F], [G]: \mathcal{A} \to \mathcal{U}$ are two objects in the fibre at $\mathcal{A}$. A *compositional witnessing* is a choice of witnesses $\iota_{F,F'}: F \cong F': \mathcal{A} \to \mathcal{U}$ where $F, F' \in [F]$ such that $\iota_{F',F''} \circ \iota_{F,F'} = \iota_{F,F''}$, $\iota_{F,F'}^{-1} = \iota_{F',F}$ and $\iota_{F,F} = id_F$. Given such for $[F]$ and $[G]$, we can define an equivalence relation on filtered colimit preserving functors $\mu: \mathbb{G}(F) \to \mathbb{G}(G)$ (as F and G run over the classes $[F]$ and $[G]$) by requiring $\mu \sim \mu'$ just in case μ and μ' commute with $\iota_{F,F'}$ and $\iota_{G,G'}$. A morphism $[\mu]: [F] \to [G]$ in $\mathcal{LFP}(\mathcal{A},\mathcal{U})$ is given by a choice of compositional witnessing for $[F]$ and $[G]$ together with such an equivalence class $[\mu]$. (For clarity we now drop the brackets $[-]$). Further we require $\pi_F = \pi_G \circ \mu$, where π_F and π_G are the (projections for the) covariant Grothendieck fibrations of F and G. Now recall from Lemma 6.5.20, μ is specified by a family of continuous functions $(\mu_A \mid A \in \mathcal{A})$. If $H: \mathcal{A}' \to \mathcal{A}$ in the base $\mathcal{LFP}$ then the reindexing functor

$$H^* : \mathcal{LFP}(\mathcal{A}, \mathcal{U}) \longrightarrow \mathcal{LFP}(\mathcal{A}', \mathcal{U})$$

is defined by the assignment

$$(\mu_A \mid A \in \mathcal{A}): F \to G \quad \overset{H^*}{\longmapsto} \quad (\mu_{HA'} \mid A' \in \mathcal{A}): FH \to GH.$$

(iii) Let $\mathcal{A}$ and $\mathcal{K}$ be objects of $\mathcal{LFP}$ and $\pi_{\mathcal{A}}^{\mathcal{K}}: \mathcal{A} \times \mathcal{K} \to \mathcal{A}$. Define a functor

$$\forall_{\mathcal{A}}^{\mathcal{K}} : \mathcal{LFP}(\mathcal{A} \times \mathcal{K}, \mathcal{U}) \longrightarrow \mathcal{LFP}(\mathcal{A}, \mathcal{U})$$

as follows. If $F: \mathcal{A} \times \mathcal{K} \to \mathcal{U}$ is an object of $\mathcal{LFP}(\mathcal{A} \times \mathcal{K}, \mathcal{U})$ then we have to give a functor $\forall_{\mathcal{A}}^{\mathcal{K}} F: \mathcal{A} \to \mathcal{U}$ in $\mathcal{LFP}$. If $f: A \to A'$ is any morphism in $\mathcal{A}$ we define $\forall_{\mathcal{A}}^{\mathcal{K}} F(A) \overset{\mathrm{def}}{=} \forall_{\mathbb{S}}(F(A, -))$ where $\mathbb{S}$ is the set of fp-generators for $\mathcal{K}$, and

$$\forall_{\mathcal{A}}^{\mathcal{K}} F(f): \forall_{\mathcal{A}}^{\mathcal{K}} F(A) \to \forall_{\mathcal{A}}^{\mathcal{K}} F(A')$$

is defined by setting

$$\forall_{\mathbb{S}}(F(A, -)) \xrightarrow[\quad\quad\quad\quad\quad]{(t_S \mid S \in \mathbb{S}) \overset{(\forall_{\mathcal{A}}^{\mathcal{K}} F(f))^l}{\longmapsto} ((F(f, id_S))^l(t_S) \mid S \in \mathbb{S})} \forall_{\mathbb{S}}(F(A', -))$$

and

$$\forall_{\mathbb{S}}(F(A', -)) \xrightarrow[\quad\quad\quad\quad\quad]{(t'_S \mid S \in \mathbb{S}) \overset{(\forall_{\mathcal{A}}^{\mathcal{K}} F(f))^r}{\longmapsto} ((F(f, id_S))^r(t'_S) \mid S \in \mathbb{S})} \forall_{\mathbb{S}}(F(A, -))$$

where $t_S \in F(A, S)$ and $t'_S \in F(A', S)$. Now we have to define $\forall_{\mathcal{A}}^{\mathcal{K}}$ on morphisms. Suppose that $\mu: F \to G$ is a morphism of $\mathcal{C}(\mathcal{A} \times \mathcal{K}, \mathcal{U})$. Then $\forall_{\mathcal{A}}^{\mathcal{K}} \mu: \forall_{\mathcal{A}}^{\mathcal{K}} F \to \forall_{\mathcal{A}}^{\mathcal{K}} G$ is given by the family $((\forall_{\mathcal{A}}^{\mathcal{K}} \mu)_A \mid A \in \mathcal{A})$ where

$$(\forall_{\mathcal{A}}^{\mathcal{K}} \mu)_A : \forall_{\mathbb{S}}(F(A, -)) \xrightarrow[\quad\quad\quad]{(t_S \mid S \in \mathbb{S}) \mapsto (\mu_{(A,S)}(t_S) \mid S \in \mathbb{S})} \forall_{\mathbb{S}}(G(A, -))$$

where of course $t_S \in F(A, S)$ and $\mu_{(A,S)}: F(A, S) \to G(A, S)$.

PROOF   The proof of this result is in essence very similar to that of Theorem 5.6.17, and of course makes use of the preceding results in Section 6.5. $\square$

EXERCISE 6.5.22   Write down some of the details of the proof of Theorem 6.5.21.

6.6   Classifying Hyperdoctrine of an ωλ×-Theory

DISCUSSION 6.6.1   The intuition behind classifying $\omega\lambda\times$-hyperdoctrines is the same as for all the other classifying structures in this book. Given an $\omega\lambda\times$-theory Th, the classifying hyperdoctrine can be thought of as the "smallest" such categorical structure in which Th can be soundly interpreted. In order to give a formal definition we need to define an $\omega\lambda\times$-functor, which can be thought of as a structure preserving mapping between $\omega\lambda\times$-hyperdoctrines.

Given $\omega\lambda\times$-hyperdoctrines $\mathbb{C}: \mathcal{C}^{op} \to \mathcal{CCat}$ and $\mathbb{D}: \mathcal{D}^{op} \to \mathcal{CCat}$, an $\omega\lambda\times$-*functor* $(\alpha, F): \mathbb{C} \to \mathbb{D}$ is a morphism of indexed categories satisfying

• F is a cartesian closed functor $\mathcal{C} \to \mathcal{D}$ sending U in $\mathcal{C}$ to V in $\mathcal{D}$,

• the components $\alpha_I: \mathbb{C}I \to \mathbb{D}FI$ are strict cartesian closed functors for every object I of $\mathcal{C}$, which agree with the action of F on objects of $\mathbb{C}I$, and

• for all objects I and K of $\mathcal{C}$,

$$\alpha_I \circ \forall_I^K \ = \ \forall_{FI}^{FK} \circ \cong^* \circ \alpha_{I \times K}$$

where $\cong: FI \times FK \to F(I \times K)$ because F preserves finite products.

Let $\mathbb{C}: \mathcal{C}^{op} \to \mathcal{CCat}$ and $\mathbb{D}: \mathcal{D}^{op} \to \mathcal{CCat}$ be $\omega\lambda\times$-hyperdoctrines, and let Th be an $\omega\lambda\times$-theory with model $\mathbf{M}$ in $\mathbb{C}$. Further, suppose that $(\alpha, F): \mathbb{C} \to \mathbb{D}$ is an $\omega\lambda\times$-functor. Then there is a model $(\alpha, F)_*\mathbf{M}$ of Th in $\mathbb{D}$ defined by the clauses

• $[\![G]\!]_{((\alpha,F)_*\mathbf{M})^{op}} \stackrel{def}{=} F([\![G]\!]_{\mathbf{M}^{op}})$ where G is any ground kind of Th,

• $[\![O]\!]_{((\alpha,F)_*\mathbf{M})^{op}} \stackrel{def}{=} F([\![O]\!]_{\mathbf{M}^{op}}) \circ \cong :$

$$\Pi_1^n F[\![K_i]\!]_{\mathbf{M}^{op}} \to F(\Pi_1^n [\![K_i]\!]_{\mathbf{M}^{op}}) \to F[\![K]\!]_{\mathbf{M}^{op}}$$

where $O: K_1, \ldots, K_n \to K$ is any operator symbol from Th (possibly $n = 0$), and

• $[\![f]\!]_{((\alpha,F)_*\mathbf{M})^{tm}} \stackrel{def}{=} \cong^* (\alpha_{[\![\Delta]\!]_{((\alpha,F)_*\mathbf{M})^{op}}}([\![f]\!]_{\mathbf{M}^{tm}}))$ where $f: \Delta; \Phi_1, \ldots, \Phi_n \to \Phi$ is a function symbol of Th and Δ has length n (possibly $n = 0$).

Then the *classifying $\omega\lambda\times$-hyperdoctrine* of Th is an $\omega\lambda\times$-hyperdoctrine $Cl(Th)$ for which there is a *generic* model $\mathbf{G}$ of Th in $Cl(Th)$ with the following universal property: Given any other model $\mathbf{M}$ of Th in some $\omega\lambda\times$-hyperdoctrine $\mathbb{C}$ there is (up to isomorphism) a unique $\omega\lambda\times$-functor $(\alpha, F): Cl(Th) \to \mathbb{C}$ for which $\mathbf{M} = (\alpha, F)_*\mathbf{G}$. It is easy to see from the definition that such a classifying hyperdoctrine is determined up to equivalence of indexed categories (and it is also clear that the indexed functors which form the equivalence must be $\omega\lambda\times$-functors).

THEOREM 6.6.2   Suppose that we are given an $\omega\lambda\times$-theory Th. Then we can construct a classifying $\omega\lambda\times$-hyperdoctrine $Cl(Th)$ with a generic model **G** of Th in $Cl(Th)$.

PROOF   The methods used in the construction of such classifying categories should now be quite familiar, and the basic techniques for the construction of a syntactic $\omega\lambda\times$-hyperdoctrine are no exception. We shall give the basic details of the proof, leaving the reader to flesh out the ideas. Let us write $\mathbb{C}: \mathcal{C}^{op} \to \mathcal{CCat}$ for the $\omega\lambda\times$-hyperdoctrine $Cl(Th)$.

The objects of $\mathcal{C}$ are the kinds K of Th. Morphisms $K \to K'$ in $\mathcal{C}$ are equivalence classes of proved operators under the relation of derivable equality. More formally, consider pairs $(X\!:\!K, \Phi)$ for which $Sg \; \triangleright \; X\!:\!K \vdash \Phi\!:\!K'$. Define an equivalence relation on such pairs by setting

$$(X\!:\!K, \Phi) \sim (Y\!:\!K, \Psi) \qquad \text{iff} \qquad Th \; \triangleright \; X\!:\!K \vdash \Phi = \Psi[X/Y]\!:\!K'.$$

A morphism $K \to K'$ is then an equivalence class $(X\!:\!K \mid \Phi)$ of such pairs, and composition of morphisms is given by substitution of raw operators.

The objects of the fibre $\mathbb{C}K = \mathcal{C}(K, Type)$ are by definition morphisms $(X\!:\!K \mid \Phi)\!:\!K \to Type$ in $\mathcal{C}$. Morphisms $(X\!:\!K \mid \Phi) \to (X\!:\!K \mid \Psi)$ in $\mathcal{C}(K, Type)$ are equivalence classes of proved terms under the relation of derivable equality. More precisely, consider for a fixed K triples of the form $(X_1\!:\!K, x_1\!:\!\Phi_1, M_1)$ where here M_1 is a raw term. We can define an equivalence relation on such triples by setting

$$(X_1\!:\!K, x_1\!:\!\Phi_1, M_1) \sim (X_2\!:\!K, x_2\!:\!\Phi_2, M_2)$$

just in case

$$Th \; \triangleright \; X_1\!:\!K \mid x_1\!:\!\Phi_1 \vdash M_1 = M_2[X_2/X_1][x_2/x_1]\!:\!\Psi_1$$

for some raw operator Ψ_1. Then a morphism $(X\!:\!K \mid \Phi) \to (X\!:\!K \mid \Psi)$ is an equivalence class

$$(X\!:\!K \mid x\!:\!\Phi \mid M)$$

of such triples, where M is a raw term for which $Th \; \triangleright \; X\!:\!K \mid x\!:\!\Phi \vdash M\!:\!\Psi$. Composition of morphisms is given by substitution of raw terms.

Given a morphism $(Z\!:\!K' \mid \Theta)\!:\!K' \to K$ in $\mathcal{C}$, the reindexing functor

$$(Z\!:\!K' \mid \Theta)^* : \mathcal{C}(K, Type) \longrightarrow \mathcal{C}(K', Type)$$

is given by substitution of raw operators. Thus for any morphism

$$(X\!:\!K \mid x\!:\!\Phi \mid M)\!:\!(X\!:\!K \mid \Phi) \longrightarrow (X\!:\!K \mid \Psi)$$

in $\mathcal{C}(K, \textit{Type})$ we have

$$(Z: K' \mid \Theta)^* \, (X: K \mid \Phi) \overset{\text{def}}{=} (Z: K' \mid \Phi[\Theta/X])$$

and

$$(Z: K' \mid \Theta)^* \, (X: K \mid x: \Phi \mid M) \overset{\text{def}}{=} (Z: K' \mid x: \Phi[\Theta/X] \mid M[\Theta/X]).$$

The functor $\forall_K^{K'}: \mathcal{C}(K \times K', \textit{Type}) \to \mathcal{C}(K, \textit{Type})$ is given by

$$\forall_K^{K'}(Z: K \times K' \mid \Phi) \overset{\text{def}}{=} (X: K \mid \forall Y: K'.\Phi[\langle X, Y \rangle / Z])$$

on any object $(Z: K \times K' \mid \Phi)$ of $\mathcal{C}(K \times K', \textit{Type})$, and by

$$\forall_K^{K'}(Z: K \times K' \mid z: \Phi \mid M) \overset{\text{def}}{=}$$
$$(X: K \mid x: \forall Y: K'.\Phi[\langle X, Y \rangle / Z] \mid \Lambda Y: K'.M[\langle X, Y \rangle / Z][xY/z])$$

on any morphism

$$(Z: K \times K' \mid z: \Phi \mid M) : (Z: K \times K' \mid \Phi) \longrightarrow (Z: K \times K' \mid \Psi)$$

of $\mathcal{C}(K \times K', \textit{Type})$. It is routine to prove that $\mathbb{C}$ is an $\omega\lambda\times$-hyperdoctrine, using the rules of Th.

The generic model $\mathbf{G} = (\mathbf{G}^{\mathbf{op}}, \mathbf{G}^{\mathbf{tm}})$ is defined by setting $[\![G]\!]_{\mathbf{G}^{\mathbf{op}}} \overset{\text{def}}{=} G$ on ground kinds G (and thus $[\![K]\!]_{\mathbf{G}^{\mathbf{op}}} = K$ for any kind K),

$$[\![F]\!]_{\mathbf{G}^{\mathbf{op}}} \overset{\text{def}}{=} (Z: \Pi_1^n K_i \mid F(\mathsf{Proj}_1(Z), \dots, \mathsf{Proj}_n(Z)))$$

for any operator symbol $F: K_1, \dots, K_n \to K$ of non-zero arity n, and $[\![C]\!]_{\mathbf{G}^{\mathbf{op}}} \overset{\text{def}}{=}$ $(Z: \textit{Unit} \mid C)$ for a constant operator $C: K$. One can prove by induction that $\mathbf{G}^{\mathbf{op}}$ is a model of Th^{op}. We also put

$$[\![f]\!]_{\mathbf{G}^{\mathbf{tm}}} \overset{\text{def}}{=} (Z: \Pi_1^n K_i \mid z: \Pi_1^m \Phi_j \mid f(\mathsf{Proj}_1(z), \dots, \mathsf{Proj}_n(z)))$$

where $f: \Delta; \Phi_1, \dots, \Phi_m \to \Phi$ is a function symbol and the context Δ is given by $[X_1: K_1, \dots, X_n: K_n]$, and $[\![k]\!]_{\mathbf{G}^{\mathbf{tm}}} \overset{\text{def}}{=} (Z: \Pi_1^n K_i \mid z: \textit{unit} \mid k)$ if $\Delta; k: \Phi$. One sees by induction that $\mathbf{G}^{\mathbf{tm}}$ is a model of Th^{tm}.

If $\mathbb{D}: \mathcal{D}^{op} \to \mathcal{ACat}$ is any other $\omega\lambda\times$-hyperdoctrine in which there is a model $\mathbf{M}$ of Th, we can define an $\omega\lambda\times$-functor $(\alpha, F): \mathbb{C} \to \mathbb{D}$ essentially by applying the structure $\mathbf{M}$. Thus $F: \mathcal{C} \to \mathcal{D}$ is given by

$$(X: K \mid \Phi): K \to K' \longmapsto [X: K \vdash \Phi: K']_{\mathbf{M}}: [K]_{\mathbf{M}} \to [K']_{\mathbf{M}}$$

and $\alpha_K: \mathbb{C}K \to \mathbb{D}[K]_{\mathbf{M}}$ is defined analogously for each object K of $\mathcal{C}$. It is easy to prove that $(\alpha, F)_*\mathbf{G} = \mathbf{M}$. The remaining details are omitted. $\square$

6.7 Categorical Type Theory Correspondence

DISCUSSION 6.7.1 Just as we have done for the other simpler type theories in this text, we show that any $\omega\lambda\times$-hyperdoctrine arises as the classifying $\omega\lambda\times$-hyperdoctrine of some $\omega\lambda\times$-theory. We begin by constructing such a theory from a given hyperdoctrine, and then prove a syntax/category theory correspondence.

PROPOSITION 6.7.2 For any $\omega\lambda\times$-hyperdoctrine $\mathbb{C}\colon \mathcal{C}^{op} \to \mathcal{CCat}$ we can define an $\omega\lambda\times$-theory $Th(\mathbb{C}) = (Sg, Ax)$ for which there is a canonical model of $Th(\mathbb{C})$ in $\mathbb{C}$.

PROOF The ground kinds of Sg^{op} are copies A of the objects A of $\mathcal{C}$ and there is an operator symbol $F\colon A_1, \ldots, A_n \to A$ for each morphism $F\colon A_1 \times \ldots \times A_n \to A$. There is a function symbol

$$f : \Delta; \phi_1(\vec{X}), \ldots, \phi_m(\vec{X}) \longrightarrow \phi(\vec{X})$$

for every morphism $f\colon \phi_1 \times \ldots \times \phi_m \to \phi$ in a fibre $\mathcal{C}(\mathcal{A}, U)$. It should be clear what happens if either n or m are 0. A structure $\mathbf{M}$ is given by setting $[\![A]\!]_{\mathbf{M}^{op}} \overset{\mathrm{def}}{=} A$ (at a ground kind A) and so on. There are also function symbols which assert appropriate isomorphisms between syntax and its denotation (such as $I_K\colon [\![K]\!] \to K$ for all kinds K); the reader can provide the full definition. The axioms of $Th(\mathbb{C})$ are given by those operator and term equations-in-context which are satisfied by this structure, which is thus a model of $Th(\mathbb{C})$ by definition. □

THEOREM 6.7.3 Let $\mathbb{C}\colon \mathcal{C}^{op} \to \mathcal{CCat}$ be any $\omega\lambda\times$-hyperdoctrine. Then the $\omega\lambda\times$-functor $Eq\colon Cl(Th(\mathbb{C})) \to \mathbb{C}$ arising from the universal property of $Cl(Th(\mathbb{C}))$ applied to the canonical model of $Th(\mathbb{C})$ in $\mathbb{C}$ is one half of an equivalence of indexed categories.

PROOF The $\omega\lambda\times$-functor Eq^{-1} is defined by taking the categorical structure in $\mathbb{C}$ to "syntactic copies" in $Cl(Th(\mathbb{C}))$, for example $F\colon K \to K'$ in the base category of $\mathbb{C}$ is mapped to $(X\colon K \mid F(X))\colon K \to K'$ in the base of $Cl(Th(\mathbb{C}))$. Once the definition of Eq^{-1} is given the details are lengthy but routine—see the proof of Theorem 5.8.3. □

DISCUSSION 6.7.4 Theorem 6.7.3 is the basis of the slogan

┌─ **Categorical Type Theory Correspondence** ──────────────┐
│ $\omega\lambda\times$-hyperdoctrines are a representation of the notion of $\omega\lambda\times$-theories which │
│ is syntax independent.   │
└───┘

EXERCISE 6.7.5   State a completeness result for the categorical semantics of $\omega\lambda\times$-theories and sketch a proof of it.

6.8   *Pointers to the Literature*

Some of the connections between higher order polymorphic type theory and higher order logic are discussed in [CE87]. This paper contains a description of the algebraic complete lattice model presented in this chapter of "Categories for Types." For those readers who are interested in looking at the categorical semantics of highly expressive type theories which are perhaps somewhat more complicated than those of this book, see [HP89]. This paper presents the so-called Calculus of Constructions along with a full account of its category-theoretic models. Further details of higher order polymorphism and associated models can be found in [See87]. The notion of kind given in this paper is a little more restricted than that of our Chapter 6, but the syntactical theories considered are slightly more complex in the sense that they involve a richer class of operators and terms.

Bibliography

[AL91] A. Asperti and G. Longo. *Categories, Types and Structures : An introduction to category theory for the working computer scientist.* Foundations of Computing Series. The MIT Press, 1991.

[Bar84] H. Barendregt. *The Lambda Calculus: Its Syntax and Semantics.* Studies in Logic and the Foundations of Mathematics. North Holland, 1984. Volume 103.

[Bir67] G. Birkhoff. *Lattice Theory.* Coll. Publ. XXV, American Mathematical Society, Providence, RI, 3rd edition, 1967.

[Bou48] N. Bourbaki. Algèbre (éléments de mathématique, livre ii), chapitre 3. *Actualités Sci. Ind.,* 1044, 1948.

[BW90] M. Barr and C. Wells. *Category Theory for Computing Science.* International Series in Computer Science. Prentice Hall, 1990.

[Car86] L. Cardelli. A polymorphic lambda calculus with type:type. Technical Report 10, Systems Research Center, 130 Lytton Avenue, Palo Alto, CA, 1986.

[Car89] L. Cardelli. Typeful programming. Technical Report 45, Systems Research Center, 130 Lytton Avenue, Palo Alto, CA, 1989.

[CE87] T. Coquand and T. Ehrhard. An equational presentation of higher order logic. In *Summer Conference on Category Theory and Computer Science.* University of Edinburgh, Scotland, U.K., September 1987.

[CGW87] T. Coquand, C. Gunter, and G. Winskel. dI-domains as a model of polymorphism. Technical Report 107, University of Cambridge Computer Laboratory, 1987.

[CGW89] T. Coquand, C. Gunter, and G. Winskel. Domain theoretic models of polymorphism. *Information and Computation,* 81:123–167, 1989.

[Chu40] A. Church. A formulation of the simple theory of types. *Journal of Symbolic Logic,* 5:56–68, 1940.

[Coh79]   P.M. Cohn. *Algebra*, volume 2. John Wiley and Sons Ltd., 1979.

[DP90]   B.A. Davey and H.A. Priestley. *Introduction to Lattices and Order*.
            Cambridge Mathematical Textbooks. Cambridge University Press,
            1990.

[EM42]   S. Eilenberg and S. Mac Lane. Natural isomorphisms in group
            theory. *Proc. Nat. Acad. Sci. U.S.A.*, 28:537–543, 1942.

[EM45]   S. Eilenberg and S. Mac Lane. General theory of natural equiva-
            lences. *Trans. Amer. Math. Soc.*, 58:231–294, 1945.

[Fre64]   P. J. Freyd. *Abelian Categories*. Harper and Row, 1964.

[Fre67]   G. Frege. Function and concept. In P. Geach and M. Black, edi-
            tors, *Translations from the Philosophical Writings of Gottlob Frege*.
            Blackwell, Oxford, 1967.

[GHK+80]   G. Gierz, K.H. Hofmann, K. Keimel, J.D. Lawson, M. Mislove,
            and D.S. Scott. *A Compendium of Continuous Lattices*. Springer-
            Verlag, 1980.

[Gir86]   J.-Y. Girard. The system F of variable types fifteen years later.
            Theoretical Computer Science, 45:159–192, 1986.

[Gir89]   J.-Y. Girard. *Proofs and Types*. Cambridge Tracts in Theoretical
            Computer Science. Cambridge University Press, 1989. Translated
            and with appendices by P. Taylor and Y. Lafont.

[Gra71]   G. Gratzer. *Lattice Theory: First Concepts and Distributive Lat-
            tices*. W.H. Freeman and Co., San Francisco, 1971.

[Gra78]   G. Gratzer. *General Lattice Theory*. Birkhäuser, Basel, 1978.

[HP89]   J.M.E. Hyland and A.M. Pitts. The theory of constructions: Cat-
            egorical semantics and topos-theoretic models. In *Categories in
            Computer Science and Logic*, volume 92 of *Contemp. Math.*, pages
            137–199, 1989.

[Joh82]   P.T. Johnstone. *Stone Spaces*, volume 3 of *Cambridge Studies in
            Advanced Mathematics*. Cambridge University Press, 1982.

[Joh87]   P.T. Johnstone. *Notes on Logic and Set Theory*. Cambridge Uni-
            versity Press, 1987.

[Kan58]   D.M. Kan. Adjoint functors. *Trans. Amer. Math. Soc.*, 87:294–329, 1958.

[Lam80]   J. Lambek. From λ-calculus to cartesian closed categories. In J.P. Seldin and J.R. Hindley, editors, *To H.B. Curry: Essays on Combinatory Logic, Lambda Calculus and Formalism*. Academic Press, 1980.

[Law63]   F.W. Lawvere. *Functorial Semantics of Algebraic Theories*. PhD thesis, Columbia University, 1963. Summary appears in Proceedings of the National Academy of Science, 50:869–873, 1963.

[LS80]   J. Lambek and P.J. Scott. Intuitionist type theory and the free topos. *Journal of Pure and Applied Algebra*, 19:215–257, 1980.

[Mac48]   S. Mac Lane. Groups, categories and duality. *Proc. Nat. Acad. Sci. U.S.A.*, 34:263–267, 1948.

[Mac50]   S. Mac Lane. Duality for groups. *Bull. Amer. Math. Soc.*, 56:485–516, 1950.

[Mac71]   S. Mac Lane. *Categories for the Working Mathematician*, volume 5 of *Graduate Texts in Mathematics*. Springer-Verlag, 1971.

[Man76]   E. Manes. *Algebraic Theories*, volume 26 of *Graduate Texts in Mathematics*. Springer-Verlag, 1976.

[McL91]   C. McLarty. *Elementary Categories, Elementary Toposes*, volume 21 of *Oxford Logic Guides*. Oxford University Press, 1991.

[ML]   P. Martin-Löf. Constructive mathematics and computer programming. In Logic, Methodology and Philosophy of Science, IV, 1979. Published by North-Holland, 1982.

[ML71]   P. Martin-Löf. A theory of types. Technical Report 71-3, University of Stockholm, 1971.

[ML72]   P. Martin-Löf. An intuitionistic theory of types. Technical report, University of Stockholm, 1972.

[ML84]   P. Martin-Löf. *Intuitionistic Type Theory*. Bibliopolis, Napoli, 1984.

[NPS90]   B. Nordström, K. Petersson, and J.M. Smith. *Programming in Martin-Löf's Type Theory*, volume 7 of *Monographs on Computer Science*. Oxford University Press, 1990.

[Pie91]   B.C. Pierce. *Basic Category Theory for Computer Scientists*. Foundations of Computing Series. The MIT Press, 1991.

[Pit87]   A.M. Pitts. Polymorphism is set theoretic, constructively. In *Summer Conference on Category Theory and Computer Science*. University of Edinburgh, Scotland, U.K., September 1987.

[Sco69a]   D.S. Scott. Models of the lambda calculus. Unpublished manuscript, 1969.

[Sco69b]   D.S. Scott. A type theoretic alternative to CUCH, ISWIM, OWHY. Unpublished manuscript, University of Oxford, 1969.

[Sco70a]   D.S. Scott. The lattice of flow diagrams. Technical Report 3, Oxford University Programming Research Group, 1970.

[Sco70b]   D.S. Scott. Towards a mathematical theory of computation. In *4th Annual Princeton Conference on Information Sciences and Systems*, 1970.

[Sco71]   D.S. Scott. Continuous lattices. Technical Report 7, Oxford University Programming Research Group, 1971.

[Sco76]   D.S. Scott. Datatypes as lattices. *SIAM Journal of Computing*, 5(3):522–587, 1976.

[Sco82]   D.S. Scott. Domains for denotational semantics. In *ICALP 1982*, volume 140 of *Lecture Notes In Computer Science*, pages 577–613. Springer-Verlag, 1982.

[See87]   R.A.G. Seely. Categorical semantics for higher order polymorphic lambda calculus. *The Journal of Symbolic Logic*, 52(4):969–989, December 1987.

[SS71]   D.S. Scott and C. Strachey. Towards a mathematical semantics for computer languages. Technical Report 6, Oxford University Programming Research Group, 1971.

[vD89]   D. van Dalen. *Logic and Structure*. Universitext. Springer-Verlag, 3rd edition, 1989. Corrected Third Printing.

[Vic89]   S. Vickers. *Topology via Logic*. Cambridge Tracts in Theoretical Computer Science. Cambridge University Press, 1989.

Index

Printed in the United States
By Bookmasters